MANAGING & ORGANIZATIONS

Sara Miller McCune founded SAGE Publishing in 1965 to support the dissemination of usable knowledge and educate a global community. SAGE publishes more than 1000 journals and over 800 new books each year, spanning a wide range of subject areas. Our growing selection of library products includes archives, data, case studies and video. SAGE remains majority owned by our founder and after her lifetime will become owned by a charitable trust that secures the company's continued independence.

Los Angeles | London | New Delhi | Singapore | Washington DC | Melbourne

Clegg • Kornberger • Pitsis • Mount

MANAGING & ORGANIZATIONS

An Introduction to Theory and Practice

FIFTH EDITION

Los Angeles | London | New Delhi
Singapore | Washington DC | Melbourne

Los Angeles | London | New Delhi
Singapore | Washington DC | Melbourne

SAGE Publications Ltd
1 Oliver's Yard
55 City Road
London EC1Y 1SP

SAGE Publications Inc.
2455 Teller Road
Thousand Oaks, California 91320

SAGE Publications India Pvt Ltd
B 1/I 1 Mohan Cooperative Industrial Area
Mathura Road
New Delhi 110 044

SAGE Publications Asia-Pacific Pte Ltd
3 Church Street
#10-04 Samsung Hub
Singapore 049483

Editor: Kirsty Smy
Development editor: Nina Smith
Editorial assistant: Martha Cuneen
Assistant editor, digital: Chloe Statham
Production editor: Sarah Cooke
Copyeditor: Sharon Cawood
Proofreader: Neil Dowden
Indexer: Silvia Benvenuto
Marketing manager: Alsion Borg
Cover design: Francis Kenney
Typeset by: C&M Digitals (P) Ltd, Chennai, India
Printed in the UK by Bell & Bain Ltd, Glasgow

First edition published 2004
Second edition published 2008
Third edition published 2011
Fourth edition published 2016
This fifth edition published 2019

Library of Congress Control Number: 2018951147

British Library Cataloguing in Publication data

A catalogue record for this book is available from the British Library

ISBN 978-1-5264-6009-7
ISBN 978-1-5264-6010-3 (pbk)
ISBN 978-1-5264-8796-4 (pbk & interactive ebk) (IEB)

Contents

Your Guide to using this book

This free interactive eBook provides a range of learning resources designed to help you understand key management concepts and how to apply these in practice to help you succeed in your studies.

Interactive icons appear throughout the book to let you know that extra learning resources are available. You can study on the go and use these resources on your laptop, tablet or smartphone.

To access these, just log in to your FREE interactive eBook and click on the icons for:

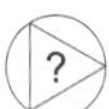

What Would You Do? videos

Watch authors Stewart and Tyrone discuss and debate real-life scenarios and provide useful pointers for your own decision making.

Videos

Watch online videos from TED Talks and YouTube to get a better understanding of key concepts.

Weblinks

Go further and expand your understanding of each topic with weblinks to key organizations and online articles.

Further reading

Access free SAGE journal articles to help you delve deeper and support your assignments.

Multiple Choice Questions

Test your knowledge and prepare for your exams with multiple choice questions.

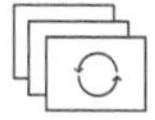

Flashcards

Test your understanding and revise key terms with glossary flashcards.

See the inside front cover of this book for download instructions

Not a fan of eBooks?

The interactive eBook provides the most seamless way to move between your textbook and the digital resources, but you can also access them here:

https://study.sagepub.com/managingandorganizations5e

FOR LECTURERS

A selection of tried and tested teaching resources have been honed and developed to accompany this text and support your course.
Visit **https://study.sagepub.com/managingandorganizations5e** to set up or use your instructor login to access:

- **An Instructor Manual** providing ideas and inspiration for seminars and tutorials, and guidance on how to use the exercises and case studies in your own teaching.
- **PowerPoint slides** for each chapter that can be adapted and edited to suit your own teaching needs.
- **Testbank questions** offering a wide variety of multiple choice, short and long answer assessment questions to use with your students.
- **Additional case studies** to enhance students' understanding.

About the Authors

Stewart R. Clegg is Distinguished Professor of Management and Organization Studies at the University of Technology Sydney. He has published widely in the management, organizations and politics literatures in many of the leading journals. He is a Visiting Professor at EM-Lyon, France and at Nova School of Business and Economics in Lisbon, Portugal. Widely acknowledged as one of the most significant contemporary theorists of power relations, he is also one of the most influential contributors to organization studies.

Martin Kornberger is an undisciplined mind: he received his PhD in Philosophy from the University of Vienna in 2002 and has since held positions in strategy, organization theory, marketing and design at universities in Australia, Austria, Denmark, Sweden, the UK and France. With one foot in the library and the other in the laboratory, his research and teaching focus on the discovery of ideas and practices that stretch the imagination of managers and scholars alike.

Tyrone S. Pitsis is Professor of Strategy, Technology & Society at Durham University Business School. He is also Director of the Global Doctor of Business Administration programme between Durham and emlyon. His research is at the intersection between strategy design, innovation and complex projects, with a focus on transformative technologies. He is consistently rated as one of the top teachers and is a sought-after speaker. He has been the recipient of several awards for his research and was also awarded the Practice Theme Committee of the Academy of Management leadership award for his contribution to AOM's strategic aims of promoting and recognizing the impact members make through their scholarship. Having worked since he was 14, Tyrone originally began his working life as a chef, starting off as a kitchen hand and working his way up to executive chef in award-winning restaurants and hotels. He now cooks as little as possible but still loves to eat. Aside from his family, Tyrone could not imagine life without music.

Matt Mount is Assistant Professor of Strategy and Innovation at Deakin Business School, Melbourne. He received his PhD in Management Science from the University of York. He is an expert in areas of strategy and innovation process and his research has appeared in top academic and practitioner journals such as *MIT Sloan Management Review, Regional Studies,* and *California Management Review* among others. He is member of the Editorial Board for the *Journal of Management Studies* and regularly reviews for journals such as *Organization Science, Research Policy, Strategic Management Journal,* and *Journal of Product Innovation Management*. He is also an active strategic management consultant, working on a number of large-scale projects and serving on the advisory board for international organizations.

Acknowledgements

The fifth edition could not have been completed without some acknowledgements being due. On this occasion, we would like to thank the following people for their invaluable assistance and feedback on this new and revised edition of *Managing and Organizations: An Introduction to Theory and Practice*. Good colleagues offer good feedback and as we developed these new chapters we received excellent advice from Miguel Pina e Cunha, Armenio Rego, Ace Simpson and Marco Berti. Administratively, we were extremely ably directed by Nina Smith and Sarah Cooke at Sage and assisted by Lisa Be in Sydney. We appreciated being advised on an error in the fourth edition, that no longer recurs, which was pointed out to us by Mateusz Piotrowski and Carolyn Downs. To all these people – and to any that we might inadvertently have overlooked – many thanks!

Part One

MANAGING PEOPLE IN ORGANIZATIONS

INTERACTIVE EBOOK ICON KEY

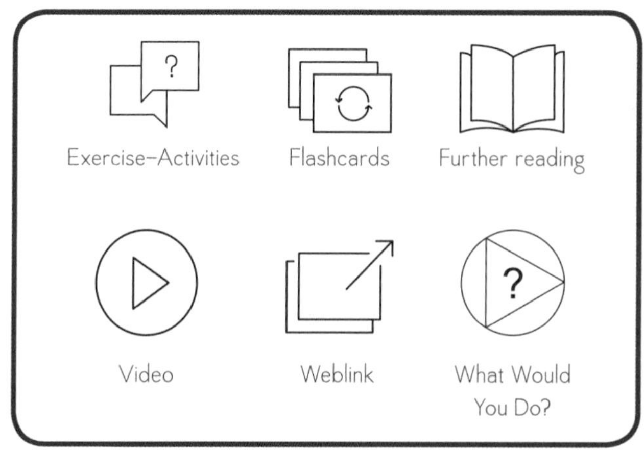

MANAGING AND ORGANIZATIONS

OPENING, THINKING, CONTEXTUALIZING

LEARNING OBJECTIVES

This chapter is designed to enable you to:

- identify the impact that changes in the contemporary world are having on *managing* and *organization*
- be introduced to trends in the digital organizations in which much contemporary *managing* and *organization* occurs
- understand *managing* and *organization* as sensemaking
- grasp the managerial rationalities that constitute much contemporary *managing* and *organization*
- familiarize yourself with some significant global shifts for future *managing* and *organization*.

BEFORE YOU GET STARTED

'When digital transformation is done right, it's like a caterpillar turning into a butterfly, but when done wrong, all you have is a really fast caterpillar.'

George Westerman | Principal Research Scientist with the MIT Sloan Initiative on the Digital Economy

INTRODUCTION

This introductory chapter seeks to familiarize you with some of the major trends of recent times that pervade the context of contemporary managing and organizations. Some of these will be familiar; others you may not have thought about. Managing and organizations are dynamic elements of the contemporary world, changing rapidly. Little stays the same, other than the processes that underline what managers do. What managers do is to make sense of these changes and other stimuli in the environments in which they find themselves. Doing this is called sensemaking. Sensemaking is one of a number of closely allied terms, including sensegiving and sensebreaking, which are constitutive of managerial work, irrespective of its substantive content.

We can differentiate between *managing as a practice*, as something that we do, and *organizations as goal-oriented collectives*, in which we are *organized*. To be organized means being an element in a systematic arrangement of parts, hopefully creating a unified, organic whole. Management is the process of communicating, coordinating and accomplishing action in the pursuit of organizational objectives, while managing relationships with stakeholders, technologies and other artefacts, both within as well as between organizations.

It would be both wrong and dangerous to consider management as a neutral activity that can simply be considered in terms of its capacity to deliver objective gains in productivity/efficiency. It is also a socio-political activity, which implies the need to adhere to societal, political and ethical responsibilities.

CONTEMPORARY MANAGING AND ORGANIZATIONS IN A CHANGING WORLD

You might think that there is a great deal of difference among organizations doing different things – organizations with different missions. For instance, the mission of schools and universities is to educate people; charity organizations support people in need; while church organizations nurture spiritual life and provide ritual for life's points of transition, such as marriage and death. Some of these organizations will be for-profit organizations – that is their mission. Others will be not-for-profit organizations, while others still will be supported through taxation as a public service. There is growing consensus that the practices involved in organizing share a high degree of commonality. In this view, the differences in mission are subordinate to the practices involved in managing and organizing. It is these practices that this book will inform you about.

EXTEND YOUR KNOWLEDGE

READ THE ARTICLE

In Bromley, P. and Meyer, J. W. (2017) '"They are all organizations": the cultural roots of blurring between the nonprofit, business, and government sectors', *Administration & Society*, 49 (7): 939–66, which is available at the companion website https://study.sagepub.com/managingandorganizations5e, the authors argue that the distinctions between what were once seen as individual sectors are blurring and it is increasingly difficult to distinguish between these historically separate entities because of global cultural shifts characterized by a growing emphasis on science. The scientific emphasis renders the world subject to systematic principles and to the expansion of individual rights, responsibilities and capacities. Focusing mainly on non-profits, this approach suggests that all sectors are changing in similar ways in the current period.

Organizations are tools: they are purposive, goal-oriented instruments designed to achieve a specific objective. A tool, traditionally, is an extension of human agency: a hammer enables a hand to hammer, a screwdriver to screw and an iron to iron. The tool extends the power of the human agent using it. Organizations extend human agency, as Perrow (1986) argues. As such, for those who are able to control them, organizations are practical tools for accomplishing their goals. Sometimes these goals can be benign, such as healing the sick, housing the homeless or assisting refugees in finding a home. At other times, especially where the interests of the rich and powerful are in control, these goals can be more particularistic, as Barley (2007) argues.

In the large organizations of the post-war era, people were managed through their career aspirations. An inability to fit in, to comport oneself in the appropriate way or to simply blend in, especially in terms of politics and gender, was a sufficient reason for a person's career aspirations and fitness for available opportunities to be questioned and restricted. A journalist, William H. Whyte, captured the spirit of the times in a bestselling book, *The Organization Man* (Whyte, 1956). Whyte observed executive behaviour that was risk-averse because no single individual was responsible for any decision. Consequently, career progression meant authority and a career for life as long as one kept one's nose clean. Not only did large-scale bureaucracies create managerial careers that employed many millions (mostly men), but these corporations also produced technological innovations in abundance, such as computers, fibre optics and satellites. These innovations would creatively destroy much of old corporate America, with the rise from the 1980s onwards of the new economy of **digitalization**, creating the world that we now live in.

Digitalization is the use of digital technologies and of data (digitized from non-digital sources or originally created as such) to manage organization processes.

Many of the jobs of the future are likely to be created and filled by **digital nomads**. The BBC in May 2018 had a Business Briefing programme dedicated to digital nomads – young people armed with a laptop and connected to Wi-Fi who can move around doing their work wherever the fancy takes them – usually in warmer places that are less expensive to live in, with good beaches and surfing, such as Portugal. Indeed, Lisbon is the capital of cool in digital terms in Europe. Some nomads housesit for a few months and then move on to another opportunity to do it again, elsewhere, or perhaps using Airbnb. Of course, being highly mobile, with no fixed abode, digital nomads create problems for tax authorities: they can contrive not to be anywhere long enough to be liable for taxation and it is very easy for them to 'fly under the radar' of national tax authorities, especially in the European Union (EU), where borderless travel and the free movement of labour mean that there is little in the way of control of passage. Additionally, the BBC note, they tend to distort local housing markets,

Digital nomads are mobile workers armed with a laptop and Wi-Fi, connecting anywhere and choosing mobility rather than a fixed abode.

driving up rents and conversions to Airbnb in cool inner-city areas, such as the Alfama in Lisbon (Bloom, 2018).

READ MORE ABOUT DIGITALIZATION

It is not only that there are new types of workers, such as these digital nomads. Even organizations, who are the clients of such workers, are changing, irrespective of their mission, as a result of the possibilities afforded by digitalization. For instance, charities earn money through using call centre staff and robot dialling in cheap labour markets. The public-sector administration of activities such as replacing driving licences and passports is now conducted online. Tablet devices stuck on tables are replacing wait staff; checkout workers in supermarkets are being replaced by self-service machines; even jobs that involved many hands, such as miners, truck and train drivers and dockers, in shifting ore from mines to port to ships are now more often one integrated and automated process. Robots are carrying out mundane work, providing opportunities for open/platform-based collaboration and transactional management that facilitate a market-based form of coordination, making organization less reliant on hierarchies, and – as a consequence – on long-term relationships with a trusted workforce.

WATCH AN INTERVIEW

There are policy implications for digital developments that might seem surprising. The objective of policy should be gradually to make labour more expensive. More expensive labour is not only a personal good for those that receive it but is also an institutional good. In the face of rising costs, those industries that thrive only because of low-cost labour will either be outsourced to countries where workers have fewer rights and protections, or increasingly adopt robotics and artificial intelligence (AI). Bill Gates has suggested that such productivity-enhancing devices should be taxed. The main argument against taxing robots is that it might impede innovation, but this is the case only if the option of a low-cost workforce is available: limit the opportunities for that through earnings legislation and enforcement and the objections would be dissolved. Enterprises that in the past relied on the super-exploitation of low-cost labour would either die as they were priced out of the market or would adjust structurally through increasing investment in productivity enhancements that would improve working conditions, wages and productivity. To the extent that they decamp elsewhere, all well and good: they will, in all probability, lift average wages where they land and, provided there is an active labour market policy funded in part by an exit tax on de-campers, the overall level of skill formation and domestic income may be raised.

Organizations in the digital age are switching from managing through 'hard power' in the form of imperative commands to 'soft power' through indirect methods, such as induction into an organizational culture, training and strategy workshops, or leadership courses. The targets of these more subtle management tools are not old-style blue-collar shopfloor workers, a diminishing breed in advanced economies, but highly skilled knowledge workers whose complex skills cannot be easily supervised. They will be people like you, practising skills that you may not even have thought of at present. Your future career may well not have been invented yet. Things are not what they used to be and this is true of managing and organizations as much as anything else.

The stress on managing through practices such as organizational culture is not new. Top managers embraced Peters and Waterman's (1982) arguments about how to hone the organization tool through leadership and culture, as did many scholars who produced studies on the keys to excellence in organizations (e.g. Athos and Pascale, 1981; Deal and Kennedy, 1982; Kanter, 1984, 1990). They argued that improvements in productivity and quality would accrue when corporate cultures systematically align individuals with formal organizational goals.

The idea of the organization as a culture not only had private-sector resonances; it also became a theme for reforming the public sector. In government and public sector circles, the view of organization as a cultural tool was led by something called **new public management**. The adoption of new public management started in the early 1980s; its reforms were informed by neo-classical economic theories relating to marketization and increased adoption of private-sector management techniques.

New public management replaces public sector bureaucracy with public managers and citizens with customers, managed by targets and audits.

Across Anglo-American polities, there has been an underlying assumption that private-sector business management is better than its equivalent in the public sector (Box et al., 2001; Kettl, 1997; Light, 2006; Nigro and Kellough, 2008; Thayer, 1978). It is widely seen as being the only tool in the box. The quest for efficiency and effectiveness in the public sector along the lines of the private sector was evident (Arnold, 1995; Kettl, 1997; Light, 2006; Nigro and Kellough, 2008; Pautz and Washington, 2009). Rather than use a traditional organization theory of bureaucracy, such as that of Weber (1978), the reformers of the new public management were inspired by classical microeconomic theories that had a strong 'normative influence' on public-sector reforms (Box et al., 2001: 611; Nigro and Kellough, 2008).

WATCH AN EXPLANATION

Microeconomic theory anchored in a 'market-based model' advocated downsizing government, applying private-sector management principles to public-sector administration, viewing citizens as customers, divorcing policy making from administration implementation and viewing government as akin to a 'business within the public sector' (Box et al., 2001: 611; Kettl, 1997). Influenced by right-wing 'think tanks' and two popular texts, *Reinventing Government* (Osborne and Gaebler, 1992) and *Banishing Bureaucracy* (Osborne and Plastrik, 1997), the reinvention movement of public-sector reform (Brudney et al., 1999; Brudney and Wright, 2002; Calista, 2002) flourished.

At roughly the same time that public sectors were being urged to abandon bureaucracy and adopt private-sector efficiencies, the decline of bureaucratic corporations was being charted by Davis (2016a), noting that the number of American companies listed on the stock market dropped by half between 1996 and 2012. These corporations were, as he says, once an integral part of building the middle class, offering millions of people lifetime employment, a stable career path, health insurance and retirement pensions – the civil benefits of well-designed bureaucracies – the latter two especially important in a non-social democratic society with minimal citizenship rights, such as the USA. Many famous corporate names from the past have become bankrupt and those that survive mostly employ fewer people than was the case. Davis (2016b) argues that this decline in corporate jobs is a root cause of contemporary income inequality, as well-paid jobs in career bureaucracies with clear routes to promotion were eviscerated.

The decline varied from country to country; in the UK, large-scale companies that had been created through government fiat, such as British Leyland and British Steel, both of which were 'nationalized' to become 'publically owned', were neither sufficiently integrated nor efficient enough to compete against more robust, better-invested-in and managed, as well as larger, foreign competition. As national champions, they became political footballs kicked around by union leaders, politicians and ideologues with little understanding of the strategies and skills required to make these concerns successful.

Favourable economic policies for the rich, such as low taxation, minimal control of offshore accounts as tax havens, the ease of intergenerational wealth transmission through inheritance laws, free mobility of capital and anti-union laws, all implemented as part of a neo-liberal agenda, to minimize regulation and maximize markets, have been widely adopted in the English-speaking world. These translated into the rhetoric of trickle-down economics in Australia and the UK, for instance. In the most recent example of this policy – at the time of writing – the Trump administration in December 2017 signed into law significant change to the American tax system, which includes a permanent 40 per cent corporate tax reduction, substantial rate cuts for the wealthy and modest (and, in some cases, non-existent) temporary cuts for the majority of the population.

At the same time that governments practised austerity for the masses, they have praised tax cuts for the elites on the grounds that lower income taxes would encourage economic activity and the benefits would be distributed in the form of enhanced employment opportunities and a trickle-down effect of increased wages paid by more successful businesses. Ruiz, Peralta-Alva and Puy (2017), in an important International Monetary Fund (IMF) paper, argue that tax cuts do not work as expected. Looking at longitudinal data from the USA, they argue that while lowering tax rates for the rich stimulates the economy, it does so at the great cost of increased inequality. The IMF study modelled the impacts of tax cuts on a US-style economy and found that income-tax cuts reduced tax revenue across the board. While growth was stimulated by increased employment and wages, it did not offset revenue lost from lower marginal tax rates. More growth occurs when cuts are made to the highest level of taxes but high-income tax cuts 'lead to increased spending on goods and services, which in turn could improve wages for those lower-income earners who provided those goods, but it would also cause prices to rise and would need to be paid for by either other tax increases or cuts to government spending' (Jericho, 2017). Economic growth occurs but at the cost of increased inequality as those on lower- and middle-class incomes adjust to rising prices by consuming less. If the tax cuts are targeted at middle- and lower-class incomes, there is less overall growth but reduced income inequality, as those from lower-income households are able to spend more on life's necessities.

Linked to these findings is another IMF article, from the journal *Finance and Development*, by Ostry, Loungani and Furceri (2016), that argues that 'austerity policies not only generate substantial welfare costs due to supply-side channels, they also hurt demand – and thus worsen employment and unemployment'. So the combination of tax cuts and austerity is toxic for national economies and the majority of people. Where taxes are lowered for the wealthy and corporations, then government deficit increases substantially which serves as a pretext for government spending to be cut. The latter has prevailed and organizational wellbeing has suffered in consequence.

WHAT WOULD YOU DO?

Diagnostically, the predominant view held by politicians influenced by neo-liberal economics was that the state, and the public expenditure that supported it, had become too large. The desire was for a smaller state to be achieved by cutting public expenditures. As the largest fraction of these expenditures went to support elements of the 'social wage', such as unemployment benefits, welfare and related expenses, these policies led to an increased rhetoric opposed to government spending in these areas, as well as a policy focus targeted at levels of public-sector debt reduction. Rather than growing the size of the surplus through government investments that would lift economic activity and thus increase tax receipts, as would have been the prescription of Keynes, the focus was very largely on the expenditure side of the equation.

What would you do if you were a policy maker?

Do you think that there might be feasible alternatives to managing debt by cutting social and welfare expenditures?

CONTEMPORARY ORGANIZATIONAL CHANGES

The upshot of the political and economic changes that occurred from 1980 onwards was a significant shift in the wages/profits share of the economy; for instance, in Australia less than 10 cents in the dollar of GDP goes to workers (Patty, 2017). People who are employees have lost out, big time, to people who are shareholders. Also amongst the losers were state employees staffing large-scale public-sector bureaucracies largely centred on the processing of people and information. These organizations suffered from a shortage of investment, efficiency drives and ideological attack for their lack of market disciplines. This is where neo-liberal economics bit hard: given that market metaphors were privileged in their rhetoric, state expenditure was stigmatized. Reliance on non-market and non-individually secured resources was positioned as a sign of moral failure, of weakness. In the private sector, market disciplines were increasingly channelled, rhetorically and practically, through a theory that developed during the period of neo-liberal economic dominance. This theory was known as principal agency theory and became a key tenet of managerial rationality.

Principal agency theory (Jensen and Meckling, 1976) has a fundamental premise that the provision of capital by shareholders is a risk-based endeavour in which the risks can be minimized if the agents that are managing individuals' capital at a distance are also themselves shareholders. Having principals and agents aligned with a common interest in share values, it is argued, will create more efficient organizations because they are focused on the privileged goal of increasing shareholder value. While these ideas initially flourished in the USA, they became widely applied in the design of shareholder capitalism in the newly emerging 'gangster capitalism' of the ex-Soviet and state socialist economies, in which previous apparatchiks of the state bureaucracies practised kleptocracy and cronyism on a grand scale as they rewarded themselves for their previous incumbency and 'good' connections with huge bundles of shares in the newly-privatized industries.

With the fall of the wall in Berlin and the demise of the Soviet system, there was an air of triumphalism in the West after 1989. Capitalism, seemingly, was vindicated as the only game in play. Fukuyama (1992) saw the signs as positioning liberal democracy and a society of markets as the most rational and evolved form of human government. Advisors flocked east to bring the capitalist revolution (Berger, 1987) to the citizens of formerly totalitarian states. As the state, as the principal agency in social life, was reformed and markets were created, new principals and agents were introduced into the mix, drawing on notions that had been brewing in the USA and the UK during the neo-liberal era.

Jensen and Meckling's (1976) influence derived from a quasi-scientific rationale for de-institutionalizing the corporation into nothing but a nexus of contracts that existed to create shareholder value. The process was one of wish fulfilment. Corporations that were quite obviously social institutions were being invited to deconstruct. '[T]he 'nexus' imagery served as a useful provocation, a lever to bust up the unwieldy and shareholder-hostile conglomerates built up over the prior decades. This was a theory perfectly designed to legitimate a bust-up takeover wave' (Davis, 2016b: 509). Agency theory, theorized in a small and, at the time, seemingly inauspicious article in an insignificant journal, spawned changes in practice on a grand scale. The consequences, in terms of the deconstruction of the corporate model of employment relations as a norm in the dominant global economy, have been profound.

The growth and application of agency theory to practice over the last 40 years or so, particularly but not exclusively in the financial sector (Mallaby, 2010), has seen agents become rewarded as principals that don't even have to risk their own capital. In tying their agency to that of the principals, they have voted themselves stock options, thus becoming significant principals in their own right. In most companies in the USA, the CEO tends to enjoy a considerable imbalance of power compared to the nominal authority of the board that appoints the CEO and to which they are legally accountable. Hence, the growing control of CEOs in governance on company boards has vested them with an ability to set, up to a point, their own salaries as well as to nominate stock options.

The immediate post-war period saw some equalization in income across the board in the USA, the UK, France and elsewhere but, historically, the period proved to be exceptional. During the period from the end of the Second World War to 1980, a number of factors inhibited the tendency to increasing inequality. These included proactive measures such as the progressive taxation of capital income and wealth as well as the physical destruction of capital as a result of the war; innovation and economic growth also decreased the concentration of wealth by enriching previously non-wealthy individuals. The post-war period up until the 1980s was an exceptional era in which the rate of return on capital (after tax) was less than economic growth, hence the reduction in income inequality. From the 1980s things changed, especially in the USA.

Drawing on Davis and Mishel (2014), we can see that after 1979 those earning more than 99.9 per cent of all wage earners, the top 1 per cent of US executives and the top 0.1 per cent of US households saw their income shares double in the period to 2007. Since 2007 profits have reached record highs while the wages of most workers (and their families' incomes) have declined (Mishel, 2013; Mishel et al., 2012). From 1978 to 2013, CEO compensation, adjusted for inflation, increased 937 per cent. Not only was this rise more than double stock market growth, it was 90 times greater than the 10.2 per cent growth in a typical worker's compensation over the same period. In 1965 the CEO-to-worker compensation ratio was 20-to-1, increasing to 29.9-to-1 in 1978, growing to 122.6-to-1 in 1995, peaking at 383.4-to-1 in 2000, and was 295.9-to-1 in 2013; if Facebook is included, whose executives are extraordinarily well-compensated, the ratio rises to 510.7-to-1.

CEO compensation has grown far faster than that of other highly paid workers: they earn more than 99.9 per cent of other wage earners put together. CEO compensation in 2012 was 4.75 times greater than that of the top 0.1 per cent of wage earners, a ratio 1.5 times higher than the 3.25 ratio that prevailed over the 1947–79 period. CEO pay grew far faster than pay of the top 0.1 per cent of wage earners not because of the greater productivity of executives but because of their ability to set the terms of their remuneration: their relative power.

CEO compensation grew strongly throughout the 1980s but exploded in the 1990s and peaked in 2000, increasing by more than 200 per cent between 1995 and 2000. Chief executive pay averages peaked at around $20 million in 2000, a growth of 1,279 per cent from 1978. This increase even exceeded the growth of the booming stock market, the value of which increased 513 per cent as measured by the S&P 500, or 439 per cent as measured by the Dow Jones Industrial Average from 1978 to 2000. The most recent report (Mishel and Schneider, 2017) looking at CEO compensation notes that in terms of stock options realized in 2016 CEOs in America's largest firms made an average of 271 times the annual average pay of the typical worker. Compared with the annual earnings of the average very-high-wage earner (an earner in the top 0.1 per cent), CEOs in a large firm now earn, on average, 5.33 times more.

What is known as 'shareholder value' is the rationale behind this inequity – placing emphasis on short-term share-value performance as a measure of success and aligning the interests of managerial 'agents' with the 'principals' holding shares, by making stock options a part of the overall remuneration. The increasing inequality might be best documented in the USA but the effects are wider, especially in the other Anglophone neo-liberal economies. The implications of these neo-liberal models are especially acute for developing countries and emerging economies because the dominant models are neither capable of generating the large number of corporate jobs that were the basis for post-war development in the major OECD economies nor of sustaining efficient state sectors.

In 2016 the data shows that just 62 people owned as much as the poorest half of the world's population, down from 388 in 2010 and 80 in 2015. As the Oxfam Canada (2016) publication, *An Economy for the 1%*, shows:

> [T]he wealth of the poorest half of the world's population – that's 3.6 billion people – has fallen by a trillion dollars since 2010. This 38 per cent drop has occurred despite the global population increasing by around 400 million people during that period. Meanwhile the wealth of the richest 62 has

increased by more than half a trillion dollars to $1.76tr. Just nine of the '62' are women.

Source: The material from 'An Economy for the 1%' (Oxfam Canada, 2016) is reproduced with the permission of Oxfam, Oxfam House, John Smith Drive, Cowley, Oxford OX4 2JY, UK. www.oxfam.org.uk. Oxfam does not necessarily endorse any text or activities that accompany the materials.

As Bauman (2013) argues, the richness of the few does not benefit the many, a sentiment shared by Freeland (2013), who argues that we are now living in the age of the global plutocracy, as a result, in part, of `lower taxes, deregulation, particularly of financial services, privatization, weaker legal protections for trade unions', all of which `have contributed to more and more income going to the very, very top'. According to Freeland, the main reasons for the rise of the new global plutocracy, however, are the twin elements of 21st century globalization and the digital technologies that enable it. From sparks of innovation with algorithms and applications entrepreneurs can become extremely rich extremely quickly through being able to be born globally with minimal friction.

WHAT WOULD YOU DO?

WHAT WOULD YOU DO?

The wealth amassed by the elites has not 'trickled down', neither nationally within specific states nor globally, in the relations between states. In terms of world inequality, the extremely wealthy are becoming holders of more concentrated wealth, while the poor, both nationally and globally, are becoming relatively, and in some cases absolutely, poorer: 'Moreover: people who are rich are getting richer just *because* they are rich. People who are poor get poorer just *because* they are poor' (Bauman, 2013).

What would you do if you were a policy maker? Think of the issue, especially, in terms of corporate taxation policy.

Do you think that cutting corporate tax rates creates more wealth for investment that trickles down through increased employment?

DIGITAL ORGANIZATION

An increase in knowledge-intensive work means that organizations have to employ – and manage – different kinds of employees. Brains not brawn, mental rather than manual labour, are the order of the day. Employees need to be capable of working with sophisticated databases, software and knowledge-management systems. These have to be related to customer and client requirements, often on a unique and tailored basis that deploys a common platform while customizing it for specific requirements. Thus, technical and relational skills will be at a premium.

Tacit knowledge enables you to speak grammatically or ride a bike: you can do it but it would be hard explaining how to a novice.

Knowledge-intensive work, according to Alvesson's (2004) research, depends on much subtle **tacit knowledge** as well as explicit mastery. In such a situation, working according to instruction and command will not be an effective way of managing or being managed, especially where the employee is involved in design and other forms of creative work on a team basis, often organized in projects. In such situations, increasingly common in contemporary work, 'because of the high degree of independence and discretion to use their own judgment, knowledge workers and other professionals often require a leadership based on informal peer interaction rather than hierarchical authority' (Sandberg and Targama, 2007: 4). As we will explore in Chapters 4 and 5, some of the old theories and approaches to leadership and project work need updating.

Knowledge workers, almost universally, are digital workers. The digital economy is a terrain with rich pickings for those who know how to exploit it. For instance, in the digital economy Facebook friends and likes are a valuable field because they comprise a network premised on assumptions of identity and, as Lakoff (2014) notes, people vote and buy in terms of their identity, their values and those they identify with. Messaging and websites that affirm that sense of identity as they disaffirm the identity of those significant others that one opposes and that oppose one have become commonplace. In such a context, whoever has the most resources of money, domain names, data, bots and technology has stacked the best odds for effecting closure to their advantage.

Electronic media buttresses digitally enhanced 'tribalism', in which boundary maintenance is accomplished through the network of like-minded feeds that occupy the targeted groups' social media and preferred websites, creating what Merleau-Ponty (1964) referred to as a bubble. As Bauman (2017: 50) suggests, it is the emotional significance that is important. What provides legitimacy is inscribed within the digital bubble and the shared imagined experiences of those who subscribe to it. What are produced are bubbles of highly situational emotionality in which reason, in the classical sense, has little purchase because legitimacy increasingly is inscribed in a shared sense of emotionality rather than a shared rationality. These bubbles can also be exploited commercially through building brand loyalty, as Apple has done so well.

The emergence of a digital platform economy enables broad recourse to a market type of governance by organizations, using spot contracts, dramatically reducing transaction costs and making it easier to assess the contribution of providers. Today, the digital economy employs far fewer people than the old corporates: for instance, Uber has over 160,000 'driver-partners' in the USA but recognizes only about 2,000 people as actual employees. The sharing economy is not an employing economy – at best, it develops self-employment and self-exploitation. Freedom and participation in the platform economy come at the cost of a reduction in responsibility and accountability for those who are the contractors/platform managers. The rise of 'freelancing' platforms can enable subjects who might otherwise be excluded from the market to accumulate experience and visibility, at the cost of a commodification and marketization of everything. The main contractors in the platform economy neither acknowledge nor bear any responsibility for the wellbeing of their providers. In the platform economy, the transaction the providers enter into is everything: if transactions dry up, so does the money.

There is also a parallel 'currency' to that of money, based on vanity and popularity, which automatically assesses the 'value' of an organization or individual's contribution. Money does not have to be invested in resources for editorial selection as the audience selects what is 'worthy', while the platform provider extracts value from the generated 'traffic'. Individuals are offering their labour not in exchange for money but for visibility, public approval, 'likes' and 'fame'. However, these assets appear to be very perishable: the owners of the game keep on accumulating hard currency and the surplus value they appropriate increases, since they can pay a great portion of the labour cost with the contemporary equivalent of 'beads for the savages'. Contemporary expressions of this are the rise of the **gig economy** and the employment of unpaid interns, seeking favour, rather than wage earners.

Gig economy participation in a labour market characterized by the prevalence of short-term contracts or freelance work as opposed to permanent jobs.

Considerable opportunity arises from within the digital economy. An increasing reliance on input and meta-data from users and customers means that organizations now have to handle the blowback that comes with the ability of critics and opponents to ironize or critique strategic choices made with marketing strategies. Managerial fiat can be widely and easily challenged. New media generate sharing, idea creation, participation and criticism that dissolve distinctions between organizations with their strategies and environments as objectively external determinants. The boundaries of the firm dissolve. New media can enable both discerning customers and ardent critics to become involved in framing or even co-producing management's strategic choices. It affords a powerful source of pressure for different conceptions of good strategy that can directly reach customers, users, employees and suppliers.

Control is increasingly distributed across a network of actors, including new media and their users. It is a diminishingly private sphere of management control alone. Hackers can seize an organization's social media projections; they can critique, ridicule and ironize them, and they can disrupt them through sabotage. Equally, digital affordances mean that distinct organizations can work together, provided there is trust, empathy and commitment on all sides. Boundaries, choices and control are all shifting in the direction of increasing fluidity and plurality. Moreover, it is evident that, in these days, if we are bereft of our digital devices and their affordances, we are less than fully human – McLuhan's (1964) hypothesis that the media become extensions of our nervous systems holds even more so than when first formulated. The nature of being an individual is changing as anyone can be connected anywhere, anytime through social media. On the one hand, social media can build rapid momentum in mobilizing blocs of voters or consumers; on the other hand, it can be used as a means of distraction and appeasement. We use digital devices to make us members of those communities we co-create and share; they network our proclivities, interests and desires; they create the digital bubbles in which we live. These networks evolve as communities over time (Fosfuri et al., 2011).

WATCH A VIDEO ABOUT HOLOCRACY

Digital affordances have been the means through which some organizations, such as Zappos, an American shoe manufacturer (see the case study later in the book), have embraced self-management, known as 'holacracy'. Behind Zappos' endorsement of self-management stands a company called HolacracyOne, which has been developing organization design based on self-managing circles since 2007. In holacracy, vertical hierarchy is replaced with overlapping and concentric circles dedicated to specific functions in which circle members can pursue other projects if the circle's work is completed. There might be an overall circle of marketing, for instance. Within this circle, there might be a team dedicated to improving user experience – the UX team.

Digital affordances are important for holacracy. In an interview, Tony Hsieh (2017), CEO of Zappos, talked about how the organization had developed self-management on a digital platform:

> Our org chart is available in real-time online and changes probably 50 times a day, and every one of our 1,500 employees can transparently view what every employee's purposes and accountabilities are. We have self-organized governance methods and meetings that happen on a regular basis, and it's all browsable and updateable online, along with, occasionally, policy updates – all of which enables any employee to contribute to the evolving structure of the organization. (*McKinsey Quarterly*, October 2017)

These digital affordances align with a definite organizational approach that seeks to empower all 1,500 employees to be 'sensors' – active sensemakers – who can bring the gap between what is and what is possible to the attention of the other sensemakers in the organization. Deeply embedded in Zappos, according to CEO Hseih, are core values that were crowdsourced internally and refined. These help make common sense in interpreting the gaps between the actualities and the possibilities. There is a strong sense of purpose at Zappos as well, aligned with an internal market for ideas and innovation: 'different internal teams become customers of each other. We're building an internal currency as well as the internal tools and systems to support an underlying infrastructure to allow for multiple participants, fast feedback loops, and things like crowdsourced participation', says Hseih. To make the internal currency more engaged and active, employees are concentrated in spaces for conviviality, where chance encounters can occur, ideas swapped and projects started.

Kallinikos (2006) argues that digital technologies allow tasks that were previously embedded in the 'fixed space' of traditional organizations (for example, accounting, inventory management, production operations or financial management) to be dissolved and recomposed as 'informatised' modules or services (Kallinikos, 2006: 96), such as Zappos' circles became. Digital technologies are implicated in an historic shift dissolving bureaucratic organization. The major advantage of digital technologies for business and organizations is their virtual possibilities for disaggregating existing designs. Increasingly, organizations are able to segment activities that are critical to their competitive advantage and to specialize elsewhere those that are not in low-wage-cost countries, or by substituting machines for human intelligence.

Machine intelligence is based on algorithms. What algorithms do most easily is to capture and replicate routines; that is why algorithms increasingly replace human labour in, for example, booking flights or hotels, or searching for basic information. Algorithms are better than laborious, slower and less skilled human energy at accomplishing routine tasks. What happens to the people whose jobs are displaced? Basically, they will have to participate in education and training that boosts their skill formation, or fall by the wayside as labour surplus to contemporary requirements.

Algorithms afford no room for critical reflection or for adjustment based on the acknowledgement of the (often unforeseen) consequences of our actions such as the distortions of the gig economy. Hence, they represent the purest form of technically rational management. On the other hand, human management (may) involve emotions, such as compassion, which emerge as a safeguard against the effects of the separation between decision, action and (moral) consequences.

Algorithms, built by extraordinarily creative mathematicians, can disrupt and transform whole industries: Uber is the most obvious example. Even more dramatically, intelligent machines can use inference based on patterns established by machine learning in big data. How these patterns are identified may well be inscrutable to the expert programmers who initially programmed the machines. The machines are just too smart. The merger of physical, digital and biological technologies is already producing a new breed of robots, which are discussed in a fascinating Ted Talk by Leila Takayama.

WATCH THE TED TALK

The clearest example of what artificial intelligence means comes from the outcome of a series of Go games, the traditional East Asian game. Unlike chess, which machines can be programmed to play through deductive logic that is based on the explicit rules of chess, Go is a game with an almost infinite number of possible moves. The winners of Go games have highly intuitive pattern recognition that they use to play their moves. The game in question occurred on 15 March 2016 when a Go grandmaster, Korean Lee Sedol, lost a Go tournament 4–1. What was remarkable was that he was not beaten by another grandmaster but by an AI program designed by Google engineers, called AlphaGo. AlphaGo was a smart intelligence – an arrangement of artificial networks analogous to neural networks – that developed its Go strategy by playing millions of games against itself and building a repertoire of pattern recognition in unsupervised learning.

What are the implications for future organizations? Two researchers, Frey and Osborne (2017), argued that half the jobs in the US economy were likely to be eliminated by algorithms for big data based upon pattern recognition that can readily substitute for labour in a wide range of non-routine cognitive tasks (Brynjolfsson and McAfee, 2011; Phillips, 2013). Combined with the fact that advanced robots are gaining sensemaking capabilities and manual dexterity, the nature of work across industries and occupations is likely to change dramatically. On this basis, they identified nearly 50 per cent of existing jobs as being under threat of routinization and disappearance within a decade.

The modelling that Frey and Osborne (2017) conducted predicted that most workers in transportation and logistics occupations, the bulk of office and administrative support workers, labour in production occupations and a substantial share of employment in service occupations, the site of the most recent US job growth (Autor and Dorn, 2013), are highly susceptible to computerization, the growth in the market for service robots (Phillips, 2013) and the concomitant gradual diminution of any comparative advantage human labour might have in tasks involving mobility and dexterity (Phillips, 2013; Peters, 2017).

READ MORE ABOUT ADOBE

Adobe hosted a colloquium on the future of work in early 2018 that is available on the Internet, in which a range of views exploring possible futures can be heard. The discussion takes off from the premise that profound advances across physical, digital and biological realms are ushering in the Fourth Industrial Revolution (4IR) which, unlike previous eras, is not driven by a single technology but by the convergence of developments in AI, machine learning, biomedical technology, virtual reality and other areas.

MANAGING AS SENSEMAKING

For the past 40 years or so, the predominant sense of what an organization should be has been modelled on lean and efficient private-sector organizations that are profit-oriented. In organizations modelled as thus, managing involves top management teams seeking to set a common frame within which organization members, customers, suppliers, investors, and so on, can make common sense of the organization – what it is and what it does. This is called **sensemaking**.

sensemaking is the process through which individuals and groups explain novel, unexpected or confusing events

Weick (2008) defines sensemaking as the ongoing retrospective development of plausible images that rationalize what people are doing.

Sensemaking, or the process through which individuals and groups explain novel, unexpected or confusing events, is critically important in the study of organizations (Maitlis and Christianson, 2014). We are constantly making sense, revising past rationalizations in the light of new information, knowledge and events that were not previously available to us. Sensemaking brackets and labels as the flow of events is broken into blocks of 'sense' that can be categorized and described with language. Meaning is constructed in an ongoing process where past experience informs the present (Maitlis and Christianson, 2014). Sometimes organization leaders bring new phenomena to the attention of people; at other times, events are so disruptive it is impossible not to register the phenomena that they bring to attention. Interaction with others is essential to constructing a shared view, if coordinated action is to occur through shared scripts and coterminous accounts (Steigenberger, 2015).

Considering the definition of sensemaking given in the margin above, we can explore each of its terms in a little more detail:

- *Ongoing*: We are always making sense – we never stop doing so, even when asleep – our dreams are ways of making sense of deep issues that we must deal with in our wakeful moments. Our sense of what we are experiencing is always of the moment – fleeting, experiential, changing and contextual.
- *Retrospective*: We make sense of something as it is elapsing and we are constantly reviewing the sense we make in terms of additional sense data.
- *Plausible*: We never make perfect but rather provisional sense, sense that is good enough for the matter and people at hand. It allows us to go on with what we are trying to do. While accuracy may be desirable, reasonable constructions that are continuously updated work better as directional guides, especially when things are changing fast.
- *Images*: We often work with representations of things – models, plans and mental maps – as we navigate our way around unfamiliar territory. We hear what the other is saying and try to accommodate it to things we already know and carry round with us as our stock of knowledge.
- *Rationalize*: We rationalize the meaning of things that are confusing to make them clearer and justifiable.
- *People*: Although organizations contain many things that act which are not people – such as computers and keypads – it is people who do the sensemaking.

- *Doing*: We do things through thinking and action, which define one another. Weick uses a rhetorical question, 'How can I know what I think until I see what I say?' The point he is making is that when people act they discover their goals, which may be different even when we think we are dealing with the same cues. Enactment is the key: what I enact may be very different from what you enact.

In doing sensemaking, the identity of the person making sense is important: who the person is, their role and the legitimacy that others attach to their capabilities for making sense will frame the reception of the sense made. Sense will be enacted through storytelling, usually expressed as a narrative account of experience, perceptions and sensemaking (Weick, 1995). Such narratives are usually shared and constructed in conversations with others as a *social activity* (Hernes and Maitlis, 2010; Maitlis, 2005).

In organizations, managers want to try and have their employees make the same sense. However, you make individual sense of what's happening around you. You use your sense data – sight, sound, touch, taste and smell – to assemble impressions of unfolding events and then use your cognitive capacities to make a pattern from the data. The sense you make is always *your* sense but you never do so in isolation. You use many cues to make sense: past experience, what others say they think is happening, likely stories that you are familiar with that seem to fit the pattern that appears to be forming, and so on. People will not use these cues in a uniform way, because they are individuals and, as a result, people can make wildly different senses from the same set of cues. A significant part of managing is to try and cue people in similar processes of pattern making to fit clues and cues together and make common meaning out of them. Managers create a frame, enabling things to be connected together to make coherent sense. Once we have the frame, we can make sense. Managing entails **framing**.

Framing By framing we decide on what is relevant from the infinite number of stimuli, behavioural cues, sense data and information that surround us.

A frame is a term that comes from the cinema: a director frames a shot by including some detail and omitting other detail. A frame defines what is relevant. All managing involves framing: separating that which deserves focus from that which does not. One thing that managers have to do all the time is to differentiate between the relevant and the irrelevant.

Framing involves the creation of devices that assign meaning to organizational situations (Fairhurst, 1993). Framing entails the ideational use of metaphors, the repetition of stories, the citing of traditions, the articulation of slogans and the material creation of artefacts to highlight or contrast a particular organizational issue (Deetz et al., 2000). Framing is what leaders do, especially when they are seeking to reframe in the case of organizational change (Fairhurst and Sarr, 1996). Framing mobilizes followers through the judicious use of images, symbols and language. Framing occurs not only through sensemaking but also through sensegiving and sensebreaking.

Sensegiving attempts to influence the sensemaking of others so that others come to accept a preferred meaning.

Sensebreaking occurs when organizational members disrupt existing sense in order to make alternative sense.

IN PRACTICE

Darkest hour

A recently released movie, *Darkest Hour*, directed by Joe Wright (2017), captures some of the most famous framing in British history. The occasion was 4 June 1940, with the evacuation of British and allied French troops from Dunkirk in full swing in the face of an overwhelming advance by German troops. The scene was set in the House of Commons when the prime minister, Winston Churchill, rose to make a statement in which he said the following:

READ THE FULL SPEECH

We shall fight them ...

Even though large tracts of Europe and many old and famous States have fallen or may fall into the grip of the Gestapo and all the odious apparatus of Nazi rule, we shall not flag or fail.

We shall go on to the end, we shall fight in France, we shall fight on the seas and oceans, we shall fight with growing confidence and growing strength in the air, we shall defend our Island, whatever the cost may be, we shall fight on the beaches, we shall fight on the landing grounds, we shall fight in the fields and in the streets, we shall fight in the hills; we shall never surrender, and even if, which I do not for a moment believe, this Island or a large part of it were subjugated and starving, then our Empire beyond the seas, armed and guarded by the British Fleet, would carry on the struggle, until, in God's good time, the New World, with all its power and might, steps forth to the rescue and the liberation of the old.

The framing that Churchill produced communicated the current predicament and set an agenda for possible futures (Fairhurst, 1993).

Questions

1. Who do you think were the audiences for this speech, in addition to the MPs to whom it was addressed?
2. What are some of the reasons that you think it was as effective as it was in stiffening the resolve of a country that, at this stage, was alone in the European theatre in its struggle against Nazi Germany, as neither the Soviet Union nor the USA had yet entered the war on the Allied side?
3. What sensebreaking and what sensegiving was it providing?

Leaders often employ sensegiving during strategic change (Gioia and Chittipeddi, 1991) and this was obviously part of Churchill's intent. In part, he also sought to defeat, by sensebreaking, those in his government who entertained the prospects of a treaty with Germany and a negotiated surrender.

Churchill was breaking the sense made by prominent proponents of appeasement in his government, such as Lord Halifax and his predecessor as prime minister, Neville Chamberlain, who in the lead-up to the outbreak of war had favoured allowing Hitler to extend German territory through occupation. In the speech cited, he reaffirmed his commitment through unequivocal sensemaking in favour of 'no surrender'. In emergency situations, such as the UK faced in 1940, the real sense of emergency aids common sensemaking. In such situations, a leader's role is to make, break and give sense to events. Churchill did all three. In terms of sensebreaking, Churchill broke any sense of appeasement as a strategy, a position that he had long argued for as a relatively lonely voice in Parliament. He made sense of the defeats in France in such a way that did not see them leading to ultimate defeat but to further fighting on the part of a country that would never surrender. He gave sense by signalling to the USA – the New World – that it should join the struggle. Leader sensegiving shapes processes of organizational sensemaking and the process of constructing accounts by directing attention to specific cues (Maitlis and Lawrence, 2007).

Sensemaking has both social and cognitive elements (Maitlis and Christianson, 2014). Issues such as the performative role of emotion in strategic conversations are important (Liu and Maitlis, 2014). A leader's sensemaking has a strong emotional element (Helpap and Bekmeier-Feuerhahn, 2016; Maitlis et al., 2013). The stentorian tone and physical embodiment of Churchill's voice, sonorous and deep, conveyed emotionally the gravity of the situation and the steeliness and resolve of the response. Emotion matters in sensegiving: information served up dispassionately, perhaps in a text, is very different from information transmitted with theatrical skill, performative ability and dramatic intent – qualities Churchill had in depth.

IN PRACTICE

The Crown

Organizations that endure, that enjoy longevity, have the opportunity to draw on deep wells of past sensemaking to ensure their continuity with the past, at least rhetorically, and to guide their progress into the future – as long as the future is not subject to disruption by disjunctive radical innovation. We usually call the kind of sensemaking such organizations rely on 'tradition'. The enactment of tradition is central to historically long-lived organizations, such as monarchies, churches, universities and also some businesses. Some of you may have seen the television series dealing with the British monarchy after the death of George VI and the ascension of Queen Elizabeth II to the throne, called *The Crown*. In the earlier episodes, where the young Elizabeth is coming to terms with the complex role that she must now occupy as the heir to the throne, there is considerable emphasis placed on the role and indeed the sanctity of tradition in defining the institution of the monarchy. Courtiers are the vital organizational agents who translate theses traditions for the young queen who finds herself as much constrained as empowered by her elevation in status.

Review

Review episode 7, series 1 if it is available to the class. Pay particular attention to the role played in relation to the new queen by Sir Alan Frederick 'Tommy' Lascelles, her private secretary. Note the title of the episode: it successfully weaves together several thematically related conflicts in different areas of the new queen's life. Of particular interest is her attempt to define what her power and her role actually consist of when it comes to questions of protocol and hierarchy. The queen is trying to negotiate between old systems of tradition and new ones that don't even fully exist yet. Tommy is the custodian of the institution in which the queen strives to be more than a cipher and their power relations mirror a reality other than the organizational ritual.

Question

1. What are the organizational and power relational implications of the role Tommy Lascelles plays?

Tradition is one basis for sensemaking, as MacLean, Harvey, Sillince and Golant (2014) found when doing archival and oral history research on organizational change at Procter & Gamble from 1930 to 2000, focusing on periods of transition. They examine historical narrative as a vehicle for sensemaking by top managers and find that the past is constantly used as a recurrent lever of strategic manoeuvres and re-orientations. Executives (re)interpret the past to author the future, ensuring ideological consistency over time, much as do the courtiers that attend the monarch. Another is to assert the legitimacy of rational sensemaking, in accordance with professionalized knowledge, compared with other points of view, as we shall explore next.

MANAGERIAL RATIONALITY

When managers claim to be able to make decisions that deny legitimacy to other forms of knowledge based on their generalized managerial competence, this is termed **managerialism**. Managerialism often seeks to justify the application of managerial techniques to all areas of society on the grounds of managers' expert training and exclusive possession of managerial knowledge (Klikauer, 2013: 2–3). The belief in management as a means capable of solving any problem elevates the necessity of management into an **ideology** of the modern world.

Managerialism claims managers manage on the grounds of exclusive education and the possession of codified bodies of knowledge.

Managers that espouse the ideology of managerialism assume that organizations should be normatively integrated by a single source of authority, legitimacy and decision-making embedded in the managerial hierarchy that controls the organization. Hence, despite the fact that organizations often have multiple sources of official formal meaning, they seek to constrain sensemaking within only the managerial frame. For instance, many organizations contain members who are represented by unions, which will formulate views that may well conflict with that of management. In a pluralist organizational setting, it is recognized that

An **ideology** is a coherent set of beliefs, attitudes and opinions. The meaning is often pejorative, with a contrast drawn between ideology and science.

management and the unions will often hold competing but legitimate views on an issue. Unions are formal organizations that need to be managed; just as other organizations, they use IT, maintain websites and offer benefits and services to members.

Economic rationalism argues that markets and prices are the *only reliable* indices of value, delivering better outcomes than states and bureaucracies.

Managerialism is essentially a construct that emerged in profit-making organizations as an expression of **economic rationalism**.

For many students and teachers in business schools, the whole point of sensemaking in business organizations is to be economically rational, signified by making a profit. Profit is what accrues to the owners of organizations after all the costs of using **capital** have been met, such as interest charged, debt repayment, wages and salaries, supplier costs and taxes.

Capital is an asset owned with the intention of delivering a return to the owner, implying a complex set of relations of ownership and control.

It is not just financial capital that needs to be managed, however. As well as *financial capital*, required to ensure that an enterprise is a 'going concern', there is also, very importantly, *symbolic capital* (above all, that intangible thing called 'reputation') as well as social capital that refers to whom you know and how you are known rather than what you own or what you know; social capital is the set of relations and knowledge embedded in those relations that you are able to mobilize. For instance, in business schools students not only learn from the formal curriculum but also make social contacts that they can relate to later in their business career. It is through this knowledge and the tools that are learnt in the classroom as well as the contacts made that management students will become accomplished sensemakers, running organizations with broad-based know-how and know-who.

READ THE ARTICLE

EXTEND YOUR KNOWLEDGE

In Andreas, S. (2018) 'Effects of the decline of social capital on college graduates' soft skills', *Industry and Higher Education*, 32(1): DOI: 0950422217749277, which is available at the companion website https://study.sagepub.com/managingandorganizations5e, the author argues that through building social capital, college students gain the cultural and behavioural information and sensitivity they need to learn soft skills. She sees a worrying decline in this learning occurring, due to the decrease in building social capital through face-to-face interaction.

Metaphors frame sensemaking by using terms other than those of the subject under discussion to describe that subject, such as aiming for the 'premier league'.

Capital is literally liquid assets; social capital is a **metaphor**. Creating a metaphor always involves the literal meaning of a phrase or word being applied to a new context in a figurative sense. Metaphors influence the way we describe, analyse and think about things. As Morgan (1986) has argued, it is the metaphor of the machine that is most preponderant in its application to managing and organizations. So, when rationality is attributed to managers and organizations, it is often done in terms of machine-like properties, such as 'the organization runs like clockwork'. Managers commonly use metaphors in practice. One study, by Latusek and Vlaar (2015), found that the common metaphors in use by a cross-national selection of managers, in respect of their day-to-day interactions in relationships with suppliers and clients, was to see them as if they were performing acts, playing games and fighting battles.

Other research has pointed to the ways in which employees are increasingly exhorted to become 'brand ambassadors' for their organizations. These metaphorical phrases provide linguistic framing for internal branding and simultaneously convey conflicting messages to different stakeholder groups. These metaphors describe internal branding as empowering employees to be autonomous and encouraging them to take control over the brand, while also pointing to a hidden value system that values brands higher than employees. The metaphors in use reflect a value system in which the financial value of brands is paramount.

EXTEND YOUR KNOWLEDGE

READ THE ARTICLE

In Müller, M. (2017) '"Brandspeak": metaphors and the rhetorical construction of internal branding', *Organization*, 25 (1): doi/abs/10.1177/1350508417710831, which is available at the companion website https://study.sagepub.com/managingandorganizations5e, the insidious organizational use of seemingly innocuous metaphors is explored.

Most organizational life is lived through highly professionalized routines. Organizations that are highly professionalized host many different forms of specialist knowledge, each with their specific rationalities. Consider the example of hospitals, places that can be surprisingly dangerous for patients. One reason for this is that the patient's body becomes the point of intersection of many different professional practices, such as radiography, anaesthetics, operative care, post-operative care, and so on. At each handover point, there will be inscriptions – readings, charts, data printouts, briefings – that are passed from one team to another. Unfortunately, these present lots of opportunities for people to make different sense of the situation. Sometimes inscriptions will be misunderstood, sometimes improperly read or communicated, at other times they will be faulty, and sometimes just plain wrong. Organizations are full of handover situations: when inspection comes into play; when training takes over; when memos are sent and instructions issued from one subunit to another. All of these offer ample opportunity for recipients to make plausible sense of incomplete details – and, hopefully, not have to be subsequently accountable for the sense that they did or did not make at the time (Weick and Sutcliffe, 2003).

Relationally, sensemaking, sensegiving and sensebreaking are different ways of mediating the flow of sense data that provides your informational environment. Sensemaking is the formulation of accounts of what's going on; sensegiving is the strategic attempt to frame others' perceptions to accord with the sense that you are making; and sensebreaking is the strategic attempt to disrupt existing flows of sensemaking and sensegiving. Sensemaking, sensegiving and sensebreaking have all become popular topics in the management literature, especially sensegiving, perhaps for the reason that it maps on to leadership competencies most evidently. Leaders are expected to frame the sense that others make, recruiting and enrolling them as followers in their sensemaking. Sensegiving has been researched in academic environments (Gioia and Chittipedi, 1991), amongst business leaders (Maclean et al., 2012), within a British division of a multinational company (Balogun et al., 2015) and in a corporate spin-off (Corley and Gioia), amongst many studies too numerous to enumerate. There are numerous studies of middle managers managing change by sensegiving (Balogun, 2003; Hope, 2010; Huy, 2002; Rouleau, 2005). Sensemaking and sensegiving amongst employees have been researched in various contexts: animal shelters (Schabram and Maitlis, 2017), a design consulting firm (Stigliani and Ravisi, 2012), a Fortune 500 retailer (Sonenshein and Dholakia, 2012), an empowerment programme for nurses (Bartunek et al., 2006), practices of communication professionals (Cornelissen, 2012), ethics training (Brown et al., 2008); and a number of articles seek to make sense of sensemaking by surveying the literature (for example, Brown et al., 2008, 2015; Helms Mills et al., 2010).

Sensemaking is a particularly acute issue in moments of crisis. The origin of much of the sensemaking literature was in Weick's (1993) analysis of the Mann Gulch Incident, in which some firefighters lost their lives because they did not drop their tools in the face of a forest fire moving at speed towards them. Dropping their tools would have enabled them to run for cover behind a ridge. Sensemaking continues to be a concern in crisis situations. Certain occupations have a strong need for accurate sensemaking, for instance in monitoring equipment upon which split-second life and death decisions need to be made. Pilots are a case in point, as analysis by Berthod and Müller-Seitz (2017) explores in the analysis of a brief failure of one item on the display of the information system (IS) on Flight AF 447, wreaking havoc in the coordination between the pilots and the aircraft, leading to the loss of all 228 lives on board.

READ THE ARTICLE

EXTEND YOUR KNOWLEDGE

In Berthod, O. and Müller-Seitz, G. (2017) 'Making sense in pitch darkness: an exploration of the sociomateriality of sensemaking in crises', *Journal of Management Inquiry*, 27 (1): 52–68, which is available at the companion website https://study.sagepub.com/managingandorganizations5e, the authors explore how the instruments supposed to ensure our safety and make organizations more reliable can lead a team to destruction. Reliance on instrumentation in highly automated systems can develop an attitude of 'mindful indifference' (i.e. the capacity for experienced operators to distinguish problems that could turn into critical ones from problems that can be tolerated on account of the overall system reliability) that provokes emotional distress, focusing the pilots' attention on the machine, instead of triggering an organizational process of sensemaking, in a crisis situation.

Organizations are full of plausible stories – rumour, gossip, official statements, business plans and websites – each making sense in its own way but none necessarily coherent with the others. People talk all the time at work. Much of what they say is formal: the transmission of instructions and information; the making and taking of orders; the analysis of data and artefacts; debating issues in meetings, or making speeches and presentations. Yet, *even more is not formal*, which is to say that it is neither constitutive of, nor mandated by, the occupational and organizational roles that organization members fill, such as gossip, which is, nonetheless, a vital part of organizational life. The gossip surrounding the 45th incumbent of the most important organizational role in the world, president of the United States, is a case in point.

READ ABOUT TRUMP & GOSSIP

Stories are a major medium of communication, circulating and changing with the telling. Managing means implementing schemes, themes and dreams for the future, contained in the official stories, the business plans, the missions and visions. These are some of the tools of management. Managers use many tools to get things done: accounting systems, resource planning models, and so on. These tools are designed to be rational instruments to aid managing. But management tools only work insofar as they are made sense of. If managers are not successful in positioning their tools as decisive in sensemaking, then it may well be stories circulating smears, fears and nightmares that define the future.

Sometimes tools work smoothly and paper over the little cracks that may occur in different understandings of a situation. However, while trying to fix everyone's sensemaking on management's terms is a powerful device, it can create a fair degree of cynicism and contestation on the part of other stakeholders when managerial interpretations are argued to be the only ones that count. An example of this is when presidential accusations of unwanted sensemaking are termed 'fake news'. The adage 'If you cannot bring good news, then don't bring any', makes a good concluding line to a song (Dylan, 1967) but a bad assumption for a senior manager to make, especially a president.

Omniscience is a not a wise claim for any manager to make. The most rational managers never have perfect knowledge of alternatives. They do not have a calculus for every action nor can every action be accounted for in quantitative terms. Some actions have value that is expressed morally, ethically and socially rather than economically, as matters of instinct or habit. Most organization and management theorists are sceptical about the capacity of human decision-making to be utterly rational. Instead, they prefer to see people as only ever rational within the bounds of their knowledge and ignorance; that is, they see people characterized by **bounded rationality**.

Bounded rationality means producing satisfactory rather than optimally rational decisions, a process referred to as 'satisficing', meaning accepting decisions that are both sufficient and satisfying.

Conditions of uncertainty are often characteristic of decision-making situations. In situations of uncertainty, individuals act inconsistently (and thus other than wholly rationally). We discuss this further in Chapter 3. The crucial thing is to *appear to be rational* by having all of the symbols of rationality in place.

Managerialist rationality places managers in control, symbolizing that they know what they are doing and positioning them as authoritative. Sometimes, as some feminist critics suggest, managerial rationality seems a peculiarly masculine view of the world (Ferguson, 1984), which we discuss in terms of gendered communication in Chapter 9. The rational attributes of decision-making are equated with male characteristics in contrast to the way that women have been represented as being emotional, capricious, unsystematic and irrational (also see Calás and Smircich, 2006).

A belief in rationality can become a self-fulfilling prophecy, a myth of rationality: if what managers define as rational is resisted then the resistance simply shows the irrationality that has to be reformed (Fleming and Spicer, 2008). For instance, when managers implementing reforms encounter widespread **resistance to change**, they tend to see the resistance as irrational. Resistance serves as additional evidence for managers of the rightness of the reforms being resisted and so

Resistance to change consists of those organizational activities and attitudes that aim to thwart, undermine and impede change initiatives.

a vicious cycle of more control generating more resistance often ensues. Hence, it is not surprising that resistance to change is a widely observed phenomenon in organizations. Such resistance can be overt, in the form of wildcat strikes, campaigns or other forms of collective action, or it can be covert, through attempts at undermining change programmes by the widespread adoption of cynicism, irony and ambivalence.

Resistance can sometimes be thought of as an attempt to assert an alternative rationality. Claims to management knowledge that position it as rational often assume all other claims are merely the promotion of sectional, self-interested and irrational strategies. A unitary view of organizations is a major strategy in promoting managerial rationalities. Often, the argument is that where there is resistance, more work must be done in building commitment on the part of HRM (see Chapter 5); otherwise, people would not resist! According to this view, if reason prevailed there would be total commitment and no resistance.

People make sense through their understanding of the world, their interpretations of other people and those things that populate their world. Some of the categories and devices that are used for making sense will be shared with other members of the organization and some will not. Some will be regarded as legitimate by the organization while others will not. Organization members will build their practices on their understandings (Baunsgaard and Clegg, 2013). Rationalities will always be situated in different practices and accounts, some of which will have far more legitimacy in certain contexts than will others. From this perspective, plural rationalities that do not necessarily agree will be the norm.

Many managers manage as if the world depicted and represented in their view of rationality was actually as controlled and controllable as they think is the case. Rarely, given the ingenuity that different stakeholders bring to sensemaking, can this illusion be sustained, because we rarely share a common sense. Employees, customers and suppliers work from different interests. Doing this makes managing a highly politicized and contested activity. One reason it is highly politicized and contested is that management is always dealing with change; things never stay the same.

GLOBAL SHIFTS

One implication of the growth in artificial intelligence, as Takayama suggests, is the development of much more team-based working in which robot intelligence is an integral part of a team that is often project-based and globally connected, whose members require skills of empathy, the ability to listen and learn from others and to be creatively curious. Rather than leadership skills being the preserve of an elite of authorities, they will need to be flexible elements of the way different team members' work.

Associated with organizational decomposition is a parallel spatial decomposition. The global division of labour, the associated asymmetry of power relations and the social systems hosting them are the result of an always-unfolding spatial process (Löw, 2009). Each long wave cycle of accumulation is associated with a spatial configuration, a global pattern of interdependent technologies, infrastructure, institutions, networks and social relations and ideologies that structure the distribution and direction of global flows of capital and labour (Albrecht, 2014).

Spatially, we have been accustomed to a long cycle of US dominance, with the two post-war countries of Germany and Japan sharing in the profits.

Times are changing: the new centre of manufacturing employment in the global economy is tilting towards Asia, especially China and its semi-periphery states in East Asia. Europe and the USA are ceding centrality, once again, to Asia (Darwin, 2007). The global realignment of the economic centre, peripheries and semi-peripheries means that the major regions of capitalist investment are no longer in the Western world but are in Asia, under the conditions of capitalisms that differ markedly from those of the liberal and social democracies of the West. Global changes have local effects. Wages have stagnated or gone down in the West for over three decades as hundreds of millions in Asia and Eastern Europe have entered the global workforce. Such a massive increase in the supply of labour, which depressed wages in the core countries of the advanced economies, was great news for capitalists but not so good for most people outside the metropolitan cities of the global economy. Adding to these pressures is the cult of disruptive entrepreneurship that threatens the livelihood and serenity of millions who work in the 'gig economy', providing only an 'entrepreneurial option', one that, in practice, is the equivalent of either a lottery ticket or a disguised precariousness.

Meusburger (2006) argues that symmetric social relations of power, dominance and control manifest themselves in spatial disparities. Both functionally and symbolically, knowledge and power tend towards spatial concentration, whereas low-skilled routine activities in production and administration show a trend towards dispersion and decentralization. The former comprise the core components of the global spatial economy, not only in terms of the financial and related capabilities concentrated in the major global cities but also in terms of design capabilities. Design and capital dominate and locate in the cores; networked and subcontracted manufacturing populates the margins in a network society. Managerial rationality laces the network together.

There are consequences for jobs when much of the routine is extracted and repositioned through artificial intelligence. The remaining core staff will need to be more skilled than before. They will be working in technological environments subject to rapid and radical change. They will be globally connected, working with people remotely as well as face to face, from many different languages, ethnicities, cultures and religions. New competencies and skills will be required. Managing will mean more developmental work oriented to renewing staff's specific skills and general competencies, rather than issuing imperative commands and generally exercising authority over lower skilled labour. Managing will mean negotiating the use and understanding of new technologies, contexts and capabilities, and facilitating the understanding of those who will be operating with the new tools and environments. Sensemaking will be increasingly digitally and technologically mediated.

Digital technologies and a growing international division of labour between economies specialized in services and production make the world economy increasingly globalized. Competition is based less on traditional comparative advantage as a result of what economists call 'factor endowments', such as being close to raw materials, and more on competitive advantages that arise from innovation and enterprise. Global competition goes hand in hand with outsourcing in industries, as firms exploit technology to disaggregate 'back-office' routine functions and locate them in cheaper labour markets, as we discuss in Chapter 15.

Just as much service work has been disaggregated into lower value-adding elements such as call centres that can be located anywhere, or has been transformed by machine intelligence. Much of what was once produced by a domestic blue-collar labour force in the heartlands of Europe or the USA is now produced globally, often in China, in contexts in which machines and humans do most jobs together in a combination of high machine learning capabilities with highly skilled personnel (Manyika et al., 2017).

One consequence of the shifting international division of labour is that employment and organizations in the developed world are increasingly based on the production of services rather than goods. Material things – such as computers, clothes and household goods – are being produced in the developing world, while the most developed parts of the world economy switch to services, such as financial services. In the developing world, peasants are rapidly becoming factory workers; in the developed world, there has been an explosive growth in what is referred to as knowledge work, done by knowledge workers in knowledge-intensive firms. Chief among these are global IT firms, consultancy, law and accounting firms, as well as the universities, technical colleges and schools that produce the new knowledge workers.

For the past 200 years, Europe and North America have dominated the global world but now civilizations and cultures that have, for the past two centuries, been marginal and minor players on the world stage are now at its centre. The capitalist development of countries such as China and India, with over one third of the global population, as well as other newly emerging states such as Indonesia and Brazil, will transform our future. If the future managers reading this book want to have stimulating and successful careers, they are as likely to be forged in these countries as in Europe or North America. The managers that you will become will have to be truly global in experience and outlook.

Doing business internationally in real time, enabled digitally, produces ample opportunity for cultural *faux pas* and misunderstanding. Work groups may be working in serial or in parallel with each other on projects that are networked globally. Global organization means managing diversity: it means developing appropriate ways of managing people who may be very different from each other – from different national, ethnic, religious, age, educational, social status and gender backgrounds (Ashkenasy et al., 2011). One consequence of globalization and diversity is that HRM must be both increasingly international and equipped to deal with diversity, as we will see in Chapter 5.

Diversity is increasingly seen as an asset for organizations: people with diverse experiences can contribute more varied insights, knowledge and experience than can a more homogeneous workforce. (In the terms that we use in Chapter 9, we can say that it is a good thing to introduce more polyphony into organizations but it can also introduce more conflict: see Chapter 7.) An evident reason is that if a business wishes to sell globally it must understand all the specificities of the local markets into which it seeks to trade. One good way of doing this is to ensure that the organization has employees that understand that market. Moreover, in certain markets, such as the Middle East, where etiquette and rituals are of considerable importance in everyday interactions, it is enormously beneficial to have employees that have an intuitive cultural understanding rather than learning through making costly mistakes. Moreover, as we will see in Chapter 14, organizations whose members are not representative of the populations the organizations draw on and serve risk being seen as discriminatory in their recruitment policies. There are ethical issues concerned in managing diversity as well.

Time and space are two fundamental coordinates of the way we relate to the world and the ways in which we do so are socially constructed. Today, the concern is with the simultaneity and immediacy of access to global web spaces at any time. Today, with a computer, camera and broadband connection any organization member can simulate immediacy with anyone anywhere in the world similarly equipped. In such a situation, time and space are eclipsed. Organizations can be global, navigating anywhere. Digital communication, rather than face-to-face meetings by appointment in the same space and time, gives the technologies and objects that mediate interaction far more importance than they had in the pre-digital era.

Immediacy through the eclipse of space presents problems. Work is much more accountable and transparent as others can be online anytime, anywhere, challenging the understandings that the other has developed. Often, these understandings will be embedded in a sense made in a cultural, linguistic, religious, ethnic, age and gendered context that is simply foreign to partners elsewhere. Great cultural sensitivity, as well as a capacity to handle circadian rhythms, is needed in the interest of global business. In such contexts, there will be a great deal of doing by learning as managers seek to make sense of others whose cues are not only unfamiliar but often mediated by the limitations of digital communication. Managing communication in these circumstances poses special challenges, as we will see in Chapter 9.

Communication differs enormously across generations. Older generations can remember when the phone was a luxury that was installed and had pride of place in the home. Middle-aged people may recall the excitement of having an early mobile phone. Millennials would hardly regard talking as the prime or only means of direct communication: Snapchat, Instagram and even old-time Facebook all offer alternative models of communication that eclipse space instantly. As we will see in Chapter 2, the issues of commitment and motivation are increasingly central to managing. The Millennial generation has been seen to be more cynical than its predecessors and less likely to accept rhetoric from management that is not backed up by actions. Using traditional management control and command devices will not work well to manage people who desire to be creative and innovative, as we explore in Chapter 11.

If there is one value that binds disparate generations together, it is the sense that previous generations have really made a mess of the planet; green values are very strongly held by Millennials, with saving the environment through sustainability high on the list of value preferences. Consequently, as we discuss in Chapter 12, issues of corporate social responsibility, especially those addressed to sustainability, are high on the values agenda. Such changes pose major implications for how organizations attract, select, retain and treat employees, as we see in Chapter 5.

IN PRACTICE

Have you ever wondered why some companies seem more politically engaged than others? When campaigns demand that a company change its practices, corporate executives tend to weigh up the costs and benefits of complying. They may estimate the risk they face to their brand image against the benefits of mitigating this risk and improving this image. Costs include shifting and monitoring their supply chains. Benefits may include accessing new markets and enhancing the marketability of the brand.

The ways in which they engage with activists will also be influenced by the corporate culture of the company. Is it a company that engages with political issues? A company that prides itself on its attitude to sustainability?

READ MORE ABOUT ACTIVISM

Finally, when the activists bring issues to the company, on whose desk do they land? Is there a Department of Corporate Social Responsibility (CSR)? If there is, does it wield much influence?

The answers to these questions will vary. But we can intuitively see why companies that have engaged with activists in the past are more likely to do so again in the future.

For one, companies are more at risk of activist 'attacks' if they have previously responded, even in other issue areas. They are on the activists' radar. This happened with Nike, which has been experiencing renewed pressure from activists who suspect the company is slipping back towards poor practices.

The same goes for Tiffany. The company's proactive response to blood diamonds made it a prime candidate for leading the charge against dirty gold – and a prime target for the activists planning the campaign (though, in this case, Tiffany beat them to it).

Companies that have also responded to past issues probably go on to boast about their sustainability credentials, making them susceptible to accusations of hypocrisy if caught backsliding. They will already have analysed sourcing strategies and supply chains, so they have the systems in place when new issues pop up. They are also more likely to have a CSR department – or consider it important enough to be handled directly by the CEO. And their corporate culture is more likely to include sustainability concerns, as they have now become part of the company's practices.

Perhaps most significantly, their leadership is more likely to reflect this corporate culture, as culture and leadership enjoy a mutually constitutive relationship of sorts. People are important, and having these people within the firm becomes more likely.

While the details will differ among individual companies, past engagement with activists can make future engagement more likely. The role of activists in driving the expanding role of business in global environmental politics becomes clear.

Business and activism

Corporations and activists are collaborating through these battles, building institutions – from CSR to certifications – within firms and across industries to tackle environmental problems. They are finding solutions to some problems and, in doing so, shifting expectations about the role and responsibility of the private sector and those who work within it. This is a good thing.

But corporations are also largely dictating the terms of their response. Activists are rarely able to force companies to do their bidding. Business is simply too powerful and consumers too complacent. This means that sustainability is made to fit within the parameters of their business models, and not the other way around.

In the hierarchy of priorities, the needs of markets are too often placed above those of people and the planet. And this can be a very bad thing indeed.

So, while there is a case for cautious optimism here, there is an even stronger case for continued vigilance when evaluating this expanding role of business in global environmental politics. And that means a strong case for continued activism.

READ THE ARTICLE

In the terms of Aguinas, H. and Glavas, A. (2017) 'On corporate social responsibility, sensemaking, and the search for meaningfulness through work', *Journal of Management*, https://doi.org/10.1177%2F0149206317691575, which is available at the companion website https://study.sagepub.com/managingandorganizations5e, activists introduce extraorganizational sensemaking into the arena of the organization. Thus, they are a source of innovation.

Question

1. Using Bloomfield's (2018) article from *The Conversation* (boxed above) and Aguinas and Glavas (2017) as guides, can you explore an industry in which activists have succeeded in making organizations more responsive to corporate social responsibilities?

CONCLUSION

The evidence is in on the neo-liberal economic experiment and it is overwhelming: almost everywhere in the developed world it has produced an economy that is more polarized and more prone to crisis and run by less regulated organizations. One effect of the loss of bureaucratic regulation in the private sector has been the diminution of opportunities for well-paid careers, while in the public sector the impositions of austerity and the slow war waged on welfare and bureaucracy have seen the erosion of standards and opportunities. Increased inequality results as the range of middle-class occupations supported by bureaucracies diminishes, while benefits and salaries going to the wealthiest increase disproportionately. The changes are often assumed to be inexorable – the result of the market, efficiencies, economic rationality, globalization, and so on. They are, however, always the result of 'strategic choices' (Child, 2002 [1972]) made by those people comprising political, public and private elites.

USING MANAGING AND ORGANIZATIONS

The basic themes of this text are now established. In this book, as we have foreshadowed, we will introduce you to the main lines of contemporary management and organization theory, and we will situate these in the major changes marking the present-day world. These, we will argue, make the ideal of the wholly rationalistic organization ever more difficult to believe in principle and secure in practice; nonetheless, that does not stop organizations and management from trying to do so effectively. Organizations go to great lengths to try and ensure that stocks of knowledge are shared as widely as possible within the organization, as we will see in subsequent chapters, and do so in ways that are reflected in each of the subsequent chapters:

1. Creating induction programmes that socialize individuals into an organizational frame of reference (Chapter 2).
2. Training individuals in teamwork and group work (Chapter 3).
3. Hosting leadership development, coaching and training for common understanding (Chapter 4).
4. Building highly rationalistic HRM plans and seeking to implement them (Chapter 5).
5. Emphasizing strong, common cultures and rules to frame everyday behaviour in the organization (Chapter 6).
6. Managing organizational conflicts, so that the goal-oriented elements of organization can come to fruition, despite countervailing tendencies, schisms and frictions in an organization (Chapter 7).
7. Managing power, politics and decision-making so that plans are implemented, not resisted, and so sectional and specific interests are well aligned with rational plans (Chapter 8).
8. Communicating these rational plans, their culture and other messages to organization members (Chapter 9).
9. Capturing all of what their members know and embedding it in management systems as they try and practise organizational learning (Chapter 10).
10. Managing change, introducing and effectively using new technologies, and ensuring innovation (Chapter 11).
11. Incorporating new mandates arising from social issues and concerns articulated by new stakeholders and influential social voices, such as sustainability, ethics and corporate social responsibility (Chapter 12).
12. Implementing global management principles in the organization and designing the structure of the organization to fit the contingencies it has to deal with, such as size, technology or environment (Chapters 13 and 14).
13. Managing to manage globally, to manage globalization and to deal with the added complexities that managing in a global world entails (Chapter 15).

SUMMARY

In this chapter, we have staked out the territory that the book covers:

- Managing and organizing is very dynamic – its world never stays still – so innovation, change and tension are characteristic of the way that events pan out.
- Managing and organization is never done in isolation from broader social trends and contexts, which is why it is important to contextualize how it is being done.
- No organization or manager today can escape the effects of digitalization.
- Managing and organizations today are increasingly either global enterprises or related to them as suppliers, markets, customers, employees or shapers of others' environments.

EXERCISES

1. Having read this chapter, you should be able to say in your own words what each of the following key terms means. Test yourself or ask a colleague to test you.
    - Globalization
    - Digitalization
    - Organizations
    - Values
    - Managing
    - Identity
    - Rationality
    - Hierarchy
    - Metaphors
    - Sensemaking
    - Tool views of management
    - Corporate social responsibility
    - Organizations as tools
    - Neo-liberal economics.
2. Why do organizations seek to forge common sensemaking?
3. Why do organizations become globalized?
4. What do you think are some of the major changes that are shaping the contemporary world and what do you think their impact is on management?
5. What are the implications of digitalization for future employment opportunities?
6. In what ways are managers typically rational?
7. Why might new CEOs seeking to turn around an organization have recourse to sensebreaking?
8. What are the major obstacles to cultivating sensebreaking in a workforce?

TEST YOURSELF

REVISE KEY TERMS

Review what you have learned by visiting:
https://study.sagepub.com/managingandorganizations5e or your eBook

- **Test yourself with multiple-choice questions.**
- **Revise key terms with the interactive flashcards.**

TEST YOURSELF

CASE STUDY

This is a very simple case study to get you started. Think about the last organization that you were a member of for some time. It might have been a school, a church or an employing organization.

(Continued)

(Continued)

1. What were its main routines?
2. How were these organized in terms of some of the factors that might frame organizations? Think about factors such as how standardized, timetabled or ritualized the flows of time and organizational effort are in the organization in question.
3. What were the characteristic markers of identity of the different people and groups in the organization?
4. What were the goals of the organization?

Resources

Check out the companion website **https://study.sagepub.com/managingandorganizations5e** for a list of web resources related to this case study.

ADDITIONAL RESOURCES

- If you want to find out more about 'sensemaking', the entry in Clegg and Bailey (2008) *The Sage International Encyclopedia of Organization Studies* is useful.
- The Swedish theorist Nils Brunsson has written three excellent books on problems with the rational model of organizations: *The Irrational Organization* (1985), *The Organization of Hypocrisy* (1989) and *Mechanisms of Hope* (2006). Together they form a remarkable trio of organization analysis at its best. There is an interview with Nils Brunsson at the companion website: https://edge.sagepub.com/managingandorganizations5e
- Christopher Grey's (2017) *A Very Short, Fairly Interesting and Reasonably Cheap Book about Studying Organizations*, London: Sage, is a good and brief introduction to the field.
- Anne Cunliffe (2014) *A Very Short, Fairly Interesting and Reasonably Cheap Book about Management*, London: Sage, in the same series as Grey's book, is also a good introduction.

READ ABOUT DIGITAL TERMS

- What do all these digital terms mean? Read www.i-scoop.eu/digitization-digitalization-digital-transformation-disruption to understand the difference between digitization, digitalization and digital transformation.

READ THE REPORT

- A November 2017 report from the Brookings Institute takes a macro view of the implications of digitalization for the US workforce: you can access it at www.brookings.edu/research/digitalization-and-the-american-workforce.

- Globalization has been a hot topic for at least the last 20 years. Some think that the era of the Trump 'trade wars' and the decision of the UK to adopt Brexit signal the end of the era of globalization. Thomas Sigler, in *The Conversation*, provides sober reasons for thinking otherwise: https://theconversation.com/trump-and-brexit-wont-kill-globalisation-were-too-far-in-73688.

READ THE ARTICLE

MANAGING INDIVIDUALS

SEEING, BEING, FEELING

LEARNING OBJECTIVES

This chapter is designed to enable you to:

- develop an understanding of how psychology contributes to organizational behaviour
- describe the process of perception and understand how it can affect performance at work
- outline how values drive individual behaviour
- outline a range of personality theories
- explain how positive psychology can improve people's workplaces.

BEFORE YOU GET STARTED...

A few words from the great William James (1842–1910), American philosopher and psychologist:

> The greatest discovery of my generation is that human beings can alter their lives by altering their attitudes of mind.

INTRODUCTION

It is not an over-dramatization to say that those of us alive today live in a world of unparalleled uncertainty. In the last few years, we have seen a succession of natural disasters ranging from destructive floods and earthquakes to human-made catastrophes, including the escalation of geo-political conflict and shifts in economic power trending towards the east, threats of trade wars, global financial meltdowns and increasing civil unrest across the world. At the same time, we have seen incredible advances in technology, particularly in artificial intelligence, robotics and communications technology, which are transforming not only the ways in which we do business but also how we relate and communicate within and between societies. As organizations face the unparalleled levels of complexity and uncertainty that arise from such challenges, they must become more agile and responsive, not only to survive but also to lead and capitalize on the opportunities available to them during turbulent times. As a current or future manager and leader, you have enormous challenges ahead of you.

In organizations today, a 'one size fits all' management approach will not work. Contemporary managers can no longer rely on hierarchy and nominal roles to manage people; there is no longer a divine right to manage, and so managing has become an increasingly difficult, political and challenging endeavour. It is so for one very good reason: people are complex. It is imperative, therefore, that managers are acquainted with some of the core ideas that have originated from psychology and are now applied to managing and organizations, often in taken-for-granted ways.

The term **psychology** is derived from the Greek word 'psyche', meaning one's own thoughts and feelings or their 'being', and the English suffix 'ology' derived from the Greek logos, meaning reason, which in English is rendered as 'ology', denoting a field of study. **Psychology** is the study of our being or more simply the study of the human mind and behaviour.

The astute reader of this book will notice that with each chapter we gradually but surely move away from **psychology** towards sociology, anthropology and politics as we increasingly situate the managing and the managed people in a broader context. In this chapter, we will predominantly take a psychological perspective to explore the core ideas central to managing individuals. Psychological properties can be analysed at both an individual and a group (social) level, both of which are critical to managing people at work. We will explain the basic psychological concepts and principles we believe are central for managing individuals in organizations and will go on to look at teams and groups in Chapter 3. For now we will discuss perception and cognition and these affect how we behave and think about things. We humans are not the perfectly designed creatures some would have you assume; how we perceive things, what we attend to and ignore, how we interpret people and make decisions about them is prone to many types of biases. For this reason, understanding the process of perception is critical in helping us become better managers. But, first, let us discuss psychology and relate it to work more generally.

Second, we will take a close look at values because they are the fundamental building blocks for managing culture, diversity and communication (all topics covered in detail throughout this textbook). You need to consider how yours and others' values are formed and how they can drive us throughout our working lives; how they bind us but also how they separate and differentiate us from others and how they can lead to conflict between people and societies. Third, personality is important because it is seen as the essence that makes each of us who we are, determines how we behave and shapes how we feel. We ask, 'Can we categorize people as types, or are each and every one of us unique individuals?' Finally, we close the chapter by looking at emotions from a 'positive psychology' (PP) perspective. We will concentrate on a topic, the pursuit of which is enshrined in at least one nation's constitution. Before we explore these fascinating topics, let us first build an understanding of psychology and its application at work. (See Talk #2: Introduction to managing people in organizations, by Dr Tyrone S. Pitsis.)

WATCH THE TALK

PSYCHOLOGY AT WORK

Psychology first explicitly emerged in Greece more than 2,500 years ago when philosophers tried to explain the nature of the self, the soul and personality. The word psychology has a classical etymology.

Psychology seeks to answer the question: 'Why are we the way we are?' It concerns itself with all aspects of the workings of the mind (such as perception, attention, thought, memory and affect at the intrapersonal and interpersonal levels of analysis), and also with understanding the brain's development, its possibilities, degradation and limitations.

The application of psychology at work has mainly occurred through the fields of applied industrial and organizational psychology (Kozlowski et al., 2017). However, more generally it is in the field of **organizational behaviour** that theory, research and practice in psychology have been applied to organizational life. OB involves understanding, researching and addressing organizational behaviour phenomena from a multidisciplinary perspective, primarily including psychology but also drawing on sociology, anthropology, economics and political science to name but a few.

Organizational behaviour (OB) refers to the study of human behaviour in organizational contexts. OB is an applied discipline that concerns itself with individual-level, group-level and organization-level processes and practices that inhibit or enable organizational performance.

At certain times in our lives, we will ask an existential question about ourselves: Who am I? What do I stand for? We can all answer such questions to a degree but how we answer them depends on our beliefs about human nature, the way in which we make sense of the world and our place within it, what we understand our values to be, which relationships we prize, what we count as successes and failures, and so on. Over the last 100 years or so, there has been a great deal of theory, research and practice in psychology that seeks to address such questions about who we are. Our intention in this chapter is to guide you to what you need to know in relation to psychology at work.

In almost all fields of psychology, two main themes drive theory and research. The first theme centres on the nature versus nurture debate. At issue is whether we are genetically encoded to be the way we are, such that how well you achieve things in specific spheres of life will depend on your genetic dispositions – your personality, ability to be a leader, to be caring or aggressive. The second theme focuses on the idea that we come into this world *tabula rasa* – that is, with a clean slate – and that our personality is something that is socially constructed as we learn to manage ourselves and become the kind of self we want to be. From this perspective, we learn to become leaders, influenced by social contexts such as the socioeconomic status of our families, our culture, social support systems, the environment in which we grow up, our schooling, and so on.

The opposing view of nature versus nurture frames much of what you will learn in the field of organizational behaviour because psychology informs much of organizational behaviour theory, research and practice. Some theorists and researchers hold dearly to one or the other view. Some think it is all in the genes, while others think that genetic potential is extraordinarily malleable and a great deal depends on the environment in which we develop. Others prefer more moderate, integrative theories about what makes us who we are – a view that we share. Our view is that we are born with some aspects of what constitutes us as a person but that much of who we are is learned over time and that context has a profound impact on our development as human beings. How you approach the question of nature and nurture influences how you manage people, how you manage yourself and behave at work, as well as the underlying assumptions that you make about how people might, or might not, behave at work.

An important theme that has emerged in organizational behaviour theory and research suggests that nurture is overridden because of the fundamental drives that underpin human nature. Such ideas are derived from Charles Darwin and his theory of evolution, in particular the importance of behaviours that perpetuate the survival of the species. Some evolutionary arguments stress the 'selfish gene' perspective: that we are programmed for competition in a fundamental struggle to perpetuate our genes over those of others. Others stress that fitness and survival depend far more on the fact that we are social animals seeking affiliation and human relations; hence, we are more committed to cooperation than competition to ensure our survival as a species. These two related but somewhat opposing views of evolution underpin many of the ideas in management research and theory today.

Many management scholars and theorists use Darwinian theory to validate and substantiate their claims about human nature as being based in a competitive instinct and struggle. Evolutionary psychology has made substantial inroads into management research and theory such that it is now steeped in the Darwinian tradition of 'survival of the fittest'. Yet, despite this belief in survival of the fittest, some of those who believe in it as a competitive concept are the first to claim a liver or a kidney transplant when their survival is at stake! In the ideal world of survival of the fittest, of course, such individuals would be left to die because they are simply not fit enough. Conversely, some of those who believe that the fittest survivors are those best able to cooperate are the first to complain when their taxes are raised to provide more public goods.

Before Darwin published *On the Origin of Species by Means of Natural Selection, or the Preservation of Favoured Races in the Struggle for Life* in 1859, Adam Smith (1961 [1776]), a political economist and philosopher of the Scottish Enlightenment who is credited with being the father of capitalism, argued that progress and economic growth occur because human behaviour is based on self-interest, which is best served by the operation of free and unfettered markets in the supply of goods and services. For example, if we as consumers want more leisure time and express a preference for this through our purchasing decisions in markets – maybe by buying vacations and appliances rather than saving money – then business people who market vacations or innovations in labour-saving devices will be rewarded. We buy and sell in markets that achieve balance between the supply and demand of goods such that, in the long term, efficiencies will prevail, with a price mechanism maintaining equilibrium. By being self-interested, we create demand preferences that markets emerge to meet; these markets benefit all of society because they create a self-regulating economic system where benefits trickle down by way of jobs, economic growth, prosperity and innovations.

Fundamental self-interest does not necessarily provide welfare or products or services that cannot be privately owned to generate income and so, the argument goes, government must become involved in providing such public goods. When a 16-year-old single parent has produced a baby and needs some support to sustain herself and her child, no business will assist her because there is no profit in giving resources away unless someone is paying them to do so. Hence, government typically provides social security and basic support. Of course, in doing so, in the long term, this is a subsidy to business in general because it enables the reproduction of another recruit to the next generation of workers and consumers. It is not surprising that social responsibility and economic, social and environmental sustainability have long been perceived as the duty of government to regulate or as a task for charity and other 'do-gooders' (see also pp. 386–397).

The views of Adam Smith have certainly been influential. Look at any newspaper story on corporate behaviour to see parallels with notions of survival of the fittest, the centrality of self-interest and the primal pursuit of economic wealth as the end of human activity. Today, this bundle of beliefs assumes that self-interested economic action is the only rational basis for human behaviour. Hence, it is a small step to arguing that our rationalities are formed this way as a constitutive feature of our human nature. Using Darwin and Smith as authorities, some scholars, such as Nicholson (2000), would argue that competition is genetically a human predisposition. Despite the global financial crisis of 2008, which continues to be felt over two decades later, one of whose effects was to raise questions concerning the viability of unfettered market behaviour, we still see behaviours being lauded that stress a return to business as usual, with exorbitant CEO salaries and payouts, together with a continuation of gender and racial inequalities in management ranks as well as resistance to sustainable, corporate social responsibility.

All ideas, such as the survival of the fittest through competition or cooperation, as well as debates about nature and nurture, underpin and are underpinned by our beliefs or working theories about how the world, and the things within it, operate. Our values and beliefs are integral to all these working theories and assumptions about work, organizations and society. These values, beliefs and assumptions are inherent in the workplace and become an important component of the management of people and organizations. Psychology provides part of the answer to understanding and dealing with the tensions and opportunities that present themselves in the workplace. For now, we will discuss perception and cognition and how these affect how we behave and think about things, especially at work.

WATCH THIS TED TALK

PERCEPTION AT WORK

In general terms, all management starts from **perception** because we manage what we think we perceive to be happening.

Perception is the process of receiving, attending to, processing, storing and using stimuli to understand and make sense of our world. The stimuli can be experienced through any and all of the senses such as sight, sound, smell, taste and touch.

Figure 2.1 represents a basic model of information processing: the model shows in a simplified way the perceptual process of how we deal with stimuli in our environment. Let us use an example in order to help us make sense of this model. Let us assume you are at a party, and the music (*stimulus A*) played has been excellent all night. You notice one of your fellow students (*stimulus B*), whom you find very attractive, is alone and you go over and strike up a conversation – you find you both have so much in common that you attend to every word (*attention*). So much so that you forget about the music, even though your absolute favourite song is playing (*filtering*) – filtering can be intentional or subconscious and essentially is the same thing as *selective perception*, or the process of selectively gathering and processing information that is consistent with one's values, beliefs and attitudes. The more you listen to the person, the more you find you have in common, the more attractive they appear to you, and the more they reinforce what you believe about their attractiveness, and so this information that is selectively attended to is stored and processed in relation to existing schemas (*organization*). The cognitive process of organization happens through schemas – which can be thought of as sets of cognitive constructs developed through social interactions that organize our thoughts, feelings and attention (Baldwin, 1992; Epstein and Baucom, 2002).

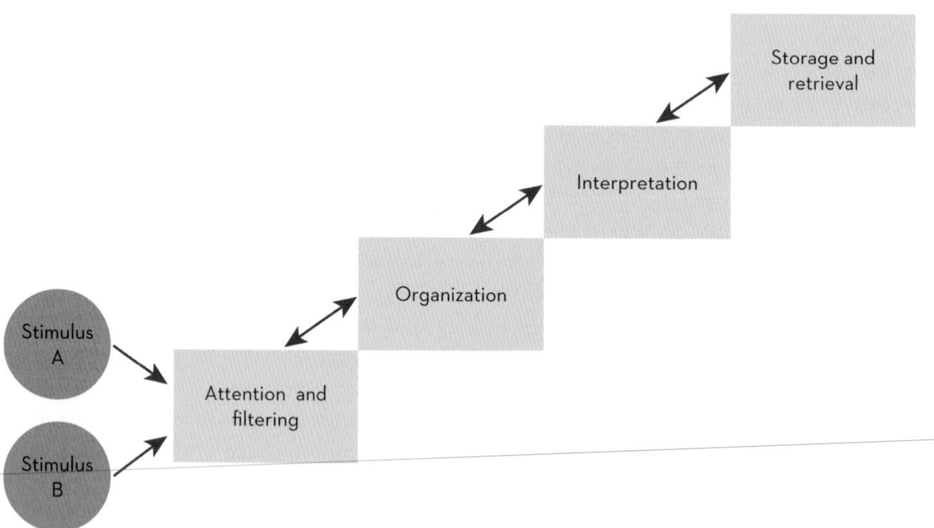

FIGURE 2.1 A basic information-processing model of perception (adapted from from Reed, Cognition, 8E. © 2010 South-Western, a part of Cengage, Inc. Reproduced by permission. www.cengage.com/permissions)

The next step in the model is *interpretation* – all the information you have gathered and organized about this attractive person (attractiveness, smiling, common interests, body language) has been grouped into a set of schemas that comprise a possible relationship (be it sexual or loving), and so you *store* all this information as reality or as representative of what you are experiencing. The problem is that people interpret stimuli in different ways, and sometimes not in the same way you do. What you did not notice is crucial: what you did not notice was that this person found you friendly and recognized you from the lectures – it was not romantic interest but simple affability that the person exhibited towards you. But, to be sure, they utter those words you never expected to hear: 'Oh, here is my partner. I'll introduce you, you'll really get along'. All that information you stored about a possible love interest is *retrieved* and reinterpreted. What you once thought 'real' is no longer real, and so you must re-analyse and update your information as you come crashing back from a momentary alternative reality. Of course, some people don't do this and still hold on to the original belief – in this example, if you did this you would probably find yourself charged with stalking or being labelled 'a creep'.

Schemas are a very important component of the perceptual information-processing story told above because in many ways they underscore much of what we cover in this chapter – our values, personality and emotions can all be linked to schemas (also referred to as schemata or scripts). Schemas are used to structure and organize information that we experience in our social world and are often hierarchical (my car is a Mini Cooper, a Mini Cooper is a small car, a car is an automobile, an automobile is a vehicle, a vehicle is a mode of transport). There are several types of schemas, including **person schemas** and **self-schemas**.

Person schemas are structures of meaning that affect thinking, planning and behaviour concerning others. Within person schemas, there are idealized person schemas that serve as prototypes with which we compare all other persons (see Horowitz, 1991).

You may perceive yourself as an open, honest and hard-working person and so it is not surprising to you that your employer also finds you hard working: self-schemas are critical in our personality and include idealized self- or projected self- (ideal self-) schemas. That is, a schema forms the 'ideal' type of what a person strives to be or with which they compare themselves.

Self-schemas are specific self-conceptions we hold about ourselves, which we believe are self-descriptive and highly important to possess (Fong and Markus, 1982; Markus, 1977).

Other kinds of schema include script, social and role schemas. We all have several scripts, deriving from **script schemas**, and these scripts allow us to function in our daily lives – we have scripts for going to a restaurant, scripts for going to university, scripts for how we ride our bikes, and so on (Schank and Abelson, 2013). In all these situations, there are *conditions* (such as going to the restaurant because you are hungry, you have money for food and the restaurant has food), *standard roles* for main actors (you are the star playing the lead role of customer) and supporting actors (waitress, chef and other customers), *props* (tables and chairs, etc.) and *results* (the main actor has less money, but is no longer hungry) (Reed, 2009). We develop these scripts from **social schemas** and **role schemas**.

Script schemas refer to schemas about how we operate in our world and understand and remember information.

Social schemas, as the name suggests, refer to our social knowledge (such as knowledge about public affairs, laws, politics, media and the arts, and anything else socially important).

Once our schemas become established, they become increasingly difficult to change and falsify; that is, we tend to pay attention to information that reaffirms or fits our schemas, rather than questioning our schemas whenever we experience information that contradicts them (Reed, 2009). As an example, read the following sentence:

> THE HAMUN BRIAN IS SO AZAMING,
>
> AS LNOG AS THE FRIST AND LSAT LTETER IS THE SMAE
>
> YUO WLIL MKAE SNESE OF THE SNETECNE!

This sentence is an example of how schemas are organized and influence perception through selective perception. Your brain will automatically complete information for you so that things will make sense – most people will see 'The human brain is so amazing …'. However, if you read the sentence exactly as the letters appear you will find most of the sentence is nonsense. What you think you see and what is actually there are two different things. This example tends to only work with people who possess good English language skills. The brain reads the first and last letter, matches it to the words on either side and quickly calls up language scripts that fit the general idea of the passage. 'The hamun brian' makes no sense (unless you actually know someone called Hamun Brian), so your brain searches for the closest match – 'the human brain'.

Role schemas refer to schemas about appropriate and inappropriate behaviour in specific contexts (for example, a woman's role as a mother, daughter, professional, wife, friend).

For social cognitive psychologists, schemas are, as already mentioned, the underlying constructs that contain information about our values, how we perceive ourselves as people, how we perceive others, how we adjust and respond to change, how we operate in our social world, and how we experience our emotions, make sense of our attitudes, opinions, prejudices and assumptions (Augoustinos et al., 2014). Schemas are so powerful that they are one of the most important components of cognitive-behavioural therapy. Schema therapy is used to uncover and deconstruct the underlying thought processes and structures of people and treat depression and anxiety by replacing destructive schemas with more psychologically healthy schemas (Giesen-Bloo et al., 2006; Young et al., 2003). Schema therapy can even be used to understand better how we might negotiate peace between conflicting parties (Leahy, 2011). We will revisit schemas in this context when we look at personality and also the pursuit of happiness; let us now look at how perception and schemas can be problematic, especially in workplace contexts.

There is probably no better example of how schemas structure our understandings, beliefs and values than the science versus religion, evolution versus creationism debate. The argument for and against intelligent design (ID) is one of those debates. There has been a growing and powerful movement within the USA, which seeks to include ID as a core part of the education curriculum. At best, the proponents of ID want it taught along with Darwinian evolutionary theory; at worst, they want it to totally replace teachings on evolution. The main argument is that God (an intelligent entity) designed the world and humans and that much of this design can be scientifically tested and supported to (a) prove God exists, and (b) prove evolutionary theory is wrong. Here is an example of the arguments used:

> The Christian world view begins with the Creation, with a deliberate act by a personal Being who existed from all eternity. This personal dimension is crucial for understanding Creation. Before bringing the world into existence, the Creator made a choice, a decision: He set out a plan, an intelligent design. (Colson and Pearcey, 1999: 55)

In March 2011, a Republican State Representative for Texas, Bill Zedler, introduced the Bill HB 2454, which was aimed at protecting the rights of people to teach ID.

Science, of course, rejects the ideas espoused in ID, and organizations and institutions such as the National Science Teachers' Association and the US National Academy of Science have responded by claiming that ID is not a science; in fact, some call it junk science. In 2017, the *New York Times*' Clyde Haberman wrote a thought-provoking article accompanied by an informative video. (You can read the article and watch the video at www.nytimes.com/2017/11/19/us/retro-report-evolution-science.html.) With the election of President Donald Trump, creationists have become emboldened by his support for some of the ideas against the core assumptions of science – such as 'facts' created by 'experts'. Hence, it is safe to assume that the ID argument will not go away anytime soon.

READ THE FULL ARTICLE

It seems that some people do not necessarily rely on facts or evidence in making up their minds about things, but rely more on commonly held beliefs that are experienced and interpreted as being true, despite the weight of evidence against them. Common errors in how people perceive the world appear to be rife.

PERCEPTION AND COMMON ERRORS

Stereotyping is the process of grouping objects into simplistic categories based on one's generalized perceptions of those objects.

Armed with a basic understanding of perception and the perceptual process and structure, let us now define and explore some common errors we make in judgements, interpretations, assumptions and beliefs about our social world, the people within it and our place in it. We will first deal with **stereotyping**. In reality, while many textbooks present stereotyping as an error, stereotyping serves as an important process for dealing with information in a timely manner and is not always negative.

Stereotyping occurs most commonly in the absence of enough social cues in order to make an informed assessment (Schneider, 2004; Kawakami et al., 1998). Stereotypes are problematic when what we stereotype is complex, as most people and their social groups tend to be. Think of the terms 'Jock', 'Nerd', 'Greenie', and so on – these are all stereotypes. The most common issues concerning stereotyping centre on culture and race. Examples of language around stereotyping include overt statements that are perceived as fact but are still false and covertly racist: 'The Irish love potatoes', 'The English don't bathe', 'Americans are loud and obnoxious', and 'Chinese drive badly'. Alternatively, and most often, stereotyping can be racist and overtly offensive: 'Mexicans are lazy', 'Arabs are terrorists', and so on.

IN PRACTICE

In 2017, the *Wall Street Journal* reported how female software engineers at Facebook were more likely than male coders to have their code rejected. While Facebook agreed that women are underrepresented in the industry, they did not believe that the rejection of coding was related to gender. Read this well-written piece on the issue by Nick Statt, published in The Verge in 2017 (www.theverge.com/2017/5/2/15517302/facebook-female-engineers-gender-bias-studies-report), then answer these questions:

1. Do you believe gender bias is in practice here? Or is there a different explanation?
2. In your opinion, how would you explain the gender differences in coding acceptance rates?
3. How might Facebook address this issue of lower coder acceptance rates for its female employees?

Stereotyping also concerns people's roles based on gender. For example, currently in Australia, the UK and the USA, there is still a gender gap in terms of equal pay – even after over 100 years of the women's rights movement. While the situation is definitely improving (although mainly for white, Western women) due to greater access to education, employment law, and so on (Kassenboehmer and Sinning, 2014), women are paid on average approximately 80 per cent of what men earn for the same role and position (Iyer and Ryan, 2006; Kee, 2006;

Taylor, 2006). When we ask our management students in the classroom about their opinions concerning such gender pay inequity, those opinions vary; some students argue that because women can become pregnant they are not a good investment and so should be paid less. Others argue that the inequity occurs because of sexist, male-dominant culture, which has no place in modern society. Research suggests that mothers are *perceived* to be less competent and less committed to their work, even though there is no evidence to support such a stereotype: most surprisingly, it is women who were more likely to perceive mothers in this way (Abendroth et al., 2014; Benard and Correll, 2010).

So, in a workplace, why don't we simply get people to think about how they are stereotyping people, such as women or ethnic groups and get them to stop or suppress stereotyping? In studies of prejudiced people, it was found that while suppression works in the short term, it tends to work only with highly motivated individuals who want to stop stereotyping people. In the long term, even when people are motivated they tend to revert back to stereotyping (Wyer, 2007). Indeed, people with unprejudiced beliefs tend not to stereotype, irrespective of whether they are motivated to do so or not (Wyer, 2007), and even when they lack social cues they still tend to avoid stereotypes (Kawakami et al., 1998). Such individuals can contribute to positive workplaces and positive identity construction (see Dutton et al., 2010). Seeking out more information about others, learning about other cultures and subcultures, knowledge and experience of other people, discussion and open communication, and practising empathy and compassion are all ways we can avoid stereotyping people. In short, the more we interact with people of different cultures, experiences and walks of life, the greater the range of social schemas that we can draw upon, and the less likely we are to make ill-informed or ill-conceived short cuts based on limited information.

The concept of the **self-fulfilling prophecy** was originally conceptualized by the sociologist Robert Merton (1957) to refer to the process by which a person who holds a belief or expectation, irrespective of its validity, causes it to come true because they behave and act as if it is true.

The next perceptual error arises from **self-fulfilling prophecies**. The self-fulfilling prophecy affects both how we perceive others and how we act when we interact with them, but it also affects how we perceive and act ourselves. One of the most famous studies of self-fulfilling prophecy was Robert Rosenthal's and Lenore Jacobson's (1992) seminal work on the 'Pygmalion effect' – an experiment that would in all likelihood not be allowed in today's world. In their experiment, the researchers randomly selected 20 per cent of students from 18 different classrooms and told the teachers that these chosen students were gifted, and that these students would show improvements in academic ability over time. The students were returned to class and by the end of the year the students did show significant improvement.

What caused this improvement? Teachers treated the gifted students differently because they were perceived as gifted. These students sat closer to the teachers, were given more attention by the teachers and were, generally, treated differently to the non-select group. The 'normal' students were perceived as less bright and these students were given less time to answer questions and had certain qualities attributed to their behaviour because they were differentiated. The implication for managers is that we can easily allow our self-fulfilling prophecies to cloud our judgement about people, so we may label some people as performers and team players and others as non-performers or not team players – we therefore start to treat people differently and the prophecy becomes fulfilled. In order to avoid such self-fulfilling prophecies, we need to be careful that how we judge people is based on sound information, is done accurately and uses critical reflection, equity and fairness. The concept of the **halo effect** was first developed by psychologist Edward Thorndike (1920) and refers to the process by which, if we ascribe certain characteristics to a person in one situation based on one trait, we tend to apply those characteristics to that person in other situations and to other traits.

As with the self-fulfilling prophecy, the halo effect also involves a bias in judgement that affects behaviour. An example of the halo effect, relative to managing people, might be the expectation that because a person who works for you is highly skilled in his job and performs well, he will also be highly skilled as a manager of people. As a result, you promote him to a supervisory level only to find he is incapable of managing the team you authorized him to lead. In terms of behaviour at an organizational level, the halo seems to be rife. Hype surrounding businesses that are perceived to be successful creates a halo around them: think of Google, Apple and Pinterest. For example, Cisco was one of the most popular companies and was often used as an exemplar of how businesses should operate – until of course Cisco developed financial problems (Rosenzweig, 2014). Similarly, a former large American company, Enron, had been awarded a number of accolades, even up to its historic collapse, so the halo effect reminds us that we should be sceptical and careful about how we use examples as proof of success.

The **devil effect** refers to generally ascribing negative interpretations of people based on one negative trait in one situation.

Interestingly, a similar but less covered concept in management is the **devil effect** – which is essentially the opposite of the halo effect. Consider a former prisoner who cannot get a job when he divulges this information, even though he has done his time – what do you think the chances of getting a job would be? Virgin CEO Sir Richard Branson sought to turn around perceptions of ex-prisoners by creating an employment and management development programme for ex-prisoners within Virgin with great success.

READ MORE ABOUT VIRGIN

The final two perceptual errors we are prone to make are attribution errors and cognitive dissonance. Let us begin with attribution error; in order to do this, we should first discuss attribution theory.

Attribution theory addresses how we explain away our own behaviour and the behaviours of others based on two general types of attribution. Attribution theory involves three general components, with **internal/external attributions** being one of those.

Attribution theory, in its simplest definition, refers to how people 'attribute' cause to their own and other people's behaviour (Heider, 1958).

Internal attribution refers to attributing the cause of an individual's behaviour to internal or dispositional factors such as being mean or being generous.

Another component of attribution is stability: if we perceive the attributed causes to be *stable*, then we would expect the same result from that behaviour next time. Conversely, if the attributed cause is *unstable*, then we would expect the outcomes to vary next time. The final component is controllability: if we believe the situation is *controllable*, then we would assume that next time we could control the outcome; if the situation is *uncontrollable*, then we believe it probably cannot be altered, irrespective of our efforts (see Weiner, 1980, 1992, 2014). Research shows how we attribute negative motivations to people we disagree with and more favourable perceptions to those we agree with. Thus, if we agree with a war, or with gay marriage, for example, we are more likely to attribute positive motivations to people who also support those perceptions and attitudes and we are also more likely to be attracted to them and they are more likely to be attracted to us (Greifeneder et al., 2011).

External attribution refers to attributing the cause of an individual's behaviour to external or situational factors – such as race, religion, colour of skin or gender.

EXTEND YOUR KNOWLEDGE

Read 'A woman's place is in the ... startup! Crowdfunder judgments, implicit bias, and the stereotype content model' by Michael Johnson, Regan Stevenson and Chaim Letwin (2018) in *Journal of Business Venturing* (https://doi.org/10.1016/j.jbusvent.2018.04.003), which you can find at the companion website https://study.sagepub.com/managingandorganizations5e. Sometimes bias can work in reverse; in this article, the authors explore how female entrepreneurs are more likely to be funded than men in a crowdfunding context because they are stereotypically seen as being more trustworthy than men.

The **fundamental attribution error** is the tendency to make internal attributions when explaining the causes of the behaviour of others.

Within attribution, we are prone to two key errors. The first is the **fundamental attribution** error.

When we see someone fail or behave in certain ways, we believe it is due to their personality, attitude or disposition. For example, over recent years research has shown that when discussing rape crimes people apportion blame to the victims of rape due to their choice of clothing, their being under the influence of drugs and/or alcohol and therefore not in control of their own behaviour, or their choice of profession (e.g. being a prostitute), rather than to external causes such as the criminal, the criminal act and the anti-social behaviour of another person (Vanderveen, 2006). Related to attribution error is the notion of **self-serving bias**.

When a **self-serving bias** comes into play, people attribute their own successes to internal causes and their failure to external causes.

Let us say you go for a job interview in which you are successful: you may believe that you got it because you did well in the interview, that you have all the skills and abilities necessary, such that you can do the job. Conversely, let us say you missed out on the job – you may attribute your failure to the poor interview questions, or to someone on the interview panel not liking you, or you felt the questions were stupid, or guessed the position had already been filled internally. The concepts of fundamental attribution error and self-serving bias are important to reflect on when managing people, especially when we are making judgements about behaviours based on assumed internal attributions. Practising empathy, by putting yourself in other people's shoes or trying to understand their perspective and trying to account for the external causes of behaviour, is a good way to avoid attribution errors.

Cognitive dissonance refers to the anxiety and discomfort we experience when we hold inconsistent and conflicting sets of cognitions (or schemas).

The final perceptual error is **cognitive dissonance**.

Most commonly, we do not experience dissonance until we experience conflicting or disconfirming information. For example, a devout person may question their faith after experiencing tragedy in their life; they may question their belief in God, and their religion. They may ask, 'Why would God do this to me?' Similarly, Albert Einstein developed his theory of relativity but when his theories were used to develop weapons of mass destruction he felt anxiety and regret – his assumption was that his theories would lead to new forms of power generation, not the possible destruction of humanity and the death of millions (Braun and Krieger, 2005).

Leon Festinger (1957) was one of the first people to develop and study cognitive dissonance theory. Along with a number of colleagues, Festinger studied the behaviour and cognitions of a cult that claimed to know the date that the world would end, believing that the world would end by flooding. A number of people were convinced and joined the cult, some of whom were totally committed, others less so. After the date of doom passed and there was no flood or destruction, what do you think happened? Those people who were on the periphery believed they had been conned, or left the cult. But a number of people became even more committed to the cult, claiming that it was actually their faith and prayers that stopped the floods.

READ ABOUT COGNITIVE DISSONANCE

When experiencing cognitive dissonance, therefore, people will either seek to reconcile their feelings of anxiety and discomfort by changing their beliefs, or reinterpreting the information that contradicts their beliefs (Festinger, 1957; Festinger and Carlsmith, 1959). There are some interesting implications that emerge out of cognitive dissonance. Let us say you choose to study a subject, and you find the subject really difficult and you struggle and put lots of effort in – you pass but do not do so well. Now let us also say you study another subject that you find very easy, you don't need to study hard and you still do exceptionally well. What dissonance theory shows is that the first case creates dissonance because you choose a subject and find it difficult; you therefore reduce dissonance by saying 'even though it's a hard subject, I really am getting a lot out of it, so it's worth it'. Conversely, your emotions concerning the subject that you did well in are less intense. Cognitive dissonance is important when we give feedback to people because their commitment to the task, their beliefs, opinions and expectations will determine how they react to the feedback.

Interestingly, we rarely question what we know, how we came to know it and what we think we know about things, because we take things such as our knowledge, experiences, values and belief systems for granted; as a result, we selectively perceive and reinterpret what we experience to fit what we already know (Kahneman, 2011; Weick, 2004). The pre-eminent psychologist and Nobel Prize winner Professor Daniel Kahneman, along with his close collaborator the late Amos Tversky, has over his lifetime provided some excellent insights into the cognitive judgement errors we make under conditions of uncertainty. In his critically acclaimed book *Thinking, Fast and Slow* (2011), he brings together core ideas that emerged out of the decades of research conducted by him, his colleagues such as Paul Slovic and Amos Tversky, and other leading researchers. Kahneman (2011) presents an interesting and powerful metaphor that sees the brain as containing two systems. Table 2.1 summarizes the core features of these two systems of the brain. This is our own representation of the core features of the two types; we recommend you read the book to get deeper insights. Daniel Kahneman sought to counter the idea in economics that humans are rational beings, have stable tastes and behave in a mainly self-interested way. He also questioned the assumption that emotions somehow cause us to make errors in judgement. Rather, Kahneman argues that people are neither 'fully rational' nor self-interested and that their tastes and preferences can and do change.

EXTEND YOUR KNOWLEDGE

READ THE ARTICLE

If humans are, as Daniel Kahneman's work suggests, prone to irrational rather than rational decisions and humans are also prone to take short cuts to decisions and these decisions are biased, what might happen if we actually changed the taken-for-granted way in which we make sense of gender? What if we dehumanized gender? Ashley Martin and Michael Slepian (2018) explore this very idea in their article, 'Dehumanizing gender: the debiasing effects of gendering human-abstracted entities', published in the *Personality and Social Psychology Bulletin* at doi.org/10.1177/0146167218774777. In their article, they argue that rather than de-gendering humans to reduce gender bias and stereotyping, it may be better to dehumanize gender.

TABLE 2.1 A summary of Daniel Kahneman's (2011) System 1 and System 2 thinking

System 1	System 2
Intuitive: system 1 is intuitive and automatic in that you have little control over what you see, hear or feel as you respond to a stimulus. For example, reading these words is automatic.	Deliberate: we must consciously engage system 2 and think about how we come to a judgement. For example, studying is effortful and deliberate.
Fast and effortless: system 1 makes judgements quickly and without much cognitive effort.	Slow and effortful: because system 2 is not automatic, it requires cognitive effort and time. Often, the conditions under which we make decisions rarely allow for time, or we cannot put in the effort.
Emotional: system 1 feels and can make judgements based on these feelings.	Rational: system 2 'thinks' it's the boss, and makes rational judgements. However, it is system 1 that really is the boss and influences the results of system 2 much more than we have ever given it credit for.
Error prone: system 1's speed and intuition can be prone to errors under conditions of uncertainty.	Lazy: system 2 is lazy and often system 1 dominates because of the cognitive effort required for system 2 judgements under uncertainty.
2 + 2 = ? System 2 can instantly and intrusively make judgements about things – which allows us to be experts and proficient.	27 x (157/47) = ? System 2 kicks in when system 1 cannot readily find the answer or make a judgement. However, it tends to 'give up' or make mistakes because of the high levels of cognitive resources being used.
I like chocolate more than coffee: system 1 often concerns issues of taste and distinction, and can change.	I must make a chocolate soufflé: system 2 often concerns itself with difficult or complex tasks.

Kahneman argues that system 1 is quick to process things, is intuitive and is 'the boss' and draws upon system 2 when more complex problems are faced. System 2 is methodical, effortful and on the whole rational. However, system 2 is also lazy and will take short cuts. As an example, look at the following maths problem and solve it in your head (do not use paper or a calculator):

$$2 + 2 = ?$$

Now look at the following problem and solve it in your head:

27 x (157/47) =

What did you notice as you tried to solve these two problems? One was easy, effortless and mainly intuitive – you could not easily give the wrong answer to the first problem. However, the second problem might have caused you to concentrate much more and there was, unbeknown to you, a very strong physiological and mental response (trust us, as you tried to complete the second problem, your blood pressure rose and your pupils dilated). In both cases, system 1 called on system 2, but because the second problem required significant cognitive effort on your part, system 2's resources were severely taxed or depleted (or what Kahneman calls ego depletion). Ego depletion means that when you are doing complex tasks or faced with complex problems, your cognitive resources are taxed quite heavily – hence there is a greater propensity for cognitive errors to occur, or for you to give up or be distracted. Interestingly, your 'self-control' or self-regulating behaviour is also diminished, hence you are more likely to eat or behave badly, be rude or make offensive comments, and take short cuts. There is an engaging and interesting presentation on system 1 and 2 thinking by Kahneman himself on YouTube, which we recommend you watch.

WATCH THE KAHNEMAN VIDEO

The process of perception is important and it shows that we can often make errors. Often, these errors occur because our ideas are based on unreflexive beliefs about things and we make assumptions or inferences based on these systems of beliefs rather than being better informed.

IN PRACTICE

Dealing with cognitive errors is increasingly becoming a central concern for developing leaders and managers. Our friends at Mind Tools have kindly given us permission to reproduce an extract from an article on cognitive errors and ways to deal with them on our online companion website. Test yourself and visit the site. For each of the errors, read the definition and the example, and before you read the section on 'how to avoid' the error, ask yourself how you would avoid the error and compare your response with the advice given.

READ THE FULL ARTICLE

VALUES: MANAGING ME, MYSELF AND I

For many scholars, **values** can be thought of as the building blocks of culture (Howard, 1988). However, values can also be understood within the context of people management; to form, sustain and improve relationships with people, or to motivate people, we must understand what is and what is not important to them. Values not only drive behaviour but also affect, and are affected by, how we perceive and make sense of our world. To a great extent, management is about managing people in a coordinated way to ensure that organizational outcomes are realized, while also ensuring that one's own and others' values are met.

Values are a person's or social group's consistent beliefs or sets of schemas about something in which they have an emotional investment.

Understanding values is a fundamental attribute for managing today. Moreover, we should also have an understanding and appreciation of how our values filter information and create knowledge, colouring the world we perceive just as tinted lenses do. Not everyone sees things the same way.

Although there are many theories and approaches to values, here we look in detail at Shalom Schwartz's (1992, 2014) account of the role that universal values play at the personal level.

WHAT ARE VALUES?

Schwartz (1992, 1994, 2014, 2017) defines values as desirable goals, varying in importance, serving as guiding principles in people's lives. People are social animals living in a state of tension between values associated with their individuality and values associated with social conformance (Aronson, 1969). Values can create tension because some values that drive our behaviour as individuals are not consistent with others that regulate our behaviour socially.

For example, superstar football players earn more money in a week than most people earn in a lifetime. They have the means to have whatever they desire and to live a lavish lifestyle in competition with other fit, wealthy young men. Not surprisingly, these young men express both highly competitive and team-based values. Sometimes their competitive values as young men competing for success can clash with social norms. In addition, sometimes the team norms of sharing with your teammates may conflict with social norms respecting the individuality and privacy of others, particularly as one comes into contact with others from outside one's field who are, nonetheless, relatively overawed followers. A number of high-profile cases of sexual assault by professional sportsmen underscore this point. For instance, from a social values perspective, one might see young football players as overpaid, oversexed and undereducated louts, whereas from an individual values perspective, they are supercompetitive and thus appropriately rewarded, but they have some problems adjusting to societal rather than team values.

FOOTBALL PLAYER CASE 1

Values have a personal component and a social component. Sometimes what we value as individuals might not be valued by society and vice versa – the interaction of personal (self-schema) and social values (social schema) can result in tension because values are something people feel strongly about. Typically, individuals become very upset when they feel their values are being threatened or compromised.

In essence, this is where the role of a manager is most difficult – in managing and sharing understanding about values, whether they are those of a co-worker, a customer, a superior or other organizations. Understanding values is critical in aligning organizational behaviour and managing people.

Schwartz (1992) identifies some values as '**trans-situational**'.

Trans-situational values refer to the idea that irrespective of the situation in which you find yourself, your values do not easily change so that you take them with you wherever you go.

For instance, if you value life and freedom above all else and one day you see a march protesting about your country going to war, it is likely that you will support this protest. Another day, you may be at the football stadium watching your team produce another amazing victory. At this time, your values for life and freedom may not be at the forefront of your thoughts but does this mean that you no longer value life and freedom or hold them any less important? In relation to the 'What would you do?' case above, even though a person works to earn money, a person may forgo a profit and even a job, if the actions are counter to their core values.

WHAT WOULD YOU DO?

WHAT WOULD YOU DO?

You run a small boutique advertising business in the IT industry, employing 12 talented people. After several secret meetings, you recently decided to take on a major tobacco company, Robin & Batman Tobacco (RBT), as a client. This is a lucrative contract and while you feel a little uneasy that you will help sell cigarettes, you make the announcement the next morning to all staff, thinking that they will be happy, given you have a profit-share system in place. That afternoon, four of your employees come into your office and say that if you take on RBT, they will have to leave the company. What would you do now, and what should you have done?

Values appear to have a strong motivational aspect. Rokeach (1968, 1973) argued that values guide our behaviours throughout life. Accordingly, Schwartz (1992) identified a number of motivational value types organized according to sets of associated values. He identified ten universal values that he believed all people would hold in common. Some of these values are mutually exclusive, but most are what Schwartz calls 'continuous', meaning that they overlap. Because values overlap, people behave or respond differently to certain things in life. Study each of the representations of Schwartz's value types in Table 2.2 for a moment and look at their associated values.

TABLE 2.2 Schwartz's values by type and their associated meanings

Value type	Description	Associated values
ACHIEVEMENT	Valuing of personal success by demonstrating one's competence according to social standards	**Success** (goal achievement) **Capability** (competence, effectiveness, efficiency) **Ambition** (hard work) **Influence** (the ability to influence people and events)
BENEVOLENCE	Preservation and enhancement of the welfare of people with whom one is in frequent personal contact	**Helpfulness** (working for the welfare of others) **Honesty** (genuineness, sincerity) **Forgivingness** (willingness to pardon others) **Loyalty** (faithful to friends, group) **Responsibility** (dependable, reliable)
CONFORMITY	Restraint of actions, inclinations and impulses that are likely to upset or harm others and that might violate social expectations or norms	**Politeness** (courtesy, good manners) **Obedience** (dutiful, meet obligations) **Self-discipline** (self-restraint, resistance to temptation) **Honouring** parents and elders (showing respect)

(Continued)

TABLE 2.2 (Continued)

Value type	Description	Associated values
HEDONISM	Pleasure and sensuous gratification for oneself	**Pleasure** (gratification of one's desires) **Enjoyment in life** (enjoyment of food, sex)
POWER	One's social status and prestige, control or dominance over people and resources	**Social powe**r (control over others, dominance) **Authority** (the right to lead or command) **Wealth** (material possessions, money)
SECURITY	Safety, harmony and stability of society, of relationships and of self	**Family security** (safety for loved ones) **National security** (protection from enemies) **Social order** (stability of society) **Cleanliness** (neatness, tidiness) **Reciprocation of favours** (avoidance of indebtedness)
SELF-DIRECTION	Independent thought and action	**Creativity** (uniqueness, imagination) **Freedom** (freedom to think and act) **Independence** (self-dependence, self-reliance, self-sufficiency) **Curiosity** (exploring) **Choice of own goals** (selecting own direction in life and being free to choose)
STIMULATION	Excitement, novelty and challenge in life	**Daringness** (risk-taking) **A varied life** (challenge, novelty, change) **An exciting life** (stimulating experiences)
TRADITION	Respect, commitment and acceptance of the customs and ideas that traditional culture or religion provides	**Humility** (modesty, self-effacement) **Acceptance** of one's portion in life (submission to and acceptance of one's life circumstances) **Devotion** (holding to religious faith and belief) **Respect for tradition** (preservation of time-honoured customs) **Moderation** (avoiding extremes of feeling or action)
UNIVERSALISM	Understanding, appreciation, tolerance and protection for the welfare of all people and for nature	**Broad-mindedness** (tolerance of different ideas and beliefs) **Wisdom** (a mature understanding of life) **Social justice** (correcting injustice, care for the weak) **Equality** (equal opportunity for all) **A world at peace** (being free of war and conflict) **A world of beauty** (beauty of nature and the arts) **Unity with nature** (fitting into nature) **Protecting** the environment (preserving nature)

Source: Adapted from Rohan (2000) and Schwartz (1992, 1996)

Much research supports Schwartz's views of values and has shown that we all, more or less, have the same sets of values – irrespective of culture, gender and religion (Schwartz, 1996). However, we differ in the priorities we assign to our values (Rohan, 2000; Schwartz, 2017). Value priorities refer to the order of values in terms of their importance to us as individuals. Research has shown that how values are prioritized can lead to conflict between people from the same political party when their values are prioritized differently (Keele and Wolak, 2006). How we prioritize our values has a strong influence on whether we trust or distrust institutions such as churches, governments, and so on (Devos et al., 2002). For this reason, there has been a lot of interest over the last decade in understanding values, especially in organizational settings, and Schwartz's model of values is growing in stature and popularity (Knafo et al., 2011; Lindeman and Verkasalo, 2005; Lönnqvist et al., 2006; Sagiv and Schwartz, 2000; Schwartz, 2014; Tsui et al., 2007).

A QUESTION OF VALUES

Using Schwartz's values, let us look at an example of how people might think and act according to their value priorities. Imagine a person who works for a major IT company meeting a client for the first time – let us call them Anne (the national manager of a chain of book stores) and Samantha (the customer relations manager of the IT firm). The two of them will have a lot to do with each other over the next few years as their associated companies are now in a joint venture. Let us assume Anne's values rate highly on tradition, power and conformance but low on universalism, so she respects and upholds her cultural and religious traditions and believes they are dominant, holding to the view that people who violate or threaten such traditions should be converted to her views or should be punished. Like Anne, Samantha also highly rates values of tradition and conformance but rather than having power as a priority she views universalism as a higher-order value. Take a look at the associated values for power and universalism in Table 2.2: do you think that over time Samantha and Anne will find it difficult to get along? What do you think might happen after they start discussing the issues that are important to them?

This is where values are very important because we tend to prefer people who have the same value priorities as we do; often we find it difficult to tolerate people with different value priorities. Understanding values, therefore, is very important for all of us when we must work with others. Managers, and especially leaders, are keen to align values within organizations. A core challenge is whether we can, or should, try to change people's values. While this is a perplexing and contentious issue, there is evidence that values can be changed through interventions.

Arieli et al. (2014), for example, have shown that values can be changed but it is not as straightforward as telling people, 'these are the values we value here and that we want you to display'. Their study focused on promoting benevolence values (see Table 2.2), using two general techniques (which reflect Kahneman's (2011) system 1 and system 2 thinking): one was 'automatic', covert, peripheral techniques such as priming people towards a certain value; the other is direct and 'effortful' methods of value change, such as self-persuasion. Arieli and colleagues found that when both automatic and effortful interventions were paired together, people would adopt benevolence values, maintaining them over a four-week period. While this research is only in its early stages, it does have the potential to make a significant impact on a range of approaches in management and organization research and practice. Essentially, if you want to bring about value change, you need to use both direct, active techniques and passive automatic techniques simultaneously.

PERSONALITY

Personality refers to the stable patterns of behaviour and internal states of mind that help explain a person's behavioural tendencies (Monte, 1991).

Why do managers need to know about personality, and what is a **personality**, anyway? Management, above all, is about managing people. And people, unlike machines or numbers, have individual personalities.

Most of us are already everyday theorists of personality – we make observations about people's actions and behaviours, and we categorize people accordingly, on an almost daily basis. Consider the following example. A group of friends goes to the university bar every Friday night. One friend, Jo, is always joking and making people laugh; another friend, Sal, is quiet and reserved. Jo is a 'fun' person, and people might say Jo is extroverted. Sal, however, is perceived as introverted. Their individual personalities influence how others react and behave in response to them, both in the bar and at work.

In the workplace, depending on the task, Sal and Jo's different personalities will have a profound effect on how those they work with perform their work and on the quality of their working relationships. For this reason alone, the ability to manage diverse personalities is an important repertoire for a manager's set of skills. In addition to values, personality is important in understanding why and how humans behave, think and feel as they do. People's personalities can have a strong impact on what they choose to do and how they perform at work (George, 1992) and on, how well they succeed in life (Rode et al., 2006), as well as on their academic achievement (Hendriks and Hofstee, 2011).

Traits refer to a mixture of biological, psychological, environmental and societal influences that characterize a person's thoughts and actions throughout their lives.

In this next section, we look at three broad accounts of how personality has been theorized: the trait, the sociocognitive and the humanist.

YOU ARE WHAT YOU ARE: THE TRAIT APPROACH

The **trait** approach develops from the perspective that personality is something that can be clearly identified, operationalized and measured.

The trait perspective became popular in the 1930s, when Allport and Odbert (1936) sought to identify all the traits that might describe people. To do this, they decided to consult a dictionary. They found about 18,000 words that could be used as descriptors, and subsequent psychologists have sought to reduce and condense this enormous list. The most popular approach is **factor analysis** – a statistical method used to describe variability among variables by identifying inter-correlation coefficients that indicate underlying factors.

Factor analysis is a statistical method used to describe variability among variables by identifying inter-correlation coefficients that indicate underlying factors.

Let us revisit Jo. Jo might be funny, friendly and easy to get along with; she might also enjoy experiencing new things and taking risks. Each of these traits reflects Jo's personality. Traits that cluster together in large-scale data sets are called a *factor*. In this example, the factor would be 'extraversion'.

By far the best-known trait theory using factor analysis is McCrae and Costa's (1999) 'Big Five' personality factors. The Big Five personality factor approach has been found to be one of the most reliable trait-based approaches to personality measurement (Endler and Speer, 1998; Schmitt et al., 2007). Almost every textbook on personality, organizational behaviour and management includes the Big Five, also sometimes referred to as the NEO-PI, and OCEAN. The five factors and their associated meanings are presented in Table 2.3.

TABLE 2.3 The Big Five personality factors

Factor	Description
Emotional stability	Emotional stability includes whether a person is calm vs anxious, self-satisfied vs self-pitying, secure vs insecure, emotionally stable vs emotionally unstable
Extraversion	Extraversion refers to whether a person is sociable vs. reserved or assertive vs timid
Openness	Openness refers to a person's approach to life - whether they are independent vs conforming, broad-minded vs narrow-minded, creative vs practical
Agreeableness	Agreeableness refers to how people get along with others - whether they are warm-hearted vs ruthless, trusting vs distrusting, helpful vs uncooperative
Conscientiousness	Conscientiousness refers to high vs low tolerance for risk, well organized vs disorganized, well disciplined vs impulsive

Source: Adapted from McCrae and Costa (2017) and Costa and McCrae (1999)

YOU ARE WHAT WE THINK: THE SOCIOCOGNITIVE APPROACH

The sociocognitive approach seeks to explain how learning, social behaviour and cognition compose and shape our personality. Its popularity started with the work of Albert Bandura and his concept of **reciprocal determinism** (Bandura, 1986).

By **reciprocal determinism**, Bandura meant that our personality is a product of our behaviour, our thoughts and our feelings in interaction with our environment.

For example, Samantha might come from a very quiet and reserved home. She has grown to like peace and quiet, a preference that makes up much of her personality. The fact that the bar is loud and crowded makes Sam uncomfortable, so she becomes quieter and more reserved. It is not that she is unsociable: Sam may be sociable and friendly at home but not in the bar because it is the wrong milieu for her personality.

One of the most appealing sociocognitive theories of personality is known as the *locus of control*, developed by Rotter (1966). You may remember our discussion on schemas as well as attribution theory, internal, external attributions and attribution errors – these are all concepts in locus of control. To get a feeling for the locus of control approach, consider the following example. You are walking along the street and you trip. You look back at the spot where you tripped and notice that there is a brick on the path. Do you say, 'Oh, I'm such an idiot because I didn't see that brick', or do you say, 'Aargh, what idiot put that brick there?'

In one case, you internalize your behaviour (it is your fault for falling over), and in the other you externalize (the reason you fell over is someone else's stupidity). In the former, we describe an internal locus of control, which refers to the belief that you control your own fate. In the latter, we describe an external locus of control, which is the perception that outside forces, or even chance, predominantly determine your fate – your fate is outside your control.

Internals have a high level of achievement, they are much more independent, enjoy better psychological and physical health, and have much better coping strategies (Myers, 2002). Moreover, internals perform better on most subjective and objective measures of organizational behaviour (Beukman, 2005; Spector, 1982). Interestingly, high external people cope better and are happier when they eventually enter aged care homes where life is structured and controlled (Cicirelli, 1987) and high externals tend to create a social environment with a preference for leading and being led in an autocratic way (Beukman, 2005).

Locus of control has been shown to be very important in terms of how people behave in organizations and how well they cope with uncertainty and change (Chen and Wang, 2007; Herscovitch and Meyer, 2002; Spector, 1982). Those with high internal locus of control are better able to deal with work conditions of high uncertainty and stress (Rahim, 1997), and in an interesting study Lee et al. (2014) found that external locus of control people are more likely to suffer stress and anxiety through over-using smartphones, a finding that has implications for people in jobs where smartphone use is a regular requirement. Ng and Feldman (2011) found that internal locus people are more likely to feel embedded within their organization, while external people are more likely to move because they are much more influenced by external forces.

Of course, as in all theories there are counter-arguments. While much of the research supports the idea of locus of control towards an internal or external orientation, to simplify behaviour as either internally or externally oriented is somewhat dualist. It might not be that people are either internal or external but rather are both simultaneously. Research suggests that locus of control can be altered through cognitive behavioural training methods, which suggests locus of control is something socialized and learned over time (Wolinsky et al., 2010).

IN PRACTICE

Answer the questions honestly and choose only one option (a or b) per question.

1. a. Children get into trouble because their parents punish them too much.

   b. The trouble with most children nowadays is that their parents are too easy with them.

2. a. Many of the unhappy things in people's lives are partly due to bad luck.

   b. People's misfortunes result from the mistakes they make.

3. a. One of the major reasons why we have wars is because people don't take enough interest in politics.

   b. There will always be wars, no matter how hard people try to prevent them.

4. a. In the long run people get the respect they deserve in this world.

   b. Unfortunately, an individual's worth often passes unrecognized no matter how hard they try.

5. a. The idea that teachers are unfair to students is nonsense.

   b. Most students don't realize the extent to which their grades are influenced by accidental happenings.

6. a. Without the right breaks one cannot be an effective leader.

   b. Capable people who fail to become leaders have not taken advantage of their opportunities.

7. a. No matter how hard you try some people just don't like you.

   b. People who can't get others to like them don't understand how to get along with others.

8. a. Heredity plays the major role in determining one's personality.

   b. It is one's experiences in life which determine what they're like.

9. a. I have often found that what is going to happen will happen.

   b. Trusting to fate has never turned out as well for me as making a decision to take a definite course of action.

10. a. In the case of the well-prepared student there is rarely, if ever, such a thing as an unfair test.

    b. Many times exam questions tend to be so unrelated to course work that studying is really useless.

11. a. Becoming a success is a matter of hard work; luck has little or nothing to do with it.

    b. Getting a good job depends mainly on being in the right place at the right time.

12. a. The average citizen can have an influence on government decisions.

    b. This world is run by the few people in power, and there is not much the little guy can do about it.

13. a. When I make plans, I am almost certain that I can make them work.

    b. It is not always wise to plan too far ahead because many things turn out to be a matter of good or bad fortune anyhow.

14. a. There are certain people who are just no good.

    b. There is some good in everybody.

(Continued)

(Continued)

15. a. In my case getting what I want has little or nothing to do with luck.
    b. Many times we might just as well decide what to do by flipping a coin.
16. a. Who gets to be the boss often depends on who was lucky enough to be in the right place first.
    b. Getting people to do the right thing depends upon ability; luck has little or nothing to do with it.
    c. As far as world affairs are concerned, most of us are the victims of forces we can neither understand nor control.
    d. By taking an active part in political and social affairs the people can control world events.
17. a. Most people don't realize the extent to which their lives are controlled by accidental happenings.
    b. There really is no such thing as 'luck'.
18. a. One should always be willing to admit mistakes.
    b. It is usually best to cover up one's mistakes.
19. a. It is hard to know whether or not a person really likes you.
    b. How many friends you have depends upon how nice a person you are.
20. a. In the long run the bad things that happen to us are balanced by the good ones.
    b. Most misfortunes are the result of lack of ability, ignorance, laziness, or all three.
21. a. With enough effort we can wipe out political corruption.
    b. It is difficult for people to have much control over the things politicians do in office.
22. a. Sometimes I can't understand how teachers arrive at the grades they give.
    b. There is a direct connection between how hard I study and the grades I get.
23. a. A good leader expects people to decide for themselves what they should do.
    b. A good leader makes it clear to everybody what their jobs are.
24. a. Many times I feel that I have little influence over the things that happen to me.
    b. It is impossible for me to believe that chance or luck plays an important role in my life.
25. a. People are lonely because they don't try to be friendly.
    b. There's not much use in trying too hard to please people – if they like you, they like you.
26. a. There is too much emphasis on athletics in high school.
    b. Team sports are an excellent way to build character.

27. a. What happens to me is my own doing.
    b. Sometimes I feel that I don't have enough control over the direction my life is taking.

28. a Most of the time I can't understand why politicians behave the way they do.
    b In the long run the people are responsible for bad government on a national as well as on a local level.

Score one point for each of the following:

2 (a), 3 (b), 4 (b), 5 (b), 6 (a), 7 (a), 9 (a), 10 (b), 11 (b), 12 (b), 13 (b), 15 (b), 16 (a), 17 (a), 18 (a), 20 (a), 21 (a), 22 (b), 23 (a), 25 (a), 26 (b), 28 (b), 29 (a)

The higher the score, the higher the external locus of control (maximum score is 23).

The lower the score, the higher the internal locus of control.

 Table 1, pp. 11–12, from J. B. Rotter (1966) 'Generalised expectancies for internal vs. external control of reinforcement', *Psychological Monographs*, 80: 1–28.

YOU ARE WHAT YOU GROW: THE HUMANIST APPROACH

The trait approaches to personality present humans as in some respects 'bits' of genes. You are a little extroverted, a little shy, a little critical, and so on. The humanist places our sense of self at the centre of personality. The aim of the humanist is to ensure that humans fully realize personal growth and potential in their entirety – as a whole being and not just as bits of genetic material. In its true original intent, humanism refers to a non-religious but naturalistic approach to understanding human behaviour, one that stresses being fundamentally ethical, human-centred, self-fulfilling and self-actualizing. The humanist tradition experienced its greatest growth in the 1960s as psychologists became increasingly critical of the over-reliance on objectivity in trait-based approaches to studying personality, where paper-and-pencil inventories and factor analysis de-humanized psychology. By far the best-known humanist psychologists are Carl Rogers (1967), Abraham Maslow (1968) and Albert Bandura (1977), also often regarded as a humanist psychologist.

READ MORE ABOUT HUMANISM

Most critical for Maslow and Rogers is the notion of how we express the self-concept. The self-concept refers to our thoughts and feelings about ourselves; in essence, it is our best answer to the question 'Who am I and who should I be?' We view ourselves as being in the world in a number of ways. First, we have an actual self and an idealized self, and we strive to reduce the gap between the two by becoming as close to our idealized self as possible. When we act in ways consistent with our ideal self, we have a positive self-image. If we feel there are gaps between our ideal self and actual self, we have a negative self-image.

Rogers approached personality from the perspective that we are all unique and fundamentally 'good' people, all striving for what Maslow termed *self-actualization*: that is, the desire to actualize our full potential of what we believe we could be. For Rogers, the key to positive self-image is the environment within which we grow because it provides three basic conditions enabling that growth:

- People must be *genuine*, *honest* and *open* about their own feelings.
- People must be *accepting*, in that they value themselves and others. Even one's own failings should be seen with a positive regard, or what Rogers referred to as 'unconditional positive regard'.
- The final important aspect for Rogers is empathy; *empathy* concerns how we communicate our feelings to the world and how we, in turn, share and reflect on these meanings. Empathy is very important in concepts such as emotional intelligence (see also pp. 65–66 and 164) and is an integral part of our ability to function in the social world.

Maslow and Rogers as well as to some extent, the socio-cognitivist Bandura, have some common elements in their ideas which provide us with a good framework for understanding what comprises a self-actualizing individual:

- They have peak experiences: that is, they find themselves experiencing moments of awe and these moments have added to their experiences and sense of place in the world.
- They are accepting of themselves and of others: self-actualized individuals do not judge themselves or others harshly.
- They are realist: that is, they tend not to make assumptions but rather approach new things in a logical and measured way.
- They have a high level of sociability, social responsibility and accountability: they enjoy being with others, often have a great sense of humour, are great at solving problems and helping others, at the same time valuing their privacy and solitude.
- They display a high level of agency: that is, they are autonomous, spontaneous and not easily led or controlled unless they want to be.
- They tend to place a great, if not greater, emphasis on the journey rather than the destination; however, they are still mindful of their goal.

PERSONALITY AND MANAGEMENT

Depending on the approach you use (e.g. trait, socio-cognitive, humanist), you will make different assumptions about people and, as a manager, you will engage with them in different ways. A humanist manager will seek to develop and foster their own and their employees' ability to move towards self-actualization and hence will design work and will structure relationships in which many of the core elements of self-actualization are developed – such as opportunity for autonomy, creating peak experiences, allowing room for creativity, practising empathy, and so on. The socio-cognitivist-oriented manager will be mindful of the types of people that exist in organizations. They will attend to the influence of people's locus of control upon performance at work and will be aware that one-size management does not fit all people. Externals react to feedback and interact differently from internals, for example. The trait-oriented manager will be mindful of the sorts of traits that are necessary in managing people, or best in certain customer interactions, or in certain tasks and roles.

Be warned, however, that having at least some understanding of personality does not mean that you are qualified for or capable of managing personalities or even categorizing and labelling people as certain types, or as possessing certain traits. Moreover, as you can read further in the related 'Extend your knowledge' box, there is complexity in the relationship between personality and human behaviour. Some of the sorts of personality traits we might assume have positive outcomes might actually produce negative ones, and vice versa. Being mindful and aware that there are different qualities to people, and that there are different ways of understanding people at work, and being abreast of and knowledgeable about current theory and research concerning different ways of understanding and dealing with different types of people will make you a better manager of people.

EXTEND YOUR KNOWLEDGE

To learn more about personality and our assumptions about the implications of 'good' and 'bad' personality traits at work, we recommend you read the article by Smith, M. B., Hill, A. D., Wallace, J. C., Recendes, T. and Judge, T.A. (2017) 'Upsides to dark and downsides to bright personality: a multidomain review and future research agenda', *Journal of Management*, 44 (1): 191–217. By reviewing and synthesizing work from organizational behaviour, human resources, strategic management and entrepreneurship, the authors show the darker side and brighter side of personality traits at work.

READ THE ARTICLE

POSITIVE PSYCHOLOGY: EMOTIONS AND HAPPINESS

Psychology is commonly associated with the study of the deviant and the abnormal but is becoming increasingly interested in more positive phenomena. Although the essence of positive psychology has been advocated since William James, the concept can be attributed to Martin E. P. Seligman and Mihaly Csikszentmihalyi (2000) who describe that:

> The field of positive psychology at the subjective level is about valued subjective experiences: wellbeing, contentment, and satisfaction (in the past); hope and optimism (for the future); and flow and happiness (in the present). At the individual level, it is about positive individual traits: the capacity for love and vocation, courage, interpersonal skill, aesthetic sensibility, perseverance, forgiveness, originality, future mindedness, spirituality, high talent, and wisdom. At the group level, it is about the civic virtues and the institutions that move individuals towards better citizenship: responsibility, nurturance, altruism, civility, moderation, tolerance, and work ethic. (2000: 5)

In its simplest form, **positive psychology** is the study, research and theorizing of the psychological bases for leading the best life possible through positive thinking, feelings and behaviour. In a management sense, positive psychology seeks to understand and to foster civic virtues, social responsibility, altruism, tolerance, happiness and psychological wellbeing (see Ivtzan et al, 2015; Pitsis, 2008c).

Positive psychology (PP), in the form of positive organizational behaviour (POB), is continuously growing and attracting attention in management theory, research and practice. In essence, it is an overnight success that was 100 years in the making. Historically, psychology predominantly concerned pathology and the treatment of a variety of mental illnesses. As such, its initial application to disciplines such as OB also bound management psychology to pathology. Psychology centred on abnormality below the norm and its explicit aim was to find ways to help the individual become 'normal'. Positive psychology is more interested in helping people be abnormal but above the norm. One area in which PP is internationally recognized is in the pursuit of happiness but, of course, this is only a small part of what PP scholars are interested in.

Not everyone is enamoured with positive psychology (see Ivtzan et al., 2015); indeed, some people are critical of certain sectors of the positive psychology movement. Barbara Held (2004), for example, believes that positive psychology paradoxically presents itself in a negative light. She believes that some within the positive psychology movement are negative or dismissive of ideas or views that run counter to the movement's dominant message: (a) negativity about negativity itself, which is explored by way of researching health psychology, happiness and coping styles rather than depression, and so on; and (b) negativity about the wrong kind of positivity, namely allegedly unscientific positivity, especially that which Seligman purports to find within humanistic psychology.

Happiness is something that PP seeks to spread and so it will be the focus of this final section of the chapter. Before we delve into happiness, let us briefly look at the general topic of **emotions**.

Emotions are by definition feelings in response to or expectation of an object or event. Emotions are complex and at the same time both highly personal and social.

It is often assumed that emotions arise as a result of an instrumentally irrational cognitive process and that they are thus superfluous to the rational job of managing. We now know that this is not the case and that emotions enter into a great deal of how managers manage.

IN PRACTICE

Try this interesting experiment. Take a few photos of your friends in natural settings - try and get them when they are naturally laughing or happy. Then instruct some other friend to assume a certain attitude or disposition (e.g. happiness). Record what they have chosen to enact. Load the pictures on your computer.

Now, show the pictures and hand out a list of emotions to another group of people. Ask each person to attach an emotion to a face. Also have them assess whether they believe the emotion being displayed in each picture is authentic or fake, and ask them to provide a short reason as to why they believe this to be the case.

How consistent and accurate are people in the attribution of emotions?

Note: We do not necessarily condone the consumption of alcohol at all, and accept no responsibility if you are influenced by the following story, but, when Tyrone was a psychology student, he and his friends used to play a very similar game but would have to drink shots of vodka every time they gave an incorrect answer. A bad idea!

Early works on emotions perceived them to be related to instinct and survival and so were presented as quite basic, simple displays of emotional responses to threat or courtship (such as anger, fear, sadness). However, by the late 1990s, emotion researchers and theorists had provided insights that go beyond the earlier accounts of emotions as solely tied to simple displays of emotions (see, for example, Campos et al., 2011). Cognition, rational and irrational, is a critical component of emotions and it is quite feasible that a person can feel many different kinds of emotions at any one time (Fong, 2006), or, more importantly, can mask emotions for a range of reasons such as the closeness they feel to other people, or the power status of others (Diefendorff et al., 2011). Diefendorff and colleagues found that when in the presence of people with high levels of power status, we mask strong negative emotions such as anger and emphasize positive ones, such as happiness. Clearly, humans are complex in their behaviours and emotional displays and so a simple smile sometimes means more than being just a smile: it may signal deference or subordination.

The understanding of emotions has been problematic. Ekman, for example (Ekman and Friesen, 1986), objectively studied emotions by observing facial expressions and found facial expressions to be consistent across cultures. But so what? When you smile, do you always feel happy? Sometimes we smile even though we are unhappy, or we smile back at someone in order to be friendly. We will tend to mimic the emotions of our 'in-group' – the group we affiliate with – irrespective of whether we actually feel that emotion (van der Schalk et al., 2011). We may display emotions when we find a person attractive (O'Doherty et al., 2003), or we want to sell them something (Sutton and Rafaeli, 1988), as well as for many other reasons that you might consider.

Anthropologists have shown that smiling might be interpreted as friendly and happy, yet culturally it might actually mean that the person smiling is nervous or anxious – as is the case with some Indonesian and Australian indigenous cultures. Of course, at other times a smile might actually mean a person is happy, but can you ever really know if what one takes to be a display of happiness means the person is actually happy? The ability to read and regulate emotions is a major concern for organizational and management researchers and theorists.

Being able to read people's emotions is recognized as an important social skill; moreover, the ability to manage one's own and other people's emotions has become a popular domain of interest. Most recently, the concept of emotional intelligence has become increasingly popular. Many textbooks include a discussion of **emotional intelligence**, with that discussion almost always placed under the topic of personality.

Emotional intelligence has been popularized by Daniel Goleman (1995), who conceives of it as the capacity to recognize our own emotions and the emotions of others, as well as the ability to manage our emotions in our relationships with others.

John D. Mayer, along with Peter Salovey, wrote profusely on EQ (emotional intelligence) in the early 1990s. Mayer argued that the popular literature's assertion – 'that highly emotionally intelligent people possess an unqualified advantage in life – appears overly enthusiastic at present and unsubstantiated by reasonable scientific standards' (Mayer, 1999: 1). More importantly, Mayer believes emotional intelligence is just that, a factor of intelligence, not a personality factor at all. Moreover, tests designed to measure emotional intelligence are still not as reliable as they should be, with claims that emotional intelligence leads to significant outcomes in terms of performance, or other life outcomes, seeming to be overstated, accounting for only 2 per cent to 25 per cent of the variance in outcomes. In other words, 75 per cent to 98 per cent of important life outcomes cannot be explained by emotional intelligence – even in those surveys developed by Mayer et al. (2001, 2003). Hence, all the really positive things you read about emotional intelligence should be treated with a little caution – it works, but not to the degree many authors of popular books might assume.

It should be made clear that the reading of emotions and the experience of emotions are very different things. Think about being severely depressed – the constant feelings of sadness, fatigue and lack of motivation can be severely debilitating, even lethal. Just by anecdotal logic we can assume that by no longer feeling depressed, you go about your daily life in a very different way. Emotions definitely affect certain life outcomes (when scientists use bland 'unemotional' words like 'life outcomes', they mean things like success, failure, life, death, alcoholism, drug abuse, and so on). Emotions include love, anger, hatred, shame, happiness, sadness, fear, resentment, joy. You will often hear people's moods being referred to, and for many people it is hard to distinguish between a **mood** and an emotion (Parkinson et al., 1996).

The difference between **moods** and emotions is duration - a mood is thought to last longer, and mood states can take time to develop. Emotions are seen as a response to an event, or emotional episode; the emotion subsides (sometimes within minutes) but a mood state remains for hours and even weeks.

IMAGE 2.1 A happy face and a sunny disposition

Happiness is a very slippery concept, and most people would describe it as feeling 'good' or feeling positive. It can generally be defined as positive thoughts and feelings about one's life and can range from elation (being present when your team wins a grand final at the weekend) to a general feeling of satisfaction and contentment with one's life; it includes feeling calm, contented, satisfied, fulfilled, inspired, positive and free.

SHINY HAPPY PEOPLE

There are few emotions that are as hotly debated in the social sciences as happiness. Life, business and leadership coaching firms, psychotherapists, organizations, self-help books and DVDs, and university research centres have been established around the emotion of happiness. But what does **happiness** actually mean?

The term 'good' could mean anything in a subjective sense, such as a general feeling that life is good (however good is defined), but here we consider 'good' to mean positive emotions and feelings with regards to one's overall quality of life. Veenhoven (2004; also see 2011) sees quality of life as integral to happiness. He breaks down quality of life (happiness) into two parts, which are represented in Figure 2.2. First, there is a distinction between chances of a good life (life chances) and the actual outcomes of life (life results); second, he distinguishes between environmental (outer) qualities and individual (inner) qualities.

Happiness, in Veenhoven's model, is a function of: (a) the type of environment we live in (top-left quadrant) and whether that environment provides opportunities for growth and happiness; (b) the purpose of life (bottom left) and whether we feel we have a higher purpose in life and are living according to our values; (c) life ability of the person (top right), which includes health, capabilities, adaptive ability (optimism, coping, resilience, and so on); and (d) appreciation of life (bottom right), which refers to satisfaction with life and is typically a subjective experience. Happiness, therefore, requires a positive environment, purpose and values, health and feelings of being capable and competent, as well as appreciation of and satisfaction with life (Veenhoven, 2010, 2011).

	OUTER QUALITIES	INNER QUALITIES
LIFE CHANCES	Livability of environment	Life-ability of the person
LIFE RESULTS	Utility of life	Appreciation of life

FIGURE 2.2 Four qualities of life (Veenhoven, 2004)

But why be happy? It has been argued that happiness increases productivity at work and leads to several other positive organizational outcomes. Yet, does happiness actually lead to organizational productivity?

This might seem like a simple question but it is one that has generated a very complex and hotly debated response. The fact is that, despite what you might read, we do not really have a definitive answer to this question – indeed, if we think about it, happiness may not be conducive to certain types of performance. For example, wealth is known to have a low correlation with happiness (Kahneman et al., 2006) and feelings of wellbeing but wealth does have a high correlation with good health (Bloom and Canning, 2000), which makes the health–happiness link a little confusing. However, the field of research on happiness and work-related outcomes is new and research is slowly beginning to address the issues of reliability, validity and scholarship (for a serious academic, rigorous and well-designed study, see Cameron et al., 2003). Also, we should point out that many of the studies on happiness and increased performance are quite dubious, as you might have read earlier in the blog by Professor Jim Coyne. So, we should be somewhat sceptical about the happiness–work performance link – indeed, we believe performance at work should not be the focus of happiness.

WATCH THIS TED TALK

Affective forecasting refers to the process of making basic decisions in the present based on predictions about your emotions in some future act or event.

As we bring this chapter to a close, we will consider just one last and important perspective on happiness from a sociocognitive point of view: Tim Wilson and Dan Gilbert discuss the concept of **affective forecasting** and the cognitive errors that occur in forecasting – impact bias and focalism.

Sometimes the prospect of a negative event in the future elicits negative emotion in the present, such that you might refrain from action (for example, you may

Impact bias may be considered to be the overestimation of the intensity and duration of the feelings actually experienced when we achieve that future event or goal (for example, we do complete the big project but we find few if any of us feel elated; rather, we feel exhausted and just want to go home).

Focalism is the tendency for us to focus on the first piece of information or experiences when making decisions about the future, resulting in a focal error because we place too much importance on one aspect of an event in our feelings and perceptions about an event in the future.

fear bad news from a full-body health check-up and so you keep putting it off). Of course, sometimes we also over-predict the value of positive goals because we think that the future event will elicit lots of positive feelings for us (for example, we may look forward to the completion of a major project at work and plan to go for a big night out). When we pursue things, we often make a cognitive error called **impact bias**. One cause of the impact bias is **focalism**.

Another source of impact bias may be our failure to anticipate how quickly we will make sense of things that happen to us in a way that speeds emotional recovery. In an interesting study conducted on affective forecasting, Kent Lam and his colleagues (2005) found that there are cultural differences in the impact bias process of affective forecasting. It seems that some cultures that think more holistically are less likely to be affected by focalism. The study found 'Westerners' are more likely to focalize than 'East Asians'; however, it also found that Westerners who were helped to 'de-focus' were as likely as Asians to make only moderate affective forecasts. In other words, when we are pursuing happiness, we need to be cognizant or aware of the fact that we sometimes attach too much emotional weight to that event, such that we can actually end up being disappointed when the event or goal achieved does not meet our expectations.

Realistically, how likely would it be that any future event would provide you with everlasting happiness and joy? Thus, in the pursuit of happiness we must be aware that the feeling subsides and sometimes our pursuits might not necessarily make us as happy as we once thought. Conversely, negative events are never as terrible (in terms of our ability to cope) as we think. What Wilson and Gilbert (2005) argue is that we often find ways to cope internally with situations as they arise. In the end, you create your future emotional state in the way that you approach and make sense of your place in that future.

IN PRACTICE

How happy are you?

This survey measures how happy you feel. Please read each of the following groups of statements and select the one statement in each group that best describes the way you have been feeling for the past week, including today.

1. a. I feel miserable almost all the time.
   b. I often feel miserable.
   c. I usually feel neutral.
   d. I usually feel pretty good.
   e. I feel great almost all the time.
2. a. I find life to be boring all the time.
   b. I'm pretty bored with most aspects of life.

c. I find life boring at times but at other times, it interests me.
d. I'm interested in most aspects of life.
e. I find life and living to be absolutely fascinating.

3. a. I have no direction or life purpose.
b. I'm unsure about my life direction and purpose.
c. Sometimes I feel like I know my life purpose.
d. I'm pretty clear about my life purpose and direction.
e. My life purpose and direction are crystal clear.

4. a. I have no energy and feel tired almost all the time.
b. I often feel tired and lethargic.
c. I usually have enough energy to do what I need to do.
d. Most of the time I feel energetic and enthusiastic.
e. I'm bursting with energy and enthusiasm almost all the time.

5. a. I'm extremely pessimistic about the future.
b There are times when I feel pessimistic about the future.
c. I'm not sure about the future, one way or the other.
d. I'm pretty optimistic about the future.
e. I'm extremely optimistic and excited about the future.

6. a. I don't have any close friends.
b. I have a few friends but none I really consider close.
c. I have a few good friends and family members with whom I'm close.
d. I have quite a few good friends.
e. I have lots of good friends and feel I easily connect with everyone.

7. a. I don't think I have any strengths at all.
b. I'm not sure whether or not I have any strengths.
c. I'm getting to know my strengths.
d. I know my strengths and try to use them when I can.
e. I know exactly what my strengths are and I use them all the time.

8. a. I never enjoy myself no matter what I'm doing.
b. I find it difficult to enjoy life in the moment.
c. I try to enjoy life as much as I can.

(Continued)

(Continued)

d. I enjoy myself most of the time.

e. I thoroughly enjoy every moment.

9. a. I have absolutely nothing for which to be grateful.

b. There's not much in my life for which I'm grateful.

c. I'm grateful for a few things in my life.

d. I have quite a few things in my life for which I'm grateful.

e. I'm extremely grateful for so many things in my life.

10. a. I've accomplished nothing.

b. I've not accomplished much in life.

c. I've accomplished about as much as the average person.

d. I've accomplished more in life than most people.

e. I've accomplished a great deal more in life than most people.

Score each question from 1 to 5 where (a) equals 1 and (e) equals 5 (your maximum score, therefore, should be 50 and your minimum 10).

If you scored 40 or above – you're doing extremely well; keep up the great work.

If you scored 30–39 – you're doing pretty well but might like to review the questions on which you scored 3 or below and consider how you might improve in these areas.

If you scored below 29 – you could be much happier!

SUMMARY

In this chapter, we have introduced the vast and complex field of organizational behaviour:

- Organizational behaviour represents the cohabitation of psychology with management. Our task has not been to provide you with a complete account of OB – there are other books that do that – but simply to suggest some ways in which psychology and its insights may be useful in understanding management and work.
- We have addressed perception, values and personality theory.
- We have looked at the new currents in organizational psychology, which stress positive organizational behaviour.
- We looked at the fascinating importance that emotions such as happiness have in and for organizations.

TEST YOURSELF

Review what you have learned by visiting:
https://study.sagepub.com/managingandorganizations5e or your eBook

- **Test yourself with multiple-choice questions.**
- **Revise key terms with the interactive flashcards.**

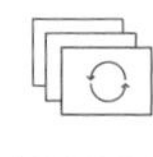

REVISE KEY TERMS

TEST YOURSELF

CASE STUDY

Oslo Philharmonic Orchestra

There is something mysterious about concert halls. All concert halls, not only the Victorian ones: dark corridors, silent signs, thick doors and the bright and alluring stage. The mystique is even more noticeable when the orchestra appears – musicians in black and white, concentrated and grave looking. After a minute or two, the first violin player (concert master) stands up. A tone is given somewhere in the ensemble – and everyone follows in tuning. Then a new silence: everyone stands up – the conductor arrives on the stage ...

- The largest orchestra in Norway, Oslo Philharmonic Orchestra, contains 109 musicians, performing as a large group, struggling and searching for a homogeneous sound day after day, concert after concert. Starting every week with a new conductor, sometimes one the orchestra already knows – even maybe the chief conductor, other times a stranger. Sometimes the teamwork pays off – in magic moments of melding together into one. But the large group is most of all 109 individuals, or even 110 including the conductor, trained towards perfection, maybe with a solo career in mind. Most of them are still in training for individual perfection, often by silent competition with the neighbouring musician at their side.
- Musicians in Oslo Philharmonic Orchestra differ widely in their career outlooks, motivations and horizons as well as their paths into their organization. Some are just starting while others are near the end of their careers. Some have moved into their present position by working up the ranks, some are fresh from music school, while others have principal positions that will last a lifetime. Not all are equally ambitious or motivated, nor are they on the same level musically, technically or emotionally. They may despise and envy one another, disagree about music and the merits of conductors, and even be in open competition with their colleagues for prestigious or better positions within their respective orchestral sections.
- The nature of work in a symphony orchestra may therefore be described as a dichotomous experience for musicians: at times, it is extremely exciting, challenging and satisfying; at other times, it is full of stress, disappointment and boredom. Orchestral musicians are highly skilled specialists who have trained from an early age. Once

(Continued)

(Continued)

in an orchestra, musicians must contend with the social dynamics of a huge group that is an amalgamation of diverse individuals, and in an organizational setting that is complex and competitive. The most mysterious part is how it is possible to make this highly specialized and individual work into an integrated and collaborating unity.

- The history of this particular orchestra goes back to the eighteenth century, under other names and forms than the orchestra we know today, formally established in 1919 as *Filharmonisk Selskap*. Famous composers and conductors such as Edvard Grieg, Johan Halvorsen and Carl Nielsen were all part of the orchestral music scene in Oslo in the eighteenth and nineteenth centuries, developing the orchestra. In more modern times, Mariss Jansons, the chief conductor for the 20-year period to 2000, is recognized by many as the most important individual in stretching the orchestra's quality and quantity of repertoire. He has also been important in stretching the management opportunity set.
- The guest conductors (on a weekly basis) and the chief conductor (leading the orchestra for about ten weeks a year) have an unquestionably important role in the orchestra's performance and development. Although there are some universal rules to the art of conducting, the conductors differ greatly in personal qualities and in musical orientation. The dominant picture of a great conductor is still the one of the lonely and gifted genius, a picture often used to describe Mariss Jansons.

We can feel the energy increase in the orchestra sometimes a week before Mariss arrives. Because we know it is going to be that good and that challenging. He forms me as a musician – by his ambitions for the orchestra and for every one of us.

- There are wonderful stories of other, greater conductors, but with less pedagogical skills. The musicians in the Oslo Philharmonic Orchestra tell stories of 'tyrannical artistic leaders' with high expectations and ambitions. Some leaders are described as having dangerous tempers and unpredictable behaviours. Individual members of the orchestra have experienced intense critique in front of the entire orchestra but there is never any noticeable protest or protection of the individual in this context. The stories of these conductors are often told with a touch of pride and as a history of success, probably because they are all willing to pay the price for an unforgettable concert. Because the musicians face a different leader every week, they must be flexible. They have to adapt to different interpretations of the same symphony and tolerate these variations. In this way, an orchestra may be one of few organized professional groups that are explicitly trained in following a leader, no matter what the circumstances.
- Everyday rehearsals and concerts on Thursdays and Fridays are held at Oslo Concert Hall, while the administrative department, with about 19 employees, is located in another building. Here you will also find the administrative director, in charge of the entire organization. The story of 'following the leader' does not, however, apply to him. In any case of non-artistic decision, the orchestra seems to follow a different logic. Outside the concert hall, every decision is based on democracy: everyone should and will be heard.

Despite the fact that it is me that has the total responsibility for this organization, I have to give the chief conductor room enough to be creative and to be an excellent performer. The rest of the year I also have to deal with a group of 109 strong individuals that feel that they have a right to be in charge - as a community. I have to live with the fact that my management room is reduced.

- During a one-year period, the chief conductor, the board leader and the administrative director all left their positions - in that order. The orchestra remained the same - 109 individuals.

Questions

1. Imagine you are recently employed as the administrative director. How will you start to establish relations and teamwork with the main artistic leader (the chief conductor)?
2. What do you think is the main challenge you have to deal with as a director?
3. What do you think are the main tensions, natural and unnatural, in an orchestra like this?
4. How can you, as a top manager, deal with these tensions?

Case prepared by Dr Grete Wennes, Associate Professor, Trondheim Business School, Norway.

ADDITIONAL RESOURCES

- Nobel winner Daniel Kahneman has written extensively on how cognitive bias affects our decision making. His 2011 book *Thinking Fast and Slow* (London: Penguin Books) will become a classic and is an engaging, easy-to-read book to get you into the topic.
- While the film is a little old, it is still as watchable almost 20 years later: *Crash* (Haggis, 2004) captures the impact of stereotypes especially in terms of race. The story follows a group of disparate characters whose lives cross over through certain events. The movie beautifully plays with our inherent bias and stereotypes based on race and gender, especially as people go about doing their daily jobs as cops, lawyers, government workers, and so on.
- *Lion* (David, 2016) is a movie that demonstrates some of the core ideas of positive psychology, as well as values and the uniqueness of our personality. The story centres on a young Indian boy who becomes lost and follows his journey from India to Australia and back as an adoptee searching for his mother and brother.
- A great book that focuses on fundamental attribution errors that we often make in our lives, and also provides some practical ways to overcome those biases, is Daniel R. Stalder's (2018) *The Power of Context*. New York: Prometheus.

MANAGING TEAMS AND GROUPS

COHABITATION, COLLABORATION, CONSTERNATION

LEARNING OBJECTIVES

This chapter is designed to enable you to:

- describe the concept of group dynamics and the process of group development
- understand the properties and processes of groups
- explain the processes through which teams are formed and the various models of team development
- understand that there is a 'dark side' to teams and teamworking in organizations
- describe toxic emotions and how to deal with them in organizations and teams.

BEFORE YOU GET STARTED...

Advice from Mahatma Gandhi:

A small group of determined spirits with an unquenchable thirst for their mission can alter the course of history.

INTRODUCTION

Our world continues to become increasingly complex and ambiguous. Resources are becoming scarcer, and globalization continues to open up exciting possibilities, while at the same time increasing the level of risk and complexity in managing organizations. With complexity comes the need to address problems in collaborative ways, where once upon a time the aim was to ensure team members were as similar as possible, current complex problems require a diversity of knowledge, skills, philosophies and practices in order to achieve success. Not surprisingly, the use of **teams** has grown because they allow greater flexibility in decision-making and adaptation to change, providing better decisions and performance outcomes than individuals operating under such contexts. Sometimes teams can be the most rewarding ways of doing things but at other times teamwork can be frustrating, riddled with conflict and even counterproductive. The reality is that every single one of us will work as part of a team at some stage in our lives – be it playing sport, doing ballet, or while studying or working. Teams and team-working is a central concern of organizational behaviour scholars because it is such an important part of life in organizations.

A **team** can be defined as two or more people psychologically contracted together to achieve a common organizational goal in which all individuals involved share at least some level of responsibility and accountability for the outcome.

In Chapter 2, we considered the problems of perception and how perceptual errors can affect our judgements and evaluations of people. These processes are even more complex in teams because we are dealing with multiple people simultaneously, all expected to be aligned to the same objectives and goals. It is therefore important for us to have a general understanding of teams, their psychological properties, how they influence us and how teams work.

We will explore our definition of teams in greater detail. Management academics like to distinguish between a team and a **group**; even though the differences between teams and groups are subtle, they are important differences in some contexts. However, in this chapter we sometimes use the terms interchangeably because in the development of psychology, all teams have traditionally been referred to as groups.

A **group** can be defined as two or more people working towards a common goal, but there is no psychological contract between them; the outcomes are less dependent on all the members working together, and there is usually no shared responsibility and accountability for outcomes.

A **psychological contract** can be defined as the assumptions, beliefs and expectations held between one person and another or within a group, organization, or some other collective entity, about the nature and function of the relationship between them.

IN PRACTICE

Eve, Theodore, Miya and Joseph all work in the kitchen of the Olive Tree café, a top-rated restaurant in the trendiest part of town. Every Wednesday they get together with the head chef to design and plan the weekend specials, decide on who will cook what meals, and so on. This weekend is Valentine's Day, traditionally one of the busiest weekends ever. The head chef points out to his team how important it is that they understand each other's roles and the menu, and stresses that they will need to work together to cope with the onslaught of diners while maintaining the highest quality of food and service. On Valentine's Day, couples from all around town leave their homes for the Olive Tree. The traffic is bad; some people are stuck in traffic, others are waiting for an hour or so for a bus and up to 45 minutes for a taxicab, while others are walking to the restaurant. Obviously, these groups of people are going to the Olive Tree for a common purpose – to eat fine food with their partner – but they are not bound by any **psychological contract**. If the people on the bus never get to the restaurant, it does not affect the people who get there by walking or driving. If, however, one of the kitchen team doesn't perform, it will affect the overall quality of the outcome (food may go out late, be burnt, be undercooked, taste bad, and so on). Thus, in this example, the Olive Tree kitchen represents a team and the customers a group.

In reality, a team is a form of work group in which people are dependent on others in their team for achieving outcomes. Interdependence among people in teams poses many challenges and opportunities to managers because it means increased saliency has to be given to managing issues such as personalities and values; coordinating behaviours; establishing direction, roles and responsibilities; and resolving conflict. Put simply, teams are not only difficult things to be part of, but they are also full of leadership challenges. To help you better understand the complexities of teams, we look at how group psychology came about, mainly in the form of group dynamics. We then consider how an individual can be affected by groups of people, as well as how and why teams are used.

TEAM AND GROUP DYNAMICS

Teamwork can be extremely difficult because it is so open to interpersonal psychological issues. Certain psychological properties of teams can attract and bind individuals, or they can orient people towards destructive behaviours, causing some managers to question the value of teams because they require substantial management time and resources. In other words, teams can demand a lot of management time and effort, mainly because when teams are used, they are not designed or managed to great effect.

The specific study of teams and especially their psychological properties is called group dynamics. **Group dynamics** is a concept popularized by Knowles and Knowles (1972) and refers to the underlying attitudes, perceptions and behaviours of groups.

Group dynamics is concerned with how groups form, their structure, processes, and how they function as a unit. Group dynamics is relevant in both formal and informal groups of all types. In essence, group dynamics is concerned with the study and analysis of any form of interaction that occurs within group contexts.

Included within group dynamics are questions about why and how teams are formed, how they develop, how they work (or do not work), how they are sustained, their challenges, and their eventual demise. So let us take a close look at group dynamics.

THE THINGS THAT BIND: WHY WE FORM GROUPS

Why do we form groups? First, let us consider the notion of safety in numbers. In evolutionary terms, forming groups rather than existing alone is a very important way in which many animals ensure survival. Ants and bees have very large, highly structured and organized societies, comprising many groups of worker ants or bees, queens and armies. Small fish in the ocean and animals in the wild (such as the impala, buffalo and zebra) all travel in large groups for safety.

In the tradition of Charles Darwin, imagine yourself as an animal aware that a predator might be waiting to make you their lunch. If there were a series of points on your journey where attack was more likely, your chances of surviving would be greater if you travelled in large numbers than if you were on your own – especially if you were fitter, smarter and could run faster than the others.

However, to say that we form groups simply to avoid getting killed is a bit too simplistic. Psychologically, being part of a group is critical to our survival in other very important ways.

Second, we form groups because of a sense of belongingness. If you pick up any psychological textbook and turn to the chapter on psychological disorders (abnormal psychology), you will notice one remarkable thing: all the disorders (regardless of their cause) are considered problems for individuals because they cannot function effectively as part of society. Being part of a group is necessary for healthy psychological development and identity. In their classic text *The Social Psychology of Organizations*, Daniel Katz and Robert L. Kahn state the following:

> By being part of something beyond the physical self, the individual can achieve a sense of belongingness and can participate in accomplishments beyond individual powers. Moreover, affiliating with others can extend the ego in time as well as space, for individuals can see their contribution to the group as enduring over time even though they themselves may not survive. (Katz and Kahn, 1978: 374)

Being part of a group, therefore, is important for our own psychological needs because it provides us with a sense of self beyond our physical life. We all belong to one form of group or another – a family, a group of friends, a work team, a student group, a union, a special interest group, a religious group, a nationality, and so on. We feel that we either belong or do not belong to those groups for myriad reasons.

With the related 'In Practice' exercise, you will notice that, for almost all of us, whether we feel part of a team or not is based on whether we are made to feel we belong, whether our interests and values are similar, and whether we fit in. Organizationally, when thinking about teamwork, the manager might design a team that cultivates the feelings in the first column and reduces the feelings in the second column. By identifying, or not identifying, with certain teams, we are effectively creating a distinction between 'us' and 'them'. Each of us is treated as either in or apart from the group. When part of a group, we, in turn, probably treat others in the same 'us' and 'them' terms.

IMAGE 3.1 Team at work

IN PRACTICE

Team feelings

Take a few moments to think about the groups you feel you belong to or are a part of. You do not need to identify these groups to anyone unless you want to – just think about them.

In the first column below, list the reasons why you feel included as part of these groups.

After you complete that list, think about the groups that you feel you do not belong to or that you feel excluded from and, using the second column below, list the reasons why you feel that you do not belong.

I feel I *do* belong because:	I feel I *do not* belong because:
______________	______________
______________	______________
______________	______________
______________	______________
______________	______________

Now, with some friends, compare and contrast your answers. What do you notice about why people felt they did or did not belong to each group? Can you see any common themes emerging? Are there any major differences?

Much research has shown that in group settings we tend to favour certain individuals when making decisions. This phenomenon is called the **in-group bias**. In-group bias occurs because one's **out group** members are perceived to possess qualities and attributes not possessed by out-group members. Such bias can be between groups (favouring your own group over other groups) and even within groups (favouring select members of your group over other members of your group) (Hogg, 1996; Turner, 1987). Creating and reinforcing an 'us' and 'them' distinction has often been used as a way of uniting teams towards performance, especially by getting a team to compete against 'other' teams, thus creating strong identification with one's own team, or in-group. Over time, strong identification with your group can lead to quite problematic relations, such as prejudice and distrust, and even hatred and anger, towards members of different out-groups (see Whitley, 1999), thus having negative conflict management consequences for the organization (Wombacher and Felfe, 2017). The more the in-group members believe that the negative attributes of the out-group are fixed and stable, the more likely they are to have negative perceptions of them because they present a greater threat (Effron and Knowles, 2015; Samão and Brauer, 2015).

In-group bias refers to the process by which members of a group favour or treat members of their own group with preference over others.

Out-group refers to those people within one's own group, or in another group, who are treated inequitably or more negatively because they are not seen as belonging to one's own in-group.

Overall, group cohesion and identification are important, but bear in mind that it can pose problems that make managing teams a complex art. We will explore managing groups in more detail later in this chapter. For now, let's look at the different types of groups that exist, and their dynamics.

TYPES OF GROUPS

Formal groups refer to those groups where people have been specifically selected and are recognized as a team in order to complete a task, innovate, solve a problem, or provide a service or a product.

Informal groups are groups that are not necessarily sanctioned or even accepted by the organization and its management, but which still play a significant role in organizational outcomes.

Closed groups have several limitations or barriers to joining, maintaining and ceasing membership.

Open groups usually have free membership and no barriers to exit, and attract people due to shared interest.

Having developed an understanding as to why we form groups, let us now look at different kinds of groups that we may experience over time. Typically there are two categories of groups in organizations – **formal groups** and **informal groups**.

An informal group forms outside the formal structuring of work roles and activities. For example, informal groups are a group of workmates who meet for lunch every week, union members within an organization, a group of workmates who play in a football team at weekends, or even a number of people who form a coalition within the organization to resist, reduce or alter the power or interests of others in the organization.

Most groups tend to be **closed groups**. For example, most teams in an organization will contain people skilled or capable in key areas. A surgical team will include surgeons, anaesthetists and nurses – all skilled in specific aspects of the surgical task. Obviously, to be part of this team you must have completed a range of university degrees in medicine, nursing, and so on. Moreover, the surgeon may belong to a national association, such as the Royal College of Surgeons, which has strict requirements in all aspects of joining and maintaining membership (including entry requirements, ongoing exams, and fees and charges). Further, being a member of such a group provides one with accreditation, as well as a certain level of prestige and professional trust within the community. Also, continued membership is not guaranteed because if a person fails to behave in accordance with the code of professional conduct and standards, the surgeon will find themselves 'struck off' the society.

Some groups are relatively open; they are called, not surprisingly, **open groups**. Some of the most common open groups can be found online. YouTube or TedX are perfect examples in which people share favourite movies, ideas and productions; in the case of TedX (or TED Talks), inspirational, educational and interesting events and presentations are provided by people from all walks of life from all parts of the world and for free. YouTube members vary from professional movie makers through to total amateurs and, as with TED Talks, come from all over the world. Of course, in reality even open teams are limited in membership in terms of available and accessible technologies, same interests, power relations, composition of the team, in terms of operating within accepted behavioural norms as we will see shortly.

Table 3.1 lists the most common types of teams used in organization.

TABLE 3.1 Types of teams in organizations

Advice and involvement teams	**Management decision-making committees, quality control (QC) circles, staff involvement teams**
Production and service teams	Assembly teams, maintenance, construction, mining and commercial airline teams, consulting teams, sales and healthcare teams
Project and development teams	Research teams, new product development teams, software development teams

Advice and involvement teams	**Management decision-making committees, quality control (QC) circles, staff involvement teams**
Action and negotiation teams	Military combat units, surgical teams, trade union negotiating teams
Functional teams	These are teams which have managerial hierarchies and specific core functions, such as a HR team, marketing team, sales team, and so on
Cross-functional teams	As organizations try to reduce silos in organizational functions, they tend to create cross-functional teams. These will involve people from several different units. These teams are typically found in advice and production and service teams
Self-directed teams	These teams tend to be highly autonomous, empowered to make decisions, often have their own budget, and do their own hiring

Source: Adapted from West (2008), with our own additions of functional, cross-functional and self-directed teams

While it is helpful to define teams in a way that simplifies how we might make sense of them, the reality is that how we actually define, classify and describe teams lacks consensus and agreement (Hollenbeck et al., 2012). As we travel throughout this chapter, you will notice that we keep adding layers to the concept of teams, but let's begin with John R. Hollenbeck and his colleagues. Hollenbeck et al. (2012) came up with 42 terms used by researchers to classify teams. They argued that while there are many variations in the categories used to describe teams, there are three central concepts that can be thought of as the building blocks for differentiating teams. These are:

1. *Skill differentiation* – refers to the degree to which team members have functional or specialized knowledge that makes each member replaceable or substitutable.
2. *Authority differentiation* – refers to how responsibility for decision-making is handled within the team: is it the responsibility of an individual member to decide, is it subgroups of the team, or the collective team as a whole?
3. *Temporal stability* – refers to the degree to which team members have a history of working together in the past and whether they expect to work together in the future.

This is a good way to think about teams in terms of these three elements; however, we do believe some elements are lacking and so we build on these elements throughout this chapter. First of all, we need to discuss the idea of social impact because it fits Hollenbeck et al.'s (2012) categories but also provides important extensions that are missing from their categorization of teams. So, let's look at some of the properties and processes in more detail because these help us in developing a good understanding of teams and hence to get a better handle on managing teams.

GROUP PROPERTIES AND PROCESSES

So far, we have considered some of the reasons why we join groups, and the kinds of groups that exist in organizations. Group dynamics research and theory have identified some key properties and processes of teams that are integral to how they perform on given tasks and also help us to make even better sense of the various types of teams in organizational and social life. In this section, we will discuss issues of social impact and group size, social facilitation, conformance and obedience, as well as the problems of groupthink and social loafing.

SOCIAL IMPACT AND GROUP SIZE

Social impact refers to the strength of ties between individuals interacting in a group, the spatio-temporal closeness of the individuals (that is, how close you are in physical distance and in time) and the size of the group.

In group work, **social impact** has been identified as an important factor in the richness and quality of communication between people interacting together (Latané, 1981; Latané and Wolf, 1981). Hollenbeck et al. (2012) do not really emphasize physical proximity and size but these are very important, especially given the growth of virtual teams: in particular, physical proximity has many implications for teams and could be added as a fourth element to Hollenbeck et al.'s list (Foster et al., 2015).

To get a better idea of how people affect and have an impact on each other, let us look at social impact a bit more closely. Social impact theory is concerned with how a social system influences people to behave and think in certain ways. In other words, how people in teams perform is a function of how well they know each other, trust each other and get along, how interrelated their jobs are in terms of space and time, how large the group is – the larger the group, the lower the social impact.

Group size is a critical component in how groups perform. Online groups, often referred to as online communities (YouTube.com, Facebook, Instagram, etc.), would be perceived typically to have a low social impact and are therefore usually seen as unable to get complex tasks completed because they lack close ties, are spatio-temporally distant and can be of an immense size – even millions of people – thus lacking the closeness one would find in a small group. This is in theory of course.

WATCH THIS TED TALK

There are exceptions to the argument that large groups lack the social impact and meaningfulness of small groups. The open source software (OSS) phenomenon is testament to this statement. OSS is a form of software development where the underlying 'code' is openly visible and non-proprietary, such that it is open to contributions from huge numbers of globally distributed software engineers and hobbyists that can access it freely and work on developing improvements. The popular web browser Firefox, developed by the Mozilla Foundation, is probably an example of an OSS solution you are familiar with or have used. This concept of engaging large numbers of individuals in a quasi-team formation is now being popularized through the term crowdsourcing. Crowdsourcing is defined as the act of taking a task once performed by the firm and outsourcing it to a large, usually undefined, crowd of users through advanced online technology (Howe, 2006). Organizations such as Starbucks (https://ideas.starbucks.com) and Dell (www.ideastorm.com) are now slowly shifting their attention towards external crowds to source new ideas and work on distinct tasks. Research, theory and discussion on crowdsourcing will explode over the next few years.

The size of a team is very important. In terms of social impact, large groups usually find it more difficult to communicate and coordinate interpersonal behaviours and actions towards group goals and objectives. Conversely, the task is also a critical component because a team that is working on a complex and demanding task but is too small in size will be stretched beyond the limits of its abilities. Similarly, a team that is too large, especially one working on routine tasks, will perform less well and less efficiently due to overcrowding – simply put, there are 'too many chefs cooking the soup'. In an interesting study, Bertolotti et al. (2015) looked at the relationship between multiple team members (MTM) and research and development (R&D) team performance and found an inverse U shape relationship between them when we consider factors such as the use of social networks and the forms of technology used. What was interesting was the effect of the use of IM (instant messaging) as a moderator of team performance. The use of IM meant small teams performed better on tasks, but in larger teams it had the opposite effect.

According to Patrick Laughlin (2011), one of the leading researchers on teams, team composition is also a critical factor influencing team performance. He suggests that group homogeneity (a high degree of sameness of the individuals) and heterogeneity (a high degree of difference) will have differential performance effects even when the group size is the same (between three and four members). However, what is interesting is that when the homogeneous groups are made up of high abilities (they are experts, skilled, knowledgeable, etc.), they outperform heterogeneous groups. Of course, more research is needed, but one might also assume that high-ability heterogeneous groups would outperform high-ability homogeneous groups.

WATCH THIS TED TALK

This suggests ability is also a critical performance factor. So, for 'better' problem solving one would focus more on teams with high levels of ability. Indeed, Laughlin found that high-ability individuals even outperformed groups composed of two, three, four or five low-ability members. Makes sense really, don't you think? So, in short, while team size definitely has an effect on team performance, with there being various arguments on optimal team size, the reality is that much more work needs to be done to fully understand how different factors moderate and mediate the effect of team size on performance.

It appears that in face-to-face teams the 'Goldilocks' principle applies to group size – teams must not be too big, nor too small, but 'just right!'. What does just right mean? The answer to this question is not as simple as some people make it out to be. Typically, there are a number of questions that we need to consider when deciding on group size:

- *What is the nature of the task?* For example, is the task complex and ambiguous and does it demand a great amount of resources, skills, knowledge and expertise? A large group might mean a greater pool of resources, expertise, skills and knowledge. There is a trade-off in terms of group size and the available pool of talent. A large group will have a greater pool of talent to choose from than a small group; however, a large group will require clearer leadership and coordination as more people can mean greater chances of conflict.

- *What is the nature of the physical space within which the team will operate?* If space is limited, a large group will mean space is cramped and uncomfortable.
- *Is there likely to be a high turnover of staff?* A small team cannot afford for one or two people to leave, so is the team large or skilled enough to cope with drop-outs?
- *How skilled, knowledgeable and able are the team members?* High-ability teams outperform low-ability teams, irrespective of size.
- *Are team members heterogeneous or homogeneous?* Heterogeneous teams have more to offer learning; homogeneous teams have more to offer group cohesion.
- *Is the team to be self-led or will there be a formal leader established?* Large teams will find it harder than small teams to be self-led and so structures and systems will need to be implemented in order to direct large teams. Small teams tend to be better for self-led tasks as people tend to share leadership in small groups.

There is a lot of research and theory about teams, and even more written in mainstream management websites, consultancies and online resources on teamwork, however there is clearly still a lot we don't understand about team-working. So many things affect the quality of experience in teamwork and we need to look no further than social facilitation to see how individuals affect teams and how groups of people affect individuals – or, more precisely, how the process of social facilitation affects and is affected by social interactions.

SOCIAL FACILITATION

As social influence and impact suggest, groups of people have a profound effect on individual behaviour and the overall performance of the team. Social facilitation is a concept that is as old as the discipline of psychology itself. In the late 1800s, Norman Triplett observed that children fishing would wind in their reel much faster when other children were present (Myers, 2001). The phenomenon of an increase in performance in the presence of others, known as social facilitation, is similar to the effect found in the Hawthorne studies by human relations theorists. Almost always, however, social facilitation occurs around fairly simple tasks only, or tasks a person is experienced in doing. If the tasks are complex or the person performing them is a novice, social facilitation produces performance that is actually worse in social settings than when the person works alone. Thus, how you introduce and train new team members needs careful consideration and thought. Also, people who can do something competently alone may not necessarily perform competently in the presence of others. Training and experience, therefore, can be a critical aspect to successful teamwork, as all sportspeople who play competitive team sports know.

CONFORMANCE AND OBEDIENCE

In 1955, Solomon Asch published in the journal *Scientific American* what has become a classic study, in which he reported an interesting and simple experiment

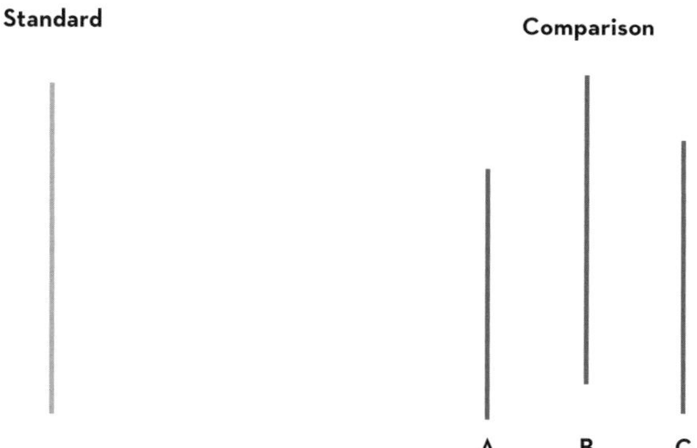

FIGURE 3.1 Solomon Asch's experiment demonstrating conformity. Which line is identical to the standard line: A, B or C?

about how groups influence individuals. Asch had prearranged a group of five people who were seated in a room. Another individual, who had been recruited for the study, would arrive at the experiment to find this group already seated at the table. The individual was told that the group consisted of other people who were recruited for the experiment. What the individual did not know was that everyone in the group was a confederate of the experimenter. After the subject (who was the real focus of the experiment) had sat down with the group, the experimenter began the study by telling the members of the group that he would show them a standard line and a set of comparison lines (similar to the lines in Figure 3.1). The group had to decide which comparison line was identical to the standard line, and each person spoke in turn, with the individual who was the subject of the experiment being asked to speak last. The process was repeated a couple of times. On each occasion, the answer was obvious, but each person in the group would answer in a way that was clearly incorrect – for example, they would all say C is identical to the standard line. Now, if you were the individual who was the real focus of the study, how do you think you would answer? You think you would say B, would you not? Well, do not be so sure, because over the course of the experiment approximately one-third of the individuals agreed with the group – even though all the information available showed that the answer was incorrect.

WATCH ASCH EXPERIMENT VIDEO

Often, of course, conformity is absolutely necessary. Imagine a workplace in which no one conformed to the rules concerning health and safety, for instance, and no one followed policy on decision-making. Imagine the chaos; you would be in a workplace that looked a lot like the Wild West with its lawlessness, bandits and outlaws. Even so, many people tend to follow or conform blindly to the group even when what the group is doing is clearly wrong. Conformity might help explain why so few people resist their organizations and why a group may tolerate or engage in unethical and socially irresponsible behaviours (see also Chapter 13 for an in-depth discussion on ethics and responsibility).

WATCH ZIMBARDO EXPERIMENT VIDEO

Groupthink refers to the tendency of members of a group to seek and maintain harmony in a group, at the cost of ignoring or avoiding important decisions that may disrupt harmony.

GROUPTHINK

Similar to conformity, **groupthink** is a term coined by Irving Janis, who was intrigued by how teams would sometimes arrive at devastating decisions – even when the teams appear to be prestigious, well educated or carefully selected (Janis, 1982). Since Janis's study, many researchers have found that groupthink occurs across broad levels of an organization. Even when a senior leadership team is made up of experts of equal power and status, it can become too strong. When this occurs, the team reinterprets information so that members can avoid any thinking that might disrupt the strong team culture, sometimes leading to a belief that, together, the team can overcome any obstacle faced (Clegg et al., 2002), but, of course, sometimes such thinking can actually help teams overcome obstacles, such as a team that strongly believes in the vision and mission of what it is trying to achieve (Pitsis et al., 2003).

While groupthink often means people are trying to avoid conflict through cohesion, and that a lack of conflict can mean a team is in trouble, groupthink can also cause a team to spiral into depressive thoughts. At least that is what Granstrom and Stiwne (1998) suggested when they expanded upon Janis's notion of groupthink. They considered how groupthink leads to depressive team behaviours and thoughts, and identified some symptoms and methods for overcoming depressive groupthink. Their work suggests that behaviour in organizations, particularly in team contexts, can have a very negative effect on people and can cause groups of people to feel shared negative emotions and have shared negative experiences. Later on, we look into this idea in greater detail when we discuss toxic emotions (pp. 97–101).

READ THE ARTICLE

EXTEND YOUR KNOWLEDGE

Read the following article on how political skill influences team performance: Lvina, E., Johns, G. and Vandenberghe, C. (2018) 'Team political skill composition as a determinant of team cohesiveness and performance', *Journal of Management*, 44: 1001–28. You can access the article at the companion website https://study.sagepub.com/managingandorganizations5e

To avoid groupthink, the team might encourage people to voice their opinion by establishing that any critique of the team's decision is welcome and encouraged, or a team can allocate a role of devil's advocate in which one or two people actively question ideas in an informed and critical way. One especially effective way to avoid groupthink is to encourage reflective learning by sending team members on reflective retreats in which they discuss and interrogate the process of decision-making in their team.

WHAT WOULD YOU DO?

WHAT WOULD YOU DO?

No space for groupthinking at NASA

By far one of the most famous cases of groupthink is Esser and Lindoerfer's (1989) analysis of the *Challenger* space disaster. On a freezing day in 1986, NASA engineers instructed key NASA administrators to abort the take-off of the Space Shuttle *Challenger* because conditions were unsafe. NASA had a proud history of leading the space race, a very strong culture of invulnerability and success, cohesion and close personal contact. There was extreme pressure on this flight to succeed due to future funding issues, time pressures and world expectations. After the instruction to abort, the engineers and other members of the NASA team involved in the launch finally made what appears to be a unanimous decision to continue with the flight. It ended in tragedy, with the crew all being killed in an explosion shortly after take-off.

Once the federal inquiry began, a number of team members started to try and apportion blame across the organization.

Tragically, groupthink can be so pervasive that even accidents such as the *Challenger* disaster have little effect on enacting change. In 2003, we saw similar events at NASA when the Space Shuttle *Columbia* broke up during its re-entry into Earth's atmosphere, killing all aboard.

Knowing what you now know about social facilitation and about management, what advice would you give NASA in order to avoid such examples of groupthink in the future?

SOCIAL LOAFING

Social loafing has been colloquially known as shirking, bludging, free riding or laziness – and it is a phenomenon that we have all experienced in one way or another (and in our experience, especially in student groups working on assignments). Most simply stated, it refers to a situation in which members of a group exert less work effort than their peers. One of the reasons that people exert less effort in some group situations is that people feel less accountable for their behaviours when they know other people will pick up the slack (Harkins and Szymanski, 1989). For instance, when everyone around you is applauding a performance, you do not need to do so demonstratively because your applause will neither add much nor be missed if it cannot be heard (though if everyone at a performance thought this way, what would happen?)

There are many reasons why people might appear to be social loafers in an organizational setting, such as lack of confidence, being poorly matched to the job, or having personal problems such as family relationship or health issues. However, although social loafing is a concern, especially for student teams doing an assignment, in a team at work it is quite unlikely that people will be able to loaf socially for a long period of time without other team members seeking to correct the situation. Theoretically, one would assume that social loafing would be much less likely to exist in work teams because team pressures can be a powerful source of conformance (Barker, 2002 [1993]). Hence, in some ways, conformance and obedience can cancel out social loafing.

Even when social loafing does occur, it is easy to counter by, for example, ensuring that team members have clear roles, responsibilities and accountability. Also, you can ensure that there are clear goals set for individuals and the team, and that team and individual performance are measured. When team rewards are based on individual contributions, allow team members to decide how members will be punished for the failure to perform. Furthermore, ensuring people are aligned in terms of their moral and ethical attitudes and that tasks are meaningful can also reduce the motivation to social loaf (Mihelič and Culiberg, 2018). In general, do not use teamwork for simple, routine or meaningless tasks or in situations in which the whole team is dependent on the performance of only one or two members. For example, many department stores use sales teams; however, in sales there are often one or two individuals that have the ability to close or complete sales transactions. In such situations, a team is only a team by name. It is probably more effective to use individuals in competition with each other rather than a team that relies on cohesion and the equal input of many individuals.

Of course, we are not suggesting more complex teamwork makes it less likely that social loafing will occur. Research has shown that when teams work on non-linear tasks (that is, tasks that require people to do tasks concurrently and revisit some tasks because they require continuous improvement – such as the design of sophisticated software – or complex decision-making) it is often the case that social loafers will coexist with active members of the team. Often, the management response to the existence of social loafing is to tighten managerial control; however, rather than using a dictatorial team-management style, cooperation in ad hoc decision-making groups can function robustly and efficiently, even more than greater command and control (Kameda et al., 2011). This implies that social loafing is not simply people being lazy, who need to be forced into doing more work; rather, it is a more subtle practice and has many reasons for being.

DEVELOPING TEAMS

In this section, we investigate how teams form and develop, and differentiate between stage and process models of team development. We then place emphasis on the social psychology of team roles because knowing our roles and responsibilities in team settings is crucial to performance. We then move on to some practical discussion of managing teams.

TEAM FORMATION

First, let us take a look at the stages of team development. West (2008) identified four key dimensions upon which all teams can be differentiated – and you will notice some similarities with Hollenbeck et al.'s (2012) categories. First, *degree of permanence* refers to the duration that teams are expected to operate as a team. The temporal life of teams can vary from quite short assignments to long-term tasks. For example, project teams may be formed for tasks that can vary from a few weeks to several years. Other teams may be required to work together in short shifts, such as a team of chefs in a restaurant or a team of airline cabin and cockpit crew who are together for only a few hours.

Second, teams vary in terms of expectations of skill levels required over time. Consider a specialist medical team that provides care to expectant mothers with medical complications – not only are the required skill levels high, but they must also be constantly developed to keep up with technological changes and improvements in the knowledge of care and treatment of a variety of medical complications. Other teams may require few skills other than knowledge or experience around a given topic (as is the case with a jury).

Third, autonomy and influence refer to the level of real power and influence possessed by the team members. A team of five 17-year-old McDonald's staff may have little autonomy and influence in what gets done and how it is to be done, whereas McDonald's top executive team is very powerful.

Finally, teams differ in terms of the nature of the task involved. Tasks can be routine, as would be the case on a car assembly line, whereas a senior leadership team may develop the strategy for a company for the next two decades.

We will add a fifth dimension that is not included in West's list, that of spatio-temporal context. By spatial context, we mean that members of a team may interact in close physical proximity or they may interact from distant or remote physical locations. By temporal context, we mean that people may operate in synchronous time (at the same time) or in asynchronous time (at different times). For example, an emergency disaster response crew will work together in close proximity at the disaster site, at the same time, sharing not only space but also time. Conversely, a virtual team of engineers may be globally dispersed, working at different times of the day via computer-mediated communications (email, virtual collaborative software) and in different time zones. Some of the engineers might never have met face to face. Teams that operate in this way are often referred to as **virtual teams**.

Virtual teams are teams that operate across space, time and organizational boundaries in order to complete a project. Typically, they use computer-mediated communication technologies and collaborative software in order to communicate and share information.

Virtual teams are predominantly knowledge based in that each member contributes their knowledge, expertise and experience to the specific task at hand.

So, to summarize, according to West (2008), all teams can be differentiated based on four key dimensions:

1. Degree of permanence.
2. Skills/competencies.
3. Autonomy and influence.
4. Level of task, from routine to strategic.

And we added a fifth, that of:

5. Spatio-temporal context.

EXTEND YOUR KNOWLEDGE

Read the article: 'The "virtual team player": a review and initial model of knowledge, skills, abilities, and other characteristics for virtual collaboration', by Julian Schulze and Stefan Krumm (2017), in *Organizational Psychology Review*, 7: 66–95, which you can find at the companion website https://study.sagepub.com/managingandorganizations5e

READ THE ARTICLE

TEAM STAGES

One of the most famous models of team development is Tuckman's (1965) stages of group development. As an educational psychologist, Tuckman was able to observe how people operate in teams, and develop a theory of team development that identified four key stages that all teams go through. These are the forming, storming, norming and performing stages of group development. Later, Tuckman collaborated with Mary Anne Jensen and together they added a final stage called 'adjourning'. Table 3.2 represents each of the stages and summarizes the key characteristics of each stage.

Many books that describe Tuckman and Jensen's (1977) stages of group development critique the model as outdated because it assumes team development occurs in a linear, functional manner. Another reason the model is critiqued has been because it is prescriptive, in that it is telling us what 'should' happen, rather than descriptive – about what is happening. However, the power of the model is not to be found in terms of the 'stages' of group development but rather in that it provides us with a relatively simple framework for understanding that certain things are happening at certain stages and that these influence the effectiveness of the team. For example, knowing that everyone is operating to the same norms around deadlines, quality of work, values, and so on, might be integral to successful task completion. In this sense, by thinking about the stages and what goes on in each stage, managers can identify and reflect on what is happening and what things need to be considered during each stage.

TABLE 3.2 Stages of group development

Stage	Characteristics
Forming	As the name suggests, as people form groups they tend to try and avoid conflict and seek to gain acceptance by others. The group seems to lack a sense of urgency as people try to get to know one another but in reality a lot is happening at this stage of group development. People are actually sizing each other up, working out status, power and roles. However, because this is an early stage of group development, there is little action as people avoid issues and actions that might create conflict
Storming	Eventually, the group will have to disband, fade away or move towards action. Once these things start happening, people begin to vie for position, they align with in-group members and conflict may start to emerge as people attempt to deal with contentious issues relating to group outcomes and processes. Individuals in the group can only remain nice to each other for so long, as important issues start to be addressed. Sometimes members work towards cohesion in order to get things done but a lot of problems concerning group dynamics emerge at this stage. Sometimes issues are repressed but continue to fester until they explode into overt conflict. It is here that the third stage, norming, begins to evolve
Norming	At this stage, people start to get an understanding of their roles and responsibilities, what they can and cannot do, how they do it and who does it. Once norms are established, new members must abide by these norms or face becoming outcast and being pushed out of the team. These norms become embedded and taken for granted and, once established, become very difficult to change. It is therefore important to ensure the norms reflect the intentions of what the group was established to achieve
Performing	Once the team has established its norms and a sense of cohesion is achieved, the team is ready to perform. If you remember earlier, we defined a team as one in which people are interdependently linked. That is, the task requires all people to perform in order for the team's outcomes to be realized. A team can only reach the performing stage when people are able to work well together, know and trust each other, and care enough about each other and what they are doing to adapt and change as needed in order to get things done. A performing team is identifiable when people are comfortable in airing their concerns, and the team members work through problems and issues without severe conflict

Stage	Characteristics
Adjourning	In the adjourning stage, the team has completed its tasks and everyone should be basking in the glow of a job well done. People exchange ideas about the tasks, say their goodbyes, or find ways to stay in touch with team members, and must cope with a sense of 'break-up' and loss that they experience as the team dissipates. Of course, some teams such as project teams only adjourn in the sense that they have completed their given task but remain a formal team that goes on to work on new projects

WHAT WOULD YOU DO?

Look at each stage of group development in Table 3.2, then read the mini-scenario below and indicate what stage of team development the scenario is referring to.

A manager has asked a small team of people to prepare a proposal for a new system for staff in the organization to nominate when they plan to take a holiday through a negotiation process. Discussion comes to how a decision will be made when two or more staff members nominate the same dates for their preferred holidays. Two team members have a strong disagreement over whether people should be allowed to toss a coin to decide on who gets the chosen holiday dates, or whether the person who has had the longest tenure at the organization is given priority.

Q1 Is this scenario reflective of the forming, storming, norming or performing stage of group development? Why?

After much discussion and in-fighting, the team has decided that from now on all ideas will be voted for in an anonymous ballot. Where ideas are given the same number of votes, the decision will be handed over to the manager.

Q2 Is this scenario reflective of the forming, storming, norming or performing stage of group development? Why?

TEAMWORK AS A REFLEXIVE PROCESS

While the team stages help us to understand what might be happening at different stages of group development in order to make the team more effective, in reality the process of team-working is much more complex. One interesting way to think of teamwork is to view it as an ongoing process of **reflexivity**.

Reflexivity is the process of thinking about the effect of one's role, assumptions and behaviour on a given action or object, and of considering the effect that the action has on how we continue to think and behave.

Reflexivity is similar to a journey in which we start off a certain way, act out certain things and then stop to think about how we acted and how the action affects future action. For example, let us say you and a friend are in a team together, and let us say that your role is to provide information for making decisions on allocating funding to certain departments, and your friend's role is to ensure that the meetings stay on track and on time. You might find that you always go way over your allotted time, constantly finding yourself being cut off by your friend. Moreover, you find that the rest of the team members agree with your friend, that you waste too much time and that your presentations should be shorter and better organized. You may get very angry and storm out but after a while you may calm down and accept that there are certain things you can do to be better prepared to present the most important information during those meetings. So, you do this and in the next meeting people commend you on a job well done, saying that the changes in the structure of your presentation are much easier to follow and to understand. Through reflexivity, you performed a task, reflected on the task, changed what you did and performed the task again.

While Tuckman and Jensen's (1977) model paints a picture of teamwork and team formation as a linear process in which we can isolate and identify where a team is in terms of its stages of development, others argue that team-working should be thought of as a complex and dynamic process (West, 2008; Wiedow and Konradt, 2011). For example, when we work in teams a great deal of cognitive processing and sensemaking are going on. How do we work together as individuals? Are we getting along? Do we know how to do the job? Are our expectations realistic? Do we have the required resources and people? And so on. Such questions do not get asked in a static way, but evolve and continue throughout the life cycle of the team's development. As all this processing goes on, each team member is constantly adapting, changing, processing and integrating what they know, do and think in relation to the task at hand – in this sense, teamwork involves a high level of team task reflexivity (Hedman-Phillips and Barge, 2017; West, 2008). By team task reflexivity, we mean that a team will be effective not so much by adhering to certain rules around stages of team development but that team members reflect on their task objectives, strategies, processes and environments and adapt and improve these aspects of their functioning in order to achieve their outcomes.

West (2008) identifies a number of problems that teams face if they are not reflexive about how they are performing tasks, including that non-reflexive teams may:

- tend to comply unquestioningly with organizational demands and expectations
- accept organizational limitations and only operate within these limitations
- fail to discuss or challenge organizational incompetence
- communicate indebtedness and dependence on the organization
- rely heavily on organizational direction and reassurance.

A reflexive team will tend to improve how things are done and challenge behaviours that are not conducive to task performance and the betterment of team outcomes.

TEAM ROLES

One final but critical aspect of teams that we need to cover is the issue of team roles. In teams, people are usually quick to take on specific roles in order to get things done. For example, consider a team designed to run a major event. A person will be in charge of budgeting and finance, another person in charge of operations management, another of marketing, another of catering, and so on. Each person has a specific role, and as each person performs their role in a synergistic way, the event is able to happen. Now let us say one person, the person doing budgeting, lets their role slip; then the project will probably fail as people lose track of costing and invoices do not get paid, and so on. Each role in the team is critical for success.

Not all roles are prescribed and often we can find ourselves taking on certain emergent roles. A team leader, for example, may not be formally identified, but one may emerge over time in order to lead the team (Ellis, 1988). Furthermore, different people have an orientation to different roles. A person may be a good people person and enjoy dealing with issues around relationships, or conversely they may not be comfortable dealing with people but have an excellent ability to ensure jobs get done.

These person and task roles underpin some seminal work on team roles developed by Meredith Belbin. Belbin (1993, 2000) offered a model of team roles that identified typologies of the roles that individuals adopted as they worked as part of a team. He later developed an inventory, the Belbin Team Roles Self-Perception Inventory, which sought to measure and identify the types of roles people play in teams. Table 3.3 lists and describes Belbin's team roles and the weaknesses of each role. Can you identify yourself in any of these?

While Belbin's typology appears to provide an original and interesting way to establish and understand such roles, research has been quite varied in its support. Some researchers argue that the Belbin team roles have no validity or reliability and that it makes little sense to use these as explanations of team roles (Fisher, 1996). Others have provided research that supports Belbin's team roles and suggests that such team roles actually exist in various formats and do vary across teams (Driskell et al., 2018; Senior, 1997).

Despite the contention and contestations, we believe the roles add value not because they are 'proven' as clear and distinct roles, but because they simply provide a frame from which we can make sense of team roles. For example, anecdotal experience tells us that each of these roles is important in getting things done. People have to generate ideas, others might be better at getting things done, and others may be good at playing devil's advocate and finding problems or pointing out limitations to the ideas. So, rather than view these as real, measurable and distinctive roles, we use them more as a sensemaking tool. They can be used as a basis for discussions when you are managing a team to get people to talk about their roles, what they will do and how they will behave.

TABLE 3.3 Examples of team roles

Role	Description	Weaknesses
Plant	Creative, imaginative, free-thinking. Generates ideas and solves difficult problems	Might ignore incidentals and may be too preoccupied to communicate effectively
Resource investigator	Outgoing, enthusiastic. Explores opportunities and develops contacts	Might be over-optimistic and can lose interest once the initial enthusiasm has passed
Coordinator	Mature, confident, identifies talent. Clarifies goals. Delegates effectively	Can be seen as manipulative and might offload their own share of the work

(Continued)

TABLE 3.3 (Continued)

Role	Description	Weaknesses
Shaper	Challenging, dynamic, thrives on pressure. Has the drive and courage to overcome obstacles	Can be prone to provocation and may sometimes offend people's feelings
Monitor evaluator	Sober, strategic and discerning. Sees all options and judges accurately	Sometimes lacks the drive and ability to inspire others and can be overly critical
Teamworker	Co-operative, perceptive and diplomatic. Listens and averts friction	Can be indecisive in crunch situations and tends to avoid confrontation
Implementer	Practical, reliable, efficient. Turns ideas into actions and organizes work that needs to be done	Can be a bit inflexible and slow to respond to new possibilities
Completer/Finisher	Painstaking, conscientious, anxious. Searches out errors. Polishes and perfects	Can be inclined to worry unduly, and reluctant to delegate
Specialist	Single-minded, self-starting and dedicated. They provide specialist knowledge and skills	Can only contribute on a narrow front and tends to dwell on the technicalities

Source: Text and Table 3.3 reprinted with permission, Belbin, R.M. (1993) *Team Roles at Work*. Oxford: Butterworth-Heinemann and Belbin, R.M. (2000) *Beyond the Team*. Oxford: Butterworth-Heinemann.

Often, problems occur due to role ambiguity and role conflict. Role ambiguity refers to the fact that people's roles have not been adequately established and understood. When people experience role ambiguity, they experience anxiety and tension because they are uncertain as to what they should be doing. For example, if people in a team are all doing the same thing and some things are not getting done, then we might assume that people are not clear about their roles. To avoid role ambiguity, it is important that we are clear about who does what, who is responsible for getting certain things done and what happens and who is responsible when things do not get done.

Role ambiguity often leads to role conflict, especially when one person believes another team member is encroaching on their role and responsibilities. Indeed, role ambiguity can often make it very difficult for newcomers to teams and organizations to function properly (Slaughter and Zicker, 2006). Imagine you get a new job and think it is fantastic and on your first day you are placed in a team. Imagine your surprise when you join the team and you are uncertain about what it is that you are actually meant to be doing. Moreover, imagine that what you end up doing actually clashes with what another member is doing. What do you think the outcome may be? Would you or your new workmate be angry? As the new person, how do you think you will be treated? Getting team role clarity is crucial in order to ensure team performance; this is irrespective of whether the team roles emerge, or whether they are prescribed. Conversely, other researchers have found that role ambiguity can be positive in team contexts where dual leaders exist, such as in project-based organizations. This is because the ambiguity can act as an impetus for actors to better define their role and position from others within the team (see, for example, Ebbers and Wijnberg, 2017).

The question of the roles people play has long been an area of research and theory. Role theory is derived from sociology and social psychology and is concerned with how people come to behave, think and feel in relation to their socially sanctioned roles. Roles are complex and varied and are always socially defined and experienced. People expect others to fulfil certain roles in society and when they come into contact with people they will make a judgement as to the roles people will play in different contexts, based on certain individual and group characteristics. The implication of this is that the role you are generally expected to play in society is a function of what social groupings you are believed to belong to. Notice here the parallels with the discussion on stereotyping and attribution error that we covered in Chapter 2. Now let us consider gender roles.

GENDER ROLES

Traditionally, occupations have been characterized as either masculine (male) or feminine (female). For example, certain job roles are seen to be feminine, such as nurse, childcare worker, seamstress and it is expected that women will mainly occupy these jobs. Other roles are perceived as masculine and tend to be dominated by men (construction worker, miner, motor racing driver, and so on). After a while, it becomes accepted that such gender roles are a social fact and we take it for granted that males and females tend towards certain jobs.

Of course, most of these gender roles are socially constructed to fit in with strongly paternalistic and male-dominated institutions. Slowly but surely, more women are becoming professionally qualified and increasingly entering the workforce and doing jobs that were traditionally the bastion of males, with many women also setting up their own businesses. Men too are increasingly entering female-dominated careers such as nursing and childcare. As this becomes increasingly popular, perhaps one day there will not be the taken-for-granted assumption that certain jobs are for women and certain jobs are for men.

TEAM CONFLICT AND THE DARKER SIDE OF TEAMS

As scholars and curious practitioners, we should always approach what we read, see and hear with a level of healthy scepticism. This is not to denigrate or reject ideas but to reflect on them and at least consider them from more than one perspective or position. This is the essence of critical thinking. In this section, we want to consider teams and teamwork a little more critically. There is a dark side to organizing and in teams that can result in misery, misfortune and even death (Linstead et al., 2014).

Much of what we have talked about so far concerns itself with how teamwork results in better performance – and this has some major implications in terms of how we think about and make sense of teams. The assumption is often that teams are people working together to achieve a goal and the emphasis is on the 'working together'. If they don't perform or 'work together', it is because they are not operating effectively due to individual psychological and sociological factors – that is, due to there being something wrong with the team member or the way teams are structured. It is then often argued (be it overtly or more subtly) that a manager's job, if not his or her duty, is to ensure people get along and do their job. Of course, there is no doubt we all want our teams to perform. However, we must also look at some of the more controversial sides of teams. Sometimes teams can be horrible contexts to work in for a number of reasons.

Elsewhere in this book, we discuss some well-established approaches to management–employee relations (see Chapter 5). Two key perspectives are the scientific management (or Taylorism) and human relations traditions. Scientific management essentially takes a very instrumental view of management–employee relations. The manager is assumed to know the best method or 'one best way' of getting the job done: a team will have no role in deciding what gets done and how it is to be done outside perhaps how much gets produced. Moreover, the use of teams in which people work closely together in a social group to complete tasks is avoided, if not frowned upon. Scientific management emphasizes clearly demarcated lines of management and worker roles, and states that work should be hierarchically divided; that is, workers and managers must be clearly separated.

The human relations approach partly grew out of resistance to the ideas inherent in scientific management and emphasizes the role of teams, and the importance of social relationships in affecting workplace performance. Groups are seen as a critical part of the human relations philosophy, which includes notions such as: people want to be liked, respected and valued; management's role is to ensure that people feel part of the team; all staff and teams should be involved in decision-making and exercise self-direction, and management should clearly define the objectives and expected outcomes, seeking input or buy-in from staff when making such decisions (Mayo, 1946).

Teams are important for the human relations school but the focus has been subject to criticism. Some influential theorists, researchers and authors argue that many organizations have unreal expectations of teams; in fact, they say, it can take up to ten years for an organization to transform itself into one with effective teams (Greenberg and Baron, 2003). Others are even more critical, such as Professor Graham Sewell (2001) who argued that the idea of teamwork is often accepted without question as a 'good thing' based on the legend that we have always worked in teams. Such ideas can have the effect of downplaying individuality and individualism. Hence, if someone chooses not to be part of a team, or prefers to work alone, they can be labelled as problematic and 'not a team player'. However, as discussed in Chapter 9, Sewell points out that teams, especially self-directed or autonomous teams (no formal leaders), can often involve powerful forms of surveillance – or what Sewell calls horizontal surveillance. What can be more powerful than being monitored by your own peers and colleagues? In this way, weaker or non-performing team members can be monitored, and coerced into performing or leaving through immense social pressures.

Similarly, groups in organizations can also evolve into gangs. A gang in this sense means a closed group that operates in often illegal or illicit ways, and can use bullying or very strong forms of violence and dangerous rituals and practices to test loyalty. Think of street gangs as an example. In a very interesting piece on the dark side of teams, Mark Stein and Jonathan Pinto (2011) have us think about the 'gang'-like aspects of work organizations. Studying organizations such as Enron and Lehman Brothers, they argue for the existence of 'intraorganizational ganging dynamics'. It is not far-fetched to think about how certain powerful teams act like gangs and 'gang' together to protect and serve their own interests.

In this way, we should constantly be asking questions about the ethical and ideological issues inherent in teams, including how workers may be bullied, dehumanized, humiliated or co-opted into behaving in ways not only against their own interests and values, but even their personal safety and wellbeing. For an example of just how dark organizing and teamwork can be, refer to an excellent special issue of *Organization Studies* edited by Professor Stephen Linstead, Garance Maréchal and Ricky W. Griffin (2014).

TOXIC HANDLING IN TEAMS

One certainty in life is that almost all of us must work for one reason or another, and for most of our lifetime. A fact of that certainty is that we are likely to spend more time with our work colleagues than with our own families. When we work as part of a close team, the emotions we feel and perceptions we have can be almost as intense as if it were a family relationship.

Fortunately, some of us will be lucky enough to work in jobs we love, working with people we get along with really well. Such jobs fill us with excitement and a sense of self-esteem, provide important social interaction, help build our sense of self-identity and provide us with monetary and other forms of wealth.

Unfortunately, for many people this is less true – work can be a miserable, dangerous, unfulfilling and even lethal place of existence. Moreover, we sometimes have to work with people that we find frustrating, challenging and difficult. Frost and Robinson (1999) systematically reflected on the impact and coping strategies that emerge from such situations in an influential article in the *Harvard Business Review*. They were concerned with how to address what happens when organizations do bad things to good people. The article begins by discussing the impact that a new CEO had when brought in by the corporate board of a public utility. According to Michael, an employee in the utility, the CEO was authoritarian and insensitive to the needs of others:

> He walked all over people ... He made fun of them; he intimidated them. He criticized work for no reason, and he changed his plans daily. Another project manager was hospitalized with ulcers and took early retirement. People throughout the organization felt scared and betrayed. Everyone was running around and whispering and the copy machine was going non-stop with resumes. No one was working. People could barely function. (Frost and Robinson, 1999: 96)

However, as we soon learn, Michael was not just a passive observer of these bullying behaviours – he played a vital role in helping the organization and its members to absorb and handle the stresses that were being created. Frost and Robinson termed these stresses 'toxins' and noted that Michael became a 'toxic handler' in the organization. According to Frost, toxic handlers are individuals within organizations 'who take on the emotional pain of others for the benefit of the whole system ... like psychic sponges for a family or work system ... they pick up all the toxicity in the system' (2003: 3–4). The toxic handler, therefore, plays a very important role in organizations. Managers deal with toxic emotions at work every day in the role of toxic handlers, as well as sometimes being the source of toxicity (Anandakumar et al., 2007).

The following excerpt from Frost's book *Toxic Emotions at Work* provides a graphic sense of one particularly unpleasant way that a manager created toxic emotions at work:

> Ryan was a senior manager who kept two fishbowls in the office. In one were goldfish, in the other, a piranha. Ryan asked each of his staff to pick out the goldfish that was most like themselves (the spotted one, the one with deeper color, and so forth). Then, when Ryan was displeased with someone, he would ask that person to take his or her goldfish out of the bowl and feed it to the piranha. (Frost, 2003: 35)

Think about the symbolism that Ryan is trying to communicate. You are as insignificant as a fish, swimming around in the fishbowl, and as long as I like you and you do what I expect of you, you will survive. The minute you do otherwise, you cease to be a survivor and will be eaten alive by the piranha. You are dispensable and will remain only while you are useful. What kind of working environment might such behaviour create and sustain? Employees might be productive, but the environment would be one based on fear and distrust. Many managers manage people in this way. They inadvertently, and sometimes purposefully, create toxic conditions at work by managing through fear and anger.

Frost characterizes the emotional pain that undermines hope and self-esteem in people at work as a toxin. To explain how managers create toxicity in the workplace, he identified seven deadly 'INs' of toxic emotions (Frost, 2003: 36). A description of these INs appears in Table 3.4.

TABLE 3.4 The seven deadly INs of toxic emotions

INs	Description	Possible effect on groups
Intention	Managers who intentionally seek to cause others pain. They can be abusive and distrust staff. They manage through control, fear and constant surveillance. They lead through punishment and fear	Reluctance of team members to question decisions that may not be in the best interests of the organization and team outcomes. Team members become socialized to believe teams should be managed in a similar way to the 'intentional' manager. Can promote aggression and conflict and push out people perceived as 'soft'
Incompetence	Managers who lack the skills and abilities for effective people management. They may be excellent in technical skills but lack the necessary people skills. They are inconsistent in their decisions and lack integrity. Conversely, they may lack faith in their employees' abilities and skills, so they try to control every decision their employees make	The team may have direction in terms of tasks but lack cohesion due to poor people-management skills. The team may display low levels of trust, and avoid responsibility and self-directions. Low levels of empowerment and autonomy make it extremely difficult for the team to operate as a team

INs	Description	Possible effect on groups
Infidelity	Managers who do not value the trust and confidence of their employees and who betray any discussion made in confidence. Or, such bosses may make promises (e.g. a promotion) and never deliver, and some may take the credit for other people's work	High turnover of team members, low levels of motivation and desire to achieve outcomes. If outcomes are achieved, it is in spite of the managers rather than because of them. Typified by high levels of resentment of management
Insensitivity	Managers may lack social intelligence. They have no idea, and do not care, how others feel. Such managers may also have no idea how others feel about them. They may be unable to regulate their own emotions and behave in inappropriate ways	Feelings of resentment, anger, pain and disenchantment are rife. Team members are uncertain as to what mood a manager will be in
Intrusion	Managers who expect employees to forego their own social or family lives for their work. They expect people to work long hours, weekends, and so on. They work long hours and expect everyone else to do the same - even if it is to the detriment of the person's family life	Burnout rates, stress and anxiety will be high as people try to keep up with the workload. Feelings of guilt and resentment will be rife. Team members may be overly critical and judgemental of other team members if they are not putting in the same hours as others
Institutional forces	Toxicity can become embedded within the policies, procedures and rules of the organization, especially when people are expected to act in ways antithetical to their own values and beliefs. Similarly, toxicity can be seen in organizations in employees that may not live by the organization's vision, mission and policies. Imagine what it would be like to work in the police force and to blow the whistle on corruption when many of the police leaders are corrupt	Can promote unethical behaviour and collusion among team members, encourage groupthink and team cohesion at the expense of ethical behaviour
Inevitability	Some toxicity is inevitable and cannot be anticipated or controlled - for example, the death of a co-worker, a change in the world economy, or a terrorist flying a plane into a building. Sometimes, managers must cause pain in the short term to ensure growth in the long term. Inevitable toxicity can become a problem only in terms of how it is handled and managed in the context of the preceding INs of toxicity	Can devastate a team if a member dies or similarly if members are downsized. Sometimes a team may be under-resourced due to budgeting, which can cause high levels of anxiety and resentment

Source: Adapted from Frost (2003: 36-50)

Looking at these toxic emotions, we can see that in most organizations some level of toxicity is unavoidable. However, the skills of toxic handlers ultimately make toxic emotions at work either disastrous or enabling. Think about situations in your life in which you have either handled toxic emotions or caused them.

Here is an example of a team situation that illustrates how toxic workplaces operate. Many of Frost's (2003) seven deadly INs are clearly evident in this case. When Tyrone was much younger, around 15 years old, he was employed as part of a team working in a kitchen. Two middle-aged brothers (whom we will call Nick and John) ran the café in a very unethical way. Many of the staff, including Tyrone, were working illegally because Nick and John had not registered their staff with the tax department. Knowing that Tyrone and the others were young and inexperienced, Nick and John would have them work extremely long hours without breaks, did not pay pension and other compulsory contributions, never logged overtime and did not provide appropriate training – after all, they had no training themselves (to use Frost's terms, an example of *incompetence*). If employees questioned these conditions, they were either ridiculed or fired (*intention*). One day, Tyrone cut his finger very badly while working, slicing the tip off. John took him to the hospital but instructed Tyrone to say it happened while Tyrone was visiting John at home and that if he said otherwise, he would be fired (*insensitivity*). After about two weeks, Tyrone returned to the café, where he was told he was no longer needed. He received neither severance pay nor the previous two weeks' pay. Six months later, Tyrone complained to the Industrial Relations Commission that he had been underpaid, unfairly dismissed and exploited. Interestingly, only two other team members supported Tyrone on the issue; the rest of the team decided to keep quiet and keep working. Eventually, however, Nick and John filed for bankruptcy, never paying a cent to anyone and got away with behaving in unethical ways (*institutional*). In this situation, the team's reluctance to respond to the toxicity ended badly for all involved.

Each of the toxic emotions that Frost identifies can have devastating effects on people. The seventh deadly IN is inevitability and refers to the pain that comes from natural and human-made disasters. A team of al-Qaeda terrorists flew two airliners into the World Trade Center twin towers on 11 September 2001. The aim was to cause as much pain as possible to the USA and its allies. However, out of that pain also emerged great bravery and teamwork. The bravery of the teams of men and women of the New York Fire Department is now legendary. However, the NYFD had to deal with immense organizational pain and managers had to be trained and skilled in dealing with high levels of emotional anxiety, depression and post-traumatic stress disorder. So what is the point of toxic handling? The management of toxic emotions is a critical component of managing people. More importantly, we do not need disasters on a grand scale to cause toxicity at work because many managers, as Frost points out, are quite capable of creating a range of toxic environments.

Stein (2007) has shown how toxicity can be rife in the workplace. He shows how toxicity in organizations is not necessarily only caused internally by poor leaders or managers and colleagues but also by customers. Clearly, toxicity at work can take many forms and working in a bad team can be one of the most toxic experiences you can have at work. Practising compassion at work might seem a bit too soft and not really the role of managers. However, Kanov et al. (2004) show that doing the 'soft' stuff can actually be the hardest thing we can do as we relate to and work with others in teams and organizations generally. Compassion at work can alleviate many of the toxic emotions that organizations and managers create and which we have dealt with throughout this chapter. The problem is, as Frost has shown us, that practising compassion and handling toxicity at work are costly in human terms.

Typically, toxic handlers fulfil vital but often formally unrecognized tasks for their organizations. Often, they burn out doing it. Think of them as filters that help remove the toxins that the organization or particular members in it can create. Although they may help to cleanse the organization, their doing so carries profound personal costs – they have to hear, share and bear the misery and pain that the organization imposes on those it employs. Often, because the sources of the toxicity are people in formally authoritative and senior roles in the organization, there is little that they can actually do to rectify the situation. If organizations reward or are run by thugs, bullies and the diplomatically challenged, expect toxicity to be pervasive. The best remedy is compassion but this commodity is often a tender, precious and vulnerable bloom, easily trampled by the foolhardy insensitivity of others, especially those in positions of formal authority.

IN PRACTICE

READ THE FULL ARTICLE

Read this great article by Mark de Rond from Cambridge University, UK on teams and happiness in *The Conversation*, available at https://theconversation.com/when-colleagues-kick-off-or-why-a-successful-team-is-not-always-a-happy-team-35302

Thinking about what he says, how do you think Professor de Rond's article differs from the assumptions made in the ideas of toxic emotions at work?

Do you think 'unhappy' teams are more productive? Is this productivity sustainable?

Think about these questions on your own, then compare and contrast your answers with your peers.

Clearly, some levels of conflict are necessary but common sense tells us that teams that get along most of the time, not all the time, will perform better than those that don't. To learn more about this, refer to Chapter 8.

EXTEND YOUR KNOWLEDGE

READ THE ARTICLE

Read this seminal article on team conflict: O'Neill, T. A., McLarnon, M. J. W., Hoffart, G. C., Woodley, H. J. R. and Allen, N. J. (2018) 'The structure and function of team conflict state profiles', *Journal of Management*, 44: 811–36; you can access the article at the companion website https://study.sagepub.com/managingandorganizations5e

SUMMARY

In this chapter, we have defined teamwork and emphasized the importance of teams within organizations and the organizational challenges of managing teams:

- Teams are an important form of mobilizing people at work that stimulate human relations that are productive, cohesive and aligned to organizational outcomes.
- Team outcomes are influenced by dynamics such as group size, cohesion and social facilitation, conformance and obedience.
- Teams develop in different ways and through different stages depending on what organizational tasks they are formed to work on. Complex task-oriented teams often develop in non-linear, dynamic ways.
- Managing teams requires an understanding of issues such as groupthink and social loafing, as well as other more toxic downsides, and ways of overcoming such obstacles.

EXERCISES

Q1, Storming, because members of the team are jockeying for position and dominance of ideas; Q2, Norming, because an agreed process that the team will follow has emerged and has been agreed.

1. Having read this chapter, you should be able to say in your own words what each of the following key terms means. Test yourself or ask a colleague to test you.
   - Teams
   - In-group bias
   - Groups
   - Out-group
   - Group dynamics
   - Closed group
   - Crowdsourcing
   - Open group
   - Team roles
   - Formal group
   - Social facilitation
   - Informal group
   - Toxic emotions
   - Role conflict
   - Toxic handling
   - Social loafing
   - Groupthink
   - Virtual teams.
2. What are some of the similarities and differences between face-to-face teams and virtual teams that a manager should know about when managing teams?

3. Try to think of – and write down – a few scenarios in which either you were a toxic handler or you might have caused toxicity in a team context. They need not be work related; they might be in a social group, at a party, at a sports match, or whatever you can think of and prefer to talk about. Thinking about your examples, which of the seven deadly INs of toxicity apply? Be sure to clearly identify which IN applies.

TEST YOURSELF

Review what you have learned by visiting:
https://study.sagepub.com/managingandorganizations5e or your eBook

- **Test yourself with multiple-choice questions.**
- **Revise key terms with the interactive flashcards.**

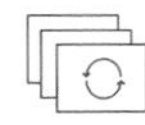

REVISE KEY TERMS

TEST YOURSELF

CASE STUDY

Trustworthiness, teamwork and the RAF debrief

Trust between team members has been said to offer a means of competitive advantage resulting from, among other benefits, increased productivity and higher quality decision-making. In line with Mayer et al.'s (1995) seminal definition, such organizational benefits derive from ongoing reassurances of peer trustworthiness as team members evaluate each other's competence, benevolence and integrity. Thus, competence to 'do a job well' is cited as just one of three core components requisite to being deemed 'trustworthy' alongside benevolence (showing concern for others) and integrity (adhering to a code of agreed ethical principles, encompassing honesty and fairness). More practical approaches have explored institutional accountability mechanisms which allow team members to demonstrate trustworthiness. As such, the underlying assumption has frequently been that trust unilaterally confers advantage as a cherished organizational treasure. However, is there ever a negative side to trust?

In order to address this question, we first consider an established accountability mechanism used within the Royal Air Force (RAF): the debrief. Reliant on organizational assurances that admitting to mistakes would not have serious professional ramifications, we consider the impact of this obligation to systematically 'own up' to mistakes on teamwork and co-member trustworthiness assessment within an RAF squadron. Second, we view a crew scenario and ask whether such accountability mechanisms can both unintentionally contribute to and guard against too much trust.

The debrief process – a post-'sortie' meeting which takes place back at the RAF base, immediately after landing – was described by a member of the team, as follows:

(Continued)

(Continued)

> We have a long debriefing process where we actually talk about things when we get back: what we did and how we could have done it better, whether we were happy, who did what, whether that was right, whether we could have done that a different way. So actually we are brutally honest with each other and it is an integral part of what we do.

Although this team was contractually bound to adhere to the institutional requirement to debrief, there was an expectation of collegiate accountability among members and full participation in the debrief process was deemed a vital signal of trustworthiness. Many commented that the importance of openness was emphasized throughout their training: 'it's sort of drilled into us from an early stage, the idea that you work as a crew and therefore you need to be open and honest with each other'. However, to return to our earlier question, can such a process of engendering team trust ever inadvertently lead to 'too much trust'?

One bright July day, the crew members were out on a mission, tasked with collecting various loads from a number of locations in the nearby area. The crew had been working together for more than three years, were all fully and openly participating in the debrief process and cited this as engendering utmost confidence in the trustworthiness of each team member. As per organizational procedure, the pilot was relying on the crew to direct while lowering the aircraft into position. Since the crew had been on many such routine outings together, the pilot no longer stopped to question the crew regarding the aircraft's proximity to surrounding obstructions, both trusting the co-team members to make that judgement and fearing that constant checking would be detrimental to the team dynamics. On this occasion, unbeknown to the pilot, the aircraft was deliberately taken beyond the organizational restrictions while picking up a load in a non-emergency situation. The team debriefed as normal but later the pilot was held to account over being in breach of the limits set out in the flight regulations. Although the aircraft was not damaged, this was viewed as a warning sign of 'too much trust' within the team.

The relevance of the debrief process for not only documenting mistakes, and ensuring that they are used as learning opportunities, but also recognizing instances of 'too much trust' was further explained by a flight safety officer. She talked about debriefing as a formalized system for both 'maintaining high levels of trust' and 'guarding against reaching a point of complacency' with regards to safety regulations:

> I think trusting too much can sometimes lead to complacency because people are human and make errors; so I think if you trust people without thinking, 'Oh I'll just check that', the one time you don't check it is the one time actually they've forgotten to do it. So I think it's trust to a certain level and then once you get past that sort of level of 'yea, he always does that', then it becomes complacency.

In conclusion, the act of debriefing served to formalize accountability within this team context. This process was in place not only to help maintain ongoing trust among team members – as full participation was a signal of trustworthiness – and to iron out mistakes, but also to recognize instances of too much trust which had the potential to lead to compromises in safety.

1. What are the advantages and disadvantages of trust within this team context?
2. When might regulation be used as a replacement for trust in an organizational setting? Under what conditions would this be a better option than measures to 'increase team trust'?

3. Consider institutional accountability mechanisms that have the potential to build/ undermine/damage team trust. Why is this the case?

Case prepared by Dr Susan Addison, Newcastle University Business School, Newcastle upon Tyne.

ADDITIONAL RESOURCES

- A movie about bonding, social facilitation and cohesion with a difference is *Fury* (2014) by David Ayer. It follows a five-man crew led by Brad Pitt as they try to achieve insurmountable goals. A new recruit has to learn to bond with the team and learns fairly brutally the tensions and complexity of working (or not working) as part of a team, of roles and psychological contracts (you are here to kill or you get killed).
- Another war film but it is brilliant: Oliver Stone's (1986) *Platoon* is a story about the devastating effects of team conflict and social influence on behaviour. As two leaders start to fight a personal war during the Vietnam conflict, soldiers begin to pick sides and eventually they are fighting and killing no longer only the 'enemy' but also each other. The movie is a strong symbol of how individuals can subvert team goals in order to meet their own interests and how team members can easily find themselves in the in- and out-groups, and suffering from groupthink.
- Some excellent, well-written and informative books written by some of the world's leading experts on teamwork are: West et al. (2003) *International Handbook of Organizational Teamwork and Cooperative Working*, and West (2003) *Effective Teamwork: Practical Lessons from organizational Research – Psychology of Work and Organizations*. Both books are excellent resources for understanding the psychology of teams, how teams are best designed and managed, the problems faced in teamwork and how problems can be minimized and controlled. We also strongly recommend *The Captain Class* by *Wall Street Journal* deputy editor Sam Walker (2017) – available as a Kindle book at Amazon, published by Ebury Digital. Using years of experience and analysis of sports teams, Walker provides some excellent insights into what makes a successful team.

MANAGING LEADING, COACHING AND MOTIVATING

TRANSFORMATION, INSTRUCTION, INSPIRATION

LEARNING OBJECTIVES

This chapter is designed to enable you to:

- define what is meant by leadership
- critically evaluate the main approaches to leadership theory
- identify newer perspectives on leadership, including the SERVANT model
- understand the assumptions underlying motivation theories and their relevance to leadership and coaching, including the value of self-leadership
- appreciate the growing importance of positive psychology and building positive psychological capital through authentic leadership.

BEFORE YOU GET STARTED...

A word from Plato: 'The heaviest penalty for declining to rule is to be ruled by someone inferior to yourself.'

–Plato, *The Republic*

INTRODUCTION

At face value, leadership appears to be a straightforward domain of interest. Almost anyone can think of a leader and can provide a definition of leadership or make feelgood statements about what a leader is, does or should do. However, after you go past leadership at a superficial level, it is one of the most complex, problematic and time-consuming domains of management and organization theory.

Leadership as a domain of interest has become an unnecessarily complex, confusing and contradictory concept. Attempting to present old and new leadership theories in one chapter is challenging. First, there are the differences of opinion in terms of what leadership is. Is leadership, as the *trait* theorists argue, a question of unique traits that people are born with, like their height, weight, intelligence and personality? Or is leadership, as the *behaviourist* school argues, specific ways of behaving that make you either an effective or an ineffective leader? Or is leadership *situational*, where different situations create different leaders? Or is leadership *contingent* upon the interactions between leaders and the led? Or is leadership a *socially constructed* concept? Or is there no such thing as leadership per se, only what members of specific organizations make of it in retrospect?

In this chapter, we introduce you to these ideas as well as the concepts of coaching, self-leadership and motivation. We close the chapter by discussing some positive psychological perspectives on leadership that argue that leadership should primarily be about inspiring and fostering positive change.

In its simplest definition, **leadership** is the process of directing, controlling, motivating and inspiring staff towards the realization of stated organizational goals.

A **leader**: (a) leads people as a ruler; (b) inspires people as a motivator and (c), facilitates or guides them as a coach and mentor.

DEFINING LEADERSHIP

What is **leadership**? The *Collins English Dictionary* defines a **leader** as 'a at person who rules, guides, or inspires others', and the process of leading as 'to show the way by going with, or ahead … to serve as the means of reaching a place' (Hanks, 1986: 476). This simple definition falls a little short because it underplays the complexity inherent in the social relations and complex environments within which leadership, as a practice, happens. Katz and Kahn (1978: 527–8) believe leadership is commonly viewed:

> as the attribute of a position, as the characteristic of a person, and as a character of behaviour … Moreover, leadership is a relational concept implying two terms: The influencing agent and the persons influenced … Leadership conceived of as an ability is a slippery concept, since it depends too much on properties of the situation and of the people to be 'led'.

Leadership may thus be seen as a product of one's position; as a set of personality traits; as a set of observable behaviours; as dependent upon the situation in which it is exercised as well as contingent upon how the leader and the people being led react to and interact with each other. Obviously, leadership may be all of these many things, consequently not surprisingly, it is one of the most overtheorized, overresearched and empirically messy areas of management and organization theory, with a clear lack of unity of perspectives or approaches. The problem is that people can come up with words to describe a leader, what a leader is or does but few can say *why* these words describe a leader. Have a go at guessing the leader in the related In Practice task.

IN PRACTICE

Who am I?

To help students cope with the complexity of the topic of leadership, let us play a guessing game called 'Who am I?' The aims of the game are to help you think about: (a) the qualities and life events that make someone a leader, and (b) how no one theory or concept adequately accounts for leadership. Read the following series of facts about a famous leader and consider the leadership qualities inherent in these facts to come up with an answer:

- I was regarded as a good *artist* and had a flair for sketching and watercolours yet I was rejected by a prestigious art school.
- I then joined the armed forces and was awarded a prestigious medal for *bravery*, yet some of my officers claimed I would never be a suitable leader of men.
- After the war, unhappy with how my country was being run and eager to prove my detractors wrong, I joined a small political party and became a great orator able to *inspire* others.
- At the time that my ideas became popular, my country was plagued by *poverty and economic recession.*
- I was soon imprisoned as a political agitator but it was in prison that I helped grow my political party, and I wrote one of the most influential books in history.
- After leaving prison, I was given charge of my political party, and we went from a handful of members to hundreds and thousands of followers - many of whom abandoned senior positions in opposition parties to join me because they could see I was committed to changing how things were done in my country forever and they wanted to *follow* me.
- I eventually became *leader* of my country and one of the most influential figures in history. Indeed, all around the world I continue to *inspire* many followers even though I am long since dead.

Now, think about the clues and consider the qualities - artistic, brave and ambitious. He was able to write books and change society from within a prison and to attract followers even from his opposition. So, who am I?

The main aim of the 'Who am I?' exercise is to encourage you to reflect critically on the term leadership. The answer to the question 'Who am I?' is, of course, Adolf Hitler. In each clue are fundamental aspects of the leadership concept: character, behaviour, situation and contingencies. Although we often see

WATCH THESE TED TALKS

leadership as composed of factors that make us feel good, sometimes leaders are not always enlightened, humane and oriented to personal growth; they are sometimes tyrants more concerned with their own egos than those of their followers, adept at practising domination, power and delusional self-interest. Therefore, it is necessary to think beyond leadership as a simple construct and to reflect critically on what leadership might mean.

Students often ask, 'What's the point of all this theory? Who cares if leaders are born or made?' Our answer is that leadership theory is critical for our understanding of the role individuals can play in shaping society and its organizations. More importantly, *leaders can and do change society*, so it is imperative that they do so in a socially responsible and ethical way (see also pp. 133–135). Only if we understand the theoretical underpinnings of those leadership perspectives in use by particular writers and leaders can we adequately reflect on and answer appropriate questions about leadership. Moreover, the theory you subscribe to will underpin your own approach to leadership – after all, you may one day be a leader, and what you believe about leadership will influence your approach to what a leader is, what a leader does and how a leader does it. Conversely, learning about different theories may cause you to reflect on and to question your own beliefs.

THE EVOLUTION OF LEADERSHIP THEORY

LEADERSHIP AS TRAITS

> Great leaders plant trees whose shade they know they will never sit in.
> (Translated Greek proverb)

The trait approach to leadership assumes people are born with qualities that are stable across time and situations, and which differentiate leaders from nonleaders. For a long time, trait theorists believed that leadership depended on certain physical features and personality characteristics. To investigate leadership, trait theorists would consider a wide range of demographic variables such as age, gender, height, weight and ethnicity, to name a few. They also looked at certain personality characteristics similar to those found in the trait approach to personality (see also pp. 56–57). Such key demographic and personality variables were believed to differentiate truly exceptional leaders from mere mortals, which is why trait theory has also been known as the 'great person theory' (Barker, 2001). According to House et al. (1996), the difference between those of us who emerge as outstanding leaders and those of us who are always destined to follow is an undying drive for achievement, honesty and integrity, and an ability to share with and to motivate people towards common goals. Such people have confidence in their own abilities as well as intelligence, business savvy, creativity and an ability to adapt to ever-changing environments (also see Kirkpatrick and Locke, 1991).

Doubtless many people believe in the great person theory. That is, they believe that certain physical features and personality characteristics will make you a leader. If this were true, the teaching of leadership would help only those with a predisposition towards leadership: the rest of us might as well either pack up immediately or perhaps enrol in a course teaching us how to be better subordinates.

In reality, however, there is little conclusive evidence to support the notion that leaders are wholly born with special traits that non-leaders lack. In fact, those who argue for the great person approach tend to miss the point – that is, many characteristics they believe to be critical to successful leadership have been made important through social norms and culture. Consequently, when testing to see if some trait makes you a better leader than someone else, it becomes quite difficult to cancel out the noise: that is, the impact of socialization and environment. If we look at leadership in most organizations, leaders tend to be taller rather than shorter and, more often than not, are male. To be consistent, these trait theorists would argue, because most leaders of major corporations are male, it must be an important trait in successful leadership. Also, in places such as the USA, Australia, the UK and much of Europe, most of them are also white, usually well educated in elite schools and institutions, and often from wealthy backgrounds. In fact, it makes a huge difference if you can choose your parents carefully! Of course, you cannot, but it is clear that a major factor that propelled leaders such as President Donald Trump to their positions of leadership was that their fathers had already founded dynasties and amassed substantial fortunes. Sure, if you are non-white or female, you can still make it, but it will be much harder for you, and you will have to expend more energy on the leadership attributes you have available or can cultivate.

The trait theory of leadership, despite its shortcomings, has played a critical role in the evolution of leadership theory and research (Zaccaro, Dubrow and Kolze, 2018), and, as we improve methods for studying leadership, the trait approach should enjoy somewhat of a renaissance. Whether you agree or disagree with it, many have used it to critique and to reflect on what it means to be a leader. Thus, even though the empirical evidence is somewhat inconclusive, its strength has been to at least create some kind of discourse and scholarship in leadership as a concept to be investigated.

EXTEND YOUR KNOWLEDGE

READ THE ARTICLE

There is a resurgence in trait-based approaches on leadership that are both informative and amusing. Read the following article: Knapen, J., Blaker, N. and Van Vugt, M. (2018) 'The Napoleon complex: when shorter men take more', *Psychological Science*, 29 (7): 1134–44. The study looks at how certain traits (in this case height) impact how leaders behave in certain social situations. It also shows that there are gender differences. Are you short or tall? What do you think about the findings of this study? What else may explain what is going on in this study? https://study.sagepub.com/managingandorganizations5e

To try to overcome the objection that many leadership traits that are assumed to be innate are actually based on norms and culture, newer theories have chosen to look at what leaders *do* rather than what traits they *have*. Some see leadership as situational or contingent upon many factors. Others see leadership as a socially constructed phenomenon – that is, what a leader is, and what a leader does, changes as society changes over time or as we move from one culture to another. Next, we visit these different perspectives of leadership, beginning with the behavioural school.

LEADERSHIP AS BEHAVIOUR

The behavioural theory of leadership is not concerned with the traits or characteristics that make someone a successful leader; it is concerned only with observable behaviour. Thus, for behaviourists, you either act like a leader or you do not. This is an important departure from trait theory because it implies that if we can observe how leaders act, we can codify and measure this behaviour, find out ways to teach it and help to develop future leaders. A critical concept that is common to all behavioural theories of leadership is the notion that there are two underlying behavioural structures that characterize leadership – an orientation towards the following:

- interacting with and relating to other human beings
- the task at hand, or the technical side of work.

You will find these two behavioural orientations in just about every theory you read about, even those outside the behavioural school. Though the terms used by these theories vary, they refer to the same fundamental distinction. The terms used include: employee centred/task centred; relationship behaviour/task behaviour; concern for people/concern for production; and consideration/initiating structure.

Blake and Mouton (1985) developed the most recognized behavioural study of leadership at the University of Texas. The approach was later expanded upon by Blake and McCanse (1991) and is referred to as the *leadership grid* or the *managerial grid* (see Figure 4.1). The grid is divided into two dimensions. On one axis is the *concern for production* and on the other axis is the *concern for people*. Depending on their responses to standardized questions, a person is rated by an accredited psychologist on both dimensions on a scale from 1 to 9 (or low to high). The ideal position is to be high on concern for production and concern for people (9,9), or what Blake and Mouton (1985) refer to as *team management*. However, very few if any ever score 9,9 on their first try, so leaders are helped to develop their concern for people and their concern for production skills so that they reach the ideal position on the grid. Leaders that score 1,1 are said to practise *impoverished management* because they lack a concern for both people and production, so their ability to manage will be quite poor. Other styles include *country club management* (1,9), where there is a high concern for people while the concern for production is forgotten or ignored, so people being happy and having fun is more important than getting the job done. (These styles can be seen in action in the hit TV show *The Office*, if you have seen it; if not, do so as it is brilliant.) Conversely, a person may be concerned with only production, or what Blake and Mouton call *task management* (9,1), and then there is *middle-of-the-road management* (5,5).

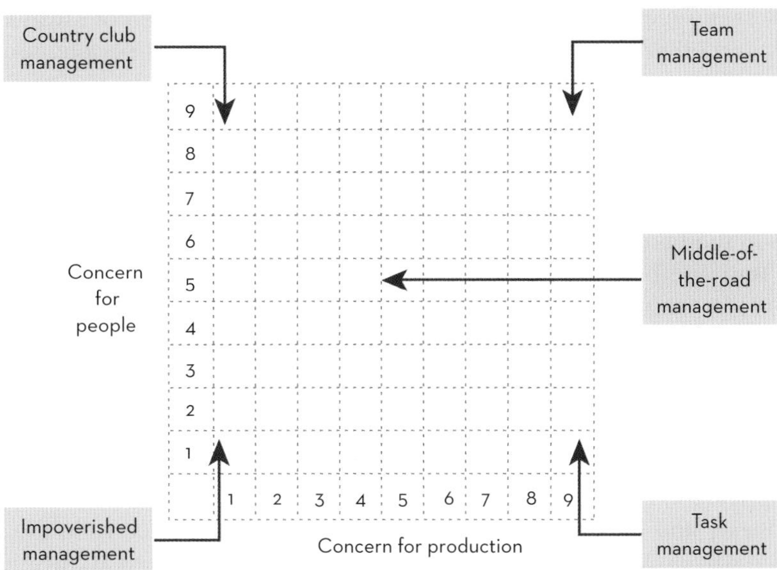

FIGURE 4.1 The managerial grid (adapted from Blake and Mouton's (1985) registered model)

As with the managerial grid, all major leadership theories seem to emphasize, first, *consideration*, or the extent to which leaders take into consideration subordinates' feelings, needs, concerns and ideas; and, second, *initiating structure*, or the extent to which leaders are task oriented and focused on ensuring that subordinates do what is required through autocratic direction, control and surveillance. These two styles tend to be presented as being independent of each other, so a leader can be high or low on initiating structure and high or low on consideration, and it was long held that superior leadership was characterized by being high–high on both dimensions. However, there is little research to support the notion that effective leaders are only those high on both initiating structure and consideration (see, for example, Nystrom, 1978). As a result, researchers began to compare and contrast effective and ineffective leaders.

Again, in keeping with the theme of orientation towards person versus task, Likert (1979) argued that *employee-centred* leaders were more successful than *job-centred* leaders – mainly because job-centred leaders tended to be overly concerned with achieving efficiency, cost reduction and deadlines, rather than with people's needs and goal achievement. However, common sense says that an overemphasis on people might compromise the completion of tasks and getting the job done, just as an overemphasis on tasks can alienate people and affect motivation and job satisfaction. It is therefore more likely that both dimensions are equally important, and this is the argument underlying the managerial grid. The managerial grid is more a behavioural training tool than a leadership theory: it emphasizes the need to *develop* a person's ability to manage both people and tasks.

The managerial grid appears to imply that all outstanding managers must have special skills for dealing both with the job and with people. Yet throughout history we have seen people reach the heights of leadership who are not always expert in tasks and others who are not always expert in managing people. Moreover, if you consider some of the people who have inspired you, we are sure that at least some of you will mention people who are no longer alive or people you have never met. It is a bit hard to manage people and tasks when you are dead or you never have face-to-face contact with your followers, so something else must make leaders be regarded as effective or ineffective besides merely what they do in the here and now.

The trait and behavioural approaches must not be totally discounted. Some situations, for example, call for high concern for people, whereas others call for high concern for production, and others call for both. However, leadership can also be thought of as being situational and contingent. The behaviourist usually is interested only in observable behaviour and ignores often unobservable intentions. We can never know people's thoughts and intentions other than through social cues, and these can be masked behind observable behaviour that, on face value, appears to be exemplary.

If honesty and integrity are inherited traits necessary for elevation to leadership, then why do so many people reach leadership positions and attain enormous material wealth, power, influence and control, only later to be revealed as crooks and charlatans who sometimes even use their 'leadership' to try to avoid the wrath of the law? Why are the attributes that one group of people see as exemplary regarded as evil by others? For example, some compare Adolf Hitler, Benito Mussolini, Osama bin Laden and Saddam Hussein to Satan, but presumably their many followers viewed them as great leaders – if not, then how did they attain such influential leadership positions? Was everyone that followed them also evil?

SITUATIONAL AND CONTINGENCY THEORIES

Some recent approaches to leadership argue that leadership emerges out of the situation. The same person who may emerge as a leader in one situation may find him- or herself unable to cope, let alone lead, in a different situation. Anecdotally, evidence suggests that there is some merit to the situational argument. For example, prior to the 9/11 attack on New York City, the former mayor of New York, Rudolph Giuliani, was known mainly for his strong stance on crime in New York. He implemented a 'three strikes and you're out' policy for repeat criminals which led him to have many critics.

However, during the 9/11 attacks, Mayor Giuliani took a strong leadership role – indeed, the moment made the man. The mayor's leadership was seen as so strong that he even eclipsed the then President George W. Bush, and the world watching the events that unfolded in New York could easily have been forgiven for believing that Mayor Giuliani was the leader of the USA. Now he is counsellor to the leader of the USA.

We have chosen to group together the situational and contingency approaches, even though some people prefer to separate the two. There are subtle differences between them, but we believe that these differences are not enough to make them distinct schools of thought. Underlying contingency theories is the notion that leadership is all about being able to adapt and be flexible to ever-changing situations and contexts. Contingency leadership theories have made one of the most important contributions to the evolution of leadership theory because leadership effectiveness is seen as being less dependent on innate traits or observable behavioural styles and more dependent on the context of leading, such as the nature of work, the internal working environment and the external economic and social environment (Fiedler, 1964). Two main contingency leadership theories are discussed here: House's (1971) path–goal theory and Hersey et al.'s (1996) situational leadership model.

PATH–GOAL THEORY OF LEADERSHIP

Perhaps the contingency theory that has been most studied and tested is Robert House's path–goal theory of leadership. According to House (1971; see also House and Mitchell, 1974), effective leaders motivate employees by helping them understand that their needs and expectations can be fulfilled through the performance of their jobs. The better an employee performs, the greater the need fulfilment. Moreover, the path–goal theory emphasizes that an ability and commitment to providing employees with the psychological and technical support, information and other resources necessary to complete tasks is integral to the leader's effectiveness.

The path–goal theory has been extended, developed and refined, and it is probably one of the most influential leadership theories around (House, 1996; Jermier, 1996). The path–goal theory is more advanced and complex than any of the theories we have looked at thus far because it lists four leadership styles and a number of contingencies that lead to leadership effectiveness. Table 4.1 lists and describes each of the four main leadership styles.

TABLE 4.1 Path–goal leadership styles and descriptions

Style	Description
Directive	The directive leader clarifies goals, what must be done to achieve them, and the outcomes of achieving the goals. They use rewards, discipline and punishment, and are mostly task oriented
Supportive	The supportive leader shows concern for the needs – especially psychological – and the aspirations of people at work. They provide a supportive and enjoyable working environment
Participative	The participative leader actively seeks and encourages the input and involvement of staff in decision-making and other work-related issues
Achievement-oriented	The achievement-oriented leader, as the name suggests, expects from people the highest commitment to excellence both at a personal and an organizational level. This type of leader believes that work should be challenging and that people will strive towards achieving these goals by assuming responsibility
Networking	The networking leader knows how to play the political power games to acquire resources, achieve goals, and to create and maintain positive relationships. (For more on power and politics, see also pp. 254–265.)
Values-based	The values-based leader is skilled in creating, sharing, and inspiring vision, and in ensuring that the organization and its people are guided by that vision and the values related to that vision

Source: Adapted from House (1996) and Jermier (1996)

However, you will notice that we have added networking and values-based leadership as two more issues that have emerged from House's (1996) and others' work (see, for example, Jermier, 1996; O'Toole, 1996; House et al., 2004). We believe that these will be increasingly important additions to House's original work because they move the leadership theory away from solely being interested in person-to-person relations to include relationships at team, organizational and interorganizational or network levels.

READ THE ARTICLE

EXTEND YOUR KNOWLEDGE

Intrigued by the election of Donald Trump and the demise of Hillary Clinton, Goethals (2017) explores the leader-follower dynamics and how Trump was able to capitalize on in-group and out-group hostilities (see also Chapter 3: 79–81) to ascend to the White House. Read this fascinating article on Trump's leadership ascendency: Goethals, G. R. (2017) 'Almost "nothing new under the sun": American politics and the election of Donald Trump', *Leadership*, 13 (4): 413–23.

An effective leader adjusts and adapts their style according to the situation and can use one or more styles as needed. However, the effectiveness of the leader ultimately depends on two broad sets of contingencies. The first concerns employee-relevant contingencies, such as the employee's competencies, knowledge, skills, experience, and even their personality, such as whether they have an internal or external locus of control (see also pp. 57–61). The second concerns environment-relevant contingencies, such as the nature of teams and the structure and nature of the task, just to name a few.

SITUATIONAL LEADERSHIP MODEL

Hersey et al.'s (1996) situational leadership model's intellectual appeal resides in its emphasis on the subordinates' readiness and willingness to be led by others. As with path–goal theory, it is up to the leader to use the appropriate style after they have established what kind of people work for them. The most appropriate leadership style depends on the amount of emotional support followers require in conjunction with the amount of guidance that they require to do their jobs – in other words, the follower's readiness.

Hersey et al.'s (1996) situational leadership model is to contingency theory what the managerial grid is to behavioural theory: it is more a training and consulting tool than a theory per se. The situational leadership model and other contingency theories depart from the trait perspective but share many elements of the behavioural approach. Where contingency approaches differ from the behavioural approach is in concentrating attention on factors outside the actual person leading. Later, we discuss contingency-based views that argue that leaders may be substituted for processes, technology and policies, and can even be made obsolete in the workplace.

TRANSACTIONAL, TRANSFORMATIONAL AND CHARISMATIC APPROACHES

We now look at three relatively recent approaches to leadership that incorporate all the leadership theories we have discussed thus far. The leadership theories presented in this section are still much more in line with the trait, behavioural and contingency schools. From the perspective of some views of leadership, neither Adolf Hitler nor many other political and organizational leaders would be viewed as positive leaders because they lack those humanist ideals that underpin positive psychology (see also pp. 63–67), whereas, in the ideas presented here, Hitler and many other violent and brutal leaders could still be defined as leaders and listed along with Nelson Mandela, Mahatma Gandhi and the Dalai Lama as examples of charismatic and other types of leaders, such as transactional and transformational leaders. While you may hear about these terms often, what do they actually mean? Well, charismatic leadership is a leadership type that emphasizes the articulation of a vision and mission that promise a better life. Sometimes such leaders develop a cult following. They have a motivating effect on people and are able to create grand visions about an idealized future. They are able to unify people towards that vision and to foster conditions of high trust. Transactional leadership epitomizes the initiating structure, concern for production and task-oriented themes of the behavioural leadership literature. Interactions between people are viewed as transactions – where reward and punishment are meted out in relation to the completion of a task or project. Transactional leaders adhere to organizational policies, values and vision and are strong on planning, budgeting and meeting schedules. Finally, transformational leadership, as you can probably guess by the word itself, epitomizes consideration and concern for people and similar relations-oriented themes. The leader engenders a sense of higher purpose and can have transformative qualities. They are the opposite of transactional leaders because they deal mainly with abstract and intangible concepts such as vision and change.

Charismatic leaders can create the impetus for change. However, they can also be volatile and inconsistent and can be blinded by their own vision (our 'Who am I?' exercise earlier in this chapter shows that Hitler had many charismatic leadership qualities, yet we do not think that you would want someone similar to Hitler to be your boss). Transformational leadership is an agent of change. Transformational leaders are the ideal people to have during major organizational change because they have the visionary component of the charismatic leader, but also have staying power and provide energy and support throughout the change process. If the transformational leader has a weakness, it is that organizational life is not always about constant change, so the effectiveness of a transformational leader can be short-lived. After the change occurs, another type of leadership style might be more appropriate. The transactional leader may be more useful during periods of homeostasis, when you want things to run smoothly.

Reading through the multitude of textbooks on management, you could be forgiven for thinking that 'leadership' and 'followership' are distinct concepts:

a leader is a person who provides direction and inspiration towards achieving goals, whereas a follower is a person who does not ask why but only how; a leader says something, whereas a follower does that which is said. What tends to be underemphasized is that inherent in many of the perspectives on leadership is a lack of explanation about how exactly a good follower becomes a good leader and whether there actually is a difference between followers and leaders. A heart specialist is working in a large hospital under a management team, but would we say the specialist is subordinate to them? Just because you are in a leadership position does not make you a leader any more than being in a subordinate position necessarily makes you subordinate.

Typically, in the army, leadership is predicated on good followership, and it is the good follower who is given the opportunity to climb the ranks from private to corporal to sergeant, and so on. Perhaps it is best to think of the leadership–followership relation as a fluid one. On some occasions, a skilful leader often serves people and organizations best by following the innovation, inspiration or interpretation of one of the followers; on another occasion, a leader may lead best by subordinating personal attitudes to those of superiors, peers or subordinates in order to retain influence or carry a decision.

To become a leader in many fields, you are required to do your apprenticeship under a master, often for many years. So, might not good leadership also require an ability to be a good follower? More important, is there actually a difference between followers and leaders other than the labels attached? Perhaps leadership theorists and researchers should become more active in asking such questions. Such issues will become pertinent when we look at leadership substitutes and neutralizers, as well as the postmodern and dispersed leadership approaches, later in this chapter.

READ MORE ABOUT LEADERSHIP

From the perspective of situational contingency arguments, in some situations you need a transactional leader to hold the ship steady, at other times you need a charismatic leader to create a vision and inspire the need for change, and sometimes you need a transformational leader to foster and manage the change process through to completion. Still, there are risks. Transformational leaders may end up believing too literally in their own hype; they might really think they are the heroes that their strategies seem to position them as being, effortlessly changing minds, actions and paradigms.

More recently, Bass and Avolio (2000; 2003) have developed the idea that leaders can be both transactional and transformational – or what is referred to as full-range leadership (Antonakis and House, 2002, 2004; Kirkbride, 2006). Full-range leadership includes transformational and transactional components, as well as passive-avoidant leadership characteristics – or non-leadership to be more precise. According to Bass and Avolio (2000), the ideal leader will be high on both transformational and transactional components, and low on the passive-avoidant ones. The next most favourable outcome is to be a high transformational leader, followed by a high transactional leader. The least attractive outcome would be to be low on transactional and transformational, and high on passive-avoidant. Table 4.2 provides an overview of each of the styles and their associated constructs.

TABLE 4.2 The full-range leadership model

Transformational	
Idealized Influence (Attributes)	Perceived by others as transformational, optimistic, open, and energetic
Idealized Influence (Behaviours)	Risk-taking, leading from the front, leading by example with purpose, integrity, and consistent with values
Inspirational Motivation	Envisions change, highly symbolic, clear strategic vision and mission articulation and symbolism, articulation of visions, hopes, and desires
Intellectual Stimulation	Encourages innovative thinking, encourages people to question what they know and think, especially their reliance on outdated or overused methods and processes
Individualized Consideration	Supportive, sensitive to members' concerns, high EQ, mentors and develops others (even to the detriment of self)
Transactional	
Contingent Reward	Recognizes the contribution of others, is able to reward and motivate by linking into especially intrinsic, but also extrinsic motivations; clarifies expected outcomes and what will be delivered and how performance will be rewarded
Management-by-Exception (Active)	Monitors performance, solves problems as they arise to maintain performance
Passive-Avoidant	
Management-by-Exception (Passive)	Part of transactional leadership but tends to avoid monitoring performance; only reacts if problems become serious or problematic
Laissez-faire	Tends to let things pan out and sort themselves out. It really refers to non-leadership and the abdication of responsibility. Avoids decisions and defers judgement to others or to a later time in expectation that the problem will go away

Source: Adapted from Bass and Avolio (2000, 2003)

NEW PERSPECTIVES ON LEADERSHIP

A critical question and challenge for leadership theory and research is whether *leadership* is merely a term or, alternatively, something that actually exists. Will there come a time when leaders can be substituted, if not made obsolete, in organizations? Some contingency theorists argue that such a time is here. Others, such as the post-modernists, turn the term leadership on its head, painting a picture of leaders as servants. So, let us look at both of these perspectives a little closer, starting with the contingency view of *leadership substitutes* and *neutralizers*. Before we visit these approaches, a quick word: leadership as a concept has come under constant bombardment – with statements such as 'Leadership is dead' – even from the contingency theorists. However, we should remember one thing: many of these approaches, but especially contingency theory, fail to account for the fact that leaders can and do change the situation and the environment within which they operate – and they often do so intentionally. That is, leaders can sometimes control contingencies. In this way, they can actually use the contingent variable to control or to increase their effectiveness – and they do this in quite subtle and pervasive ways.

SUBSTITUTES AND NEUTRALIZERS

Some contingency theorists, such as Kerr and Jermier (1978), argued long ago that situational variables could act as substitutes for leaders, thus rendering the leader irrelevant. Let us look at an example to help illustrate how such a theory works. You might work as part of a self-managed work team (SMWT). In a SMWT, teams have full autonomy and control of all aspects of their work, so each team member might be involved in all decision-making about rostering, goal-setting, performance measurement and evaluation, setting of wages, and so on. There could be high levels of trust, shared responsibility, interdependence and support. A leader, be it transactional or transformational, is not required. Similarly, you may identify more with a profession (say psychology) and have high levels of autonomy, be motivated, capable and high on self-efficacy (a belief in one's ability and competence to complete tasks). For a team or individual equipped with the right resources, as well as knowledge of what needs to be done and by when, a leader can be a hindrance rather than a benefit.

LEADERS AS SERVANTS AND THE POSTMODERN CONDITION

The study of leadership is continually producing ideas of leadership that are constantly evolving and becoming more sophisticated and while we continually seek to search for new models or theories to explain and make sense of the concept, elements of all the approaches we have looked at so far endure (Lord et al., 2017). However, as the boundaries between leaders and followers blur, the focus on 'the leader' in the more traditional theories highlighted earlier in this chapter become increasingly problematic; this will become especially so as technology, artificial intelligence and deep-learning, simplification and automation advance. When leadership skills and responsibilities are dispersed or shared throughout an organization through technology, or leadership is substituted or neutralized, an emphasis is placed on the process and practice of leadership and not on the attributes or style of a unique person or set of persons – the 'leaders'. In short, *dispersed leadership theories* – theories that move leadership away from an individual person – may imply that leadership is something that many people can do and actually do; therefore it is not a fruitful basis upon which to differentiate people at work. Furthermore, viewing leadership as a relational process suggests that the leader–follower relationship is no longer of central importance to the study of leadership (see, for example, Gordon, 2002), but rather the ability to be critically reflexive about one's own practices and how these practices relate to and impact on others are more important (Gambrell et al., 2011). Such views suggest that the boundaries that once differentiated 'the leader' from 'the follower' are becoming very grey – a follower is a leader is a follower is a leader, and so on, *ad infinitum*. This has opened the door to postmodern concepts, so it is appropriate to review at least one postmodern perspective on leadership – that of Boje and Dennehey (1999).

WATCH THIS TED TALK

FROM PREMODERNISM TO POSTMODERNISM

Postmodernism applied to organization studies has many critics. While some criticisms are valid, many are based on incorrect assumptions, partly because postmodern theories can be somewhat confusing, and even convoluted. Postmodernism has its roots both in French philosophy and in architecture, but it was American cultural theorists Fred Fiedler (1964) and Susan Sontag (1961) who did most to bring postmodernism into view and provide the impetus for its spread into art, cultural studies, history, philosophy, sociology, psychology and, most recently, organization theory. Put simply, what is seen as true or false is a result of power relations and dominant discourses, which present 'truth or reality' in ways that are framed through systems of power. For example, for many, profit is more important than environment, which is reflected through policies, practices, the media, and so on.

Postmodernity is subtly different from the idea of postmodernism. Postmodernism is underpinned by the idea that reality is constructed, and that there are multiple realities in which what comes to be known as real or truth is talked into being. The critical idea in postmodernity, however, is that the idea of capitalism has spread into every area of society and into every part of the globe, such as the media, education, health, sport, the arts, sciences, almost everywhere. In this sense, there is a pre-capitalist (premodernity) period prior to the Industrial Revolution, a capitalist (modernity) era that came about through industrialization and the growth of global production, and a hyper-capitalist (postmodernity) era. In postmodernity, absolutely everything becomes about consumerism, even selling books like this. Many argue that we are now in the hyper-capitalist era – or in postmodernity (for an excellent account and discussion of this, see Nicol, 2009).

Postmodernism blurs the boundaries of how we understand and make sense of leadership, stressing that leaders are servants of the types of leadership that others recognize as leadership in discourse. Put simply, leaders become servant to the qualities that people characterize as leadership: they are therefore talked into leadership. Let us go through Boje and Dennehey's (1999) approach, in which each letter in the word SERVANT is given a special significance, to get some of the flavour of the postmodern approach from their analysis:

S is for *servant*. The leader is the servant to the network. Leaders serve people and the people, in turn, serve customers. For a long time in the past, leadership was about differentiating oneself so that a leader would be different from a follower. In a postmodern perspective on leadership, leaders seek to rid the world of such differentiation; the leader articulates the servant conceptions of what the leader should be. Think of the CEO who dresses down and on Fridays works on the shop floor with the other workers.

E is for *empowers*. The leader empowers participation in social and economic democracy.

R is for *recounter of stories*. The leader tells stories about the organization's history, heroes and future.

V represents being *visionary*. Leaders without vision, the reasoning goes, offer nothing, and people's hopes perish. At their best, visionary leaders should articulate a clear concept of what it is that followers are already committed to and believe in.

A is for being *androgynous*. Androgyny means no gender; the leader must be able to speak in both male and female voices.

N is for *networker*. The leader manages the transformation and configuration of the diverse network of teams spanning suppliers to customers.

T is for *team builder*. The leader mobilizes, leads and dispatches a web of autonomous teams.

Boje and Dennehey provide a description and comparison of premodern, modern and postmodern leaders, as shown in Table 4.3. They explain their model in terms of the stages of premodernity, modernity and postmodernity: each typified by different forms of leadership. Their approach is novel and creative, but take a closer look at the table. Can you see any parallels with transformational, transactional and charismatic leadership? Also, can you see some link to behavioural and contingency theory? Note how Boje and Dennehey conceive leadership almost from the perspective of a behavioural style.

TABLE 4.3 Premodern, modern and postmodern leadership

Premodern leaders Leader as master	Modern leaders Leader as panoptic	Postmodern leaders Leader as servant
Master. Head of the work institution Owner of the slaves, serfs, and tools	**Panoptic**. Leader does the gaze on everyone, Big Brother style Bentham's principle of the Panopticon is central here: power should be visible and unverifiable (see also pp. 422–423)	**Servant**. The leader is the servant to the network. Leaders serve people who, in turn, serve customers Differentiates self from the people
Authoritarian. Enforces unquestioning obedience through authoritarian rule over subordinates	**Authoritarian**. Final evaluator of performance and quality	**Empowers**. The leader empowers participation in social and economic democracy
Slave driver. A leader oversees the work of others A real taskmaster	**Network of penal mechanisms**. Penal mechanisms are little courts for the investigation, monitoring, and correction of incorrect behaviour and then the application of punishments and rewards to sustain normalcy and reinforce leader's power	**Recounter of stories**. Tells the stories of company history, heroes, and futures **Visionary**. Without vision, we perish **Androgynous**. Male and female voices
Elite. Leaders are regarded as the finest or most privileged class and usually are drawn from such classes	**Organizational**. Lots of divisions, layers, specialties, and cubbyholes to cellularize people **Pyramid**. Leader sits at the top of the pyramid **Top**. The head boss, the top of the hill, and the highest-ranking person	**Networker**. Manages the transformation and configuration of the diverse network of teams spanning suppliers to customers

Premodern leaders Leader as master	Modern leaders Leader as panoptic	Postmodern leaders Leader as servant
Ruler. Leaders govern and rule over other people	**Inspector**. In charge of surveillance, inspection, and rating of everyone else	**Team builder**. Mobilizes, leads, and dispatches a web of autonomous teams
	Centralist. All information and decision flows up to the centre and back down to the periphery	

Source: Adapted from Boje and Dennehey (1999)

Moreover, if leadership transforms through time, something must be accounting for that transformation from master to servant; are time and place the contingent factors? Also, are the nature and expectations of those of us who were once led changing as we access education, gain instant information through the Internet, and use the new technologies to receive greater exposure to contrasting views of political, social and economic current affairs?

POSTMODERN LEADERSHIP, EMPOWERMENT AND NEUTRALIZERS

Let us take a postmodern look at empowerment and leadership and contrast this with contingency views of leadership. Empowerment addresses the power inequality inherent in subordination. We are subordinate because someone or something is in a relational position of power over us. Empowerment, therefore, concerns releasing the shackles placed on us by those who have power over us in the workplace. Employees are empowered when they are given control of organizational decision-making, as well as many other aspects of their work life, and by the use of SMWTs.

By empowering people, you are lowering their reliance on and need for leaders to rule over them and to be constantly monitoring them. Followers, through empowerment, start looking more like leaders.

However, what if you manage a small music store and you employ students who work on the weekends while studying law or medicine? They come to work because it is fun, they like listening to music and many of their friends come in on the weekends. (Maybe you have read Nick Hornby's novel *High Fidelity* (1995) – which was also made into a film (Frears, 2000) – in which the sales staff are interested in only those customers who are as cool and knowledgeable as the sales staff think themselves to be.) Such people do not mind working in low-status jobs because one day they know they will be wealthy doctors or lawyers. But although they are having fun, customers find they are extremely poor salespeople – they are rude and ignore customers in favour of their friends, and they take your business for granted. You know they do not need the job, and the unemployment rate is so low that people can walk in and out of low-skilled jobs like these.

Because of all these contingencies, your ability to lead actually *neutralizes* your leadership ability. So rather than being able to substitute your leadership through contingent variables, such as empowerment of your friends, your leadership becomes impotent. Obviously, neutralizers can be viewed in a more negative light than substitutes. Indeed, substitutes can be very useful tools of empowerment and can free up your time for other duties, whereas neutralizers cancel out the benefit or effectiveness a leader might have.

Coaching is the process of developing and enhancing employees' job competencies and capabilities through constructive suggestions and encouragement.

Mentoring is the process of passing on job expertise, skills and knowledge in order to develop a protégé.

LEADERS AS COACHES AND MOTIVATORS

LEADERS AS COACHES

Great leaders create great leaders, not more followers. (Greek proverb)

Increasingly, an important function of leaders, particularly transformational leaders, is the ability to coach and mentor people at work. While leadership has long been of interest to organizational behaviourists, **coaching** and **mentoring** are more recent domains of research and theory. Coaching refers to the process of developing a person's own knowledge and skill sets in order to improve on-the-job performance. While coaching at work concentrates on achieving excellence in organizational outcomes and objectives, more recently life coaching has become an increasingly common 'profession'.

Coaching differs somewhat from leadership because a coach is not a person who directs people; rather, a coach 'develops' the individual's knowledge and skills. Coaching psychology emphasizes the importance of psychological health, and so it has strong connotations with positive psychology. Even so, the ability to coach is now becoming a core challenge for good leadership.

Unlike coaching, mentoring is an ancient process of development that goes back at least to the ancient Greeks. It can be much more intensive than coaching, and often involves master and student, although mentoring can also include the mentoring of groups. In reality, everyone has a mentor at some stage in life. The mentoring relationship naturally occurs in our lives, even though we may not realize it – with our parents, teachers, bosses, sports coach, and so on.

Dubrin (2005) identifies 12 key areas in which a person must be proficient in order to be an effective coach. By developing these skills in one's self, one will be able to develop and enhance other people's strengths and leadership capabilities. According to Dubrin, these critical areas include building trust, showing empathy, employing active listening, using influence, setting goals, monitoring performance, giving feedback, encouraging positive actions and discouraging negative ones, training team members, helping people solve problems and managing difficult people.

WHAT WOULD YOU DO?

WHAT WOULD YOU DO?

In Australia, in 2015, a report was published showing that Australia has some of the poorest (in terms of capabilities not wealth) leaders in the world. Visit the Centre for Workplace Leadership where more recent information on this report is provided: www.workplaceleadership.com.au/sal/key-findings-study-australian-leadership.

In 2014, Professor Peter Gahan wrote the article 'Why Australian workplaces need much better leaders' (https://theconversation.com/why-australian-workplaces-need-much-better-leaders-23354) which captures the problem nicely, even though it was written before the report. Of course, these problems are not isolated to Australian leadership but we could argue that if things are bad in the USA, the UK, China and elsewhere, they are worse in Australia. Read the article by Professor Gahan and then complete the task below.

There are two parts to this task: first you must work alone, and then you must discuss your results with your group:

- Part 1: Visit the article by Professor Gahan using the link above. Consider what you have learned about leadership in your course and through this chapter – what is the problem according to Professor Gahan? How might you address the leadership challenges facing Australia? How do you think your own country compares to Australia? If you are in Australia, how do you think it compares to other parts of the world (you will need to do a bit of research – use Google, etc.).
- Part 2: Form small groups and compare your results. Come up with a group response to the question, 'What would you do to fix Australia's leadership challenge?'

LEADERS AS MOTIVATORS

Part of the role of the leader as mentor or coach is the ability to motivate and inspire. There is not a single theory or approach to leadership that fails to recognize that a fundamental quality of leaders – irrespective of whether leadership is seen as innate, learned, situational, or whatever – is an ability to inspire and motivate people.

Motivation is defined as the psychological processes that drive behaviour towards the attainment or avoidance of some object.

While the psychological concept of **motivation** is over 100 years old, it has been applied to organizational and management contexts only since the 1950s. It has been a topic of philosophy and theoretical debate for centuries in one way or another. Motivation is necessary whether you are to lead yourself, to lead others, or to be led by others. It is therefore important to visit briefly some approaches to motivation and see how they are relevant to you as a leader. We discuss two key approaches to motivation – the process and content theories – and two key motivation concepts – intrinsic versus extrinsic motivation. Rather than talking about individual motivation theories, we explore the assumptions behind the theories and how such approaches might specifically relate to leadership.

One of the oldest ideas in motivation is the opponent process theory of motivation. This idea has its origins in research on perception in the 1880s and was extended by Ewald Hering in the 1970s (Hering, 1977). A short time later, this idea was extended to motivation, providing a physiological basis to motivation and emotions by Solomon and Corbit (1978) who showed how hedonism (pleasure or pain seeking and avoiding behaviours) works in the same way. As such, these ideas have been applied to motivation and leadership (see the article by Hollenbeck et al., 2014). Simply put, the opponent process theory of leadership states that if a leader is stimulated in a positive or negative way, he or she will have an opposite reaction once that stimulus is removed

READ MORE ABOUT OPT

(Hollenbeck et al., 2014). The idea here is that the human system will tend towards homeostasis – that is, a tendency towards an equilibrium state – hence, when we experience anything that makes us feel good or bad, once removed we will tend towards a 'normal' way of being. This is, of course, unless we keep experiencing the positive or negative event – which means we will then move to a different equilibrium state (which can be a new positive or negative equilibrium state). Less technically, we can become happier or depressed. Clearly, a lot more research and development is needed in this area, and its long-term viability as a leadership theory is yet to be put to the test.

One of the best-known perspectives on leadership and motivation is McGregor's Theory X and Theory Y. McGregor (1960) developed his work on Theory X and Theory Y after observing the main approaches used by people when managing and motivating people. According to McGregor, how we approach the way we motivate people is strongly influenced by our beliefs about human nature. McGregor argued that managers could be grouped in terms of their assumptions concerning the way people behave towards work

Theory X orientation assumes that people are lazy, require structure, direction and control, and want to be rewarded with money for a job well done.

Theory Y orientation assumes that people crave responsibility and autonomy, want to be treated with respect and are driven towards self-actualization (Pitsis, 2008a, 2008b).

The concepts of **Theory X** and **Theory Y** are extreme opposites and it would be hard to find an organization that epitomizes either theory in its extreme form. McGregor developed these ideas in the 1960s when most corporate organizations approached a Theory X style of management. McGregor was a humanist psychologist and so he believed in an ideal world in which people come before profit. Much of motivation theory evolved out of the humanist school of psychology, and its main interest was to find those motivational processes that would lead to a psychologically healthy society.

Today we might say, if we take an overly cynical view, that much of motivation is about ensuring that people behave in the organization's best interest (Rousseau, 1996) – even if it is not in one's own interest. There has been a clear shift away from motivation theory's original objective, which was first and foremost about the psychological wellbeing and esteem of individuals, not about how much harder we can make them work.

For many centuries, philosophers have contemplated why we do the things we do. For instance, in the eighteenth century, Adam Smith held the view that we are motivated by self-interest. Smith (1961 [1776]) believed that self-interest was a central concept leading to the wealth of nations. As people set up companies to become wealthy, they create jobs, which provide income to people and tax revenue to government, which would be spent on health, education, security, and so on.

Contemporary approaches to motivation focus on the satiation of needs – we all need food, love, shelter and safety, for instance. When you do not have these things, you are 'pushed' to go out searching for them. There are many negative consequences if we do not satiate our needs – for example, starvation, loneliness, illness, injury or death. In organizational behaviour, theories that focus on needs are known as **content theories of motivation**.

Content theories of motivation refer to those 'contents' within us that drive or push us.

One of the most famous content theories of motivation is Maslow's (1970) hierarchy of needs (see Figure 4.2). According to Maslow, there is a hierarchy of needs; as we meet the needs within each tier of the hierarchy, we can move on to meet the next level of needs. The hierarchy begins with typical physiological needs, such as the need to satiate hunger and thirst; second in the hierarchy are safety needs, such as shelter and security; third are the needs to belong, love and be loved; fourth are esteem needs that are met by professional or other achievements, respect and recognition. At the top of the hierarchy is the self-actualization need, or the need to live the happiest and most fulfilled life possible, the achievement of which usually requires us to realize our fullest potential.

The self-actualization component of Maslow's theory is its most critical part because it was embedded in his philosophy of life. Yet, if you look at almost any organizational behaviour textbook, you will find fleeting mentions of Maslow's theory as an early and outdated theory of motivation, criticized on the grounds that it assumes that motivation is hierarchical. Such thin criticisms and misrepresentations of Maslow's life work ignore his notion of *eupsychian management* (Maslow, 1965) and the fact that it was not Maslow who represented his theory as a pyramid (for an excellent discussion on this and on the broader history of management thought, see the excellent book by Cummings et al. (2017) *A New History of Management*). Maslow coined the term 'eupsychia' for his vision of utopia, which, he argued, society should aspire to; with this vision, he attempted to refocus attention on motivation back to psychological wellbeing. Maslow believed that leadership should promote, support and maintain psychological wellbeing at work by basing the structure of society and its organizations on virtues, which, in turn, would filter into broader society and the community. He saw leadership in organizations as integral to helping people self-actualize. Yet, if you look at Maslow's hierarchy of needs theory in any organizational behaviour textbook, it will not tell you that Maslow was driven to try to understand why some self-actualized people were what he called 'fully functioning' and how to capture and foster such positive virtues in society at large.

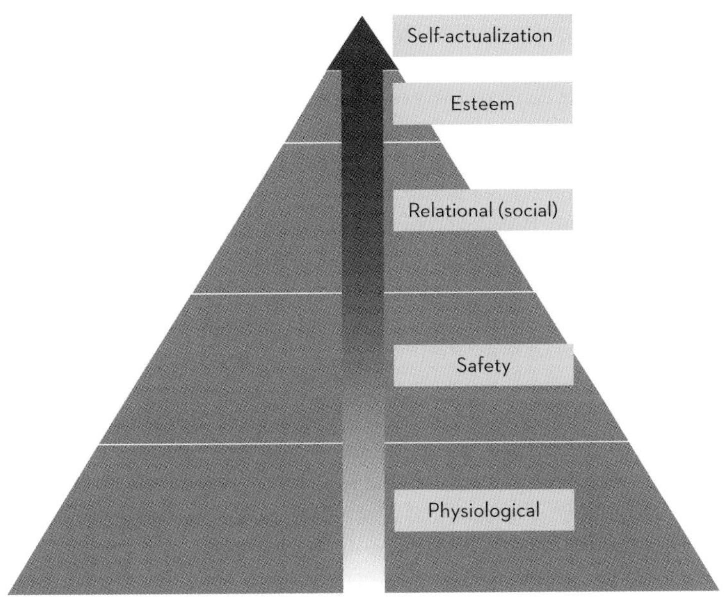

FIGURE 4.2 Maslow's hierarchy of needs

In essence, 50 years ago, Maslow thought about issues that still dominate much of leadership education and theory today. If people have to worry about where their next meal will come from, or where to sleep, or whether they have family support, how can they realize their full potential? The fundamentals of Maslow's arguments remain humanist despite their grounding in early work that he conducted on primates.

Process theories of motivation concern themselves with the processes that are involved in motivation. Some argue that the process is one of expecting that behaving in a certain way will realize certain outcomes.

Content theories do not sufficiently explain why people are motivated to behave in certain ways. To answer such questions, we need to consider **process theories of motivation**.

Proponents of process theories assume that you are more likely to behave in certain ways if: (a) your effort leads to your expected level of performance, (b) your level of performance gets the results you expect, and (c) you value such outcomes. Such assumptions are typical of a particular type of expectancy theory, known as expectancy theories of motivation (see, for example, Georgopoulos et al., 1957).

Another process theory, equity theory, extends the expectancy argument by adding that we also compare our inputs and outcomes to other people's inputs and outcomes (see Adams, 1963; Mowday, 1991). Equity theory – or social exchange theory – is by far one of the most dynamic and influential process theories. As an example, let us say that your rock band has been playing for ten years now but has never gained the recognition and rewards you believe it deserves, even while others become pop stars 'overnight' through *The X Factor* or one of its many clones globally. You compare your effort, performance and outcome to theirs and realize that the world is damn unfair. You give up being a musician in disgust and start working in a music store, managing medical and law students who really do not need the job, money or hassles, living out the alienated *High Fidelity* lifestyle.

Unlike many process theories, equity theory does not assume a rational process. If we were rational, we would expend effort only when we think it will lead to an outcome that we value and we would not expend effort when it leads to outcomes that we do not value. The theory acknowledges that sometimes our motives are hidden or subconscious (Adams, 1963). Why do people murder? Why do some leaders hide unethical and corrupt behaviour? Why do some people avoid effort? Why do some people put themselves in danger for other people? Why do some of us stay in a job or a relationship that makes us unhappy, sometimes for many years? Human behaviour is not always a rational and linear process. Often, we find ourselves doing the very things that do not make us happy, and we, in turn, expect those working for us, or with us, to suffer the same existence. Perhaps a more fruitful way of thinking about motivation is to think about *extrinsic* and *intrinsic* motivation. Intrinstic factors such as self-expression, interest and enjoyment drive intrinsic motivation. You might feel motivated to finish reading a book because you are interested, work because you find a job stimulating or change jobs because you want the challenge. On the flip side, extrinsic factors such as the promise of reward or threat of punishment would drive extrinsic motivation. You might feel motivated to finish reading a book to meet a deadline, work because you need the money or change jobs because you are certain you will be fired. Obviously, you could think of more examples, but it should be clear by now that *intrinsic motivation* refers to those internal states that drive us towards behaviours that directly meet self-actualization and belongingness needs. On the other hand, *extrinsic motivation* refers to those internal states that drive us towards behaviours that directly meet esteem needs.

TABLE 4.4 Examples of intrinsic and extrinsic motivation

Intrinsic	Extrinsic
Behaviour motivated by intrinsic factors such as self-expression, interest, and enjoyment	Behaviour motivated by extrinsic factors such as the promise of reward or threat of punishment
Motivated to finish reading because you are interested	Motivated to finish reading to meet a deadline
Working because you find the job stimulating and enjoyable	Working because you need the money
Changing jobs because you want the challenge	Changing jobs because you are certain you will be fired
Motivated to work in difficult jobs that challenge you	Motivated to work in difficult jobs to get the pay rise
Study to improve yourself	Study to get a high-paying job

Source: Adapted from Deci and Ryan (1987); Myers (2001: 451-2); Ryan and Deci (2000)

Theoretically, the two types of motivation are not mutually exclusive; however, notice that we used the word 'directly' in the previous sentence. In other words, sometimes money is important, even for an intrinsically motivated person, but it can simply be a means to an end – for example, to save enough money to realize your life dream of starting your own little restaurant. So, as a leader you have to know whether people – including you – are extrinsically or intrinsically motivated and not assume that all people are always intrinsically or extrinsically motivated by the same things. Moreover, much research suggests that the overuse of extrinsic motivation can kill or thwart intrinsic motivation (Deci and Ryan, 1985, 1987).

Self-determination theory (SDT) is a theory of motivation that emphasizes our intrinsic need to be seen as competent, liked and free from the control of others.

WATCH THIS TED TALK

MOTIVATION: A QUESTION OF SELF-DETERMINATION

Ryan and Deci (2000) became increasingly dissatisfied with traditional conceptions of motivation theory – especially those theories with an emphasis on instrumental goal achievement. They therefore developed a comprehensive theory of motivation that is linked to personality and self-regulation. This theory is called **self-determination theory (SDT)**. SDT places great importance on the social context in thwarting or facilitating psychological wellbeing and health:

> people's inherent growth tendencies and innate psychological needs … are the basis for their self-motivation and personality integration, as well as for the conditions that foster those positive processes. Inductively, using the empirical process, we have identified three such needs – the needs for competence (Harter, 1978; White, 1963), relatedness (Baumeister and Leary, 1995; Reis, 1994), and autonomy (deCharms, 1968; Deci, 1975) – that appear to be essential for facilitating optimal functioning of the natural propensities for growth and integration, as well as for constructive social development and personal well-being. (Ryan and Deci, 2000: 68)

A critical component of SDT is that emphasis is placed on social context. As is stated in the quote above, the need for competence, relatedness and autonomy all occur in social contexts.

In many ways, SDT is an exciting and promising field of motivation theory and research that we believe will make a significant contribution not only to leadership and organizational behaviour, but also to psychological health and wellbeing. SDT assumes that we are active organisms, who inherently strive towards psychological growth and development, seeking to master ongoing challenges and to integrate our experiences into a coherent sense of self. All this requires a supportive social environment in order for us to function effectively, to ensure our active engagement in life and our psychological growth (see Deci and Ryan, 2000). When people feel they have achieved high levels of self-determination, they are believed to be operating at high levels of psychological health and wellbeing because they feel more competent, social and free (Thrash and Elliot, 2002; Vansteenkiste et al., 2004).

READ THE ARTICLE

EXTEND YOUR KNOWLEDGE

The following article: Fuller, B., Marler, L.E., Hester, K. and Otondo, R. F. (2015) 'Leader reactions to follower proactive behavior: giving credit when credit is due', *Human Relations*, 68: 879–98, provides some nice insights into SDT and the effect of leadership on proactive behaviour. You can access the article at the companion website https://study.sagepub.com/managingandorganizations5e

Try the self-determination scale in the In Practice box, developed by Kennon M. Sheldon (1995). It has been shown to be a reliable and valid predictor of psychological health and wellbeing (Sheldon et al., 1996). A high score on the two constructs in the scale (less than 10 on both) indicates high levels of self-determination.

The SDT is an important motivation theory underpinned by principles of positive psychology. It is therefore appropriate and important that we consider an increasingly popular aspect of the positive psychology of leadership: that of authentic leadership and positive psychological capital.

IN PRACTICE

The Self-Determination Scale

Scale description

The Self-Determination Scale (SDS) was designed to assess individual differences in the extent to which people tend to function in a self-determined way. It is thus considered a relatively enduring aspect of people's personalities, which reflects (1) being more aware of their feelings and their sense of self, and (2) feeling a sense of choice with respect to their behaviour. The SDS is a short, 10-item scale, with two 5-item subscales. The first subscale is awareness of oneself, and the second is perceived choice in one's actions. The subscales can either be used separately or they can be combined into an overall SDS score.

Instructions

Please read the pairs of statements, one pair at a time, and think about which statement within the pair seems more true to you at this point in your life. Indicate the degree to which statement A feels true, relative to the degree that statement B feels true, on the 5-point scale shown after each pair of statements. If statement A feels completely true and statement B feels completely untrue, the appropriate response would be 1. If the two statements are equally true, the appropriate response would be 3. If only statement B feels true, the appropriate response would be 5, and so on.

1. a. I always feel like I choose the things I do.

   b. I sometimes feel that it's not really me choosing the things I do.

   Only A feels true 1 2 3 4 5 **Only B feels true**

2. a. My emotions sometimes seem alien to me.

   b. My emotions always seem to belong to me.

   Only A feels true 1 2 3 4 5 **Only B feels true**

3. a. I choose to do what I have to do.

   b. I do what I have to, but I don't feel like it is really my choice.

   Only A feels true 1 2 3 4 5 **Only B feels true**

4. a. I feel that I am rarely myself.

   b. I feel like I am always completely myself.

   Only A feels true 1 2 3 4 5 **Only B feels true**

5. a. I do what I do because it interests me.

   b. I do what I do because I have to.

   Only A feels true 1 2 3 4 5 **Only B feels true**

6. a. When I accomplish something, I often feel it wasn't really me who did it.

   b. When I accomplish something, I always feel it's me who did it.

   Only A feels true 1 2 3 4 5 **Only B feels true**

7. a. I am free to do whatever I decide to do.

   b. What I do is often not what I'd choose to do.

   Only A feels true 1 2 3 4 5 **Only B feels true**

(Continued)

(Continued)

8. a. My body sometimes feels like a stranger to me.
   b. My body always feels like me.

Only A feels true	1	2	3	4	5	**Only B feels true**

9. a. I feel pretty free to do whatever I choose to.
   b. I often do things that I don't choose to do.

Only A feels true	1	2	3	4	5	**Only B feels true**

10. a. Sometimes I look into the mirror and see a stranger.
    b .When I look into the mirror I see myself.

Only A feels true	1	2	3	4	5	**Only B feels true**

Scoring information for the SDS

First, items 1, 3, 5, 7, 9 need to be reverse scored so that higher scores on every item will indicate a higher level of self-determination. To reverse score an item, subtract the item response from 6 and use that as the item score (so if you scored 5 for question 9, subtract this number from 6 and you get 1). Then, calculate the scores for the Awareness of Self subscale and the Perceived Choice subscale by averaging the item scores for the 5 items within each subscale. The subscales are: Awareness of Self: Questions 2, 4, 6, 8, 10; Perceived Choice: Questions 1, 3, 5, 7, 9. Scores greater than 10 on both reflect a high level of self-determination.

This survey first appeared in Sheldon, K. M. (1995) 'Creativity and self-determination in personality', *Creativity Research Journal*, 8: 25–36.

POSITIVE PSYCHOLOGY OF LEADERSHIP

BUILDING POSITIVE PSYCHOLOGICAL CAPITAL THROUGH AUTHENTIC LEADERSHIP

To be a leader is a huge moral responsibility because executive leadership can easily overwhelm reason. A large body of work is emerging that emphasizes and distinguishes leadership by behaviours and *cognitions* (or ways of thinking). Such approaches have emerged out of the traditions of positive psychology (see also pp. 63–67) and place virtues such as strength of character, wisdom, authenticity and humanity before all else. Remember that many of the traditional theories of leadership do not differentiate between leaders such as Hitler and Obama. As such, wisdom, authenticity and humanity are strong values that allow us to make sense of leadership as 'doing good'.

As the work of Milgram (1971) has shown, these values are extremely important. Milgram was intrigued as to why people would follow some leaders to the point where they would engage in atrocious behaviour. As a person of Jewish ancestry and as a social psychologist, Milgram was especially interested in why

Germans, and many others, blindly followed the Nazi quest to exterminate all Jews. How could leaders have so much power and influence over people? Was there something specific about those followers that made them obey the Nazi leader's orders? Or could any one of us become violent, murderous, blind followers given the right conditions? Milgram designed a study in which people were asked to give various levels of electric shocks to individuals (who unbeknown to the participants were actors in the experiment). The participants thought the experiment was about punishment and learning; however, after administering mild shocks to the actors, Milgram asked participants to give extremely high, lethal shocks to people. Over two-thirds of respondents were willing to give the highest dose, even when the participants themselves appeared emotionally distressed.

READ ABOUT MILGRAM EXPERIMENT

As Milgram (1974: 4–5) so eloquently noted a few years after his original study was published:

> ordinary people, simply doing their jobs, and without any particular hostility on their part, can become agents in a terrible destructive process. Moreover, even when the destructive effects of their work become patently clear, and they are asked to carry out actions incompatible with fundamental standards of morality, relatively few people have the resources needed to resist authority. A variety of inhibitions against disobeying authority come into play and successfully keep the person in his place. Sitting back in one's armchair, it is easy to condemn the actions of the obedient subjects. But those who condemn the subjects measure them against the standard of their own ability to formulate high-minded moral prescriptions. That is hardly a fair standard. Many of the subjects, at the level of stated opinion, feel quite as strongly as any of us about the moral requirement of refraining from action against a helpless victim.

Increasingly, especially since the positive psychology movement but even before that, there has been a concern for developing and unashamedly biasing the concept of leadership towards doing and being good. Tomkins and Simpson (2015), for example, promote the idea of caring leadership based on Heidegger's philosophy of care. Martin Heidegger was a German philosopher and one of the greatest thinkers in pragmatic philosophy and phenomenology. According to Leah Tomkins and Peter Simpson, caring leadership is concerned with the affairs of the world and the efforts of others. The caring leader takes responsibility for the ramifications of their interventions, balancing the urge for certainty of outcome and visibility of contribution with the desire to encourage and enable others. The authors critique transactional and transformational leadership because of their under-reliance on agency (people's freedom to act upon the world). In a Heideggerian view, caring leadership has little to do with compassion, kindness or niceness; it involves and requires a fundamental organization and leadership of the self.

Luthans and Avolio's (2003) concept of the **authentic leader** differs from the type of leader encountered in Nazi Germany and the Milgram experiment. Their authentic leadership development exemplifies many of the qualities espoused by positive psychology. According to Luthans and Avolio (2003: 242–3), authentic leaders are transparent. Their intentions seamlessly link espoused values, actions and behaviours.

Authentic leaders have the qualities of transformational leaders but also work on moral and ethical grounds; possess great self-awareness, integrity, confidence and self-control; and are positive, optimistic and resilient.

Authentic leaders inspire, transform, mentor and develop (Gardner et al., 2005). The authentic leader might be the perfectly designed leader to achieve Maslow's eupsychian philosophy that we discussed earlier.

WATCH THIS TED TALK

EXTEND YOUR KNOWLEDGE

Watch this Tedx talk by Professor Francis Frei (2018) – listen carefully about what she has to say about authenticity. What do you think about authenticity? Can we ever truly be and should we be, authentic? www.ted.com/talks/frances_frei_how_to_build_and_rebuild_trust/transcript?language=en

The authentic leader, by definition, should be able to realize when she or he makes a mistake or inadvertently does wrong and will then take responsibility, accept accountability and seek to amend the situation. In addition, a very important aspect of the model is that authentic leadership occurs within a context in which leaders are able to empathize with subordinates and to reflect cultural, moral and ethical standards in their approach to management, so the authentic leader is not only a way of being and a way of seeing but is also situational. A critical aspect of the authentic leader is the ability to develop **positive psychological capital (PsyCap)** (Gardner et al., 2005; Luthans et al., 2002, 2007).

Positive psychological capital (PsyCap) refers to positive states such as hope, resilience, optimism and self-efficacy through leadership and organizational behaviour that is oriented towards the positive psychological wellbeing and health of its members.

Fred Luthans and his colleagues have done most to develop and apply the concept of PsyCap. According to Luthans et al. (2007: 542–3), PsyCap refers to an individual's positive psychological state of development and includes: (1) self-efficacy – the confidence to take on and put in the necessary effort to succeed at challenging tasks; (2) optimism – making a positive attribution about succeeding now and in the future; (3) hope – persevering towards goals and, when necessary, redirecting paths to goals in order to succeed; and (4) resilience – the ability to bounce back and succeed in the face of problems and adversity.

Luthans and Youssef (2004) argue that the role of psychological capital leadership is to develop and enhance employees' psychological strengths. These strengths of self-efficacy, optimism, hope and resilience have been shown to be important in performance and satisfaction at work (Luthans et al., 2007). Leadership can play an important role in building psychological capital by acknowledging that everyone brings their life experiences with them to the workplace and that current workplace events shape an employee's confidence, hope, resilience and optimism (Bagozzi, 2003; Luthans, 2002; Luthans and Avolio, 2003; Luthans and Youssef, 2004). We have all worked for organizations where the building of PsyCap was the last thing on lists of priorities. Our anecdotal experience – that is evidence based on our own life experience – shows that such organizations are detrimental to happy, functional, productive and healthy working lives, and they can stay dysfunctional for a very long time. PsyCap has been shown to reduce levels of workplace incivility, and also to buffer people from the negative effects of incivility (Roberts et al., 2011); to promote servant leadership behaviours (Searle and Barbuto, 2011) as well as improving performance (Peterson et al., 2011).

To believe that such positive ideals can be attained as absolutes (or universal truths) is not only idealistic but, in our opinion, unrealistic and unattainable. Now, by no means should this imply that we should not try to strive for organizational and leadership behaviour that espouses positive psychological capital. However, to do so requires a change in the dominant sources of leadership wisdom.

SUMMARY

In this chapter, we have looked at the main approaches to leadership, coaching and motivating people:

- What leaders do and what they say have profound effects on the world. Leaders influence others and can make life fulfilling, enriched and empowered (of course, they can also make it empty, shallow and powerless). There have been many different theories of leadership, the main currents of which we have considered.
- Leadership is an extremely complex and value-laden domain of theory and research. Is a leader, as the trait theory suggests, made up of inherent characteristics? Behavioural theory sought to refocus leadership away from traits to how a person behaves - that is, whether or not one's behaviour makes one a leader.
- Moving on from the behaviourists, theorists concluded that situational/contingent factors were influential in determining what made leaders and, more importantly, what made them effective.
- Leaders were then conceptualized as charismatic and transformational, with an ability to envision, to inspire and to implement change. Others may be transactional in that they know how to be exemplary managers. Of course, if full-range leadership theory is correct, the best leaders are both transformational and transactional.
- The dispersed and postmodern approaches to leadership attempted to turn leadership around. The leader has changed over time, from premodern to modern to postmodern. The postmodern leader is a SERVANT.
- No matter which leadership theory we look at, motivation emerges as a critical concept. Leaders must be motivated, but they must also motivate others by inspiring, envisioning and empowering.
- Intrinsic and extrinsic motivation are important as a way of understanding motivation and leadership, and we emphasized the growing influence of Deci and Ryan's self-determination theory.
- Positive psychology is an important and evolving field. Authentic leaders are able to develop positive psychological capital.

EXERCISES

1. Having read this chapter, you should be able to say in your own words what each of the following key terms means. Test yourself or ask a colleague to test you.

   - Leadership
   - Coaching
   - Self-leadership
   - Leadership traits
   - Leadership behaviour
   - Leadership styles
   - Transformational leadership
   - Transactional leadership
   - Charismatic leadership
   - Servant leadership
   - Authentic leadership
   - Positive psychological capital
   - Positive psychology
   - Motivation
   - Extrinsic motivation
   - Intrinsic motivation
   - Self-determination theory
   - Maslow
   - McGregor
   - Theory X and Theory Y.

2. What does it mean to say 'true leaders create more leaders, not more followers'? How far do you agree with this statement? Give reasons for your answer.
3. How practical is it to argue that leadership can be substituted or neutralized? Can we create leadership substitutes or neutralizers in any industry or organization? Why or why not?
4. Choose two perspectives or theories of leadership – the one you liked best and the one you liked least. Compare your choices with those of your peers and try to find out why you and your peers chose those theories or approaches. What was it about the theories that you liked or disliked? What were their strengths and weaknesses? Take note of how and why you and your peers differed or agreed.
5. Set up a class debate titled 'In the end, when you want to motivate people, all that matters is money – everyone has a price!' Have one team argue for the statement and one team against. Both groups should use current motivation research and theory to state their claims.
6. How might a leader be able to inspire people through the principles espoused by self-determination theory?
7. What is coaching and why is it a critical component of leadership?
8. Is it realistic to assume that the concept of positive psychology can be applied in the business world? Why or why not?

TEST YOURSELF

Review what you have learned by visiting: https://study.sagepub.com/managingandorganizations5e or your eBook

- Test yourself with multiple-choice questions.
- Revise key terms with the interactive flashcards.

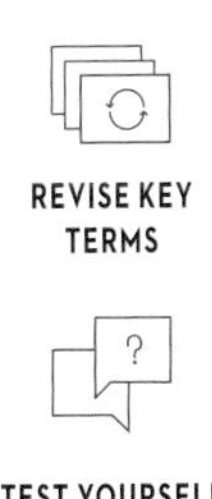

CASE STUDY

Authentic leadership at CLIF Bar organization

Introduction

This case is about the CLIF Bar organization, and is presented from the perspective of the third person. It demonstrates authentic leadership which is a concept based in: (a) self-awareness; (b) balanced processing (i.e. seeking alternative, even contradictory, viewpoints); (c) transparency and disclosure of relevant information; and (d) morally based ethical actions. Authentic leadership is applying individual leader authenticity, which at the core represents being true to one's self, to the broader scope of leadership experiences that impact a leader's constituencies and organization. The case below will illustrate these points.

The story

In 2006, CLIF Bar was a private company with estimated annual revenues of about $150 million and about 170 employees. Yet, there was a moment when it almost became another product line of a large mega corporation and another countless blip across the C-SPAN screen. It was a 'moment' that can be described as authentic leadership that changed the course of the future for the owner, employees and customers of this unique company.

After large corporations bought two key competitors in the industry, an offer was made by a third large corporation to purchase the CLIF Bar company in the year 2000. It was an outstanding offer that was sure to make both owners extremely wealthy to the extent that they would never have to work another day in their lives.

On the day of signing the contract, however, Gary Erickson, one of the owners, felt a sense of panic, so he decided to take a walk to consider his 'epiphany'. In that moment, being aware of his innermost thoughts, he realized he did not want to sell the company. He decided he was not going to give in to all the rational reasons that 'experts' gave him for selling the business, the primary one being the fact that key competitive products were recently bought by corporations with large marketing budgets; it was argued that CLIF Bar would never be able to compete at that level and would wither away under the force of immense competition. But on this day, Gary listened to his conscience and made a decision that went against these experts, including

(Continued)

(Continued)

the co-owner of CLIF Bar, who would now have to be bought out. Gary defied the odds and decided to back out of the deal of a lifetime. He went on to buy out the other owner for over $60 million, even though he only had $10,000 in his bank account at the time.

In this case, his leadership paid off. The company has since grown from about $40 million in sales to $150 million, even while competing with mega corporations. Most recently, CLIF Bar became a leader in business sustainability by offering the nation's first incentive programme to pay cash to employees who purchase clean-burning bio-diesel cars, helping employees buy high-mileage hybrids, and offering a variety of rewards to those who leave their cars at home altogether.

Gary Erickson has demonstrated authentic leadership by aligning his actions with his conscience when he chose to back out of the sale at the last minute and follow his 'inner voice'. He trusted his own wisdom over the advice of the other highly experienced business people involved. Not only did he succeed in sustaining the revenue growth of the company over time, but CLIF Bar continues to create innovative ways to be a company that values and takes actions towards sustaining the planet.

In retrospect, he could have been wrong about the future-earning potential, but he would still have been right about himself. His level of self-awareness regarding his inner morals and values led him to maintain and grow one of the best-known outdoor food brands in the USA. Although authentic leadership in this example was clearly demonstrated by a major decision, that decision took years to carry through and required a repeated focus on core values during that time. As a result, the company continues to thrive and lead other companies in social responsibility initiatives.

CLIF Bar has recently instituted policies intended to make it more ecologically sustainable – for example, switching to organic ingredients and cutting down on plastic use and rewarding employees for getting to work on foot, by bicycle or by public transportation. The company also began offering employees up to $1,000 annually to make eco-improvements to their homes. In April 2009, CLIF Bar joined Business for Innovative Climate and Energy Policy, a coalition of companies including Nike, eBay and The North Face, with the goal of passing progressive climate and energy legislation. In 2010, the company moved into a new headquarters in the EmeryTech Building in Emeryville, California that was renovated and redesigned for sustainability, with photovoltaic panels, solar thermal panels, reclaimed wood, plants and other biophilic features. In 2012, the company announced that thenceforth '100 per cent of cocoa ingredients for CLIF Bar will be sourced from Rainforest Alliance Certified farms', in order to ensure that neither slave nor child exploitation produced their crops. In April 2013, Kevin Cleary was named CEO of the company; co-owners Gary Erickson and Kit Crawford became co-chief visionary officers.

The vision expresses itself in building company facilities including an on-site gym, rock climbing wall, two yoga room/dance studios, and massage rooms, on-site showers, free counselling and life coaching. Employees can bring their dogs to work and get two and a half hours of paid exercise each week with free personal training. Perhaps not surprisinglsy, CLIF Bar & Company has been consistently named as one of the Best Places to Work.

Questions

1. What do you think the moral of the story is?
2. Would we still call it effective leadership or even authentic leadership if CLIF Bar had gone bankrupt instead of increasing in revenues? Why?

3. How is CLIF Bar's authenticity expressed in its employment and environmental policies? What do you think the advantages of these policies might be in business and in life?

You might want to check out Erickson (2007) available at **http://clifbarfamilyfoundation.org/About-Us/Our-Story** and learn a bit about the foundation and also about Gary and Kit, the people behind the idea.

Case prepared by Tara S. Wernsing, Gallup Leadership Institute, University of Nebraska-Lincoln; James B. Avey, Assistant Professor of Management, Central Washington University, and updated by Tyrone Pitsis in 2018.

ADDITIONAL RESOURCES

- Check out this great website created by Dave Wraith on leadership and the movies. It contains lots of discussions about films, as well as other great resources on leading: www.movieleadership.com
- A great travel companion book for the aspiring and inspirational leader of the future is Robert C. Stone's (2015) *Circle of Wisdom: A Path for Life, Mind and Leadership*, on CreateSpace Independent Publishing Platform. However, we recommend this book to any leader. Stone is a psychotherapist and academic specializing in post-traumatic stress disorder, so his views on leadership urge a more mindful and compassionate form of leadership.
- Another great book on leadership is John Anotnakis and David D. Day's (2018) *The Nature of Leadership*, 3rd edition, Thousand Oaks, CA: Sage. This book has chapters by some of the leading and upcoming thinkers on leadership research, theory and practice and gives you a detailed and in-depth coverage of all things leadership.
- While none of us (the authors) are fans of war, a powerful but great film about leadership is *Hackshaw Ridge* (Gibson, 2016). This is a true story about Private First-Class Desmond T. Doss. Doss finds himself conflicted about his values as a pacifist but also his belief in defending the freedoms of democracy. He enlists to fight in the Second World War and goes into the frontline of battle, never picking up a gun.
- Finally, make sure you check out the exciting Global Leadership and Organizational Behaviour Effectiveness (GLOBE) project. This project seeks to identify the necessary skills, capabilities, competencies, cognition, behaviours and structures that are necessary for organizations to prosper in a global world. It involves over 170 researchers from over 61 cultures around the world using a range of quantitative and qualitative methods to examine the interrelationships between societal cultures, organizational culture and organizational leadership. GLOBE is by far the most comprehensive research project on cross-cultural leadership (http://globeproject.com/globe_2020).

MANAGING HUMAN RESOURCES
DIVERSITY, SELECTION, RETENTION

LEARNING OBJECTIVES

This chapter is designed to enable you to:

- describe the origins and meaning of human resource management
- understand the key concepts in human resource management and how they affect organizational practice and performance
- understand the main methods and approaches to recruitment, selection, retention and development used in the main functions of human resource management
- describe the 'hard' and 'soft' approaches to human resource practices and policies
- appreciate the role of government in influencing human resources policy.

BEFORE YOU GET STARTED...

Some words from a Marx Brother:

> I don't care to belong to a club that accepts people like me as members. (Groucho Marx)

INTRODUCTION

'Why do you want to work for us?' It is likely that almost all of us will be faced with this uninspiring question at least once in our working lives. Other typical questions include: 'What are your strengths and weaknesses?', 'Why did you leave your last job?', 'Can you work as part of a team?', and so on. These questions are not simply friendly banter: they are underpinned by specific intentions. Think for a moment: why would a possible future employer ask you these things? It is not because they want to date you (well, usually not!). It is because they want to determine if you are the right person for the job. Having the 'right' people is one of the most critical success factors for any organization. Given that staffing is one of the biggest costs in any organization, it is therefore not a surprise that so much money, time and effort are spent on attracting, selecting and retaining the right people in organizations. Once the domain of large corporations, an increasing number of small- and medium-sized organizations are finding it necessary to invest in human resources (HR) departments and professionals.

Human resource management (HRM) is the process and practice of managing and advising management on the recruitment, selection, retention and development of staff in an increasingly complex legal and social environment, with the aim of achieving the organization's objectives as they are made sense of by its managers or consultants.

Human resource management (HRM) concerns a broad range of practices and processes that include:

- attracting and selecting employees in line with the strategic direction and intent of the organization
- managing and facilitating the career development and advancement of employees
- dealing with and keeping abreast of current rules, laws and legislation in industrial relations and other policy areas such as occupational health and safety legislation, equity and diversity, and anti-discrimination laws
- ensuring that there are uniform procedures and company HR policy information available to staff and management on all aspects of employment.

Most large organizations will have a department dedicated to human resources. However, most people work in small- to medium-sized organizations, many without a HR department. The HR manager in small organizations is usually also the business owner, manager or supervisor, typically with a wider span of duties and responsibilities and a much smaller HR budget. Even so, many of the HR challenges that large businesses face are the same as those that face small businesses. For example, it is just as important that a small business is able to attract and retain talented staff. More importantly, in the case of workplace accidents, where employer negligence is involved, it can often be easier for government departments and legal entities to pursue the small-business owner than large-company executives. Moreover, there is little doubt that organizations that have strong, well-managed and well-run HR departments outperform those that do not.

WATCH THIS TED TALK

In this chapter, we will explore the contextual aspects of HRM that shape the way people are recruited, selected, retained and treated once on board the organization. HRM is a complex and difficult part of organizational practice: HR managers and their teams must understand a plethora of government laws, rules and regulations in areas such as equity and diversity (anti-discrimination and affirmative action), occupational health and safety, and industrial relations laws (both domestic and international). Not only must HR managers be knowledgeable about all these things, they must also have a strong awareness of what is happening in society – for example, generational differences are believed to have major influences on why and how people work. Knowing all these things, and transforming all this knowledge into understandable, easily accessible and practical information, is easier said than done.

If you were to ask any executive or business owner what they find most challenging in running their organization, it is likely that they would respond that finding and selecting the right staff is one of the biggest challenges. However, once you find people, you need to keep them. Herein lies one of our biggest challenges as managers – how do we actually keep people? A good HR manager will ensure practices, processes and policies exist that maintain the interest of employees and provide opportunities for staff development. So, we will focus on the areas of recruitment, selection, retention and development of staff; but, first, let us delve a little deeper into the history and main themes of HR.

HR ORIGINS

HR practices have been studied implicitly by anthropologists for over two centuries as they investigated work practices in ancient times. For example, it has been found that many Anglo-Celtic people were named after what they did for a living – Smith, Cook, Miller and Taylor are not simply surnames but also job titles: people were, quite literally, what they did for a living.

In ancient times, people often did the same job for life: sometimes they were born into a trade and often people would follow in their father's footsteps. Some jobs required a lifetime of learning, practice and experience before they could be mastered and young people would enter apprenticeships where they would receive close mentoring. In many respects, apprenticeships have changed very little over the centuries and the model used to train people has remained strong. Young stonemasons, jewellers, glassmakers, chefs and other craftspeople were bound to their masters through apprenticeships, often having to live with their employers until they mastered their trade. Today, the apprenticeship system of staff training and development remains. Even in academia, if you intend one day to be an academic you will find the apprenticeship model is alive and well when you do a PhD.

HRM GROWS UP

The *theory/study* of HRM is relatively new as a discipline in its own right. HRM was introduced as an area of study as part of the Harvard University MBA and later at the Michigan Business School in the 1980s. Often, you will hear people refer to 'hard' and 'soft' HR models; in reality, they are inadvertently referring to the Michigan and the Harvard schools of HRM respectively. The notion of 'hard' and 'soft' approaches to HRM is an integral component of all HRM practices, so it is important that we appreciate and understand what is meant by these two terms. To comprehend fully these two HRM schools of thought and to understand the meaning of the terms 'hard' and 'soft', let us look at two seminal approaches – Frederick Taylor's scientific management and Elton Mayo's human relations approaches to management (both approaches are discussed in greater detail in Chapter 9). More so than most topics in this textbook, HRM is underpinned by variations of scientific management or human relations approaches – especially in regards to staff training and development, and performance measurement and reward. While we cover these topics in greater detail shortly, they are important underlying concepts in HRM theory and practice. Table 5.1 summarizes the key points of both approaches to HR practice.

These two underlying themes of soft and hard HR practices can be seen in the Harvard and Michigan models. The models can also be matched to Douglas McGregor's conception of Theory X and Theory Y orientations to managing people (see Chapter 4 for more details). Theory X refers to managers who take a hard orientation towards managing and motivating people at work, and Theory Y refers to leaders who take a soft orientation (Pitsis, 2008a, 2008b).

TABLE 5.1 Hard and soft HRM practices and philosophies

HRM practices	Hard	Soft
Assumption about managing people	Staff will work to rule if not managed correctly. Emphasis is on the individual and on management control. People are a specific kind of resource and should be managed as such. Emphasis is on the strategic match of people to the organization's objectives	Staff are looking for self-fulfilment and meaning in work that comes from social relations. Emphasis is on teamwork and participative collaboration. Management should focus on creating fulfilling and meaningful workplaces that encourage autonomy and self-management. People are assets. Emphasis is on the value of viewing the organization as comprised of multiple stakeholders, staff being one of these interested stakeholders
Selection orientation	Selection should focus on the best people for the task. The emphasis is on the fit between person and task	Selection should focus on people who can enhance the organization and bring in new knowledge and expertise. More important than the fit between people and task is the fit between person and organization
Retention orientation	The retention of staff is less important than maintaining productivity and efficiency. Low-level jobs are easier to fill, so staff retention is not an underlying concern	Retention is achieved through building social networks in the organization. Commitment to and identity with the organization are critical
Training and development orientation	People must receive the best training specifically for the task at hand, but all training and development must be specific to the task. The best training available should be used on the best people	Personal and organizational development is key. Using the knowledge and intellect of staff will benefit the organization. If people are not right for the task, design tasks or find them jobs that are right for them

HRM practices	Hard	Soft
Performance orientation	Management ultimately drives and sets performance outcomes. Almost always measured at the individual level and always on the meeting of specific job-related outcomes. Poor performance is due to poor management control of employees	Performance outcomes are usually decided as a team. Performance evaluation is measured not only on task performance but on the ability to work as a team player. Hence, tasks that are not directly related to the specific job might also be part of measured performance outcomes, e.g. social responsibility by volunteering time to charity events
Motivation orientation	Theory X orientation: mainly extrinsic rewards, such as monetary rewards in the form of bonuses paid for exceeding set targets. Time in lieu also used as a motivator (also see Chapter 4)	Theory Y orientation: mainly intrinsic rewards such as promotion, recognition and opportunities for self-development, self-actualization and self-management (also see Chapter 4)
HR model	Michigan model	Harvard model
Alignment to management philosophy	Scientific Management (i.e. Frederick W. Taylor)	Human Relations (i.e. Elton Mayo)

Source: Adapted and extended from Price (2004). Reproduced by permission of Cengage Learning EMEA Ltd.

The **soft model of HRM** takes a humanistic approach; typically soft HR managers have a Theory Y orientation, which emphasizes that people are intrinsically motivated.

In the **hard model of HRM** managers tend to have a Theory X orientation and believe that most people would rather not be at work; for this reason, management monitoring and control are integral, and typically extrinsic rewards such as pay raises and bonuses are used.

In the **soft model** of HRM, it is assumed that work is an integral part of life and should provide a fulfilling, empowering and positive experience for people. People will be attracted to jobs that provide opportunity for growth and advancement; they will stay in jobs that invest in them as valuable assets.

In the **hard model** of HRM, it is assumed that people do not want empowerment: they simply want to be told what is required of them, given the resources and training to achieve these requirements, and be remunerated if they go beyond those requirements. People will be attracted by good pay, clear objectives and unambiguous job duties.

Before considering the main functions of HRM, let us cover one very important concept underpinning HRM practice – 'humans' as 'resources'. The online encyclopaedia, Encarta, describes resources in a number of ways. Two of the most interesting and most commonly shared ideas of resources are:

- **backup supply** – a reserve supply of something, such as money, personnel or equipment
- **corporate assets** – any or all of the resources drawn on by a company for making profit, e.g. personnel, capital, machinery or stock.

On the face of it, these definitions look benign. However, we need to deconstruct their meaning and origins. When we take a closer look at the 'reserve supply of something', in our case the 'something' refers to personnel. As a corporate asset, personnel are used 'by a company for making profit'. Personnel are of course humans, or more precisely human resources, yet it can sound as though they are merely an item on a corporate shopping list, along with other items such as money, equipment, capital, machinery and stock. One could imagine a large warehouse somewhere, full of pencils, pens, envelopes and boxes of copy paper, and, just below that, perhaps some nicely packaged humans. Of course, we are only joking, well sort of – most organizations do store people in a warehouse (offices) for a large part of the day (a fate awaiting most of us). However, the concept of humans as resources has very important implications for the notion of HRM because there are some very basic assumptions underpinning the notion of humans as resources.

Historically and abhorrently, some humans were thought of as resources that could be bought and sold as slaves and for hundreds of years slavery was the most profitable trade in the world economy. Indeed, the British, French and Dutch prospered greatly from the slave trade. Sadly, slave labour still exists today across the world.

It was not only the slave trade that reinforced the treatment of humans as nothing more than resources. The wealthy industrialist classes in the UK, France, Germany, Spain, the Netherlands and other capitalist nations helped to create a large working class. Economies were structured in terms of a division between the owners of capital and those whose only resource was the ability to provide their labour power by renting some of their time and labour to a capitalist for a wage.

At this time, many nations saw an increase in the union movement, as unions were created to counter the increasing power of industrialists and owners of capital, and to ensure a fair wage for a fair day's work. Unionists believed that the main aim of union organization was to ensure that humans were not treated simply as resources but as human beings with lives, families, aspirations, and so on. For many in management, and some management theorists – including those within both the scientific management and the human relations schools – unions were seen as more of a source of disruption and conflict in organizational life.

One might be sceptical about the intentions of HRM and its role in people's – those human resources – working lives. You do not have to search far or wide to experience cases of people being treated as nothing other than a resource. Often, companies pursue programmes of mass redundancies in order to influence stock market prices and every day there are cases of unfair dismissal, discrimination and exploitation, even in some of the biggest and most successful companies.

Yet, while it is certainly true that the exploitation of people occurs on a day-to-day basis, it is also true that many organizations proclaim that their people are their greatest asset: mainly because it is true. Some of these companies have experienced phenomenal growth, even in times of great competition and challenge, and we will visit some of these throughout this chapter. The point to be made here is that the desire to treat humans as valuable 'assets', rather than as expendable 'resources', gives HRM a very important role within organizations – especially as unionism continues to decline, partly in the face of governments' aggressive neo-liberal economic policies on industrial relations which privilege individual over collective contracts. So, it is time now to visit the HRM core functions that are central to the success and growth of organizations.

HRM IN PRACTICE: THE CORE FUNCTIONS

The core HRM functions have the potential to influence significantly the performance and outcomes of organizations (Becker and Gerhart, 1996). HRM is more than simplistic and cost-efficient bureaucratic ways of finding, hiring and monitoring the performance of people; the HRM functions should be active and central to innovating and meeting the greatest challenges facing all organizations' quest for talent (Björkman et al., 2014; Boudreau and Lawler, 2014). In this chapter, we provide you with an easy to read and understand introduction to the core HR functions. We do so because understanding these functions, as a manager, is very important as it provides you with knowledge that will complement the people and organizational management skills and knowledge that you are acquiring as you study. So, now let us focus on the recruitment, selection, retention and development of people in organizations.

RECRUITING PEOPLE

Recruitment refers to the processes and practices used to attract suitable employees to the organization. It involves searching for and obtaining potential job candidates in sufficient numbers and quality so that the organization can select the most appropriate people to fill its job needs (Shen and Edwards, 2004: 816).

Demographic changes associated with globalization, migration and generational changes have critical implications for the ability of employers to attract talented, qualified staff to their organizations, especially as the demand for talented and qualified staff is global. No longer are organizations competing against only their local competitors for staff, they are competing against large international corporations and international governments offering the promise of higher standards of living, higher wages and career prospects. As jobs are going global, so too is recruitment and it has become a multi-million dollar business. In addition, sustained global economic growth has created staff shortages in several countries' sectors. This applies in the case of white-collar knowledge workers and blue-collar (trade) workers, which includes plumbers, electricians, chefs, firefighters and police officers. Furthermore, as with the selection stage, one should pay particular attention to the relevant equity and diversity acts, laws and legislation when recruiting. As such, one of the critical aspects of effective HRM is the ability to design appropriate **recruitment** methodologies.

The process of recruitment requires that the organization and the HR manager know what they are looking for in terms of skills, knowledge and capabilities and that these things match what is required for the job. Importantly, effective recruitment should be targeted appropriately.

The Uncle Sam poster is one of the most recognizable images, if not all over the globe, then definitely in the English-speaking world. Indeed, every nation has its version of Uncle Sam, such as the old COO-EE! posters used in Australia and 'The 'Empire Needs Men' posters from the UK for the First World War. These posters were integral to the recruitment of men into the army at a time when many young people were being killed in the war, and many more were needed to wage a 'total' war, thus recruitment was crucial.

Today, HR managers and departments have a variety of tried and trusted recruitment strategies at their disposal. These include job ads in local, city, suburban, national and even international newspapers, recruitment and employment agencies, government employment agencies, the Internet and e-recruitment websites, internal communications, specialized industry publications and associations, through to personal and social networks and networking (Twitter, Instagram, LinkedIn, etc.), word of mouth, and even via serendipity (that is, by good fortune). In the recruitment stage, the applicant is provided with a realistic job preview (RJP). This specifies critical, essential and desirable job criteria. The unique aspect of the RJP is that the employer lists both positive and negative aspects of the job. More recently, innovative multimedia approaches have been used, such as video or YouTube presentations, to provide a realistic sense of what working in the target job would be like. Incumbents present both the positives and negatives about the job and the applicant is provided with first-hand experience of the ins and outs of the working environment(s). The RJP provides the applicant with detailed glimpses into the job and so it is likely that being transparent about the virtues and less virtuous aspects of the job ensures that the successful applicant knows what to expect (Adler, 2011; Boyce et al., 2013). In other words, the RJP creates a strong psychological contract between the new employer and employee because it is based on reality rather than on false information (Adler, 2011; Guest, 2004; Robinson et al., 1994). Realistic job previews have been shown to correlate with low staff turnover and to increase productivity compared with other methods of recruitment (Hom et al., 2017; Phillips, 1998; Weiss and Rupp, 2011). The more realistic the previews are, the better the results – for example, the more accurate and detailed the rewards of the job are, the better the outcomes such as the quality of candidates applying and their perceptions of person–job fit (Verwaeren et al., 2017).

IMAGE 5.1 We want you as a new recruit!

IN PRACTICE

Below is an example of a job-duty statement with key selection criteria. Assuming you were going to apply for this position, how would you respond to the criteria? The more essential and desirable criteria you can account for in your application, the better the chance of being shortlisted. However, you would still need to perform well in interviews and other possible selection hurdles (for example, doing a teaching presentation to faculty). When responding to such criteria, a common error people make is to simply repeat the criteria, when it is advisable to give clear examples to substantiate your claims.

Key selection criteria – academic staff

UTS: human resources

Senior Lecturer in Organizational Behaviour

Skills and attributes

- Ability to work in a team.
- Good oral and written communication skills.
- An enthusiasm for research and teaching.
- Good rapport with students, staff and members of the community.
- Flexibility as regards patterns and location of teaching (days, evenings, block release at either or both campuses or in off-campus settings).
- Capacity to develop industry links and obtain research funding.

Knowledge

- Demonstrated knowledge of management and organizational behaviour theory and practice.
- Practical knowledge of management and the principles of organizational behaviour.
- An understanding of and ability to apply the principles and practices of effective teaching.
- An understanding of and ability to apply equal opportunity in the workplace.

Qualifications

- Doctoral degree in management or a related discipline.

Experience required

- Teaching experience with evidence of good teaching performance.
- Evidence (such as research papers) of a capacity to undertake high-quality research that will lead to journal publications in the field of management and organizational behaviour.
- Demonstrated capacity to contribute collaboratively to at least one of the research strengths of the School of Management.
- Experience in teaching in the area of leadership and/or management consulting is desirable.
- Well-established research and publication record in the field of management/organizational behaviour, including evidence of publications in high-quality, refereed international journals.

Selection refers to the tools, methods and criteria upon which people will be, and are, selected for a given position, and includes job applications, interviews, tests and measurement. Selection is related to the recruitment stage of the HRM function.

SELECTING PEOPLE

In reality, **selection** and recruitment are not entirely distinct functions. Both require high levels of synthesis between: (a) the nature of the job(s) being filled; (b) the skills, qualifications, capabilities and attributes required of the prospective employee(s) and (c), the skills, qualifications, capabilities and attributes of the people available in the job market. Where recruitment concentrates on attracting the right person for the job, selection concentrates on choosing the right person based on a range of selection techniques and methodologies.

In order to aid selection, the HR manager will ensure that a clear job–duty statement has been written. Job–duty statements must include a list of the essential criteria and desirable criteria required or expected of the applicant. The essential criteria are those aspects of the job – the knowledge, skills, expertise, abilities and capabilities – critical to the job's performance. The desirable criteria are those extra aspects that, while not critical, are looked upon favourably by potential employers.

With well-designed job–duty statements, applicants are able to ascertain whether they would be appropriate for the position. They then have to demonstrate that they are the ideal candidate by writing a job application in which they address each and every criterion specifically and with practical examples – in this example, not just by saying 'I do lots of research, and I enjoy it so I am a really good researcher'. Rather, the applicant would write something like:

> As demonstrated by my publications in journals such as *Organization Science*, *Organization Studies* and *Journal of Management*, my best research paper awards at the Academy of Management, as well as my papers under current or second review in journals such as *Academy of Management Review*, *Human Relations* and *Journal of Organizational Behavior*, I am able to publish research in reputable journals of significant impact. My first publication in *Organization Science* investigates … blah blah blah.

Applicants should address each and every essential and desirable criterion in detail in order to demonstrate that they clearly meet the criteria.

The essential and desirable criteria: (a) help the potential employer to develop a set of measures, or weights, in order to rate and rank a potential employee and (b), give potential employees an indication of how well they might fit the job. The better the applicant is able to articulate how they meet those criteria, the more 'ticks' they get. For jobs where several candidates apply with similar qualifications, experience and performance outcomes, the task of selection becomes more difficult. A number of selection tools and techniques are available that aid the process of selecting appropriate candidates. These tools include:

- *The job application*: Unless the job applicant is applying from within the organization, the job application is usually the very first contact a prospective employee will have with their potential employers. The good job application usually includes: (a) a letter covering the applicant's key strengths and highlighting achievements; and (b) a curriculum vitae addressing the essential and desirable criteria, as well as including relevant biographical data such as educational and work history, membership of professional associations, as well as extracurricular activities such as volunteering, sports, and so on. Of course, there is the possibility that people will exaggerate their successes in résumés. As a result, security and information checks are now becoming big business, which adds to the cost of the selection process.

- *The job interview*: Successful applicants usually receive a telephone call, a letter or an email stating that they have been shortlisted for the position and are invited to attend an interview. Some organizations also let applicants know if they were unsuccessful, but many do not because of the volume of applications. The job interview is almost always formal, with prepared questions, and usually includes an interview panel. The questions will always centre on the core aspects of the job. For example, assume we own a marketing company and we are interviewing two people for the position of marketing manager. After reviewing our essential criteria, we developed a range of questions aiming to highlight the applicant's knowledge, experience and abilities in both marketing and managing projects. Let us say a critical criterion of success in marketing management is the ability to meet tight deadlines. We would ask these people for concrete examples of how they meet deadlines under pressure, as well as how they prioritize deadlines. Now let us say the first person answered, 'Well, I was at university and I always handed in my assignments pretty much on time', and the second person said, 'Well, last year I was handed two major accounts by my boss; both were scheduled for completion in the same week. So I met with both clients over lunch and we discussed their expected outcomes. I used reverse planning and carefully implemented a number of contingency plans along the way.' Who would you employ? (Hint – it is not the first person!)
- *Tests and measurement*: Increasingly, organizations are using more advanced and some would say invasive tests. Most of us will be expected to do one test or another at some stage in our professional careers. Tests include personality tests such as the Big Five Personality Factors (see Chapter 3), intelligence tests, tests of general aptitude and cognitive abilities, psychometric tests, even mental health tests. In some organizations, people undergo bio-feedback, lie-detection tests, even DNA and drug tests, and today a number of knowledge-intensive companies (i.e. consultancies) conduct a whole range of selection methods.

READ ABOUT SELECTION METHODS

Research suggests that the use of such selection tools is a good predictor of performance of staff (Borman et al., 1997), especially so when multiple selection tools – what is now increasingly called multiple hurdles – are used appropriately (Mendoza et al., 2004). Moreover, both qualitative and quantitative techniques are useful in selecting staff, as long as the tools are well designed and appropriately used (Ehigie and Ehigie, 2005). Some organizations now use a range of innovative techniques such as 'role plays' and other simulation exercises to select staff. Some

READ THIS ARTICLE

even use approaches similar to those used in the popular television show *The Apprentice*, where Donald Trump or Lord Alan Sugar places a number of young 'talented' people through a series of gruelling situations until they are left with the successful candidate. However, there are some real challenges facing organizations in the use of such tools because such tools tend to focus on standardizing people based on assumptions of homogeneity (sameness) in a world of diversity (Newell and Tansley, 2015), and even the nature of the environment such as its stability or volatility can impact the benefits of multiple recruitment techniques (see Kim and Ployhart, 2018).

We therefore cannot leave this topic without raising some serious questions about selection tools. The first concerns equity and diversity. Organizations have been successfully sued because their selection techniques were judged to be discriminatory against certain people (Holly, 2003; Landy, 2005). For example, intelligence tests have been shown to have a cultural bias; additionally there are also issues of English-language skills, education levels, and so on. If a person can show they were discriminated against because of the selection tools used, this can be very expensive for the company (Gardiner and Armstrong-Wright, 2000; Landy, 2005). Second, measurement and testing explicitly involve the total subjugation of the individual to strangers – sensitive and powerful information is collected on people, before they are even members of the organization. In this sense, there are some serious ethical questions that need to be asked about how personal information is used, shared, stored and destroyed. While the topic is becoming of increasing interest, there is still a dearth of research and literature, which should be a general concern to all people using such approaches, especially in global contexts (Newell and Tansley, 2015; Ryan and Ployhart, 2014), and particularly as we try to find and attract people who are innovative and will offer something different that could be the difference between success and failure (Boudreau and Lawler, 2014).

IN PRACTICE

Online? Employers are watching you!

Do you use Instagram, Twitter, Facebook? What you post can one day come back to haunt you because employers are increasingly checking out your social media profile and your posts. Read this excellent opinion piece by Jonathan Margolis from July 2017 in the *Financial Times*: 'Be careful with social media - employers are watching' www.ft.com/content/5b8bb3b0-6aca-11e7-b9c7-15af748b60d0

After reading this piece, what do you think about employers looking at your social media to determine whether you should be recruited or not? Discuss this with your friends and classmates. What do they think? Clearly, what we do today, even as relatively free college or university students or as private citizens, can have implications for us in the future when we use social media as a form of communicating.

RETAINING AND DEVELOPING PEOPLE

Retention refers to the practices and processes used to retain staff, and often includes **staff development**, which refers to the procedures and policies designed and implemented to enhance and update the skills, knowledge and capabilities of staff in relation to their career and their job.

If the right people have been appointed by the HRM process, then it is crucial that they should be **retained** and allowed opportunities for **staff development**.

This final HRM function addresses the processes and practices of retaining and developing an organization's best assets – its people. In most industrialized countries, it is now generally well recognized that employers can no longer offer job security and so a range of retention and development methods will prove the key not only to retaining and developing talent but also to attracting talent to the organization (Lawler, 2005). Indeed, staff will actively seek out and participate in training and development when jobs are challenging and the organization values career progression (Tharenou, 1997) and in turn, investment in retaining and developing people through training and development, for example, can aid knowledge transfer and organizational learning that benefits the organization (Sprinkle and Urich, 2018).

There are two interrelated aspects to retention and development: retention consists of the methods and approaches used to keep talented people in the organization in some way – such as awards, promotions and remuneration; development concerns the methods and approaches used to enhance, transform and better utilize staff knowledge, skills and capabilities – such as training, mentoring and education.

In an organizational context, developing people most often means providing them with training and education that assists them in entering and finding their way around the organization and familiarizing them with the job (*orientation*); skills training that aids in learning and updating skills required for the technical aspects of a job; and management or leadership development programmes that help develop employees' managerial and leadership skills. Such forms of development can be via on-the-job training, which includes coaching, apprenticeship and mentoring programmes; off-the-job training, which includes formal courses and programmes, delivered in-house or by independent training and education institutions, as well as online and through other training and development methods such as role plays, scenarios, and so on.

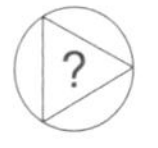

WHAT WOULD YOU DO?

WHAT WOULD YOU DO?

Consider a scenario in which the company you work for pays less than the competitors; however, it has an excellent reputation for corporate social responsibility (CSR) or 'doing good'. You are offered a promotion and pay rise by a competitor with fewer CSR credentials and reputation. Would your current employer's approach to corporate social responsibility make you more likely to want to stay, or would the prospect of more money and a promotion make you leave? Think about it for a few minutes; maybe even discuss it with your classmates or study group if you have one.

According to research by Tim Devinney and his co-authors (2015), a company's CSR reputation was less important for potential job applicants than remuneration, time demands and salary: so it is more likely than not that you would go for the better paying job and promotion. Of course, we should point out that Devinney et al.'s study was on MBA students' preferences; those who might be working in an organization with excellent CSR credentials might answer in a very different way. What do you think?

In a similar vein, distinguished Professor Edward E. Lawler III argues that organizations should forget about loyalty contracts and instead move towards 'value propositions' that are tailored to the types of employees being sought, and also promote continued development and improvement in order to sustain one's edge. Through the use of value propositions, Lawler believes organizations should strive towards virtuous spirals in their HRM practices and processes:

> Organizations need to offer skills and a performance-based substitute for the loyalty contract that motivates selective retention and high performance. It needs to stress that continued employment is based on performance and having the right skill set for the organization's business strategy. It also needs to stress that people are rewarded for performance and skill development. When this is translated into the right combination of reward system practices, people will be motivated to excel and those who excel will be motivated to stay because they will be highly rewarded. This is the foundation of the virtuous spiral, in which both sides win and create success for each other. (2005: 14–15)

Lawler identifies some organizations that have promoted the virtuous spiral. These include Microsoft and Procter & Gamble in which large stock options are provided to employees, as well as generous professional and self-development programmes. Southwest Airlines has long been a preferred employer. Southwest was one of the only airline companies in the USA to thrive in the face of a downturn in air travel and chaos post-9/11, a time that saw major airlines file for bankruptcy – including United Airlines and American Airlines.

Many organizations realize the importance of play at work and space in which to relax. Google is renowned for attracting some of the brightest minds from all over the world from a range of professions such as computer programmers, designers, marketers and even philosophers. It retains the best staff by offering them work that is challenging, fun and also in line with the values of sustainability. Imagine working somewhere where you can take your pets, eat for free, play during work times and even have a nap when you want, as Google's corporate website demonstrates.

Of course, one has to be extremely careful regarding the type of value propositions that companies such as Google try to create and reinforce through 'virtuous' spirals. By way of experiment, look at images of Google on their website: what kinds of people do you think it would attract? What sorts of people do you think it is looking for? Back in 2004 Google had an age discrimination suit filed against it, and the suit focused on the 'youthful' corporate culture branded by the organization and reinforced through its HR practices. A former Google executive claimed wrongful termination because he did not fit in with Google's youthful culture (Shah and Kleiner, 2005). Google won the case in 2006, but the man appealed and the alleged claims about age discrimination at Google will not die down easily (see the article 'Google to hundreds claiming age discrimination: you can't fight us together' by Ethan Baron in *The Mercury News*, 3 May 2018). The lesson is that those very things that are designed to attract and retain certain types of talent can sometimes result in litigation (Hurley-Hanson and Giannantonio, 2006). According to Lawler:

> organizations that link skill development with continued employment – and rewards with performance – handle change more effectively than others. In a sense, you might say that they create 'mobile' human capital; people

> who realize that they must continue to learn, develop, and perform in order to maintain their positions and careers. Today, organizations need mobile capital. Getting stuck with obsolete human capital is just as big a negative as getting stuck with outdated equipment and materials. (2005: 15)

Such claims are all well and good but one should be extremely careful in referring to humans as obsolete capital – perhaps the former Google executive felt he was deemed obsolete capital because of his age? Fortunately, Google, in many ways and with very few exceptions, is an exemplary organization with excellent working conditions, training and development programmes, employee benefits and remuneration (Effron et al., 2003; Menefee et al., 2006).

Much of Lawler's early arguments concerning HR were underpinned by the economics of Milton Friedman, in particular that an organization must ensure that making money is its first and most critical objective; employees should only be retained if they fit such a value proposition. More recently, however, Lawler and his colleagues have moved entirely away from the arguments that organizations should be driven by performance at the expense of sustainability and corporate social responsibility, going as far as to argue that there needs to be a complete 'reset' in management thinking in relation to what constitutes performance (Lawler et al., 2011: Ch. 1). Of course, many of us in the Critical Management Studies and Positive Organizational Studies fields have been arguing this for years (so we commend Professor Lawler for his 'reset').

Inherent in arguments about training and retaining staff is the principle that the organization should only seek to retain staff that are deemed talented and worth the effort (no obsolete human capital allowed here!) and develop staff that will be willing to increase effort and performance. Of course, this begs the question of the measurement of performance. Performance measurement/evaluation is one of the most difficult things to do because there is no consensus on defining performance. Moreover, as many jobs move away from manufacturing or producing goods, in favour of knowledge work and service provision, it becomes increasingly difficult to conceptualize and operationalize performance and much work still has to go into considerations of the validity and especially the ethicality of performance appraisal. To be sure, we are not saying that performance measurement and appraisal will not work: indeed, there is evidence to suggest it can (Schleicher et al., 2017; Smither et al., 2005). Rather, we are saying that how it works may not be a reliable measure and basis upon which to reward and retain staff (Atkin and Conlon, 1978). Table 5.2 outlines some of the more common appraisal systems used and some of their more common shortcomings.

EXTEND YOUR KNOWLEDGE

Those of you interested in a relatively up-to-date review of the current state of play in performance management and appraisal will gain a lot of value out of this article by Deidre Schleicher and her collegues: Schleicher, D. J., Baumann, H. M., Sullivan, D. W., Levy, P. E., Hargrove, D. C. and Barros-Rivera, B. A. (2017) 'Putting the system into performance management systems: a review and agenda for performance management research', *Journal of Management*, 44 (6): 2209–45. You can find this at the companion website https://study.sagepub.com/managingandorganizations5e

READ THE ARTICLE

TABLE 5.2 Common performance appraisals, their use and their limitations

Performance appraisal interview	Very common. This is used as a formal session where the employee meets with their supervisor or manager to discuss the employee's work plans for the next reporting period and their performance over the previous reporting period. In this session, they will agree on certain performance outcomes on given tasks and duties, the employee's weaknesses and strengths, and desires and intentions for development and training, and will often include a question on perceptions about management and supervisors. An appraisal will be given in terms of whether the employee is progressing well or has certain limitations and weaknesses, as well as recommendations for development and growth	• Evaluations can be open to halo effects where evaluations are tainted by an emphasis on one or two talented individuals rather than on the specific performance of the individual being appraised • Errors and bias can occur if the person evaluated is attractive or a member of the in-group (friends) or out-group (foes) • Can be used as a political tool for pushing problem or difficult people out of the organization rather than as a true appraisal of performance • Supervisor may not have sufficient knowledge and training to conduct interviews, nor possess sufficient knowledge about the employee's job and tasks
360° and 180° feedback	The least common approach. It involves a survey completed by the employee and a range of people, including peers, direct reports (180°) and subordinates (360°) and can also include customers and other stakeholders. The survey provides multiple ratings and multiple evaluations on the target person's performance at work. Often, these measure the ability to manage and deal with people, job knowledge, competence, strengths and weaknesses, and so on	• Can be biased towards overtly positive ratings or overtly negative ratings • Can sometimes cause conflict and resentment as, while 360° feedback is anonymous, the target often guesses or thinks they can guess who provided the ratings. Can sometimes even lead to a 'witch hunt' to identify the negative raters • Often, 360° feedback surveys are generic, off the shelf and not tailored specifically to the organization's needs • Raters might be inexperienced in rating people and using such surveys • Can be expensive and require data input, low-level statistics, and analysis
Behaviourally Anchored Rating Scale (BARS)	The BARS, like the GRS below, is a behavioural appraisal. The BARS involves a range of critical incidents centred on specific aspects of a job. The incidents are presented as behavioural statements concerning performance on each task. A person is rated in accordance with the behavioural statement that most closely describes that person's performance on each job-related task on a scale that provides options at opposite extremes. (E.g. 1 = a details person, who checks over the minutiae; 9 = a big-picture person, with very little or no eye for detail)	• Underplays or ignores cognitive aspects, especially of the rater, and there is no significant evidence that BARS is better or worse than any other rating system

Graphic Rating Scales (GRS)	The employee will be rated on a number of behavioural variables: these can include attendance, job knowledge and customer service, quality of work, corporate citizenship behaviours, presentation and personal appearance, and so on. The person will be rated or ranked and measured against a baseline score. Bonuses, promotions and other benefits are usually tied to performance appraisal scores	• Evaluation criteria may become obsolete or redundant between the time performance targets were set and when they are evaluated • Similar issues to BARS and performance appraisal interview

Sources: Nathan and Alexander (1985); Tziner et al. (2000)

Overall, we may say that while there are many limitations to performance management, measurement and appraisal, they do have a role in assisting HRM decisions. Indeed, we would be the first ones to say that there is nothing worse than staff effort and hard work going unrecognized and unappreciated by employers. However, many performance measurement systems are poorly designed and inappropriately used and applied. Error and bias in ratings have commonly been reported as under-recognized (Newell and Tansley, 2015; Ryan and Ployhart, 2014). There can be legal ramifications when performance measurement systems fail to accommodate diversity (Arvey and Murphy, 1998; Atkin and Conlon, 1978; Olson and Hulin, 1992; Spector, 1994; Watkins and Johnston, 2000), and the systems are often used more as a tool of managerial control and subjugation than as a system that benefits the employee in any real way.

HRM IN CONTEXT

HRM AND STRATEGY

A key function of HRM is to assist the business to meet its strategic objectives. Earlier in this chapter, we outlined the soft and hard approaches to HRM. While the Harvard and Michigan models are presented as the main HR models, in reality four general schools of thought evolved about HRM at around the same time. In addition to the Harvard and Michigan schools, Price (2004) lists two other important HRM schools of thought that have influenced the way in which HRM is understood, practised and taught: these are the Warwick and the Schuler schools. Importantly, the Schuler school is named after Professor Randall S. Schuler who emphasized the critical role that HRM plays in strategic management. His work since the 1980s has sought to emphasize that, although the practice of HRM and the practice of strategic management are interrelated, most strategic management scholars under-emphasize the role that HRM plays in business strategy (Jackson et al., 2014; Schuler and Jackson, 2000; Schuler and MacMillan, 1984; Tarique and Schuler, 2010). From Schuler's work emerged the important but debated concept of strategic HRM, an area of research and practice which will continue to grow and change in very important ways over the next few decades as business leaders realize that successful people and successful strategy are interrelated and interconnected in ways historically under-recognized and understood (Beach, 2015; Becker and Huselid, 2006).

In the formulation stage, **strategic HRM** can contribute to the organization's objectives by ensuring that all key HRM functions such as the recruitment, retention and development of staff are consistent with the business strategy. In the implementation stage, HRM can contribute by ensuring that people understand the key strategic intentions and objectives, and ensuring that people are abiding by those strategic intentions through a measurement of performance consistent with those objectives.

Strategic management is a broad managerial function, usually formulated, implemented and evaluated by the senior leaders within an organization. Strategy is more than just planning and executing, it is about change and leading from the front (Hamel, 2002; Hamel and Prahalad, 1996). According to Porter (1987, 1996), strategic management is what gives businesses competitive advantage because it differentiates them and what they are doing from other businesses. Traditional approaches to strategic management, such as those proffered by Porter and others, involve a vision of the future of an organization, then formulating, setting and selling a clear plan, a set of objectives and measurement systems for the organization's future. The strategic plan is sold to staff, customers and other stakeholders in order to help the business realize its vision.

According to Schuler and Jackson (2000), strategic management is comprised of five core practices that can be divided into strategy *formulation* and strategy *implementation*. They argue that these core activities can be directly transposed onto the key HRM functions of the business as strategic HRM. The strategic activities relating to formulation include: (a) deciding what business the company will be in, formulating a strategic vision and generating a set of values and a general strategy; (b) identifying strategic business issues and setting strategic objectives; and (c) crafting a set of strategic plans of action for meeting the objectives. The activities relating to implementation include: (a) developing and implementing the strategic plans of action for functional units; and (b) evaluating, revising and refocusing for the future. For Schuler and Jackson, **strategic HRM** is closely tied to strategic functions of strategy formulation and implementation.

EXTEND YOUR KNOWLEDGE

READ THE ARTICLE

Read the article 'Strategic management and the person' by Thomas C. Powell (2014) *in Strategic Organization*, 12 (3): 200–7, which you can find at the companion website https://study.sagepub.com/managingandorganizations5e. In the article, Powell takes issue with strategic management's movement away from a focus on humans, and calls for a return to a human-centred focus (which is really what strategic HRM is meant to be about).

There is common sense in ensuring that HR and corporate strategy are well aligned. However, the notion that one can plan for and measure strategy, let alone design the entire HRM function around that strategy, is grandiose. The notion assumes: (a) that the rational model of strategy is what actually gets implemented and (b), that external events are knowable, controllable and manageable. In practice, however, the likelihood is that what is implemented are the various, contested, understandings of this model that people in different parts and levels of the organization possess. Specifically, there is debate around the idea that one can plan for and measure the performance of things that have not yet happened. That is, the contexts within which organizations operate are exemplified by uncertainty (unknowable events) and ambiguity (differences in understanding and perception about events and objects). Strategic management is therefore a process that 'happens' as it unfolds in real time and space (Brunson, 2006; Carter et al., 2008; Clegg et al., 2017).

Those of you who go on to specialize in HRM will invariably study strategic HRM and it is likely that you will then come across debates about measurement of performance in line with strategic imperatives. Perhaps in some courses you will even debate whether HRM actually is strategic. In our experience, most HR departments simply implement what they are told to by company executives, and so it is the executives who are being strategic, something evident in the fact that relatively few boards include the HR director, nor do HR managers often present to the board and say, 'This is the strategy we believe the company must take, here is our ten-point plan to implement it, now let us go do it!' In most cases, HR does not have a strategic role in an organization, which is not to say that it should not and cannot, especially in public organizations (Beach, 2015). The debate on the role and effectiveness of strategic HRM in affecting organizational performance is young and inconclusive but it promises to be a growing and interesting area of research and study (Brewster, 1995; Guest, 2011; Jackson et al., 2014; Lawler, 2005; Schuler and Jackson, 2000), especially as alternative strategic management perspectives that challenge the dominant rational scientific approach to strategic management enter the fray (see Clegg et al., 2017).

HRM AND ENVIRONMENTAL COMPLEXITY

A complex and challenging aspect of the HR function is the need to remain up to date with the constantly changing legal, political, technological and social environment. In this section, we will discuss a number of areas where HRM can provide critical knowledge and information regarding all aspects of managing people at work, specifically in areas that concern their employment.

Environmental complexity has a considerable impact on the core functions of HRM, such as recruitment, selection and retention. However, what is often underplayed is the way in which organizations can alter and create the very environment they seek to adapt to. Here we will consider issues such as the changing nature of the workforce, issues of diversity and gender, equal employment and affirmative action or positive discrimination, and occupational safety and health.

All these things, either alone or in tandem, can significantly affect the ability of an organization, large or small, to function effectively. For this reason, the HR manager and their team – if fortunate enough to have one – have a key role to play in the organization. Whether those responsible for HR have their own department in a large organization, or whether they are a small-business owner with a handful of staff, understanding and accounting for the environmental complexity and uncertainty caused by social, economic, ecological and political factors are crucial. The HR manager not only provides advice to other managers and staff on these issues but also implements organization HR policies and procedures that reflect and help account for these complex issues.

DEMOGRAPHIC CHANGES: 'TALKING 'BOUT MY GENERATION'

HRM requires management of the critical areas of employee recruitment, selection, and training and development in a way that is consistent with an organization's objectives. However, the organization does not exist in isolation from its context or the environment within which it operates. Because HR is fundamentally about people – irrespective of whether it is hard or soft oriented, or whether HR strategy can be planned, or whether it evolves in response to events as they occur – everything to do with people has an impact on HR practices and processes. One of the most important concerns for organizations is the changing nature of the workforce. Here we will discuss selected key areas. The discussion will be by no means exhaustive; rather, we cover these to ensure that we can all appreciate the complexity, challenges and opportunities available in managing HR. The areas we will focus on are:

- assumed generational differences between people that affect their attitudes, perceptions and expectations about work
- the knowledge, skills and education levels of people currently in the workforce and the job market
- types and levels of immigration and migration central to government immigration policy.

Let us begin with generational differences. One often hears people talk about Generation 'X', Generation 'Y', 'Baby boomers', 'Millennials', and so on. Some organizational theorists have asserted that generational differences will have profound effects on organizations (Conger, 2000), but others argue that the idea that generational differences have had a profound effect on organizational behaviour is still yet to be sufficiently proven (Parry and Urwin, 2011). Even so, many researchers have shown that generational differences not only exist but also have important implications for HR practice (Benson and Brown, 2011; Burke, 1994; Lyons et al., 2005; Smola and Sutton, 2002). Benson and Brown (2011) show that one uniform HR policy cannot adequately account for the differences in work- and life-related values identified with each different generation. Hence, HR policy has to be sensitive to and reflective of the values of the varied generations. So what does it mean to differentiate generations, to think of them as characterized by different types of behaviour, and why do they differ? Essentially, every generation has claimed to have difficulty understanding the next.

Different age groups experience events that shape their lives in different ways; these can be local or world events that occur as events in a specific period of people's lives. The Great Depression, the Second World War, the 1960s period of social experimentation and protest, the 1980s and the advent of economic rationalization, of corporate greed, downsizing and high unemployment, periods of rapid economic growth, the Internet and, of course, 9/11 and the associated War on Terror – all these things leave an imprint on people's psyche. But smaller events also shape people – the proliferation of new technologies, changes in expectations about leisure time and work/life balance, improvements in education and health care, and so on. All these things transform people in implicit ways, and therefore also have an impact on their attitudes and expectations around work. Table 5.3 lists some of the generations and some of their implications for HRM practice and policies.

TABLE 5.3 Managing the different generations from an HRM perspective

Generation	Description	Implications for HR practice
Baby boomers	Born between 1946 and 1964. Almost all baby boomers will retire from full-time employment in the next 15 years. Typically, they grew up in times of post-war economic prosperity, and (except in the USA) most enjoyed free access to almost all services such as education, health, and so on. They are hard-working and committed and some have high incomes and savings - especially those whose children have left home. Many have families and mortgages and work hard to pay for these. They usually have strong relationship skills and drive. They can be resistant to change and to differences of opinion between people. They also tend not to handle negative feedback very well, and they tend to avoid conflict	The implication for HR is the need for policies on retirement and redundancy. As they retire, a knowledge/skills gap will be left that HR will need to address. Much work has to be done to ensure organizations are ready for the boomer retirement. Mentoring programmes and knowledge transfer can be used in positive ways to ensure boomers are involved in workforce transitions. Perks and benefits that will attract and retain boomers include help in financial planning for retirement and semi-retirement programmes where boomers' knowledge and skills continue to be utilized
Generation X (Baby busters)	Born between 1965 and 1980. There are fewer Generation X-ers than baby boomers. Typically, Gen-X grew up in times of economic downturn, high unemployment and corporate collapse and greed. They tend to have low savings and prefer having a social life. Work/life balance is very important. They are usually quite self-sufficient and technologically savvy, quite adaptable to change, creative and resist control and authority. They also tend to lack experience, have poor people skills and can be overly cynical. Gen-X will fill the leadership and management gap left by baby boomers and will experience tensions in overtaking boomers and handling Gen-Ys	A shortage of younger people poses serious problems in attracting and maintaining a competent, qualified workforce. Gen-X will be the leaders and managers of the future. They will place emphasis on family and so flexible scheduling will be an expectation; they are not 9-5 people and do not react well to monitoring and control because they believe in working smarter not longer. They thirst for development support, such as time off and financial support to study, not just in areas deemed relevant by the business. Both X and Y will prefer to work as part of projects rather than in specific positions in an organization. Thus, project-based work will be used increasingly. Gen-X require technologies in their jobs, will use the Internet to help in decision-making and problem-solving, though are more sceptical about information than are Gen-Y
Generation Y (or Millennials)	Born after 1981, Gen-Y will soon overtake both X and boomers. This generation is considered to have a much less serious attitude to work, preferring working to live, rather than living to work. They are believed to have little concern about jobs for life and like Gen-X will move jobs several times in their careers but at a much higher rate than Gen-X. They have grown up with technology and so using it is second nature to them. They rely	Because of Gen-Y's ambition and reluctance to 'do time' in order to be promoted, they can be very difficult to manage and motivate if their career is perceived to be developing slowly. They are less independent than Gen-X and require closer supervision and attention. As the largest workforce of the future, they will need to be recognized as an important asset and so HR practices and policies that reflect Gen-Y values and expectations need to be formulated. This includes flexible working times, policies of work/life balance, group- and

(Continued)

TABLE 2.3 (Continued)

Generation	Description	Implications for HR practice
	on family more so than Gen-X and tend to be optimistic, positive and prefer to work in groups or in collaboration with others. They lack experience and patience in learning, and can be naive in relating to others	team-based work, and both extrinsic and intrinsic motivation such as free food and drinks. Policies will need to concentrate on attracting and retaining staff through a number of soft HR policies and practices. Both Gen-X and Gen-Y will expect cutting-edge communication technologies, but will also need assistance in developing their people-management and communication skills. Gen-Y are especially open to technologies, particularly the Internet, to locate information for problem-solving and decision-making – this can pose challenges to organizations given the high level of misinformation on the Internet

Sources: Nowecki and Summers (2007); Proffet-Reese et al. (2007); Wikipedia

FIGURE 5.1 Stuffing the head full of different knowledge

THE CHANGING FACE OF KNOWLEDGE

Knowledge comprises that which is part of the stock of ideas, meanings and more or less explicit understandings and explanations of how phenomena of interest actually work, or are structured or designed and relate to other phenomena: facts, information and skills acquired by a person through experience or education.

Let us now look at issues around the **knowledge**, skills and education levels of the workforce. It is not just generational differences that pose challenges to HRM practice and policy. The changing nature of the workforce in terms of education and skill is also a critical factor. A better educated workforce means people can be better informed about many issues relating to work and the quality of working life. We have already seen (in Table 5.3) how Gen-X and Gen-Y are especially technologically savvy, though of course the use of technology is only a small part of what people do at work. The nature of knowledge and concomitant skills expected of people has transformed over time. Figure 5.1 represents the changing knowledge and skills of people in society over time. In Western civilizations, most societies were structured around agriculture and artisan crafts such as tool-making, weapon-making, pottery, art, and so on. The demand for people with knowledge, skills and abilities was concentrated around farming and artisan craftwork. However, as the Industrial Revolution gained impetus there was a change in the expectations of knowledge, skills and abilities as there was a giant leap in economic growth. Industries based on mass production, heavy mining, heavy transport (such as trains and ships), with many other technological and scientific innovations, taking the place of agricultural and artisan work. As we will discuss in Chapter 14, mass production brought with it standardized, routinized and formalized work. Thus, workers were no longer expected to be skilled artisans; rather, they were trained to do specialized, repetitive tasks.

By the 1990s, information technology (IT) professionals were being paid exorbitant amounts of money as the IT bubble kept expanding. University courses and degrees and specialized IT colleges appeared from everywhere to meet the demand for people seeking IT qualifications. In many ways, the IT rush was similar to the Gold Rush era of the USA, Australia and South Africa. Around the turn of the century, the Western world was said to have entered the stage of knowledge work and the growth of knowledge-intensive firms. It is likely, given that you are studying a management and organizational behaviour textbook, that you are or will be a knowledge worker yourself one day, as we are, as the authors of this book, and that you will work in a **knowledge-intensive firm**.

Knowledge-intensive firms create value by solving their clients' problems through the direct application of knowledge. Whereas knowledge plays a role in all firms, its role is distinctive in knowledge-intensive firms. Rather than being embodied in the process or product, knowledge resides in experts and its application is customized in real time based on clients' needs (Sheehan, 2005: 54).

EXTEND YOUR KNOWLEDGE

Read the article 'Human capital is dead: long live human capital resources!' by Robert Ployhart and his colleagues (2014) in a special issue on Strategic Human Capital in the *Journal of Management*, 40: 371–98, which you can find at the companion website https://study.sagepub.com/managingandorganizations5e. It provides a novel approach to making sense of human capital compared to the dominant economic views of human capital as strategically linked to market efficiencies.

READ THE ARTICLE

Once, knowledge-intensive firms included only consulting companies, legal firms and other organizations where the outcomes were professional advice for organizational problems. Increasingly, however, even traditionally non-knowledge-intensive firms have moved to trading and promoting their knowledge. Most organizations in a variety of industries now involve at least some level of knowledge-based work, be it in banking and finance, tourism and travel, education, pharmaceuticals, food, and so on.

Mats Alvesson (2004: 139–41) argues that knowledge-intensive organizations, more than most, must acknowledge that people are critical to their growth and success. He offers two interesting concepts that he believes are critical ideas in HRM and in how people are employed and treated at work:

1. Human capital advantage (HCA) – HCA refers to the employment of talent and the advantage that the organization derives from that talent. For this reason, high levels of effort and expenditure should go into the recruitment, selection and retention of exceptional and talented staff. The knowledge, skills and qualities of these talented people lead to desirable organizational outcomes.
2. Human process advantage (HPA) – HPA refers to highly evolved processes that are difficult to imitate, such as systems of cross-departmental

> cooperation, executive development, and so on. The aim of HPA is to set up the preconditions for organizational functioning and synergy between people and processes. This can include job design, policies, and so on. The emphasis is on process delivering outcomes rather than the specific knowledge of employees delivering outcomes.

According to Alvesson, effective HRM requires both HCA and HPA, but many companies prioritize these differently – not least because HCA is costly. Most try to design and implement work systems and processes that transform effort into specific, preordained outcomes.

Alvesson (2004: 137–9) argues that knowledge work and the growth of knowledge-intensive firms pose significant challenges to HRM practice and policy. He believes that most current HR practices are inappropriate for attracting and retaining knowledge workers and that the primary aim of HRM should be to enhance the appeal of the organization to talented staff. That is, the key to organizational excellence is to attract excellent employees, to retain them and to develop and draw on their talent. Indeed, research supports Alvesson's idea, showing that an emphasis on human capital advantage allows organizations to be more innovative (Camelo-Ordaz et al., 2011).

WATCH THIS TED TALK

WATCH THE INTERVIEW

EXTEND YOUR KNOWLEDGE

Another transition in knowledge and skills can be seen in Figure 5.1, where it is represented by the symbol of the heart. The heart represents the growing emphasis on the ability of people to practise empathy and compassion at work, to exhibit high levels of emotional intelligence, communicate effectively and work closely with other people (Cooney, 2011). In many ways, knowledge workers will also require an ability to relate from the heart. One of the leaders in this area was the late Professor Peter Frost. We have an excellent interview with Professor Frost at the companion website https://study.sagepub.com/managingandorganizations5e, in which he discusses how matters of the heart are the essential skills and attributes required of leaders and employees of the future.

Often, you will hear arguments that women will be better suited to such new 'emotional roles' at work because caring, empathy and relationship-building are all feminine-type roles. How often have you heard people say that women are better listeners and communicators than men? Often, research supports such findings; for example, there has long been a strong correlation between gender and helping behaviours and altruism (Mesch et al., 2006; Piliavin and Unger, 1985), arguing for women's superior communication skills over men:

> there is some evidence that many women are exceptional global people for the following reasons. One, they tend to approach relationships and negotiations from a win-win strategy that results in success for both sides … Two, women tend to be more formal, show more respect, and take care in

establishing relationships than men. Three, women tend to be better listeners and more sympathetic than men. (Abbott and Moran, 2002: 78)

Such claims should be viewed with some scepticism because often there is a role expectation that women and men will behave in certain ways. Moreover, much of the research conducted on gender difference involves people rating men and women on different variables. The ratings attract a halo effect in that women are often rated as being more helpful and altruistic than men simply because they fulfil a specific gender role such as mother, wife or girlfriend (see Hendrickson-Eagley, 1987). We are not saying that these attributes are not important in the workplace, or that being emotionally sensitive, an excellent communicator and listener, and so on, are not critical skills and knowledge to possess. They are, and employers will increasingly demand such knowledge, skills and abilities as businesses emphasize relationships and collaboration more and more. Our point is that too much emphasis is placed on the idea that men and women are fundamentally different and naturally inclined towards one form of employment than another – rather, people fill specific roles in life, and act and are perceived to act in accordance with these roles (Fletcher and Sydnor Clarke, 2003; Rees and Sprecher, 2009). It is not that there are really differences in sex but rather socialized differences – and so it is no less important that men should be expected to develop and possess emotional skills and knowledge (see also the discussion of gender roles in Chapter 2).

INSTITUTIONAL SHAPING OF HRM

The picture we have painted so far is that HRM is a difficult and challenging endeavour, in which generational changes and the transition towards knowledge work have increasingly complicated its role. However, in many ways these changes are what give life to the growth and interest in HRM as a domain of research and practice. One more area that we will now discuss has far-reaching and significant implications for the practices and policies enacted by HR managers. Through public policy, government shapes society and therefore the workforce in a wide range of areas. Here we consider only three: diversity and equal opportunity, occupational safety and health, and industrial relations law. We begin with diversity and equal opportunity. The demographic transformations that we described earlier in this chapter directly and indirectly implicate organization policy on issues of workplace safety, and gender, equity and diversity. Let us take a look at gender, equity and diversity first.

EQUITY AND DIVERSITY

One of the most important and politically charged aspects of HRM practice is dealing with issues of gender, equity and diversity. Let us start with **diversity**.

The most common form of diversity is cultural diversity, and given that organizations are more or less comprised of members of society, one would expect that they would reflect the diversity in that society – or so the theory goes. Most industrialized countries in the world have relied heavily upon immigration in order to grow prosperous. Some new countries, established on the traditional lands of an indigenous population, such as the USA, Canada and Australia, are almost entirely comprised of migrants.

In an organizational context, **diversity** can most simply be defined as variety in geography, culture, gender, spirituality, language, disability, sexuality and age.

The sources of the migrant population have transformed with time, which has provided such countries with a culturally diverse society.

The most significant wave of new migrants occurred immediately after the desolation of Europe in the Second World War. Many of the Jewish people who survived the horrors of Hitler's Nazi regime fled Europe for the USA, Australia, or to join the new state of Israel, on land previously controlled by the British as protectors of the Palestine Mandate and settled by several different peoples, predominantly Palestinian. Post-war Europe saw Italians, Greeks and Yugoslavians (as they were called then) also flee Europe for the relative wealth, safety and opportunities available to them in relatively free and democratic countries such as the USA, Canada, Australia and New Zealand. Later, war and despotic regimes in Vietnam and Cambodia respectively saw a large intake of South-East Asian refugees, while the war in Lebanon also saw a flow of Middle Eastern migration. Interspersed between them came migration from Third World nations and nations experiencing civil unrest, such as China, India, Pakistan, the West Indies, Sudan, as well as South Africa and Zimbabwe (for excellent accounts of international migration, see Castles and Miller, 2003; Jupp, 2002; Kupiszewski and Kupiszewska, 2011).

Diversity is not restricted to cultural diversity. Take a moment to study Table 5.4. Clearly, diversity poses great challenges for HRM. On the one hand, it is a complex, emotionally charged and legally and socially explosive area of organizational behaviour. On the other hand, it can be a source of growth, competitive advantage and creativity. Indeed, if there is one thing that organizations cannot afford to get wrong it is their approach to HR processes and practices concerning diversity.

TABLE 5.4 The key diversity categories: their descriptors and HR implications

Category	Descriptors	HRM practice implications
Geography	Affinity to or identification with a particular geographic location, which may include, but is not limited to, the following: country, region, state, county, vicinity, rural, urban, suburban	Some organizations offer travel allowances and other reimbursements Some organizations, either voluntarily or by law, must employ people from specific geographic locations - sometimes this is done via negotiation in order to operate on private or public land. (For example, diamond mining giant Argyle Diamonds actively employed and trained indigenous residents from Western Australia)
Culture	Cultural diversity refers to an individual's affinity, or identification with, a particular cultural dimension - ethnicity, nationality, colour, and so on	Organizations must have policies on cultural diversity such as anti-discrimination policies, conflict resolution and complaints handling, equal employment opportunities. Some organizations are required by law to enact positive discrimination and affirmative action
Gender	Gender diversity is usually limited to male or female. However, today we have a more complex understanding of gender	In theory, there must be equal employment opportunities for both males and females Organizations are not allowed to discriminate on gender grounds

Category	Descriptors	HRM practice implications
		Some organizations include maternity leave, and the expectation is that the organization will not discriminate against the employment and promotion of women based on the fact that they have children – remember, we did say, in theory Many organizations also have sexual harassment training and clear policies on sexual harassment
Spirituality	This refers to religious and/or spiritual affiliations which include Christian, Muslim, Jewish, agnostic, atheist, denominational and non-denominational	Most larger organizations must not discriminate, nor allow their staff to discriminate or exclude people based on spiritual beliefs
Language	This refers to an individual's linguistic identity, which can be monolingual (speaks only one language), bilingual or multilingual (speaks two or more languages)	Some organizations with a high number of immigrant staff have a policy of translating HR material, signs, and so on into the dominant non-English language In fact, some organizations actively seek out bilingual and multilingual people due to increasing globalization and the cultural diversity in society
Disability	Disability identity refers to an individual's identification with some type of visible and/or invisible impairment, which can include physical, mental, visual and hearing	An organization, except where certain abilities are absolutely necessary to perform the task, such as eyesight for an airline pilot, should not discriminate against people with a disability Where a person acquires a disability while in employment, some organizations actively seek out alternative roles and tasks for the individual (e.g. as the police do when they place an officer on 'light' or 'desk' duties after the officer has been injured)
Sexuality	This refers to sexual orientation which includes heterosexual, homosexual, lesbian, bisexual, transsexual (sex change) and transvestism	As with gender, it is often unlawful to discriminate against people based on their sexuality; however, this protection is limited, as policies and laws vary from state to state and country to country
Age	This refers to a person's identification with a particular age category, generation, and so on, such as twenty-something, thirty-something, baby boomers, Generation X, Y, etc.	In many countries, in theory, employers cannot discriminate based on age

Source: Adapted and extended from Hopkins (1997: 5)

Gender inequity is a highly emotive issue typified by a variety of arguments and perspectives. Consider pay inequity between the genders across different business sizes. Table 5.5 lists the percentage difference between males and females in the same or similar jobs across various industry sizes over the last seven years. While there are slight improvements here and there, the gender inequity gap in pay seems to still not have been addressed. Ironically, in the UK, it is more

WATCH THIS TED TALK

because the real wages of men have declined, than women being paid more. Notwithstanding this, the gender pay story is the same for most other countries, especially for Australia and the USA, where women are paid less than 85 per cent of what males earn for the same job, qualifications and experience (*The Guardian*, 17 October 2017; NBC News, 10 April 2018). Even in Germany and Sweden, women face an array of stereotypes that reinforce pay inequity (Lilja and Luddeckens, 2006). However, things are changing and in 2018, for example, Iceland made it illegal for businesses to pay men more than women (see Osbourne, 2018).

TABLE 5.5 The gender pay gap for all employees by business size and year, UK, ASHE, 2011–17

							Percentages (%)
Size/Year	2011	2012	2013	2014	2015	2016	2017
1 to 9 employees	16.5	15.8	15.4	14.8	14.1	14.2	12.6
10 to 49 employees	20.2	20.5	20.5	19.6	21.5	20.0	20.4
50 to 249 employees	21.3	19.3	20.5	20.1	20.6	21.0	19.3
250+ employees	21.5	20.7	20.6	19.7	19.7	19.2	19.3

Source: Office of National Statistics, 2018 (Gender pay gap statistics: www.ons.gov.uk)

WATCH THIS TED TALK

While inequity continues today and several initiatives are being implemented to counter inequity, it is clear that change is happening extremely slowly. Often, people may rationalize pay inequity as being the result of women's choices, such as choosing not to advance their careers or to work full time because of family commitments, or that, because women bear children, their employment is a financial risk which should be accounted for in wage levels (Lilja and Luddeckens, 2006). A related defence of the gender pay gap is that people in positions of power tend to be men and so bonuses and pay are based on the individual's effect on organizational performance: if women are not in positions where they are measured on performance, they will not receive bonuses and hence will have a lower income (Roth, 2006). While publicly many people and organizations deplore such inequity, the reality is that this inequity continues to exist. Of course, migrant women are doubly disadvantaged when it comes to pay because migrant workers who do not speak the language of the country they have migrated to are paid significantly less than other workers – irrespective of gender (Boyd and Pikkov, 2005; Kung and Wang, 2006).

When considering the diversity categories, descriptions and HR implications we presented earlier, we need to attend to one very important fact. The nature of HR policy on diversity cannot be separated from government policy and ideology. For example, if a government favours 'cultural integration' and assimilation, it expects that migrants will forego their cultural past and integrate fully within the dominant culture. If a government values multicultural diversity, then it will ensure diversity is preserved. Some countries, such as Canada (see the case study at the end of this chapter), take the 'perfect neutrality' approach, in which the aim is to ensure that all forms of diversity are fully protected and all discrimination is eradicated. Most governments, however, will ebb and flow between cultural diversity and cultural assimilation – depending on the mood of the constituents, the country, the prospect of an election (if one is allowed) and, ironically, the spiritual disposition of those in charge (such as Christian fundamentalists, Islamists or Zionists) with their specific views on homosexuality, gender roles and disability.

Fortunately, many developed-nation governments in the OECD appear to value almost all the categories of diversity we covered earlier. However, there are many more governments around the world that have scant regard for human rights of all kinds. Many governments, especially those in the industrialized world, have a range of laws, acts and regulations upholding and reinforcing the principles of equity and diversity and equal employment opportunities. Moreover, global organizations such as Amnesty International, the United Nations Human Rights Council, and GlobalVision also oversee the policies and practices of governments and organizations in terms of issues of equity and diversity. In the additional resources section at the end of this chapter, you will find some outstanding government web links to equity and diversity in the USA, the UK, Sweden, Australia and other countries.

WHAT WOULD YOU DO?

WALMART UP AGAINST THE WALL – TAKING DIVERSITY SERIOUSLY?

Court approves class-action suit against Wal-Mart, by Steven Greenhouse, published in the *New York Times* online (7 February 2007)

READ THE FULL ARTICLE

Almost every few days in early 2007, a new magazine article or news story emerged concerning the HRM practices of the massive US-based company Walmart. See, for example, 'Court approves class-action suit against Wal-Mart' by Steven Greenhouse (2007), which you can find online at www.nytimes.com/2007/02/07/business/07bias.html. Or, alternatively, click on the icon in the interactive ebook to go straight to the web page.

- Knowing what you now know about HR and equity, what HRM policies and procedures might have avoided such outcomes for Walmart?
- What advice would you give Walmart in relation to HRM practices for the future?

In the workplace context, equity means that people will be treated fairly. As a general rule, governments that value equity and diversity all have certain elements in common; these include protection against discrimination based on gender, sexuality, culture, language, religion, disability and age in the workplace. These include, but are not limited to, protecting people from:

- being denied an interview or employment based on any one or more of the above

Affirmative action attempts to address long-standing and institutionalized discrimination against people of diverse backgrounds – on the basis of gender, race, and so on – by discriminating in favour of people perceived as belonging to categories that are disadvantaged.

- being denied promotion or advancement due to one or all of the above
- experiencing persecution, ridicule and/or harassment based on one or all of the above.

One of the most controversial HR policies enacted by governments is **affirmative action**.

Affirmative action (or positive discrimination) originated in the USA, specifically in the Thirteenth, Fourteenth and Fifteenth Amendments and in the 1966 Civil Rights Act. The main aim was to address the damage done as a result of slavery and racism against African-Americans and by gender stereotypes to women. Today, affirmative action applies to all categories of diversity in order to reinforce the American ideals of fairness (Crosby et al., 2003). In Australia, affirmative action was applied especially to reverse the bias against indigenous people as well as women and is enacted in a number of laws and acts. Many of these are administered by the Affirmative Action Agency and include the Affirmative Action (Equal Employment Opportunity for Women) Act 1986. While Australia and New Zealand were the first countries to allow women to vote, indigenous people in Australia, similarly to African-Americans, had very few rights until the 1960s.

Many people, for no other reason than gender, colour, ethnicity and so on, were and continue to be excluded from many jobs in favour of white males (in the West that is; there is similar discrimination against white people in some Asian and African nations). The main application of affirmative action is aimed at influencing organizations to review employment policies for discriminatory practices. The next most commonly reported policies relate to companies' efforts to assist employees to balance the competing roles of work and family. Very few affirmative action policies seek to challenge traditional patterns of employment, and policies that seek to 'fix' people into certain positions are even less commonly reported by organizations (Sheridan, 1998).

According to the National Organization for Women, affirmative action is often opposed because it is seen to promote reverse discrimination, in that if a white person and a black person or a woman apply for a job, the black person or woman must get it. Such an understanding, which is quite prevalent, is somewhat of a myth because both the black person and the woman must possess the relevant skills and qualifications. Despite negative perceptions in some parts of society, research has found that affirmative action produces positive benefits and is predominantly based on merit (Crosby et al., 2003; Hideg and Lance, 2017). Moreover, when explained in a way that connects with people's values of fairness, equality and opportunity, positive discrimination policies tend to be supported by the broader public (Does et al., 2011; Hideg and Lance, 2017).

Overall, equity and diversity are important, we maintain, and the principles espoused by proponents of equity and diversity are the cornerstone of a free, open, progressive and democratic society, the practical test of which is how any society treats not only its own citizens but also those who seek citizenship. Whether you become an executive officer, a supervisor or an HR manager, these things should feature in any and all aspects of your organization's HRM decisions, practices and processes.

OCCUPATIONAL SAFETY AND HEALTH

Occupational health and safety (OHS) refers to legislation, policies, acts, practices and processes that are aimed at protecting all workers from injury and death in the workplace.

Death and injury have a variety of causes, including chemicals, gases, equipment failure, risks associated with the nature of the work (mining, emergency services, military, etc.), employee or employer negligence, incompetence or mental illness, violence (by colleagues or customers) and ergonomic design flaws (Collins and Schneid, 2001; Tehrani and Haworth, 2004). These are issues of **occupational health and safety (OHS)**. As with equity and diversity, OHS is also legislated. Its simplest expression is found in the many safety notices that abound in the workplace.

Violation of OHS legislation has two extremely negative impacts: first, it results in death or injury; second, it can result in criminal proceedings, fines and even imprisonment for management, including the HR manager. In the event of a death or an injury, management can be personally liable if it can be shown not to have implemented and understood the relevant health and safety legislation in the workplace – irrespective of whether the business is large, medium or small. The HR manager, along with management in general, must design and implement OHS management systems, processes and training in accordance with OHS legislation.

All OHS acts and legislations are framed around the following:

- preventing death and injury at work
- dealing with events that can or have caused death or injury
- dealing with compensation paid to the family or next of kin of the deceased, or paid to the injured person(s)
- dealing with the occupational rehabilitation of the injured person(s).

Any management system must adequately account for each of the areas listed.

OHS laws, acts and legislation are complex and can be confusing. Fortunately, governments provide excellent resources and training that HR managers can use to help design, implement and enforce their OHS management systems (see, for example, in Australia: The Australian Safety and Compensation Council, www.ascc.gov.au/ascc; in the UK: The Health and Safety Commission, www.hse.gov.uk/aboutus/index.htm; in the USA: Department of Labour: OHS Administration, www.osha.gov).

THE INDUSTRIAL RELATIONS CLIMATE

The issues most commonly dealt with under the banner of **industrial relations (IR)** include: claims for improved working conditions (occupational safety and health, working hours, and so on); claims for better pay and reward systems; the nature of the notification of redundancies and discrimination or unfair dismissals and disagreement on the promotion of employees. However, the definition we have provided in the margin may be a little too broad since not everything associated with the employer–employee relationship comes within the scope of IR. Most countries have an IR commission or government department that deals with a number of issues pertaining to employer–employee relationships and the IR climate.

Industrial relations (IR) refer to the relationship between employers and employees.

Table 5.6 provides links to the relevant government departments and commissions that deal with IR issues. This list is not comprehensive, as individual jurisdictions – states, local councils, counties and boroughs – might also have IR powers and responsibilities. We list the main federal and commonwealth bodies that include resources and material on IR laws, acts and other relevant issues. We are certain that you will find these links will enable you to access some very interesting reading. (If you are not from one of the countries listed, we welcome an email from you telling us where you are from, with a link to the equivalent government body that deals with IR in your country.)

Our aim is not to deal with specific acts and pieces of legislation because IR legislation varies between countries. Rather, in this section we will deal with two broad but interrelated themes integral to the IR climate: unions and employment relations. Though these may vary across different national boundaries, there are certain issues that are shared irrespective of the nation where you reside.

TABLE 5.6 Government organizations that deal with IR

Country	Organization	Web link
Australia	Department of Employment	www.employment.gov.au/workplace-relations
India	Ministry of Labour and Employment	http://labour.nic.in/content/innerpage/acts.php
New Zealand	Department of Labour	www.dol.govt.nz
Norway	Ministry of Labour and Social Affairs	www.regjeringen.no/en/dep/asd/id165
Sweden	Ministry of Employment	www.sweden.gov.se/sb/d/8281
UK	Department of Business Innovation and Skills	www.gov.uk/government/organisations/department-for-business-innovation-skills
US	Department of Labor	www.dol.gov

Notes: Most of these countries also have independent IR commissions to handle IR matters and disputes between employees/unions and employers/employer associations; all sites last accessed March 2015.

UNIONS

Unions can be defined as an association of wage-earning employees mobilized and organized in order to represent their constituents' interests. These interests can often be counter to the interests of employers, but not always necessarily so.

Unions are closely associated with IR and employer–employee relations. They tend to be politically charged organizations and are often perceived, sometimes correctly, as being in direct opposition to the interests of employers and employer associations. However, many organizations achieve excellent performance results when they work with unions (Appelbaum and Hunter, 2005; Kochan et al., 2009; Reardon, 2006). Unions have had to transform their activities and the way they relate to organizations, governments and non-unionized labour. The old hard-line adversarial approach that once typified unions has mellowed. This has occurred mainly because of a decline in union membership around the industrialized world (Bronfenbrenner, 1998) but also because of aggressive government policies implemented by political parties such as the Republicans in the USA, the Conservatives in the UK and the Liberal Party in Australia. (It should be noted, however, that the relationship between social democratic parties and trade unions has also changed in recent years, with policies of economic labour market deregulation also pursued by nominally social democratic parties.) In the USA, union membership has declined from a peak of 35 per cent in 1954 to 12.9 per cent today (Reardon, 2006: 171). The decline is similar in Australia (Burchielli, 2006) and throughout the UK and much of Europe (European Industrial Relations Observatory Online, 2004).

The issues on which unions represent their members include wage negotiations, conditions of employment, penalty rates and working hours, as well as OHS pension and superannuation. Unions also assist members in a range of other employment-related areas such as unfair dismissal and advice on corporate HR practices and policies. Today, many smaller unions have amalgamated or been consumed by large unions and are represented by mega trade union organizations such as the AFL-CIO in the USA, ACTU in Australia and the TUC in the UK. Because unions were traditionally associated with programmes such as that outlined in Marx and Engels' *Communist Manifesto* (1998 [1848]), organized labour has always been treated with suspicion, if not contempt, by many businesspeople and conservative governments (but not all). In view of the decline in union numbers around the world, it may be that the general population also finds unions irrelevant and overconfrontational in orientation. However, the unions' decline has coincided with a remarkably long boom in these economies. Unfortunately, most people do not realize what the unions have achieved in their long and often acrimonious opposition to business owners. Wins have included overtime pay and reduced working hours (Trejo, 1993), paid holiday leave (Green, 1997), paid maternity and paternity leave (Baird, 2004). In the USA, unions have influenced policies that have transformed societies – for example, the Public Accommodation Act of 1964, the Voting Rights Act of 1965, equal employment opportunity legislation, anti-poverty legislation and the Occupational Safety and Health Act of 1971 (Freedom and Medoff, 1984).

WATCH THIS TED TALK

Despite the decline in union membership, some organizations have found that cooperating with unions can actually improve the performance and commitment of employees to the organization's cause. This may apply even when open-book management is used (see, for example, Clegg et al., 2002). 'Open-book management' means that the finances of the organization are transparent to all stakeholders, including the union. This is not a new approach: Brazilian millionaire businessman Ricardo Semler, between 1980 and 1990, turned his organization around with soft HR approaches (he was a Harvard MBA graduate); at Semler's business, the unions were actively involved in the running of the business and open-book management was also used (Semler, 1993). Evidently, finding ways to work with unions can actually benefit the organization.

Semler's idea to involve unions in a proactive way in his business has gained considerable attention over the last few years, but the idea is quite old. It dates from the Scanlon Plan of the 1940s (also known as Gainsharing). Joseph Scanlon was a former steelworker and union leader, and later Massachusetts Institute of Technology graduate, who believed union–employer cooperation was the key to growth and prosperity for society. A large body of work has supported the Scanlon Plan and its overall beneficial environment of cooperation between key stakeholders (Collins, 1998; Hatcher and Ross, 1991; Schuster, 1983, 1984). Scanlon became increasingly interested in how unions, employees and employers could participate for win–win outcomes. He advocated that the best way to do this was to involve unions and employees in key decision-making. It should not be forgotten that at the time that Scanlon was doing this, the dominant management model was the Theory X orientation to employee–employer relations.

More recently, the literature and research on participatory approaches to OB have downplayed the role of unions. However, those true to the original Scanlon Plan ensure that unions are incorporated. Indeed, such approaches might provide an excellent way for unions to regain some lost ground. However, many critical management scholars who subscribe to the neo-Marxist models of management–employee relations in terms of labour process analysis would argue that even participatory management should be viewed with great scepticism. They argue that words such as 'empowerment', 'gainsharing' and 'participatory management' are nothing more than new managerial words of control and subjugation (Hancock and Tyler, 2001; Howcroft and Wilson, 2003; Voronov and Coleman, 2003). It seems that in some ways people can sometimes feel that they are damned if they do, damned if they don't, when they attempt to address the quality of working life.

EMPLOYMENT RELATIONS

In this final section on the IR climate, we will look briefly at a specific HRM issue that we believe is critical in the current economic climate: the nature of employment contracts. As we said earlier, we will not go into specific IR labour laws here. Rather, we provide a general theme that underpins all labour contracts between employees and employers – collective or individual contracts. Table 5.7 indicates the main features, strengths and weaknesses of each type of negotiated contract.

As Table 5.7 indicates, there are both positives and negatives in individual and collective agreements. In reality, presenting a table like this underplays the serious implications and ideologies underlying these two approaches. The argument for and against **individual agreements** versus **collective agreements** is a war of political and economic ideologies about the nature of work and employment. We will leave it up to you to decide whether you agree with one or the other, or neither of these.

Individual agreements, as the term suggests, refer to the process of individuals negotiating the terms and conditions of their work, including pay, rewards and remuneration, and so on.

Collective agreement refers to a written agreement, made between the employer and the employees, which sets out the terms and conditions of employment. Usually it is made between a union, as a body representing employees, and an employer. Collective agreements are typical of social democratic approaches to industrial relations.

The movement towards individual contracts, while being advocated as positive and in the interests of talented employees, raises some serious issues that need to be addressed. First, the individual contract is, as Lawler (2005) believed contracts should be, one based on the objective of getting rid of 'obsolete capital'. Over time, the USA and Australia have watered down the ability of unions to seek collective agreements on members' behalf. Part of the reason for this is obviously to ensure employers are not committed to maintaining employment levels when they experience downturns. Downsizing, outsourcing, permanent and temporary lay-offs typify the US, Australian and to a lesser extent UK markets. In Sweden, as with many other North European and more social democratic countries, 90 per cent of employees are protected by collective agreements, many of which include job security (*Landsorganisationen I Sveirge*, 2006). Indeed, recent research shows that countries that actively avoid policies of downsizing and lay-offs, but are typified by companies that value and actively seek to create job security, are actually outperforming countries that do not (Eichengreen, 2007; *New York Times*, 25 February 2007).

TABLE 5.7 Types of negotiated contract; their strengths and weaknesses

	Individual agreement	Collective agreement
Details	Contract of employment, wages and conditions that are negotiated between the employee directly with the employer	Contract of employment, wages and conditions that are negotiated collectively, usually between union and industry or company representatives
Strengths	1. The individual agreement is believed to provide employees with greater power to negotiate for higher wages and other conditions Employees are given flexibility in sacrificing unused benefits in favour of more desirable ones (e.g. sacrifice holiday or sick pay for pay rises). An employee can choose to use a bargaining agent to represent them; the agent can be a family member, a union representative, and so on 2. Employers are less bound to cumbersome legalities around termination based on poor performance and other work-related discipline matters. Employer's risk is reduced because they are able to deal with employees on a case-by-case basis, allowing the employer to downsize or lay off staff (temporarily or permanently), during economic downturns or for other financial matters	1. The individual can rely on the knowledge, skills and expertise of union delegates to negotiate wage levels and conditions. The employee knows the conditions and wages are fair because they are usually applied across the industry 2. Employer is able to deal with issues at a broader collective level; because agreements are collective, wages and conditions will be standard across the board
Weaknesses	1. Individual agreements override any collective agreement and once an individual agreement is set, collective bargaining gains no longer apply to the employee who signed an individual agreement. Can be highly inequitable because those with the knowledge, education, experience and disposition to negotiate effectively do well in the employer/employee negotiation. Those who lack such attributes, skills, knowledge and experience can be taken advantage of 2. Union power and influence become eroded, and employee legal protection is significantly reduced with the onus of proof placed on the individual employee	1. Collective agreements can be legal and managerial nightmares for employers, especially when they employ both unionized and non-unionized labour 2. The individual has little negotiating power outside accepting the award, wages and conditions for their job and their industry

Source: The information in this table is derived from the various government websites listed in Table 5.6.

In a democratic and free society, certain core human rights issues are taken seriously: they include equity, diversity and justice. Such values should not be forgotten when performing the core HR functions we covered in this chapter because to do so would be not only unethical but also often unlawful. Of course, in practice they are often forgotten: sometimes organizations get away with it, and sometimes they do not and end up in tribunals or the courts. However, in a world that is undergoing such rapid transitions, where the Internet provides endless sources of information (some of which, at least, is valid!), people are more knowledgeable and inquisitive about how they should be treated at work. If people are going to expend effort, apply their talents, capabilities, knowledge and skill for an employer, money is no longer the main motivator. Organizations must be thoughtful and reflexive in how they attract and retain talent and we would expect that those organizations that do so would prosper.

SUMMARY

In this chapter, we have considered how organizations manage their human relations:

- HRM is a complex task: it deals with how people are recruited to the organization, how they are selected, retained and developed.
- While at face value recruitment, selection, retention and development seem like straightforward tasks, they are in fact extremely complex and sometimes controversial processes. We have considered some of the main issues in their practice.
- HR and HRM do not occur in a vacuum; the HR manager cannot simply assume that anything goes, because HR occurs in specific contexts undergoing constant change
- Government policy, industrial relations, unionization, social attitudes, globalization, demographic changes, immigration, technological changes, amongst others, all affect the ability to perform and implement the major HR functions.

EXERCISES

1. Having read this chapter, you should be able to say in your own words what each of the following key terms means. Test yourself or ask a colleague to test you.
   - Human resource management (HRM)
   - Hard and soft HR
   - Recruitment
   - Performance review and assessment
   - Equity and diversity
   - Realistic job preview
   - Benefits and remuneration
   - Human process advantage
   - Human capital advantage

- Affirmative action (positive discrimination)
- Selection
- Training and development
- Humans as resources
- Workplace regulations and legislation
- Strategic HRM
- Knowledge workers
- Occupational health and safety
- Unions
- Industrial and employment relations
- Collective bargaining
- Enterprise bargaining.

2. What are some of the main contextual issues that HR managers must account for in their everyday practices?

3. What are the core HRM functions and how might they have an impact on different aspects of organizational performance?

4. This exercise assists in writing realistic job previews. Draw a table with two columns and in one column write 'good' and in the other write 'not so good'. Now, if you work, think about your job; if you don't work, think about the task of being a student. Assume you want to leave work or university and you have been told you can leave as long as you find a replacement. List all the positives and negatives of the job by using the appropriate 'good' and 'not so good' columns. Once you have listed all these, write a job ad using the realistic job preview. Compare your realistic job preview with others in your class. What differences and similarities do you find?

5. With your peers, discuss critically the following statements:

- 'Maternity leave makes it too easy for women to opt for getting pregnant at the expense of the organization.'
- 'Should women and men have equal pay? Why and under what conditions would inequity in pay be justified?'
- 'Do affirmative action and positive discrimination work? Why or why not?'

6. In groups, discuss the performance appraisals used at work or university. How well do these systems work? Are they fair? How would you design a performance appraisal system for students studying this subject at university or college?

7. Divide into two teams; team 1 will follow the scientific management model of HRM and team 2 will follow the human relations model. Assume you are the co-owner of a medium-sized company that deals in the production and export of electrical components for plasma HD TV sets. You have a staff of 25, and you are seeking to hire

(Continued)

(Continued)

another five people. Read through your team's allocated column – i.e. scientific management (hard) or human relations (soft) – in Table 5.1, and then, as a team, design your HR policies in terms of each area of the HRM practice orientations. Once you have completed this, both teams should present their models and compare and contrast the differences in approach.

8. Debate: Unions are a waste of time and money!
9. Choose two teams of three, plus one moderator and one timekeeper, with the rest of the class to act as the audience and judges. Organize a debate between two groups with one group for the affirmative ('unions are a waste of time') and one group for the negative ('unions are not a waste of time'). It is best to have a week to prepare, do some research on unions and bring along facts and figures. Perhaps your teacher may even purchase a reward of some sort for the winning team!

REVISE KEY TERMS

TEST YOURSELF

TEST YOURSELF

Review what you have learned by visiting:
https://study.sagepub.com/managingandorganizations5e or your eBook

- **Test yourself with multiple-choice questions.**
- **Revise key terms with the interactive flashcards.**

CASE STUDY

Midwestern Health System (MHS) and Cisco as exemplars of compassionate human resource practices and policies

Suffering is fundamental to human experience. Often, it is triggered by such events as illness, accidents, death or the breakdown of relationships. As organizations are places of human engagement, they are invariably places that harbour feelings of joy and pain and reactions of callousness or compassion in response to another's suffering (Dutton et al., 2002). The emotional and social cost of human suffering in organizations includes loss of work confidence, self-esteem and health; as well as toxic relations involving reduced employee cooperation (Frost, 1999, 2003). The financial and social cost is astronomical, even in the wealthiest nations on earth (Margolis and Walsh, 2003).

Awareness of the power of compassion to lessen and alleviate human pain (Kanov et al., 2004; Lilius et al., 2008) has led to growing interest in compassion in organizations under the banner of Positive Organizational Scholarship (POS). Compassion is defined by POS scholars as a three-fold process of noticing another person's suffering, feeling empathy and responding in some way to alleviate the pain (Dutton et al., 2006; Frost et al., 2006).

Human resource departments in organizations that strive to be compassionate actively promote compassion both by encouraging compassionate co-worker relations, establishing systems and policies to ensure that employees' pain is recognized, acknowledged and responded to with compassion, and by developing compassionate leadership.

Compassionate co-worker relations

Human resource departments can promote compassionate co-worker relations by encouraging co-workers to recognize, feel and respond to each other's pain through kind words, providing comfort with flowers and cards, hospital visits, open listening, help with home and office work, and financial support (Frost et al., 2006). Examples of such supportive employee relations are found among the employees at MHS.

Several years ago at MHS, an employee with seven children required bypass surgery but didn't have enough money to take leave from work for the period of operation and recovery. Neither did he have insurance coverage to provide this support. In a show of support, a co-worker set up a tax trust fund and other co-workers from among the 75 who worked in the lab submitted donations (Frost et al., 2006). In less than a week, $5,800 was collected, more than enough to cover the employee's time off work. Afterwards, co-workers expressed feelings of pride to be working among people who care. This example demonstrates the provision of tangible support in compassionate co-worker relations. Yet, support does not have to be tangible. Just knowing that someone cares is often all that matters. When another MHS employee struggled to work while attending to her critically ill mother, her co-workers daily asked after her welfare and enquired if they could do anything to help (Dutton et al., 2007). She later explained that most of the time there was nothing they could do but knowing they cared and were eager to help boosted her spirit. She further stated that it enhanced her relationships with her co-workers, which she described as irreplaceable.

Compassion can be expressed towards others at all levels of social relations - colleagues of equal hierarchical status, junior employees, as well as senior supervisors. When the dog of a senior supervisor at MHS was diagnosed with cancer, her staff showed great compassion by enquiring after her pet's welfare and listening each day as she revealed greater detail of the illness as well as 'happy' stories from her healthy days (Dutton et al., 2007). When the supervisor called in one day to say she would be late as her dog had just passed away, the staff made a collection and sent flowers. Sharing such a moving experience brought them all closer together as friends beyond their professional roles.

Compassionate policies and systems

Human resource departments can further promote compassion within the organization by establishing policies and systems that legitimate, reflect and ensure the enactment of a culture that underscores and supports values of dignity, commitment to others, respect, equality, the importance of members, and so on (Frost, 1999). It further supports beliefs that people are more than their professional identity, that humanity should be displayed and that members are like family (Dutton et al., 2006). Finally, it is reinforced by outcomes of the practices of compassion such as trust, quality connections and positive emotions, creating social resources based on a conceptualization of the organization as one that cares (Dutton et al., 2007).

(Continued)

(Continued)

The fulfilment of compassionate organizational values and policies is executed through the development of compassionate support systems. When a Cisco employee visiting Japan had a medical emergency and couldn't find any English-speaking health-care support, Cisco designed a network system to provide medical assistance to Cisco employees travelling abroad (Dutton et al., 2002). The objective was to ensure that no Cisco employee would again feel so forsaken and alone in a frightening situation. This system has proven invaluable on many occasions. During a period of civil unrest in Jakarta, Indonesia in 1998, employees found themselves in the middle of the conflict zone. Cisco used its networks to organize an ambulance that could travel unimpaired through the city streets, to collect employees and drive them hidden under blankets to a waiting airplane at a deserted army airstrip and fly them to safety.

Systems can also be established to build the organization's capability for compassion by recognizing and rewarding compassionate acts (Dutton et al., 2007; Frost et al., 2006). The MHS had in place such a system by way of a monthly newsletter entitled 'Caring Times', which was distributed to the entire hospital staff (Dutton et al., 2007). The newsletter contained stories of MHS staff performing compassionate, caring behaviours.

Questions

1. Describe the HR approach used by MHS and Cisco.
2. How was compassion embedded within MHS and Cisco?
3. What might be the result, in terms of positive psychological capital, of the HR approaches used in this case?

Case prepared by Ace Simpson, UTS School of Business, University of Technology, Sydney.

ADDITIONAL RESOURCES

- There are some great movies on issues about work and employment: Kevin Smith's (1994) *Clerks*, Colin Higgins' (1980) *Nine to Five*, and Mike Judge's (1999) *Office Space*, plus the classic *On the Waterfront* (1954) and *Waiting for Superman* (2010).
- A classic IR film is John Ford's *How Green Was My Valley* (1941), which traces 50 years in the lives of a close-knit clan of Welsh coal miners. As the years pass, the Morgans try to survive unionization, a lengthy strike and a mining accident; meanwhile, their hometown and its venerable traditions slowly disintegrate.
- There are also some fantastic situation comedies on TV, such as *The Office*, and some all-time classic episodes concerning work in *The Simpsons* and *Futurama*.
- www.hrmguide.net is an excellent resource for students and practitioners of HRM. The site is full of the latest information and ideas in

HRM, and provides some excellent links to a number of valuable and interesting web sites.

- For our American readers, the US government's Equal Employment Opportunity Commission is an excellent resource: go to www.eeoc.gov.
- For our Australian and New Zealand readers, there is an excellent equity and diversity toolkit with lots of great links and resources: www.dss.gov.au/our-responsibilities/settlement-and-multicultural-affairs/programs-policy/access-and-equity/multicultural-access-and-equity-policy-toolkit.
- For our UK readers, there are some excellent resources on government websites: www.gov.uk/discrimination-your-rights/types-of-discrimination, www.opsi.gov.uk and www.direct.gov.uk/en/Employment/index.htm.
- For all our 'wherever you are' readers, the International Labour Organization has some fantastic resources and information: go to www.ilo.org/skills/lang--en/index.htm.
- This YouTube video of President Obama talking about CEO pay inequity shows how important the problem is: www.youtube.com/watch?v=TXFBW4ObxWE

Part Two

MANAGING ORGANIZATIONAL PRACTICES

INTERACTIVE EBOOK ICON KEY

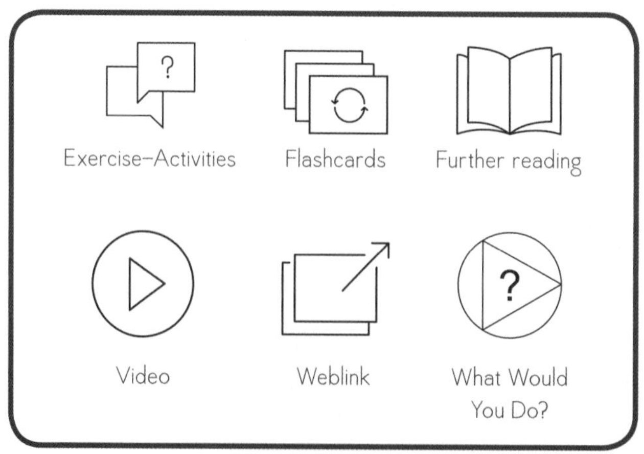

MANAGING CULTURES

VALUES, PRACTICE, BEING

LEARNING OBJECTIVES

This chapter is designed to enable you to:

- recognize that organizational culture is important, complex and multi-level
- understand that a common view of organization cultures regards it as a managerial tool capable of use in different organization designs
- realize that culture is in part orally communicated through the stories that circulate and the assumptions taken for granted
- distinguish between views of culture as organizationally integrated, differentiated or fragmented
- appreciate and critique arguments that postulate that there are 'national cultures'.

BEFORE YOU GET STARTED...

> 'Trump is empowering a conservative political culture that celebrates everything that patriotic Americans should fear: the cult of strength, open disdain for truthfulness, violent contempt for the Fourth Estate, hostility toward high culture and other types of 'elitism', a penchant for conspiracy theories and, most dangerously, white-identity politics.'

So says Brett Stephens, on 'Donald Trump's fatal culture of governance': www.afr.com/opinion/columnists/why-i-am-still-a-nevertrumper-20171230-h0bm94#ixzz5BqdReNoP

INTRODUCTION

Every organization has a culture. The White House organization under President Trump is the subject of our opening quote. Whether you are a Trump fan or not, or whether you agree or disagree with the quote, what it points out is the way that a leader can set a certain framework of culture for an organization. As we shall see, culture plays a large part in managing and organizations. In investigating framing, we need to ask whether organizations *have* a culture or *are they a culture* or do they comprise *multiple cultures*? What role do *leaders* play in *framing cultures*? Do nations have *a culture* or are they *multicultural*?

WHY IS ORGANIZATION CULTURE IMPORTANT?

There are many recent manifestations that strongly state the case for the importance of organization culture. The #MeToo movement has been reacting against male CEOs, such as Harvey Weinstein, who presumed to have the right to sexually harass those with whom they worked in their organization. Weinstein is but one case of a culture of presumed entitlement, arrogance and domination; across the Atlantic, in the City of London, the 2018 Presidents Club dinner, held in The Dorchester Hotel, proved to be the last one ever as two undercover reporters from the *Financial Times* revealed that the 130 young women who had been hired to wait on tables as scantily clad 'hostesses', with instructions to be so clad, were harassed, propositioned and molested by some of the men-only 'presidents' – powerful City folk – who seemed oblivious to the abuse they were committing. In the Presidents Club case, language was used not only to represent but also to embody the role of 'hostesses', with symbols of short, tight little black dresses and high heels conveying a uniform appearance of sexiness, amidst artefacts of power: the presence of powerful men in a powerful institution in a wealthy and powerful arena, one of the world's most privileged hotels.

The sense of privilege attaching to some members of the upper echelons of the power elite is evident in their regard of organized misogyny as an entitlement. In this case, as the *Financial Times* (2018) and Marriage (2018) reported, the 'display of male entitlement was linked to institutions and individuals at the centre of the British establishment. Major business leaders were present, publicly listed companies bought tables, and respected children's charities were to be the beneficiaries'. Responsible organization cultures do not insist employees should be dressed in a uniform way, stipulating short, tight black dresses, high heels and black underwear, or that they sign five-page non-disclosure agreements that they are not allowed to read or keep. Wealthy and powerful men, such as members of the Presidents Club, Harvey Weinstein and, allegedly, President Trump, frequently use non-disclosure agreements to silence those who witness them embarrassing themselves.

Culture in organizations conceived as a sphere of privileged symbols, language and artefacts has a complex history that stretches back long before organization theorists began to study it. Consider Image 6.1, showing Traitor's Gate at the Tower of London – the place where unfortunate individuals deemed to be traitors, having been transported by barge up the River Thames, entered the tower to await their execution (or, if they were lucky, imprisonment). Many of Henry VIII's courtiers and two of his wives – Anne Boleyn and Catherine Howard – saw that gate close behind them before they lost their heads to the executioner's axe. Traitor's Gate stands as a stark reminder of what might be the consequences of perceived deviance in an organization ruled by an absolute authority, such as the Tudor monarchy of Henry VIII.

Today, there are still a few CEOs who seem to imagine that they can behave like Tudor monarchs. Many examples were provided at the trial of Lord Conrad Black, the ex-newspaper magnate, convicted on charges of fraud, being accused of using organizational finances as if they were his personal property. Referring to the 'greed of Conrad Black and his complete disregard for his shareholders', Hugh Totten (a partner for the New York law firm Perkins Coie) commented, 'It makes him look like some English Tudor monarch rather than the CEO of a public company with responsibility to shareholders' (Bone, 2007: 45).

IMAGE 6.1 Traitor's Gate: the symbol of the Tudor monarchy's organizational culture of control

Tellingly, really great companies do not seem to be like a Tudor court, ruled by absolutist authority, capable of committing injurious social actions: they prize collaboration, building social as well as financial capital, boundary spanning and initiative and certainly would not tolerate harassment. What differentiates the cultures of organizations and institutions that tolerate and indeed implicitly encourage harassment and those that do not is their organization culture.

WHAT COMPRISES ORGANIZATION CULTURE?

Culture represents the totality of everyday knowledge that people use habitually to make sense of the world around them through patterns of shared meanings and understandings passed down through language, symbols and artefacts. In the Presidents Club case, the men were dining on a menu that featured Scottish smoked salmon and 34-day-aged USDA Black Angus beef fillet with onion rings and mac 'n' cheese, with dessert being a deconstructed black forest gateau. You might find that menu appealing if you are not a vegetarian but what about these delicacies in the 'What would you do' feature below?

WHAT WOULD YOU DO?

Given that we all need to eat to live, it is particularly interesting to consider the cultural rules that surround food. All societies have rules about what is edible and what is not. How do *you* feel about chicken's feet, a delicacy in Hong Kong; Witchety grubs, an Australian Koori treat; grasshoppers, deliciously deep fried in Mexico; dog, a perennial favourite in Korea and some other parts of Asia; rats, sometimes on the menu in China (www.chinadaily.com.cn/china/2007-07/16/content_5435896.htm); cow's stomach lining (tripe), popular both in the north of England and in many parts of Continental Europe; or horsemeat, a German delicacy?

What would you do as a guest? Would you eat the culture you were offered?

In understanding what culture is, we need to be able to consider:

1. *Norms*: ways of acting underlain by tacit and unspoken assumptions and informal rules, which people negotiate in their everyday interactions. The Presidents Club clearly displayed misogynist norms.
2. *Identity*: through comparison with those whom you see as alike and those whom you see as different, as members of distinct groups, you learn and position who you and others are in terms of culture. At school, it could have been jocks and swots; at work, it could be suits and creatives; at the Presidents Club, hostesses and corporate men.
3. *Deviance*: a way of clearly establishing what cultural norms are is by breaking them and others letting you know that you have done so. You are more likely to be told when you are breaking cultural norms than when you are practising them, something that the Presidents Club members learnt in January 2018.
4. *Artefacts*: organizations are full of material elements such as the overall architecture, pictures, office spaces and material objects that all have social meaning and are a key part of culture. At the Presidents Club, the hostesses' uniforms were a key symbol.
5. *Transcendence*: in organizations, culture is always transcendent – it encompasses some collective of individuals, but not necessarily *all* people, as many corporate responses to the Presidents Club story protested.
6. *Subcultures*: in many organizations there will likely be subcultures, which may run counter to the official overall culture; in the Presidents Club

case, the 'men-only' guest list made it clear that there was no place for high-achieving women in a man's world: their gender made them a subculture.

7. *Practices*: culture comprises what is done everyday, which is one reason not only why culture as lived experience can be hard to change but also why different groups create and value different elements of culture, creating cultures in the plural: the practices of inebriated corporate executives constituted their relaxed attitude to gender relation mores.
8. *Design*: culture is often explicitly 'designed' by organizations or their consultants as an official or formal culture. Many organizational practices are oriented towards reinforcing this official culture. At the Presidents Club, the hostesses were obliged to wear a specific uniform, the symbolism of which was highly visual, and to sign non-disclosure agreements by design before the event.
9. *Process*: although often explicitly defined, culture is necessarily a living thing, a complex of stories that are historically related and emergent, sometimes held together by traditions, rituals and customs. One of the encouraging aspects of the *Financial Times*' exposure is the realization that this kind of boys' club behaviour has no place in contemporary organizations: as the expose concludes in the final paragraph, 'When company leaders exclude and degrade women, investors and stakeholders make their fury felt.'

IN PRACTICE

Becoming a graduate

Universities are replete with culture and not just the kind that you find in books: they are alive with traditions, rituals and customs, as you will no doubt encounter on Graduation Day when the final passage from being a student to becoming a graduate is marked by the rites of ceremony, processions, symbols of authority such as the university mace, the different gowns that different degree holders are entitled to wear, and the traditions that structure the presentation of degrees.

Question

1. Can you identify other aspects of university organization culture marking your time in the institution?

APPROACHES TO ORGANIZATIONAL CULTURE

The earliest approaches to organizational culture referred to it using a term from the psychological literature, *organizational climate*. Schein (2002) argues that this term was a precursor to the concept of organizational culture. As Ashkenasy (2003) demonstrates, these roots in the psychology discipline are pervasive in discussions of organizational culture.

WATCH CORPORATE CULTURE VIDEO

Organizational culture comprises the deep basic assumptions, beliefs and shared values that define organizational membership.

Schein (1997) offers the most popular definition of **organizational culture**. He defines it as the deep, basic assumptions and beliefs that are shared by organizational members. Culture is not only displayed on the surface; instead, for the most part it is unconscious and hidden beneath the surface, similar to an iceberg. To clarify the various components of culture in organizations, Schein differentiates between three levels of culture that we can illustrate using the metaphorical image of a plan in which outer walls surround the core of basic assumptions, the hardest to reach area. (Figure 6.1).

FIGURE 6.1 The levels of culture as an iceberg according to Schein

Espoused values are consistent beliefs about something in which there is an emotional investment, articulated in speeches, writings or other media.

Basic assumptions subconsciously shape values and artefacts, forming around fundamental views on the nature of humans, human relationships and activity, reality and truth.

Level 1 consists of artefacts, including visible organizational features such as the physical structure of buildings and their architecture, uniforms and interior design. This level is easily observable but does not reveal everything about an organization's culture other than the more evident and malleable aspects of the organization's environment.

Level 2 comprises **espoused values**. Values represent a non-visible facet of culture that encompasses the norms and beliefs that employees express when they discuss organizational issues. A mission statement or a commitment to equal employment opportunities is part of this level.

The deepest culture – the **basic assumptions** hidden beneath artefacts and expressed values – is found in level 3. It includes the basic assumptions that shape organizational members' worldviews, beliefs and norms, which guide their behaviour without being explicitly expressed. It is the most influential level because it works unacknowledged, shaping decision-making processes almost invisibly, hidden beneath the surface. It is hard to observe and even harder to change. Nonetheless, it is the level that carries the most potential for transformation. (Notice the Freudian influence on these conceptions of culture in terms of unconsciousness and hidden depths.)

IN PRACTICE

Organizing children's homes

READ THE FULL REPORT

All religious organizations have strong value commitments that proclaim their faith. Despite this, many members of many organized religions have in recent years been found guilty of major breaches of those values, including sexual and physical abuse. One such case, by no means the only one, concerned the Salvation Army in Australia. As was reported in the Report of Case Study No. 33, The response of The Salvation Army (Southern Territory) to allegations of child sexual abuse at children's homes that it operated, from July 2016, reporting to Commissioners Justice Jennifer Coate, Mr Robert Fitzgerald AM and Professor Helen Milroy of the Royal Commission into Institutional Responses to Child Sexual Abuse (childabuseroyalcommission.gov.au), abuse was rife in some of the homes for children that the institution organized.

Extracting from the report on pages 8, 13, 14 and 18 we can summarize the following.

> From 1894 to 1998 The Salvation Army operated children's homes across what it termed its Southern Territory ... During the life of the Institutions, there were no guidelines, orders or regulations, policies or procedures that regulated the appointment of employees, officers or managers to the homes. In particular, at the time that the Institutions were in operation, there were no legal or other requirements for specific qualifications or for police checks (page 8).

What did the Report establish?

> We are satisfied that many former residents of the Institutions run by TSAS did not report their complaints of sexual abuse at the time it was occurring because:
>
> - they did not think there was anyone to tell
> - they did not think they would be believed
> - they were threatened with physical harm
> - when they did attempt to report the sexual abuse, they were accused of telling lies.
>
> We are also satisfied that some former residents were physically punished after telling officers or employees of The Salvation Army about their complaints of

(Continued)

(Continued)

> sexual abuse and this stopped them from disclosing any further incidents of sexual abuse (page 13).

What was the Salvation Army's formal organization culture expressed in policies and procedures in these homes during that period?

> Before 1990, aside from the Orders and Regulations for Soldiers of The Salvation Army (and its ancillary volumes, collectively referred to in this report as the Orders and Regulations), The Salvation Army had no practice of maintaining written policies and procedures for its social welfare programs. In particular, the Royal Commission heard evidence that between 1940 and 1990 The Salvation Army did not have any specific policies or procedures on how to respond to complaints of sexual abuse in any of the homes it operated. We are satisfied that before 1990 The Salvation Army had no policies or procedures which governed how to handle and respond to complaints of sexual abuse received in respect to its institution (page 14).
>
> In respect to each of the examples discussed, The Commissioners concluded that, in failing to take action against its staff and officers who were breaching Orders and Regulations prohibiting the mistreatment of children, TSAS provided a culture in the Institutions in which:
>
> - Children felt afraid to report sexual abuse.
> - Children felt powerless to resist the maltreatment.
> - The staff and officers whose behaviour was in breach of Orders and Regulations were able to, and did, continue the prohibited behaviour (page 18).

Questions

1. In practice, what recommendations do you think the Commissioners should make to ensure that the culture is not replicated in any institutions in the future?
2. What would be the necessary steps in the redesign of the culture in such institutions to minimize harm in future?

CULTURE IN PRACTICE

CULTURE AS A TOOL

In the contemporary study of organizational culture, a split has opened up between those who maintain a focus on organizations as rational instruments, or tools, and those who see them more anthropologically as patterns of culture oriented around norms, claims to legitimacy, and the symbolism and artefacts that embedded these claims and counter-claims.

The tool view came into focus from the early 1980s. US business was reeling from the onslaught of Japanese imports in areas previously dominated by American firms, such as TVs and automobiles. Japanese firms were attributed with advantages that derived from organizationally cohesive cultures compared to more conflictual American cultures. In determining a way of fighting back, business consultants recognized an opportunity by proselytizing aspects of US organizations' culture in terms of its potential for moulding individuals and collaborative relations for competitive advantage. Consultancies mushroomed that claimed to be able to build organizational cultures akin to communities or tight-knit 'clans', replete with images of mutual support, solidarity and commitment (see Clegg, 1990, for an outline of the broader arguments about culture at this time).

The researchers who initially did most to popularize the strong culture approach were Peters and Waterman (1982). Tom Peters and Robert Waterman, two consultants from McKinsey & Company (the multinational consulting firm) who had links to Stanford's Graduate School of Business, offered an account of culture based on an instrumental view of the relation between managerial practice and management knowledge. They promoted the concept that culture is a strong and unifying tool. It is worth looking at the web pages of any of the big consulting firms, and keying in 'culture', to see the tool view in use today.

READ MORE ABOUT CONSULTING

Peters and Waterman's (1982) work translated ideas from quite subtle and complex organization theories to apply them to practical exigencies. The origin of these theories was the sensemaking perspective of Weick (1969, 1979, 1995). As Colville et al. (1999: 135) argue, this was reflected in *In Search of Excellence* through the insights that 'fundamentally … meanings matter' and 'mundaneity is more scarce than people realize' (1999: 136).

WATCH PETERS' EXCELLENCE TALK

Peters and Waterman had a nice story to tell. Integrate everyone into one managerially designed and approved culture of excellence and superior performance will be the outcome. Subsequent researchers (e.g. Denison, 1990) supported this idea. However, as critics were not too unkind to point out, many of the so-called excellent companies had in fact become far less successful within 18 months of *In Search of Excellence* being published. The change in their circumstances did not slow the roll-out of the rhetoric of excellence in management-speak, however. It proliferated rapidly. Soon, nearly every manager and wannabe manager could be heard talking about how important searching for excellence was and many management consultants were only too happy to help design a culture to make this happen.

In Search of Excellence propelled culture to centre stage in corporate analysis, resulting in related research referred to as *excellence studies*. The message was simple: great companies have excellent cultures. Excellent cultures deliver outstanding financial success. What makes a culture excellent are shared core values and presuppositions that are acted on. In addition to other books, such as *Corporate Cultures: The Rites and Rituals of Corporate Life* (Deal and Kennedy, 1982) and *Organizational Culture and Leadership* (Schein, 1997), the new emphasis made culture a popular and acceptable topic in business. Excellence studies stressed how a pattern of learned and shared basic assumptions framed organization members' perceptions, thoughts and feelings.

Put simply, culture as a tool encompassed the following questions:

- How were things done in particular organizations?
- What was acceptable behaviour?
- What norms were imparted to new members?
- What norms were members expected to use to solve problems of external adaptation and internal integration, and which ones did they actually use?

Despite *In Search of Excellence* being a huge commercial success, it is, analytically, too one-dimensional, too focused on culture as just one aspect of organization life, too focused on the stories of top managers and thus serving somewhat as propaganda for the managerial elite and their views of the way culture should be. But millions read it.

If we go back to consider Schein's views, not just using the metaphor of an iceberg but thinking of the different levels as targets that have variable degrees of difficulty to score in we can see how they may be difficult to manage. While it is relatively easy to introduce a new uniform or artwork to an organization, thus changing the artefacts, the bullseye of values is much more difficult to hit. New CEOs can espouse values and issue mission and vision statements, as level 2 initiatives; however, their impact may be limited if employees do not take them seriously, treat them hypocritically or cannot recall them. Such devices, when introduced by leaders, can easily be subject to the criticism that the pious words do not match up with real actions – that the statements are those of a hypocritical organization (see Lagace, 2006 [https://hbswk.hbs.edu/item/corporate-values-and-employee-cynicism], reporting on Cha and Edmondson, 2006).

In fact, the articulation of mission and vision values can inadvertently give rise to employee disenchantment, despite the good intentions of leaders and followers. Employee sensemaking triggered by strong organizational values can increase the risk of attributing leader hypocrisy, leading to employee disenchantment in a process Cha and Edmondson (2006) call the hypocrisy attribution dynamic. Strong statements of values may increase followers' experience of meaning at work but also increase the risk of subsequent disenchantment when behaviours do not match values. More recent research bears this view out: Guiso, Sapienza and Zingales (2015) researched what dimensions of corporate culture were related to a firm's performance and found that proclaimed values appeared to be irrelevant. It is, perhaps, not surprising that value proclamations in mission and vision statements have little impact on performance if they are treated, with reason, as hypocritical precisely because they do not mirror practice.

WHAT WOULD YOU DO?

WHAT WOULD YOU DO?

You are a manager. You are trying to complete an urgent report for your boss. One of the people that report to you comes to you with a complaint against another member of the team. What would you do? What do you think would be the implications of what you would do for the organization's culture?

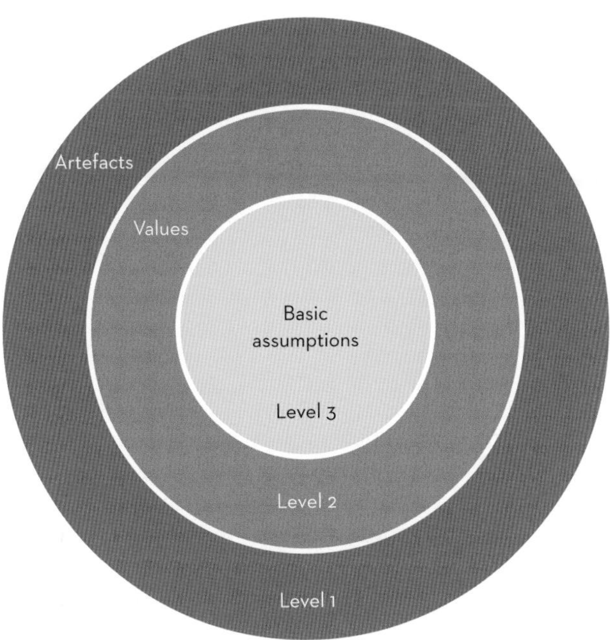

FIGURE 6.2 The levels of culture as targets, according to Schein

DESIGNING CULTURE

Management practitioners often seek to use culture and control to try and frame the subjectivity of their employees – to try and get them to see things with the same set of relevancies that they have as managers. We see this most readily in some accounts of quality management, such as the Six-Sigma movement popular in Japan and much of East Asia (Kono and Clegg, 2001). Principles such as *seiri* (putting-in-order), *seiton* (arrange properly), *seiketsu* (cleanliness), *seiso* (cleaning) and *shitsuke* (good behaviour), seen in many plants of Japanese corporations, seek to govern not only the workplace but also the comportment of employees in the workplace (March, 1996).

Much contemporary organizational culture discourse represents a desire by management to enlist workers' cooperation, compliance and commitment to create an *esprit de corps* with which to limit human recalcitrance at work. The rhetoric of control, coupled with a new vocabulary of teamwork, quality, flexibility and learning organizations, constitutes culture management projects that seek to create culture as a mechanism of soft domination (see also pp. 274–7) through cultural change programmes (Casey, 1995; du Gay, 2000a; Jacques, 1996).

Organizational culture that prescribes norm-defined management techniques and habit-inducing routines seeks to create an obedient and disciplined consciousness around those sets of beliefs and values that the organization favours. Usually, these promise a new corporate personhood, a new corporate subjectivity and even a new corporate embodiment: think of highly designed conceptions of organizational culture that frame what it means to be an organization member.

WATCH THE CARMAZZI VIDEO

EXTEND YOUR KNOWLEDGE

For insight into a hyper-consulting view of building an integrative culture, watch the 2017 video 'Organizational Culture - The 5 Pillars Change with Arthur Carmazzi' on YouTube (www.youtube.com/watch?v=RVo8VduckdY) which is not intended as a parody of organizational culture consulting - but succeeds in being so.

For Casey (1995), a designed culture has the following characteristics:

1. Individual enthusiasm manifested in the values of dedication, loyalty, self-sacrifice and passion. These values translate into use of the organizationally approved forms of language, including buzz-terms, as well as a willingness to be part of the team at work, in play and recreation (joining in at the pub, for instance), and putting in long hours at work – where you earn your salary from 9 to 5 and your promotion from 5 to 9.
2. A strong customer focus, where customers are not just the end-users but employees, and other significant stakeholders are thought of as customers.
3. Management discourse characterized by a language of team and family inclusive of everyone – even if they would prefer not to be a part of the team or family.
4. Finally, there is public display of the designer culture. There will be many artefacts, such as websites, that display images of the culture, such as team photos, team awards, employee of the month, and such like.

Owners and senior managers who have a paternalistic relation to their employees will urge them to be part of the organization family. The use of family metaphors – 'we're all one big happy family here' – is particularly inappropriate. The family metaphor is widely used to try and represent an organizational culture, as, for instance, when people talk of disloyalty when an employee criticizes the firm or approaches another organization for a position – almost as if they were having an affair! Of course, the whole notion of the organization being metaphorically aligned with a family is suspect. Are managers then parents and employees children? Here is our advice: beware of employers suggesting that the organization in which you work is like a family!

ORGANIZATIONAL CULTURE: A TOOL THAT TRAVELS

Organizational culture is an extremely versatile tool: for instance, it can be used to create the appearance of not only a corporate culture but also a familial culture. By the twenty-first century, the corporate culture phenomenon that had characterized 1980s management in the Western world had reached the shores of China where it influenced the management of some of the largest Chinese business firms. Arriving in China, its destination completed a strange journey of over half a century. The concept of corporate culture evolved, in part, from early research by Edgar Schein into the 'brainwashing' of captured GIs by the PRC-backed North Korean army during the Korean War. In studies of the experiences of such people during the Korean War defections, Schein (1961; also see 2006) concluded that 'brainwashing' was an inappropriate concept to account for the renunciation of US citizenship by these captured GIs; in fact, the Chinese term for the practice was more appropriately translated as 'thought reform'. The Chinese captors were able to elicit public anti-American statements from prisoners by placing them under harsh conditions of deprivation with the offer of more comfortable conditions for recanting. The prisoners did not actually convert to Communism but rather behaved as though they did in order to avoid further extreme physical coercion. Moreover, the few prisoners that were influenced by Communist indoctrination did so as a result of motives and personality characteristics that existed before imprisonment. Those who were vulnerable to a need for certainty, especially if certainty was presented to them in attractive terms, with unpalatable alternatives, were most easily disposed to profess what was offered to them.

Schein (1961) realized that whatever form of indoctrination was being attempted, indoctrination methods were quite similar: the message might be different but the process was essentially the same. From this insight he developed the following views. First, he deduced that group and organizational forces are stronger than individual forces and that once an individual feels psychologically safe, he or she can accept new information either through identification with others or by scanning the environment for new solutions. Schein (2010) argues that change occurs by 'cognitive redefinition' through:

- semantic change in old concepts
- change in 'adaptation level' or judgement standards as to how a given behaviour or perceived object is to be judged
- the introduction of new concepts and meanings.

It was these insights that contributed to Schein's famous work on corporate cultural change as a threefold process encompassing change in artefacts, behaviours and values. Where artefacts reinforce centrally directed messages, and where behaviours model these messages, then values, the subconscious of collective culture, may change. Even if they do not, where behaviours change, the more ambiguous the situation, the more the individual will rely on the perceptions and judgements of others, especially where these are socially and personally reinforced and confirmed.

If people can be persuaded to embrace a particular belief system as if it were their own, there is a reduced need for explicit forms of surveillance because their behaviour will be self-guided in the appropriate directions, therefore requiring minimal oversight (Tourish, 2013: 56). The key is the blocking of any questioning, reflective or reflexive attitudes, or, in other words, restricting the capacity of subjects to think for themselves (Stacey, 2012: 83).

While the imprisonment of US citizens during the Korean War is clearly not analogous with the context of most contemporary organizations, Tourish (2013), basing his table on Schein's (1961) theory, identified nine techniques that could be used, irrespective of the message, for creating cultural cohesion (see Table 6.1).

TABLE 6.1 Techniques for cultural cohesion

Technique	Description
Reference group affiliation	People identify with those they are organizationally close to as a way of reducing anxiety about belonging
Role modelling	Organizations develop systems of role modelling and mentoring so that members learn appropriate behaviour
Peer pressure	A focus on team working, shared rewards and shared consequences intensify peer pressure to conform
Identity alignment	Repetition of core elements of organizational identity, often conveyed in mission and vision statements
Performance assessment	Employees are assessed based on their conformity with strategy and its practice
Reward systems	Conformity with expectations is rewarded
Communication control	Organizational messaging is tightly controlled
Work/life balance	Organization members are expected to work longer hours and expend greater effort as a means of demonstrating conformity and commitment
Psychological safety	It is stressed that conformity and commitment to organization values is expected and required as the right thing to do

Source: Adapted and extended from Price (2004). Reproduced by permission of Cengage Learning EMEA Ltd.

An article discussing the adoption of these techniques of persuasion in the People's Republic of China notes their widespread use as a part of cultural framing in key institutional areas of contemporary Chinese organizational life. The major institution promulgating this cultural framing is the Chinese Communist Party (CCP). The Party increasingly promotes and extols traditional Chinese cultural values through a policy and administration of deliberately designed corporate culture within its state-owned and private enterprises as well as in educational institutions.

Hawes (2012) traces the early application and adaptation of Western corporate culture in a growing literature on corporate culture in China. Hawes' (2012) search of the *China National Knowledge Infrastructure China Academic Journals* database revealed a steady increase in the number of articles with corporate culture in their titles published by Chinese academics and management consultants (Table 6.2).

TABLE 6.2 References to corporate culture in Chinese sources

Year	Number of corporate culture references
1986	10
1991	177
1996	696
2001	1,144
2008	3,661
2018	5,590

Source: China Academic Journals Full-text Database

Besides being a popular topic in Chinese management literature, corporate culture discourse has strongly influenced management practices and the vast majority of China's top 300 corporations have, according to Hawes' survey, set up corporate culture programmes and referenced their firms' chosen cultural values and the ways they attempt to implement their values among employees and managers as part of their websites.

The emphasis on 'culture' in Chinese corporations aligns with the Chinese government in its vigorous sponsorship of national corporate culture conferences as well as its subsidy of culture training for executives. The rationale articulated by the CCP is that 'building an advanced corporate culture is a significant factor in strengthening the Party's hold on power, in forcefully developing a progressive socialist culture, and in building a harmonious socialist society' (State-Owned Assets Supervision and Administration Commission of the State Council, 2005). Corporate culture building is intended to improve the quality of management, strengthen internal cohesion and build competitiveness, while organically integrating with Communist Party doctrines.

The shift to consolidating corporate culture as a basis for collective identity recognizes that it is more effective to build culture by organization rather than seek to conquer the whole of society from a single centre of command. It is a shift from a form of state to organizational corporatism (Callick, 2013; Hawes, 2012). The process is carried out in phases, initially being launched in state-owned enterprises followed by private firms throughout China, as Chan and colleagues (2018) demonstrate.

EXTEND YOUR KNOWLEDGE

READ THE ARTICLE

Management and organization in contemporary China is a fascinating and important area for analysis, given that the Chinese economy is now globally dominant. In the following article: Chan, A., Clegg, S. and Warr, M. (2018) 'Translating intervention: when corporate culture meets Chinese socialism', *Journal of Management Inquiry*, doi/abs/10.1177/1056492617696888, which is available at the companion website https://study.sagepub.com/managingandorganizations5e, the management practices of contemporary Chinese organizations are explored in detail, with a focus on organizational culture, its design and transmission.

THE CULTURE OF CULTURE

CULTURE FROM AN ANTHROPOLOGICAL PERSPECTIVE

Whereas contemporary anthropologists seek to study a culture as it is, without influencing it in any way, managers assume that culture can be designed according to the dictates of the manager. Management consultants make a lot of money out of implementing culture change programmes and yet research findings suggest that 90 per cent of culture change programmes fail (Carr et al., 1996). Not surprisingly, more anthropologically oriented researchers are horrified at the instrumental, naïve and managerialist appropriation of culture as a tool. From a more anthropological perspective, they are inclined to see culture as a practice in terms of a more conflict-oriented, fragmentary view, questioning the unitary assumptions of managerialist approaches.

Anthropologically, culture refers to something that the organization *is*, its 'nature', its being. Organizations don't have cultures that can be changed by design but are cultures in which there is a 'sense of commonality, or taken for grantedness ... necessary for continuing organized activity so that interaction can take place without constant interpretation and re-interpretation of meaning' (Smircich, 1985: 64). Above all, culture implies that organizations have a rich and deep symbolic life. One way that we learn the nature of this symbolic life is through organization stories.

ORGANIZATIONAL STORIES AND MANAGEMENT SPEAK?

Stories are an important part of organizations; often, they circulate as gossip, sometimes as part of the informal legends, sagas and mythologies of the organization and characters deemed important in its history. Stories may be transmitted orally through storytelling, although they can be recorded and become a text that is part of the official story – think of how Silicon Valley companies such as Apple and Hewlett-Packard, which started off in garages and grew to become global corporations, celebrate their origins in stories about their founders' humble beginnings in inauspicious surroundings. Research on corporate cultures has used stories about top leadership that circulated widely in the organization as data. Phenomena such as organizational myths and legends are thus as important for research as common behavioural patterns or the new corporate values that senior management wishes to inculcate (Schein, 2002).

Every organization is the repository of many stories. Organizations are characterized by complex differentiations of work titles and divisions; departments and hierarchical levels organize responsibilities and relationships, often determining who can do what, where, when, in what ways, with what degrees of freedom in terms of the disposition of time, dress, demeanour and other aspects of identity. Typically there will be strong differences in terms of meanings, values and symbols between people distributed amongst these complex differentiations. In addition, organizations employ people of varying ages, genders, classes, skills and professional knowledge, all of which tend to 'produce and sustain cultural variety and fragmentation rather than overall organizational cultural unity and coherence' (Alvesson and Svenningsson, 2008: 39).

Many subcultures exist within organizations outside of the official culture engineered and sanctioned by management, beyond the knowledge and control of management. The existence of such subcultures (and every organization has them) suggests that the ideal of an integrated managerially sanctioned culture is a myth. Culture is not just the formally approved ways of doing things; it is also the sly games, informal rules and deviant subcultures of lower-level employees against supervisors, and supervisors against lower-level employees, women against men and men against women, and creatives against management types as well as management types against creatives (Burawoy, 1979; Rosen, 2002; Young, 1989).

CULTURE AND CLARITY

LISTEN TO AN EXAMPLE

The ex-*Financial Times* business journalist Lucy Kellaway, while she still practised journalism, gave awards each year for what she called heights of corporate 'jargon' and 'guff'. You should listen to her examples – they are really bad – and, in consequence, really funny. Her final award in 2017 was for eBay's claim that

> 'We are passionate about harnessing our platform to empower millions of people by levelling the playing field for them.' Bingo! In fewer than 20 words it combined five previous years' winners, only to say nothing at all. With a heavy heart, I award eBay my overall Golden Flannel Award.

It is possible to speak clearly and effectively and communicate important messages about organization culture in doing so.

WATCH MARTIN LUTHER KING SPEECH

WATCH JULIA GILLARD SPEECH

WHAT WOULD YOU DO?

The culture of language – especially organizational and management language – matters. There are few great speeches by politicians and business leaders – indeed, the author has never heard a great speech by a business leader – but the few that there are shine like a beacon of clarity in that sea of sludge that passes for managerial and leaderly discourse. Two that stand out are speeches by Martin Luther KIng and Julia Gillard.

Question

1. In terms of organization culture, what are the key elements in these two speeches?
2. What similarities are there between them?

Culture in organizations and between people in them cannot be ignored. It might not be as manageable as consultants suggest but it has to be understood. Clear language use by managers is an important element in providing sense for others as well as making sense of what others are saying and doing. Managers need to be practical ethnographers, able to understand what's going on, and what's going on will not always be positively designed culture.

The ways that we make sense of the social realities of everyday working life in organizations can be thought of as texts. Various accounts and stories abound, with which we seek to enrol and influence others who are trying to do the same to us – they want us to accept their versions of affairs just as we might be committed to our versions. Many different accounts circulate in organizations. Some of these we are familiar with; others we are aware of as fragmentary accounts, and some are unknown to us. The official accounts may be well known and are often dismissed, rightly, as weasel words, as corporate guff, but there are also absolutely clear unofficial and often downright scurrilous accounts circulating as well, such that one might be foolish to believe just the official story. It is a

Antenarrative is the process by which already existing narratives link to other accounts to make a 'living story'.

fragment of what's going on but not the whole story: indeed, it is often designed to cover the whole story in linguistic sludge, clag and gruel. The fragmentary **antenarratives** that abound in the organization, perhaps commenting and speculating on the more formal accounts, often have the virtue of clarity rather than being deliberately constructed to be as opaque as possible.

David Boje (2001, 2008) has written extensively about antenarratives and how stories circulate as either literal texts or discourses that are text-like. Such stories are often fragments, lacking clear beginnings, middles and ends. They have the capacity to spiral out of their progenitors' control, dynamically changing meanings as they do so, pulling in other hitherto unrelated stories, creating a hetroglossic effect of many voicings that are not necessarily in accord or easily translated the one to the other.

Such stories are all social constructions with the texts reflecting different accounts that we reflect on in various ways. These texts – whether formal or informal in their production – are fabricated as bricolage made up from whatever materials and resources organization stories provide. Using these resources, different organizational members will seek to talk some particular sense into being and, in doing so, the sense of other accounts or ideas is denied or questioned. The organization is thus a complex of living stories.

Obviously, managers will try and frame, steer, nudge the sensemaking about stories that occurs in organizations. Doing so is a subtle skill, one not easy to practise. It is much more than making pronouncements or telling people what the culture is. It is about being sensitive to different accounts, trying to explain preferred stories in simple and clear terms and trying to win assent to them. It helps if the stories are plausible, of course, not just the imaginings of out-of-touch executives or consultants who have only a partial, incomplete understanding of the situation.

Organization change (see Chapter 11) is usually an open, continuous and unpredictable process, without any clear beginning or ending, rather than being tightly scripted and controlled. Management obviously plans change but in implementing whatever is planned it will invariably be the case that plans are reinterpreted and altered in unanticipated ways. Organizational reality is invariably more chaotic and complex than organizational planning allows. Resistance, politics, negotiation, conflictual sensemaking and misunderstandings are normal (Balogun, 2006; Dawson, 2003; Pettigrew et al., 2001). Consequently, organizational change is rarely a matter of carrying out a sequential list of steps successfully.

Buchanan and Badham (2008) are the primary realists when it comes to organizational culture change programmes. Such initiatives, they propose, are characterized by the following. It may not be overtly admitted but organizational life is inherently political despite rational arguments being advanced to defend or oppose cultural change programmes when they are on the agenda. Accounts of why things should change or stay the same will invariably be presented as being in the interest of the organization; being par for the course, that almost goes without saying. Underlying the seemingly rational surface of organizational agreement, there will be political motives, agendas and behaviours. On the surface, this may not be apparent; beneath the surface is where the reality resides.

Although rarely acknowledged as such either by many managers or many management theorists, politics are an integral part of everyday organizational life.

Sometimes the politics are tough, negative and conflictual but there is another face to politics, one that is positive, empowering and transformational. It all depends on the culture. If the culture is premised on zero-sum games in which one side wins and another must lose, the former will tend to prevail. Where the culture is more inclusive, participatory and democratic, there is the possibility of empowerment that does not necessarily disempower others.

Planned organizational change programmes invariably run up against the complex realities of cultural heterogeneity, as we have discussed, which managerial change models often do not take seriously enough. The message of the change programme will often lead to diverse responses that are embedded in and reinforce existing sources of differentiation and fragmentation – even when the intent is to overcome these by creating a more unitary culture. The stratification of levels of culture that Schein identifies tend to make risky any change programme's plans for a designed culture. An overwhelming sense of different identities with their diverse organizationally embedded constructions of meaning and sensemaking makes planned change unfolding smoothly, 'according to plan', something that is a rare occurrence. How diverse people make sense in a complex organization cannot be assumed to follow managerially espoused organizational plans and values, especially if these are opaquely expressed in meaning light jargon; there will always be situational meanings in play.

IN PRACTICE

In early 2018, the international UK-based company, Carillion plc, a major construction and outsourcing company, collapsed into liquidation. Carillion had a very positive organizational culture, according to its website. Read about its organizational culture and then read about some other versions of its organizational reality at the other two sites.

READ MORE ABOUT CARILLION

Question

1. Thinking about Carillion's values, in reality how well and for whom primarily were these implemented?

CULTURE: INTEGRATED, DIFFERENTIATED AND FRAGMENTED

By now it should be clear that there is a fair degree of ambivalence and controversy about the nature of organizational culture. Martin (2002), in a classic contribution, distinguishes between three perspectives on organization culture that stress one or other of *integration*, *differentiation* or *fragmentation*. The integration perspective is most amenable to the tool view; the differentiation perspective points out structural obstacles to the use of the tool; while the fragmentation perspective stresses that the use of any tool is always embedded in practice.

Integration characterizes a situation in which everyone shares the same culture and there are no contrary cultures or ambiguities about the culture.

INTEGRATION PERSPECTIVE

The excellence studies made perfect sense to managers because they provided generic solutions that seemed to be capable of being applied to many problems that could now be reclassified as culture issues. The great strength of the excellent culture perspective was that it seemed to promise the dissolution of all that friction and resistance that managers know they often produce routinely, as a normal part of their work. In the place of conflict, it offered **integration**.

Indeed, some analysts refer to the strong cultures model as an integration perspective. According to Martin and Frost (1996), integration theorists defined *culture* as a phenomenon that was consistent and clear, including in their evidence only manifestations of it that accorded with definitions of a unified culture, thus excising all the plural and non-integrative aspects of the culture.

Integration theorists define *culture* as 'organization-wide agreement with values espoused by top management' (Martin and Frost, 1996: 608). Often, they suggest, such agreement was assumed by researchers only after the views of top management had been sampled! When decisions were not overtly biased by sampling decisions to exclude the likely sources of dissenting views, they were often made to exclude any data that seemed to suggest a weak or fragmented culture as an inconsequential margin to the central cultural values. Martin and Frost (1996: 608) are scathing:

> [E]ach 'strong' culture was a monolith where every manifestation reinforced the values of top management, employees complied with managerial directives, and preferences were assumed to share these values, and there was, apparently, only one interpretation of the meaning of events shared by all. These studies were designed so integration research would find what it was looking for.

IMPLICATIONS OF INTEGRATION PERSPECTIVES

Many anthropologically inclined researchers were critical of the integrationist findings because they systematically excluded resistance, subcultures and countercultures from their analysis. These critics saw the integrationist concept of dominant cultures as one that stressed a unitary perspective because it privileged the views of managers of the organization against those for whom a subculture, or even subcultures, might be more important (Willmott, 2002 [1973]). Only one culture – the official culture – was envisaged. Subcultures may form around the status attributes of the workforce (such as ethnicity, gender, class and skill) or on the basis of spatial markers (such as where people work and the conditions under which their work is performed). Sometimes, there may be a well-organized counterculture centred on a union or an ethnic subculture, reinforced by a strong sense of community among co-workers. Often, this is the case among those who do blue-collar, dangerous work, including dockers, miners and construction workers.

The integration theorists countered that if you went looking long enough and hard enough for such things as subcultures, you would be sure to find them, especially, the critics continued, if the research consisted of 'focused, non-random samples of lower level employees' and if the process involved 'ignoring (or not searching for) evidence of values shared on an organization-wide basis' (Martin and Frost, 1996: 608). Integrationists hold that, if properly conducted with appropriate skill, even ethnographers could come to see that deep fundamental values might be shared by a majority of organization members (Schein, 1997).

Ethnography understands organizational life as it happens from the point of view of understanding what and how everyday meanings and understandings are socially constructed.

Predictably, with such disagreement between researchers surfacing in the public arena, the idea that culture might be a quick fix for corporate ills became harder to market. The committed ethnographic researchers were never very interested in the market, anyway. They saw themselves as more akin to anthropologists who practised long-term participant observation and brought tales from the field to the public arena (Van Maanen, 1988). For such researchers, resistance to an imposed organization culture was not an attribute of insufficient socialization and deviance but a part of the forming of cultures.

LEARN MORE ABOUT ETHNOGRAPHY

Smircich (2002) was particularly critical of the approach to data collection by functionalist researchers. Typically, they had little deep knowledge of the culture that they wrote about, knowledge that should be gained from **ethnography** and the use of anthropological methods (e.g. living in and mingling intimately with the community being researched). Usually, they just administered a questionnaire with a series of questions and Likert-scale response sets. One consequence was that the studies of excellence often ended up being accounts of the espoused values of the top management as if they were the values characterized throughout the organization, rather than being a study of the values actually used by all managers in practice. Thus, these 'excellent' cultures were more often than not top managerial wishes, the fulfilment of which was empirically questionable because the ethnographically rich data that might address it had often not been collected. Much of the best work on organizational culture consists of organizational ethnographies.

DIFFERENTIATION PERSPECTIVE

Martin (1992) became particularly concerned with the lack of concordance between researchers from different perspectives using different methodologies. In the perspective that she classified as 'integration research', discussed previously, the a priori assumptions were that culture was the vehicle of integration for organizations; consequently, that was what was researched. In the perspective that she called **differentiation perspective**, the assumption was that more than one culture was likely to be the norm; thus, researchers started with a predisposition to see plural cultures rooted in different experiences within organizations.

The **differentiation perspective** does not expect organizational cultures to be monolithic but holds that there are plural conceptions of culture with tensions existing among them.

Organizations may have members who share strong values about basic beliefs with some, but not all, of the other members of the organization. There will be cliques and cabals, relatively separate lunch networks and distinct coffee circles. When these groups are sufficiently clearly articulated in terms of cultures, we refer to them as *subcultures*, which are occupational and professional groups that reflect different interests, tastes and habits; such subcultures develop alongside whatever may be the formally acknowledged organizational culture. Subcultures coexist with other cultures and can become dominant if they can unify adherents through the use of resources, symbols and other forms of meaning, and may even become dominant and legitimate when they reflect a cohesive group and defend plausible ideas. Where they challenge legitimate values, they might become a counterculture engaged in oppositional activities.

IMPLICATIONS OF DIFFERENTIATION PERSPECTIVES

The problem with the differentiation perspective, suggest its critics, is that if you expect difference and resistance a priori then you will probably find it. Moreover, if the expectation is that there are irreconcilable interests between different genders, religions, ethnicities or classes, then this is not very useful to the manager who has to manage these tensions. Sure, it gives them some intelligence about what the issues are that they might expect but it doesn't promise a solution. On the other hand, it should forearm managers with a degree of scepticism for the highly integrationist solutions and assumptions that are often offered to them by consultants and senior executives out of touch with the realities of the office or shop floor. From this perspective, a little basic sociology should make for better-informed and less naïve managers. If their expectations are that conflicts and tensions are likely to be structurally deep-seated, they won't be surprised when they meet examples in practice.

The best ways of dealing with tensions caused by structural sources of differentiation, such as ethnicity, class and gender, is to acknowledge the differences, try to be transparent about the difficulties that occur, and maintain open management that is inclusive, in part by ensuring that the different interests all gain representation in important meetings, committees, project teams, and so on.

FRAGMENTATION PERSPECTIVE

Cultures may be simultaneously somewhat integrated and somewhat differentiated and also somewhat fragmented. An organizational culture might be *integrated* when it reflects a wide consensus, *differentiated* when it is confined to separate subcultures, or *fragmented* when there is little consensus and the situation is essentially ambiguous. Although Martin suggests that these conditions can be found simultaneously at *a given time*, they also provide a framework for depicting changes in organizational culture *over time*, such as in Gouldner's (1954) classic study of a gypsum plant. We could easily describe that study's events in terms of a shift from an integrated culture of community to one that became differentiated due to top management change and then fragmented by unexpected strike action in response to management's changes.

From any perspective that sees organizational culture as more akin to fluid processes than stable value systems, measuring culture would be meaningless. We can understand its fluent and changing nature better through ethnographic case studies. Chan (2003: 313) argues that the 'treatment of culture as a fixed, unitary, bounded entity has to give way to a sense of fluidity and permeability'. He suggests that earlier studies of organizations as essentially 'negotiated orders' (Strauss et al., 1963) are better guides to managerial behaviour. Rather than seeing the organization as a fixed pattern, managers should instead look at the ways that the members of the organization use its resources (including conceptions of its values and culture) constantly to negotiate the sense of what it is that they are doing in and as an organization. In this view, the members of the organization create culture from the mundane, everyday aspects of their work and often use the managerially approved dominant culture as a resource in doing so but not always in ways that would be approved within its rhetoric (Linstead and Grafton-Small, 2002).

Chan (2003) suggests that culture should be thought of as a way of accounting for what has been done in and around an organization, as a way of making sense of what has been experienced. Thought of in this way, culture is far harder to engineer than the strong-culture perspective suggests. Rather than being just a matter of replacing one set of normative assumptions with an alternative set, producing yet another mission and vision statement, culture consists of loosely negotiated, tacit ways of making sense that are embedded in specific situations in the organization, rather than an all-enveloping structure that somehow contains all who are members. Because culture is overwhelmingly situational, culture is usually quite fragmentary, forming around certain emergent issues and then dissolving. Often, managers take different sides on these issues and are thus themselves divided.

These views are known as the **fragmentation perspective**. The fragmentation approach shares very little with the normative integration theorists, who argue for the benefits of a strong culture, and the differentiation proponents, who say that a strong culture equals a dominant culture, and a dominant culture is one that subordinates differentiated subcultures.

The **fragmentation perspective** sees culture as neither *clearly* consistent nor *clearly* contested but shifting and fragmentary as issues arise and different coalitions of interest form.

The picture represented by fragmentation perspectives is likely to be one that represents contradictory and confusing cultures battling for the soul of the organization as well as those of its employees. Individuals are likely to exist in a state of competing cultural commitments, where they are constantly under competing pressures to identify themselves and their organization with rival conceptions of an appropriate cultural identity. In such a situation, 'consensus is transient and issue specific, producing short-lived affinities among individuals that are quickly replaced by a different pattern of affinities, as a different issue draws the attention of cultural members' (Martin and Frost, 1996: 609, citing the work of Kreiner and Schultz (1993) on emergent culture in R&D networks as an example).

IMPLICATIONS OF FRAGMENTATION PERSPECTIVE

Managers schooled in the fragmentation perspective should expect the realities they manage to be complex and ever changing, in process, liquid rather than carved in stone. The good news is that the deep-seated tensions that the differentiation perspective sees may be more fluid than imagined. The bad news is that you never know which issues will emerge as points of coalescence of local interests in antipathy to formal policies and strategies. From this perspective, organizational cultures are unpredictable and a pest. They sow confusion for managers rather than being aids to efficient management.

Organizational cultures overlap and are only partially understood in terms of common sensemaking. Culture is not about a clear, sharp image of corporate and individual identity; it is about ambiguity. Confusion is normal; asking questions about clarity is not. Culture is an artefact of the methods used to investigate it and the assumptions that make such an investigation possible. Realistically, if you cannot define culture clearly, and the people whose culture it is supposed to be do not know what it is, it can hardly be the cure for corporate ills. One implication is that an organization can change over time from being integrated, differentiated or fragmented. Suzana Braga Rodrigues (2006) presents a rare historical and contextual account of an organizational culture undergoing substantial change over a period of years. By focusing on a long slice of time, she provides insight into Martin's (1992, 2000, 2002) views of cultural integration, differentiation and fragmentation as they unfold politically over time. Most studies of organizational culture have been cross-sectional and therefore unable to explore in any depth the questions of how and why culture changes in the direction of differentiation or otherwise over time.

Rodrigues shows that institutional forces interact with internal political actors in organizational culture change. Institutions empower or disempower certain categories of actor and create or deactivate the rules that foster alliances and different social formations. When a powerful group or leading coalition supports an organizational culture, it tends to be integrated; where there is incapacity by the leading group to satisfy the interests of other groups, fragmentation is likely. The more institutionalized an organization's environment, the more likely it will be that institutional agencies will influence its prevailing culture. In such environments, where external institutional actors control the leadership's mandate from above, power and legitimacy do not necessarily cohere. The dynamics of culture change are seen to centre on the confluence of internal political forces with external institutional parameters. Cultural change is a multifaceted and multilevel process. Whether change pushes culture in organizations in the direction either of cultural integration or differentiation depends on the legitimacy of internal coalitions and their capacity to sustain integrative ideals.

CULTURES NOT CULTURE

As young people enter the workforce after graduation, they have to adjust to the organization cultures in which they find themselves. Not surprisingly, they do not always do so in the same ways. The range of identities adopted lends support to the fragmentation thesis: in the same situation, the organization culture appears quite dissimilar in fragmentary ways that, nonetheless, are coherent in themselves. For example, rapidly changing institutional and organizational conditions make professional identity today highly contextually specific. Professionals are increasingly employed in contemporary organizations conceptualized as 'hybrid settings' (e.g. doctors working in national health services), in which the 'hybrid worker' is one who is simultaneously a professional and a bureaucrat (i.e. unquestioningly obeying authority) and also enterprising, the kind of person that values individual initiative, judgement and risk-taking (Bardon et al., 2012). In such settings, professional workers may struggle to balance their multiple and often conflicting identities: on the one hand, they identify as culturally integrative in terms of being the professionals they trained to become in professional training; on the other hand, their professional training has to be accommodated to a professionally managed organization in which the norms of the profession and the norms of management do not always cohere.

Professionals such as physicians, architects, accountants and lawyers, whose senses of existing identities are deeply entrenched, appear to face distinct identity challenges associated with the diffusion of managerialism into organization cultures, which research suggests professionals tend to negatively construe (e.g. Joffe and MacKenzie-Davey, 2012). Individual workers negotiate these tensions in their everyday work by engaging in 'identity work' through which they actively 'construct their identities in a manner that preserves a positive understanding of who they are' as their self-concept (Wei, 2012: 446). Given the complexity of the formation of multiple professional identities in many large and complex professional organizations, it should not be surprising if there is a tension between professional and managed identities. Identities are 'practical projects of everyday life' in which individuals strive to be 'able to exercise creative potential within the constraints imposed by social structures' (Coupland et al., 2008: 331). Not surprisingly, the result of this is to produce distinct patterns of culture that are both differentiated and fragmented.

Professionals increasingly face a range of fragmentary and often contradictory discourses, practices and logics (Bardon et al., 2012). In such conditions, reconciling contradictions and tensions in an overall sense of a common culture to 'affirm' workplace identities does not account for the complex challenges individuals face. Professionals' identity work may lead to multifaceted outcomes. Managers must expect that, in practice, managing means they will have to deal with fragmentation. Fragmentation in culture is to be expected when we are trying to capture a certain reality. Social realities are always already textual, composed in words and deeds by different people with different interests. All conceptions of what an organizational culture is will necessarily suppress, silence and marginalize some elements that some other account might instead privilege. That is, culture acts as a structure around individual behaviour: it constrains what actions you might take and encourages you in particular actions over others – as a result, formal, official cultural texts are powerful forces within organizations. They can be used as frames, points of reference, political tools and orienting devices. People can seek a sense of their self within the documents and texts that imply or state the organizational culture, but there is no reason to expect that they will only find direction in the officially approved texts.

New officially produced documents and texts are often produced by organizations to mark significant changes, such as a merger. These texts are endeavours at fostering cultural integration between two evidently separate and different cultures: clearly, on what we already have learnt, the attempt may be to integrate them while retaining elements of distinction in each or to differentiate them, to preserve their pre-existing cultural characteristics. There are other options: one might dominate the other in an attempt at assimilation or marginalization of the other culture. Van Marrewijk, a cultural anthropologist, chose to make a longitudinal analysis of cultural change through the process of a merger between a Telco and an Internet start-up (van Marrewijk, 2016). The Telco was aiming for innovation through the takeover; however, as it sought to assimilate the culture of the start-up – loose, informal, cyber-punk and anarchic – it ended up dominating and subordinating the innovative culture with its bureaucratic rules-based engineering culture, driving the innovators out elsewhere where they were not so constrained. Striving for cultural integration emptied the merger of the very capabilities that had animated the decision to merge in the first place.

MEASURING NATIONAL CULTURES

If it is a big assumption to think that organizations have a singular culture, how much bigger is the assumption that countries have a singular national culture? And that it can be measured? Some researchers argue that we *can* measure an organization's culture and its effects on performance (see Gordon and DiTomaso,

1992). One prominent researcher along these lines is Ashkenasy (2003), for whom values are the core component of organizational cultures. He says that conceptions of organizational culture are more reliable when they can be measured rather than just described and argues that the concept of a value system allows you to do this. Hofstede (1980) goes one step further: he says that you can measure the values of a national culture.

Geert Hofstede, the writer best known for having measured national culture in terms of values, studied only one organization – but he studied it in over 40 countries! In the second edition of his book *Culture's Consequences: Comparing Values, Behaviors, Institutions and Organizations across Nations* (2001), it was confirmed that the previously unidentified organization that Hofstede reported on in the 1980 edition was the multinational company IBM. He describes culture as 'mental programming', as 'software of the mind', as 'subjective'.

At base, Hofstede's views rely on a definition of values defined as invariant and stable preferences that manifest themselves in any situation, despite other contingencies; these values, it is assumed, are universally shared by the population of a given country, which makes the values recognizably coherent and thus 'national' in character. It is because of their fundamental character that, as in Schein's hierarchy of culture, they frame behaviour and shape artefacts. These values can be elicited by statistical analysis producing the mean scores of answers to self-response survey questions from a small organizational sample of a national population and can be factor analysed as 'dimensions' on which various nations may be contrasted.

Hofstede is a cultural determinist: for him the national culture will determine the shape of the organizational culture. While the population of a nation can be differentiated on many grounds, Hofstede claims that, nonetheless, a national population shares a unique culture. His empirical basis for this claim, however, is a statistical averaging of the principal data – questionnaire responses from IBM employees. It is as a statistical average based on individuals' views, which he calls a 'central tendency' (1991: 253), or 'an average tendency' (1991: 253). In other words, it is a statistical artefact. It has no real root in practice other than an averaging out of data and construction of a mean to represent its totality.

Hofstede's data drew on a data bank of 75,000 employee attitude surveys undertaken around 1967 and 1973 within IBM subsidiaries in 66 countries, which he analysed statistically. He found that the data demonstrated that there were four central dimensions of a national culture, such that 40 out of the 66 countries in which the IBM subsidiaries were located could be given a comparative score on each of these four dimensions. Hofstede (1980, 2001) defines these and some subsequently composed dimensions as follows:

1. *Power distance*: 'the extent to which the less powerful members of organizations and institutions within a country expect and accept that power is distributed unequally' (2001: 98).
2. *Uncertainty avoidance*: 'the extent to which the *members* of a culture feel threatened by uncertain or unknown situations' (2001: 161).
3. *Individualism versus collectivism*: Individualism 'stands for a society in which the ties between individuals are loose: Everyone is expected to

look after him/herself and her/his immediate family only. Collectivism stands for a society in which *people* from birth onwards are integrated into strong, cohesive in-groups, which throughout people's lifetime continue to protect them in exchange for unquestioning loyalty' (2001: 225).

4. *Masculinity versus femininity*: Masculinity 'stands for a society in which social gender roles are clearly distinct: Men are supposed to be assertive, tough, and focused on material success. Femininity stands for a society in which social gender roles overlap: Both men and women are supposed to be modest, tender, and concerned with the quality of life' (2001: 297).

The first four definitions were based on questionnaires from IBM employees. In 1991, drawing on research in Hong Kong and Taiwan, he had added a fifth dimension:

5. *Long-term orientation versus short-term orientation*: 'Long-term Orientation stands for the fostering of virtues oriented towards future rewards, in particular, perseverance and thrift. Its opposite pole, Short-term Orientation, stands for the fostering of virtues related to the past and present, in particular respect for tradition, preservation of "face" and fulfilling social obligations' (1991: 359).

In 2010, Hofstede et al. (2010) renamed the fifth dimension *pragmatic versus normative*, and added a sixth dimension:

6. *Indulgence versus restraint*: Indulgence stands for a society that allows relatively free gratification of basic and natural human drives related to enjoying life and having fun. Restraint stands for a society that suppresses the gratification of needs and regulates it by means of strict social norms.

READ MORE ABOUT HOFSTEDE

Hofstede arrived at the original and subsequent national patterns by averaging the means of data collected on individuals in terms of national samples. Consistent patterns were established in terms of national variation – variation according to the means, which were, of course, statistical devices for representing the sum of individual variance. The upshot would be similar to saying that the average Dutch person is taller than the average Chinese person; the statement accepts that the average is a summary device. The average tells you nothing about what any particular Dutch or Chinese person's height may be any more than it informs you about the values they hold. An average of values, although it is economical, is about as meaningful as an average of height. Just as there would be wide variance in the height of any given population, so there would be wide variance in the values of that population, a point that is well established in McSweeney's (2002) critique. As he says, Hofstede assumes that it is national cultures that produce the variance in his data but provides no evidence to support the assumption; any other classification made on the basis of another assumption would have done just as well – or as badly – as an explanatory device.

To accept Hofstede's analysis is to assume the cultural homogeneity of nations – that lines on a map inscribe a unitary, patterned and consistent common culture.

In the vast majority of cases in the contemporary world, this is hardly feasible. Neither are there few singularly ethnically, linguistically and culturally homogeneous countries among the major nations in the world, nor do their boundaries necessarily circumscribe a constant space. For one thing, boundaries change politically. Indeed, one of the countries that Hofstede (1980) treated as a unitary cultural space in his study, Yugoslavia, no longer exists as such – precisely because it was not a unitary cultural space in the first place, as indicated by the horrors of the 'ethnic cleansing' and associated mass murders in the early 1990s that were its major contribution to world affairs. For another thing, in many contemporary countries, modern identities are much more likely to be plural than singular, as shown in hybrid, hyphenated identities such as Anglo-Indian, Viet-Australian, and so on. Will the diversity that the organization's members display in their everyday life not be reflected as diversity in the organization as well?

Citizenship is not a very strong predictor of a common cultural identity as the battles for Scottish independence, the deadly struggles between Shia and Sunni citizens in countries such as Iraq, and the assertion of Catalonian nationalism in Spain, would suggest. The 2016 referendum in the United Kingdom on whether or not the UK should remain part of the European Union led to 2 per cent of the votes being for independence over continued membership. The UK is one country but the referendum results and the debates that ensued around the referendum suggest that it would be a grievous error to assume that the one country was characterized by value concordance. For example, Scottish desires for independent nationhood, reflected in the EU referendum votes, revealed that the construct of the UK submerged some very strongly divergent values. Elsewhere, as we have seen with the complex and current civil wars in Syria in the Middle East, citizenship can be a mask for a fragmented reality of religious beliefs and non-beliefs, linguistic differences and plural ethnic cultures.

It is difficult to see that Hofstede has much to offer managers, other than a nostalgia for times when, in most countries, you could rely on a bunch of similar men running things in their interests. You could argue that it is precisely because organizations are able to pick and choose who joins them – through human resource management practices – that they may be said to have specific national cultures (but the countries they operate in also have equal employment and anti-discrimination laws!). In other words, they might select people to fit what they think of as a national culture. Contrary to this viewpoint, however, many organizations have been torn apart by bitter internal conflicts, even when professionally managed by people with the same citizenship, which makes the idea of their having only one culture seem questionable. Considering 'nation' as the primal source of identity only makes sense as a piece of political rhetoric, as when a politician talks of national identity – which usually has both an inclusionary and an exclusionary focus.

National culture is certainly not as integrated as Hofstede suggests; indeed, Hofstede's position is ultimately one of romantic conservatism: conservatives insist that every state is based on a notion of a national culture. Historically, such notions feed into and from totalitarian nationalist fantasies. In its extreme form, it leads to a view of the predominant cultural space in which the members of other cultures (the 'others') who live in the same space must either respect the terms that the dominant culture prescribes or accept exclusion or, in extreme cases, be 'ethnically cleansed'.

Geert Hofstede's *Culture's Consequences* is well represented in controversies on the web. For instance, there is a site which includes summaries of Hofstede's work and critiques of it, the most useful of which is McSweeney's (2002) article from *Human Relations*, which is called 'Hofstede's model of national cultural differences and their consequences: a triumph of faith – a failure of analysis'.

READ THE ARTICLE

EXTEND YOUR KNOWLEDGE

Brendan McSweeney is Hofstede's most persistent critic. You can check out his most recent foray against Hofstede in a chapter in the book *Transculturalism and Business in the BRIC States: A Handbook* (Sánchez and Brühwiler, 2015), entitled 'Globe, Hofstede, Huntington, Trompenaars: common foundations, common flaws' (McSweeney, 2015). In this chapter, he extends his critique to include not only Hofstede but also other arguments that stress that 'national culture' shapes the behaviour of the populations of discrete national territories (countries) both within and outside of organizations (e.g. the decisions and actions of managers and consumers), by also addressing the multi-authored Global Leadership and Organizational Behaviour Effectiveness project (GLOBE) as well as the lesser-known work of Fons Trompenaars.

THE GLOBE VIEW OF NATIONAL CULTURE

The GLOBE project, conducted by Robert House and his international team of collaborators (House et al., 2004), was initiated to investigate one fundamental question: How is culture related to societal, organizational and leader effectiveness? The research project developed measures of culture for different countries, industries and organizations, focusing on what it termed both current practices and values. Its results were based on data from about 17,300 middle managers from 951 organizations in the food processing, financial services and telecommunications industries in 58 countries. Its results compare cultures in terms of their values and practices, and in terms of the leadership style of different cultures.

GLOBE built on findings by Hofstede (1980), Schwartz (1994), Smith (1995) and Inglehart (1997). The variables that they use to differentiate cultures are the following – some of which you will recognize from Hofstede's studies.

TABLE 6.3 The GLOBE Project

Variable	Description
Power distance	The degree to which members of a collective expect power to be distributed equally
Uncertainty avoidance	The extent to which a society, organization or group relies on social norms, rules and procedures to alleviate the unpredictability of future events

(Continued)

TABLE 6.3 (Continued)

Variable	Description
Humane orientation	The degree to which a collective encourages and rewards individuals for being fair, altruistic, generous, caring and kind to others
Institutional collectivism	The degree to which organizational and societal institutional practices encourage and reward the collective distribution of resources and collective action
In-group collectivism	The degree to which individuals express pride, loyalty and cohesiveness in their organizations or families
Assertiveness	The degree to which individuals are assertive, confrontational and aggressive in their relationships with others
Gender egalitarianism	The degree to which a collective minimizes gender inequality
Future orientation	The extent to which individuals engage in future-oriented behaviours such as delaying gratification, planning and investing in the future
Performance orientation	The degree to which a collective encourages and rewards group members for performance improvement and excellence

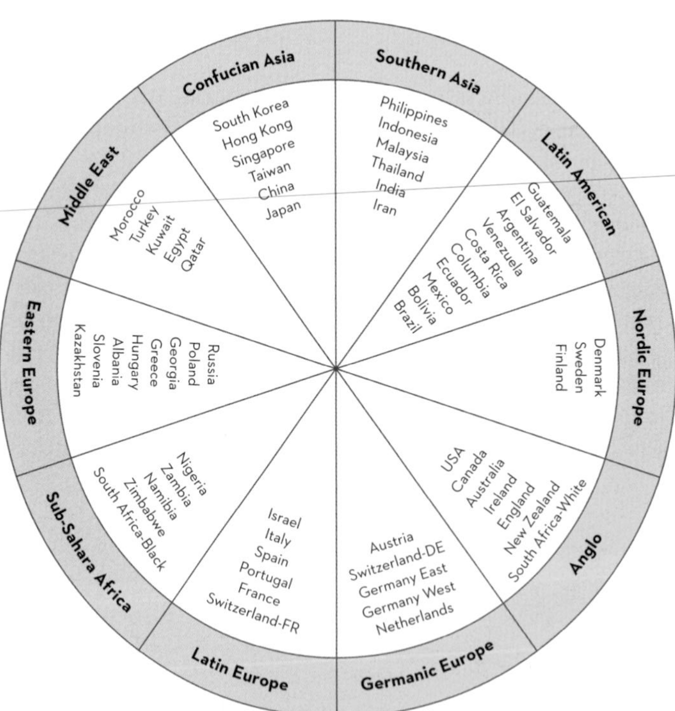

FIGURE 6.3 GLOBE's distribution of culture clusters

The GLOBE data placed 60 of the 62 societies into culture clusters, similar to those identified in other, previous studies (Inglehart, 1997; Ronen and Shenkar, 1985; Schwartz 1999). A cluster is defined by the cultural similarity of scores on the variables, with cultural difference increasing with the distance that the clusters are apart. For example, the Nordic cluster is most dissimilar from the Eastern European cluster (See Figure 6.3).

As we discussed in Chapter 3, the data also related leadership styles to cultural differences. Hofstede (2006) argues that the essence of the GLOBE findings is captured in his findings, as a result of subsequent re-analysis. While GLOBE is impressive for its industry, collaborations and findings, the same caveats that have been raised about Hofstede's work apply here. Assumptions of national unity of culture and lack of consideration of regional and multi-cultural differences and the aggregation of individual level data to provide a spurious national score, all apply. Given these caveats, the findings are useful for orienting international business people to the likely cultures that they might meet on their travels. However, deep immersion and ethnographic experience should provide better orientations in the longer term.

SUMMARY

In this chapter, we have introduced some key ideas about organizational culture and its discussion in management and organization theory:

- The integrative view of organizational culture, spurred by the remarkable commercial success of *In Search of Excellence* (Peters and Waterman, 1982), has long been dominant in management, emphasizing the importance of a strongly shared culture.
- More recently, ethnographers have suggested that it may be quite normal for some organizations to have neither a strong nor a dominant culture. On the contrary, culture may be characterized by differentiation and fragmentation.
- All experiences of culture in organization, even those that are planned as part of the roll-out of a major change initiative, will be characterized by complex, multi-voiced reactions, interpretations and resistance as well as conformance. Planned change is not impossible but is best thought of as a direction rather than a blueprint.
- Sophisticated managers will be flexible in the ways that they seek to understand and possibly manage culture.
- While the idea of a national culture is usefully understood as an orienting device, when it is applied in complex multicultural contexts it should be thought of as indicative only, not predictive.

EXERCISES

1. Having read this chapter, you should be able to say in your own words what each of the following key terms means. Test yourself or ask a colleague to test you.

   - Culture
   - Levels of culture
   - Organizational culture
   - Integration perspective
   - Differentiation perspective
   - Fragmentation perspective
   - Antenarrative
   - Living stories
   - National culture
   - Hofstede dimensions
   - GLOBE dimensions.

2. What are the three levels of culture, and how do they operate?
3. What are the distinctive artefacts of your university organization? How are they used?
4. What are the values of your university organization? Identify them from web pages and then ask colleagues if they know what these values are. If, as we suspect, they don't know, what are the implications?
5. What are the management arguments for a strong culture?
6. What are the differences between the integration, differentiation and fragmentation accounts of culture?
7. How useful is the construct of national culture? What are its drawbacks?
8. Look at the students around you; think of your conversations with them and discussions in class. To what extent can the variance between their value statements be considered reflective of a 'national culture'?

REVISE KEY TERMS

TEST YOURSELF

TEST YOURSELF

Review what you have learned by visiting:
https://study.sagepub.com/managingandorganizations5e or your eBook

- **Test yourself with multiple-choice questions.**
- **Revise key terms with the interactive flashcards.**

CASE STUDY

SEC enacting organizational culture

In the 1980s, 'culture' operated as a kind of 'open sesame' concept in management theory. Subsequently, it has been heavily criticized. Despite the critics, the concept of culture continues to be widely used by managers and consultants. It signifies processes of importance in organizations that other concepts do not capture so well. A project of 'managing culture' was devised in collaboration with the Scandinavian engineering consultant company SEC.

Cultural merging

SEC was in a heavy growth period, after mergers and acquisitions of a number of firms. The reasoning behind the mergers was to position the company for the purpose of delivering complete solutions to large engineering projects, which were getting increasingly higher shares of the total project market. The challenges of creating and realizing practical synergies after mergers and acquisitions are all too familiar from the literature. In 83 per cent of large mergers, the stock price of the combined organization did not rise above those of the single entities.

SEC identified challenges with diverse organizational cultures and work practices in the different companies it had acquired for realizing its ambitions. For example, some of the companies comprised highly specialized, mono-disciplinary, engineers with a much sought-after expert status, and which subsequently had a wide geographical area as their 'field' of work. On the other hand, some companies comprised highly transdisciplinary engineers with work practices targeted at complex and often local projects where they had responsibilities for more or less the totality of the project. Thus, the project was initiated with the slogan of 'accelerated cultural integration'. In collaboration between key members of the company and our team of researchers, we defined the work tasks implied in the slogan in terms of barriers and enablers for knowledge exchange. The project subsequently focused on methods, concepts and approaches for accelerated cultural integration after and during the new company mergers and acquisitions.

Rituals of cultural exchange and dissemination

The underlying premise was that faster (than the natural cadence of time would have achieved 'left to its own' social evolution) cultural integration would enable conditions for improving, and lowering the costs of, knowledge sharing. A guiding principle in the project was that culture cannot be dictated through directives and decisions, but rather is enabled through communal practices of everyday work. The basic methods of the project were twofold; first, to facilitate process meetings where top management and local project workers met in all the locations where SEC had offices; and, second, to follow closely through interviews two specific projects that SEC was accomplishing at the time, and on the basis of them make two so-called 'learning histories'. We had about 15 process meetings and 20 interviews with top management, middle management, project leaders and project members. Both in the real-life gatherings and in the learning histories, we focused on what we called the 'fruitful

(Continued)

(Continued)

dilemmas' that SEC employees were facing in daily work activities. Through the 'dilemma doorway', the process meetings provided arenas for people to meet, get to know each other, and exchange different perspectives on significant phenomena and challenging themes. The learning histories, with their intimate project practice focus, provided a possibility to lay down traces and 'sedimentations' in the company from the discussions, perspectives and practices that the process meetings and the two project cases spurred. Through this work, two critical 'sets of oppositional stories' displaying core dilemmas in the company surfaced. We conceived these two 'sets of oppositional stories' as two of the most important myths that were guiding different practices and thus constituting key cultural knowledge in the company.

'Heart surgery – the cheaper the better?'

One of the most important activities in project-based companies like SEC is undoubtedly the process of acquiring and initiating new projects. SEC, like similar companies, lives on project acquisitions, accomplishment and satisfactory deliverances, and stories of project creations have naturally a significant place in story-telling practices and thus in the reproduction of the cultural in the company. The learning histories from SEC focused, to a large extent, on what might be called the myth of 'project initiation' that, in the specific case of SEC, was labelled 'Heart surgery – the cheaper the better?' Basically, the dilemma of project initiation as unfolded in the myth and displayed in the learning histories stretches along an axis from an understanding of project acquisitions as highly formalized procedures answering 'invitations for tenders' from potential customers, on the one side, to an understanding of acquiring projects through a history of reputation and trust with 'good customers' and intimate personal relationships, on the other.

'The flying engineers'

Much of the focus in the discussions in SEC project meetings (which we considered as enacting rituals enabling cultural exchanges) evolved around aspects of 'the ideal organizational structure' of the company, and practical consequences of the form chosen. Again, dilemmas were at the core, not surprisingly, given the challenges of knowledge sharing after mergers and acquisitions (M&A) in a distributed environment comprising several large and small former companies, 'inhabited' by engineering experts of different disciplines. For example, the leader of one of the divisions in SEC on several occasions, when discussing priorities, strategies or challenges, said, 'we cannot make the flying of engineers a business idea!' The contention received mixed applause. Some groups and individuals consented to it, notably the specialized high-status experts, while others expressed their absolute disagreement. The saying pinpointed some of the dilemmas pertaining to the myth concerning the existence of 'the ideal organizational form'. In the joint dialogic unfolding of this myth during the project, company members increasingly realized that whatever organizational form you choose to realize, you gain some and you lose some. And, like cultural practices that never can be reduced to static structures, you move on.

Questions

1. Is it possible to 'manage culture' at all, or is this a contradiction in terms?

2. Based on your own experience, discuss possible approaches to 'managing culture'.
3. What does culture consist of in this case?

Case prepared by Emil A. Ryrvik, Department of Sociology and Political Science, Norwegian University of Science and Technology (NTNU).

ADDITIONAL RESOURCES

- For an approach to organizational culture that reflects a more anthropological perspective, you can consult Henry Stewart Talks, a series of online audio-visual seminars on Managing Organizations, edited by Stewart Clegg, and choose Talk #9: Managing Cultures, by Professor Stephen Linstead of York Management School, UK, if your university supports access to this resource.
- Both the late Peter Frost and Joanne Martin, whom we have discussed in this chapter, can be seen in short interviews at the companion website https://study.sagepub.com/managingandorganizations5e
- *Rogue Trader* (Deardon, 1999) is a film that makes particularly interesting viewing, if seen in conjunction with another classic business movie *Wall Street* (Stone, 1987), as an illustration of an organizational culture premised on absolute selfishness and ruthlessness. It is interesting to analyse how the culture at Barings allowed Nick Leeson to do what he did: the articles by Stein (2000) and Greener (2006) provide useful pointers.
- We can learn something about organization culture by following the #MeToo movement. Research #MeToo in your country: what policies are being debated related to organizational cultures based on sexual harassment and bullying? What does the available evidence suggest debate considers criminal, what is defined as legal but intolerable in a workplace, and what cultural practices are tolerated in the workplace? What experiences can you bring to the debate?

#METOO

- Silicon Valley culture is lionized for its innovative potential globally, with many imitators in many countries. But what constitutes this famous Californian culture? Accenture, the global consulting company, found out.

READ MORE ABOUT ACCENTURE

- Hofstede's model has come under renewed and empirical founded criticism of late: see Minkov (2018), who uses a far more robust set of data than the Hofstede measures to substantially revise their global applicability.
- One of the earliest accounts of national culture grounded it, historically, in a common religion as a form of communication that was widely shared by a populace, providing its members with a grammar of motives, situated accounts and reasons for action. The classic study is Max Weber's

(1976) analysis of *The Protestant Ethic and the Spirit of Capitalism*. More recently, Sundback (2018) has revisited the role of religion in national culture by looking at the five Nordic countries as a whole. What binds them together is obviously not a national culture – they are five separate nations with complex and overlapping histories – so much as a common religion. Concentrating on the established state religion makes it easy to treat the five Nordic countries as a whole. Martin Luther's sixteenth-century separation from Roman Catholicism in these countries became a decisive and dominant social movement for centuries afterwards, argues Sundback (2018).

MANAGING CONFLICT

CONFLICT, CLASHES, CONCILIATIONS

ELISABETH NAIMA MIKKELSEN AND
STEWART CLEGG

LEARNING OBJECTIVES

This chapter is designed to enable you to:

- appreciate that organizational conflicts are normal phenomena
- explore different accounts of the role of organizational conflict
- understand the functions of conflict within organizations
- identify how conflicts may be managed
- explain how shifting conceptions of organizational conflict lead to different practical implications.

BEFORE YOU GET STARTED...

A new twist on an old proverb:

> Conflict is the spice of life...

INTRODUCTION

Realistically, despite all the talk of teamwork, working as one big family and the importance of a common culture, organizations have to handle conflict, as wise consultants know. Diverse assumptions underlie the analysis of organizational conflict. First, conflict can be seen as dysfunctional, which is the most frequent lay view that deplores the fact that people at work cannot get along with each other. Such views often lead to highly judgemental, normative views that regard conflict as something that should be avoided at all costs. Second, and more analytically, there has been a shift in focus from normative prescriptions of what disputants should do in conflict situations to focusing on what is actually done in practice. Third, there has been a realization that conflict is a normal organizational phenomenon and should be treated as such. (See Talk #10: Organizational Politics, by Professor Richard Badham of Macquarie Graduate School of Management, Sydney, Australia, one of a series of online audio-visual seminars on Managing Organizations, edited by Professor Stewart Clegg.)

WATCH THE TALK

WHAT IS ORGANIZATIONAL CONFLICT?

Organizational conflict results from the expression of the actual or perceived opposition of needs, values and interests between people working together.

Traditionally, in the broader social sciences if not always in management and organization studies, an analytic focus on **organizational conflict** owes a great debt to Marx's (1976[1867]) views. For Marx, conflict is something always born of the contradictions of class struggle. Few scholars would endorse these views today, regarding them as too reductionist, as insufficiently complex to grasp the full range of identities that might mobilize people and their conflicts. Nonetheless, Marxist views became incorporated in a diluted form in contemporary 'conflict sociology' (Collins, 1975).

The abundance of historical literature on conflict has mainly dealt with controlling, avoiding and eliminating social conflict (Rahim, 2010). Classical philosophers such as Plato and Aristotle shared an interest in conflict based on the need to maintain order in a society. Both Plato and Aristotle assigned conflict a pathological status: viewing it as a threat to the success of the state and arguing that the state should be responsible for keeping conflict to an absolute minimum (Shipka, 1969). Later, seventeenth-century social contract theorists, such as Thomas Hobbes and John Locke, suggested that government's central role was to control conflict so as to establish order in social relations. By the nineteenth century, however, major philosophical contributions from the dialectical perspective inspired by Hegel (1975) and continued by Marx (1976[1867]) identified conflict as the necessary engine of social change.

LEVELS OF CONFLICT

Current perspectives on organizational conflict in organization and management replay those of 1950s functionalist sociology (Coser, 1956), dealing primarily with whether conflict is a negative phenomenon – that is, destructive and disruptive – or if conflict can be a constructive process that has positive consequences (for such a debate about conflict, see, for example, De Dreu, 2008; De Wit et al., 2012; Tjosvold, 2008b).

Putnam and Poole (1987) analyse three levels of conflict: interpersonal, intergroup and inter-organizational. De Dreu and Gelfand (2008) synthesize the literature about sources and effects of conflict across different levels of analysis: individual, group, organization and national culture (see Table 7.1).

TABLE 7.1 Levels of conflict

Conflict	Disputants	Sources of conflict
Interpersonal	Individuals - often dyads	Competition; incompatibility; interpersonal relational tensions
Intergroup	Teams or informal groups	Work-related disputes due to ambiguity, rivalry, competitive pressures of reward systems
Inter-organizational	Different organizations	Different organizational interests; different national cultural stereotypes; different categories of identity such as expatriates versus locals

Much of the organizational conflict literature has an intra-organizational focus, as we shall see. Some of this is planned; some not. In terms of planned conflict, the 'rank and yank' employee evaluative system used at Enron, but commonplace in organizations across the world, deliberately creates conflict. Each year, the bottom 5 per cent of employees in performance evaluations know that they will be fired and a new group hired, which is seen as overall improving the organization's pool of capabilities: it certainly creates conflict by instituting as a norm the rhetoric of market competition and competitive advantage. This rhetoric draws on Darwinian notions of survival of the fittest and assumes organizational life to be a dog-eat-dog environment where each individual is a competitor only concerned with their own self-interest. Not surprising then is the commonplace occurrence of bullying as a form of interpersonal conflict, especially as harassed superordinates strive to push for ever more from those subordinate (Riemer et al., 2013).

We should not overlook the many inter-organizational sources of conflict that can occur in the modern world in which extensive supply chains are the norm. Occasionally, in the business press or in regulatory moves, we can glean some insight into these conflicts. Writing in *The Conversation* in 2013, Professor Christine Parker discusses how the duopolistic structure of the supermarket industry in one country, Australia, predisposes the organizational field to being one of profound inter-organizational conflict. The main reason is the extreme disparity in power between the players in the field.

READ THE FULL ARTICLE

Suppliers claim that Coles and Woolworths require them to make payments above and beyond that negotiated in order to stock their products and that the supermarkets impose penalties that do not form part of any negotiated terms of trade. Suppliers also claim that the duopoly does not pay the prices agreed and that they discriminate in favour of their own home-brand products.

These tactics may be unattractive, even uncivilized. But they are exactly what we should expect when two retailers hold 80 per cent of the grocery market. Coles and Woolworths likely have a bevy of lawyers ready to show that their terms were set out in contracts that suppliers freely agreed to; any deviations were the rogue acts of individual bad apples. The supermarkets will argue that this is nothing more than robust competition in the interests of lower prices for consumers.

Parker goes on to discuss and denounce the strategy of squeezing suppliers on price to deliver what they say consumers want, which is cheap, reliable, accessible food. But it is food that is industrially produced, that sustains an industrialized system of animal cruelty and exploitation about which consumers are kept in the dark. She cites the case of 'free range eggs' that, on investigation, are far from being what they claim to be on the box. Analytically, the key point is that the system that has been established with the duopoly of supermarkets in the driving seat is one of extreme market power concentrated in the hands of the two firms that control a great deal of the market. Consumers have little choice and suppliers are ground down to the lowest common price denominator because the duopoly is able to operate in this way. The supermarkets claim the system is functional, delivering low-cost produce to customers; the suppliers claim that it is forcing them to use extreme industrial farming methods and exploit their animals and crops in consequence; consumers who are aware and have the resources of time and money to do so go and shop at farmers' markets instead. Most have neither the resources of time nor money to be able to do so. Hence, organizational conflict, orchestrated through downward pressure, is normal.

CONFLICT: GOOD OR BAD?

READ ABOUT ORGANIZATIONAL CONFLICT

The lay view of organizational conflict is one that often rebukes it as a distraction, as unnecessary organizational politics. A shift from a view that saw conflict as inescapably negative to a functional view of interpersonal conflict occurred from the 1950s to the late 1970s. Conflict slowly became seen as a productive force, if the right kind of conflict occurred and was handled correctly, rather than as a breakdown in organizational harmony and a deviance from a position of blissful equilibrium. Conflict was now viewed as a potentially productive force because it could improve performance, innovation and decision-making in organizations.

Drawing on Barley (1991), Morrill (1989) and Wall and Callister (1995), we can see conflict research moving away from a view of it as dysfunctional – as breaches of harmony in organizational life (Fink, 1968; Mack and Snyder, 1957; March and Simon, 1958) – to viewing conflict as constructive and potentially beneficial for the organization if the right kinds of conflict occur (De Dreu and Van de Vliert, 1997; Jehn and Mannix, 2001; Tjosvold, 2006). These views are examples of management and organization scholarship coming into increasing accord with the classical sociological analysis associated with Simmel (1955) and Coser (1956).

Much conflict research focuses normatively on what makes one type of conflict better than another in organizations in order to reduce conflicts that are 'bad' for the organization and stimulate 'productive' conflicts. Conflict is seen as an instrumental means to achieve authoritatively sanctioned ends. The focus is on how to manipulate the system to reduce conflicts perceived as bad and to stimulate other types of conflict deemed constructive for increasing performance, effectiveness, creativity and innovation. Accordingly, by distinguishing between conflicts seen as detrimental to organizational functioning and conflicts that are functional and productive, they emphasize instrumental aspects of the 'right' kind of conflict for the achievement of goals. A widespread focus within the field is on how to reduce or stimulate conflict depending on the situation and the kind of outcome desired by management.

THE BRIGHT (FUNCTIONAL) SIDE OF CONFLICT

In spite of the early tendency to view conflict as dysfunctional, an increasing number of researchers began pointing to its positive dynamics and consequences. Coser (1956) published his now classic book on the *Functions of Social Conflict*, greatly influenced by Simmel (1955), in which he contended that conflict is not always socially destructive but rather an essential mechanism in the positive evolution of society. Subsequent theorists such as Pondy (1967, 1992) and Thomas (1992) also contributed to a changing view of conflict in organizations. Pondy (1967) argued that conflict is neither good nor bad but must be assessed in terms of its individual and organizational functions and dysfunctions. However, underlying his analysis of conflict remained the notion that it disturbs the 'equilibrium' of the organization, an assumption implicit in nearly all studies of organizational conflict at that time: conflict represented situations of ambiguity, which were to be eliminated for cooperation to take place.

FUNCTIONAL CONFLICTS

THE DARK (DYSFUNCTIONAL) SIDE OF CONFLICT

Early modern works on organizational conflict largely regarded conflict as a dysfunctional phenomenon. There was a tendency to regard conflict as 'altogether bad' (Fink, 1968: 445), as 'a breakdown in standard mechanisms of decision-making' (March and Simon, 1958: 112), and 'as basically different from "co-operation"' (Mack and Snyder, 1957: 212). In fact, because conflict was often depicted as part of a conflict–cooperation dichotomy, where one is defined in terms of the absence of the other, conflict situations were considered best kept under control through elimination (Mack and Snyder, 1957). Conceptually, conflict was associated with self-interested intentions that deliberately undermined the collectively defined goals of others (see, for example, Boulding, 1957; Fink, 1968). Sometimes competition was regarded as a species of conflict but most often conflict was treated as a subset of competition since it was assumed that all cases of conflict would involve some level of competition.

By contrast, some other writers (see, for example, Katz and Kahn, 1978; Mack and Snyder, 1957; Schmidt and Kochan, 1972) criticized the ambiguous distinction between concepts of conflict and competition. These researchers sought to limit the concept of conflict by conceptualizing it narrowly as overt behaviour or social interaction processes occurring after the perception of mutually incompatible goals or values. According to this view, conflict is conceptualized as an 'overt behavioral outcome [...], that is, the actual interference or blocking' (Schmidt and Kochan, 1972: 363). The interference must be deliberate and goal-directed by at least one of the parties involved and it may be passive or active. In this view of conflict, perception of goal or value incompatibility is central and even seen as a necessary precondition for conflict.

Katz and Kahn argued that whether a conflict is characterized by great anger or not, by real or imagined differences of interest, by hostile acts or misunderstood gestures, while these are all aspects that might be important in understanding a conflict, they do not define it. Conflict is 'the collision of actors' (1978: 613), in a distinct behavioural conceptualization of the phenomenon. There has to be an observed clash where two bodies collide in social terms. Schmidt and Kochan term this a 'behavioral conceptualization of the process of conflict' (1972: 359). Theoretical assumptions underlying the notion of conflict as a distinct behavioural phenomenon viewed conflict in terms of competition, either because of goal incompatibility or as a result of overt struggle.

In 1992 Pondy argued that 'conflict is not only functional for the organization, it is essential to its very existence' (1992: 260). Pondy's conception of conflict in organizations epitomized an emerging shift within the field of conflict research from viewing conflict as dysfunctional to viewing it as potentially constructive and even productive if the right kind of conflict occurred. Thomas (1992) also saw conflict as being potentially constructive, inspiring much research to distinguish between dysfunctional and constructive conflict. This led to the establishment of a conflict typology framework, identifying task, relationship and process conflict (see Table 7.2).

TABLE 7.2 Types of organizational conflict

	Task conflict	**Relationship conflict**	**Process conflict**	**Intrapersonal conflict**
At issue	Resources, policies, pressures, judgements, interpretations	Personal issues, different preferences, dissonant values	Task definitions, delegation, role prescriptions	Ethical decisions where there is a question of alignment between the organizational and individual sense of ethicality
Outcomes	Motivates agreed outcomes; functional conflict	Lowers trust and performance; dysfunctional conflict	Instrumental for the achievement of goals	Organizationally dysfunctional but personally validating where a conflict leads to whistleblowing

TASK-RELATED CONFLICT

Task-related conflict concerns 'disputes about the distribution and allocation of resources, opposed views with regard to the procedures and policies that should be used or adhered to, or disagreeing judgements and interpretations of facts' (De Dreu and Beersma, 2005: 106). Relationship conflict involves 'irritation about personal taste and interpersonal style, disagreements about political preferences, or opposing values' (2005: 106).

WHAT WOULD YOU DO?

You have been in your current job for nearly three years. Recently, someone that you used to work with, who was a subordinate in the previous job, who has been working elsewhere, has joined the organization, partly as a result of your sponsorship. Now you find yourself reporting to him, and for reasons that are not immediately obvious he starts to try and provoke conflict with you by using his executive position in a way that is clearly designed to be a threat to your interests and to those that you represent in the organization. What would you do?

Questions

Would you:

1. Confront and complain?
2. Accept the changed reality and do as directed?
3. Launch a formal grievance procedure in line with HR protocols?

Explain why you would choose this course of action and how it should be managed.

Disagreements about personal issues often represent ego threats because the issues in relationship conflicts are strongly interwoven with self-concepts (De Wit et al., 2012). Process conflict is closely related to task conflict: whereas task conflict has to do with the actual task, process conflict concerns the process of task accomplishment in terms of how resources and duties are delegated and how the task is done (De Wit et al., 2012; Jehn, 1997). The concepts of task and relationship conflict are widely used in conflict research and are therefore well-established concepts in the literature. Process conflict is accepted as an important concept but although investigation and understanding of it are growing (see, for example, Behfar et al., 2012; De Wit et al., 2012; Greer et al., 2008), application of the concept is still limited.

Generally, task conflict is considered less threatening to one's personal identity than is relationship conflict, involving fewer negative emotions. More importantly, it is agreed that task conflict motivates team members' search for optimal decisions and solutions (Olson et al., 2007). Jehn and Mannix, for example, argue that '[m]oderate levels of task conflict have been shown to be beneficial to group performance on certain types of tasks' (2001: 239). Newer research into the benefits of task conflict has focused specifically on how this type of conflict may improve group outcomes (Bradley et al., 2012).

Task conflict is seen as more likely than other types of conflict to be constructive due to its ability to enhance decision-making quality, individual creativity and innovation, task commitment and member satisfaction, as well as work team effectiveness, by stimulating discussion and preventing premature consensus (Behfar et al., 2012).

RELATIONSHIP CONFLICT

Relationship conflict, by contrast with task conflict, is more likely to affect identification and trust negatively (Jehn et al., 2008) and is seen to interfere with performance by lowering effectiveness, creativity and innovation (Farh et al., 2010). Relationship conflicts are more difficult to manage (De Dreu and Van Knippenberg, 2005) and poorly managed relationship conflict is regarded as having the most negative long-term consequences for individual health and wellbeing (De Dreu et al., 2004). Although there appears to be some debate within this area of organizational conflict research over whether task conflict is beneficial or not and under which circumstances the benefits of task conflict in groups may be reaped, a common distinction is to view task conflict as constructive and relationship conflict as dysfunctional.

It is from a perspective on the dysfunctionality of relationship conflict that peace negotiator William Ury (2010) starts. He argues that all conflicts have a duality as oppositions define them: it is opposing sides, values, interests and points of view that define a conflict. However, he seeks to affirm what he calls the `third side', which is always present if not always visible in any conflict. As he says, `the third side of the conflict is us, it's the surrounding community, it's the friends, the allies, the family members, the neighbors'. In relationship conflicts in organizations, it is the non-conflictual parties trying to get on with their work that are not really interested in who is right or wrong in the dispute: they would just like to see more focus on getting things accomplished rather than getting even. Ury stresses that we must beware of being in the moment, reacting in haste to words and actions that themselves might be intemperate, so that the loss of perspective rapidly escalates on all sides, anger rises, and incautious words cause lasting damage.

What Ury encourages us to do is to gain some perspective on the heat of battle. Battles do not go on forever and it is rare that there is an outright winner and loser. Often, there is a negotiated peace or truce, an acceptance of the other. That is where we need to arrive in dealing with relationship conflict – what Ury (2010) refers to as 'getting from no to yes'. Where conflicts between staff and management are defined as private problems that must be resolved and managed individually, although the organization is not responsible (Bartunek et al., 1992; Martin, 1992) it should be able to broker a resolution.

WATCH THE TED TALK

It should not be assumed that role conflicts are necessarily bad; in some cases, they can be deliberately designed to foster creativity and innovation, as our next 'Extend your knowledge' feature argues. It answers a question that many of you must have speculated about when watching a favourite movie: what is the difference between a producer and a director?

READ THE ARTICLE

EXTEND YOUR KNOWLEDGE

In an article published in 2017: Ebbers, J. J. and Wijnberg, N. M. 'Betwixt and between: Role conflict, role ambiguity and role definition in project-based dual-leadership structures', *Human Relations*, 70 (11): 1342–65, which is available at the companion website https://study.sagepub.com/managingandorganizations5e, project-based organizations in the film industry are investigated. Usually, these organizations have a dual-leadership structure, based on a division of tasks between the dual leaders - the director and the producer - in which the former is predominantly responsible for the artistic and the latter for the commercial aspects of the film. These organizations also have a role hierarchically below and between the dual leaders: the first assistant director. This organizational constellation is likely to lead to role conflict and role ambiguity experienced by the person occupying that particular role. Although prior studies found negative effects of role conflict and role ambiguity, this study shows that they can also have beneficial effects because they create space for defining a role expansively that, in turn, can be facilitated by the dual leaders defining their own roles more narrowly. The study also shows the usefulness of analysing the antecedents and consequences of roles, role definition and role crafting in connection to the behaviour of occupants of adjacent roles.

PROCESS CONFLICT

Coser (1956), Pondy (1967) and Thomas (1992) were among the first to offer a new perspective on organizational conflict, seeing it as a normal process that needed managing. Conflict could be seen as instrumental for the achievement of goals, and this view is summed up in Tjosvold's (2006: 92) statement that 'it is through conflict that teams can be productive and enhancing and leaders effective'. From the 1980s onwards, research in organizational conflict concentrated either on task-related conflict or relationship-related conflict, categorizing conflict on the basis of its content and its sources and essentially regarding conflict as a 'thing' in itself.

IN PRACTICE

WATCH THE TED TALK

Stimulating conflict might sound odd to you - why would you want to do that? Well, one reason might be precisely to ensure that innovation is robust. Basic scientific method helps us appreciate this with the story of Dr Alice Stewart, as written by Margaret Heffernan (2012) in TED Talks in a piece called 'Dare to disagree'.

Dr Stewart managed to win a small grant to do research into a hard problem in the 1950s: the rising incidence of childhood cancers. While most disease is associated with poverty, the children who were dying were drawn largely from affluent families. The answer seemed evident from the data that she collected: by a rate of two to one, the children who had died had had mothers who had been X-rayed when pregnant. She rushed to publicize her findings in *The Lancet*. Despite the initial excitement her findings provoked, it took 25 years before the - British and American - medical establishments abandoned the practice of X-raying pregnant women. The data was out there, it was open, it was freely available, but nobody wanted to know. A child a week was dying, but nothing changed. Openness alone can't drive change.

(Continued)

(Continued)

Alice Stewart knew that she was right because she had a fantastic model for thinking. She worked with a statistician named George Kneale, who defined his role as being to prove Stewart wrong. He actively sought disconfirmation: different ways of looking at her models, at her statistics, different ways of crunching the data. He saw his job as creating conflict around her theories. It was only by not being able to prove that she was wrong, that he could give Dr Stewart the confidence she needed to know that she was right.

Questions

1. In science, peer review and critique are custodians of the correctness of interpretations of data. In business, managerial prerogative often makes peer review and critique more difficult, although 360° reviews are an attempt to do something equivalent. What are the pros and cons of this form of peer review?

READ ABOUT 360 REVIEWS

2. An alternative to personal 360° reviews is for the organization to host a digital space on which comments can be posted. What might be the pros and cons of these comments being attributed or anonymous?

A number of takeaways emerge from the story of Alice Stewart. The first, as argued in Chapter 3, is to find people who are very different from us to create teams, by resisting the neurobiological drive to prefer people similar to ourselves; instead, seek out people with different backgrounds, different disciplines, different ways of thinking and different experience, and find ways to engage with them. Second, this means that most organizations do not really think deeply – because they can't. And they can't because the people inside of them are too afraid of conflict. Third, open information and networks are essential but we have to develop the skills and the habit and the talent and the moral courage to use them.

EXTEND YOUR KNOWLEDGE

READ THE ARTICLE

In an article published in 2017: Mikkelsen, E. N. and Clegg, S. 'Conceptions of conflict in organizational conflict research: toward critical reflexivity', *Journal of Management Inquiry*, http://journals.sagepub.com/doi/abs/10.1177/1056492617716774, which is available at the companion website https://study.sagepub.com/managingandorganizations5e, the authors of this chapter expand their discussion of organizational conflict. They note that diverse and often unacknowledged assumptions underlie organizational conflict research. Distinct ways of conceptualizing conflict in the theoretical domain of organizational conflict are identified. Three distinct and essentially contested conceptions are found to frame studies of conflict at work. They argue that organizational conflict research can benefit from a more reflexive approach and emphasize how philosophical and political assumptions about conflict frame knowledge production within the field.

INTRAPERSONAL CONFLICT

Intrapersonal conflict between peers can be the most difficult of all to deal with as it is so often based on what had once been affinities. For an intrapersonal conflict to matter, there has to have been some point of connection in the past. Often, the conflict can be over something that occurs organizationally, such as a performance review or evaluation, which is interpreted through a more personal lens. At other times, the organizational forms of behaviour can be used by one party to settle a grudge or a score, perhaps a long-held jealousy about the other party. These intrapersonal conflicts, because they are so close to one's identity based in relationships, are the most difficult to resolve. Where there is mutual animosity, it is difficult to reconcile by a third party that can find little objective basis for what are deeply held sentiments.

Summarizing, a functionalist view of organizational conflict emphasizes it as a constructive and even productive force, rather than being dysfunctional, if the 'right kind' of conflict can be managed. Whereas early modern organizational conflict research regarded conflict as dysfunctional and focused on ways to remove it, many analysts began to see conflict as intrinsic to human relationships. Seeing conflict as intrinsic, the conceptual distinction between dysfunctional and constructive conflicts led conflict research to focus on the reduction of dysfunctionality and the stimulation of those conflicts considered productive and beneficial for the organization. Normative conflict research flourished, which was especially useful in cross-cultural contexts. As Ury (2010) recommends, we need to keep the 'third side' in view in any conflict.

POWER, POLITICS AND CONFLICT

MANAGING CONFLICT

NORMATIVE APPROACHES

A majority of the normative school was inspired by Deutsch's theory of cooperation and competition (1949, 1973) and Deutsch's (1973) definition of conflict as incompatible activities, where one person's actions interfere or get in the way of another's action. Within this strand of research, dominant notions of conflict conceptualized it as a distinct behavioural phenomenon because it was presumed to include a blend of cooperative and competitive motives that were manifested in activities: whether protagonists in conflict believed their goals to be cooperative or competitive would affect their expectations, interactions and resolutions of conflict.

The normative school emphasizes prescriptive approaches to conflict resolution, often by identifying practical steps that the disputants should take to deal with conflict, its causes and consequences (Deutsch, 1973, 1990; Hocker and Wilmot, 1991). Such steps might include, for example, disputants acknowledging the conflict, distinguishing between interests and positions, and listening attentively and speaking to be understood by each other, as we have seen in Ury's (2010) Ted Talk. Process interventions such as workshops, interpersonal interventions to resolve conflicts (e.g. Blake et al., 1964; Walton, 1969) and collaborations have been recommended as 'best practice' ways of dealing with conflicts (e.g. Thomas, 1976). Eiseman (1978) and Gray (1985), in particular, encourage disputants to think about conflict from the opponent's position in order to be able to focus on what could be jointly achieved. Tjosvold (1985) advised disputants to be open-minded and recommended that cooperative goals could be established through open discussion of opposing views (Tjosvold et al., 1992).

In the heat of the moment, disputants sometimes resort to violence (Coser, 1967; Kriesberg, 1992). This is rare, although one often encounters public notices in service organizations such as hospitals, surgeries, pharmacies and border control points, warning of penalties for intimidation or violent and threatening behaviour, and there are infrequent but well-reported instances of disgruntled workers coming to the workplace and dispatching summary revenge, in terms of their grievances, from the barrel of a gun, especially in those countries where the right to bear arms is considered more sacrosanct than the killings that this right enables. Nonetheless, most conflict does not end in violence and disputants usually engage in the prescriptions offered by organizations and the legal framework.

Short of visceral hatred, conflicts can be managed if not entirely resolved. The success of reconciliation in South Africa after the end of apartheid and reconciliation in Northern Ireland are practical testament to these possibilities. Nelson Mandela's great achievement in South Africa after apartheid ended was to avoid communal bloodshed and revenge. In Northern Ireland, after the 'Troubles', the internecine conflict between Catholic and Protestant forms of social organization, including discrimination in patterns of housing and employment, and the organization of armed paramilitary militias on both sides of the conflict, ended with the 'Good Friday' agreement of 10 April 1998, providing a framework for power sharing and the end of hostilities.

WATCH THIS EXPLANATION

IN PRACTICE

Mediation, conciliation and arbitration

Conflicts in organizations can often turn toxic. Animosities can simmer and build. Resentments curdle. In such circumstances, if managers are unable to help the parties conciliate, they will try to defuse the conflict through referring the parties to either mediation, arbitration or conciliation services, either sourced in-house or brought in from outside. There are some important differences between the three ways of resolving a conflict and it is important to understand them. Most of the steps involved in conciliation and arbitration are founded in the belief that it is through the disputants' changed behaviour that conflict may be dealt with – or possibly resolved. The focus is on what can be achieved jointly or collaboratively. Conflict management, from this perspective, concerns getting the strategy for personal conflict management right so that conflict will lead to productive outcomes.

Question

1. In practice, what are the differences between mediation, conciliation and arbitration?

VOICING AND SILENCING CONFLICT

Complex organizational systems are pluralistic (Denis et al., 2001), constituted by agents with conflicting interests by virtue of the overall social relations (of capital, power, privilege, discipline, knowledge, etc.) connecting them. These conflicting interests result in observable contradictions made visible through specific events. Contradictions operate at multiple levels, connecting institutions, organizations, teams and individuals (Seo and Creed, 2002). Oppositions can be explained as resulting from a processual plethora: for example, the specialized and differentiated interests of shareholders, which conflict with those of other stakeholders (Bower and Paine, 2017); a reinforcement of exploitation that exacerbates the need for exploratory competencies (March, 1991), and so on. Organizations are thus not ordinarily singularly or unilaterally voiced phenomena; instead, organizations can be thought of as being comprised of multiple voices (Jabri et al., 2008).

In their discussion of dialogue as everyday communicative practice, Barge and Little (2002) use the idea of 'voice' to characterize conversational positioning within organizational life. They argue that

> given that organizational life is composed of multiple, often conflicting voices, people are constantly making choices about whether to privilege one voice over another at a particular moment, whether to merge various voices together or to keep them separated, and whether to position voices in ways that promote agreement or maintain an opposition. (Barge and Little, 2002: 387)

Three forms of voice are identified. The first is a singular voice, which privileges a particular idea, perspective or thought and enlists others to support that particular idea. The second is the unified voice, where distinct voices of organization members are integrated to form a common voice such that one individual voice does not dominate. Organization members in unified voice, a frequently desired state, are like members of a choir singing the same verse, same melody line and an identical rhythm in unison. The third voice is the blended voice. This voice does not merge several voices into a unified sound but rather sustains the multivocal nature of different ideas, perspectives and thoughts in various and competing 'voices'. Blended voice may be more or less dissonant. The more atonal the blend, the more conflictual it may seem: as composers after Schoenberg (McDonald, 2008) realized, music does not have to be tonal. Nor do organizations.

The task for organization members is to create constructive multivocal oppositions that are generative in nature and keep the organization moving forward, as opposed to blocking movement (Barge and Little, 2002: 389). When teams brainstorm solutions for problems or play with alternative ways of framing issues, they are engaging in positive polyphony (i.e. simultaneously combining a number of parts, each forming an individual melody and harmonizing with each other) because the different solutions or frames coexist with one another and may actually serve as the inspiration for additional solutions or frames (Barge and Little, 2002: 389), which Putnam, Fairhurst and Banghart (2016) call a 'more-than' response. Multivocality is a way to keep incommensurate positions in play (Putnam et al., 2016), as it recognizes and sustains the diversity of perspectives and voices (Janssens and Steyaert, 1999). Multivocality is not necessarily always received positively; sometimes, different voicings are interpreted as being resistant to the dominant voice of managerial authority.

Sometimes resisters are silenced and sometimes they silence themselves by intentionally refraining from action. Sometimes there might be a general reluctance to convey negative information because of anticipated consequent discomfort. Employees are often encouraged to hold the view that the only news that bosses want to hear is good news (see Ryan et al., 1996). Oftentimes, employees do not want to 'rock the boat' or create conflict (Redding, 1985; Sprague and Rudd, 1988). Some organizations develop cultures of silence (Morrison and Milliken, 2000) in which there is an awareness of what issues and topics should not be broached.

Silencing conflict can create a variety of problems. Silence has been implicated in a range of organizational pathologies, including Watergate (Harvey, 1974), the *Challenger* launch disaster (Vaughan, 1997), the *Columbia* accident (Gehman et al., 2003), a large collection of corporate scandals (e.g. Enron, WorldCom), industrial accidents (Bhopal, BP Texas City) and public sector organization failings (Pidd, 2014).

Scandinavian management has long been held to be a bastion of relative democracy in organizational design and management. Such design is regarded as being particularly well suited to address the challenges companies and organizations face in the knowledge society. The style is network-oriented and motivating, with managers seeking to empower employees to act independently. In Scandinavia, this is achieved by companies managing with goals and values rather than through a strict emphasis on control and hierarchical chains of command.

Scandinavian management strives to be democratic management. It is the short power distance characterizing relatively egalitarian relations between people that makes it easy to create a flat organization structure, an idea that was condensed for many Scandinavians in the 1985 publication of *Riv Pyrmiderna* by Jan Carlsen, meaning 'Tear down the pyramids'. A relatively flat structure breaks down the barriers between management and staff. Democratic managers enter into discussions with subordinates to achieve consensus but these discussions are not a talkfest but are results oriented. Democratic managers strive to be both relation-oriented and goal-oriented, to co-create productivity, employee happiness and collegiality among staff. In this way, the result is regarded as improved staff efficiency, better risk-taking and a feeling of accomplishment.

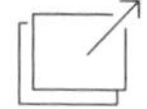

SCANDINAVIAN MANAGEMENT OF CONFLICT

IN PRACTICE

In Scandinavian management, the core values are care and trust, with great responsibility delegated to individual employees. One reason for this is the generally high education level in which Scandinavians are, from childhood, taught to think independently and critically. This Scandinavian culture is thought to promote more creative workplaces in which the flat power structure means that the short distance from top to bottom strengthens the flow of ideas through the organization. One's position in an organization does not determine who wins a debate or decision: it is the arguments that decide what is best, one consequence of which is that there are more opportunities for open discussion and debate. Democracy strengthens openness and trust in organizations, promoting employee wellbeing and motivation, critical for creativity and innovation.

Mads Øvlisen, former CEO of Novo Nordisk, a pharmaceuticals maker, describes his experience with the American model:

> Already in my time in the USA, the terrifying thing for me was that the people, who are a company, did only what was expected of them and not what they were capable of. I did not want to work in an American company. It was a type of military organization that was completely hopeless. One that decided how much time you used, when you were promoted, what you said to whom and whom you addressed. A hierarchy I simply could not use.

Scandinavian management, at best, is based on a leadership style that thinks strategically long term, cultivates employees' personal development and is strongly relation-oriented. Scandinavian culture, with its emphasis on egalitarianism, helps promote qualities that are positive in connection to the democratic style of management practised.

The risks associated with being a Scandinavian manager, according to the report, include falling into laissez-faire management. Too much freedom for employees and too much camaraderie between managers and employees can be corrosive for an organization. Laissez-faire management offers great freedom but being friends with everyone is not necessarily the best basis for sustainable management. It can lead to the delegation of responsibility and authority, not to improve the business so much as to minimize managerial work. This can lead to them being focused on procedural work, being conflict-shy, with no clear goals for the organization, which consequently lacks direction. In avoiding conflict, the innovative clash of creative ideas can be lost. What distinguishes democratic from laissez-faire management is not only delegating but also following up on delegation, to ensure that employees meet standards.

Scandinavian management concerns relation-oriented management that compensates for the absence of a highly hierarchical structure. Studies have shown that managers who advance most quickly are more relation-oriented and goal-oriented in their management style. The employee has freedom within specific areas, with clear accountabilities and responsibilities. The manager acts as a personal coach rather than a higher authority.

More American styles of authoritarian management are creeping in with bottom-line focused management that in the long term may undermine the competitive advantage of a more democratic style of organizing. If a more American-inspired management model makes in-roads, we will probably see greater use of more measurable management tools with clear pay-offs for the employees who perform. But in that connection, managers must be aware that even if that increases productivity, it is not a management method that can be used to lead knowledge workers in a company that must survive by being creative. The challenge is to strike a balance between strong relation-oriented management and a strong profit focus. Innovation and creativity is the vital link.

Questions

1. How democratic in practice are Scandinavian organizations in general? Pick an organization such as IKEA or some other well-known Scandinavian organization and

(Continued)

(Continued)

check out what their employees really think about them, using the online tool https://au.indeed.com/Best-Places-to-Work?from=headercmplink&attributionid=jobsearch.

2. Contrast what the employees say with what the website of the organization in question has to say about working there: is the Scandinavian model for minimizing organizational conflict and maximizing organizational democracy and creativity borne out?

CONFLICT STYLES

Research on conflict management is commonly characterized by numerous descriptions of the disputants' management options. Almost exclusively, the focus is on psychologically assessing the use of five specific conflict management styles: forcing/dominating, avoiding, accommodation/obliging, problem solving and compromising. These five styles have their origin in work by Blake and Mouton (1964), who developed their theory of leadership effectiveness that proposed a graphic portrayal of leadership styles through a managerial grid. The grid depicted two dimensions of leader behaviour – 'concern for production' and 'concern for people' – and became a fundamental inspiration for researchers working with organizational issues. Within conflict management research, the basic ideas of grid theory were adopted and spurred the development of a two-dimensional measure of conflict management and negotiation. Later, the two dimensions from the grid theory were redefined into 'concern for self' versus 'concern for others' (Rahim, 1983) and 'concern about other party's outcome' versus 'concern about own outcomes' (Pruitt, 1983). These two orthogonal dimensions framing the five styles of personal conflict management have dominated empirical research into how conflict is handled (see Chapter 4).

Conflict has been seen primarily as occurring at the interpersonal level, limited to relations between individuals or groups in organizations (Barki and Hartwick, 2004). At this level, the conventional view is that conflict needs to be acknowledged and verbalized by those who are involved in it for it to exist and thus its expression can be measured. Accordingly, the preferred methodology for investigating conflict is survey instruments designed to measure conflict intensity and conflict levels (see, for example, Behfar et al., 2012; Jehn, 1995; Jehn and Mannix, 2001; Shah and Jehn, 1993) between individuals and groups as well as staff and management's conflict management styles (see, for example, Kilmann and Thomas, 1977; Rahim, 1983, 2002, 2010). Relationship conflicts are often seen to be at the basis of managing problems in cross-cultural situations. In situations where there are managers and employees from different cultural contexts, as often happens when expatriate managers are on assignment in foreign subsidiaries, these relationship conflicts can be more frequent because the managers and employees, literally, are living in different cognitive worlds.

Conflict management instruments include, for example: the Conflict MODE Instrument by Kilmann and Thomas (1977); the OCCI (Organizational Communication Conflict Instrument) by Putnam and Wilson (1982); ROCI-II (Rahim Organizational Conflict Instrument II) by Rahim (1983); the Dual Concern Model by Pruitt (1983); and the ECI (Employee Conflict Inventory) by Renwick (1975).

Empirical studies in conflict management have examined relationships between the five styles of handling interpersonal conflict and the big five personality factors (Antonioni, 1998), the effectiveness of decision-making in workgroups (Kuhn and Poole, 2000), moral development (Rahim et al., 1999), gender and organizational status (Aquino, 2000; Brewer et al., 2002), team role preference (Aritzeta et al., 2005) and cultural differences (Kim et al., 2007; Morris et al., 1998). In each case, empirical data is involved: all conflict management behaviour is fitted into whatever grid is in use. The grid defines and confines the knowledge derived from sensory experience and observation.

As conflict researchers began to study the management of real-life conflicts, a shift occurred within conflict research. Survey instruments were developed to measure styles of conflict management, consolidating a great number of techniques into approximately five styles. Generally, the goal is to make conflict productive rather than to eliminate all conflicts. Research has focused widely on strategies for personal conflict management to result in productive outcomes.

Wall and Callister (1995) criticize the two-dimensional scope of instruments used for measuring the de facto management of conflict: 'The use of a two-dimensional instrument has generated two-dimensional thinking, and the discussion or investigation of five styles has conduced many researchers into thinking these five are all-inclusive' (1995: 539). Other conflict scholars (e.g. King and Miles, 1990; Knapp et al., 1988; Kolb and Putnam, 1992; Kuhn and Poole, 2000; Olekalns et al., 2008, Somech et al., 2009; Womack, 1988) have additionally criticized conflict-management measurement instruments for using the individual as the unit of analysis. Treating the individual as the sole benchmark for conceptualizing conflict and for determining how conflict will develop often relegates consideration of the organizational context in which the conflict occurs to the distant background.

In attempts to move beyond the two-dimensional conceptualization of disputants' conflict management styles and to capture how conflict is not only an individual or dyadic phenomenon but also a social and cultural phenomenon, some conflict scholars began emphasizing the social and cultural embeddedness of conflict (Barley, 1991; Kolb and Putnam, 1992). With this shift to a concern with embeddedness and groundedness, a third major shift in organizational conflict research was signalled, which moved beyond the traditional view of conflict as dyadic interactions existing in the two research factions focusing on interpersonal conflict and conflict management, and embraced an understanding of conflict as an organizational phenomenon.

Morrill (1989) and Barley (1991), in particular, emphasize how the focus of mainstream organizational conflict research has broadened to no longer focus only on psychological and functionalist analyses of the different types of conflict and different styles of conflict management, assuming conflict to be an individual or dyadic phenomenon, emphasized by the first two shifts, but now also includes studies that emphasize how social relations, organizational culture and structure shape the forms that conflict and conflict management assume, including a focus on informal conflict management.

While much of organizational conflict theory concerns interpersonal and intergroup levels of analysis, often conglomerated into the term 'interpersonal conflict' (Barki and Hartwick, 2004), there is additional concern today with conflict relationships occurring across organizational levels (De Dreu and Gelfand, 2008; Sheppard, 1992; Tjosvold, 2008a) and between organizations where conflict is viewed as being complicated by power differences. Whereas research has engaged in discussion over how measurements of individuals' strategic choices for conflict management exclude the interconnectedness between disputants (e.g. King and Miles, 1990; Knapp et al., 1988), conflict scholars have recently called for a shift in focus from analysing the individual in conflict to recognizing that individuals act in dyads or groups (Olekalns et al., 2008). Accordingly, organizational conflict research must explore conflict in dyadic interactions, at whatever level they occur.

Social psychological studies of conflict use experimental studies and survey instruments as the main methodologies to investigate negotiation as a means for resolving conflict. While these approaches have clearly been important for understanding specific aspects of conflict and conflict management, there seems to be an implicit assumption in the literature that all conflicts, whether individual, group or inter-organizational, tend to follow the same principles of interaction dynamics premised on person-to-person dyads (Barley, 1991). Accordingly, the dyadic level of analysis is taken to represent all organizational conflict. Conflict can be somewhat more complicated, as we shall see.

INTER-ORGANIZATIONAL CONFLICT

Barley (1991) and Kolb and Putnam (1992) view conflict as more than an individual or interpersonal event. Instead, they view conflict as a social and cultural phenomenon, where conflict behaviours are shaped by the organizational context in which they occur. Observers of inter-organizational conflict agree that conflict is a natural part of inter-organizational interaction (Assael, 1969; DiStefano, 1984; Evan and MacDougall, 1967; Gray and Purdy, 2014; Putnam and Poole, 1987; Tidström, 2009). Conflict may arise between organizations that compete for customers and resources such as external support and skills (Barkan, 1986; Zald and McCarty, 1979), or interrelate as producer, distributer or customer in distribution channels (Pruden, 1969; Reve and Stern, 1979; Stern et al., 1973). Organizations that work together in projects, partnerships and various forms of networks are particularly prone to developing inter-organizational conflict over differing objectives, coordination issues or values (Alter, 1990; Gray, 1985; Gray and Purdy, 2014; Kumar and van Dissel, 1996; Molnar and Rogers, 1979; Vaaland and Håkansson, 2003). Research providing insights into conflict between organizations has focused on sources of conflict in inter-organizational relationships.

High interdependence between organizations comprises a significant source of conflict because with no common authority it may be very unclear who decides what the dividing line of task and responsibilities among the organizations should be. Organizations may therefore bring differing aims and expectations to the exchange relationship about how allocations of resources and functions between them will occur (Kumar and van Dissel, 1996; Molnar and Rogers, 1979). Moreover, similarity between organizations, particularly overlapping client constituencies and shared operating sectors, can be a source of conflict because comparable interacting organizations may find it difficult to separate responsibilities and prerogatives in their relationship and may consider their services as competing rather than synergetic (Molnar and Rogers, 1979).

Power imbalances between organizations are often significant sources of conflict because they can undermine trust in the inter-organizational relationship and inhibit some partners' influence over the joint domain in which they are all working (Gray, 1985; Hardy and Phillips, 1998; Purdy, 2017; Vaaland and Håkansson, 2003). Front workers, who are directly involved in inter-organizational interaction, and who represent the more powerful organization, may be less compromising and collaborative when interacting with front workers of less powerful organizations (Callister and Wall, 2001). A more balanced power distribution is crucial for direction setting and for organizations to develop positive working relationships. Incompatible goals and incompatible systems and routines are also viewed as significant causes of conflict between organizations, which may lead to role confusion among staff interacting across organizational boundaries and even headhunting (Tidström, 2009). Differential identities may also provoke and prolong conflicts among organizations (Lewicki et al., 2003). Finally, the legal-political context can be a source of conflict, particularly when organizations are forced to interact or work together because inter-organizational hierarchies may exert constraints on the way that linkages between organizations are defined and developed (Molnar and Rogers, 1979; Putnam and Poole, 1987).

Topics such as the facilitation of knowledge sharing (Panteli and Sockalingam, 2005) and control mechanisms for task coordination and appropriation concerns (Dekker, 2004) have received much attention in discussions of networks. Inter-organizational collaboration research (Huxham and MacDonald, 1992) has focused particularly on domain formation (Trist, 1983) and cross-sectoral collaboration (Gray, 1996, 2008) to identify factors and processes that lead to effective collaboration. In terms of inter-organizational coordination (Alexander, 1993; Orton and Weick, 1990), the search for determinants of well-functioning coordination has undergone foundational changes from viewing coordination as a matter of designing and planning (Mintzberg, 1983; Thompson, 1967; Van De Ven et al., 1976) to studying the role of meaning in coordinating collective action between organizations, emphasizing a floating, interactive and relational form of coordination (e.g. Reff Pedersen et al., 2011; Weick, 1993).

CONFLICTS IN CONTEXT

Analysts within the field of organizational conflict have argued that the context of conflict is a critical variable in assessing conflict in organizations and requires the examination of different sources of conflict – for example, the allocation of work between entities, power and resource distribution, rules, norms and values existing in the organizational systems (Gray et al., 2007; Kolb and Bartunek, 1992; Morrill, 1989, 1995; Sheppard, 1992). Rather than assuming that conflict is a special case to be treated in special ways, it is assumed to be part of the social fabric in organizations. Conflict occurs as part of the routines of work and the norms for handling it that are embedded in everyday organizational activities (Bartunek et al., 1992; Dubinskas, 1992; Friedman, 1992; Friedman and Antal, 2005; Gadlin, 1994; Tucker, 1993; Van Maanen, 1992).

The conception of 'conflict [as] part of the social fabric of organizations' (Bartunek et al., 1992: 217) implies that interpretations of issues and problems that make up a conflict must be understood within the context in which the conflict occurs, highlighting the role that social context and social process play in shaping the form and trajectory of a conflict. Murnighan and Conlon (1991), for example, found that interpretations, together with many other factors such as experience, culture and goals, influence and underpin the disputants' approaches to conflict management. Accordingly, within this domain of conflict research, conflict is assessed as an organizational phenomenon embedded in social processes framing how conflict is recognized and made sense of and how it is handled within the organizational system (Brummans et al., 2008; Mikkelsen, 2013; Putnam, 2004). Such social processes are seen as equally important to our understanding of the strategies used in conflict management.

By introducing a **dispute** perspective to organizational conflict, conflict research seeks to capture the complex interaction of players, issues, context, and dispute processes.

Within this strand of conflict research, preference is given to the term **dispute** instead of 'conflict'. The change in language stems from a desire to be dissociated from existing descriptive and normative approaches to organizational conflict (Kolb and Putnam, 1992).

The assumptions that underlie this development of conflict research constitute conflict as a social construction because the focus is on how conflict is given definition and shape within an organizational setting as disputants take action. An article by Felstiner et al. (1980) on 'Naming, blaming, and claiming' laid the foundation analysis of conflict as a social construction by arguing that conflict, as a thing in itself, is meaningless: '[D]isputes are not things: they are social constructs. Their shapes reflect whatever definition the observer gives to the concept' (1980: 631–2). In a comment on his study of conflict management among the British police force, Van Maanen (1992) similarly articulated the importance of meaning in conflict: 'Meaning is so critical because there is absolutely nothing inherent in the notion of conflict that is strictly independent of human observation and the making of meaning' (1992: 55).

Conflict seen as a **social construction** emphasizes the role that the social context plays in its interpretation and conceptualization.

Attention should be given to how disputants interpret a specific conflict, how they talk about the conflict and how the conflict is acted out at different times and in different places. Consequently, conflict should be seen as a performance in which the involved parties and third-party observers attach different meanings that may change over time and which can be talked about in any number of different ways. Observers of organizational relationships using the concept of conflict as an analytic category are not captive to any parties' particular definition of the situation; instead they focus on the **social construction** of conflict.

By assuming conflict as omnipresent and normal, scholars working within this frame do not see conflict as necessarily overtly understood by all participants to its expression but acknowledge that conflict can be expressed in subtle ways (Bartunek et al., 1992; Martin, 1992; Morrill, 1995). Conflict is therefore not always assumed to be visible nor is it always acknowledged or verbalized.

The conceptualization of conflict as a social construction is underpinned by qualitative research methodologies inherent in a constructivist research paradigm. Qualitative researchers aim to attain an insider's view of the phenomenon of conflict in order to reflect the definitions that participants use. Conflict, from this perspective, is embedded in mundane human interaction as organizational members go about their daily activities. Conflict is embedded in the cultural and structural context. From a constructivist perspective, conflict should be studied as an organizational phenomenon, which means that conflict and the forms it may take are shaped by the context in which it occurs.

A good example of conflict being studied in context is the discussion by Courpasson et al. (2012) of resisters at work. They observe instances of productive resistance by branch managers against headquarters' strategies that have the effect of generating conflict that is productive. The notion of productive resistance refers to those forms of protest that develop outside of institutional channels (such as unions) and are concerned with concrete activities that aim to voice claims and interests that are usually not taken into account by management decisions. In this case, the productive resistance began when branch managers met and discussed their distaste for a centralized policy initiative; they organized and came up with an alternative that was eventually accepted and implemented in the organization. Productive resistance's goal is to foster the development of alternative managerial practices that are likely to benefit the organization as a whole. Because of the case marshalled by the branch managers against some instances of managerialism that did not make sense in the context to which it was being applied, the organizations came to reconsider their strategies and refined them in line with the resisters' views.

Resistance is not just an oppositional structure of action that encourages actors to isolate and to think of themselves as organized exclusively around their specific interests and values, thus shaping resistance as 'misbehaviour' (Ackroyd and Thompson, 1999). Resistance is rather more an ongoing social and material accomplishment, something to achieve, constituted and sustained by the work of actors who overtly engage in a given struggle. To be productive, resistance requires more than a legitimate claim, a strong leadership, extensive resources and wide collective mobilization, as most theories of resistance would suggest (Spicer and Böhm, 2007), including those studying powerless resisters (Scott, 1990). Resistance also requires a true competence in 'resisting work', encompassing an ability to generate compelling social and material productions defined as successful when they temporarily displace normal power relations.

WHAT WOULD YOU DO?

WHAT WOULD YOU DO?

You utterly oppose a strategic management initiative. You talk to other colleagues at the same rank as you in the organization and find that your views are widely shared. How would you organize amongst yourselves to try and produce a different outcome? What would be the crucial steps that you would take?

SHIFTING VIEWS OF CONFLICT

Early works on organizational conflict viewed conflict as dysfunctional, often depicting it as part of a conflict–cooperation dichotomy. Accordingly, conflict was conceptualized as a distinct behavioural phenomenon because it was found to be visible in the breakdown of the relationship and in one party's deliberate interference with the goals of the other party, resulting in the blocking of cooperative dynamics.

A functional view of organizational conflict sees it as a positive rather than a negative aspect of organizations and emphasized how conflict can be a productive force rather than a dysfunctional breakdown. As normative ideas about conflict management receded, researchers began studying the de facto management of conflict. The traditional view of conflict as comprising dyadic interactions came under increasing challenge to include a conceptualization of conflict as a more meso-level organizational phenomenon.

The move towards viewing conflict as constructive emphasized that conflicts can result in positive dynamics and positive consequences for organizations. Much conflict research has embraced a functionalist view of organizational conflict that focused on how to reduce those conflicts that are bad for organizations and stimulate productive conflicts.

Given the focus on what makes one type of conflict better than another in organizations, the research objectives are irremediably normative because they aim to reduce conflicts that are 'bad' for the organization and stimulate 'productive' conflicts. Doing so is profoundly difficult, even where it is considered analytically desirable, because the nature of any conflict varies with the 'here and now' (Schutz, 1967) from which it is viewed. Nevertheless, the theoretical underpinnings of this shift bear witness to the current widespread conceptualization of conflict as an instrumental means to achieve something else existing within the domain of organizational conflict.

Research about what should be done assumes that managing conflict includes a blend of cooperative and competitive motives. While cooperative or competitive interests each yield different processes of conflict handling, this blended approach emphasizes how conflict is manifested in activities, revealing theoretical underpinnings that regard conflict as a distinct behavioural phenomenon. The move to focus on what is done in real-life conflict management and the development of survey instruments to measure actors' conflict management styles emphasizes strategies for personal conflict management that lead to productive outcomes. Theoretically, these approaches regard conflict in purely instrumental terms as a means to authoritatively sanctioned ends. The goal is to make conflict productive for the organization because it can surface innovative or neglected ideas; it can introduce new issues and actors to decision-making arenas, questioning values that are taken for granted in organizations that have become complacent.

A majority of normative and functional conflict research explores conflict in dyadic interactions with an implicit assumption in the literature that the dyadic level of analysis represents all organizational conflict. Theoretical underpinnings of conflict as a dyadic phenomenon follow the same principles found in normative and functional conflict research: that is, if the 'right' kind of conflict is attained and managed correctly, conflict can be used to the organization's advantage. The shift to viewing conflict as an organizational phenomenon emphasizes two important aspects of how conflict should be conceptualized: its embeddedness in the context of social relationships and the meaning that is attached to it. Accordingly, with this shift conflict is conceptualized as a social construction because in itself, as an event, any conflict is meaningless and is only given shape and definition in and through social interaction and organizational, group and individual labelling.

It is clear that the study of organizational conflict has undergone three major shifts that have established diverse traditions of theorizing, creating specific grounds for contestation: the first theoretical shift, from viewing conflict as dysfunctional to the pursuit of order to viewing it as constructive, created contestation over the *functional* essence of the term; the second theoretical shift, from normative prescriptions to descriptions of what disputants actually do in conflict, generated contestation over the *descriptive* essence of the term; the third theoretical shift, from psychologically oriented analyses to studying conflict as a practice that occurs as an organizational phenomenon, generated contestation over the *performative* essence of the term. While these shifts have occurred separately over periods of several decades, each of them has broadened and generated new strands of conflict research.

Conflict is one of those 'essentially contested concepts' that Gallie (1956) noted, along with power (Lukes, 2005). To say it is essentially contested is to propose, with Garver (1978: 168), that:

> The term essentially contested concepts gives a name to a problematic situation that many people recognize: that in certain kinds of talk there is a variety of meanings employed for key terms in an argument, and there is a feeling that dogmatism ('My answer is right and all others are wrong'), scepticism ('All answers are equally true (or false); everyone has a right to his own truth'), and eclecticism ('Each meaning gives a partial view so the more meanings the better') are none of them the appropriate attitude towards a variety of meanings.

The many different definitions of conflict arise from diverse epistemological, methodological and theoretical positions and are an inevitable consequence of diverse social science practices. These different positions involve endless disputes that cannot be settled by 'appeals to empirical evidence, linguistic usage, or the canons of logic alone' (Gray, 1977: 344). Essentially, contested concepts are evaluative, creating inherently indexical and complex concepts depicted in mutually incommensurable terms by positions that index different assumptions and traditions of theorizing. Because of this, there is no one best instance of an essentially contested concept although, in terms of their interpretative breadth and depth, some will be better, more useful, than others (Swanton, 1985).

The many different definitions of conflict are not a problem because they obstruct generalizability; the problem is rather the failure to be specific about which meaning of 'conflict' is being referred to in any specific case. It is this failure to be clear about terms rather than the absence of agreement on a common definition of conflict, which creates conceptual ambiguity and obscures conceptual advancements in conflict research. Each incommensurable theoretical position is rooted in significant philosophical presuppositions about what conflict is and what it means for the organization. Moreover, each theoretical position embraces distinct methodological orientations for researching conflict and holds distinct objectives for yielding scientific knowledge about conflict.

CONFLICT THEORY AND AUTOPOIESIS

Methodologies rest on assumptions about the real status of the phenomenon under study, constituted by an applied ontology and epistemology (Hatch and Yanow, 2008; Johnson and Duberley, 2000). Having established that different conceptual positions concerning the nature of conflict are constituted by contestable differences, a significant question remains: why are these differences not explicitly discussed in the conflict research literature? We believe that this relates, first, to

Autopoietic systems reproduce and maintain their functioning. In the realm of ideas, certain intellectual positions develop their own forms of inclusive and exclusionary reference.

the fact that organizational conflict research is overwhelmingly embedded within existing and foundational theoretical frameworks that are reinforced through an **autopoietic** system.

Approaches to organization conflict have been so diverse, and so resolutely embedded in their differences, that, despite seemingly addressing the same phenomenon, they seem to be constituting it in different ways that are reflective of the systems of thought and research that generate them. Hence, there has been a reproduction of theoretical positions developed from positivist or objectivist research paradigms, the two dominant frameworks of conflict types and conflict management styles (see, for example, Jehn, 1995; Kilmann and Thomas, 1977; Rahim, 1983). Second, in practical terms, the field has been overridingly normatively preoccupied with the instrumental outcomes of conflict. The upshot is, as Tjosvold (2008) argues, that current conflict definitions and research reinforce 'popular misconceptions rather than challenging them' (p. 448).

In the past, there has been an almost total separation between the two major research strands that work with conflict types and conflict management approaches or styles, respectively. Although these two main research strands take a particular interest in conflict and its management at the interpersonal level of analysis, they are largely independent research areas. We have only recently begun to see studies that combine these research areas by examining the relationships between conflict management styles and conflict types (see DeChurch et al., 2013; Leon-Perez et al., 2015). As evidence of the latter, the literature on the positive versus negative effects of conflict has been meta-analysed no less than four times (DeChurch et al., 2013; De Dreu and Weingart, 2003; de Wit et al., 2012; O'Neill et al., 2013) since the turn of the millennium due to contradictory findings on the direct effects of task conflict on team outcomes such as productivity and performance. An overriding interest in the instrumental outcomes of conflict diverts attention from conceptual debate and those more sophisticated theoretical developments that capture the complex and dynamic nature of conflict. There is little discussion of multiple or contrasting interpretations of conflict within the different research strands.

We have provided insight into the context and dynamics of conflict research. Our examination of conflict research literature clearly reveals that much of modern conflict research views conflict and conflict management as a matter of types and styles, simplifying conflict rather than understanding it as a complex and dynamic phenomenon.

Conflict research is never a philosophy-free enterprise, isolated from ontological commitments, whose diversity leads to different ways of conceptualizing and engaging with conflict. Ontologically, there is a division between those who see social order as the primary value in organization and those who stress that, without conflict, innovation and change would not occur. Although ontological commitments are rarely openly displayed within organizational conflict research literature and may often even be unrecognized by individual researchers, they are a key feature of the theoretical assumptions that influence how researchers make things intelligible.

In as much as managers read different accounts of organizational conflict and ontological commitments are implicit in them, they may develop views about conflict whose partiality they are unaware of. Good managers really do need to be aware, reflexively, of the assumptions that guide their behaviour. More often than not, they will start from a premise that conflict is not a good thing, that it is dysfunctional. Wise managers should not be so simple. They should be smart enough to realize that conflict that can be productively contained and directed can lead to innovative outcomes that might not otherwise have materialized.

EXTEND YOUR KNOWLEDGE

READ THE ARTICLE

In de Graaf, G., Huberts, L. and Smulders, R. (2016) 'Coping with public value conflicts', *Administration & Society*, 48 (9): 1101–27, the authors start their analysis from the premise that good governance involves managing conflicting values. They ask and answer three questions: which public value profiles do public administrators have, which value conflicts do they experience, and which coping strategies are used? The article presents two case studies of a municipality and a hospital to show six different value clusters to which administrators adhere. They identify which value conflicts are typically experienced in various public sector organizations and which different coping mechanisms are used. You can access the article at the companion website https://study.sagepub.com/managingandorganizations5e

Think about the absence of conflict, a situation where social harmony prevails, something that is often assumed to be a good thing. An organization devoid of conflict would be a place in which, because nobody ever conflicted with others, nothing would ever be learned, views would never be challenged; in fact, to all intents and purposes nothing much would seem to happen because everything would run on agreed routines.

March (1991) suggests that organizations tend to need both exploration and exploitation: exploration of what they don't know and exploitation of what they do know. Failure to balance these can lead to either stasis in the case of too much exploitation of what is already known, or chaos as too much exploration and not enough exploitation throw the possibility of developing orderly routines out of the window. Usually, these points are made with regard to innovation (see Chapter 11) but they also pertain to organizational conflict. If there were not champions of different ideas prepared to express their differences with those in organizational authority, then the conflict of ideas would not occur. Without conflict between different ideas and those whose ideas they are, whether internal members of the organization or external stakeholders, change would not occur (see Chapter 11).

External sources of conflict are especially productive. They may come from another company that wants to take over an organization in order to redirect its energies, or they could from social movements or organizations that fundamentally question the organization's values. In the former case, where there is a hostile takeover, conflict is usually guaranteed. To the extent that shareholders, unions and other interested parties such as communities have a voice, then the arguments about the future of the organization will be extremely valuable as different scenarios are contested. The overall stock of knowledge about what might happen, its value and probable consequences are advanced through the conflict of different interests and ideas.

While we agree with Coser's (1956) argument that conflict may provide the impetus for positive developments and change, our examination of the conflict research literature clearly reveals that, instrumentally, there is less concern with the actuality of conflict and its lived experience and more with its managerial manipulation for authoritative ends. Much of it would be of little use in addressing complex cases such as the Adani mine case that we highlight next, in part because of the difficulty in finding neutral ground from which to analyse. Adani, an Indian company, is trying to fund a huge open cut mine in Queensland on land that is adjacent to the Barrier Reef and in an area of highly productive farmland. A coalition of interests has formed against the mine. A poll of 3312 people, conducted by pollsters ReachTEL on 25 January 2018 and commissioned by the Stop Adani Alliance, found 65.1 per cent of Australians opposed or strongly opposed Indian mining company Adani building the new coal mine in Queensland (Massola, 2018). As the related 'In practice' demonstrates, conflict is an essentially contested concept.

WATCH THE DOCUMENTARY

IN PRACTICE

Controversial mining in Queensland

A television documentary, produced by ABC's *Four Corners*, 'Digging into Adani', is well worth watching to capture the full complexity of the inter-organizational conflicts that are occurring around the Adani mining project and how they are creating unusual and unexpected alliances. Green groups, local farmers, banks, political parties and marine biologists all oppose the mine on different grounds. The green movement is opposed to further fossil fuel extraction on the grounds of its contribution to global warming, as well as the dangers to the Barrier Reef of enhanced sea traffic shipping dirty coal. The banks, failing to see the commercial viability of the project in an era where coal consumption is in decline, have declined to loan it money. Farmers, who raise beef cattle in the surrounding land of central Queensland, oppose the mine because of its effect on groundwater. In this drought-prone region of Central Queensland, farmers fear the project could contaminate the groundwater they rely on for their cattle. Not only that, the farmers have joined ranks with the Green movement in opposing the mine; the Greens opposing it because it is one of the most water-intensive methods of generating electricity. About 200 litres of fresh water is required for each tonne of coal produced and Adani has stated that it will use 12 billion litres of water annually.

In the face of this opposition, it is, perhaps, surprising that Adani is still championing the project as well as the federal government. Adani's interest is fairly clear: the proposed coal mine makes up half the book value of the parent company, Adani Enterprises. Admitting defeat would be halving the value of the company and doubling its debt to equity ratio overnight. Additionally, and perhaps more significantly, the coal-loading terminal that the company built to export the coal to India, needs the mine to be able to export coal in the future. The federal government's support is less clear. In part, it may be because of a commitment by the conservative parties that form the government to support fossil fuels as an opposing point of difference to the Green opposition. However, other explanations have been countenanced:

> The most plausible explanation is simply politics and political donations. There is no real-time disclosure of donations and it is relatively easy to disguise them, as there

> is no disclosure of the financial accounts of state and federal political parties either. Payments can be routed through opaque foundations, the various state organisations, and other vehicles.
>
> Many Adani observers believe there must be money involved, so strident is the support for so unfeasible a project. The rich track record of Adani bribing officials in India, as detailed by Four Corners, certainly points that way. But there is little evidence of it.
>
> In the absence of proof of any significant financial incentives however, the most compelling explanation is that neither of the major parties is prepared to be 'wedged' on jobs, accused of being anti-business or anti-Queensland.
>
> There are votes in Queensland's north at stake. Furthermore, the fingerprints of Adani's lobbyists are everywhere. (West, 2017)

The future of the Adani mine project is still in the balance but it presents a fascinating case of inter-organizational conflict in which external parties, by forcing conflict through resisting the organization's rationales, are fostering social change. Adani is just one of a number of ecological and climate change related issues that are reshaping the fortunes of mineral resource extraction of coal in Australia. Whether these conflicts are regarded as functional or dysfunctional, or positive or negative, is entirely dependent on the values that one brings to the conflict. Much as with many inter-organizational conflicts, it is difficult to occupy a neutral ground.

Questions

1. In practice, what is your understanding of the value basis of the conflict over Adani?
2. Should the mine go ahead in your view?
3. What factors influence your decision?

SUMMARY

In this chapter, we have introduced some key ideas about approaches to conflict in organizations:

- There are different levels of analysis of conflict, ranging from those between individuals, through conflicts between groups, to inter-organizational conflicts.
- Three main approaches to different types of organizational conflict can be identified: the first takes a negative normative view – conflict is a bad thing and should be minimized. The second says that, in the right circumstances, conflict may be a good thing – that is, it can be functional for organizations. The third perspective tries not to be normative and seeks to be more analytically descriptive,

(Continued)

(Continued)

focusing on the social construction of organizational conflict.

- With the emergence of the realization that conflict was not necessarily dysfunctional and negative, a focus on a conflict typology framework, identifying task, relationship and process conflict, developed.
- The conciliation and arbitration approach was introduced as well as the idea that there is a third side to any conflict.
- The five styles of personal conflict management developed from Blake and Mouton's theory of leadership effectiveness have been outlined. Overall, the shifts in conflict thinking – from a view of it as dysfunctional to seeing it as constructive, from a normative to a descriptive view, and from seeing it as principally a dyadic phenomenon to one that is organizational – have been outlined.

EXERCISES

1. Having read this chapter, you should be able to say in your own words what each of the following key terms means. Test yourself or ask a colleague to test you.
    - Organizational conflict
    - Conflict resolution
    - Dysfunctional view
    - Task conflict
    - Normative view
    - Relationship conflict
    - Third side
    - Arbitration and conciliation
    - Process conflict
    - Silencing
    - Values conflicts
    - Autopoiesis.
2. What are some of the main ways that organizations can use to minimize the probability of organizational conflicts? (Hint: recall Chapter 6, Managing Cultures.)
3. What are the positive aspects of organizational conflict?
4. What reasons can you advance for the proposition that progress depends on conflict in and between organizations as much as in and between states?
5. Is the absence of conflict the sign of a happy and healthy organization? Justify your reasoning by reference to the literature.
6. Compare what you know about Scandinavian and American approaches to managing conflict: what are the significant differences?
7. In your opinion, informed by relevant literature, are capitalist enterprises and organizational democracy compatible?

8. In a succession of board meetings, no conflict between members is observed. What are some different reasons why this might occur? Is consensus rather than conflict a good thing, normatively, in board deliberations?
9. Is resistance to organizational authority expressed in conflict justifiable? Under what conditions?

TEST YOURSELF

REVISE KEY TERMS

TEST YOURSELF

Review what you have learned by visiting:
https://study.sagepub.com/managingandorganizations5e or your eBook

- **Test yourself with multiple-choice questions.**
- **Revise key terms with the interactive flashcards.**

CASE STUDY

READ THE FULL REPORT

The following case study is drawn from a wider study, the report of which is available as van Marrewijk, A., Ybema, S., Smits, K., Clegg, S. R., and Pitsis, T. S. (2016) 'Clash of the Titans: temporal organizing and collaborative dynamics in the Panama Canal megaproject', *Organization Studies* (Special Issue on Temporary Organizations), 37 (12): 1745–69, which is available at the companion website **https://study.sagepub.com/managingandorganizations5e** It would be advisable to read the full article before attempting the case.

Collaboration in common projects between different organizations, different cultures, both organizational and national, is never easy. Tensions can develop between efficiency criteria and institutionalized policies and programmes that may be ceremonially adopted. Organizations maintain ceremonial conformity by developing loose coupling between formal structures and actual work activities. The nature of these loose couplings in practice may be hinted at in constitutive documents that create the project organization but are rarely specified in advance. The reasons are that plans and projects always have to be enacted in practice.

A case in point was the *Panama Canal Expansion Program* (PCEP) megaproject. The *Autoridad del Canal de Panamá* (ACP) hired US consultancy firm CH2M Hill (CH) jointly to manage the megaproject execution. Instead of the division of roles expected and customary for the consultants in which the programme manager (CH) led the execution and was responsible and accountable for the project outcomes (and the client organization deferred decision-making to the consultant project managers), the in-situ role in this project was that the client (ACP) was formally in charge of the project and the programme manager was assigned the role of mentor. This discrepancy between the contract requirements and

(Continued)

(Continued)

traditional project management roles resulted in what were, on occasions, tense negotiations and organizational conflict.

For ACP, the alliance was one of subcontract; for CH it was one in which they were hired as autonomous project managers. The actual statement of the foundation of the alliance stated that, in performing programme management services, the programme manager would work in close coordination with the ACP's existing personnel to form a unified team capable of delivering the programme in accordance with ACP's requirements. The key elements here are the notion of 'close coordination', 'ACP's existing personnel', a 'unified team' and 'accordance with ACP's requirements'. A great deal depends on how one reads these terms. In large part, interpretation depends on past experience and the dispositions that are thus created. For CH, used to running international projects globally from the command seat, with various national partners, in English, creating a unified team seemed obvious. It meant simply working to well-tried project principles with which they were deeply familiar, adopting these as project routines and expecting everyone to be or become familiar with them rapidly. For ACP, proudly Panamanian and Spanish-speaking, experienced in running the canal since its repatriation, the key elements were interpreted as stressing 'ACP's existing personnel' and 'accordance with ACP's requirements'. From this perspective, the ACP personnel not only set the requirements but their personnel were there to ensure a continuity of command and control. Some of the older staff had worked under American control in the past and were not unhappy to do so again, while for many of the staff it would be a new experience.

The project owner ACP did not find it easy to impose roles on CH consultants for whom the role of mentor, with ACP as the trainee, was radically new to them. The perceived discrepancy between ACP's expectations and actual experience triggered a constant negotiation over role enactment in a context of ambiguous hierarchies. Contractually, ACP was the project owner and therefore had clear authority and power. However, right from the outset of the project, ACP not only maintained its right to formal authority but also cast itself in the role of novice, having to learn from its counterpart and 'chaperone', CH, as mentor. In this situation, the hierarchy was temporarily turned into a mentor–apprentice relationship, which triggered colonial sentiments among some ACP employees.

A discourse of harmonization, equal relationships and a 'One Team One Mission' slogan, referencing historical roles in the Panama Canal operations, made hierarchies even more ambiguous. The everyday practices showed a mixture of different hierarchies at play. Project participants struggled to find satisfactory conditions for collaboration. In the daily execution of the Third Set of Locks project, each CH expert was coupled to a senior ACP employee to stimulate learning experiences. Consequently, coordination practices depended on individual actors' gender differences, personal compatibility, language and individual characters, resulting in one-to-one collaboration that could be more or less difficult or smooth.

The collaboration in the project organization was thus a case of conflicting interests and identities and attempts to harmonize. The collaborating partners stood opposed or side by side in terms of formal authority versus expert power, apprentices and their tutors, Panamanians versus Americans. The power asymmetry between the two was remarkably diffuse and ambiguous. At times, ACP made decisions with CH coming in second best. At other times, CH made the actual decisions and ACP, despite its formal authority, signed the paperwork to formalize decisions. The egalitarian, hierarchy-denying slogan 'one team, one mission' was supposed to smooth out hierarchical differences and to remedy potential frictions. However, the ambiguity - being able to draw on one's formal position while lacking the expertise to legitimate this position (ACP) or, vice versa, playing an expert role while lacking formal authority (CH) - seemed to frustrate both parties.

Questions

1. In a temporary project organization in which two organizations with different cultural backgrounds and competencies come together under a one mission-orientation, is it best to establish at the outset which partner is dominant?
2. In what ways did the cultural differences between the partners exacerbate the conflicts that occurred in this project and how might these have been minimized?

ADDITIONAL RESOURCES

- Organizational conflict is a staple of drama. Recent examples include *The Crown*, the Peter Morgan (2016) production, the series about the reign of Queen Elizabeth II, in which conflicts in her marriage and in her role as a monarch are explored, as well as political conflicts in the cabinets of the various prime ministers with whom she has dealt – in the first series between Churchill and Eden.
- Another recent movie that deals in organizational conflict is *Miss Sloane*, directed by John Madden (2016); it has a complicated plot in which inter-organizational politics is central, with a fascinating plot twist at the end of the story. If we detailed the plot, we would spoil the ending.
- In terms of bibliographic resources, the *Handbook of Conflict Management Research* edited by Oluremi B. Ayoko, Neal M. Ashkanasy and Karen A. Jehn (2014) is the obvious place to start. It is a seminal treasure trove of references.
- In terms of novels, the John Le Carré series about George Smiley offers great insight into organizational rivalries in MI6, especially the most recent book, *A Legacy of Spies* (2017). Le Carré is one of the few writers to make intra- and inter-organizational politics a central feature of his narratives; as an ex-spy it is assumed that he knows what he is writing about very well. Finally, another classic is C. P. Snow's (1964) *The Corridors of Power*, a novel that has conflict over nuclear deterrence at its core.
- As we shall see in Chapter 14, when we discuss organizational designs, the degree of conflict is likely to vary with the level of employee democracy and participation or exclusion from decision-making. In Scandinavia, these levels of democracy and participation are high. There are evident consequences for the ways that organization conflicts are managed: see the web page of the Danish Centre for Conflict

READ ABOUT THE CENTRE

Resolution for insight into how conflicts might be well managed, at http://mva.org/membership/member-benefits/danish-centre-conflict-management, where both short courses and testimonials from organizations that have used these services are available.

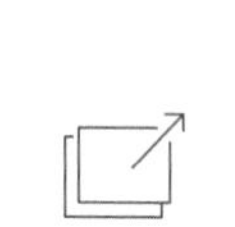

GO TO HRM SOCIETY TOOLS

- The Society for Human Resource Management maintains an informative web page at www.shrm.org/resourcesandtools/tools-and-samples/toolkits/pages/managingworkplaceconflict.aspx, which provides an overview about how employers and employees can manage and resolve workplace conflict. It contains recommendations for building appropriate culture and managing conflict if it arises, and discusses employee communication and metrics pertaining to the management and resolution of workplace conflict.

MANAGING POWER, POLITICS, AND DECISION-MAKING IN ORGANIZATIONS

POWER, AUTHORITY, DECISIONS

LEARNING OBJECTIVES

This chapter is designed to:

- introduce the topic of organization politics and understand how power, legitimacy and uncertainty have been seen as related
- address why organizations have politics and recognize its normalcy in organizational life
- explore the organization of surveillance and resistance
- critically consider the practice and ethics of empowerment
- introduce you to how decision-making in organizations operates.

BEFORE YOU GET STARTED...

A consultant's experiential viewpoint:

> I always thought politics was a dirty word at work, but it's reality, it's reality and it's not ... being sneaky, it's just ... making sure that, you know, your people that are going to help you go where you need to go, [are] aware of you and know what you do, so it's ... talking about what you've done, your achievements, to the right people. (Young consultant in a global company)

WATCH ORGANIZATIONAL POLITICS VIDEO

INTRODUCTION

Understanding office and organization politics is an important skill for all managers that underlies and shapes the formal structures of rationality and authority in which organizational life is situated. Some textbooks paint organizations and managing as really rational enterprises; sometime, perhaps, they can be but more often than not they harbour often conflictual and always power relations. If managers never met opposition, didn't have rivalries, had bosses that were really *au fait* with what was happening in the organization, exhibited perfect knowledge and had perfect interpersonal skills and perhaps interacted only with perfectly working machines and devices, there would be no need for organization politics. Dream on! Managers do not have the luxury of not being able to manage politics – as Clegg et al. (2006a: 3) put it in relation to the key topic of this chapter: 'power is to organization as oxygen is to breathing'.

Organization politics refer to the networks between people in and around organizations that entail power relations.

ORGANIZATION POWER AND POLITICS

We have seen that organizations are made up of formal and informal rules that coordinate social actions and relations amongst different people. We have seen that various kinds of conflict are endemic to organization. We have seen that organizational cultures are rarely wholly integrative but also display tendencies to differentiation and fragmentation. Knowing these things, we should not be surprised that **organization politics** are ubiquitous.

WATCH DECISION MAKING VIDEO

At the centre of organization politics is the simple fact that organizations are composed of relations of power. Power is the concept that encompasses the mechanisms, processes and dispositions that try, not always successfully, to ensure that people act in ways that accord with senior management intent as it is communicated through various devices: instructions, documents, websites, actions. Hence, power should be one of the central concepts in both management practice and theory.

Authority is expressed in terms of the chance of specific commands being obeyed by a specifiable group of people.

Max Weber is recognized as the 'founding voice' on power in organization studies. He distinguished between key terms such as **authority**, which requires the consent of those being managed, and domination, which characterizes situations where the legitimacy of authority is not granted to superordinates by those subject to existing power relations. Weber saw power as a pervasive aspect of organizational life, as people in management sought to execute actions through imperative commands – orders – that may or may not be resisted. The imprimatur of authority attaching to management was a great asset in securing compliance from subordinates.

The most common definition of **power** is that it is the chance for someone to realize their own will, even against the resistance of others.

The existence of **power** is routinely explained as occurring when an A does something to a B to cause B to do something that B would not otherwise do. However, power is more complex than just the push and pull of attraction and repulsion, command and control. It also involves the structuring of dispositions and capacities for action, as well as action itself.

Organizations operate within complex internal and external networks of interests and opportunities, which make 'social and political skills vital to managerial success' (Douglas and Ammeter, 2004: 537). Yet, most studies of organizational behaviour make little or no reference to politics and political behaviour. Typically, it is seen as something done either to resist managerial authority or as an example of maverick management: where self-interested action by individual managers prevails, acting with the sole objective of advancing their own career interests. Any organizational benefit may be coincidental or secondary. 'Politics' is frequently conflated with 'politicking' (Mintzberg, 1985), which is seen as something disreputable. Perhaps for this reason, as organization theorists began to think and write about power, they did so in terms that often saw it as illegitimate.

LEGITIMACY

As organization theorists began studying the empirical workings of organizations, they noticed that some members of organizations were able to exploit seemingly impersonal rules for their own ends. The prevalent conception identified organization hierarchy with **legitimacy**, which bestowed authority.

Legitimacy attaches to something, whether a particular action or social structure, when there is a widespread belief that it is just and valid.

The legitimacy of authority is often contrasted with the illegitimacy of power. Authority inheres in the rights of office bestowed by position in an organizational hierarchy. It is often assumed that if an office holder in an organization sought to have subordinates do as they were bid or expected to, this is not part of a power relation. Where authority is present, the assumption is that power relations were absent. Hence, by a process of reversal it is easy to think that where power was present authority is absent. For this reason, it seemed the norm to equate power with the illegitimacy of action while, by definition, authority would define legitimate action. Power as illegitimate is thus seen as an aberration, a perturbation of the normal structure and state of affairs. Consequently, whatever it is that office holders commanded within the boundaries of their role rights it is not power; any contrarian action, whether individual or collective, would automatically be an exercise of illegitimate power. Thus, when actions were identified that seemed to subvert or bypass the official hierarchy of authority, they were labelled illegitimate – they were not authorized.

Power works best when it is seen least. If people already want to do what is expected of them, there is no need to exercise overt power. If **organizational legitimacy** can be created for individual actions, if they are seen as 'desirable, proper, or appropriate' (Suchman, 1995: 574), the chance of opposition is greatly reduced because a meaningful context has been created in which actions can be accepted and justified (Edelman, 1964, 1971).

Organizational legitimacy is the 'generalized perception or assumption that the actions of an entity are desirable, proper, or appropriate within a social system' (Suchman, 1995: 574).

In managing and organizations, the arbiters of legitimacy are never those who claim authority. Authority is always bestowed by significant others rather than the actor the status of whose action is in question. Such significant others can be subordinates or superordinates, customers, suppliers, government, and so on. Legitimation lowers the probability of resistance, as Blau (1964: 199) recognized when he noted that 'stable organizing power requires legitimation ... The coercive use of power engenders resistance and sometimes active opposition'. Legitimation is achieved through what Pettigrew (2002 [1977]) called the 'management of meaning' – a double action because it seeks to create legitimacy for one's initiatives as it simultaneously seeks to delegitimize those it opposes.

Within organizations, signs of legitimate authority are things such as office size, depth of carpet, room furnishings, location in the building, having an executive assistant as a gatekeeper controlling access to the office and its incumbent, the views from the office window, the dress styles of its incumbents: all have been seen as symbolic markers of legitimate authority. Symbols of authority have to be recognized for them to be effective.

UNCERTAINTY AND POWER

The proximity of power and uncertainty has been much explored in organization theory. A common view is that when an organization experiences uncertainty in areas of organizational action, if a person has organizational skills that can reduce that uncertainty, they will derive power from such expertise. In other words, this view states that despite formal hierarchies, prescribed organizational communications and the relations that they specify, people will be able to exercise power when they control or have the necessary knowledge to master zones of uncertainty in the organizational arena.

Thompson (1956) researched two US Air Force bomber wing commands, comprising both flight and ground crew personnel, and found that the technical competency vis-à-vis safety issues put the ground crew in a strategic position to exercise 'unauthorized or illegitimate power' (Thompson, 1956: 290), because they controlled the key source of uncertainty in an otherwise routinized system. Crozier (1964) also found control of uncertainty to be a central resource. Female production workers in a French tobacco factory were central to its workflow-centred bureaucracy. Male maintenance workers were marginal, at least in the formal representation of the organization design. Production workers were paid on a piece-rate system that depended on machinery working to earn the maximum. Work stoppages made the production workers extremely dependent on the maintenance workers, whose expertise could rectify breakdowns. Consequently, the maintenance workers possessed a high degree of power over the other workers in the bureaucracy because they controlled the remaining source of uncertainty in the system. Maintenance workers' technical knowledge could render the uncertain certain and the non-routine routine. There was also an issue of gender; the male maintenance workers used their expert knowledge as a masculine device over and against the female production workers. Strategic contingencies theory (Hickson et al, 2002 [1971) developed a theory of power related to the control of uncertainty. Michel Crozier subsequently revisited the links between power and uncertainty as a critical resource (Crozier and Friedberg, 1980) in which power was played out in daily struggles over the rules of an uncertain game.

STRATEGIC CONTINGENCIES AND RESOURCES

Hickson et al. (2002 [1971]; also see Hinings et al., 1974) sought to measure power in organizations conceptualized as comprising four functional subunits (Figure 8.1). The major task of the organization was conceptualized as coping with uncertainty. The theory ascribes the differing power of subunits to imbalances in the way they did this. Those subunits least dependent on others could cope with the greatest systemic uncertainty and were the most powerful when the subunit was not easily substitutable by another and was central to the organization system. In reality, each subunit was typically a hierarchy with a more or less problematic culture of consent or dissent.

Similar to strategic contingencies theory is the resource dependency view. This derives from the work of social psychologists such as Emerson (1962) and related work by French and Raven (1968). The focus is on how managers in organizations secure the flow of resources essential for organizational survival. 'As such, the theory recognizes that organizations act not only in response to, but also upon,

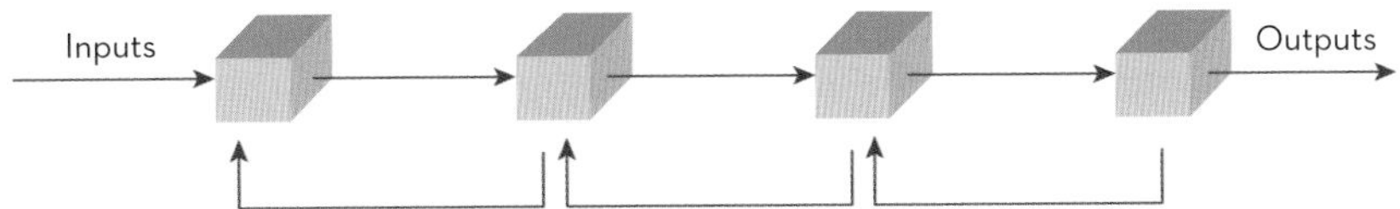

FIGURE 8.1 An organization conceived as made up of subunits

their contexts. Specifically, organizations strive to influence organizations upon which they are dependent for scarce and critical resources. These actions are frequently political' (Greenwood, 2008: 1383).

Pfeffer and Salancik (2002 [1974]) hypothesized that power would be used in organizations to try to influence decisions about the allocation of resources such as raw materials, capital, information, authority or any other essential resource. Resources have to be procured and secured from a network of other organizations. While the organization is thus *dependent* on other organizations, rationally it will strive not to be over-dependent. To be so places it at risk, as a hostage to the actions that these other organizations might undertake or fail to undertake: banks may not advance loans, for instance, because the organization is perceived as being already over-indebted. Organizations respond to resource contexts by *adaptation* (i.e. through internal changes to strategies or operations) and/or by *domination* (i.e. through efforts to control the environment).

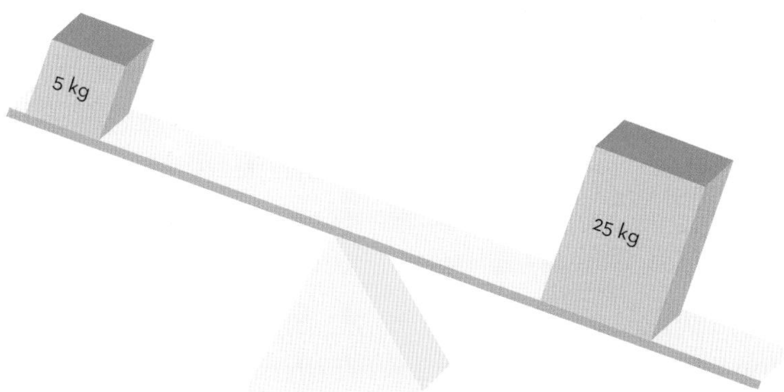

FIGURE 8.2 A zero-sum conception of power

Using archival data on decision-making in the University of Illinois, Pfeffer and Salancik (2002) confirmed their hypotheses, suggesting that power is a positive-sum game for those that have control of critical resources – using the power these resources bestow, they can acquire yet more resources, to leverage more power. Those that have resources attract more resources and thus more power. It is assumed that there is a fixed or zero-sum amount of power to go around (Figure 8.2).

There is no doubt that uncertainty – as well as the other contenders for strategic resource status – can be a source of power but not in a context-independent way.

What counts as a resource can be made to count only in specific contexts. For instance, box cutters, which are used for cutting paper and cardboard, are not usually thought of as powerful resources – or at least they were not until 9/11. Then, in the hands of determined terrorists, they were responsible for what has now passed into history. So, if information, uncertainty – or box cutters – are to count as resources for power, they will do so only in specific contexts.

IMAGES 8.1a and 8.1b Power resources in context

To the extent that specific resources are related to power in a general way, without regard for context, they are not very helpful. Anything can be a resource in the right context – the context is what is important. Thus, possessing scarce resources is not enough to deliver power over and above that formally authorized; one also needs to have an explicit knowledge of context (Hickson et al., 1986; Pettigrew, 1973, 2002 [1977]) and how to use resources accordingly. The stress on resources as bases of power is, we think, too simple, as the case of the box cutters demonstrates.

WHY DO ORGANIZATIONS HAVE POLITICS?

The process of mobilizing (or demobilizing) power is the process of politics. What do organizational politics arise from, according to Pettigrew (2002 [1977])?

1. The management of meaning. Actors in political relations seek to legitimate the ideas, values and demands that they espouse, while simultaneously

denying or decrying those that they seek to oppose. Thus, power is ultimately deployed in games of organizational symbolism. It is wrapped up in myths, beliefs, language and legend – the stuff of organizational culture.

2. Structural divisions in the organization between different component elements and identities, and the different values, affective, cognitive and discursive styles associated with these. Think of the differences between the creative types in an organization and the accountants.
3. The complexity and the degree of uncertainty attached to a central dilemma (as we have seen from previous theory). Being able to control uncertainty that is hardly of much significance will not deliver power.
4. The salience of issues for different actors and identities in the organization. If the issue isn't one that concerns the top management team, it is probably a poor basis for a power claim.
5. The external pressure coming from stakeholders or other actors or organizations in the environment. If important people externally are pushing an issue, those within who can resolve it will become more empowered.
6. The history of past politics in the organizations in question.

Consequently, power and organizational politics are central to much of what normally goes on in organizations, as Buchanan and Badham (2008) argue. Organizations comprise a series of 'turf wars' between different branches, divisions, departments, occupations and cultures. Organizations contain different arenas in which many and varied games are in play, whose rules shift and overlap with variable clarity.

Buchanan and Badham (2008) noted that politically unskilled managers fail. Managers have to be good at 'power steering'. Power steering uses skills to influence decisions, agendas and participation in organizational politics (Bacharach, 2005: 93). Mintzberg identifies various commonly occurring political games.

TABLE 8.1 Political games in organizations

Insurgency games	**Played by lower-status participants against the dominant elites**
Counter-insurgency games	Played by the dominant elites against the insurgents
Sponsorship games	Played by patrons and clients
Alliance-building games	Played among peers who implicitly seek reciprocal support
Empire-building games	A political actor or subsystem seeks to capture others and enrol them as subordinate to their interests
Budgeting games	The objective is to secure resources
Expertise games	The games of strategic contingency
Lording games	Relatively powerless players seek to 'lord it' through using what they claim to be their legitimate power over those who are supplicant or lower in status; think of family politics between elder and younger siblings

(Continued)

TABLE 8.1 (Continued)

Insurgency games	**Played by lower-status participants against the dominant elites**
Line vs staff games	Each side uses legitimate power in illegitimate ways in games of rivalry
Rival camps games	Alliance or empire-building games develop into rival blocks that face each other in zero-sum games similar to those witnessed in international relations between competitive countries or blocks of nations. People in organizations that cannot manage their power relations, because they cleave around fundamentally opposed worldviews, will end up spending more time fighting each other than seeking to find common purpose against competitor organizations. Only very large organizations or those with no competition can survive sustained complex politics for long
Strategic candidate games	Those in power seek to ensure the succession of preferred candidates as vacancies arise
Whistle-blowing games	Participants, usually lower-status ones, seek to expose malfeasance or illegitimacy outside the organization to effect internal policy or strategy changes
Young Turks games	Organizational authority is preserved, while a coup unseats its present incumbents to institute a regime change

In a piece that will be fascinating for any football fan, Chadwick (2013) analyses why 'managerial sackings in football seem to be the norm'. There are several reasons why these sackings are so prolific and, not surprisingly, they turn out to correlate quite highly with the political games that Mintzberg analyses. Sackings may be performance-related:

> but they can also be due to employee unrest ('the manager had lost the dressing room'); divergent interests ('the club and the manager didn't see eye-to-eye on several issues'); timing considerations ('after the first ten games, the club thought it best to make a change'); strategic orientation ('we needed the manager to focus on bringing on the next generation'); cultural incompatibility ('the manager and the club take different views on how to bring success to the club'); recruitment and selection problems ('the club doesn't feel that the manager is the right person at this time to take us forward'); and so forth. (Chadwick, 2013)

In organizations generally, just as in football, politics are normal and serve many orderly functions. They can be the harbinger of a need for realignment (Donaldson, 1999), the midwife to change (Pettigrew 1985; Pettigrew et al., 1992), the source of renewing innovation (Frost and Egri, 2002) or, sometimes, the instrument of death (Havemann, 1993). Thus, political games are to be expected – they are neither aberrant nor deviant. The types that Mintzberg specifies are not mutually exclusive, of course, and may often overlap and interlink, typically finding expression in several major forms in the political arena, which vary with the duration and intensity of conflict (Table 8.1). Success in power games is exhilarating, an anti-depressant (Robertson, 2014). It can also induce the condition of impaired judgement, indispensability, risk

READ THIS ARTICLE

blindness and emotional nullity, often referred to as 'hubris', after the term that the ancient Greeks used to refer to arrogance and contempt for others' opinions, a term which Brown (2012) uses to discuss the staging of the invasion of Iraq by George W. Bush and Tony Blair.

SURVEILLANCE AND RESISTANCE AS ORGANIZATIONAL POLITICS

Hardy and Clegg (1999: 375) suggest that 'organizational structures and systems are not neutral or apolitical but structurally sedimented phenomena. There is a history of struggles already embedded in the organization'. In management and organization theory, organizational politics increasingly became defined as the unsanctioned or illegitimate use of power to achieve unsanctioned or illegitimate ends, as argued by Mintzberg (1983a, 1984), Mayes and Allen (1977), Gandz and Murray (1980), and Enz (1988). From this perspective, organizational life reduces to a morality play about efficiency: either members do what they are scripted to do in their formal organization roles in the terms that authorities determine for them, or, if they do not, they are effecting **resistance**, behaving illegitimately. Being moral and being efficient become identical actions in a well-designed system.

Resistance attempts to challenge, change or retain existing societal relations, processes and/ or institutions of domination, exploitation and subjection at the material, symbolic or psychological level.

The central tension in organization is that between resistance and obedience (Clegg et al., 2006a; Courpasson, 2000 [2002]). On the whole, from the perspective of management control, obedience is a far more productive result of policies than resistance. Excessive use of coercion and force invites resistance. Power can be used to prevent conflict by shaping:

> [P]erceptions, cognitions, and preferences in such a way that [people] accept their role in the existing order of things, either because they can see or imagine no alternative to it, or because they view it as natural and unchangeable, or because they value it as divinely ordained and beneficial. (Lukes, 1974: 24)

Power is able to achieve these effects to the extent that it is effectively subsumed through legitimation within an integrated system of cultural and normative assumptions. Given the integrated system of cultural and normative assumptions and an efficient organizational apparatus, goals can be achieved. Authorities create legitimated rules that are reinforced by clear and credible threats to career, rewards, status, employment, and so on. Hence, analysis of power in organizations needs also to focus on the subtle mechanisms through which obedience is produced – **soft domination**.

Soft domination entails the administration of rules providing managerial discretion to managers while reinforcing the strength of centralized authorities through highly defined systems of authority (Courpasson, 2002).

Soft domination is based on the appearance of equality in the organization among peers and the reality of a pervasive system of controls. Chief among these are instrumentally legitimate techniques such as human resource management, audit, and holding managers accountable to plans, making managers responsible, rendering them surveyable, exercising surveillance over them. What sustains senior management and limits organizational members, ultimately, is the political concentration of the power of control combined with the regular use of credible sticks (e.g. formal warnings) and carrots (e.g. performance-related pay) deployed within clear rules.

READ THE ARTICLE

EXTEND YOUR KNOWLEDGE

In the following article: Brannan, M. J. (2017) 'Power, corruption and lies: mis-selling and the production of culture in financial services', *Human Relations*, 70 (6): 641–67, which is available at the companion website https://study.sagepub.com/managingandorganizations5e, many of the themes of the chapter thus far come together. The central issue is an ethical question: how is mis-selling reproduced in retail financial services organizations? The organizational dimensions of mis-selling, specifically how new employees are introduced to and subsequently enact mis-selling behaviour when not explicitly encouraged to do so, are analysed.

Dialectics refers to the contradiction between two conflicting forces, where each shapes the other, often against the pressure that is being exerted.

Organizations incorporate 'structures of dominancy' (Weber, 1978), invariably saturated and imbued with power, distilled deep in the structure, culture and history of the organization, 'normalizing' power relations so that they hardly seem like power at all. Just as normal is resistance to these when they become evident to those subject to them. The **dialectics** of power and resistance offer a window on the corporate world that is too rarely viewed (Fleming and Spicer, 2007).

Behind the many facades of contemporary corporate life – the visions, missions, websites, spin doctors, consultants, coaches, culture, corporate scripts ('have a nice day'), uniforms, corporate attitude and attire – are people sometimes feeling trapped by roles, sometimes playing – ironically, cynically, creatively – with the demands that are made, sometimes exercising the right to voice that which provides them with existential identity. The reality of life contained and constrained by the corporation contains many corporate and contested dialectics of power, resistance and struggle as normal states of affairs.

Rather than contemporary dialectics being played out in set-piece industrial struggles, the norms of the Fordist era, typified in the British miners strike of 1985, replete with mass mobilizations of police and unionists, and the orchestration by the state and judiciary (Buckley, 2015), in neo-liberal times the struggles are more sotto voce and local, being centred on what Foucault called governmentality, which represents a shift from coercive governance to self-governance (Marks, 2000). The term merges two words – governance and mentality – a means of ruling and a way of thinking (Müller et al., 2014). Governmentality is based on active consent and a subjugation of subjects rather than oppression or external control. Governmentality is an alternative to policing and is often referred to as self-policing or self-surveillance (Sewell, 1998). It is also conceptualized in terms of subjectification where the governed become subjects of the exercise of covert power (Fleming and Spicer, 2014). Governmentality can also be categorized as a soft power as it achieves outcomes through attraction, seduction and other types of soft power (Clegg et al., 2006). The personal ambitions of the governed become enmeshed with those of organizations and their top management teams. For the latter, the intent is managerial control; the former are designated as the targets of this governmentality, designed to create willing subjects. Consequently, the forms of resistance engendered tend not to be organized industrial battles as in the Fordist era.

EXTEND YOUR KNOWLEDGE

READ THE ARTICLE

In an article published online first: Raffnsøe, S., Mennicken, A. and Miller, P. (2017) 'The Foucault effect in organization studies', *Organization Studies*, http://journals.sagepub.com/doi/abs/10.1177/0170840617745110, which is available at the companion website https://study.sagepub.com/managingandorganizations5e, the different ways in which organizational scholars have engaged with Foucault's writings over the past 30 years or so are traced. Four overlapping waves of influence are identified: (1) Foucault's *Discipline and Punish*, bringing organizational discipline and techniques of surveillance and subjugation into focus as power practices; (2) a focus on how, in practice, discourses constitute ways of seeing and acting; (3) Foucault's work on governmentality, which investigated how governmental technologies operate on subjects in different institutional and organizational contexts; and (4) Foucault's work on asceticism and techniques of the self, oriented to the ways in which subjectivity is constituted.

Sharp and colleagues (2000) observe that power and resistance are always mutually constituted and 'entangled' in complex ways. There are two characteristic types of resistance in contemporary times. First, new forms of transnationally networked collective, overt and intentional resistance (Amoore, 2005; Castells, 2010; Hardt and Negri, 2004; Juris, 2008) that is occasional and spectacular, occur at staged events such as global business meetings of the World Trade Organization, with the resistance often organized digitally through social networks and expressed through a form of theatre. The use of V for Vendetta masks by the movement known as Anonymous is a case in point. These forms of social movement resistance are characteristic of the digital era, with flash mobs able to assemble speedily and surreptitiously, confronting authorities with various degrees of violent and non-violent resistance, depending on the politics of the movements involved.

Second, the majority of the literature (see Johansson and Vinthagen, 2016) emphasizes not forms of collective action but that which is more individualized, less organized, less overt and more attendant to local power relations in the organizations in question. These forms of resistance tend to be performative and embodied, articulating issues embedded in everyday organizational life, and manifest through phenomena such as distancing (Collinson, 2003), cynicism (Fleming and Spicer, 2003), humour (Fleming and Spicer, 2002) and gendering (West and Zimmerman, 1987). That they may start local does not mean they stay that way. The #MeToo resistance started local, with a few people who articulated resistance to the sexual predations of one powerful Hollywood man, Harvey Weinstein, and grew into a much more visible and organized mobilization. These forms of resistance can assume a creative, performative and productive exercise of power, as in the case of the 'black dress' solidarity of women attending the 2018 Golden Globe Awards (Wiseman, 2018).

IN PRACTICE

'Rice bunny' (米兔), pronounced as 'mi tu', is a nickname given to the #MeToo campaign by Chinese social media users. The #RiceBunny hashtag, accompanied by emojis of rice bowls and bunny heads, is used by Chinese women to expose sexual harassment – often in conjunction with other Chinese hashtags, such as #IAmAlso (#我也是) and #MeTooInChina (#MeToo在中国).

The adoption of nicknames and emojis is not just a public relations strategy designed to increase the popularity of the campaign, it also serves as a tactical response to circumvent online censorship.

Similar practices of using homophones and images are widely used in China as a form of coded language to avoid censorship on social media. Internet censorship is a major challenge for the #MeToo campaign in China. Internet users have reported numerous instances of posts and chat pages relating to the topic being removed.

How #MeToo came to China

On 1 January 2018, Luo Xixi – a Chinese citizen who now resides in Silicon Valley – decided to bring the #MeToo campaign to social media in her home country. She began by publishing a 3000-word post on Weibo, revealing a secret she had kept to herself for 12 years. While studying for her PhD at Beihang University in Beijing, she was harassed by Chen Xiaowu, a renowned professor and Luo's former supervisor.

Luo's post received millions of views, and was widely circulated through both state media and social media. The university and education authorities quickly responded to the scandal by sacking Chen Xiaowu.

Encouraged by the triumph of Luo's allegations against Chen, more women from China broke their silence and shared their own accounts of sexual harassment at the hands of university professors.

As several victims of university sexual harassment have revealed, predatory teachers often used coursework scores, scholarships and even the outcome of degrees to lure or blackmail students.

But mistreatment is not unique to male professors and female students. In late December 2017, a male PhD student, Yang Baode, was found drowned in a river in Xi'an. His girlfriend later published an open letter on social media claiming that Yang committed suicide after years of abuse from a female supervisor. According to her statement, and the results of the university's own investigations, during Yang's PhD study he was forced to become a servant to his supervisor, watering her plants, going shopping with her and picking her up from parking lots.

READ THESE ARTICLES

Popularity is the kiss of death for any civil movement in China. The Chinese government is known for preventing online activity from growing into collective action - especially demonstrations - no matter how politically innocent in nature.

The article by Meg Jing Zeng suggests that, even under the conditions of authoritarian state censorship that exist in contemporary China, resistance is possible through the use of social media. Other feminist writers, such as Jessica Megarry, writing in *The Conversation* on 29 October 2017 (https://theconversation.com/why-metoo-is-an-impoverished-form-of-feminist-activism-unlikely-to-spark-social-change-86455), would disagree: 'hashtag activism', she writes, 'represents an impoverished form of feminist activism, containing few possibilities for sparking real social change'. Against this use of social media, Megarry argues for consciousness raising:

> Consciousness raising involved women meeting regularly in small groups of around ten – sometimes for years on end – to talk about their experiences, find connections between issues, and understand the scope of men's control over their personal lives.
>
> For these activists, a male presence in either consciousness raising or the broader movement was inconceivable. Men, they believed, would influence the direction of conversations and monopolise discussions with their own concerns. Many democracy theorists stress that women-only spaces such as these are vital to successful movements for social change. They were non-negotiable for Women's Liberation activists.

Questions

1. In practice, where would you stand in this debate: is hashtag activism a potent form of organizational politics or merely a form of gestural politics?
2. Is gender apartheid the only way to create more gender equity, given the masculinist hegemony of most institutional and organizational spaces?

TOTAL INSTITUTIONS

Information Panopticon Instruments such as closed circuit television (CCTV), speed and security cameras are forms of surveillance that have been referred to as the .

Extended electronic surveillance has been seen as the hallmark of high modernity, of a world in which surveillance is insidious, making the majority of people increasingly transparent to others who may not be transparent to them (Bogard, 1996; Lyon, 1994; Poster, 1990; Robins and Webster, 1985; Sewell, 2002). Zuboff (1988) introduced the **Information Panopticon** as a key term (also see Chapter 13). The electronic eyes of the Information Panopticon are numerous. They are aimed at all of us as generalized bodies caught in their eye. We are aware of their existence in creating a normative environment – but it becomes a matter of choice as to whether we allow them to target us specifically. Our deviance defines their acuity, unless we are in total institutions, such as a prison, where their vision defines our deviance.

Total institutions are organizations organized on the basis of, in principle, constant surveillance, on the principle of inclusion and enclosure.

The Canadian sociologist Erving Goffman used anthropological research to investigate how authority was configured in **total institutions**.

People within total institutions are cut off from wider society for a relatively long time, leading an enclosed and formally administered existence. In such contexts, the organization has more or less monopoly control of its members' everyday lives. Goffman's argument is that total institutions demonstrate in heightened and condensed form the underlying organizational processes that can be found, albeit in much less extreme cases, in more normal organizations. The range of total institutions is very broad, ranging from elite boarding schools to prisons as well as long-stay hospitals, amongst many other organizations.

What the very different types of organizations comprising total institutions have in common is that each member's daily life is carried out in the *immediate presence* of a large number of others. The members are very *visible*; there is no place to hide from the surveillance of others. The members tend to be strictly *regimented* and often wear institutional clothing such as uniforms. Life in a total institution is governed by *strict, formal, rational planning of time.* (Think of school bells for lesson endings and beginnings, factory whistles, timetables, schedules, bugle calls in the barracks, and so on.) Hence, members of total institutions are not free to choose how they spend their time; instead, it is *strictly prescribed* for them. It is because of this that members lose a degree of autonomy because of an all-encompassing demand for *conformity to the authoritative interpretation of rules.*

Total institutions seek to minimize polyphony and difference from the presence of competing and conflicting voices. As Bauman (1989: 165) suggests, '*the readiness to act against one's own better judgement and against the voice of one's conscience is not just the function of authoritative command, but the result of exposure to a single-minded, unequivocal and monopolistic source of authority*' (emphasis in original). Total institutions – organizations that presume to exercise strong cultural control over their members, to the extent that they diminish pluralism – squeeze the space in which civility, reflection and responsibility can thrive. As Bauman (1989: 166) urges, 'The voice of individual moral conscience is best heard in the tumult of political and social discord'.

Clegg and colleagues (2006), writing about 'The Heart of Darkness', following the work of Goffman (1961) and Bauman (1989), renewed organization theory interest in total institutions. The renewed interest gave rise to a number of studies of historic examples. Amongst these are a series of investigations of total institutions in the era of Pol Pot's Khmer Rouge Kampuchea (Cunha, Clegg and Rego, 2010; Cunha, Rego and Clegg, 2011; Clegg, Cunha and Rego, 2012; Cunha, Clegg, Rego and Lancione, 2012; Clegg, Cunha and Rego, 2013; Cunha, Rego and Clegg, 2014; Cunha, Clegg and Rego, 2015; Cunha, Rego, Silva and Clegg, 2015) as well as analyses of the Holocaust in organizational terms (Clegg, 2009; Maarti and Fernández, 2013) and of the Magdalene Laundries in Eire (Simpson et al., 2014). The importance of these extreme examples of organizations as total institutions cannot be under-estimated because they serve to present in an extreme form practices that are much more widespread organizationally, a point that is made especially clear in the 'twenty ways of constructing total institutional power relations' in Clegg et al. (2006: 177–9).

The **Information Panopticon** privileges organizational elites by making it possible to consolidate various sources of electronic information about the many who serve the organization (Robey, 1981). Sewell (2002 [1998]) argues that electronic surveillance supplements, rather than replaces, earlier forms of surveillance. Its basic thrust is to make people in organizations more accountable and less autonomous.

The Information Panopticon is often used in conjunction with policies whose avowed purpose is quite opposite to these intentions. Sewell concentrates on teamwork. Teams operate with two dimensions of surveillance: vertical and horizontal. Vertical surveillance focuses on the aberrant: aberrant waste, time, quality, and so on. To define the aberrant, you must first define the normal, which is usually done by establishing performance norms on a statistical basis that enables the aberrant to be immediately transparent – it stands out as a deviation from the norm of time taken, quality produced, or waste accumulated. Electronic forms of monitoring of performance make the norms more transparent and are supported by peer review through horizontal surveillance. Although electronic and traditional forms of surveillance reinforce the vertical dimension, which seeks to make the subject of surveillance their own monitor, the horizontal dimension causes us to monitor each other. Panopiticism explains only some vertical aspects of this group scrutiny (Hetrick and Boje, 1992).

EMPOWERMENT, EXPERIMENTS, EMANCIPATION, ETHICS

One of the major strategies of normalization is to practise empowerment. Thus, much recent management theory has been written in praise of teamwork and against bureaucratic hierarchies, because it is believed that this is the way to minimize the expression of power. Neither the presence of teams nor the absence of hierarchy means an end to power. More recently, there has been a shift in focus from bureaucracy to a consideration of more empowered alternatives. But, as we will see, **empowerment** is not necessarily all it is cracked up to be – it can mean even tighter control.

Empowerment means transferring power to the individual by promoting self-regulating and self-motivating behaviour through self-managing work teams, enhanced individual autonomy, and so on.

Teamwork is not usually thought of as a mechanism of power, but recent theory has suggested that it is (Barker, 2002 [1993]; Sewell, 2002 [1998]). Indeed, as Sewell notes, teamwork is usually associated with the rhetoric of empowerment, trust and enhanced discretion. Sometimes it is even referred to as 'giving away' power. There has been a flood of popular management books whose message is cast in terms of this normative rhetoric, as an analysis by Barley and Kunda (1992) has demonstrated. These books often espouse single-answer solutions for harried managers: TQM (Total Quality Management), organizational learning, lean production and BPR (Business Process Re-engineering) are among the recipes that Sewell notes.

Teamwork does not abolish politics. Rather, it relies on what Barker (2002 [1993]) terms '**concertive control**' as its horizontal mode of surveillance. The forms of power at work help create the types of subjects that work there (Foucault, 1983; Knights and Vurdubakis, 1994; Townley, 1993, 1994). The Information Panopticon seeks to make each worker the governor of what they do at work, aware as they are of the supervisory gaze. Barker begins his account with a brief snatch of interview data with an employee called Ronald, who is reported as saying that he is more closely watched under a new team-based work design than when he was closely supervised by a manager. The team is a stricter supervisor than his supervisor had been!

Concertive control occurs where the sense of responsibility to the members of the team impels you to work intensively and to not let them down.

Concertive control, argues Barker, is what occurs when organizations become post-bureaucratic, when they adopt decentralized, participative and more democratic designs, a strategy that has long been promoted by more liberal management theorists such as Follett (1941) and Lewin (1951). Popular writers such as Kanter (1990), Peters (1988) and Drucker (1998) promote the benefits of 'unimpeded, agile authority structures that grow out of a company's consensual, normative ideology, not from its system of formal rules' (Barker, 2002: 183). The argument is that 'cutting out bureaucratic offices and rules' will 'flatten hierarchies, cut costs, boost productivity, and increase the speed with which they respond to the changing business worlds' (Barker, 2002: 183). Employees collaborate to develop the means of their control. Barker does not see the rise of self-management as antithetical to power relations. He charts the shift in management style from more hierarchical to self-managing teams (see Table 8.2).

TABLE 8.2 Barkers self-managing teams

Hierarchical management: hierarchically ordered supervision	**Team management: shift to self-management**
The supervisor has precise supervisory responsibilities	The supervisor is replaced by a team of 10–15 people, who take over the responsibilities of their former supervisor
The supervisor gives instructions	Self-managing employees gather and synthesize information, act on it and take collective responsibility for their actions
Management relies on formal rules and authority expressed in terms of disciplines that seek to reinforce this authority	Management provides a value-based corporate vision that guides day-to-day actions by being a reference point from which employees infer appropriate action
The supervisor checks that instructions have been followed	The self-managing team guides its own work and coordinates with other areas of the company
The supervisor ensures that each employee fulfils their job description	The self-managing team is responsible for completing a specific well-defined job function for which all members are cross-trained. All members of the team have the authority and responsibility to make essential decisions, set work schedules, order materials and coordinate with other teams

Self-managing teams cut costs by laying off front-line supervisors and gaining productivity benefits from more motivated and committed employees (Mumby and Stohl, 1991; Orsburn et al., 1990; Wellins et al., 1991). When the people that you work with, rather than a supervisor, impose the limits, it is harder to disagree. It is much easier to steal some time from a supervisor or manager with whom you do not share any obvious interest, other than a necessity to work, than it is from colleagues. You all depend on each other – and that is the subtlety of concertive control. Everyone is empowered to speak – but with the same agreed-upon voice.

Ordinary people can do extraordinary things, as an experiment by Milgram (1971) shows. Milgram's research question was quite simple: he asked to what extent individuals are inclined to follow the commands of figures perceived to be in authority. His answer demonstrated that the kind of situation in which people are embedded determines, in part, how they will act. He designed an experiment in which white-coated scientists instructed ordinary people (whom we call the subjects) to do cruel and unusual things to other people (whom we call the participants) as part of an experiment in a laboratory.

In a nutshell, the subjects were instructed to administer increasing levels of electric shocks to the participants as part of a behavioural learning programme. They did so under a range of circumstances. When participants gave incorrect answers to test questions, they were to be administered a shock, with each one to be higher than the one before. (No shock was actually administered – the participants, unbeknownst to the subjects, were actually actors who performed the responses that, physiologically, would be the normal reaction to the levels of shock being administered.) When the subjects were face to face with the participants and told to administer the electric shock directly to their hands, using force if necessary, only 30 per cent of the experimental subjects did so. When the subjects could still see the participants but used a control lever that administered the shock instead of having to force the hands of the participants onto the plates administering the shock, 40 per cent did so. When the subjects could no longer see the participants but could only hear their distress as the current surged, 62.5 per cent were able to apply the current. Moving the others out of earshot marginally improved the rate to 65 per cent.

The more distance – both physically and psychologically – there was between the controllers and the controlled, the easier it seemed to be to be inhumane and cruel. The closer the relation between the controller and the supervisor, and the more removed the subject, the easier it became to continue. Obedience flows more easily when the subjects of action are at a distance. When these subjects can be transformed into objects in the controller's mind, obedience flows even more easily.

Another factor facilitating the application of the current was its incremental thresholds – once someone had committed to the action, each increase in the threshold was just a small step, just another slight increase in pain to be endured. It is not as if they started out to kill another person or cause them irretrievable injury. They just did what they were instructed to do, only they did a little bit more of it each time. Where such action should stop, once started, is not at all clear. After someone has committed to the action, especially if others are complicit, what Milgram (1971) termed 'situational obligations' arise.

Milgram (1971) made one crucial change to the experiments to test out a further hypothesis: that plurality produces space for reflection and pause for consideration. In the experiments reported thus far, there was only one expert giving instructions. He introduced another expert and instructed them to disagree with each other about the command being given. The disagreement between authorities paralysed the capacity for obedience of the research subjects: out of 20 subjects in this experiment, one refused to go further before the staged disagreement; 18 broke off after it; and the remaining subject opted out just one stage further.

Haney et al. (1973) designed an experiment in which the researchers divided a group of male American college students into two types of people: guards and inmates. They created a mock prison in a laboratory basement, using as subjects 21 healthy male undergraduate volunteers. Each person was to receive $15 a day for two weeks. Nine were randomly selected to be 'prisoners', with the remainder designated as 'guards' who were to supervise the prisoners in a rotating three-shift system. Each wore the symbolic garb of the role. Prisoners were given unflattering uniform clothing and tight caps to simulate shaven heads. Guards were put in a militaristic-type uniform and given LA cop sunglasses. Names were suppressed with norms of impersonality, and complex rules and penalties for their infraction were promulgated. Then the experiment began.

The experiment had to be aborted after less than a week. An escalatory chain of events occurred; the construed authority of the guards was enforced by the submissiveness of the prisoners, tempting the guards to further and increasingly illegitimate displays of the power that their authority allowed them to exercise, leading to further humiliation of the prisoners (Bauman, 1989: 167). Bear in mind that the subjects were all normal, well-adjusted people before the experiment began, yet after one week they were playing their roles with such conviction that the experiment had to be abandoned because of the real possibility of harm to the 'prisoners'.

IN PRACTICE

Detention centres or concentration camps?

As the world's trouble spots multiply, as some peoples become increasingly subjected to the pressures of famine, ethnic cleansing, wars of religious intolerance and the effects of military campaigns that toppled a dictator but did little or nothing to prepare a civil society in the wake of the military victory, the world is awash with millions of asylum seekers. As an island continent, Australia has a relatively small number of asylum seekers that seek to reach its shores in leaky boats run by 'people smugglers', usually sailing from Indonesia, mostly carrying people from the Middle East or Sri Lanka. Australian policy has been, for many years, to place these people in camps for processing of their claims for asylum. Over time, the policy has hardened: asylum seekers are not allowed into the country and are committed for processing to offshore detention centres. Alastair Nicholson (2014), a judge, wrote an article in which he likened these detention centres to concentration camps. As the Jesuit Refugee Service (https://jrseurope.org/advocacy?LID=725) acknowledges, such centres are global phenomena. Just keying in 'refugee detention centres' on YouTube will provide you with about 150,000 results from all over the world.

Question

1. What do you think of the ethics of putting in camps people who seek refugee status, including their children, when intercepted by authorities?

Is it possible to think of emancipation in organizations, to imagine organizations that do not dominate? Huault et al. (2014) think so. Investigating diverse literatures, they find many pleas and searches for emancipation. First, there is the 'new age' management literature, with its themes of self-discovery, freedom and rebellion (Fleming, 2009). Second, there are Critical Management Studies, which are frequently 'concerned with freeing employees from unnecessarily alienating forms of work organization' (Alvesson and Willmott, 1992: 433). Third, there are those social movements that organize for emancipation (e.g. Zanoni and Janssens, 2007). Fourth, entrepreneurs strive for autonomy in order to escape the drudgery of being under control (Goss et al., 2011; Rindova et al., 2009).

What is necessary for emancipation is the experience of inequity, of unequal distribution of opportunities for voice and recognition. In this sense, resisting means 'asserting the power of equality in every place where it is in fact confronted with inequality' (Rancière, 2009: 168; our translation). Dissensus can occur intra-organizationally but it can also be articulated outside the organization, in the wider civil society, as in the various manifestations of the Occupy movement. Another ingredient for emancipation is being able to think differently, to use a different form of sensemaking. When sensemaking is shaken up and disturbed, this occurs. Gender politics that raise feminist issues often have this effect – think of the impact of the #MeToo campaign.

In order for power to be exercised, the exerciser must choose to exert power and the subject or subjects of that power exercise must choose to obey. Where some authority establishes rules that are represented as absolutely symbolically dominant, such as the party, the nation or the leader (as in the extreme case of Hitler, the Führer, and his henchmen such as Eichmann), working according to the rules that are defined is not sufficient to justify ethical responsibility. Principles of concordance with ultimate authority as a rule for action, as either intuited or formally expressed, are an insufficient basis to ensure ethical outcomes. In a world of social relations increasingly dominated by organizations, there is an urgent necessity for ethical principles to be more widespread, organizationally, and less ritualistic, politically. And this means that managers have to be able to manage with power positively in terms of both their internal and external dealings. Here are some suggestions as to how to be able to use power but be ethical at the same time:

1. Decide what your goals should be and what you are trying to accomplish in consultation with direct stakeholders in your organization.
2. Diagnose patterns of dependence and interdependence: which individuals both inside and outside the organization are influential and important to achieving these goals?
3. What are the points of view of the important people likely to be? How will they feel about what you are trying to do?
4. What are the power bases of the important people? Which of them is the most influential in the decision?
5. What are your bases of power and influence? What bases of influence can you develop to gain more positive control over the situation?
6. Which of the various strategies and tactics for exercising power seem most appropriate and are likely to be effective, given the situation you confront?
7. Based on steps 1–6, choose an ethical course of action to get something done.

These simple steps can help us build positive, ethical power. Being a good manager means knowing how and when to use the kinds of power wisely. When using power to manage others, always remember that those you are seeking to manage will probably also be trying to manage you with power. Thus, the old adage 'do unto others as you would have others do unto you' is worth recalling. Although you may think of their response as resistance, to do so presumes a value legitimacy that may not be justified on your part. They are trying to manage your management of power through their management of the power that they can enact in the situations in which they find themselves or that they can create. Power is nothing if not creative.

Crucially, your managing with power means achieving common definition, a genuine accord, on which to base strategies, tactics and actions. Positive uses of power make things happen that would not otherwise have happened – not by stopping some things from occurring, but by bringing new things into creation, involving less force and more listening, working with, rather than against, others.

Managing with power does not always mean seeking to impose a specific meaning on an uncertain context because it entails an arbitrary structuring of others' realities. In contrast, the alternative model is often seen as one where people advocate bottom-up decision-making, seeking to listen to what others in the organization have to say. Organizations that use empowerment seek to enhance the overall systemic powers of the organization, to mobilize everyone's resources to get things done. Such use of power frequently means giving way in the organization conversation, not claiming a special privilege because of title or experience, and not being selectively inattentive to others, but listening and attending to them.

The challenge for future power theory, as Pfeffer (1992: 340) suggests, is 'to manage with power', where you recognize, diagnose and respect the diversity of interests and seek to translate and enrol members within organizational courses of action, while at the same time listening to what others are saying, modifying your position accordingly and choosing the appropriate strategies and tactics to accomplish whatever is chosen.

Sometimes, after taking all that into consideration, it still means making others do what they would not otherwise have done, against their resistance. Power can be like that. Yet, it does not have to be so. Coercive power should be the refuge of last resort for the diplomatically challenged and structurally secure, not the hallmark of management's right to manage.

DECISION-MAKING

Think of everyday language – it is in *head*quarters where decisions are made, by *heads* of departments, which the organization is supposed to follow. Decision-making is understood as management's task *par excellence* – the bureaucratic *cogito* (the thinking brain) whose decisions the corporate body should follow. Management makes decisions on strategic directions; action plans to implement them and forms of control to evaluate their effect.

Usually, the model of decision-making is described as a perfectly well-organized, rational and logical process. First, the problem is defined. Second, all the relevant information that leads to an optimal solution is collected. Third, reviewing the data, management (perhaps with the help of technocratic 'experts') develops several possible solutions. Fourth, evaluating the possible solutions carefully, management makes a decision regarding the optimal solution. Fifth, this solution is implemented in a top-down approach and evaluated constantly by management. Such constant processes of rational decision-making, supported by the latest IT equipment and an army of analysts and consultants, are meant constantly and incrementally to refine and improve an organization's processes and products. The problem of recalcitrant hands is solved by turning them into disciplined and reflexive extensions of the corporate body, able to exercise discretion, but in corporately prescribed ways.

Thus, decision-making has often been discussed as if it were a highly rational activity: a decision is seen as a rational choice based on a logical connection between cause and effect, made in the context of a rational search for solutions to something defined as a problem, for which the options can be rationally weighted and compared and the optimum decision chosen. Unfortunately, such 'rational actors' are rarely to be found outside of introductory textbooks, especially of economics; real life is a bit more complicated.

READ AN ARTICLE BY SIMON

Herbert Simon recognized that few, if any, decisions are made under conditions of perfect rationality (Simon, 1957). Issues are frequently ambiguous; information about alternatives will often be incomplete and the choice criteria unclear. In addition, others may see the issues, alternatives and choices in utterly different and sometimes antagonistic terms. And the time, energy and political will to reconcile different positions may well be lacking. Managers thus operate with limited rationality rather than complete rationality. Decision-makers can only review a limited range of factors and possibilities in making decisions because of the limitations both of the information available to them and of their cognitive and temporal ability to handle its complexity. Hence, they can only ever exercise what is known as bounded rationality – that is, a rationality that makes do within these cognitive and temporal limits rather than searching ceaselessly for all information and data that are available.

Simon (1960) makes a contrast between two types of decision that managers may have to deal with: programmed and non-programmed decisions. Programmed decisions can be made by reference to existing rubrics, are fairly easy and can be categorized as operational questions that admit of solution by applying organizational rules that subordinates can be trained to do. Non-programmed decisions have no precedents, are unfamiliar, novel and complex, and cannot be left to subordinates: they are what are sometimes referred to as messy or intractable problems.

Look at the 'In practice' example of a messy problem that CEO Gerard Fairtlough had to face in practice.[1]

IN PRACTICE

Appointing a CEO

Here is a story told from my own perspective and with the benefit of a lot of hindsight. In 1980 I led the small team that founded Celltech, the UK's first research-based biopharmaceutical company. The formation of the company was widely recognized as novel and

(Continued)

(Continued)

important. The UK was a world leader in biological science but the USA was the place where new biotechnology companies were being formed. It was hoped Celltech would reverse this trend. Celltech did turn out to be highly innovative, not only in science and technology, but also in its relations with academic research and in the openness and trust within the company, an environment right for a 'knowledge-based' business.

By the end of the 1980s, the company had been successful financially, had several key patents and a pipeline of promising projects, and it had a workforce of some 300 people, nearly half of whom were PhD scientists. Nevertheless, I found the job of CEO a demanding one and after ten years I said it was time to retire. I thought I was acting responsibly when I decided to leave. There was an obvious person to take over: my deputy, whom we will call Peter, who was very keen to get the job.

Most members of the board of directors knew little about knowledge-based businesses. Probably they were pleased to be presented with a task they found more familiar - that of appointing my successor.

The board must have had reservations about Peter as CEO, but they were not open about them. Probably they feared he would quit if he did not get the job and that this would damage the business. Whatever their reasons, the board organized a formal and lengthy search process. The process failed to produce anyone suitable and the board then announced that the search would continue for more months. Peter resigned in disgust and I said I was leaving anyway. Things looked bleak for Celltech. Then, unexpectedly, a senior person from the industry expressed interest and the board had little choice but to appoint him. In the end, he did a great job. The company continued to prosper as an independent business for ten years until acquired by a Belgian company for US$ 2.5 billion. The new owners showed their confidence in the Celltech team by putting it in charge of their whole pharmaceutical R&D.

Why did the succession process go wrong? It is clear that the board were at fault in giving Peter false hope and in asking me to go along with a phoney recruitment process. Perhaps board members had found themselves uncomfortable with their responsibility for a knowledge-based business and were too keen to demonstrate power. Perhaps Peter was too ambitious. Although I thought I was behaving responsibly, I later realized I was at fault too. I thought I was avoiding the classic mistake of the proud founder of an organization who cannot let go. But I now realize I concealed from myself that Peter was a psychological surrogate, who could continue the traditions I had established in the company. If he had become CEO, I would have felt I still had my baby.

Question

1. In practice, what lessons can be learnt from this story about power and people's motivation? How open was the process?

ORGANIZATIONAL DECISION-MAKING PROCESSES

As Miller and Wilson (2006: 470) put it, topics for decision may be complex; definitions problematic; information unavailable and/or difficult to collect; solutions hard to recognize and the process generative not so much of solutions as headaches from further problems. Most significant organizational issues involving major commitments of resources that top management teams have to deal with usually fall into this category. Problematic search, incremental solution and dynamic non-linear reiteration and redefinition of almost all the terms in the decision mix will characterize these types of activity (Braybrooke and Lindblom, 1963; Lindblom, 1959; Quinn, 1978, 1980).

Incremental decision search and solution means many small steps, which are easier to retrace if things do not go as hoped for. 'Once each small step has been taken it gives a clearer picture of what has to be done and the future becomes more focused', as Miller and Wilson (2006: 470) put it. Also, small steps are more likely to cool out resistance than big sweeping changes which will always seem obviously threatening to existing interests in a way that a smaller change – as a part of a larger iterative, emergent and unfolding design – will not.

Muddling through, as Lindblom calls it, is less scary than storming through. Common processes in muddling through include finding an initial simple impasse and further investigating it to reveal more complex political issues, from which a basic search for a solution ensues. The search is modified as the complexity and politicality of the issue start to become more apparent. Next, a basic design for a solution is advanced and then, typically, the basic design is subject to blocking moves from other interests. Finally, a dynamic design process is developed as changes are made, opponents brought on side, isolated or otherwise neutralized (Mintzberg et al., 1976; Nutt, 1984).

The muddle's decision-making process is organized according to the logic of what Cohen et al. (1972) call the 'garbage can' of situations characterized by 'problematic preferences', 'unclear technology' and 'fluid participation'. The garbage can, of course, is a metaphor. Problems, solutions and decision-makers, unlike in traditional decision theory, are seen to be disconnected. Specific decisions do not follow an orderly process from problem to solution, but are outcomes of several relatively independent streams of events within the organization. Decisions are made when solutions, problems, participants and choices flow around and coincide at a certain point. There is a large element of randomness in where they come to rest. Much as garbage in a can, what gets placed next to what is often purely random. Yesterday's papers end up stuck to today's dirty diapers just as downsizing attaches itself to profit forecasts.

WHAT WOULD YOU DO?

WHAT WOULD YOU DO?

You are a project leader. You have a multi-disciplinary project team. Your task is to devise product innovations that will influence the bottom line positively. The trouble is that the finance members of the team utterly oppose the design engineers' proposals as too costly and too experimental; the engineers utterly oppose not only the opposition of the finance members but also have to deal with the marketing people, who cannot see the value proposition in the features of the product being proposed. You are nearly half way through the time allotted to the project team to make a decision.

(Continued)

(Continued)

Questions

1. What would you do to arrive at a decision in view of the garbage can situation that you seem to be in?
2. How do you achieve purposive decision-making when all the disciplinary solutions seem to be defining the problem differently?

Starbuck (1983) similarly argued that organizations are not so much problem solvers as action generators. Instead of analysing and deciding rationally how to solve problems, organizations spend most of their time generating problems to which they already have the solutions. It is much more economical. They know how to do what they will do, so all they have to do is work out why they will do it. Just think of any consulting business – its solutions to whatever problems occur will be what it currently offers.

Hickson and colleagues (1986) looked at 150 decisions in 30 organizations; some decisions that the organizations' top managers defined as strategic were found to be resolved within a month while others dragged out over four years, with the mean time for strategic decision-making proving to be just over 12 months. Nonetheless, how the decisions were arrived at varied between three predominant processual paths, characterized by *sporadic*, *fluid* and *constricted decision-making* (Table 8.3). The more political the matter for decision, the more stakeholders tend to be engaged; the more complex the problems are, the more fluid the processes tend to be. The key stakeholders are usually intraorganizational, typically production, sales and marketing, and accounting, in the organizations that were studied.

There are two typical ways of managing implementation. Where the management team has a pretty clear idea of what it is doing, and the likely reactions of others to it, a more planned mode of implementation occurs, based on experience. Where the management team doing the implementation has less experience and is not so sure what it is doing, the receptivity of the context in which the decision is being implemented is crucial. In other words, it matters a great deal if the team can succeed in getting key people 'on-side' (Hickson et al., 2003; Miller and Wilson, 2006).

Three different ways of connecting decision-making and implementation are noted in the literature:

1. *Continuous connectedness* is provided by the key involvement of personnel usually drawn from production, finance and marketing. They see the whole phased process through, provide a memory and retain commitment as other interested parties drop out of the loop.
2. *Causal connectedness* is more complex. Three elements are crucial: the degree of contention, seriousness and endurance of the processes of

decision and implementation. High degrees of contention tend to limit familiar solutions – these are clearly not working if the contention is high – and they also indicate a context less receptive to whatever solution is proposed. Contentious decisions tend to be faster. Decisions characterized by a high degree of consensus take longer to make and implement, but there may well be a lot less firefighting afterwards (Dooley et al., 2000). The more serious the importance of the decision being made, the more specific steps will be taken in implementation.

3. *Anticipatory connectedness* involves thinking forward in terms of the future perfect tense – what we will have achieved when we have implemented the decisions we will have made. Thinking in an anticipatory way about the impact of the decision can feed back on the decision itself. If implementation of the posited and projected decision seems unlikely to be smooth, because implementation will be intricate, then the decision-making process probably needs revisiting, thus dragging out the process further. There is a form of feedback from imagined implementation to possible decision, making the decision process more protracted.

TABLE 8.3 The Bradford studies of decision-making

Sporadic processes	Fluid processes	Constricted processes
Many disruptive delays	Little informal interaction	Revolve around a central identity or figure, such as a finance or production director
Uneven quality of information	More formal meetings	Widespread consultation across a range of expertise
Many sources of information	Fewer delays	Neither as fluid nor as sporadic as the other two types
Scope for negotiation	Short cycle of decision-making	More authoritatively structured
Informally spasmodic and protracted process	Process steadily paced, formally channelled and speedy	Process carefully and narrowly channelled by the identity directing it

DECISION-MAKING AND PARADOXES

Much decision-making occurs in the face of paradox, suggests Smith (2014). The important thing is not to try and resolve paradoxes but to allow their tensions to frame dual and ongoing action. Dual commitments to both exploration and exploitation, for instance, create pressure to succeed in each domain while creating tension among business areas. In some instances, pressures to minimize internal conflict and to address external legitimacy drive leaders to choosing a single strategy rather than pursuing strategic paradoxes simultaneously, thus treating paradoxes as decision-making dilemmas rather than as paradoxes to be managed through a 'consistently inconsistent' decision pattern, in which leaders may address issues while maintaining commitments to both tensions over time (Smith, 2014).

Paradoxes denote 'contradictory yet interrelated elements that exist simultaneously and persist over time' (Smith and Lewis, 2011: 382). Paradoxes are basic characteristics and inherent features of organizational life. By definition, paradoxes resist closure (see Quinn and Cameron, 1988; Smith and Lewis, 2011). Cunha and Clegg (2018) claim that paradoxes are conceptually persistent and hence irresolvable. If paradoxes are conceptually resistant to closure, however, the more appropriate management response may be embracing, rather than resolving, paradoxes. Embracing is deemed appropriate because attending to one of the demands exacerbates the need for the other (Sundaramurthy and Lewis, 2003), or if one demand is subdued, the tension ceases to be paradoxical and resurfaces and even intensifies over time (Smith, 2014).

DECISION-MAKING AND SENSEMAKING

Some paradoxes have to be resolved, as in the following case. Allison (1971) wrote a famous case study of decision-making using the 1962 Cuban missile crisis as his topic. The Soviet Union had installed missiles on Cuba, aimed at the USA, just 70 kilometres (44 miles) away. Many people thought that the outbreak of a nuclear war was imminent as the respective leaders of the USSR and the USA faced each other off, neither willing to compromise: US President Kennedy demanded the missiles be dismantled and USSR President Khruschev argued that if NATO could ring the Soviet Union with missile bases, what was the problem with bases in Cuba? Allison suggested that the crisis looked very different depending on the type of model through which one looked at it.

If one party is looking through one model and the other party is using another model – say a rational as opposed to a political model – then the opportunities for miscalculation and misunderstanding are enormous. One side will define the matter in terms of one set of issues; the other side will define it in terms of a different set of issues. Each side will be busy organizing some issues into politics while others will be organized out, or as Schattschneider (1960: 71) put it, there will be mobilization of bias occurring, with different sides mobilizing different biases and excluding other biases. Thus, as agendas form some issues will be suppressed or poorly represented, and fall into the space of 'non-decision-making' that Bachrach and Baratz (1962, 1970) wrote about.

Non-decisions are the unspeakables of local politics, the covert issues on which it has already been decided that no action will be taken. Their existence may not even be registered as they are sidestepped, suppressed or dropped. Within organizations, the differential resources, expertise and access that attach to players in complex power relations mean that the strategy of making some issues 'non-decisions', perhaps by controlling who is given voice, or whose voice is noted, or seen as rational, sensible and useful, serves to constrain agendas in the interests of those who already occupy dominant relations of power. Like the tip of the iceberg, only those matters already acceded to be legitimate and rational make an appearance on the agenda. At its most subtle, this occurs when there is an apparent consensus about what issues are and are not, such that there is no conflict about issue definition. An apparent hegemony is created. The official view is the only view registered. Of course, this assumes that there are few opportunities for actors to create awareness about non-issues and non-decisions.

EXTEND YOUR KNOWLEDGE

You can extend your knowledge by reading the following article: Dean, D. and Greene, A.-M. (2017) 'How do we understand worker silence despite poor conditions – as the actress said to the woman bishop', *Human Relations*, 70 (10): 641–67, which is available at the companion website https://study.sagepub.com/managingandorganizations5e

READ THE ARTICLE

Dean and Greene (2017) investigate the most pervasive form of hegemony – silence in the face of evident experience and awareness of organizational disadvantage. The research investigates female actors and clergy who routinely tolerate poor quality conditions rather than express dissatisfaction. The argument picks up on Hirschman's (1970) analysis of exist, voice and loyalty as the three possible responses to disadvantageous organizational circumstances. The article considers how occupational ideologies facilitate loyalty as an adaptation to disadvantage in ways that discourage voice, in framing silence as positive, a type of loyalty they see as potentially salient in understanding silence in other occupations. Certainly, reading Dean and Greene's analysis and then looking at the testimony of BBC China correspondent Carrie Gracie's past silence about her pay – far less than equivalent male correspondents – one can see that systematic organizational disadvantage, allied with the silence of loyalty, as well as the silence of management about the discrimination in pay, maintained her allegiance.

READ THE ARTICLE

Decision-making occurs in a complex web of political relations that are constantly shifting the shape of what counts as knowledge, rationality and truth. An important part of organizational politics involves shaping the agenda, getting some issues on to it, making sure that they remain there and keeping other issues off. But remember, everyone is probably playing the same game!

One of the more difficult contexts of decision-making is when the organization is multinational and operating across diverse cultural contexts. In such contexts, decisions made at the centre often have to be adapted and made to fit at the various peripheries in terms of the specific context into which they are adopted. How do organizations manage the tension between allowing local adaptation of a management practice and retaining control over the practice?

By studying the adaptation of a specialized quality management practice – ACE (Achieving Competitive Excellence) – in a multinational corporation in the aerospace industry, Ansari, Reinecke and Spaan (2014) identified three strategies through which an organization balances the tension between standardization and variation in decision-making, preserving the 'core' practice while allowing local adaptation at the subsidiary level: creating and certifying progressive achievement levels; setting discretionary and mandatory adaptation parameters; and differentially adapting to context-specific and systemic misfits. Practices that are engineered to allow a better fit with diverse contextual specificities diffuse more readily and decision-making needs to acknowledge this rather than attempting to impose a one-size-fits-all model.

Organizations may listen or not, may work with the creativity and diversity of people's identities and the different division in the organization or they can try and standardize one set of practices. The politics of power and decision-making can be based on active listening rather than assertive denial through the instrumentality and ritual of established power. To build such organizations – ones that seek to extend the organization conversation rather than to exploit its lapses – would seem to be one of the more pressing aspects of the agenda for future managers.

SUMMARY

In this chapter, we have covered the pervasiveness of power as the most central aspect of organizational life:

- Organizationally, power is wrapped up in the velvet glove of authority but inside that velvet glove is an iron fist controlling the levers of power that authority confers.
- Power is always a relational concept, often related to control of resources - but these are always contextual
- It is important to understand the limits of power and authority, resistance and obedience and how these limits can be defended ethically.
- Organizational decision-making is a major means through which power relations are communicated.

EXERCISES

1. Having read this chapter, you should be able to say in your own words what each of the following key terms means. Test yourself or ask a colleague to test you.
   - Power
   - Resistance
   - Legitimacy
   - Domination
   - Strategic contingencies
   - Hegemony
   - Uncertainty
   - Total institutions
   - Context
   - Decision-making
   - Politics
   - Non-decision-making.
2. What power games characterize what types of organizations?

3. In what way is managing with power positive?
4. Are power and resistance inseparable?
5. Who gets empowered through empowerment strategies?
6. What is total about total institutions?
7. Where is the border between the use and abuse of power in management?
8. Why is there more to understanding power than listing its most common bases?

TEST YOURSELF

Review what you have learned by visiting:
https://study.sagepub.com/managingandorganizations5e or your eBook

- Test yourself with multiple-choice questions.
- Revise key terms with the interactive flashcards.

REVISE KEY TERMS

TEST YOURSELF

CASE STUDY

Power and megaprojects

Huge 'megaprojects' are transforming the lives of millions of people and the landscapes and cityscape in which they live. Megaprojects, conventionally, have numerical thresholds around $1 billion; however, the characteristics that elevate a project to mega-status are much more complex than simply project cost. We can define a megaproject as a unique endeavour, a project whose special conditions include higher time, budget and/or resources allocated than in similar projects. Risks, requirements and difficulties to perform it are commonly high as well. Characteristically, megaprojects are risky due to long planning horizons and complex interfaces; are carried out by fluid, dynamic and shifting project teams; have multiple stakeholders and conflicting interests. Often, they are proposed as so unusual and specific that they have a 'uniqueness bias', which leads to an escalation of commitment in their delivery and a project scope that usually changes significantly over time. Typically, these megaprojects are characterized by complex contracts, subject to highly indexical and contested interpretations, presenting many opportunities for rent-seeking behaviour by stakeholders. They are managed with overly rational expectations that lead to frequent disappointment as complexity exceeds budget and time contingencies. One consequence of these is that there is a bias towards misinformation about costs, schedules, benefits and risks; consequently, cost

(Continued)

overruns, delays and benefit shortfalls are commonplace. Given their high sunk costs, their complexity and scale, measured in terms of the numbers of people whose lives are affected, these big power adventures, when they go wrong, damage citizens' lives and have potentially hurtful effects upon large swathes of humanity and their environment.

The principle of open communication serves to limit unrestrained power, a principle that can be implemented within project management as the case under consideration demonstrates. It is a case of a megaproject that was successful and pioneered new ways of managing. It came in on time and just 4 per cent over budget and was a highly innovative project, which accomplished in two and a half years what would normally have taken seven. It was a megaproject associated with a mega-event that, from the outset, sought not to lapse into default management:

> Default managers fit easily into a recognisable and established corporate hierarchy; run on a basis of old-fashioned command and control and governance by title and status. They are usually passive, carrying out instructions that are either explicit in orders from the top or implicit in budgets, accounting timetables, and short-term targets and incentive plans. (Andrew Hill, 'On management', *Financial Times*, 11 November 2014)

The case demonstrates non-default management: management by collaboration, improvisation and inspiration. The megaproject arose after Sydney won the bid for the 2000 Olympics. By 1997, when planning of events was well under way, it became evident that for the several events that involved use of the harbour, including sailing and the triathlon, there were potential problems posed by the fact that there was mass sewerage and street detritus output into the harbour when significant rain events occurred. In 1997, judging an opportunity to implement some infrastructure development, Sydney Water, the body charged with management of Sydney's water resources, proposed constructing a 20-kilometre tunnel on the north side of the harbour which would function as a vast reservoir to hold the overflow of rainwater and the backing up of the sewer system so that the unsightly, dirty and smelly detritus did not end up in the harbour. The decision to undertake this major project in the run-up to the Sydney 2000 Olympics was taken as part of the NSW Government Waterways Project in May 1997, designed to clean up NSW rivers, beaches and waterways. Cleaning up the waters of Sydney Harbour was seen as a priority for the Olympics in 2000, given that the 'eyes' of the world would be on the city in just over three years.

With the whole world watching, it would not be a good look if the water was anything other than clean and sparkling. The problem was that they had only two and a half years to implement a project that would normally take about seven years of detailed planning, investigation of ground and subterranean conditions, securing of equipment, construction and testing. Yet, they had only two years to build the 20 km tunnel; they did not have the vital equipment – two tunnel boing machines (TBMs); there was no time for detailed geological investigation; and planning would have to be concurrent with construction. In short, high levels of risk and uncertainty characterized the project.

A further issue was that Sydney Water was one of the largest and oldest public organizations, one that had been undergoing constant change. Over ten years, since 1990, 30,000 employees had been reduced to 5,000 on the way to under 3,000 employees. The organization had been subject to various governments' demands to be leaner and more efficient, as well as become more entrepreneurial, despite diminishing resource capabilities in-house. Moreover, any project such as this was bound to be politically contentious in a state government context characterized by strongly adversarial politics between the two main political parties of Labour and Liberal. In addition, any public project would be subject to close scrutiny by commentators who were oriented towards neo-liberal economic practices: for such commentators, the public sector ought to get out of the way and allow the private sector to deliver major projects.

The norm in government work put out for tender was to drive the most competitive bargain through what are known as 'hard money' competitive contracting norms that sought to reward the offer of the lowest price for a contract by a tenderer. However, in this case there were no detailed contract specifications to work from - there was no time to produce them. Besides, faith in the competitive approach to tendering ignored the fact that a low bid, once accepted, would inevitably cost much more in practice as skilled project managers exploited the fine detail of the contractual bill of works and sought to charge for variation orders at every opportunity - the price could easily escalate. The legal profession would always be available to fix the accountabilities and responsibilities after the fact, at considerable cost.

Despite all the complications, issues and contingencies, the project was successful: on time and on budget.

What were some of the success factors? Improvisation through collaboration was important, as was the practice of open-book management: both fostered positive behaviours among partners. The partners acknowledged that ambiguity, risk and uncertainty were present productively. The normative ethos that was cultivated on the project as a part of the Sydney Olympics was also very important.

Questions

Clearly, this is a very different approach to management and power relations than we would find in the vast majority of similar cases:

1. Why do you think this was so?
2. What are the important power lessons that you take from the case?
3. What are the crucial aspects of the project's design, in your view, that created the success of the megaproject?

To answer these questions, it will help to consult Clegg et al. (2002) and Pitsis et al. (2003).

ADDITIONAL RESOURCES

- In this chapter, the focus is on organization politics, power relations and decision-making. In order to get oriented to this chapter, you might want to consult the state of the art briefings available at Henry Stewart Talks series of online audio-visual seminars on Managing Organizations, edited by Professor Stewart Clegg: please visit www.hstalks.com/r/managing-orgs, if your university makes these available to you. The relevant talks are Talk #10: Organizational Politics, by Professor Richard Badham of Macquarie Graduate School of Management, Australia and Talk #11: Managing Organizational Decision-making, by Professor Susan Miller of the University of Hull, UK.

- Following on from the discussion of the Scandinavian Way in Chapter 7, one of the distinctive characteristics of Scandinavia is the widespread adoption of democratic models in workplaces. One presentation that links 'Design, Democracy and Work: Exploring the Scandinavian Participatory Design Tradition' by Professor Pelle Ehn is available at www.cd-cf.org/video/design-democracy-and-work-exploring-the-scandinavian-participatory-design-tradition and is well worth watching for the implications for the relations between power relations and innovation.
- Many people have written about the topic of managing power in organizations, and finding just a few suggestions for further reading is hard. One place to start would be Lukes' (1974) slim volume *Power: A Radical View*, if only because of its brevity – 50 pages – as well as its elegance and lucidity. (There is a longer second edition from 2005.) If you find the previous resource interesting, you might want to try Clegg's (1989) *Frameworks of Power* and another book that he wrote with Courpasson and Phillips (2006), *Power and Organizations*, although neither is written for the introductory student.
- Probably the most interesting case study of power in and around organizations is Flyvbjerg's (1998) *Rationality and Power: Democracy in Practice*, researched in the arena of urban planning in the town of Aalborg in Denmark.
- Cynthia Hardy and Stewart Clegg's (2006) chapter 'Some dare call it power' in the *Handbook of Organization Studies* (edited by Clegg et al., 2006b) covers the field in detail.

NOTE

1. Gerard Fairtlough CBE (5 September 1930–5 December 2007) wrote this case. He was an English author, speaker and management thinker. Stewart is proud to say he was a friend. Gerard was a most impressive man who trained initially as a biochemist at Cambridge University. He worked for 25 years in the Royal Dutch Shell group, where he spent the last five years as chief executive of Shell Chemicals UK. In 1980 he founded the biopharmaceuticals firm Celltech and remained its chief executive until 1990. He was subsequently involved in the formation of a number of high-tech businesses. Fairtlough served as an advisor to several UK government and academic institutions. He was Specialist Advisor to the British House of Commons Select Committee on Science and Technology, Chair of the Advisory Panel on Science Policy Research Unit at the University of Sussex, and a member of the UK Science and Engineering Council. He also wrote management books, and was the author of *The Three Ways of Getting Things Done: Hierarchy, Heterarchy and Responsible Autonomy in Organizations* (2007) and *Creative Compartments: A Design for Future Organization* (1994), and co-author with Julie Allan and Barbara Heinzen of *The Power of the Tale: Using Narratives for Organisational Success* (2002). Gerard wrote extensively on the theory and practice of organization design and management and of innovation. He was a rare person: a gentleman and an equally brilliant manager, entrepreneur and scholar.

MANAGING COMMUNICATIONS
MEANING, SENSEMAKING, POLYPHONY

LEARNING OBJECTIVES

This chapter is designed to enable you to:

- understand organizations as communicating entities
- explain the importance of communication processes at different levels
- discuss the role of the organization in driving and structuring communication
- evaluate critically the power of communication
- appreciate why polyphony is important in organizations.

BEFORE YOU GET STARTED...

You cannot not communicate. (Paul Watzlawick)

INTRODUCTION

Organizations, first and foremost, are communicating entities; they are composed of people who are able to speak to each other and who want to speak to others. They have products to sell, news to distribute, clients to reach. Plans, change programmes and strategies all need to be communicated. Gossip, PR strategies, informal chats and jokes, as well as marketing campaigns, branding exercises, and websites communicate what an organization is all about. If you have a great business idea and a really smart plan with which to realize it but no one knows, you will not achieve anything. You need to communicate your ideas to others. For instance, you might need a bank to lend you money to kick off your project and help you through cashflow problems, or you might have to convince an investor to finance your project or recruit reliable suppliers to ensure the quality of your product. No wonder that one of the earliest treatises in organizational communication was Dale Carnegie's bestselling *How to Win Friends and Influence People* (1944).

COMMUNICATION

Communication can be defined as the exchange of ideas, emotions, messages, stories and information through different discursive means.

Communication connects all organizational activities with each other. It is a game that we all learn to play.

The process of exchanging information between two or more people or entities defines communication. Organizational communication is what occurs when an organization seeks to communicate with various audiences. These audiences may be employees, customers, investors, regulatory bodies, and so on.

IN PRACTICE

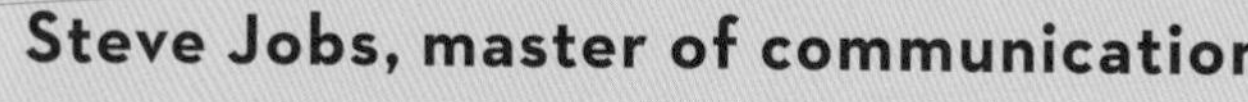

Steve Jobs, master of communication

WATCH THIS TED TALK

Communication is one of the key skills of business leaders. Take Steve Jobs, one of the founders of Apple. Early on, he recognized that communication was the key to success. When he and his team built the original Macintosh computer in 1982, they were battling against extremely tight deadlines and had to work under resource constraints. Jobs motivated his team to accomplish the seemingly impossible task to finish the project on time. In return, he engraved the names of the key designers and engineers on the inside of the computer. On the outside, the signatures were not visible; nonetheless, Jobs explained, every artist signs their artwork, and therefore his team signed their masterpiece. This was a symbolic act that soon became one of the myths surrounding Apple; the story communicated that Apple was different and irreverent: in the world of technology in which functionality was key, Jobs' idea served as a reminder that human ingenuity was still the most important ingredient in an organization. Later, when Apple was a celebrated brand, Jobs developed his story-telling skills into a veritable art. At conferences, Jobs would introduce new plans he and his team pursued or release new products. His conference appearances become such iconic events that they were labelled as 'Stevenotes'. You can find many of them if you insert Stevenotes in your search engine.

Source: Isaacson (2011)

Fascination with communication reaches back to the ancient Greek philosophers, who emphasized the importance of rhetoric. Aristotle analysed the role and power of rhetoric in public speeches and events. Following this tradition, it was 'studies of propaganda and the flow of information and mass media effects (in the first half of the twentieth century) that would lay the foundations of what is now commonly thought of as the beginning of a communication science' (Bordow and Moore, 1991: 7). The old study of rhetoric transformed into that of opinion-making, propaganda and the strategic use of information to ensure or create 'suitable' narratives that would explain and legitimize the order of things. For a state-of-the-art briefing on how to manage organizations effectively, please visit the Henry Stewart Talks series of online audio-visual seminars on managing organizations, edited by Stewart Clegg: www.hstalks.com/r/managing-orgs, especially Talk #14: Managing Communication, by James Barker.

WATCH THE TALK

In most accounts, communication is understood as a direct cause–effect relation, as an act in which information is passed from a sender to a receiver. However, in the 1950s the emerging discipline of **cybernetics** changed the field dramatically.

Cybernetics can be defined as studying feedback and other communication mechanisms in machines, living organisms and organizations.

The concept of feedback stressed that communication was not only a one-way effort from a sender to a receiver but also a reciprocal undertaking. Person A sends some information (message) to B, and this information is transported through channels (media) that might affect and change it. The message does not simply inform B, but might change B's behaviour. B's change in behaviour is noticed (received) by A, influencing future action. Put simply, communication is an interactive circle that involves sender and receiver, messages, media and feedback loops.

Early communications research used cybernetics to focus on the relationship between superior and subordinate in terms of: (a) flows of information; (b) their impact on efficiency and (c), the possible distortion of communication as it moved up and down various channels in the organizational hierarchy (Bordow and Moore, 1991). Nowadays, communication is understood not just as merely passing on information but as an active way of creating, shaping and maintaining relationships and enacting shared values, common cultures, agreed goals and the means for their achievement. Of course, in this context, the advancement of information and communication technology plays a pivotal role. With the Internet, many-to-many communication becomes, in principle, available to anyone who has access to a computer and the Internet.

IN PRACTICE

The power of mass communication

Take the example of the young activist Jonah Peretti who challenged the global sportswear brand Nike. Nike offered a customization option for some of its sneakers, where users could have their own tagline printed on the shoe. Peretti asked for the word 'sweatshop'

(Continued)

(Continued)

READ THE FULL EXCHANGE

to be printed on his trainers. Nike declined his request. You can find the full exchange by going to the *Guardian* website at www.guardian.co.uk and then searching for 'Jonah Peretti and Nike', or by clicking on the icon in the interactive eBook to go straight through to the relevant web page.

This email exchange soon caught on and went around the world, challenging Nike's million-dollar marketing machinery. Of course, without the Internet, its speed and connectivity, Peretti's critique would never have travelled around the globe.

Source: www.shey.net/niked.html; see also Kornberger (2010)

How legitimate do you consider Peretti's campaign against Nike? How legitimate do you consider Nike's refusals to accede to Peretti's requests as a customer?

Multinational companies such as Nike are fair game for critics. They spend millions providing favourable communication of their image, so it is not surprising they are subject to critical probes to uncover the reality behind the images.

Normally, different disciplines within management explore the relations between organizations and the diverse groups created, maintained and nurtured through distinct patterns of communication. These disciplines are marketing (communication with customers), public relations (communication with shareholders and stakeholders such as local communities or environmentalists) and human relations (communication with internal audiences). Bypassing this division of labour, we synthesize aspects of each discipline in this chapter to produce insight into the fascinating ways in which organizations communicate.

THEORIES OF COMMUNICATION

Organizations can be seen as multiheaded hydra (the mythical beast of Greek mythology), with many mouths speaking to different internal and external audiences. Of course, with many mouths speaking simultaneously, it is sometimes difficult to gain agreement, understand what is being said, or to remain consistently 'on message'. Organizations often suffer from these problems. Communication from one part of an organization is contradicted by a message from another. Additionally, the giant hydra does not live in a vacuum, where no other messages circulate. Instead, the environment is full of other, sometimes competing and sometimes conflicting stories: someone's got it in for the organization; they are planting stories in the press. Maybe the unions are agitating, or employees are gossiping, and the markets chatter about the stories that circulate as the hydra tries to chill out the stories it does not like or want. One site that tries to stay on message in terms of organizational communication is www.adforum.com.

IMAGE 9.1 Like games, communication is based on feedback loops: your next sentence depends on the reaction of your opponent, whose reaction depends on your action, etc.

WHAT WOULD YOU DO?

WHAT WOULD YOU DO?

On 9 April 2017, United Airlines made global news when a 69-year-old doctor, David Dao, from Kentucky was forcibly dragged off a United flight after he refused to give up his seat for an employee of a partner airline. It was announced that four existing passengers had to vacate the plane and would be reimbursed in the form of hotel vouchers and a later flight. With this offer being unsuccessful, staff members selected four passengers. However, Dr Dao refused to give up his seat as he needed to tend to patients in Kentucky the following day. Dr Dao (a paying customer) was subsequently violently removed from the plane, knocked and suffered lost teeth and a broken nose. The footage went viral and United's CEO Oscar Munoz initially defended the actions of staff and publicly called Dr Dao 'belligerent'. The stock price effect was instantaneous. What would you have done and communicated differently if you were the airline's CEO?

READ AN ARTICLE ABOUT UA

Different theories try to map this terrain. In organizational behaviour (OB) theory, the flow of instructions from the top to the bottom of an organization is supposed to ensure that employees do what management decides they should do. Within an OB perspective, there are several different emphases (Frank and Brownell, 1989). First, there is a cultural emphasis, in which communicating produces and shares common meanings and interpretations. Theorists who stress the primacy of human relations emphasize the importance of communication for a climate of openness, trust, commitment and collaboration (see also Chapters 3 and 4). Those who view OB from a power perspective understand communication as a medium through which conflicts and struggles will be played out as a means to influence and recruit others to preferred views and interests (Frank and Brownell, 1989). They do not assume that your preferences and those of others will necessarily align; in fact, they are more inclined to think they will not (see also Chapter 9).

A recent school of critical thought is referred to as *discourse theory*. From this perspective, discursive communication (including writing and speaking) informs our actions and decision-making processes. For instance, the discourse of human resource management allows you to ask certain questions, make assumptions about employees, and so on, that are entirely different from those that would be triggered by Frederick Taylor's scientific management (see Chapter 14). Think of Taylor's description of factory workers as 'hands' in the early 1900s. Thinking of them as 'hands' evokes implicit meanings including an image of a headless and heartless worker who is easily replaceable, because all they contribute is manual dexterity, which is tightly trained and controlled. This changed during the human relations movement and Elton Mayo's emphasis on emotions and feelings at work. In the 1980s, the focus shifted to workers as being human resources that can be systematically managed, trained and exploited. In each case, the particular way of speaking about workers influences the way we think about and try to manage them: in the world of an HR manager, employees are resources that should be developed, managed and harnessed. On the other hand, in Taylor's scientific management, employees were nothing but a pair of hands that were replaceable. Other contemporaries such as Henry Ford wrote over the entrance to his factory "hands' entrance". The two cases show how different labels (employees as hands or as human resources) reflect different ways of organizing and managing them. Discourse analysis argues that the differences and inequalities of the social world are directly connected to the world of language: because we use certain metaphors to make sense of the world and often do not reflect on the implications of these metaphors, they frame our way of thinking about the world and restrict our imagination. Language is the map that guides us through the world; the map does not neutrally describe the territory but actively shapes it through highlighting certain points (tourist attraction, scenic drive, etc.). In other words, language frames and sometimes even shapes reality.

Sounds complicated? It isn't. Gareth Morgan made a similar point in his classic book *Images of Organizations* (1986): if you think of organizations as machines, instead of cultures, or as living organisms, for example, it makes a big difference when you try to understand them and devise a plan of action based on that understanding.

EXTEND YOUR KNOWLEDGE

You can extend your knowledge of the role that language plays in managing and organizing by looking at Kodish, S. (2017) 'Communicating organizational trust: an exploration of the link between discourse and action', *International Journal of Business Communication*, 54 (4): 347–68; and Lauring, J. and Klitm ller, A. (2017) 'Inclusive language use in multicultural business organizations: the effect on creativity and performance', *International Journal of Business and Communication*, 54 (3): 306–24. You can access these articles at the companion website https://study.sagepub.com/managingandorganizations5e

READ THESE ARTICLES

Analysis of organization discourse suggests that the language employed in the communication within organizations shapes organizational reality. Gordon Shaw, formerly executive director of planning and international business within 3M, describes the importance of discourse in organization by using the concept of story-telling:

> Storytelling is the single most powerful form of human communication. Stories allow a person to feel and see information, as well as factually understand it. The events come alive for the listeners so that they 'see' with you and become physically and mentally involved in the story. Storytelling allows you to create a shared vision of the future ... The potential leverage in conceptualising, communicating, and motivating through the use of strategic stories (both inside and outside the enterprise) will define superior management in the future. (Shaw, 2000: 194)

IMAGE 9.2 Look at the image of a hill tribe from northern Vietnam: although the image does not speak, the dresses, the colours, the facial expressions, the posture, the fact that only women pose for photos for visitors, etc. – almost everything in the image communicates a great deal about the life of these people

EXTEND YOUR KNOWLEDGE

READ THE ARTICLE

Storytelling, done well, is a powerful tool for managing as you can see by reading Tesler, R., Mohammed, S., Hamilton, K., Mancuso, V. and McNeese, M. (2018) 'Mirror, mirror: guided storytelling and team reflexivity's influence on team mental models', *Small Group Research*, 49 (3): 267-305. You can access the article at the companion website https://study.sagepub.com/managingandorganizations5e

IMAGE 9.3 Underground

Corporate stories differentiate a company from its competitors (just as your personal story – your history – distinguishes you from anybody else) and create a shared sense of community and belonging among internal and external audiences. As organizational boundaries blur more and more, external and internal are concepts that lose their descriptive importance: employees also watch TV ads and read external messages intended for stakeholders, thus internal communication shapes how employees represent the organization to outsiders (Cheney and Christensen, 2001). Everything an organization does communicates meaning, both verbally and non-verbally (whether the organization intends or desires it to or not). It is not only glossy brochures that tell you what an organization stands for but also, much more importantly, the actual behaviour of its management and employees. In our social world, we use clothing and other artefacts to communicate who we are. Take the example of the hill tribe from northern Vietnam in Image 9.2: what does the image communicate?

The well-known saying that 'one cannot not communicate' means that even non-interaction is a form of interaction. Think of your mum who is angry with you because you did not spend time with her on Mother's Day and therefore will not speak to you. This non-communication expresses something more than words. Or think of that text message you never wrote to your boyfriend about something else that you did other than be with him. That can bring you trouble. When the girl you dated the other day does not answer your calls, she is also communicating something. It is almost impossible not to communicate.

What is true of people is also true of organizations: they communicate even when they think they do not. Consider the messages communicated by the essentially similar subway signs shown in Images 9.3 and 9.4. What do they suggest to you about the organization that each represents?

IMAGE 9.4 Metro

LEVELS OF COMMUNICATION

A conventional way of making sense of communication in organizations is to distinguish the different levels of communication. Communication can be analysed by looking at the level of personal and social involvement. Littlejohn (1989) differentiates between four levels of communication, shown in Figure 9.1.

Dyadic communication means two-party communication that can be impersonal when two people interact without direct personal contact, as well as face to face.

Whereas the first three types of communication are mainly situated in an interpersonal context (face to face, with exceptions such as a phone call or email), the fourth type is mediated through channels of mass communication (again, there are exceptions, such as 'word of mouth'). **Dyadic communication** occurs between an employee and a manager; small-group and team communication happens in meetings, brainstorming sessions, as well as workshops; finally, mass communication is at work in marketing and PR campaigns. Wherever it occurs, through whatever modes, organizational communication is a culturally driven process of sensemaking. People communicate to make sense for themselves and others; sometimes they communicate to mislead, while at other times they do so to be understood clearly. No wonder there is ample opportunity for messages to become mixed and for the wrong audience to receive or interpret an incorrect message (Watzlawick et al., 1967). Sometimes signs that communicate the same message can differ markedly; attractive communication is pretty easy to spot: compare the Underground and Metro signs.

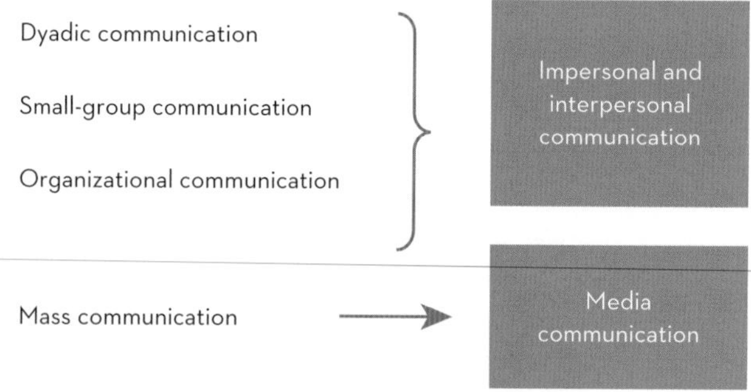

FIGURE 9.1 Levels of communication (after Littlejohn, 1989)

DYADIC COMMUNICATION: INTERPERSONAL

When the manager from production and the newcomer in the marketing department go for lunch together, or meet while smoking outside the building, they might build some understanding of each other's task that will be helpful when their company launches its next product. Sure, they may be doing other things, such as flirting, or chatting about sport or fashion, but they also get to know each other's work. They are communicating interpersonally, face to face.

Interpersonal communication refers to the direct interaction between two or more people.

Interpersonal communication is based on interdependence, where each person's behaviour is a consequence of the other's. Such behaviour can be expressed both verbally and non-verbally and have either a formally framed or informal character. A selection interview, for instance, is a formally framed organizational procedure, whereas a chat over lunch may be informal.

Every communication has an informational aspect and simultaneously tells you something about the relationship of the people involved. The manager saying to his subordinate, 'You have until Monday to write this report', or 'Would it be possible to have your report by Monday?' communicates almost the same information, but the two sentences define the relationship quite differently. Communication always has a meta-communication aspect and organization managers should be well aware of this – the way the message is projected and received is as important as the content it contains.

Communication involves multiple meanings, interpretations, distortions and omissions. It is not so much the smooth processing of information but rather the complex, interactive emergence of knowledge, meaning and narratives that drive communication. In this process, the transitions are neither additive nor linear; what you learn now may change everything you thought you knew before or will know in the future. This theme is often played out in movies such as *Sliding Doors* (Howitt, 1998), a film that showed how an accident can change the whole foundation of a relationship and of life.

Communication comprises a series of interactions seen differently by the participants (Figure 9.2). For instance, a leader with a need for control can generate resistance from employees. If the leader responds with tighter control, this is likely to generate further resistance, which may be interpreted as a lack of motivation.

IMAGE 9.5 Dyadic communication is key to human relationships. Often, it is overshadowed by multiple meanings, interpretations, distortions and omissions

Increased control can produce even more resistance and less motivation! We will encounter further examples of these dynamics in Chapter 13, when we discuss bureaucracy. When a vicious circle is in play, it is quite tricky to resolve. Both parties have good reason for their behaviour. They are part of the same interaction but they differ fundamentally in punctuating what is happening. Whereas the subordinate might argue that they are demotivated *because* of a lack of trust, the superior might stress that *due* to a lack of motivation only strictly enforced controls can guarantee a minimum of engagement. Both parties are weaving the same story, participating in the same dialogue, even agreeing on the same facts but punctuating the story differently and thus creating different realities in which causes and effects are reversed. The amplification of misunderstanding escalates in such circumstances.

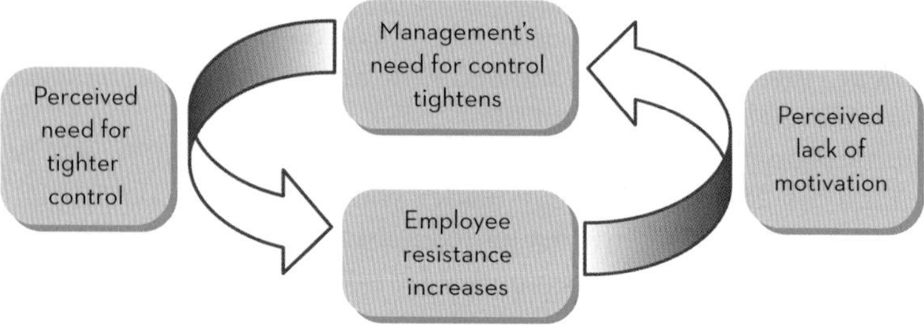

FIGURE 9.2 Vicious circles at work

IN PRACTICE

Communicative double interacts

According to Weick (1979), organizations consist of processes that he calls a double interact. Weick defines the double interact as an *act* followed by a *response* that leads to a *reaction* changing the initial act followed by a response, in an ongoing loop. Think of a typical work situation: a supervisor says that he has to control employees because they do not seem to be motivated; the employees are not motivated because they are tightly supervised and feel demotivated by the lack of trust. You can see how a vicious circle is produced and sustained. The interesting thing is that both parties live in the same world but attribute cause and effect differently. For the supervisor, tighter control is the effect, caused by low motivation levels; for the workers, tight supervision is the cause for low morale. In such a situation, both parties are right and wrong at the same time. Trapped in the ongoing loop, they can argue forever without finding a solution.

In practice, what would you do to break the loop?

An example demonstrating the double interact would be the case of a manager who tells an employee that the employee must increase productivity and quality and will be monitored more closely in the future (act). Demotivated through this lack of trust, the employee responds by taking more sick days and taking less care of quality standards (response). The manager understands this behaviour as proof of the necessity to tighten the control mechanism and reacts by increasing pressure on the employee (re-adjusted action), which leads to a drop in employee motivation, resulting in even more sick days and poorer quality! It is important to see that this vicious circle is played out in daily communication. As you already know by now, such fatal dynamics result from the complexity of communication processes (Watzlawick et al., 1967).

Can you think of any double interacts that you have experienced? How and in what ways were they double interacts? Jot them down and compare notes with your friends.

EXTEND YOUR KNOWLEDGE

READ THE ARTICLES

You can extend your knowledge of communication and its concomitants in managing and organizing by reading Rothausen, T. J., Henderson, K. E., Arnold, J. K. and Malshe, A. (2017) 'Should I stay or should I go? Identity and well being in sensemaking about retention and turnover', *Journal of Management*, 43 (7): 2357–85. You can access the article at the companion website https://study.sagepub.com/managingandorganizations5e

DYADIC COMMUNICATION: IMPERSONAL

A letter or email between you and an officer from the tax office is dyadic but impersonal.

Think of a call centre that is, by definition, an interface between customer and organization. When it puts you on hold and bombards you with uninteresting new offers while you are waiting, it is communicating how the organization that you are seeking to gain information from takes care of customer needs. Directing you through a complicated number system to the 'right' person, call centres assume that digital communication is the appropriate level of involvement. However, it is not necessarily the appropriate frame for establishing a relationship. Companies miss out on the chance to express and actively shape their relationship with consumers when they restrict themselves to such forms of communication. Also, the relationship is purely complementary: if the customer has a problem, the call centre resolves it as long as it is a standard problem – one for which it has a standard solution. However as we will see shortly, organizations can learn a great deal from their customers about what they want, how they actually use their products and what improvements they wish to see. A more dialogical style would involve customers more interactively and create stronger relationships (see also Chapter 12).

SMALL-GROUP COMMUNICATION

Group-level dynamics differ from those in dyadic communication. Think of a team with nine members. Communication is not only face to face; roles are established, subgroups formed and a different dynamic is created. A group is formed by dynamics beyond the influence of its individual members. The culture, as well as the quality of problem-solving within a group, depends on the interaction between its members. Group pressures influence their members' ways of thinking, as the phenomenon of groupthink demonstrates (Littlejohn, 1983: 237).

Groupthink occurs when a group of people used to working together end up thinking the same way (see also p. 85-7). There are six negative impacts of groupthink:

1. Groups limit the discussion of alternatives to only a few and do not consider the whole range of possible solutions.
2. Those options favoured by the majority are often taken without being revisited.
3. The group does not re-examine disfavoured alternatives.
4. Expert opinions are generally not valued more.
5. Groups are highly selective in collecting and valuing information.
6. Once a decision is made, the group is so confident that it does not think of alternatives for plan B scenarios.

Groupthink is often marked by several symptoms:

- Groups have an illusion of invulnerability.
- Groups undertake joint efforts to (post-)rationalize the actions they undertake.
- Groups tend to see themselves as inherently moral.
- Persons outside the group are branded not only as outsiders but also as less worthy in some ways – they are stupid or bad, for instance.
- Self-appointed 'mind-guards' protect the group.

The group exercises self-censorship, which ensures both uniformity and homogeneity. Thus, the negative outcomes of groupthink are enacted, reinforced and exercised in communication.

Going beyond organizations, Internet-enabled phenomena, such as crowdsourcing, can be seen as arenas for groupthink from a critical perspective. The US legal scholar Cass Sunstein (2006) argued that the cognitive limitations in processing complex information and social pressures to fit in and please others might dominate deliberations. In technology-mediated problem-solving exercises such as crowdsourcing, people might show conformity to social norms that become even stronger when they are mimicked by thousands of users (the crowd), globally.

In work situations, given that organizations rely more and more on teamwork, these tendencies to groupthink are frightening. They indicate that organizations actively have to manage communication in teams if they are to overcome these problems.

SHARED MEANINGS

Organizational communication comprises a series of recurring communication patterns that occur throughout the entire organization. In a rather awkward formula, Weick (1979) argued that organizing is a consensually validated grammar used to reduce equivocality by means of what organization members constitute as sensible interlocking behaviours. Now, this is rather a mouthful, but what we think Weick means is the following: communication takes place on the basis of shared understandings and implicit rules, which function as if they were a grammar. They produce predictable communication patterns, which organization members use to reduce the time spent worrying about the huge amount of things they do not know in order to make their tasks more manageable by focusing on the predictable. That is, they seek to reduce equivocality. The way they do this is through developing shared routines with others in the organization. These shared routines produce the interlocked behaviour expressed in and through the double interacts – different ways of sensemaking.

Placing an emphasis on consensual validation helps you understand that shared meanings form one fundamental aspect of organizations. These shared meanings are 'agreements concerning what is real and what is illusory' (Weick, 1979: 62). But meanings are not always shared. Think of organizations where the newly merged partners turn out to be sharing the same bed but not the same dreams. The merger of two companies that appeared synergistic but shared totally different cultures, styles of communication and ways of making sense – such as the Time Warner/AOL merger or Citibank and Travelers – is a case in point.

Think of a restaurant like McDonald's: what holds it together is a complex set of rules that allows all people that work and eat there to interact. When you walk into a typical McDonald's, the menu gives you several options. Ordering at the counter, you have to translate your craving into the McDonald's products and meal combinations. That is important, otherwise the person behind the counter could not tell the kitchen what to prepare next. And the kitchen could not tell the many suppliers which products to drop in next Monday. In order to make such complex chains function, every organization has particular forms, routines, practices and processes. The rules involved may be thought of as a grammar that reduces all possible combinations to a handful of legitimate ones. They all ensure that outcomes can be achieved by interlocking different behaviours and actions. Again, think of McDonald's: it could offer you an endless variety of burgers, but in order to create predictability it reduces the number to a dozen or so, throwing in a special or new choice every now and then. Of course, sometimes this grammar ossifies the organization: for instance, when McDonald's decided to add coffee and healthier meals to its product offer it had to change the way customers, employees and suppliers interacted.

All organizational reality is constituted and constructed through communication *and* miscommunication. Although formal communication programmes try to facilitate shared meaning, there will always be stories, myths and gossip circulating as well. It is important not to assume that organizations are some privileged space of shared meaning; though they may strive hard to achieve this, there are often countervailing tendencies.

EXTEND YOUR KNOWLEDGE

READ THE ARTICLE

Organizations guard what they take to be their secrets zealously: extend your knowledge of the relation between secrecy and creativity in project success by looking at Courpasson, D. and Younes, D. (2014) 'Double of quits: understanding the links between secrecy and creativity in a project development process', *Organization Studies*, 39 (2-3): 271-95. You can access the article at the companion website https://study.sagepub.com/managingandorganizations5e

Besides this internally focused communication, organizations also constantly talk to their environments and diverse stakeholders (such as suppliers, network partners, investors). Basically, organizations communicate their identity, their values and their reason for being to these audiences. Corporations seek to express a sense of what they are and, in doing so, they build strong relationships with key stakeholders. Mass communication is one (preferred) way of achieving this.

MASS COMMUNICATION

Since McLuhan (1964) coined the phrase the 'global village', the importance of mass communication has constantly increased. **Mass communication** has four characteristics: (1) it is communication to a large, anonymous and heterogeneous audience; (2) it is primarily one-way communication, meaning that feedback from the audience is restricted; (3) it is transmitted through different channels that work fast and (4), the sender is usually a big organization rather than individuals (Littlejohn, 1983). Billboard advertisements were an early form of commercial mass communication but by no means the earliest or the most pervasive in Western experience (see Image 9.6).

In contrast to the three other levels of communication, **mass communication** goes from one point to many receivers.

One of the earliest forms of explicit mass communication developed in the Christian church. In an age when literacy was not widespread, the church controlled the most powerful means of mass communication. Because the majority of the church's congregational members were non-literate, they were able to relate to iconic symbols much more easily than to sophisticated literary sources such as the Bible. The church realized this, and, as well as through the words spoken by priests to the masses as they interpreted the Bible and papal edicts, it communicated through religious art as its central representational form. The most sophisticated representational forms were the paintings and stained-glass windows of religious art, still to be seen in the churches and cathedrals of Europe. However, much more numerous and available to the populace at a local level, in their homes and everyday observances, far from the cathedrals and churches, were representations of Christ on the cross and the Virgin Mary, objects that could as easily fill a niche in the home as play a role in a procession. These were the core icons and, as such, were examples of one of the earliest and best developed forms of mass communication (see Image 9.7). These symbols played an important function. In Weick's (1969) terms, we might say that they helped to reduce equivocality about belief. Pieces of inert wood, when appropriately rendered and painted, could become holy icons, calling forth attendant rituals and behaviours.

The church was particularly effective at mass communication when there were few other organizations offering competing messages. Today, of course, most large organizations have marketing and PR departments or agencies that seek to find appropriate channels to help them reach relevant audiences and get their message across. Advertisements on TV, billboards, websites and newspapers remain organizations' preferred ways to tell the rest of the world who they are and what they have to offer. To see the world of glamorous advertisement and some outstanding ads, see the home page of the International Advertisement Festival in Cannes. While mass advertising can be costly and, as specialists argue, ineffective and inefficient, other means of interactive mass communication are therefore explored. The Internet and the Web 2.0 explosion have paved the way for new forms of communication, some of which we have already explored above.

VIEW ADVERTISING FESTIVAL WEBSITE

IMAGE 9.6 Parisian billboards add grace and style to civic space

Some theorists go even further and think of the Internet as a new form of capitalism that is built in and around communication. In this view, communication itself becomes the central resource for value creation. Think of Facebook, for example: of course, it is a means for communication but at the same time, it is an interface that translates the communication of its one-billion-plus global members into economic capital that can be utilized for targeted advertising programmes. Knowingly or not, when you push the 'like' button you work for Facebook, helping it to refine its advertising machinery. In this case, communication itself becomes the resource for value creation. In other, perhaps catchier words: if you're not paying for the product (such as in the case of Facebook or Twitter), most likely you *are* the product.

IMAGE 9.7 Christ on the cross, communicating that he died to save us from our sins

IN PRACTICE

The Twitter President: Donald Trump, President of the USA

Trump and Twitter have changed the face of politics forever. The Trump campaign and presidency have been like no other in the 230-year history of the American Republic, and have transformed the way politicians communicate with the public; often not in relation to any solid policy-related schemes or insights. Rather, analysts have suggested that Trump uses Twitter as a 'weapon to control the news cycle', as Professor George Lakoff of the University of California at Berkeley puts it, to frame ideas, divert attention, deflect attack and trial reactions.

In his first year of office, the newly elected president posted approximately 36,800 tweets. He has used Twitter most excessively to denigrate his opposition, antagonize rival world leaders, pass comment on the 'hoax' and 'con' of proven global warming and efficacy of global trade treatises, separate fact from 'fake news' and promise to 'make America great again'. Some have referred to his excessive tweeting and quick-to-draw thumbs as a vehemently childish and strong cyber-bullying presence that should be banned. In one famous response to televised claims from the North Korean leader, Kim Jong-un, of the USA being within striking range of new nuclear weapons, Trump took to Twitter to craft the following reply on 3 January 2018:

> North Korean Leader Kim Jong Un just stated that the 'Nuclear Button is on his desk at all times.' Will some from his depleted and food starved regime please inform him that I too have a Nuclear Button, but it is a much bigger & more powerful one than his, and my Button works!

More recently, however, with the seeming easing of nuclear tensions on the Korean peninsula in the formal meeting of North Korean leader Kim Jong-un and South Korean President Moon Jae-in in April 2018 in the demilitarized zone, Trump was nominated by his Republican peers for the Nobel Peace Prize, owing to his work in brokering the 'peace' between the long-standing foes. What is your take? Have Trump's tweets been an integral part of the historical meeting? How has Twitter changed the nature of global politics and the nature of communication?

Sources: Lionel Barber, Demetri Sevastopulo and Gillian Tett, 'Donald Trump: without Twitter, I would not be here – FT interview', *Financial Times*, 17 January 2018; Andrew Buncombe, 'Donald Trump one year on: how the Twitter president changed social media and the country's top office', *Independent*, 3 April 2017.

EXPLORE TRUMP'S TWITTER ARCHIVE

ORGANIZATIONAL COMMUNICATION AND ORGANIZATIONAL DESIGN

In a large and strictly hierarchically organized company, it is unlikely that the CEO will speak to people from the bottom, or that people from the bottom will be able to communicate their ideas directly to top management. Also, it is hard for different departments that are not directly linked to each other to interact. Put simply, the organizational design decides who communicates with whom directly. The more specialization, formalization and centralization, the more restricted is communication (see also Chapter 14).

Open-plan offices, shared photocopiers where people intermingle and chat, as well as corporate events where the usual sense of hierarchy is relaxed (usually when everybody is a little drunk and people may forget themselves, taking risks that only become evident when the hierarchy reinstates itself) all produce the internal flow of communication and ensure the necessary exchange that is inhibited by the formal structure. To undo these structures is the necessary precondition of rich communication processes. Following Bordow and Moore (1991), such processes have four major functions:

1. *Informative*: Communication transports information about facts and figures that are the basis for informed action. Thus, communication generates action.
2. *Systemic*: Communication is the glue between organizational members. It establishes efficiencies for social interaction.
3. *Literal*: Communication does not merely transport facts from sender to receiver but also connotes meaning and sense. In fact, communication is sensemaking.
4. *Figurative*: Communication links an organization to its wider environment. It represents an organization's identity, its mission and its purpose. Put simply, it legitimizes an organization.

Christensen and Cheney (2000) argue that the distinction between different communication disciplines such as marketing, PR and advertising is no longer easy to draw. PR functions were once specialized in their focus on an organization's contact with the public, whereas marketing tried to manage relations with customers. But when Shell, for instance, tried to sink the Brent Spar oil platform in the North Sea, it was the public who reacted quickly, loudly and impulsively. Unfortunately, this public was simultaneously its customers, so who should have reacted for Shell – the PR or the marketing department? Or take another disaster that BP is responsible for – the oil spill in the Gulf of Mexico. The difference between the public, consumers, employees and other stakeholders is increasingly blurred. Hence, different functions including PR, marketing, HR and others manage an organization's communication with its environment, seeking to get relevant information from the environment and respond to it adequately. In addition, well-informed and briefed employees can serve as employee-ambassadors in spreading the message an organization seeks to promote. General Motors, for instance, integrated internal and external communication in the 1980s as it relied on its employees (who received both commercials on TV at home and memos at the workplace) to promote an emphasis on safety (Christensen and Cheney, 2000: 248).

AUDIENCES

Communication is not just sending messages; it also involves receiving them, and different audiences are involved in the reception of meaning – which may not always be that intended. Three main audiences receive organizational communication: internal audiences (employees) targeted through **intraorganizational communication**; other organizations (partners, suppliers, etc.), who receive **interorganizational communication**; and wider society (markets, society, press, etc.).

Intraorganizational communication occurs inside an organization and typically engages organizational members.

Interorganizational communication takes place between members of different organizations.

INTRAORGANIZATIONAL COMMUNICATION

Communication can be downward, upward or horizontal, and comprises both formal and informal messages. Downward communication means the flow of communication from superior to subordinate. Such communication has several functions. It instructs employees, provides them with goals, explains how they can achieve them, gives feedback concerning their performance and seeks to build commitment.

Upward communication means the flow of communication from subordinates to superiors. It includes employees' feedback concerning rules, strategies, implementations, and so on. Employees often know most about customers, services and products, as they are in daily contact with them. Naturally, management lacks this knowledge, even though it forms the basis for strategic decision-making. So, to be good strategists at the macro level, they need to be good communicators at the micro level. A famous study conducted by MIT focused on the difference between Japanese and American ways of producing cars, which revealed that Japanese employees were more actively involved in the definition and refinement of car manufacturing process improvements (Womack et al., 1990). US industry, however, was still mainly organized according to concepts derived from Taylor, making such communications difficult. This difference in the management of communication was one of the determinants of the success of Japanese corporations during the 1980s, when they first made major inroads into US markets.

Finally, horizontal communication describes communication that takes place between different departments. Marketing, for instance, might need to know the planned product innovation for the next few years in order to align its campaign with the long-term image.

A good deal of managerial work involves providing information and facilitating communication (Mintzberg, 1973). Managers spend most of their time gathering information from other people, by talking, listening and negotiating in meetings, by informal conversation and through other media. Peters and Waterman (1982) took this idea one step further and defined a leadership style called 'management by walking around'. In essence, the manager must not only be seen around the place but also be seen to be aware of what is going on and acting on it.

An example of the power and importance of such intraorganizational communication is given by Ginger Graham, CEO of ACS, a $300 million US company. Newly appointed, she found the company in denial of the real roots of its recent failures. She wrote a plea for open and honest communication within the company (Graham, 2002). And she started to practise what she preached when, at an annual meeting, instead of saying the usual friendly things, she said, 'I've always heard about what a wonderful company ACS is, but frankly, that's not what I see'. After saying straightforwardly what everyone knew but nobody openly dared to admit, there was a huge relief in the audience and among employees that – finally – someone from top management could see and address the hot issues. What Graham did from this moment on was, in her own words, to:

> create a culture that would allow everyone in the company to feel free to tell the truth, from top managers to the people on the loading dock. Only by arming ourselves with the truth, I felt, by owning up to it, and by acting according to it, could deep-rooted problems be identified, understood, and ultimately solved. (Graham, 2002: 43)

An atmosphere of openness and honesty can be a trigger for change. All communication is important internally, even when it is addressed externally. For instance, branding and marketing communication is usually directed towards external stakeholders, but it also affects employees. Mitchell (2002) argues for the importance of 'selling the brand inside'; when done, it creates a powerful link between the services the company sells and the employees who actually sell it. If employees do not know what an organization is promising its clients, how can they live up to what is being preached? In fact, it becomes important that external and internal marketing are connected. All internally focused information is important externally: if the markets get negative reports from within a company, it will be reflected in their valuation of the firm. Check out Richard Branson's TED Talk on how to run a business: the godfather of branding provides interesting insights into management, leadership and the art of turning oneself into a mega-brand.

WATCH THE TED TALK

Mitchell (2002) provides an instance of a financial services institution that announced it was shifting from being a financial retailer to becoming a financial advisor. A year and a marketing budget later, nothing had happened. Customers did not feel that the announced shift had occurred and still seemed to see the institution in retail terms. The reason was simply that employees were not convinced by the new strategy. Marketing had targeted only customers and forgotten that there was an important internal market to convince – its own employees.

INTERORGANIZATIONAL COMMUNICATION FOR COLLABORATION

Interorganizational collaboration and networks have become increasingly important for organizations.

Like humans, organizations build relationships that sometimes end up happily ever after and, at other times, end in acrimony. Oliver (1990) distinguished six reasons why organizations might collaborate with other organizations:

1. *Necessity*: Collaboration might be based on the fact that an organization is working together with another organization in order to meet legal or regulatory requirements.
2. *Asymmetry*: Collaboration can be driven by the wish to control relevant environments. A clothes manufacturer might work closely with its suppliers in order to exercise control and power over them.
3. *Reciprocity*: The interests of two organizations might be better pursued when they join forces and form an alliance from which both benefit, such as occurs in a trade association.
4. *Efficiency*: Obviously, this motivation to collaborate is based on the idea of improving organizational performance through collaboration.

5. *Stability*: Organizations might collaborate in order to maintain a level of stability otherwise unreachable.
6. *Legitimacy*: Organizations seek collaboration in order to legitimize their own business. Shell, for instance, works together with Greenpeace, which obviously helps Shell to produce the image of a caring and responsible company.

For the growth of networks, mutual trust and consensus are decisive. This can only be achieved by communication. Two organizations working together need lots of coordination, cooperation and bargaining, which sometimes inevitably produce conflict and coercion, all of which will be played out in communication and non-communication (Irwin and More, 1994).

Successful networks rely on managed communication in which two roles are especially important – the boundary spanner and the interlocker. The boundary spanner represents and communicates an organization's goals to its environments and acquires information from the outside, which is necessary for the organization. He or she has the ability to bridge the gap between inside and outside, ensuring the flow of information across boundaries. The interlocker is a member of two organizations (say a senior manager in company A and a board member of company B) and knows things that the boundary spanner, as an outsider, would not be able to decode. Gossip, rumours and industry trends are examples of information that the interlocker can communicate because of his or her position (see also Chapter 7).

COMMUNICATION WITH STAKEHOLDERS

In **communication with stakeholders**, organizations use different distribution channels (TV, print, radio, Internet and specially organized events) to communicate what they offer. As products and services become increasingly refined and simultaneously more similar and exchangeable, organizations seek unique ways to position themselves in the marketplace. PR, marketing communication, reputation management, and branding are the organizational means for differentiation. They communicate what an organization stands for – promoting not only its products but also its core values and its identity.

Communication with stakeholders describes communication between an organization and other relevant parties (stakeholders) such as media, community groups, labour unions, politicians, etc.

As products and services change quickly and the difference between original and generic products increasingly blurs (think of the cola market with all its cheap generic brands), companies try to establish a unique identity. They create this through communications, including mission statements, corporate design (business cards, stationery, etc.), retail outlets, logos and other activities, such as sponsorship. The soft drink producer Red Bull, for instance, the biggest global energy drink manufacturer, selling more than a billion cans a year, promotes its soft drink heavily through promoting extreme sports events (www.redbull.com). The goal is to establish an image of the organization that goes beyond the characteristics of its products. Rather, the products should be promoted through this image.

COMMUNICATION AS BRANDING

When managers talk about communication, they often refer to it as the practice of branding. Olins (2000), Hatch and Schultz (2001) and one of the authors of this

A **brand** is the image an organization creates through design (e.g. its name, ads, logo), behaviour (e.g. its employees) and its products and services.

book (Kornberger, 2010) identified several reasons why branding is so influential and a key to success. First, a **brand** makes choice easier. You probably know the feeling of standing in front of a packed supermarket shelf and being completely overloaded by the information and choices you face. Market economies create choices that are paralysing when you are confronted by many interchangeable products with slight variations in packaging and product information. Powerful brands short cut the need for you to make comparisons, thus making choice easy – if somewhat redundant. Thus, branding is the conscious projection of a consistent image of itself that an organization seeks to communicate.

Second, brands help us to make up our own identity and provide us with devices to tell others who we are (or, at least, what we try to be). Just think of clothes. Wearing a Hugo Boss suit, sunglasses designed by Porsche and a Rolex instantly says a great deal about who you want to be (or be taken to be). The same goes for street-level fashion and design; they provide a source of identity. However, the icons can be quite different. For instance, see if you can identify in Image 9.8 some of the images being marketed in the selection of T-shirts hanging in the market stall, and imagine the kind of identity construction that would accompany wearing them.

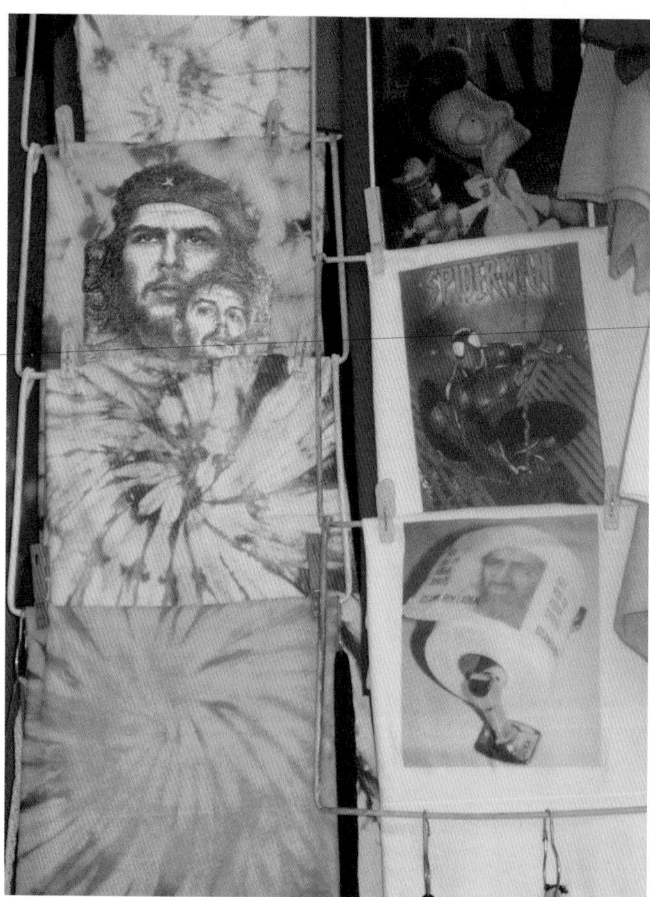

IMAGE 9.8 T-shirts in a market

From an organizational perspective, it seems having a strong brand is an asset; however, the visibility that comes with a strong brand also includes vulnerabilities; people look extremely closely at what a brand such as Nike is doing (just think back to the Jonah Peretti example) and, due to its visibility, any negative message about it travels quickly through newspapers and/or websites. At best, brands become universal signs, such as Coca-Cola, the world's most recognizable brand (see Image 9.9).

IMAGE 9.9 Do you want a Coke with that?

Branding expresses what and who an organization is. It is not just a matter of cosmetics – where stylish packaging promotes a product whose real costs are a fraction of the asking price, or packaging old ideas in new boxes – but a way of communicating the identity of the company. Think of Absolut Vodka. Its image as a company that is young, sophisticated and chic does not derive from its product but rather its products are incubated by its style. Vodka is vodka, one might say, but Absolut has managed to transform its product into a unique, recognizable and successful brand, as an icon that inspires people. It is witty, droll, iconoclastic and cool.

Icons, as Holt (2003) argues, are encapsulated myths that bring products alive. Nike, for instance, is not just in the business of selling training shoes – which are merely a vehicle for a story – because its products embody the myth of individual achievement through perseverance. In this game, products are but one way to tell the corporate myth and to provide a story that customers appreciate.

Branding is about interacting with the public and communicating your organization, its values and its contribution to society. Benetton, apart from launching campaigns that made it one of the most recognized (but also most contested) companies worldwide, also features a magazine called *Color* dedicated to issues such as slavery, prisons and refugees. *Color* is translated into many languages and sold in over 60 countries. It analyses topics and makes people aware of marginalized problems. In doing so, Benetton positions itself not just as a clothes manufacturer but also as a highly socially responsible organization that is concerned with social issues.

Successful branding involves customers and creates a relationship between them and the company. The Body Shop is an excellent example of branding. Anita Roddick, founder of The Body Shop, created a strong brand identity around the notion of a profit-with-principles philosophy. The company protests against animal testing, supports developing countries and plays an active role in women's and equality movements, to name but a few of its many activities (Joachimsthaler and Aaker, 1997). These express the company's values clearly and consistently and simultaneously motivate staff members. Benetton, on the other hand, got into trouble with its brand strategy. When Benetton started advertising using images of HIV-positive people on its billboards and picked up similar hot issues, it doubtless created brand awareness but it failed to link this awareness back to its business – selling clothes. Rather, it alienated both its target market and the retailers (Joachimsthaler and Aaker, 1997).

COMMUNICATION AT WORK

Understanding the power of communication and language enables you to utilize words to manage organizations. Take the example of employees. As a manager, you might refer to them generically as employees, but you could also call specific people, on different occasions or in different contexts, 'hands', 'human resources', 'team players' or 'stars'. Different metaphors not only affect people differently but also trigger different thoughts. Resources can be exploited and developed, whereas hands are only utilized and, symbolically, come independent of minds, brains and bodies. By using different metaphors and communicating through them, managers become storytellers that weave their own realities (see also Chapter 2). Deal and Kennedy (1982) identify three roles that stories play in organizations. First, they anchor the present in the past. They locate an organization's history and its background, which makes it possible for people to understand the current situation. Second, they maintain cohesiveness. By sharing the same stories, they provide members with a sense of community and common values. Finally, they explain why things are the way they are. Stories explain a good deal of the practices and behaviour that are displayed in organizational life. To this we might also add that they define normalcy and its range; they locate the deviant both as extraordinarily good and extraordinarily bad.

LISTENING

Communication for an expressive organization starts not with speaking but with listening. As Carl Rogers found in his experience as a psychotherapist in counselling, the main obstacle to communication is people's tendency to evaluate (Rogers,

1991). This phenomenon can be overcome by strengthening another skill – listening. Especially when people talk about emotionally charged issues, they stick to their own frame of reference and forget to understand the other's point of view. But, as Rogers suggests, change can only be accomplished by understanding *with* someone, not by understanding *about* someone.

WHAT WOULD YOU DO?

A simple technique can help you grasp the importance of listening: before you start to argue with people, summarize their points so accurately that they agree and are satisfied. Rehearse this with a friend or colleague who disagrees with you on some current issue. Listen carefully to their arguments and go away and itemize them. Think of the points of difference that you would have with that person over these issues. Marshal data and arguments that support the view that you wish to oppose their views with. Arrange to see them and then try to have a rational discussion about the points. To the extent that you are able to do this, you will have actually fully understood what they want to say – which is a much better starting point for a productive debate.

COMMUNICATION AS A STRATEGY

An example drawn from the Navistar Company illustrates the linkage of communication to strategy (Argenti and Forman, 2000). John Horne, CEO of the heavy truck manufacturer Navistar, joined it in 1993 and found the organization in a less than ideal situation. Key stakeholders (employees, unions, senior management, the financial community, media) had lost trust in the company, and the overall situation was not very pleasant. Horne decided that the way to change this was through bringing his employees on board (again) – and this happened through a well-developed communication initiative.

The first step was to visit the plants in order to engage all employees in a discussion of how to beat the competition. Soon this became a formal management task, and every month a member of senior management visited a plant. At meetings that involved some 30 workers, who talked to their colleagues about their needs beforehand, they spoke about the good things and things that could be improved. After the meeting, management published a report that included answers to the issues raised. Furthermore, assembly plant workers were invited to visit the headquarters and discuss workers' needs with the decision-makers informally and directly. Such communication practice develops joint processes of strategy making and implementing, where workers and managers learn mutually from each other.

Second, Horne started a survey of employees focusing on their specific work situations. The results of the survey were published, and an action plan was developed, including deadlines and deliverables involving union leaders, making them participants in the change process. Through these efforts and a couple of related exercises (such as a PR campaign and the introduction of leadership conferences to improve leadership), Horne put Navistar back on the road to success. He started communication processes with different audiences. Through creating a shared communicative basis, the organization enacted a common future in and through these communications (see Argenti and Forman, 2000).

POWER AND COMMUNICATION

Every way of managing involves power. Communication is no exception; it is never a neutral device to express reality. In fact, it is a powerful means to establish and reinforce organizational reality. The following story illustrates the power of communication. Thomas Watson Jr, chairman of the board of IBM, was challenged by a supervisor, described as:

> [a] twenty-two-year-old bride weighing ninety pounds whose husband had been sent overseas and who, in consequence, had been given a job until his return. The young woman, Lucille Burger, was obliged to make certain that people entering security areas wore the correct clear identification. Surrounded by his usual entourage of white-shirted men, Watson approached the doorway to an area where she was on guard, wearing not a green badge, which alone permitted entrance at her door, but an orange badge acceptable elsewhere in the plant. 'I was trembling in my uniform, which was far too big,' she recalled. 'It hid my shakes, but not my voice. "I am sorry," I said to him. I knew who he was alright. "You cannot enter. Your admittance is not recognized." That's what we were supposed to say.' The men accompanying Watson were stricken; the moment held unpredictable possibilities. 'Don't you know who he is?' someone hissed. Watson raised his hand for silence, while one of the party strode off and returned with the appropriate badge. (Peters and Waterman, 1982, quoted in Mumby, 1987: 121)

The story makes clear that regardless of power and the status within the organizational hierarchy, all members have to obey the rules equally strictly. Both Watson and the supervisor set an example of correct behaviour: Watson by organizing the right badge and the supervisor by acting strictly according to the rules. But the story also functions as a reference point for organizational members (especially for newcomers who do not yet know how the organization works in reality) and has some more subtle meanings. As the story demonstrates, everybody at IBM has to accept the rules equally. What the story does not say, however, is that these rules are established by management and people like Watson and not by the supervisor.

Mumby (1987) argues that the story has several hidden meanings that powerfully influence organizational reality. If Watson really was just another employee who has to follow rules, the story would not be worth retelling. Simultaneously, Watson is introduced as an 'ordinary' employee who can be spoken to as much as any other member of the organization, but at the same time he appears as a godlike figure in the story. Just look at the description of the two actors. The supervisor is described as a 'twenty-two-year-old bride weighing ninety pounds whose husband had been sent overseas'; her clothes do not fit her and she is nervously facing Watson. While the story paints a poor picture of her, only working because her husband is overseas, Watson appears as a mythical figure, surrounded by the kind of entourage that normally accompanies a king. Whereas the supervisor speaks, Watson, again godlike, does not speak at all – other people speak for him. And even at the point in the story where he might have spoken, he simply raises his hand and things happen. Using this ostensibly innocent story as an example, you can see the power of communication at work. It tells organizational members how they have to behave (follow rules strictly) and simultaneously it promotes and reinforces organizational power relations (Watson as a godlike figure, Burger as a woman who struggles with her job).

Communication is more powerful when it uses images instead of words and concepts. Looking at how leaders spark people through communication, a team of researchers analysed the communication style of US presidents and the inspiration felt by citizens (Roche, 2001). The results of their study were interesting. Presidents who were described as charismatic and great used image-based words to communicate their vision. They painted verbal pictures that truly inspired their fellow citizen. John F. Kennedy said in his inaugural address, 'Together let us explore the stars, conquer the desert, eradicate disease, tap the ocean depths, and encourage the arts and commerce'. Compare this with Jimmy Carter's address in which he said, 'Let our recent mistakes bring a resurgent commitment to the basic principles of our nation, for we know that if we despise our own government, we have no future'. Whereas Kennedy used lively pictures, Carter used abstract concepts that seem to remain empty and fail to create commitment. Donald Trump represents an example of a president that successfully deployed simple slogans and dystopian visions and images of the future. Put simply, image-based communication is more powerful than conceptually driven language. Instead of just talking about sustainability, for example, addressing how we can preserve the planet for our children's children would be more likely to move people.

If you watch the documentary *An Inconvenient Truth* by David Guggenheim (2006) and *An Inconvenient Sequel: Truth to Power* by Bonni Cohen and Jon Shenk (2017), featuring Al Gore's attempts to battle climate change and navigate the politics and needs of nations to broker the Paris Agreement, you will see that it is a great example of masterful storytelling. When you watch these documentaries, focus on the metaphors, the imagery and the other rhetorical devices that made it such a success – but not with Donald Trump.

Sometimes the announcement of a fact creates that very fact. This power of prerogative is humorously illustrated in an example from sport that you can find in Weick's book (1979: 1): 'The story goes that three umpires disagreed about the task of calling balls and strikes. The first one said, "I calls them as they is." The second one said, "I calls them as I sees them." The third and cleverest umpire said, "They ain't nothin' till I calls them."' As the third umpire argues, balls and strikes do not exist independently of judgement; rather, they become real only when they are pronounced as such. In philosophy, this case is discussed as performativity: it occurs when the utterance of a word constitutes a new reality. Take the example of a marriage ceremony, in which saying 'Yes' changes reality (and saying 'No' probably as well). It is through language that a new state of affairs comes into existence. Now think of more complex situations, such as rating agencies' announcements of the creditworthiness of firms or states. By stating that a state (such as Greece during the financial crisis from 2009 onwards) might face difficulties meeting its repayments, and hence downgrading its creditworthiness, two things happen: first, interest rates that the state has to pay for loans will rise, which will make it more difficult for the ailing state to recover; second, people who lose trust in the state will withdraw their money, hence triggering the crisis that the rating agencies had warned about.

In this scenario, the rating agencies' reports turn into a self-fulfilling prophecy: they become true because they have been announced.

WATCH THIS TED TALK

POLYPHONIC COMMUNICATION

Polyphony means literally the presence of many voices and hence different ideas and perspectives.

In a metaphor often used by writers and artists, organizations may be said to be similar to the Tower of Babel,[1] with its imperfect and diverse buildings, the product of people speaking many tongues. Different cultures and subcultures, each having their own voice, enact messy organization reality. Instead of forcing all people to speak one language, homogenizing the organization in monotonic communication, which would lead ultimately to the death of creativity (see also Chapter 12), management must recognize the value of **polyphony**.

Boje (2002 [1995]) has a metaphor for understanding organizations that makes use of *Tamaraland*, a theatrical production. *Tamaraland* is a play in which different acts take place simultaneously in different rooms, between which the audience is free to move. What a member of the audience encounters, as well as the sense they make of it, will vary markedly according to the route they take around the rooms. The production makes problematic notions of what it is to be a member of the audience. More importantly, however, the play disrupts notions of linearity, especially through the way in which the audience may have infinite experiences of the play by virtue of the order in which they have entered particular rooms. For Boje, *Tamaraland*, as multiplicities of meaning, outcome and experience, is a projection of contemporary organizations. His suggestion is that although organizations may well be scripted through missions, strategies and so forth, there are too many directors (i.e. finance, marketing, human resources) for only one script to be followed.

Boje suggests that we regard organizations as a meta-theatre, as a multiplicity of simultaneous/discontinuous dramas, whose sense you make as you go along. Multiple people make multiple senses and successful processes of sensemaking listen democratically to voices normally silenced. People from the periphery (newcomers and outsiders) will think more creatively because they are 'exposed to ideas and developments that do not conform to the company's orthodoxies' (Hamel, 1996: 77). Thus, rather than provide strong leadership that silences dissent, organizations should use the polyphony they have available in their narratives. 'Narratives', as Mumby suggests, 'provide members with accounts of the process of organizing. Such accounts potentially legitimate dominant forms of organizational reality, and lead to discursive closure in the sense of restricting the interpretations and meanings that can be attached to organizational activity' (Mumby, 1987: 113). Thus, narratives are not only devices of sensemaking but also a 'politically motivated production of a certain way of perceiving the world' (Mumby, 1987: 114). As we have argued using the IBM example above, stories told can also have powerful effects. Stories enact and reinforce a certain image of an organization that can influence its members almost subliminally, beneath the threshold of their awareness. Those narratives that provide the matrix for normal organizational talk, action and decision-making can, therefore, be productive or counterproductive, functional or dysfunctional. If the images are monotonic, have been conceived remotely and imposed downwards onto organization members, there is greater probability of a lesser sense of ownership, commitment and responsibility, because few opportunities for participating in sensemaking or sharing have been created. By contrast, seeking to manage organizations polyphonically means engaging in different stories that are communicated through different channels with different means at the same time. In doing so, we reduce the risk of groupthink and increase our ability to think creatively.

SUMMARY

In this chapter, we have visited the notion of organizational communication and, specifically, organizations as communicating enities:

- Organizational communication is central to managing. It ranges across many approaches to analysis, as we have seen. Key theories come from the areas of organizational behaviour and discourse theory.
- Communication occurs at different levels, including interpersonal, impersonal, small-group and mass communication.
- Managing communication means managing with power. It involves speaking, listening and meaning making from and across many different identities.
- Managing polyphony requires rethinking monotonic meaning, singular cultures and one-way communication organized in a top-down authoritative model.

EXERCISES

1. Having read this chapter, you should be able to say in your own words what each of the following key terms means. Test yourself or ask a colleague to test you.
    - Communication
    - Sensemaking
    - Identity
    - Polyphony
    - Groupthink
    - Branding
    - Public relations.
2. What are the main approaches to communication theory?
3. What, in the context of management and communication, are vicious circles and how do they happen?
4. What are the main media for organizational communication?
5. How do words socially construct organization realities?
6. What is the power of silence in the IBM story?
7. How would you manage in a polyphonic organization?

REVISE KEY TERMS

TEST YOURSELF

TEST YOURSELF

Review what you have learned by visiting:
https://study.sagepub.com/managingandorganizations5e or your eBook

- **Test yourself with multiple-choice questions.**
- **Revise key terms with the interactive flashcards.**

CASE STUDY

Managing communication

Data is an ICT communication agency. Data started out developing tailor-made applications based on inspiration from artificial intelligence computing. Within ten years, Data grew from a small core of 12 developers to more than 130 employees. As the company grew, the projects it performed got bigger and its services slightly more product oriented. With a continuously growing portfolio of projects and continuously growing size of these projects, Data needed to enhance project management skills in the organization. These skills included formal project management procedures, such as budgeting and contract negotiation, as well as softer skills, such as the management of client expectations, team motivation, and so on. A wide range of project management skills proved hard to nail down. These skills were typically tacit practices lacking clear-cut definitions, involving emotions and people skills, drawing on collages composed from a wide range of experiences. In communicating these skills, the experiences of the employees and managers, across the time and space barriers that project work placed on them, became a central issue.

One of the tools developed for this cause was Scheherazade's Divan. According to the ancient Persian tale, Scheherazade is the story-teller in the *1001 Arabian Nights*. Each night for 1001 days she tells the King of Persia a story and his waiting for the next story is what keeps her alive. Like Scheherazade, Data figured that it needed stories to stay alive, or at least to keep on growing, thus it created Scheherazade's Divan. Scheherazade's Divan is a virtual story mediator, designed as computer software that presents stories. It presents a large sample, all of them created by employees and managers in Data. These stories are comprised of different formats, such as text, cartoons, movie cuts, sound files, and so on. All employees in Data can contribute stories, and there are no predefined notions of style or content. In other words, Scheherazade's Divan is an attempt to articulate and capture some of the informal practices in the organization, nourish them and spread them throughout the organization.

One day, a programmer chose to videotape himself telling a story from a project he had just entered. The project was fairly large, the customer had recently criticized the mid-project deliveries and there had been internal friction concerning the staffing of the project. In the video, the programmer criticizes the project, identifies project members, describes the contribution of some of them quite harshly, and portrays himself as a knight in shining armour, saving the project. As he does this, he sits, laid back, by his computer, with an ironically twisted grin on his face. Less than two hours after the videotape was presented on Scheherazade's

Divan, the management team removed it. Within minutes, the whole organization knew not only that the story had been withdrawn but also that it was there in the first place. The whole organization was in a buzz; some resented the idea of censorship, some thought that the story as it was told should not have been presented in that way, and still others thought that it was correct that the story as they thought it occurred should be told.

Questions

1. The creation of Scheherazade's Divan can be explained as an authorizing of employees' knowledge and voices. Discuss the pros and cons of enabling, and authorizing, informal communication in a public space.
2. Censorship of communication is found in any workplace. Discuss the different formal and informal forms that it might take.
3. Communication such as Scheherazade's Divan was intended only for internal dissemination: is it realistic to think that what is designed for inside stays inside?

Case prepared by Kjersti Bjørkeng, NTNU, Norway.

ADDITIONAL RESOURCES

- It is probably just as well that you are familiar with some of the popular accounts of the importance of organizational communication – as they have been so influential – and none has been more influential than Carnegie's (1944) *How to Win Friends and Influence People*.
- A classic text for understanding the mass media of communication is McLuhan's (1964) *Understanding Media*. It would be interesting to take his ideas about what constitutes 'hot' and 'cool' media and apply them to some of the media that have developed since he wrote.
- In terms of critical perspectives on communication, including the nature of organizational communication as gendered discourse, the volume edited by Corman and Poole (2000) entitled *Perspectives on Organizational Communication: Finding Common Ground* is a useful, if advanced, text.
- The classic film about organizational communication is the superb early Francis Ford Coppola production *The Conversation* (1974). The context of *The Conversation* was Watergate and the fascination with the Nixon tapes and Nixon's surveillance tactics on his colleagues as well as his enemies. We see it as an organizational allegory on the centrality and difficulty of really understanding communication when the message is opaque and the intent mysterious, and the effects can be deadly. It is also an allegory on how we can use communication strategies to conceal rather than reveal.

- A more recent film in which the paradoxes of communication are highlighted is *Into Eternity*, directed by Michael Madsen and released in 2010. The documentary follows Finnish efforts to find a safe deposit for its nuclear waste for the next 100,000 years. A deep geological repository is being constructed for waste storage. One of the most interesting aspects of the documentary concerns the communication of the storage site: should large signs in all languages inform the visitor about what is stored underground? And should large sculptural structures warn the visitor about the dangers of the site? But is this not the same communication strategy as the Egyptians and their pyramids pursued – with the unintended result that their imposing structures triggered interest and that the writings on the wall are lost, after only 3,000 years? Should the site best be forgotten then? Or would such forgetting only resurface as the myth of a hidden treasure, aka Troy?

NOTE

1. According to Genesis 11, the Tower of Babel was a tower built to reach the heavens by a united humanity to reach their God. God, observing the arrogance of humanity in the construction, resolves to confuse them to prevent any further attempts. He does this by making the previously uniform language of humanity one of multiple languages, immutable each to the other, thereby preventing any such future efforts. The story is an origin-myth about the multiplicity of languages.

MANAGING KNOWLEDGE AND LEARNING

COMMUNITIES, COLLABORATION, BOUNDARIES

LEARNING OBJECTIVES

This chapter is designed to enable you to:

- explain the basic theories of knowledge management and learning
- understand the importance of these theories for organizations
- examine the benefits and shortcomings of these approaches
- understand the challenge that learning and managing knowledge poses for management
- identify organizational practices that encourage learning.

BEFORE YOU GET STARTED...

'In a learning organization, leaders are designers, stewards, and teachers. They are responsible for building organizations where people continually expand their capabilities to understand complexity, clarify vision, and improve shared mental models – that is, they are responsible for learning.'

Peter Senge

INTRODUCTION

In 1988, Arie de Geus, Senior Manager at Royal Dutch/Shell, wrote an article in which he stated: 'the only competitive advantage the company of the future will have is its managers' ability to learn faster than their competitors' (1988: 74).

When one investigates the ways in which management researchers have addressed knowledge, some distinctly different approaches are discernible. Psychologically oriented researchers have focused on different learning styles: how knowledge is acquired, how people learn and how knowledge is transferred. Sociologists have looked at learning from the more general perspective of social structures and interaction, emphasizing the influence of power, politics and ideologies. From the 1980s, with the rise of a cultural perspective on management, the importance of norms, values and rituals is more obvious.

However, knowledge really sprang into prominence when change management became linked with organizational learning. In particular, Peter Senge's bestseller *The Fifth Discipline* (1990) made knowledge a hot topic. We live in a knowledge society, in which information is paradoxically both the most valuable resource and one that constantly overloads us to such an extent that we neglect its richness and depth. In such a world, the management of this knowledge and its development (i.e. learning) becomes one of the most important concepts in management practice. Hence, almost every major consultancy has a knowledge management practice these days, in which it seeks to exploit present knowledge to develop opportunities for further knowledge. We investigate, first, where know-how might come from and then we consider the types of knowledge that might be the sources of know-how.

Knowledge: The stock of ideas, meanings and understandings and explanations of how phenomena of interest are structured and relate to other phenomena.

KNOWLEDGE MANAGEMENT

SOURCES OF KNOWLEDGE

Knowledge, **knowledge management** and **organizational learning** have become buzzwords of our age. Not only should students and adults learn, but also whole organizations and even societies are supposed to learn constantly. Lifelong **learning** seems to be the most valuable asset in an age in which information is everything and knowledge is the key to success. According to management guru Peter Senge, the distinctive feature of successful companies is their ability to learn (Senge, 1990). Companies such as General Electric, Coca-Cola and Shell use learning concepts in their organization and claim that they are the key to success. In short, knowledge seems to be the most important strategic asset of organizations.

Knowledge management: the process of managing knowledge - know-how and know-why - to meet existing and future needs.

Organizational learning: the process of detection and correction of errors.

Learning is the process of acquiring knowledge and capabilities in addition to those already known.

The concepts of learning and knowledge management have many parents, as Easterby-Smith (1997) pointed out. Usually thought of as something that individuals do, learning is often associated with specific institutions, such as a school or a university. However, recently there has been a shift of emphasis to informal and work-based learning that occurs outside these specific institutional areas and in employing organizations. In many respects, organizational learning is similar to individual learning. The idea is that organizations learn when the *knowledge* that their members have is explicitly known and codified by the organization. Organizations should seek to make as much of what their members do as explicit as possible. If members leave, the *explicit knowledge* that they developed in their jobs should stay. Two distinct streams – one from psychology and one from more technical approaches to management information – come together in this literature. The older tradition of information management emerged from library studies because, once upon a time, if you sought knowledge, it could most readily be found in books and libraries.

What previously was scarce and zealously guarded is now freely available. Knowledge in the modern world is everywhere; it is no longer under strict control by monastic authorities. Books are just one medium used to process and store technical information; information processing now includes databases and, of course, the Internet. There are many places where we can acquire and learn different approaches to knowledge. Today, you are more likely to find out what you need to know from a laptop than a book. Knowledge can take many different forms and can derive from many sources: figures, information, written instructions, stories, rumours, gossip, beliefs, and so on. Think about where people at work – in particular, decision-makers – get their knowledge. In the modern world, much of what people know comes from formal bodies of knowledge, especially science. Universities educate tomorrow's managers and, through imparting information about management research, these educational institutions seek to provide knowledge about how current issues might be resolved. Of course, universities are not the sole providers of knowledge. Fulop and Rifkin (1999) argue that the following four particularly influential sources of knowledge are far more important than scientific treatises and management textbooks:

- *Learning by doing*: The complexity and variety of managerial tasks make it hard to formalize what managers do when they manage. Thus, to obtain most of their knowledge, they learn when they are actually in the middle of managing. Common sense, reflection and informal conversations with their colleagues tell them how to react and what to do in certain situations. Such action-oriented behaviour is not always the best, however. Consider how often things get broken when you learn while you do, compared with an approach where you think before you do, and then learn. The classic example of the difficulties of learning while doing is the story of the Apollo 13 space mission, which introduced the phrase 'Houston, we have a problem' to the wider world. Here the mission, seemingly routine, was under way, when the crew and ground-based flight command had to learn and improvise their way from disaster to triumph.
- *Hearing stories*: Managers learn what their job is all about through stories that are told in the organization. Stories are good formats because they relate the core of an experience (and take the freedom to embellish it a little to make it more interesting). Accounts of how a tricky problem was solved, an important deadline was met, or a disobedient employee was disciplined, communicate the message of how things are done in the organization. Regardless of whether or not these stories are true, they form a template for managers' own experiences and help them make narrative sense of messy situations.

- *Being exposed to popular accounts*: Fulop and Rifkin (1999) refer to stories that are printed and communicated through management seminars as exemplary cases drawn from a great organizational culture. These accounts often tell how great CEOs managed to turn around large organizations and how their practices can be applied by almost everybody, everywhere, anytime. These popular accounts, sometimes communicated through the quality popular business press (such as the *Harvard Business Review*) as well as the general media, provide a clear focus on how to do things, summarizing them in case studies. Equipped with the success story of how other managers developed outstanding practice and gained standing ovations, it is intended that manager readers will be impressed.

READ THE FULL ARTICLE

- *Being curious and doing research*: As Tim Dean (2014) argues in *The Conversation* in an article entitled 'Why research beats anecdote in our search for knowledge', research drives out ignorance. It is one of the very best ways to learn. He cites the example of disease and notes that for the majority of human history disease was wrongly attributed to witchcraft, sin or unaccountable mechanisms such as 'miasma', the fog that was thought to spread cholera and other diseases. As a matter of sensemaking, given preponderant ways of making sense, these all seemed plausible and intuitive. But they were utterly wrong, thus crippling our ability to treat them. Most diseases are caused by microscopic pathogens beyond the ken of common sense and discernible only through possession of a good theory and good microscopes.

Given this research, it was with some concern that we recently read an article in *Audit&Risk* that UK business leaders rank data and analytics third after personal intuition and experience and the experience of others as the basis for decision-making, according to a new report by PricewaterhouseCoopers and the Economist Intelligence Unit. These findings were corroborated by Canadian research publicized in the *Toronto Globe and Mail* on Thursday 2 October 2014 that reported that 73 per cent of Canadian executives said they went with their gut instinct when making their last big decision. Of course, from a sensemaking perspective, we do not find these results entirely surprising; however, as researchers we find our lack of surprise at these results deeply worrying. We are supposed to be living in a world of reason, of big data, of knowledge management, yet, if these results are correct, major investment decisions are often made on a lack of data. One good aspect of the results is that the 43 per cent of executives who say that their companies are highly data-driven report the biggest improvements in decision-making over the last two years. All executives said top priority over the next two years is to make investments in the quality of data analysis to make better decisions.

TYPES OF KNOWLEDGE

Ironically, what we know about the concept of knowledge itself is actually limited. Polanyi (1962, 1983) came up with a distinction that still dominates the debate. His basic idea was that we know more than we can tell. At first, this may sound paradoxical, but think of the example of riding a bicycle: you might be able to do it, but you cannot describe this complex process in all its aspects and facets. Another example would be the rules of grammar: you must use them to communicate clearly but you probably could not spell out all the rules that you were using at any particular time. Thus, Polanyi differentiated between two types of knowledge: **tacit knowledge** and **explicit knowledge**.

Tacit knowledge is knowledge used to do things that you cannot necessarily articulate. An example is the knowledge required to ride a bike.

Explicit knowledge is knowledge consciously talked about and reflected on, usually elaborated and recorded for learning.

Nonaka (1991) and his colleague Takeuchi (Nonaka and Takeuchi, 1995) adapted the notion of tacit knowledge for management practice. For Nonaka and Takeuchi, explicit knowledge is the formalized, accessible knowledge that can be consciously thought, communicated and shared. Tacit knowledge, on the other hand, consists of personal beliefs, values and perspectives that individuals take for granted; they are not easily accessible and thus are hard to communicate. Tacit knowledge is a personal cognitive map that helps you navigate – consciously or not – through routines, practices and processes. Organizationally, it enables you to fill in the gaps between what is formally stipulated and what you actually do.

Nonaka (1991) differentiates between four basic patterns of knowledge creation, as shown in Figure 10.1. Looking at the fourfold table that he creates, we can see that, as the grid suggests, there are four major movements during which knowledge is created:

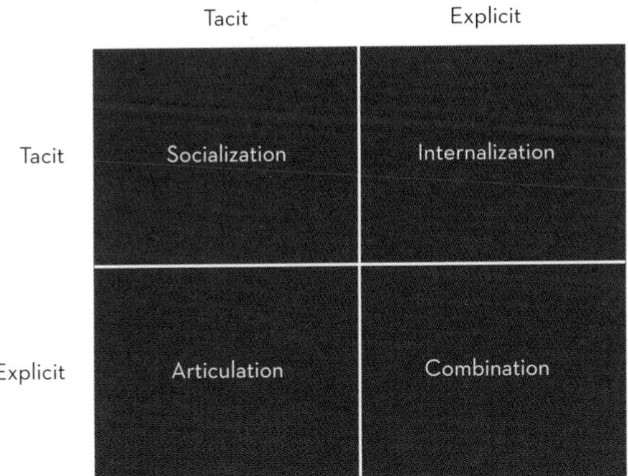

FIGURE 10.1 Nonaka's tacit and explicit knowledge dimensions

1. *Socialization (the move from tacit to tacit)*: People learn codes of conduct and rules of behaviour implicitly from other people without ever thinking about their meaning. Think of how you have learnt basic behavioural patterns: rarely will you have acquired them through reading a book and reflecting on them. Rather, you probably absorbed them through mimicking how others behave. Hence, your knowledge guides your actions but you have little awareness of why and how it does so. Often, we become aware of our own set ways of thinking and doing things when we visit

other cultures: suddenly even the simplest things that we take for granted are done differently; when we ask why this is the case, more often than not the answer will be a shrug with the shoulders rather than an explicit explanation. A good example is rules of behaviour in traffic: while the explicit traffic regulations in Ho Chi Min City and Hamburg are rather similar, the tacit knowledge you need to master traffic could not be more different.

2. *Combination (the move from explicit to explicit)*: People combine ideas they are already well aware of. You tell me the latest news in microbiology, and I tell you what is happening in microphysics. An organization allies with another and knowledges are combined (Badaracco, 1991). Such a combination can be decisive; when Sony collaborated with Apple, the two produced much more elegant microcomputers than Apple could have achieved on its own. Similarly, Sony learned a great deal from Apple, which led to the production of Sony's own array of portable computers, before quitting the PC market. Open-source platforms such as www.innocentive.com formulate problem briefs and seek solutions from outsiders who receive a reward if they manage to solve the problem. Such collaboration is based on knowledge sharing rather than on the creation of new knowledge within an organization (see also Chapter 12).

3. *Internalization (the move from explicit to tacit)*: Things that you learned once become a pattern in your repertoire; you begin to take them for granted and you forget that you learned them in the first place. If you start working in a new job in a different country, you might at first wonder why things are done the way they are done but after a while you accept them as a social fact of that society. Therefore, newcomers are often a valuable source of insights, as they have not (yet) become accustomed to the culture of an organization; they might be able to see things that could be done differently.

4. *Articulation (the move from tacit to explicit)*: Through articulating and sharing within the organization, new knowledge becomes accessible and part of official processes. For instance, the US-based product design firm IDEO developed a sophisticated research methodology that it uses to discover customer needs. One technique is simply asking the question 'Why?' several times until customers can articulate the real reason why they want to buy a certain product. For instance, you might say that you prefer a certain fashion brand because you like its style and quality. Asked why you like the brand, you might reflect and answer, 'Because my friends wear it' – which reveals that the brand is as much a symbol of being part of a community as it is a piece of clothing.

In the last decade, management theorists have increasingly suggested that tacit knowledge contributes significantly to innovation processes (see also Chapter 11). Thus, it is very important for management to attempt to organize and manage tacit knowledge, and to try to transform elements of tacit knowledge into organizationally explicit knowledge – an idea that marks the birth of the concept of knowledge management.

TACIT VERSUS EXPLICIT KNOWLEDGE

The difference between the two types of knowledge is easy to understand when you look at artificial intelligence programs. For example, the information needed to play chess is highly explicit knowledge that you can program into a computer; indeed, the computer can calculate the best move in any given situation faster than a human brain. On the other hand, it's quite difficult to instruct a computer to make small talk or be funny; the rules for what you are supposed to say, when you are supposed to laugh (even if it is just to be kind), or when something is meant to be ironic, cynical or offensive are deeply embedded social behaviours that are almost impossible to turn into explicit knowledge. If you ask a friend why they behaved in a certain way during a conversation, and the friend says, 'Well, simply because that is what you do', then you know that your friend is referring to tacit, not explicit, knowledge.

No wonder management tries to dip into the pot of tacit knowledge; whereas explicit knowledge encompasses all you can talk about, tacit knowledge is a much deeper and richer source, and knowledge management is the instrument that is supposed to allow managers to savour this rich stew. Developing this resource and aligning it effectively with change became the domain of what is known as organizational learning.

EXTEND YOUR KNOWLEDGE

You can extend your knowledge by looking at Ingvaldsen, J. A. (2015) 'Organizational learning: bringing the forces of production back in', *Organization Studies*, 36 (4): 423-44 ; and Van de Ven, A. Bechara, J. P. and Sun, K. (2018) 'How outcome agreement and power balance among parties influence processes of organizational learning and nonlearning', *Journal of Management*, http://journals.sagepub.com/doi/full/10.1177/0149206317698021, to learn about current research on organization learning that you can access at the companion website https://study.sagepub.com/managingandorganizations5e

READ THE ARTICLE

ORGANIZATIONAL LEARNING

Obviously, talking about learning touches on a rather broad field: for example, you can learn to drive a car, you can learn a mathematical formula by heart, you can learn how to play the drums, and so on. Each of these processes requires different skills, timing and involvement. Although learning something by heart goes rather quickly (and is in fact forgotten quickly because it involves repetition and lodges in short-term memory), learning to play an instrument can take years and requires that you have *talent* (an inherent potential which you either have or do not). Learning to drive a car is an entirely different kind of process from the others; it involves not only cognitive but also complex bodily skills. To be a good driver, your feet must touch the clutch and accelerator, your hands must act according to what you see and the information you are processing (about the road conditions, traffic, and so on), and you must factor in your experience of similar situations. Organizations accomplish far more complex processes than driving a car. How do they learn to fly to the moon (as NASA did), organize peacekeeping missions (as the UN does) or coordinate the activities of over 100,000 employees (such as German industrial giant Siemens, which employs 400,000 people globally).

Let us start with a simple question: what is organizational learning? In the past, managers valued only what was explicit, codified and routine, yet gradually, with the systematic development of management, they began to realize that organizational learning – similar to the skills mentioned in the previous paragraph – involves far more than meets the eye. Whereas Taylor (1967 [1911]) sought to establish one best way to do things that it was management's task to enforce, elsewhere, especially in Japan, the emphasis shifted to one of continuous improvement (Kono and Clegg, 1998). The premise was that it was not only managers who should know what was happening – other members of the organization might also know and might even be able to think of better ways of doing things. The organization could learn from the tacit knowledge, short cuts, experience and improvements introduced by its members. If all of these were captured and implemented, then they could be a powerful source of competitive advantage. That management might not, a priori, know best was a significant retreat from the position of scientific management.

Taylor's scientific management in 1911 was basically an attempt to find out what workers were actually doing so that it could be codified. Before Taylor, managers set the agenda and the objectives of what was to be done, but they did not know how workers actually achieved what they did. Often, actual practice was based on craft knowledge. Taylor wanted to change this situation; the lack of knowledge on management's side made it hard for managers to tell realistically how much time workers should take to do a certain task. Moreover, when problems suddenly occurred, management could not react because it lacked the know-how of workers. Taylor set out to change this state of affairs, trying to get the knowledge out of the workers' heads and into management's prescriptions to make it an accessible and objective phenomenon for managerial control. Taylor was convinced that knowledge was power and managers should own it; more contemporary managers, exposed to the philosophies of continuous improvement and quality management, might agree with the sentiment but not have the same expectation of monopoly rights. Knowledge can be and is generated anywhere and everywhere in the organization: often, the hierarchy of power is the exact reverse image of the hierarchy of ideas. Employees that meet customers on a daily basis and learn about their feedback often know more about potential new innovations than management which spends time in internal meetings and planning processes.

EXTEND YOUR KNOWLEDGE

READ THE ARTICLE

Jiang, Y. and Chen, C. C. (2016) 'Integrating knowledge activities for team innovation: effects of transformational leadership', *Journal of Management*, 44 (5): 1819–47.

You can access the article at the companion website https://study.sagepub.com/managingandorganizations5e

CAN ORGANIZATIONS LEARN?

Although you might agree that learning is an important concept for individuals, can entire organizations learn? Is it only the members who learn how to do things? How do organizations learn? Think of old and established organizations, such as the Catholic Church. Its liturgy has changed entirely over the centuries but the organization goes on, seemingly forever. In the Church as well as in secular organizations, what persist are the routines, practices and stories that embody and enact the organization's individual character. The specific character of an organization is formed through its routines, processes, practices and stories – put simply, those cultural facets that constitute where organizational knowledge is 'stored'. To change organizational culture – the store of knowledge – organizations must both relinquish old habits and learn new ways (see also Chapter 6). Looking at those organizations that seem best able to learn is a useful practice. What types of organizations are best at organizational learning? This is a question that Professor Simon Mosey (2014) answers. It is, he says, the airline industry, 'an industry that learns from its mistakes. It's no exaggeration to say that every plane crash makes the next flight safer.'

READ SIMON MOSEY'S ARTICLE

IN PRACTICE

How do organizations learn?

There is a simple way of imaging how organizations learn. Think of your university: there is a certain way students have to enrol – courses are described online and in brochures; electives and majors are communicated through the website; assessments consist of multiple-choice tests, group work, essays, and so on. The point is that universities have established this way of doing things over centuries. If your lecturer leaves, the university will continue to do the same thing. In fact, after about 30 years, the entire staff of your university will either be retired or work elsewhere. Still, the university will work with the same processes and routines that are now played out by other staff. On this perspective, it matters very little what individuals learn; organizations have their own way of doing things that has grown historically. In order to change this way of doing things, it is not enough to educate employees; rather, practices have to be changed and turned into new routines. In practice, if this happens, we speak of organizational learning.

The biggest enemy of learning (besides the usual suspects, such as lack of interest) is, ironically, knowledge itself. Whenever we assume that we know something, this implies that we can stop learning about it. In fact, often we think that when we know, we do not have to learn any more. We know how to ride that bike, drive that car or chant that liturgy. The problem is that we do not know how and when to know otherwise. Starbuck (1983) offers a good example: Facit, the assumed name of an organization in the 1960s that produced better mechanical calculators at lower cost than any other company in the world, failed exactly because it thought it knew what to do:

> The engineers within Facit itself concentrated on technologies having clear relevance for mechanical calculators, and Facit understood these technologies well. Top, middle

(Continued)

(Continued)

> and lower managers agreed about how a mechanical-calculator factory should look and operate, what mechanical-calculator customers wanted, what was key to success, and what was unimportant or silly ... No resources were wasted gathering irrelevant information or analyzing tangential issues. Costs were low, service fast, glitches rare, understanding high, expertise great! ... Relying on the company's information-gathering programs, the top managers surmised that Facit's mechanical-calculator customers would switch to electronics very slowly because they liked mechanical calculators. Of course, Facit had no programs for gathering information from people who were buying electronic calculators. (Starbuck, 1983: 92)

In practice, Facit's problem was exactly that it already knew a lot, which made learning seem like a waste of time. However, after the market and technology had changed, it was too late to learn the lessons that the competition had learned. Facit failed because it knew too much about what it did and had insufficient knowledge about competitors, technologies and customers.

Having read the Facit case, to what extent can this analysis be extended to other firms such as Nokia or BlackBerry? Use the web to investigate and create a case.

LEARNING AS ADAPTATION

Levitt and March (1988) as well as Argyris and Schön (1978) tackled the kinds of problems that led to Facit's failure when they thought about how organizations can learn and change. Their theories still provide the template for most accounts of organizational learning, so we explore them in detail. Levitt and March (1988) understand learning as a process of adapting to the environment that an organization is dealing with. Organizations turn past experiences into routines and learn in this way. Learning is played out as adaptation to environmental changes; think of new technologies that force organizations to explore the new opportunities they make possible. Speaking generally, such learning processes increase an organization's competence and thus are beneficial. However, Levitt and March identified what they call the 'competency trap'. It occurs when an organization does something well and learns more about it until it becomes such an expert organization that it does not see the limits of its achievements. It cannot change in response to the changes in its environment because it has become so focused on doing things its way, even when it becomes evident that the old routines are no longer working.

The example of the failure of Facit makes the point. Although Facit learned to build the best calculators in the world, it failed because it relied on its competencies. Its competencies made it blind to what it did not know. What it did not know was that electronic innovations were outflanking the knowledge basis of what it was that they knew so well. In common parlance, they were about to expire and the future would consign their technology to the junkyard. It was this phenomenon that Argyris and Schön (1978) tackled from an inter-organizational perspective when they distinguished between single- and double-loop learning – which sounds a bit knotty but is actually a quite useful distinction.

Single-loop learning means optimizing skills, refining abilities and acquiring the knowledge necessary to achieve resolution of a problem that requires solving.

Double-loop learning means changing the frame of reference that normally guides behaviour.

SINGLE- AND DOUBLE-LOOP LEARNING

Argyris and Schön (1978) were among the first researchers to focus on the phenomenon of organizational learning. In contrast to Levitt and March (1988), they researched the organizationally internal preconditions and implications of learning processes. To understand ways of learning, they differentiated between two types of learning: **single-loop learning** and **double-loop learning** (or learning I and II).

If you attend a training seminar where you learn to use PowerPoint and related programs, you will obviously learn something (even if you only learn that you do not want to learn how to use PowerPoint!). Such learning happens within a given frame of reference: the parameters are given and clearly defined, and the learning experience focuses on how to optimize (or maximize or increase) your capacity within this frame. This is an example of single-loop learning.

Double-loop learning is not the acquisition of knowledge that you need to accomplish a given task; rather, it involves rethinking the task and considering whether its accomplishment is beneficial or not. Managers in a weekend seminar discussion of the company's mission and core values are engaged in double-loop learning processes when they redefine the market for their products or the products themselves.

To put this distinction metaphorically, single-loop learning involves learning the competencies necessary to play a certain game successfully, whereas double-loop learning requires thinking and learning about what is the most valuable game to play. Single-loop learning concerns acting according to the rules of a certain game; in contrast, double-loop learning involves learning what the actual rules of the game are and how they could be changed to make another game. Single-loop learning focuses on optimizing problem-solving behaviour in a given context, whereas double-loop learning challenges the core assumptions, beliefs and values that frame the context. In the words of Argyris and Schön (1978: 2):

> When the error detected and corrected permits the organization to carry on its present policies or achieve its present objectives, then that error-and-correction process is single-loop learning. Single-loop learning is like a thermostat that learns when it is too hot or too cold and turns the heat on or off. The thermostat can perform this task because it can receive information (the temperature of the room) and take corrective action. Double-loop learning occurs when error is detected and corrected in ways that involve the modification of an organization's underlying norms, policies and objectives.

For organizations, these distinctions have important implications. Whereas single-loop learning is important to improve performance incrementally, double-loop learning questions the business an organization is in, its culture and its strategic vision. Double-loop learning represents an ability to reflect on the single-loop learning processes and to understand when fundamental change is required.

Single-loop learning is fine as long as everything stays in place so that what you are doing has a market and customers keep returning. But it is risky. It only needs some innovation elsewhere – through double-loop learning – and your customers might vanish and the market disappears. Your organization, if it is not double-loop learning, could soon be in trouble.

IMAGE 10.1 The popular Nike Air trainers

IN PRACTICE

Learning at Nike

To make these concepts more concrete, think of the example of Nike. When Nike learned how to produce shoes more cheaply through outsourcing to Asia or learned to improve the quality of its shoes by engaging athletes in their design, it was engaged in a single-loop learning process. But when Nike, thinking that its shoes were completely over-engineered for everyday use, stripped the design out of them, it began a process of double-loop learning. The result of Nike's action was that customers no longer wanted to buy the shoes because they no longer embodied the Nike spirit. Customers wanted to wear the shoes their idols wore. In facing and resolving this challenge, Nike was engaged in a double-loop learning process. In such a situation, Nike had to find out which business it was in, what its mission was and what its core value proposition was. Learning that normal customers love over-engineered sports shoes because such shoes communicate something that customers cannot get anywhere else, fundamentally changed Nike's understanding of its identity and how the company should do and be what its identity entailed (Hatch and Schultz, 2001). Put simply, to improve how you do things you engage in single-loop learning. In order to question what you do and change it more fundamentally, you will have to engage in double-loop learning.

LEARNING THROUGH EXPLOITATION AND EXPLORATION

March (2002) writes about the **exploitation of knowledge** and **knowledge exploration**. The exploitation of knowledge focuses on the repetition, precision, discipline and control of existing capabilities. The hallmark is process improvement, deepening and refining existing knowledge about ways of doing things, which is risk averse and measurement oriented; it seeks measurable improvement in performance as a result of systematically identifiable causal factors. Exploitation is aided by strongly legitimated and uncontested organizational cultures where people know and perform in highly institutionalized appropriate ways.

The **exploitation of knowledge** occurs through routinization, standardization and formalization of what is already known and done: doing it more cheaply, quickly, efficiently.

March contrasts knowledge exploitation with knowledge exploration. Knowledge exploration requires more relaxed attitudes to controls and institutional norms. Evolving and adaptive organizations need to be able to exploit and explore simultaneously. If they are only good at exploitation, they will tend to become better and better in increasingly obsolescent ways of doing things; they will find themselves outflanked. And if they are only specialists in star trekking, in exploration, they are unlikely to realize the advantages of their discoveries, as they lack the exploitative capacities to be able to do so. Organizations have to learn to balance search and action, variation and selection, and change and stability (March, 2002: 271). Organizations will most often attempt risky exploratory behaviour when they are failing to meet targets rather than when they are achieving them; however, risks are best taken when there is sufficient slack in or surplus of resources that the organization can afford to risk different ways of doing things. In many respects, however, it is least likely that risks will be taken at this time because the grooves of success are already directing the organization.

Knowledge exploration involves serendipity, accident, randomness, chance and risk-taking, not knowing what one will find.

From March's perspective, organizations that abandon what they know best in search of the new will be led only to error and failure. Only those few organizations that were able genuinely to exploit novelty – paradoxically by rapidly driving the unknown out of exploration – would survive, although not for too long.

March offers a good diagnosis of why efficient forms of exploitation are likely to continue to be reproduced as the dominant organization form. Where innovation does occur, it is likely to be rewarded only where its exploration rapidly becomes exploited. If organizations fail to exploit what they know efficiently, they will wither and atrophy. If organizations fail to explore how to do different things (double-loop learning) or the same things differently (single-loop learning), the same fate will befall them. Organizing successfully involves managing both exploration and exploitation so that they are balanced because too much of either, when pursued single-mindedly, leads to atrophy. While particular organizations may come and go, the forms that they exhibit are much less likely to display the radical discontinuities that some of the gurus of management, such as Peters, would suggest. As March says, it is tenacity more than awareness that most revolutions require.

March (2002: 275) states that '[i]maginations of possible organizations are justified by their potential not for predicting the future (which is almost certainly small) but for nurturing the uncritical commitment and persevering madness required for sustained organizational and individual rigidity in a selective environment' (2002: 275). Many organizations must fail so that the few models of difference may survive 'in a system that sustains imaginative madness at the individual organizational level in order to allow a larger system to choose among alternative insanities' (March, 2002: 276). Empirical research thus far suggests that the majority of new organization practices remain incorporated within traditional organizational forms, that organizations may embrace new technologies and practices but do not necessarily change their forms in consequence (Palmer and Dunford, 2001).

March (2002) thinks that the framework of increasingly rapid organizational change will be more likely to create rapid incremental turnover in organizational forms than radical discontinuities. In an environment demanding greater flexibility and change of organizations, these changes will tend to play out not just in individual organizations but also in terms of the population of organizations. Some organizations will be selected as efficient, adaptive and legitimate, whereas others will not survive because they do not match what the environment requires. March foresees a future of short-term organizations that are effectively disposable. These organizations will efficiently exploit what they know how to do until some other organizations emerge to do this better. Then they will die. Adaptability will occur at the population level rather than necessarily at the specific organizational level. Overall, efficiency will be served, although specific organizations may not survive. Not every organization can be a survivor.

For March's scenario to be realized, however, there has to be a pool of organizations that are discontinuously exploring learning through active imagining. Of course, without the pioneering of new forms and structures, there would be no new and more efficient mutations of organization forms to succeed those that already exist. Now, if March is right, what this probably means is a double-edged movement: McDonaldization of the efficient but relatively disposable exploiters of knowledge, with the exercise of imagination reserved for those organizations that seek to explore new forms of knowledge. What is foreseen are highly innovative science-based knowledge organizations in gleaming towers for the highly paid, skilled and educated, on the one hand, and, on the other hand, lots of street-level organizations that are exploitative and relatively impoverished, providing a poor working environment.

EXPLORATION AND EXPLOITATION

- If organizations cannot exploit what they know efficiently, they wither and atrophy.
- If organizations cannot explore so that they know how to do different things (double-loop learning) or the same things differently (single-loop learning), they wither and atrophy.
- Organizing successfully involves managing both exploration and exploitation.
- Organizations must be balanced and structurally include exploitation and exploration in the form of the ambidextrous organization, for example.
- Too much of either pursued single-mindedly leads to atrophy.

THE SUCCESS TRAP

Paradoxically, March's theory suggests that success can breed failure. The phenomenon has been described as the success trap. It arises from being too good at exploitation. Imagine an organization that keeps on repeating actions that mimic what was successful previously, and consequently develops highly specific capabilities that new ideas do not match in action, thus encouraging aversion to exploration. A good example would be General Motors, Chrysler or Ford, the giants of the US auto industry. They developed tremendous know-how in building big cars that US consumers liked – before petrol prices soared and consumers developed a sense of environmental responsibility. Asian car manufacturers were quick to respond and offered more suitable alternatives, while the former US giants failed initially to explore new green technologies and innovative car designs fit for the twenty-first century. Consequently, in 2009 General Motors, which was formerly the biggest US company, had to file for bankruptcy. Or think of the story of the calculator manufacturer Facit: it also became a victim of its own success.

In many respects, it is least likely that risks will be taken during success because the grooves of success are already directing the organization. March offers a good diagnosis of why efficient forms of exploitation are likely to continue to be reproduced as the dominant organization form. A successful organization will resource activities and promote people that contribute to that success; however, at the same time, tomorrow's winning ideas might question past recipes for success and hence implicitly undermine the organization's hierarchy and culture. Where innovation does occur, it is likely to be rewarded only where its exploration rapidly becomes exploited. The moral of this story is that organizations cannot rely only on their past experience and know-how: being in too deep a groove is dangerous. This fact has also been demonstrated to exist individually as well as organizationally. A study by Bayus (2013) on crowdsourced contributions to Dell's online 'IdeaStorm' community, for example, demonstrates that individuals' prior success tends to limit their chances of future success. That is, what aspects of information and knowledge individuals attend to become biased by past heuristics. Thus, organizations need both exploration *and* exploitation but not too much of either. The question is: how can we design for this?

In a series of articles, Charles O'Reilly and Michael L. Tushman (2004, 2008) developed the idea of the ambidextrous organization. They posit that organizations are capable of balancing the duality of exploration and exploitation by structurally separating exploratory activities from the organization's core exploitative activities. The specialist exploratory subunit possesses unique processes, structures and cultures that are specifically intended to support early stage exploration that runs in parallel with the larger parent organization that is focused on exploitation. More recent studies have started to question the efficacy of this approach in practice, however, especially for smaller organizations that lack the resources structurally to separate exploratory from exploitative activities (see Durisin and Todorova, 2012). Contemporary approaches suggest that the capacity to simultaneously explore and exploit is not only influenced by the organization's design configuration but also by the individual manager's network connections (Rogan and Mors, 2012, 2016).

EXTEND YOUR KNOWLEDGE

READ THE ARTICLE

Rogan, M. and Mors, M. L. (2017) 'Managerial networks and exploration in a professional service firm', *Organization Studies*, 38 (2): 225–49. You can access this article at the companion website https://study.sagepub.com/managingandorganizations5e

KNOWLEDGE MANAGEMENT AND ORGANIZATIONAL LEARNING

Most management theorists differentiate between knowledge management and organizational learning. For us, knowledge and learning are closely interlinked concepts, or two sides of the same coin. On the one side, knowledge management focuses on the actual creation, dissemination and transformation of knowledge; on the other, learning involves change in the existing state of knowledge. Thus, we argue that knowledge management focuses on the existing resources within an organization and learning focuses on the dynamic development of these resources. In practice, these two can work against each other: establishing routine knowledge through databases limits the potential for the organization's members to learn new ways of doing things as the established routines are privileged and these routines drive out the space and opportunity for innovation. In practice, a tension has to exist between opportunities for learning and opportunities for routine repetition.

WHAT WOULD YOU DO?

WHAT WOULD YOU DO?

You have recently joined the quality team at an aged care facility and one of your initial assignments is to devise organizational learning programmes that will help to make long-term patients more comfortable. The facility wants to build a reputation as the leading provider of aged care with a quality of experience for patients second to none. You are aware that the basic clinical requirements are being met but the facility seems to have very little evidence of being able to learn, as most knowledge seems tacit and goes when an employee or patient leaves. Given that the facility wants to improve the quality of living and the experiences for its patients and families, especially by developing ways of learning from the patients and their families and friends in improving service delivery, what would you do? Being a management major, you have learnt about 'organizational learning' and 'tacit' knowledge' in your studies: how would you translate these into an action programme to deliver what the facility wants in terms of improvements to service quality? How could you encourage single-loop and double-loop learning? What kind of knowledge would the two different learning cycles yield?

DRIVING FORCES BEHIND KNOWLEDGE AND LEARNING

In summary of the chapter so far, we can understand organizational learning as being 'best applied to organizations which are able regularly to monitor and reflect on the assumptions by which they operate, so that they can quickly learn about themselves and their working environment, and change' (Gabriel et al., 2000: 323). As we saw with Levitt and March's (1988) and Argyris and Schön's (1978) analyses, learning is about self-reflection, which triggers insights into organizational routines, beliefs and values. After these facets of an organization are understood, they are open to being changed – theoretically. But how is such learning actually accomplished and what are the driving forces behind learning? In this section, we focus on two major arenas that drive learning: communities of practice and collaborations. Whereas the first concept focuses on learning within an organization, the second explores the learning that occurs when organizations collaborate.

LEARNING IN AND THROUGH COMMUNITIES OF PRACTICE

According to Etienne Wenger, a **community of practice** represents a social learning system that develops when people who have a common interest in a problem, collaborate to share ideas and find solutions.

With his concept of a **community of practice**, Wenger (1998, 2002), a consultant and researcher, understands learning as a process deeply embedded in what he calls a 'social learning system'.

Wenger argues that learning does not happen just in the individual mind, departmental routines or organizations; rather, learning is a process that occurs in social learning systems. Consider your own experience as a student of management; of course, learning takes place (we hope!) while you are reading the lines we have written. But, equally important, you learn in the classroom when interacting with colleagues and teachers. Perhaps you might talk to a friend who is working, or think of the experiences you had in casual jobs you took during summer vacations, or maybe you already have a job – these are the resources that you use to make sense of what you hear. Or maybe you watch movies or read newspapers and link what you see and read back to what you are learning in the higher education context. When you speak to a friend who decided to study law instead of management, maybe you try to explain why you enjoy studying management and why it is important. Combined, it is all these interactions that make up what Wenger calls a 'social learning system'.

When such a system is established, it often blurs the boundaries of single organizational contexts. It creates learning alliances (between a university and an organization, perhaps), regional clusters (maybe a group of organizations in a high-tech industry, such as in Silicon Valley) and global networks (think of all those Linux users, unknown to each other, who, through cyberspace, are making the Linux system ever more robust and challenging Microsoft). Learning often takes place through the almost imperceptible networks that bind us together with others, both inside and outside the organizations in which we work. Translucent and like a spider's web, the objective of networks is to capture knowledge.

For organizations, Wenger's (1998, 2002) ideas have important implications; learning does not occur in isolated activities such as training weekends or know-how seminars offered every six months. Rather, it happens within the normal contexts that span organizational boundaries and processes and that bring many different activities together. As Wenger puts it, the interplay between the competence that an individual's institutional environment represents and an individual's own experience is what triggers learning.

IMAGE 10.2 Informal learning in progress

COMMUNITIES

Wenger's (1998, 2002) notion of communities of practice captures the actions that take place in social learning systems. Regardless of whether you look at a group of students who work together on a project, the R&D team of an organization, or a street gang, they are all communities of practice because they are the social building blocks of learning systems. It is within these communities that we define what counts as competence, whether it involves designing a successful project answer, developing breakthrough innovations, or solving a problem.

Take the example of a design firm: organizational members are dressed casually and wearing a 'cool' T-shirt with interesting prints from foreign cultures is seen as appropriate clothing. Ideas are developed in brainstorming sessions and by looking at design work from artists and other creatives. The development of products such as a new logo takes place through a playful trial and error process in which the individual designer needs creativity, passion and courage to develop something new that will not only please the client but also other, fellow designers. Now compare this with a large accounting firm such as PricewaterhouseCoopers: organizational members are dressed formally, other than on informal dress-down Friday, and values of professionalism are held in high esteem. Rather than brainstorming ideas, solutions most often come from the diligent study of similar cases, the scrutinizing of books and decisions from the high court. A good solution is one that not only respects the law but also saves the client money. In the two cases, each community of practice defines what constitutes competencies: in the case of the design firm, it is creativity, thinking outside the box and experimentation; in the case of the accounting firm, it is detailed legal knowledge, sound understanding of the client's business and reliable advice that has to hold (sometimes) all the way up the high court. According to Wenger (2002), different competencies are defined by three elements:

1. *Sense of joint enterprise*: Members need to understand and share what their particular community is about and how they can contribute to their community. Put simply, if you work for PricewaterhouseCoopers you need to understand the core values of professionalism and respect the organizational model of the partnership. If you work for a design firm, creativity and knowledge about trends is key to becoming a successful employee.
2. *Relationships of mutuality*: Communities are built and sustained through interaction between their members. Through interaction with each other, they establish relationships of mutuality. To be a member, you must be trusted as a member of this community. Put simply, if you are a member of the Mafia, or want to pass for one, you have to be prepared to live outside the law that everyone else follows. Diego Gambetta's fascinating book *Codes of the Underworld: How Criminals Communicate* (2009) provides some great examples of how undercover police agents had to commit minor crimes in order to be accepted by the members of the organizations they attempted to infiltrate. Gambetta recounts that some criminal syndicates challenge potential new members to commit a random murder – something an undercover police agent clearly could never do. The movie *Donnie Brasco* (Newell, 1997) with Johnny Depp tells the story of an undercover agent who lives through the dilemmas of mutuality in order to be accepted as part of the New York Mafia.
3. *Shared repertoire*: Over time, communities of practice produce a common history. They establish a shared repertoire of stories, languages, artefacts, routines, rituals, processes – put simply, a culture. Being a member of a community means having access to this repertoire and the knowledge of how to use it accordingly. Think of the scene in the movie *Gladiator* (Scott, 2000) in which the character Maximus, played by Russell Crowe, finally gains the acceptance of his peers by behaving, fighting and talking like a gladiator.

The social learning system encompasses many smaller communities of practice. These communities, equipped with a sense of joint enterprise, relationships of mutuality and a shared repertoire, are the building blocks of learning. Obviously, these building blocks are not good per se – just think of the shared repertoire of stories that can often be organizationally quite scathing. Shared understanding and trust are the basis for communicating about change, but, as we have seen theoretically with Argyris and Schön (1978) and practically with the example of Facit, shared assumptions can lead to homogeneity, blindness and groupthink (see also p. 297-8).

BOUNDARIES

Communities of practice must interact with other communities, which shifts the focus to the boundaries around communities. On one hand, boundaries are important because they trigger the establishment of a community. However, on the other hand, they need to be spanned and transgressed to facilitate the flow of information. The boundaries around communities of practice are less clearly defined than organizational boundaries. For instance, a community of practice can involve not only parts of an organization but also an important supplier who works closely with the organization.

READ THE ARTICLE

EXTEND YOUR KNOWLEDGE

Beane, M. (2018) 'Shadow learning: building robotic surgical skill when approved means fail', *Administrative Science Quarterly*, online 9 January 2018, https://doi.org/10.1177/0001839217751692. You can access the article at the companion website https://study.sagepub.com/managingandorganizations5e

IN PRACTICE

Walmart

A good example of close collaboration between an organization and its suppliers is the US-based retailer Walmart. Being the largest people-employing organization in the world, with about 1.6 million employees and a turnover of more than US$250 billion, Walmart can make or break the business of its suppliers. If your company produces toothpaste and Walmart decides to stock it in its almost 4,000 stores, you can be almost 100 per cent certain that your sales will increase manifold. Walmart will also help you to develop and refine your product: through access to its massive database, you can learn in which stores customers buy your product, when they buy it and what else they put in the shopping cart. Walmart will also help you to figure out the best way to package your product and how to deliver it to the Walmart supercentres from where the products are housed. Often, this collaboration becomes so close that suppliers open up offices next to the Walmart headquarters in Bentonville, Arkansas. Procter & Gamble, for instance, has several hundred employees working in Bentonville who liaise every day with their largest customer and work on improving their collaboration.

Communities of practice can evolve across organizational boundaries and can include non-organizational members. Boundary-spanning activity is important because it offers unique and rich learning opportunities. Being confronted with an outsider's perspective or challenged by someone with a different social and cultural background can trigger new insights. The clash between what you take for granted and what someone else might see in a different light can become the starting point for an innovative and creative process (see also Chapter 12).

Wenger (2002) argues that communities of practice can become hostage to their own history, and an outsider or newcomer might challenge the repertoire that makes them inert and reactive (see also p. 336). Managing the boundaries of interaction between the communities of practice that form a social learning system is thus an important managerial task. As Wenger (2002) suggests, there are three ways of managing boundaries – through people, artefacts and interaction:

1. *People*: People can act as brokers between communities of practice and span their boundaries. Think of a woman who is a board member of an organization and also works as a senior manager in another company. She lives in two worlds simultaneously and can infuse one community of practice with knowledge from the other. By doing so, she creates learning opportunities for both. Of course, brokers run the danger of being marginalized, overlooked and becoming invisible in communities because they do not exclusively and fully belong to only one community. Thus, managing their needs, expectations and experiences is an important task. Sometimes organizations explicitly seek such members – for instance, when they want to have *interlocking directors* (people who already hold a directorship in another company and can bring to bear their experience from that firm and industry to a different type of organization).
2. *Artefacts*: Objects such as tools, documents, models, discourses and processes can act as boundary spanners as well. Think of a bar in which people from different backgrounds meet and chat. In this case, a bar's preferred beer brand, the type of music it plays or the sports it broadcasts can function as a broker between different groups. As another example, some groups – such as surfies, skaters or homeboys – might be linked to each other through their preference for specific clothes and fashion items. In this case, a common interest of all three groups in Nike products – even though they might use them quite differently – creates a potential bridge that connects different communities.
3. *Interaction*: Interaction can be a direct boundary-spanning activity because it exposes the beliefs and perspectives of one community to another. Think of an exchange programme between your university and a university in another country; through the exchange programme, you are exposed to another culture. By comparing your own culture to the other one, you might learn new perspectives and change established ideas. Organizationally, this interaction happens between customers and sales staff; salespeople that form one community of practice talk to the community of users about their products and services, and complaints from customers are used to improve existing services and products or even to develop completely new ideas.

In complex interdisciplinary project teams, such as the collaboration between Swatch and Mercedes that resulted in the Smart Car, different communities of practice combine and challenge the knowledge and competencies of the others. When this is done well, it provides a rich learning opportunity for organizations, given that they accept that they cannot fully own or control these processes. As Wenger (2002) notes, organizations can participate in such opportunities, leverage them and learn from them. However, the precondition for such learning is the willingness to open up organizational boundaries and increase transparency. Hence, trust becomes an important ingredient in successful learning partnerships.

LEARNING IN AND THROUGH ALLIANCES AND COLLABORATION

Negotiating alliances and collaboration have become new ways of growing and expanding. Take the example of the airline industry. Instead of competing and pushing each other out of the market, there are two major alliances: One World and Star Alliance. Through a clever network, the companies in each alliance build on their respective strengths and compensate for each other's weaknesses. Without each airline having to fly to every destination in the world, the alliances are able to offer flights just about everywhere through their networks. And through a smart reward system (frequent flyer points), they retain customers within their network and create loyalty.

Arguably, many companies are sceptical when it comes to working across boundaries in **collaborative relations**. They are scared that their competitors could gain access to their know-how and run off with the fruits of the valuable learning they have acquired over the years. Growth is to be achieved through mergers and acquisitions rather than through networking and collaborating.

Collaborative relations: sharing resources, including ideas, know-how, technologies and staff between two or more different organizations to create a solution to a given problem.

Collaborations can trigger knowledge creation and organizational learning when organizations work closely together with suppliers, retailers, customers, universities or consultants. Or they might focus on collaboration internally among different divisions, teams and experts. The car manufacturer BMW and the car rental company Sixt, for instance, agreed on a partnership to explore innovative urban mobility concepts such as *Drive Now*. The rationale behind the deal was simple: BMW produces fine cars and Sixt has the know-how to rent cars to customers. Thus, their collaboration brings together different expertise and should enable them to combine and transform their knowledge into innovative products. It is important that both companies learn from each other and, through broadening their knowledge base, trigger innovation and change (see also Chapter 11).

From a learning perspective, collaboration is an important means to access new knowledge and transfer skills that an organization lacks. Moreover, facing the challenge of creating more and more complex products, it is hard for any organization to stay at the cutting edge in every single detail. Just think of the automobile industry; almost every part of a new car is a complex mini-project in itself, from the stereo system to the computer-controlled engine, the light aluminium subframe and even the tyres. Thus, car companies are forced to work closely with their suppliers and, in collaboration, they learn from each other. Obviously, this is a dangerous game because no one wants to give away too much information or divulge secret knowledge that competitors could use. However, without trusting and sharing, collaborations are hard to keep alive. As in every learning situation, collaboration needs an open environment in which ideas can grow and spread.

Drawing on extensive research, Tidd et al. (2001) identified three major issues that determine successful learning through collaboration. First, an organization must have the intent to learn through collaboration. Instead of trying to steal its partner's assets, it needs to see the opportunity to learn mutually. Second, it requires transparency. If cultural barriers block the flow of knowledge between companies, or if one partner refuses openness, learning cannot take place. Also, if the knowledge is more tacit than explicit, it will be harder for a partner organization to acquire it. Finally, absorptiveness, referring to the capacity to actually learn, is important.

Learning often happens through a trial and error process in which mistakes and failure provide the richest source of learning. However, normally, organizations do not embrace mistakes as opportunities for learning but as a mechanism to allocate blame: usually a scapegoat needs to be found to blame when a failure occurs. Management that sees in mistakes only the negative is likely to block organizational learning processes because it excludes mistakes from its agenda and brands as 'losers' those people who make mistakes.

David Kelley, managing director of the product design firm IDEO, has identified the blame-game as the biggest hurdle in the learning process. Therefore, at IDEO employees are encouraged to make mistakes quickly and learn from them fast. As the management guru Tom Peters (who admires IDEO for its innovativeness) has put it, the only difference between successful and unsuccessful organizations is that the successful ones make their mistakes more quickly.

ORGANIZATIONAL LEARNING AS PARADOX?

THE PARADOX OF ORGANIZATIONAL LEARNING

In mainstream texts on learning and knowledge management, learning is depicted as a more or less straightforward process. Weick and Westley (1999) would not necessarily agree with this dominant view; rather, they challenge the concept of organizational learning in its fundamentals, arguing that the term *organizational learning* is, in fact, a paradox (or, as they put it, an **oxymoron**). Just like the members of a dysfunctional family, organization and learning are things that do not seem to fit together well. As Weick and Westley argue, learning and organizing are 'essentially antithetical processes, which means the phrase "organizational learning" qualifies as oxymoron' (1999: 190). Organizing involves ordering and controlling – or, as the authors put it, decreasing variety – whereas learning disorganizes existing knowledge and increases variety. If learning is about exploring new terrain and understanding the unknown, and organizing is about exploiting routines and the already known, organizational learning is a paradox indeed. Weick and Westley suggest not that we should simply forget the concept but that we should be careful that, in using it, we make sense of its ambivalence. Put simply, learning happens when the old and the new clash and create a tension.

An **oxymoron** is a figure of speech that combines two normally contradicting terms (such as deafening silence or military intelligence).

A LEARNING ORGANIZATION IS A PARADOX

As the old proverb goes, knowledge is power. Learning means changing knowledge and therefore it also means questioning those who have power. Take the example of an employee questioning their manager: the manager might understand this as questioning their authority and react negatively. Learning – and especially double-loop learning – implies questioning the rules of the game. Of course, those who are comfortable with the current rules and those who have established these rules will be critical of attempts to change the status quo. Also, we have seen that learning implies a trial and error process that can be messy.

Organizations are made up of rules and routines that try to make the world stable and predictable. Learning challenges these rules and those who have established them. Therefore, one can argue critically that learning and organization have a paradoxical relationship!

A PRACTICAL GUIDE TO ORGANIZATIONAL LEARNING

As we have seen with March's provocative ideas of learning, learning happens somewhere between organizations exploring what they do not know and exploiting what they do know. Or, to put it another way, profound learning happens when single-loop learning (exploitation, evolution, adaptation and habit) intersects with double-loop learning (exploration, revolution and thinking outside the box). Weick and Westley (1999) analyse three ways of dealing with the complexities of exploring and exploiting. Their ideas are framed by the metaphors of humour, improvisation and small wins as moments of learning.

1. *Humour*: Jokes and funny situations provide opportunities for learning because they play with the meanings we normally associate with specific words and deeds, turning them upside down. Almost every joke pulls together things that are normally separated and, in doing so, creates a surprising element that makes us laugh. In addition, the normal social order is suspended for a moment when we are telling a joke; you might say 'just joking …' when you are telling a joke and you say something that might be true but that is not socially acceptable. (Remember, in the ancient feudal kingdoms, the only one allowed to tell the truth was the fool or the jester!) Finally, humour happens spontaneously; it cannot be planned or forecast. The funniest situations happen out of the blue. Humour carries the flexibility and richness of quick and creative response to the environment and represents a way of exploring new ideas.
2. *Improvisation*: Improvisation is another concept of learning that deals productively with the tension between learning and organizing. Actors and jazz musicians improvise, and so do employees; rather than sending people to seminars where they learn things they cannot apply back in the organization, learning on the job – improvisation – encourages people to play around with everyday patterns and to change them slightly, not necessarily radically, but *in situ*. Improvisation is always based on the interplay between past, present and future; by carefully listening and changing past rhythms, something new emerges. Also, errors play an important role within improvisation. To enable learning and development, errors are tolerated and used as starting points for future improvisation. Finally, improvisational learning is a team event, not a one-person show. It relies on the feedback of others, their feelings (rather than their rational capacity alone) and their contribution to change.
3. *Small wins*: Small wins, according to Weick and Westley (1999), are not the big revolutionary changes promised by consultants or management gurus but rather the learning opportunities that happen when you *almost* do business as usual. The researchers give the example of feminists, who sought to change laws and regulations, which turned out to be quite a

successful learning strategy. However, while working to achieve their overriding goal of equality for women, the feminists scored a small win by showing that language itself was deeply gendered (chair*man*, post*man*, and so on). This seemingly small win had a big impact, making our society learn much more about the ways in which gender is deeply embedded in how we normally do what we do and become who we are. Thus, small wins might look small, but their effect can be quite big. Again, they are moments of learning because they juxtapose order (common language) and a sense of disorder (new language), creating the space in which learning happens.

LEARNING, UNLEARNING, NON-LEARNING

As we have seen, learning is a process that is in tension with the core processes of managing and organizing. Because learning happens only when there is some freedom to experiment with actions and ideas, it challenges management practices that focus on order, predictability and control. Given this problematic relationship between learning and organizing, you might wonder whether learning is always good for organizations. If learning challenges organizations, why should they learn at all? This is exactly the question that Brunsson (1998) asks in a thought-provoking and ironic article introducing the idea of the non-learning organization. He argues that non-learning organizations are healthier than learning ones, which is an idea directly in opposition to the commonly accepted view that there is a positive relationship between learning and organizational performance. In fact, most scholars and management gurus argue that learning leads to greater efficiency and better performance.

Brunsson (1998) looks at public sector organizations and wonders whether their non-learning – the way that they keep making the same errors – is simply pathological (something bad) or whether their persistence with routines (their non-learning) is something more fundamentally positive. He starts by suggesting that if learning is as extremely positive as theorists suggest, non-learning must be dysfunctional and negative for organizations. Instead of following the mainstream argument (learning is good, therefore non-learning must be bad), Brunsson (1998) turns the order upside down and argues that non-learning can result in the following unexpected benefits for the organization:

1. *Tolerance of contradictions*: When learning organizations face contradictions, challenges or problems in their environment, they have to adjust either their behaviour or their objectives. They have to act consistently over time and constantly align their behaviour with their objectives. Non-learning organizations, on the other hand, are much more flexible. If they face an environment in which contradictions and uncertainties are the norm rather than the exception, they can still operate normally. The budget agencies, for instance, were confronted with unsatisfactory reports and asked for better reports next time. However, despite the incomplete reports, they accomplished their tasks. Non-learning organizations manage contradictions well because they accomplish what they have to do, even though they hope that things will be better next time.

2. *Organizational discretion*: Non-learning organizations are capable of benefitting from the gap between talk, action and decisions. Although they kept asking for better reports, they did their job based on the same unsatisfactory reports that they had always received. Facing this situation, a learning organization would probably become unsatisfied, and its employees would be frustrated enough to seek better sources of information, whereas the non-learning organization is able to differentiate between what it would like to have (better reports) and what it actually has (incomplete reports). Again, this makes the non-learning organization flexible, and it provides a certain kind of freedom – such organizations can be realistic in their task accomplishment and remain idealistic about the future.

In light of these positive aspects of non-learning, Brunsson argues that the non-learning organization is in fact an emancipated organization. Learning organizations have to change, adjust and align all the time, whereas non-learning organizations can deal with contradictions, inconsistent demands and gaps between ideal worlds and actual reality. They are emancipated because they can disregard the (ostensible) need for change that drives learning organizations.

THE POWER OF LEARNING

KNOWLEDGE MANAGEMENT AND SCIENTIFIC MANAGEMENT

Knowledge management practitioners like to think of themselves as conceptually new and innovative. However, as we have seen above with the example of Taylor, the focus of knowledge management is quite old; transforming tacit knowledge from employees into explicit knowledge that is owned by the company was the driving force behind the idea of scientific management in 1911. Taylor disliked the fact that the workers knew more about the actual process than he or the managers did. Workers could tell stories about why things are the way they are, and others had to accept these stories. Management lacked any better, alternative knowledge because it did not have a basic understanding of the tasks that the workers accomplished. Without such objective knowledge, how could management coordinate and control effectively? Taylor's initiative in getting the knowledge out of workers' heads and making it an object of managerial manipulation in Bethlehem Steel was a harsh way of transforming tacit into explicit knowledge. It sought to destroy the craft basis of existing know-how from the situation in prior generations, where knowledge and status were coterminous – that is, one did not become a master without having acquired the knowledge of a journeyman and an apprentice – so this separation of power and knowledge was unthinkable (see also Chapter 8).

LIFELONG LEARNING EQUALS LIFELONG EXAMINATIONS

In organizational terms, we have already talked about Taylor's approach and the way he empowered management: he simply gained knowledge that had been the workers' domain. Scientific management changed the power relations, made the worker an object of study, formalized the worker's task and made any worker exchangeable with another. The difference between Taylor's scientific management and modern knowledge management is that Taylor thought you have to codify knowledge only once, whereas knowledge management realizes that you can never stop learning or codifying – it is a lifelong process.

Given the enthusiasm for the concept of lifelong learning, it is interesting to consider one of Foucault's (1979) core arguments, which shed some light on the dark side of lifelong learning – that lifelong learning might very well imply lifelong examination. Foucault focused especially on the examination as a common practice integrating knowledge and power. Once, the integration was institutionally fairly specific: it occurred mostly at school and university. Thus, Western societies that praise continuous learning are simultaneously paving the path of lifelong learning with exams that assess the learners, given the centrality of performance measurement to contemporary management culture. As you know from your own experience, exams are powerful instruments that shape your behaviour and, by extension, your personality. Or think of the assessment centres that are widely used tools of human resource management. They are almost perfect examples of the knowledge/power link because they have the power to assess someone (using their knowledge dimension) and change them (using their power dimension).

For Foucault, the examination is such a powerful tool because it combines both a hierarchical observation and a normalizing judgement. These are the two functions of examinations. First, they make individuals visible (who is clever, who is not?) and allow the supervisor to categorize them and establish a hierarchical relation among students. Exams enable supervisors to find out who are their potential 'stars' and who is the 'deadwood'. Second, examinations make it possible to judge people and to compare them with each other. They establish a norm that enables the supervisor to categorize some as normal and those who do not comply as abnormal. Think of your class. You and your classmates might have different strengths and skills that are not easily comparable. The exam ignores these individual differences and judges everybody by the same template; it normalizes people as it ignores their differences and subjects them all to the same metric. The process of scrutiny transforms ordinary individuals into cases who are obliged to compete with each other in relation to one common standard.

Foucault analyses three mechanisms that form the heart of the examination:

1. *Visibility*: During examinations, the learning subjects are fully visible, whereas the examiners are almost absent. We see this power working through surveillance; transforming the individual into an object that is visible and that can be assessed ensures discipline. For instance, many organizations routinely test their employees and link promotion back to successful results.

2. *Individuality*: Examinations transform a group of people into individuals by making individual features comparable. Exams establish a hierarchy within a group and put each individual in their place within the hierarchy. Organizations that test their employees can create tables where they rank all employees and categorize the top 10 per cent as 'high potential'. This means that employees constantly compete among each other for the top 10 per cent.

3. *Case*: Exams transform individual characters into cases that are documented and objectified. Every individual has a history in this system that can be compared with others. Individual development can be assessed and, if necessary, corrected. Yearly or even six-monthly performance

> reviews mean that each employee is turned into a case recorded in a file where their supervisor can track the progress of learning and development and, if necessary, correct the career path.

Examinations combine the hierarchical surveillance of people with the normalizing judgement of the supervisor. This makes individuals visible, transforms each into a case and renders them open to powerful intervention. A society that understands itself as continuously learning must see its shadow as well in a never-ending series of examinations that shape individuals.

IN PRACTICE

We are assuming that you are a student at a tertiary education institution and that is why you are reading this book. As a student, you will have frequently been assessed in a number of different ways. Enumerate the different ways in which you have been assessed. Then, having numbered them, write a few points about each form of assessment that addresses these points:

- What did you learn from the assessment exercise?
- Who benefitted from this assessment?
- How well did it test what you knew?
- What do you think are the comparative advantages and disadvantages of the various methods of assessment for whom?
- To what extent does each of these methods of assessment prepare you for practice outside university?

Organizational learning is no guarantee that what organizations will learn will benefit them. Organization theorists interested in knowledge management seek to ensure that organizations learn the appropriate lessons and retain what is good while avoiding or discarding what is bad. That seems pretty straightforward, but, as this chapter has repeatedly suggested, the process is not quite as simple as it seems.

Sometimes, non-learning organizations may have an advantage over learning organizations. Learning organizations can place their members under a fearsome audit and sap their vitality; they can also codify what is unimportant and inconsequential while missing that which is profound because it is so deeply embedded in the normal ways of doing things. These issues often come to haunt organizations that downsize; thinking that they have routinized and learned everything that they need to know from their members, organizations find out too late that downsizing results not only in live bodies walking out the door but also in the departure of some deeply embedded and important knowledge that managers did not know would be missed because they did not know what they had until they lost it.

Still, as the chapter has covered, there are many ways of seeking to ensure that knowledge is managed appropriately. Most importantly, openness to error, improvisation, humour and a strategy of small wins are key to creating a learning organization

SUMMARY

In this chapter, we have considered the role that knowledge and learning play in managing and organizations:

- The capability to learn and manage knowledge is one of the most important aspects of organizations. Knowledge management is the process of managing knowledge to meet existing and future needs, and to exploit present knowledge to develop opportunities for further knowledge.
- We have explored different sources of knowledge (learning by doing, hearing stories, popular accounts). We have also discussed tact and explicit types of knowledge, and how they can be transformed from one to the other. Learning as changing knowledge is a key concept in management.
- A second key topic discussed is different types of learning. Single-loop learning basically means optimizing skills, refining abilities and acquiring the knowledge necessary to achieve resolution of a problem that requires solving. Double-loop learning describes learning as changing the frame of reference that normally guides behaviour. The dialectic between exploring new ideas and exploiting old ones (March) frames the dilemma of organizational learning.
- With the concept of 'communities of practice', we have analysed learning as a social process that occurs within social learning systems. These communities are characterized by three key features: a sense of joint enterprise, relationships of mutuality and a shared repertoire. We have explored how learning happens through collaboration between organizations and across organizational boundaries.

EXERCISES

1. Having read this chapter, you should be able to say in your own words what each of the following key terms means. Test yourself or ask a colleague to test you.
   - Organizational learning
   - Knowledge management
   - Tacit knowledge
   - Implicit knowledge

(Continued)

(Continued)

- Learning as adaptation
- Exploring and exploiting
- Single- and double-loop learning
- Communities of practice
- Collaboration
- Unlearning
- Lifelong learning
- Organizational learning as paradox.

2. Why is learning important for organizations?
3. Where does knowledge come from?
4. What does Nonaka think is the most important knowledge to manage and why?
5. What differentiates single-loop learning from double-loop learning?
6. How would you describe the paradox of organizational learning that results from exploring and exploiting?
7. To what extent does the concept of the ambidextrous organization provide a solution to the paradox of organizational learning?
8. What do communities of practice do in terms of learning?
9. Why should organizations collaborate across boundaries?
10. Why might the term organizational learning be a paradox?

REVISE KEY TERMS

TEST YOURSELF

TEST YOURSELF

Review what you have learned by visiting:
https://study.sagepub.com/managingandorganizations5e or your eBook

- **Test yourself with multiple-choice questions.**
- **Revise key terms with the interactive flashcards.**

CASE STUDY

Athena

Managing knowledge

Let us introduce Athena, a medium-sized consultancy company, employing around 100 consultants. Athena delivers custom-made software applications for its customers, primarily knowledge management and workflow support tools. The consultants work in client projects and often work from the customer's site for several weeks, sometimes months, in a row. This makes it difficult for the employees as well as the managers to share knowledge and experience across their different projects, and to keep track of the latest solutions developed. To enable the consultants to work together, and work as a team, the consultants themselves have developed a wide range of well-functioning software applications, or knowledge management tools: they have designed their own intranet and extranet, and applications for sharing project specifics like best practice exemplars and project management procedures.

The tools the consultants have developed are primarily dedicated to the articulation and spreading of codified knowledge. In addition to these efforts, Athena has made the not-so-common decision to invest in knowledge-sharing practices that cannot easily be accounted for. At Athena, the management decided to extend the lunch break, sponsor free lunch for all employees and hire a chef with the work instruction 'spoil them'. The lunch area is now in the centre of the Athena building. Entering the lunch room in the morning, the first thing greeting you is the smell of freshly brewed espresso, the second is the smile of the chef and the third is a couple of employees in the corner playing darts. If you pause for a moment, you can get a glimpse of your lunch being prepared; if you take the time to stop, which one often does, you might get the recipe.

The reasoning behind the lunch initiative was that it would encourage the employees to eat together, to talk together, to socialize. By making the lunch attractive, they wanted to tempt their consultants to come to head office more often. In other words, believing that knowledge sharing is primarily a social enterprise, a natural extension of spending time together, extending lunch and making spending time together attractive was seen as a perfect way of enhancing knowledge sharing and creating practices.

The investment has turned out to be a big success. Around noon, the lunch area gets crowded. You hear a buzz of talk about projects, slick computer designs, programming codes as well as Saturday's pub round and the lack of kindergarten availability. There is no obvious hierarchy among the lunchers and no scheduled seating; employees, managers and customers all line up for their food. There is just a big smorgasbord of hot and cold meals, the promise of a good meal and the potential for good company. On Fridays it is more crowded than ever, as Fridays are labelled 'lunch with all', and consultants working off site are encouraged to come 'home'. The Friday lunches are used for presenting important announcements and project achievements.

Questions

1. (How) Can you justify calling free lunch a knowledge management tool?
2. What types of knowledge, if any, can be said to be shared and possibly created in such an initiative?
3. Discuss what types of knowledge management efforts you would invest in if you were a senior manager.

Case prepared by Kjersti Bjørkeng and Arne Carlsen, NTNU and BI, Norway.

ADDITIONAL RESOURCES

- The formative work of Nonaka and Takeuchi (1995), drawing on ideas from Polanyi (1962), has been very influential. The concept of tacit knowledge as Polanyi develops it is not quite as easily tamed and domesticated by management as Nonaka and Takeuchi suggest (see Ray and Clegg, 2007).
- The missing dimension from most treatments of knowledge management is the way that knowledge always implicates power and is always implicated in power. The classic text is Foucault's (1979) *Discipline and Punish*, especially the graphic opening pages, in which he contrasts a gruesome execution with the rules of a model prison established in France just 60 years later. To the former belongs a fearsome vengeance, to the latter a reforming zeal – but neither vengeance on the body nor zeal towards the mind of the criminal is a practice of knowledge that we can easily understand unless we consider the regimes of power associated with them.
- In terms of films, *Terminator 3: Rise of the Machines* (Mostow, 2003) is one that comes to mind. In this movie, a machine, played by Arnold Schwarzenegger, knows what the future holds for the hero and heroine, and he has to ensure that they meet their fate. If only organizations were able to have such prescience!
- *The Right Stuff* (Kaufman, 1983), about the NASA space programme, is a good resource for organizational learning. The movie is based on Tom Wolfe's bestselling 1979 book of the same name. The film dramatically depicts the way that an organization – in this case, NASA – learned and did not learn. In a similar vein, the film *Apollo 13* (Howard, 1995) is also required viewing.
- We also suggest watching *Beyond the Brick: A LEGO Brickumentary* (Davidson and Junge, 2014), which provides insights into the fascinating story of the LEGO community of practice that innovates and learns in close interaction with the LEGO company.

MANAGING INNOVATION AND CHANGE

CREATIVITY, IMAGINATION, FOOLISHNESS

LEARNING OBJECTIVES

This chapter is designed to enable you to:

- explain the internal innovation process and its complexity in organizations
- understand the benefits and managerial challenges of innovative openness in organizations
- understand innovation cycles and dynamics of progressions
- critically analyse the different approaches for managing change and innovation
- discuss practices for organizing for innovation and change.

BEFORE YOU GET STARTED...

If I had asked people what they wanted, they would have said faster horses. (Henry Ford)

Innovation refers to the implementation of a new or significantly improved product or service or new organizational process.

INTRODUCTION

Instituting change in the organization's internal processes, practices and routines, as well as the products and services it produces, is not an easy task. Doing something new is often quite painful and difficult for managers and, by consequence, organizations, as they are often biased by past successes and seek to sustain the status quo through maintaining what they do and how they do it, which renders them myopic to future developments. Thus, organizations often find **innovation** difficult.

As this definition implies, innovation constitutes both a process and an outcome (Crossan and Apaydin, 2010). That is, it represents both a way of 'doing' within the organization embodied by different stages and innovation pathways that lead to implementation known as the innovation process, as well as a form of 'being' embodied by a particular type and outcome orientation known as innovation outcomes. Let us use a concrete example to illustrate the connection between process and outcome and highlight the distinction.

If you were asked to name the organization that initially developed and commercialized the first MP3 player, most people would say the Apple iPod. Yet, the iPod was not the first MP3 player to market; Sony was the first organization to deliver the MP3 player to the prospective consumer masses. The problem was that the market was not quite ready for this new way of delivering and listening to music at the time of initial release. MP3 was a radically new way of consuming music that allowed users to compress large music files and transfer and use them fast through the Internet. While Sony was the first player to market with this new product innovation and possessed the requisite internal knowledge and processes to produce it en masse, the Sony MP3 was essentially a failure. Why Sony's MP3 failed hinged on issues with the underlying process and complexities of developing a relevant business model prior to market commercialization. That is, the MP3 was also dependent on the establishment of a new mode and platform for accessing music and a new way of capturing value from users that were downloading music for free online from unregulated pirate sites such as Napster. Sony failed to see these other factors in the innovation process and was not capable of resolving them. Apple's successful iPod was realized owing to the co-existence and development of the relevant mechanism to deliver and capture value through its complementary iTunes platform.

As the following example illuminates, the outcomes of innovation are intimately linked with the process of innovation and one requires the other. The innovation process and the dynamics of internal change required to drive innovation are quite complex and we will delve into these concepts in more detail in this chapter which is dedicated to innovation and change.

INNOVATION AS A PROCESS

While innovations, by definition, represent unique new ideas in the form of products, services and processes that are implemented, the process that precedes their implementation from initial conception follows a remarkably similar pattern.

MAPPING INNOVATION

In 1983, the Minnesota Innovation Research Program started a longitudinal study of service, product, technology and programme innovation. The goal of the study was to analyse the process of innovation, from concept development to implementation and resulted in the book *The Innovation Journey* by Van de Ven et al. (1999). What the authors found, however, did not confirm mainstream opinion that innovation is an easily managed stage-wise, linear process of trial-and-error learning that unfolds in a stable environment. At the same time, the authors were critical of random conceptions of innovation being an 'accidental' event that is unplanned, unpredictable and unmanageable. Such an approach, they suggest, implies that you should 'turn the organization off to invent and develop innovations, and turn it on to implement and diffuse innovations when they emerge' (Van de Ven et al., 1999: 5). Rather, innovation is a complex, non-linear process in which managers create internal conditions that increase the probability of developing, leading and cycling through the innovation journey.

Such a view leaves no option for managing innovation; instead, it suggests that 'innovation management' is an oxymoron and that innovation happens not because, but in spite, of management. Although innovation challenges management's urge for planning and controlling, it is not a purely random process. Van de Ven et al. (1999) delineated a road map to innovation that encompasses the major steps of the process. It provides a rough outline of the complex, ambiguous and dynamic terrain from where discovery and creation emerge. According to Van de Ven et al., the innovation journey can be differentiated into three main stages: (1) initiation; (2) development; and (3) implementation.

THE INITIATION PERIOD

The innovation process begins as a set of apparently coincidental events, such as the introduction of a new manager, a shift in technological paradigm, a loss in market share, and so on, which set the stage for a new innovation to emerge. These early events accumulate over a period of time that trigger an internal or external 'shock' to the organizational system that garners the attention of key stakeholders. Plans are then developed to gain resources internally and to create legitimacy externally. However, these plans are marketing tools more than project descriptions.

THE DEVELOPMENT PERIOD

Once development begins, the initial idea proceeds along a planned convergent pathway, but then splits into multiple divergent pathways through cycles of exploring new directions and trial-and-error learning, where new goals are formed. This convergence–divergence cycle iterates unpredictably until a preferred direction emerges. In this stage, setbacks and mistakes are common as unexpected changes erode the basic assumption the innovation was built on. Also, criteria to assess the achievements of the project differ between resource controllers and innovation managers. People who are committed to the idea tend to see progress and new opportunities where external agents see only hesitation and dead ends. Moreover, staff changes frequently occur in the development period. Motivation and euphoria are often high at the beginning, whereas setbacks and mistakes breed more and more frustration and closure towards the end of the innovation journey.

Top managers and powerful key stakeholders (such as investors) act in contrasting ways and serve as checks and balances on each other. It is at this stage that network building with other organizations is necessary, and top management should be involved in this process to gain political support, which can sometimes lead to unintended consequences. Thus, to innovate means to build multifunctional communities of practice (Wenger, 2002), where the disparate views of various and often incoherent disciplinary knowledge can be integrated to drive innovation. In addition, project responsibility must be maintained in terms of emergent criteria that allow for both exploratory and exploitative learning, which, as we discussed in Chapter 10, requires the balancing of contradictory learning tensions between strategic emergence and strategic determination. This is because top-down plans do not easily allow new opportunities for learning to emerge and bottom-up emergence does not easily allow innovation to be integrated and incrementally cumulated.

THE IMPLEMENTATION PERIOD

The implementation and adoption of the innovation are achieved by integrating the new with that which is old, established and already known, fostering a fit within a local context and situation. Politically, the radically new and different will probably not be embraced by everybody because people have committed time and emotions to the status quo. Evolution and integration, not revolution and transformation, seem to be the keys to success.

Finally, innovations reach the end of their organizational careers – they are either released or dumped as top management and investors assess whether the innovation was a failure or a success. However, the criteria against which management assesses the innovation are often inappropriately loaded in terms of short-term financial indicators. Thus, it is important to focus on monitoring and evaluating the innovation process. This process challenges usual management evaluation, which rarely incorporates all the organizational competencies that a successful appraisal of innovation would require. Management generally involves abstract and generalized calculations. With such calculations, it is difficult to capture novelty and uniqueness. Standard budgets, deadlines and reporting protocols can all sabotage innovative efforts. Members can be transferred or let go, and crucial tacit learning can be lost from the innovation process. Formalization can be demanded and the critical detail missed. Managing innovation successfully means that organizations must manage the tension between determination and emergence to link innovation with the firm's resources and strategy.

Being innovative or producing innovations is not automatically useful or profitable. Rather, usefulness can be assessed only at the end of the innovation process and what the destination seems to be is always subject to redefinition and renegotiation as the criteria of judgement change.

LEADING THE INNOVATION PROCESS

Managing innovations requires leadership skills and involvement from the top of an organization. Van de Ven et al. (1999) established that many managers are usually involved in innovation processes, shifting among four roles:

1. Sponsors: usually top managers that can command the allocation of resources
2. Mentors: usually experienced 'innovators' that guide the process

3. Critics: those that keep the process grounded and serve as devil's advocate
4. Leaders: often executives that are able to navigate and settle disputes in the journey and issues that arise among different roles.

Each understands and acts from different perspectives, with their decision-making being influenced by the pragmatics of innovation more than long-term strategic orientations. For simple and trivial tasks, a hierarchical power and leadership structure is most appropriate, but for more complex and ambiguous innovation journeys, it is highly inappropriate, as 'directing the innovation journey calls for a pluralistic power structure of leadership that incorporates the requisite variety of diverse perspectives necessary to make uncertain and ambiguous innovation decisions' (Van de Ven et al., 1999: 15). Thus, leadership in innovation processes differs from business-as-usual management tasks. Given the ambiguous nature of the innovation process, we should recognize that it is highly unlikely that the innovation process will be smooth, rationally unfolding and bereft of politics and contestation. On the contrary, the production of consensus and a single strategic intent unifying the heterogeneous opportunities of innovation would seem to be rather more a part of the problem than the solution.

For state of the art briefings on how to manage organizations effectively, please visit the Henry Stewart Talks series of online audio-visual seminars on managing organizations, edited by Stewart Clegg: www.hstalks.com/r/managing-orgs, in particular, Talk #12: Improvising Improvisational Change, by Miguel Pinha e Cunha and Joao Vieira da Cunha, as well as Talk #5 in the series on the origins and development of management, called Innovation: The paradox of back to the future, by Johannes Pennings.

WATCH THE TALKS

EXTEND YOUR KNOWLEDGE

Naar, L. and Clegg, S. (2018) 'Models as strategic actants in innovative architecture', *Journal of Management Inquiry*, 27 (1): 26–39. You can access the article at the companion website https://study.sagepub.com/managingandorganizations5e

READ THE ARTICLE

INNOVATING THROUGH EMPLOYEES

Of course, innovation roles are not purely confined to sponsors, mentors, critics and leaders; often, creative companies employ and rely on creative people to come up with new ideas and drive the innovation process. The practices needed to manage creative staff, however, differ fundamentally from traditional management practices and are fraught with tension. Chris Bangle, when global chief of design for BMW in Munich, managed creative staff; his job was to mediate between financial and technological constraints and innovative and creative design ideas. Thus, he has to balance creativity and the commercial side of BMW. In his view, it is the task of leadership to foster innovation and achieve commercial goals (Bangle, 2001). Since innovators are usually not accountants, the logic of commerce often sounds odd to them. Yet, on the other hand, finance departments often understand the latest innovation as a fancy of the design team and regard it as a cost rather than an investment. The question is, then, how do managers deal with this tension?

Bangle's answer was to protect his creative resources and make sure that they could work without being interrupted by people who did not understand the process. In this way, innovative products could emerge – regardless of whether or not they were financially feasible. At BMW, Bangle sent his design team away from its normal work environment so that it could develop ideas without being interrupted by criticism: 'To make certain that no one could possibly trample on the seeds they were planting, I instructed the group to keep their whereabouts a secret – even from me' (Bangle, 2001: 50). In such safe spaces, away from business-as-usual constraints, creativity and innovation are born.

This solution aligns with the development period of the innovation journey discovered by Van de Ven and colleagues (1999), in which ideas fragment in cycles of convergence and divergence. To stimulate these conditions within the organization, Bangle espouses a separation of designers from their normal work where they can play and explore without constraint. Shifting the focus from design (innovation) to engineering (implementation) too quickly kills creativity. However, to make sure that creative people do not fool around forever, deadlines are imposed to ensure that playfulness and exploration find an end rather than becoming an end. These deadlines also assure managers and engineers that these processes, which to them may appear to be uncontrollable, will result in tangible outcomes. In the contemporary business environment, BMW is once again a pacemaker. BMW is moving from being a car manufacturer to being a provider of mobility – and mobility does not necessarily mean owning a car that spends most of its life parked up in various locations.

Managing innovation requires extraordinary communication skills (see also Chapter 9). The various groups must understand each other's language: innovators must understand corporate requirements, budgets and deadlines, whereas managers must let go and trust in the people involved in a process with unknown output. The art of managing innovation is to bridge this gap and create a mutual understanding. As Bangle (2001) concludes, business and creativity are not the same, but they can be directed towards the same ends. Think of the glue that created the Post-it notes that the guy at 3M developed against the orders of his boss. His boss could not see the value in this tool because he could not relate to it at all. The same point applied to the chairman of IBM when he claimed in the 1950s that there was a world market for only about five mainframe computers. Again, he simply did not understand the new concept because he could not relate to it. Or think of groundbreaking artists; how many of them had the same fate as Van Gogh, who died poor and lonely, because everybody thought his art was nothing but madness? Years later, we know better. Innovation means taking risks – and sometimes the risks may be very obvious and the destination unclear.

Innovation is much more demanding than routine. Routine can be managed mechanistically, whereas innovation needs to be managed organically. Mechanisms require only routine action (Burns and Stalker, 1961). Organic structures require members not only to enact innovation but also to make sense of the plurality of organization and network members that may be involved in many indeterminate aspects of innovation. Organicism implies the commitment of psychic energy and attention. It embodies the tension between responsibility and freedom. In innovation, people have to be free to follow the lead of the TV series *Star Trek*, 'going boldly where no one has gone before', but they also have to be organizationally responsible in terms of timelines, budgets and goals. Organizations tend to be much better at framing these responsibilities than they are at empowering creativity. Organizations must manage the tension between freedom and responsibility to balance commitment with accountability.

INNOVATION AS AN OPEN PROCESS

Innovation does not always proceed from the inside out, however. Over the last decade, the notion of open innovation coined by Henry Chesbrough (2003) has rapidly proliferated within the management and organization field, and espouses a higher degree of openness to external sources of knowledge, such as with lead-users, suppliers, competitors and, more recently, online crowds (Felin et al., 2017) who work with organizational professionals in order to bolster internal innovation processes.

Being more 'open' to external sources of knowledge and information can overcome tensions that arise between internal technological knowledge that drives the development of new innovations and specialist market knowledge. These are often separate areas within the organization, rarely communicating with each other. Thus, incorporating competencies that are not necessarily a part of the innovation team, such as lead-users and other external constituents, can create a potential tension between *control* and *innovation* (see the In Practice LEGO example). Many complex organizations concentrate best on what they can control through routines and standard operating procedures. However, concentration on control minimizes learning from innovation by filtering out new information, reinforcing past routines and focusing on foreseeable and manageable issues. It also tends to reinforce existing circuits of power within the firm, based on existing resource control (Clegg, 1989; Pfeffer and Salancik, 1978), thus reinforcing conventional sensemaking (Weick, 1995). Innovation requires organizations to rethink their business in ways that operational controls do not easily allow (Workman, 1993).

IN PRACTICE

Co-creation through lead users: innovation at LEGO

In 1998, LEGO released a new product, called LEGO Mindstorm. At the heart of it was a yellow microchip. The product became an instant hit – within three months, 80,000 sets had changed hands. There was just one small problem: the buyers were not children but adults. And that was despite the fact that LEGO marketed the product to children, not adults. Worse, these adults did not consume the product as the LEGO masterminds had anticipated. Within weeks, hackers from all over the world had cracked the code of the new toy and created all sorts of new applications: Mindstorm users built everything from soda

(Continued)

(Continued)

machines to blackjack dealers. The new programs spread quickly over the Internet and were far more sophisticated than those LEGO had developed. More than 40 guidebooks advised how to get maximum fun out of your 727-part LEGO Mindstorm set. How did LEGO react? First, negatively: consumers were meant to consume, not produce their own versions. They were not meant to challenge LEGO's in-house product developers. Confusion set in. Inaction followed. Then, after a year, LEGO started to listen to those unruly users and attempted to understand what they were doing with the product and, more importantly, the LEGO brand.

After lengthy discussions, LEGO came to understand that the community around its products was doing something interesting. First, LEGO learnt that the boisterous users were actually not a homogeneous group. While part of the LEGO community was into outer space, there was a second group who shared a love for trains and real-life modelling. The two groups could not be more different. The former was about fantasy, science fiction, humour and free building; the latter was about real-world models, suburban life, no-nonsense and precisely scaled modelling. Despite these differences, they formed a community around the LEGO brand that shared a passion for innovation. LEGO users produced physical and aesthetic add-ons such as batteries for cars and trains, or clothes for figures. Other users developed new play themes such as LEGO Harry Potter or LEGO Life on Mars, which explored new experiences for users. Finally, some LEGO fans developed new building techniques, such as new styles of buildings, models, or colour effects. Of course, community members toying around with ideas do not develop automatically marketable new products. Most of their new ideas were incremental improvements that left basic product ideas unchallenged. But about 12 per cent of all user innovations represented more radical explorations of new functionalities and new experiences. These included strategy games with multiplayer features and role-play elements, such as BrickWars. Or mosaic building techniques: rather than copying existing images with LEGO bricks, an image is translated into pixels (LEGO bricks) and then assembled digitally. Software called PixeLego has been developed and distributed for free by users to translate images into LEGO Syntax.

WATCH THIS TED TALK

It pays to empower your customers so that they can do the innovative thinking for you because they might know what they want, and what they do not want, better than do experts in a remote lab. But there is more to be learned from the LEGO case. Before you read the next section of the case, imagine you are LEGO's chief innovation manager. What organizational challenges do you think could result from co-creative, open innovation? How does LEGO have to change in order to benefit from the changing rules of the game?

Sources: Antorini (2007); Antorini et al. (2012); Kornberger (2010)

Managerial challenge of control

The control that organizations enjoy over production and distribution, however, vanishes as users short cut internal circuits of power and relate to each other more directly and there is the loss of a single authority that is usually represented by management. The new distribution of authority puts a lot at stake – including an organization's deep-seated identity. At LEGO, the identity of the organization emerges out of the brand-facilitated conversation between external communities and employees. The challenges for management are formidable: managing identity in the context of co-creation requires an organization to develop high tolerance for ambiguity, uncertainty and paradox. Brands provide the arena in which an organization's identity emerges out of the interactions between consumers and producers. A stable identity remains elusive: rather than searching for an enduring essence, organizations continuously oscillate between self-definition and definition by outsiders. The brand provides the space for this dialogue to unfold: it enables an organization to focus narcissistically on its uniqueness, and, at the same time, forces it to keep an eye on outsiders' visions. Rather than dreaming of a unified hierarchy, brands transform organization into a form of organized heresy: the search for differences becomes the core of their identity. The brand manifests itself as the interface where those different, competing and contradictory narratives clash and are, temporarily, reconciled. Rather than being the sole author of an organization's identity, the brand manager becomes the editor of a polyphonic, sometimes even dissonant, narrative.

You will find many more examples if you search for Lego Innovations on YouTube, such as the really funny Lego Death Star Canteen which has been viewed more than 20 million times.

WATCH THE LEGO VIDEO

INNOVATING THROUGH COLLABORATORS

Collaboration between organizations is usually temporary but often produces long-lasting relationships. Collaboration has intended purposes but its emergent benefits may be more important. Collaborations are dialectical systems and their stability is determined by balancing multiple tensions within systems of accountability (Das and Teng, 2000). Certain large-scale, complex, project-based tasks are rarely completed by a single organization; instead, they involve many project partners, each of which brings specialized skills and competencies to the task at hand.

The global economy is marked by the increasing importance of knowledge and creativity, which, paradoxically, places a premium on innovation facilitated by proximity. Although the modern economy is global, it is also resolutely regional; Silicon Valley is the best example. Innovative capabilities are frequently sustained through sharing of a common knowledge base, interaction through common institutions, and proximal location. Local, socially embedded institutions such as universities play an important role in supporting innovation (Leonard and Sensiper, 1998; Qiu et al., 2017). Organizations that are able to relate to one another in a proximate geographical or regional space seem better able to collaborate.

Collaborations link people and knowledge, simultaneously tying them to multiple external contacts. Knowledge circulates through internal and external networks at various levels. Achieving sustainable competitive advantage means being faster and better at innovation, which often comes down to being better connected and having more effective collaborations. Swann et al. (1999) suggest that what is important is how networks interact with knowledge: what knowledge, who has it and how it can be accessed. National and regional institutions – such as universities and research centres, as well as firms, government policies and programmes – frame regional innovation capabilities (Bartholomew, 1998; Dodgson, 2000: 25–6) because they define the availability and quality of the *what*, *who* and *how* of innovation and its knowledge networks.

One firm that is probably the world's best at putting the end-user at the heart of innovative design is IDEO. IDEO is one of the most innovative firms in the world. Go to the company website and check out the news section where you will find links to inspiring books by and about IDEO.

READ ABOUT IDEO

IDEO

INNOVATION NETWORKS AND PLATFORM INNOVATION

Many of the examples mentioned above point towards innovation networks in which new ideas flourish: indeed, innovation takes place outside of organizational boundaries in networks, communities, movements or other, more fluid forms of social organization. For instance, the Stanford-based sociologist Woody Powell and his colleagues (Powell et al., 1996) argued that the locus of innovation has shifted from firms to networks. He argued that in networks information flows more freely than in hierarchical firms. For an individual firm, this means that its position within a network influences its capacity to innovate.

A **platform** is defined as an evolving eco-system that is created from many interconnected pieces.

Other researchers think of innovation as occurring on **platforms** in which various parties co-create new products, services and experiences that contribute towards the platform's development (Cusumano and Gawer, 2002, 2008; Gawer and Henderson, 2007; Parker and Van Alstyne, 2017).

The automobile illustrates how platform innovation works: Henry Ford's story of the genius innovator is only half of the truth. Rather, Ford benefitted from and exploited a social movement that paved the way for a society in which the car would take on the status of a cultural object – sometimes even a cult object. When the first car-like vehicles were invented towards the end of the nineteenth century, people could not agree whether they were a blessing or a curse. Some called them a 'devilish contraption', while others argued that 'you can't get people to sit on an explosion' (quoted in Rao, 2009: 20). Cars were deemed expensive, dangerous, noisy, slow and unreliable. People could not even agree on a name for them – some called them locomobile, others quadricycle, and so on (Rao, 2009: 19). While it was hard to imagine a name for those new monsters, it was even harder to imagine how they could be used.

Thus, for people to become *custom*ers, people actually *buying* cars, their customs had to be changed – and this implied a deep societal change. Rao argues that one key element in instigating this social change that made the car a culturally accepted object was reliability testing. In these tests, cars competed against each other to demonstrate that they were trustworthy:

> Reliability contests were credible because each race was an event that could be interpreted as evidence of the dependability of cars by the public. Since reliability contests were public spectacles, they were emotionally charged events. Finally, reliability contests had 'narrative fidelity' because they combined the logic of testing with the practice of racing and created a compelling story. (Rao, 2009: 32)

In other words, these contests made the advantages of cars tangible and visible to a large audience; they created familiarity (custom!) with a new technology and produced stories people could relate to. Henry Ford had won one of those reliability contests in 1901 against the established producer Alexander Winton, which helped to legitimize the start-up of the Ford Motor Company two years later (Rao, 2009: 32). Rao's point is that market rebels, including those who organized reliability competitions, those who attended them and those who wrote about them extensively, created an atmosphere in which either car critics could be convinced that the car was a symbol of progress or they could be successfully marginalized.

The ecology, or ecosystem, in which the invention of the car could become a commercial success did not stop with reliability contests. John Urry (2007) argues that the car marked a radical departure from the train, which was the great nineteenth-century transport invention. While the train was public and followed a time regime set by the railway companies, the car embodied the opposite: it created and meant *freedom* (I can go where I want), *privacy* (the car as a living room on wheels) and *individuality* (from choice of model to tuning or 'pimping' up the car).

As well as cultural legitimacy, the car required a huge infrastructure to become useful: roads, highway networks, petrol stations, repair workshops, public licensing authorities, police, legal framework, insurance, and so on. In the twentieth century, entire cities have been modelled to accommodate the car – think of Los Angeles as the most often quoted example. Once such a system takes shape, innovations against the grain of the established ecology are hard to implement because so many players benefit from the status quo. The politics of the present situation prevail: in Los Angeles, they were enough to stymie any public transport rapid transit ideas for decades because of the entrenched power of the petroleum and related products lobby.

Even when we know that cars have a negative impact on the environment and make our cities dysfunctional, and that each and every year roads produce 1.2 million dead and more than 20–50 million injured people, at an estimated cost of $518 billion, the car is still *the* preferred means of transportation. The power and diffusion of the car involved a whole network of actors who had to collaborate to create the cultural and physical conditions to turn the 'devilish contraption' into a desired object and a cultural icon. Hence, the moral of the story is that successful innovation is more than just developing an idea: it needs the active shaping of a platform in which the idea can grow and create traction. This is the point that Cusumano and Gawer (2002) make. They argue that successful firms do not simply develop new products and services and compete with others in open markets. Rather, leading firms establish a platform on which new products emerge. Importantly, innovations have to build on other pieces to make sense to customers. Think back to our opening example of the MP3 player and the success of Apple versus the success of Sony; the technology relied on complementary innovations to make the core value proposition appealing to the consumer masses. Platform leaders are those companies who control or at least shape the structure of overarching systems architecture. In other words, platform leaders define the rules of the game, the size of the playing field and the entry conditions for players. Of course, to be able to control the platform is a powerful position that leads to a significant competitive advantage. A good example of a platform leader is Microsoft Windows: its ubiquitous operating system forces friends and foes to engage with its technology (Cusumano and Gawer, 2002).

EXTEND YOUR KNOWLEDGE

Adner, R. (2017) 'Ecosystem as structure: an actionable construct for strategy', *Journal of Management*, 43 (1): 39–58. You can access the article at the companion website https://study.sagepub.com/managingandorganizations5e

READ THE ARTICLE

INNOVATION AS AN OUTCOME: DYNAMICS OF PROGRESSION

The product, service, process and business model outcomes of the innovation process pursued by organizations induce dynamics of innovative progression and change. Surprisingly, the cumulative dynamics of innovation and technological progression have been found to follow remarkably similar patterns or cycles.

INNOVATION CYCLES AND TECHNOLOGICAL PARADIGMS

Ever since the pioneering work of Joseph Schumpeter (2006 [1942]) documenting the successive waves of product and process innovation that induce 'gales of creative destruction' and drive industrial progression at the cost of destroying a predecessor, research has been interested in the effects of technological change on industries, organizations and roles (Anderson and Tushman, 1990; Tushman and Anderson, 1986). It is now widely accepted that innovation as an outcome broadly follows macro-level cycles of technological change characterized by s-curved trajectories of improvement that are punctuated by eventual shifts in the underlying technological paradigm that initiates a new paradigm and renders the old one obsolete.

These s-curved trajectories represent the overall dynamics of technological progress. An innovation cycle is first initiated by the emergence of a dominant technological standard that then sets the tone for innovative progress within the parameters of the defined trajectory. Within this trajectory, innovation follows a step-wise, evolutionary path in which the dominant standard is progressed and propagated through incremental improvements (Dosi, 1984; Nelson and Winter, 1982). As progress continues to ensue and technology develops, the trajectory evolves through phases of growth, maturity and decline that create the distinctive s-curved trajectory of progress until there is a shock to the system induced by a breakthrough, radical advancement that punctuates the s-curve and starts a new one. This punctuation point represents the end of a technological paradigm that is undergirded by a dominant standard.

According to the seminal study of Anderson and Tushman, this punctuation point initiates what's known as an 'era of ferment':

> The introduction of a radical advance ushers in an era of experimentation as organizations struggle to absorb (or destroy) the innovative technology. This era of ferment is characterized by two distinct selection processes: competition between technological regimes and competition within the new technical regime. This cycle of old versus new ends with the emergence of a dominant design that instantiates the incremental evolutionary progression on the s-curve again and the cycle goes on and on. (1990: 611)

Organizations live and die by these macro-level cycles of technological progression. Technology is a ubiquitous force that shapes environmental conditions. Changes in technology are not constrained within a single industry and operate at a higher level of aggregation that results in cascading effects on organizations. These technological advances we have discussed can be classified as either *competence-enhancing* or *competence-destroying* for the organization (Tushman and Anderson, 1986). While the former may represent an order-of-magnitude improvement over prior products, they are sustaining of the underlying knowledge and skills that contribute to the development and reaffirmation of the existing trajectory. Incumbent firms seeking to maintain the status quo typically develop such innovations. Competence-destroying advances, on the other hand, create an entirely new product class that represents fundamentally new ways of doing things that render existing skills and knowledge obsolete: these innovations are typically developed by new entrants.

THE INNOVATOR'S DILEMMA

In his influential book, Clayton M. Christensen analysed the underlying managerial reasons why successful organizations (such as Kodak and Xerox) fail when they are faced with technological improvements that are not necessarily technologically discontinuous! Christensen described this failure as the *innovator's dilemma*, and asserted in his provocative thesis that this type of failure is paradoxically the result of good management:

> Precisely because these firms listened to their customers, invested aggressively in new technologies that would provide their customers more and better products of the sort they wanted, and because they carefully studied market trends and systematically allocated investment capital to innovations that promised the best returns, they lost their position of leadership. (Christensen, 1997: xii)

Christensen regards good management as the reason for failure, which he explains in the following way. Disruptive technologies are the key to innovation. However, most technologies are *sustaining technologies*, meaning that they improve the performance of existing products aligned to an existing technological trajectory rather than replace it. Disruptive technologies, on the other hand, result in worse product performance (at least in the short term) for existing products. Compared with established products, new disruptive technologies often perform at a lower level of perfection. For instance, top-end decks, tone arms and immaculate quality vinyl beat early CDs hands down for tonal warmth and resonance, though CDs did not scratch as easily and were easier to use, played more music and were portable. The CDs had characteristics valued by markets: they were smaller and they were also easier and more convenient to use. Another example of disruptive technologies was the off-road motorbike manufactured by Honda and Kawasaki. Compared with sleek BMW and Harley Davidson machines, these models were

WATCH A VIDEO ABOUT DISRUPTORS

EXTEND YOUR KNOWLEDGE

Whether MOOCs carry disruptive potential to universities is a question considered by D. J. Teece (2018) in 'Managing the university: why "organized anarchy" is unacceptable in the age of massive open online courses', *Strategic Organization*, 16 (1): 92–102. You can access the article at the companion website https://study.sagepub.com/managingandorganizations5e

READ THE ARTICLE

primitive, though they could go places that the big bikes, with their smooth finish, could not. The desktop computer was a disruptive technology relative to the mainframe computers developed by IBM.

The problem for established companies is that they generally do not invest in disruptive technologies, despite being cognizant of their existence, as they are simpler and cheaper and develop in fringe or low-end segments of the market that do not offer enough profit and margins to sustain the operations of incumbent firms. After the market is big enough to create serious profits to sustain the operations of incumbents, it is usually too costly or too late to join. Often, the established firm's best customers do not want, and cannot use, the new, disruptive technologies, and the potential customers of the new technology are unknown. Proven marketing tools and planning skills do not necessarily work under these conditions.

BEYOND TECHNOLOGICAL PARADIGMS

The organization–environment linkages do not stop at technological paradigms in corporate settings, however, and the driving force behind innovation is not always the same. There are many layers to the external environment that induce effects on the organization, including access to scientific knowledge, competent human resources, curious financial investors, educated consumers, institutional norms, as well as political, economic, socio-cultural and legal cornerstones. These parameters can only be controlled by an organization to a very limited extent, as most of them are out of the organization's reach. Think of a biotechnology company that experiments with genetically modified food. It not only needs highly trained staff from universities but also relies heavily on public opinion and the favourable resolution of legal and ethical issues that dominate the debate. None of these are implicit in the science or the organization of innovation, yet they are fundamental to its potential success.

SOCIAL INNOVATION

More recently, socio-cultural effects are driving innovation beyond corporate boundaries. The great challenges of our time – such as climate change, radicalization of cultural identities, poverty, an aging population and rapidly rising health care costs – need innovative answers if we want to solve them. But who could work on holistic, complex solutions for large-scale challenges? Governments and the public sector in general seem to be too thinly resourced and organized too much in silos to tackle these challenges. On the other hand, corporations, the drivers of much of innovation in the past two centuries, seem to be more concerned with ensuring the survival of their existing business models and annual (if not quarterly) returns for their shareholders. Neither the market nor government planning provides a satisfying answer. How, then, can we tackle the big challenges of our time? Who will be the innovators to solve these problems?

The answer that is mentioned in the corridors of power and community movements alike is: social innovation. Robin Murray, Julie Caulier-Grice and Geoff Mulgan (2010) define social innovation in *The Open Book of Social Innovation* as 'new ideas (products, services and models) that simultaneously meet social needs and create new social relationships or collaborations. In other words, they are innovations that are both good for society *and* enhance society's capacity to act'

EXTEND YOUR KNOWLEDGE

Porter, A. J., Kuhn, T. R. and Nerlich, B. (2018) 'Organizing authority in the climate change debate: IPCC controversies and the management of dialectical tensions', *Organization Studies*, 39 (7): 873–98. The article examines the dialectical -tensions in the climate change debate. You can access the article at the companion website https://study.sagepub.com/managingandorganizations5e

Subhabrata, B. B. and Jackson, L. (2017) 'Microfinance and the business of poverty reduction: critical perspectives from rural Bangladesh', *Human Relations*, 70 (1): 63–91. The article critically examines approaches to poverty reduction in developing countries. You can access the article at the companion website https://study.sagepub.com/managingandorganizations5e

READ THE ARTICLE

(Murray et al., 2010: 3). A good example of social innovation is micro-finance: in poor regions, development is often stifled through a lack of access to finance. In these regions, a small amount of money could go a long way. For big banks, it is not an attractive business though: they prefer customers with big incomes who use their credit cards and pay back their mortgage on time. The Grameen Bank Project founded by Muhammad Yunus, who was awarded the Nobel Peace Prize in 2006, is a good example of micro-finance.

READ THIS JOURNAL ARTICLE

Two emerging forces shape social innovation: (1) technology as an enabler of social networking where people share ideas and solutions; and (2) a growing concern with what Robin Murray et al. (2010) call the human dimension, which becomes more important than systems and structures. How does social innovation work? Murray and his colleagues have devised a six-step process:

1. *Prompts, inspirations and diagnoses*: Every new idea starts with the perception of a problem or a crisis. In the first stage of social innovation, the problem is experienced, framed and turned into a question that tackles the root of the problem.

2. *Proposals and ideas generation*: Initial ideas are developed and the proposal is discussed. Importantly, a wide range of ideas is taken into account.

3. *Prototyping and pilots*: Talk is cheap – so ideas need to be tested in practice. Trial and error, prototyping and testing are means of refining ideas that cannot be substituted by armchair research. The motto is: fail often, learn quickly!

4. *Sustaining*: This step includes the development of structures and sustainable income streams to ensure that the best ideas have a useful vehicle to travel. Resources, networks and practices need to be organized so that innovation can be carried forward.

5. *Scaling and diffusion*: Good ideas have to spread – hence the scaling up of solutions is key. This can happen formally, through franchising or licensing, or more informally, through inspiration and imitation.

6. *Systemic change*: The ultimate goal of social innovation. This involves change on a big scale driven by social movements, fuelled by new business models, structured by new organizational forms and regulated by new public institutions and laws.

READ MORE ABOUT SDGS

WHAT WOULD YOU DO?

All of us are committed to some social causes, such as ecology, feminism, LGBT rights or vegetarianism. Check out the United Nation's Sustainable Development Goals (SDGs). Review these issues and their underlying drivers to create ideas with regards to how organizations and other stakeholders can adequately respond. What would you do? What are the strategies that you think are best to follow and why do you think this?

MANAGING CHANGE AND INNOVATION

Peter Drucker defines innovation as the 'specific tool of entrepreneurs, the means by which they exploit change as an opportunity for a different business or service. It is capable of being presented, as a discipline, capable of being learned, capable of being practiced' (Drucker, quoted in Tidd et al., 2001: 38). Thus, innovation is an entrepreneurial tool that should be exploited. Although this is a nice definition, we suggest adding some critical reflections on the different types of change and organizational politics shaping the unfolding process.

TYPES OF CHANGE

Fundamentally, **change** refers to a transition that occurs from one state to another.

Opinions about **change** vary between researchers: some argue that change is the exception and stability is the norm, whereas others support a process-based view according to which almost everything is in flux and transformation.

Speaking generally, there are four types of change (Van de Ven and Poole, 1995):

1. *Life cycle* change: change that occurs in terms of stages of maturation, growth or aging.
2. *Dialectical* (struggle-based) change: change that occurs through the interplay, tensions and contradictions of social relations. Such change can be observed in two-party-dominated political systems such as those in the USA and the UK. Change often occurs in moves from one side to the other of the political arena.
3. *Evolutionary* change: change that occurs through environmental adaption, such as organizations that decide to develop a new online-based product owing to the proliferation of the Internet.
4. *Teleological* (vision-based) change: change that occurs as a result of a strategic vision, such as when a city government aims to host a future Olympics and creates an organization to oversee the bid.

UNFREEZING, MOVING AND REFREEZING

Kurt Lewin packaged this philosophy of change theoretically. In his model of change (Lewin, 1951), he identified three steps that are involved in changing organizations and people: (1) you have to unfreeze the current state of affairs; (2) you move things to where you want them to be; and (3) after you have succeeded, you refreeze again. This simple chain of unfreeze, move, refreeze became the template for most change programmes. Some differ in terms of how many steps they assign to each phase, but few question the underlying rationale and logic of Lewin's model (see Cummings, 2002: 265).

EXTEND YOUR KNOWLEDGE

READ THE ARTICLE

Suddaby, R. and Foster, W. M. (2017) 'History and organizational change', *Journal of Management*, 43 (1): 19–38, will help you to understand why the past is important when changing for the future. You can access the article at the companion website https://study.sagepub.com/managingandorganizations5e

PLANNED CHANGE

Recall the concept of rational management encountered in Chapter 1. As we shall see in Chapter 14, Taylor argued for a complete rational reorganization of the entire shop-floor base of the enterprise. Taylor's change initiatives were built upon two principles that have been remarkably resilient: (a) that change is accomplished through rational plans developed, implemented and monitored by management; and (b) that these change programmes are put in place to minimize future changes. Put simply, the promise is that if you adapt change ideas (from scientific management, for instance) and change your organization accordingly, you will never need to change again. This approach views change as something that is unfortunately necessary; change is undesirable because it is an interruption to the natural state of organizations, which is a stable equilibrium. The expectation is that stability will be interrupted by short periods of change, forced upon an organization either by technological progress or by new organizational processes. In any case, the environment induces change externally, and the organization has to adapt as quickly as possible to achieve equilibrium again. Business-as-usual is the ideal, with everything else being a disturbance.

A typical example of a rational approach to change is business process re-engineering (BPR), which was developed, disseminated and successfully marketed by Hammer and Champy (1993). BPR encompasses a radical rethinking and redesigning of core organizational activities to achieve higher efficiency and performance. It is based on two simple assumptions. First, BPR analyses organizational activities step by step so it can develop suggestions for improvements (such as time saving, cost cutting, and so on) on a micro level and reassemble the whole process in the most efficient way. Second, it redesigns the entire organization in accordance with these findings without paying attention to its past history or its cultural and social context.

If you think this sounds a lot like an overly rationalist approach to management, you would be correct. Even the name gives it away as an engineering rationality. However, the engineering is not very robust – roughly 70 per cent of the change initiatives made as BPR fail, which explains why BPR has been less successful in colonizing the change market than its proponents had hoped.

IMAGE 11.1 Accepting change

WHAT WOULD YOU DO?

You are a student of Management at a university – that is why you are reading this book, we assume. As such, you are on the receiving end of other people's ideas about what you should know – your instructors, the authors (including us) that wrote the books and articles that you read. Now, think about the future: what do you think *you* really want to know and what do you think you really need to know? Write it down in bullet points. Talk to others in the subject and get their views. Now workshop with the others – what would you do to change the contents and orientation of what you are learning? What are the arguments for the changed omissions and commissions?

THEORIES OF PROCESSUAL CHANGE

Process theories of organizational change reject Lewin's three-step approach. The root metaphor of unfreezing/freezing is profoundly problematic because organizations are always in motion; they never respond solely to singular design imperatives, but usually emerge from many pressures and directions, even though management change agents may be able to exercise a steering capacity (Buchanan and Badham, 1999).

The processual perspective emerged from the work of a number of writers, but there is no doubt that it was Pettigrew who had the single greatest impact. His magnum opus, *Awakening Giant: Continuity and Change in ICI* (1985), was a careful case study that challenged many of the dominant assumptions about how organizations change. The plans of change agents equipped with formal schemas were not reflected in what actually occurred. Instead, change appeared to be both incremental and evolutionary, as well as being punctuated by revolutionary and radically discontinuous periods. He saw 'change and continuity, process and structure' as 'inextricably linked' (Pettigrew, 1985: 24). Rather than stages of change being observed, processes could be seen changing in patterns produced by the interplay between the contextual variables of history, culture and political processes (Pettigrew, 1990).

ICI (Imperial Chemical Industries) went through a crisis in its traditional way of organizing. It made the decision to change its organization structure and processes. A large organization such as ICI often initiates major programmes of change but there are also changes introduced by snipers and ambushes as well as those that are planned; symbols are used to advance change as much as to retard it and rumours about boardroom manoeuvrings and executive succession, in both the organization and the wider business community, are rife. Organizational change is not unlike a long and contested campaign in which successfully positioning and maintaining the dominant myths and symbols are of vital importance. And it is the task of leadership to achieve such positioning (see also Chapter 4). In doing so, as Buchanan and Badham (2008: 231) remind us, management is a contact sport, one in which 'if you don't want to get bruised, don't play'. In the game of organizational change, it is directed and strategic change that retains the central focus, so there is little room for gifted amateurs, although many participants may well try to press sectional or local advantages in the opportunities that widespread change presents.

EXTEND YOUR KNOWLEDGE

READ THE ARTICLE

Check out the introduction and explore some of the articles in a dedicated special issue in *Organization Studies*: Smith, W., Erez, M., Lewis, M., Jarvenpaa, S. and Tracey, P. (2017) 'Adding complexity to theories of paradox, tensions, dualities of innovation and change: introduction to special issue on paradox, tensions, and dualities of innovation and change', *Organization Studies*, 38 (3-4): 303-17. You can access the article at the companion website https://study.sagepub.com/managingandorganizations5e

Contemporary perspectives, rather than seeing change as a sequence of linear events that occur and are then frozen, emphasize process and temporality. Anyone seeking to change organizations must exhibit a mastery of power and politics (see Figure 11.1). Managers usually seek to manage as if organizations were rational, even when rationality is a mere facade or veneer for mobilizing resources, allies and opponents in a political struggle for change. More often than not, organizations feature messy and ambiguous problems that stop short of drifting into chaos.

RICHARD BADHAM'S 5M FRAMEWORK

Professor Badham has been studying organizational change for over 30 years and has synthesized his approach into a useful 5M model. He defines managing change as the process of influencing others to accomplish an objective. This process unfolds along five steps (Badham, 2013):

1. *Mindfulness*: Change is difficult, messy and likely to fail; hence, at the outset of a change process, it is important to be mindful of its complexities and subtleties – including the chances of failure.
2. *Mobilizing*: This refers to achieving buy-in from important stakeholders and mobilizing their intelligence, emotions and networks in order to accomplish change.
3. *Mapping*: This action refers to planning the journey ahead – to map the route, outline potential obstacles, short cuts, and so on.
4. *Masks*: Plans need to be performed in order to make a difference. Performances, like those in theatres or concert halls, need 'masks' that transform people into performers that the audience finds engaging. In short, masks are what change makers need in order to play roles.
5. *Mirrors*: These provide learning spaces in which actors can reflect on what has happened, why and how to go forward. Especially in times of change, things are uncertain; as Badham writes: plans are hypothesis and action experiments. Therefore, feedback and learning are quintessential parts of the change process.

EXTEND YOUR KNOWLEDGE

READ THE ARTICLE

Panayiotou, A., Putnam, L. L. and Kassinis, G. (2017) 'Generating tensions: a multilevel, process analysis of organizational change', *Strategic Organization*, DOI: 10.1177/147612701773446. This article explores the importance of generating tensions and responses to tensions for driving organization change; you can access it at the companion website https://study.sagepub.com/managingandorganizations5e

INNOVATION AND CHANGE AT THE EDGE OF CHAOS

Current approaches to innovation do not put much emphasis on rational planning. Instead, they stress the politics of innovation and the balance that is necessary between freedom and the responsibility required for autonomous and disciplined

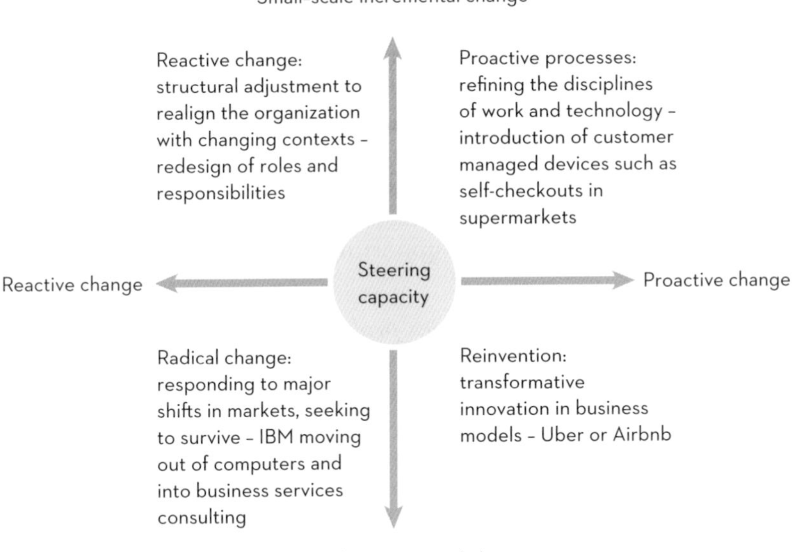

FIGURE 11.1 The capstan steering change model (adapted from Dawson, 2003: 23)

creativity. Change cannot be prescribed through one-best-way or prescriptive practices, but instead there are many different ways of achieving innovative outcomes. In fact, innovation sometimes happens while management is busy making other plans. Some writers suggest that, rather than planning and order being the normal conditions for organizations, management needs to become accustomed to **chaos**.

Chaos is a Greek word that is in opposition to cosmos (an orderly and harmonious system). Normally, chaos is related to system unpredictability.

Innovation challenges established management practices and beliefs, especially the planning and control functions. Pascale (1999) introduced four new principles derived from complexity theory that can frame the innovation process differently:

1. *Equilibrium equals death*: Remember when you first learned to ride a bike? The idea that those narrow wheels could stay balanced might have struck you as crazy until you learned that, when riding a bicycle, you can stay balanced only when you move. Organizations are not that different; as long as they move, they gain stability but after they cease to move they do not retain their balance and being an unbalanced organization in the fast-moving corporate world (like being an unsteady bicycle rider steering through fast-moving traffic) is a recipe for death. Innovation and creative breakthroughs push an organization away from equilibrium and increase the necessary variety it has to deal with. As Tim Mannon, the president of Hewlett-Packard's (HP) Printer Division, said, 'The biggest single threat to our business today is staying with a previously successful business model one year too long' (quoted in Pascale, 1999: 90). Hence, stability can be dangerous.
2. *Self-organization is important*: Organizations are capable of organizing themselves according to internally evolving principles. In managing

complex unforeseeable tasks or events such as disasters, people organize themselves, and an order evolves that is not imposed by a mastermind. Instead of acting according to a purposefully designed plan, people interact spontaneously and patterns of collaboration emerge. A good example is a soccer game: there is no hierarchal relationship between individual players, rather they are self-organized around the attractor of the ball, and bound by the rules of the game. From the perspective of the innovation process, this means that management should give up its fantasies of control and, rather, focus on supporting the self-organizing powers of a system.

3. *Complex tasks need more complex problem-solving processes*: To maintain a complex system, many apparently chaotic and unstable processes work together. Think of a high-wire performer for whom many small, ostensibly chaotic movements maintain balance on the high wire. The same goes for innovation; lots of trial-and-error steps may finally come into balance and lead to successful innovation. During the initial process of innovation, a chaotic patchwork of actions and outcomes seems to prevail, whereas, in the final stages, more orderly patterns emerge. We know what sense we make only after we have made it. As Weick (1995) says, all sensemaking – even that projected into the future – has a retrospective quality about it. The fact that we did not achieve a certain plan by the due date turns into a great step in the innovation process because it helped us realize that we were doing the wrong thing, going in a foolish direction. Without some foolishness, we would never find our way to what we can later determine is wisdom. All the mistakes on the way can be represented retrospectively as learning that will eventually be rewarded in the final successful innovation outcome (see also Chapter 12).

4. *Complex organizations can only be disturbed, not directed*: Small causes might have huge effects, and vice versa. In a complex organizational environment, changing one pattern might transform the entire company. In innovation processes, calculations about invested resources and predicted outcomes are meaningless, because what innovation will produce may simply not be calculable. Think of ideas that were truly new, such as the telephone, the Internet, or simple things such as Post-it notes; their potential for changing organizational practices and consumer behaviour could not be forecast simply because no one could imagine the impact they would make on everyday life. Thus, all that can be done is to make sure that the system does not come too close to equilibrium and that it keeps on moving, experiencing new ideas as opportunities and not as threats.

The way these four principles conceptualize innovation and change is radically different from the rational approach. They take into account the limited capacity of management to order and to prescribe, and argue for a more complex, chaotic and emergent understanding of the innovation process. Innovation that is supposed to lead to truly new outcomes and change cannot be detailed, prescriptively, in advance. The future is uncertain and the end is always near, shifting in and out of our grasp.

MANAGING THE POLITICS OF CHANGE AND INNOVATION

Innovation changes organizational power relations: 'Accomplishing innovation and change in organizations requires more than the ability to solve technical or analytical problems. Innovation almost invariably threatens the status quo, and consequently, innovation is an inherently political activity' (Pfeffer, 1992: 7). As Van de Ven and his colleagues (1999: 65) found, 'managers cannot control innovation success, only its odds through the creation of preferable conditions'. This principle implies that a fundamental change is needed in the control philosophy of conventional management practices. At its core, innovation is a journey into the unknown and thus is inherently unpredictable and uncontrollable. Most change initiatives fail, not because the ideas or concepts were not refined or smart enough, but because the actual implementation was not understood and executed perfectly – which it never will be.

IN PRACTICE

Changing

Change can be conceptualized as consisting of three different, though closely interlinked, initiatives (Hirschhorn, 2002). First, there will be a political campaign, which should create strong and lasting support for the desired change (see also Chapter 8). A second initiative will be a communication campaign, ensuring that all major stakeholders understand and share the idea of change and are committed to the principles and consequences behind it (see also Chapter 9). Finally, there will be a rationally planned campaign that makes sure that the human and material resources necessary for a successful change are available. Without paying attention to these political implications, innovative ideas cannot be turned into actionable and tangible outcomes.

Can you think of any campaign that has been oriented to you as a consumer, whether from government, business or an NGO, that follows such a three-stage model? Jot down your thoughts on it and share them with others in your study group. Compare Hirschhorn's model with Badham's 5M approach. What are the differences and what are the similarities between them? How could you criticize the two models?

Hirschhorn's focus is intraorganizational, which makes sense managerially because the organizational arena is the one most subject to managerial control. However, innovation is not something that occurs just within the firm, because the firm itself is embedded within a broader innovation system.

Recent studies of innovation demonstrate the interdependence of economic, political, social and cultural factors. Some of these factors are external to the organizations involved, as a part of the broad institutional setting, whereas others are internal, such as those that Hirschhorn focuses on. The relative degree of success enjoyed by organizations and networks of organizations in nations and regions in the global knowledge-based economy depends on the effective management of these factors. Therefore, there is a need to understand better the complex interdependencies between internal firm dynamics around the innovation process and the broader institutional settings in which the firms operate.

Institutional settings have been identified in terms of local contexts that interact with the system of innovation – including networks of organizations in the public and private sectors – to initiate, import, modify and diffuse new technologies. The concept of the system of innovation shifts the focus from an isolated firm so that it may be seen as part of a network of organizations embedded within specific contexts. The type of context may not only be identified at a regional or a local level but also include deliberately constructed virtual networks that seek to eclipse contextual specificity.

ORGANIZING FOR INNOVATION

SEARCH, ORGANIZING DISSONANCE AND ENTREPRENEURSHIP

When a shipwrecked Robinson Crusoe walked on the beach, he knew what was valuable and what was not – and he knew instantly that he had to act when he saw those footprints in the sand. Unfortunately, our world is more complex. When do we have to act? What is valuable? How can we decipher those signs showing us as much of the future as they hide? Where should we search? And how should we organize search?

Search becomes a major challenge to navigate the world. A new economy has emerged around the central concept of the search engine, replacing the steam engine, the dynamo of the Industrial Revolution. In an information society, the capacity to produce is eclipsed by the ability to find, edit and connect information and new ideas. The world of business often struggles with search. Typically, search is outsourced to the entrepreneur. In a Darwinian struggle, so the story goes, thousands of entrepreneurs worldwide explore niches and new ideas. Most fail. But some make it. Once they have made it, their search has come to an end. They stop exploring and switch to exploiting their ideas – until younger entrepreneurs make them obsolete and the process starts all over. Schumpeter (2006 [1942]) has termed this transformation creative destruction. IBM gave way to Microsoft, and Microsoft to Google, and Google to Facebook, and Facebook to Twitter, and so on. Each of those firms emerged out of entrepreneurial drive and acumen, grew into a formidable corporation and lost sight of new ideas because it focused on exploiting its capital.

In his book *The Sense of Dissonance: Accounts of Worth in Economic Life*, David Stark (2009) describes entrepreneurship as the ability to keep multiple principles of evaluation at play simultaneously and benefit from the friction between them. Rather than deciding what is valuable and what is not, the entrepreneur keeps on collecting items with different (maybe even contradicting) values and defers judgement about their usefulness. In the words of Stark, 'entrepreneurship exploits the indeterminate situation by keeping open diverse performance criteria rather than by creating consensus about one set of rules' (Stark, 2009: 16).

While it might be possible for an entrepreneur to chase several different ideas at the same time, organizations usually put a premium on efficiency and alignment. This results in a singular value system that drives the organization and enforces consensus. Remember that search requires the opposite mindset: if you search you have to be open-minded and look at each item you find from a different perspective – especially if you're not sure what you are looking for! Stark argues that organizations should actively seek different principles of evaluation, different regimes of what counts as valuable, and different mechanisms to determine what is potentially interesting and worthy for future exploration. Strategically speaking, the dilemma is obvious: in an organization that is perfectly well aligned with an environment that demands typewriters, the PC could only be perceived as negligible noise. After a long tradition of building big cars that would be filled with cheap petrol, GM, Chrysler and Ford did not value small cars built by their Japanese competitors.

Stark's question is: how to marry organization and the entrepreneur? He refers to heterarchy as the organizational form that allows diverse principles of evaluation to flourish at the same time. While hierarchy reflects a heavenly order, heterarchy is a pattern of relations between elements that are, in respect to power and authority, equal. While hierarchy relies on a singular rationality informing the organization, heterarchy accepts that there are several bounded rationalities, each of them having their own evaluation principles.

For Stark, heterarchy resembles organized dissonance. He argues that organizations with 'greater diversity in ways of doing things are more likely to have the capacity to adapt when the environment changes' (2009: 179). While dissonance might be something to be avoided, it might emerge as an organizational form that can cope best with the problem of search. Accepting polyphony (Kornberger et al., 2006) as the reality of organizational life, heterarchy is the form that allows for multiple entrepreneurial strategies that have their own evaluation principles.

BEING FOOLISH AND CREATIVE

It should be clear by this point in the chapter that innovation and change cannot be entirely planned and will unfold in largely unpredictable and uncontrollable ways. These facts might be scary and challenging for the world of management, which is used to control (see also Chapter 14). As the senior vice-president of research and development at 3M puts it:

> innovation ... is anything but orderly ... We are managing in chaos, and this is the right way to manage if you want innovation. It's been said that the competition never knows what we are going to come up with next. The fact is, neither do we. (Van de Ven et al., 1999: 181)

The statement of the 3M manager is echoed, and somehow anticipated, by James March, one of the most thought-provoking minds in the field of management and organization theory. In his playful article 'The technology of foolishness' (March, 1988), he criticizes two major building blocks of common-sense thinking that are both closely linked to the concept of rationality (see also Chapter 2). First, he tackles the idea of pre-existing purposes that inform our actions generally and change initiatives especially, and, second, he questions the principle of consistency that should link our purposes, decisions and actions so that they are aligned. March says that innovation happens not because of but despite these two principles; the problem is that goals are not given beforehand but are developed in context and are thus subject to change. He argues that sometimes we have to do things for which we have no good reasons to come up with a new objective.

A great example of this is the development of Watson, IBM's Artificial Intelligence platform. The original thread of the idea was spawned from experienced coders who wanted to build a system capable of beating master chess players. These coders worked on the idea in their spare time and experimented during lunch breaks. Watson was then developed and taught how to beat the two most successful champions of the popular TV show *Jeopardy* – check out the video. Although Watson was developed out of play with no real application in mind, it is now a core IBM business unit and is being applied in areas such as oncology and education.

WATCH THE JEOPARDY VIDEO

The call for consistent rational behaviour is counter-intuitive when it comes to innovation. March (1988) juxtaposes playfulness with rationality and argues that playfulness unleashes creativity and innovation because it emphasizes improvisation, trial and error, and the general openness to try out new things. The urge for consistency would not allow us to act in different, maybe even contradictory, ways because this course of action seems to be irrational and hence undesired. As March argues, 'we need to find some ways of helping individuals and organizations to experiment with doing things *for which they have no good reason*, to be playful with the conception of themselves' (1988: 262, emphasis added). He delineates this as the technology of foolishness, an approach that 'might help … in a small way to develop the unusual combinations of attitudes and behaviors that describe the interesting people, interesting organizations, and interesting societies of the world' (1988: 265).

In summary, March (1988) suggests that a narrowly defined notion of rationality that is obsessed with order and control might be counterproductive when it comes to the question of innovation, change and creativity. Rather, he suggests that a technology of foolishness that allows us to do playful things for which we have no good reasons might be more appropriate to explore new terrain. This technology of foolishness happened at 3M, where a chemist discovered the not overly sticky adhesive that formed the basis of the Post-it note. Playfully exploring where new ideas lead, without a purpose in mind, can lead to great outcomes; at 3M, management learned this lesson, and asks employees to devote 15 per cent of their time to working on things they fancy – a practice adopted by many innovative firms, including Google.

IN PRACTICE

The paradox of innovation and change

To paraphrase the Greek philosopher Plato (1968), innovation is a paradoxical concept: if things are really new and innovative, we would not understand them at all because they would embody a radical break with all we know. What we usually call new is not really new – it will resemble phenomena we are used to. Take a new car. Is it new because of its styling and engineering? Does it not resemble all the other cars so much that it is hardly justified to speak about innovation in this case? Thus, the paradox is that the new is either already known and established, but disguised in new clothes, or, if it is really new, it is unrecognizable and beyond our understanding. The perfect example is the invention of the telephone. Alexander Bell presented his idea to senior managers at Western Union. They listened patiently to him and, after a couple of days, Bell got a letter from them saying, 'after careful consideration of your invention, which is a very interesting novelty, we have come to the conclusion that it has no commercial possibilities ... we see no future for an electrical toy'.

Obviously, the guys at Western Union were not exactly right; within four years, there were more than 50,000 phones in the USA, and after 20 years, there were 5 million, and the patent became the single most valuable patent in history (see Tidd et al., 2001). Innovation requires the creativity of foolishness to stick with an idea beyond the stage where most people would dismiss it entirely.

What are the contemporary equivalents to the phone as innovative ideas initially not understood? Can you think of any? What were the reasons for initial non-acceptance and ultimate acceptance?

HOW TO KILL CREATIVITY

It is hard to tell how one can actually nurture creativity, but it is quite clear how one can kill it quickly. We have compiled, with the help of others' research, a practical guide for managers who want to avoid innovation and creativity (Amabile, 1998; Kanter, 1984: 204; Morgan, 1989: 54; Ordiorne, 1981: 79). Think of it as ten easy steps for sustaining routines to the point that they will eventually destroy your organization:

1. Always pretend to know more than anybody around you. Especially be suspicious when people from below come up with ideas. You know better!
2. Police your employees by every procedural means that you can devise. Insist that they stick to the rules of good old bureaucracy and fill in many forms that need to be signed by almost every senior manager in the organization.
3. Run daily checks on the progress of everyone's work. Be critical (they love it!), and withhold positive feedback, which would only encourage them to do things that are potentially dangerous.
4. Make sure that creative people do a lot of technical and detailed work. Make sure that they do their own bookkeeping, and count everything you can count as often as possible.
5. Create boundaries between decision-makers, technical staff and creative minds. Make sure that they speak different languages.
6. Never talk to employees on a personal level, except for at annual meetings at which you praise your social and communicative leadership skills.
7. Be the exclusive spokesperson for every new idea, regardless of whether it is your own or not.
8. Embrace new ideas when you talk, but do not do anything about them.

9. When the proposed idea is too radical, you can always argue that no one has done it before and that there might be reasons for this.
10. When the proposed idea is not radical enough, just say that the idea is not really new and that someone else already did it.

Of course, this list is far from being complete; there are many small practices that can be built into organizational routines that may help you effectively avoid unnecessary creativity, such as organizing endless meetings in which you discuss and rehash every new idea without actually developing any; sticking to the protocols of ways that have been successful in doing things so far; throwing lots of detailed questions on the table (cash flow in the next couple of weeks, uncertainties in your business environment, and so on); insisting that everything needs to be planned carefully before steps of action can be taken; nurturing the not-invented-here syndrome – the list is endless. Although the vast majority of organizations seem to follow the ten rules, some more creative organizations try to work with a structure that actually triggers innovation and change.

WHAT WOULD YOU DO?

WHAT WOULD YOU DO?

We have suggested ways of blocking innovation and intrapreneurial action within organizations, ways that we have encountered all too often in our careers. Now we want you to counter these barriers. You are a member of a task force that has been charged with introducing innovation and change to the governance of an organization with which you are familiar. What would you do to promote innovative ideas?

CREATIVE STRUCTURES

The creative process can be illustrated by using the example of Frank Heart, one of the core team members of the group that developed early hardware and software for the Internet. He remembers how the members of the group worked together:

> Everyone knew everything that was going on, and there was very little structure … There were people, who specifically saw their role as software, and they knew a lot about hardware anyway; and the hardware people all could program. (Cited in Brown and Duguid, 2001: 93)

These highly creative people were working in a relatively small team, driven by highly motivated people, built around self-organizing and flexible principles. Creativity, defined as the ability to combine previously unrelated dimensions of experience, flourishes in such an environment. However, this communicationintensive practice challenges companies when they start to grow; professional management structures are put in place to manage new ideas – their design, development, sales, marketing, and so forth. Brown and Duguid (2001: 94) observe that 'once separated, groups develop their own vocabularies; organizational discourse sounds like the Tower of Babel'. At Xerox, for instance, what had been intuitive to scientists turned out to be unintelligible to the engineers who were supposed to transform the idea into a marketable product. As each group told its tales, 'the scientists dismissed the engineers as copier-obsessed "toner heads," whereas the engineers found the scientists arrogant and unrealistic' (Brown and Duguid, 2001: 94).

Thus, as Brown and Duguid assert, one of the greatest challenges that innovative companies face is the step from initial innovation to sustainable growth, a challenge that can be managed only by carefully balancing structure and creativity. As we have eluded to earlier in this chapter and in Chapter 10, creativity without structure tends to grow out of touch with reality, whereas structure without creativity results in a loss of innovation.

One strategy to overcome this problem is to use structures as shelters – that is, to create sheltered zones in which innovation can occur undisturbed by routine. As the BMW example illustrated, establishing safe 'playgrounds' in which innovators can explore without being constrained by business-as-usual can help to create new ideas and trigger innovation. The risk, however, is that sheltered zones can become ivory towers. Disseminating and integrating new knowledge into everyday organizational structures and practices from a position of remoteness seem to be almost impossible.

Turning creative ideas into successful products takes more than business-as-usual concepts; the process must combine elements of structure with elements of process by building project teams that include both R&D people and process improvers, together with end-user representatives and those who will have manufacturing and delivery responsibilities for the design that is implemented. There is no point in having a great design that cannot be made, improved, sold or used. Thus, creativity becomes a major asset in the conceptualization of innovation and change. The ability to think outside the box, however, is something organizations find hard because their efforts are focused on order, control and predictability. Stacey argues that creativity is linked to instability:

> Organizations with the potential for creativity are those that are tensed by the presence of efficient formal hierarchical systems that are continually being subverted by informal network systems in which political and learning activity takes place. Creative systems are systems in tension and the price paid for creative potential is an unknowable long-term future. (1999: 75)

In conclusion, it is important to recognize that innovation is one of the hottest topics in contemporary management. Rather than view innovation, creativity and change as a rationally planned process, we concentrated on its emergent, processual and political aspects. Central to this process are what we have identified as the key tensions of innovation in organizations, which centre on making innovations happen in terms of the organization changes and creativity that are required.

SUMMARY

In this chapter, we have introduced the concept of innovation in terms of a process and outcomes, and discussed the main theories of management and organizing for innovation and change:

(Continued)

(Continued)

- Managing innovation implies a focus not only on internal innovation processes and their complexities but also on the macro-level outcomes and dynamics of innovation and change characterized by shifting technological paradigms and discontinuities that induce widespread failure through creative destruction.
- Innovation's complexity is compounded by micro-level politics and difficulties in managing for and organizing innovation internally.
- Planned change and its model of unfreeze-change-refreeze offers a simple way of understanding change. Processual theories argue that change is more complex and has to be studied as it unfolds over time.
- Recent theories explore the importance of chaos and unpredictability for the innovation process and argue that innovation cannot be planned.

EXERCISES

1. Having read this chapter, you should be able to say in your own words what each of the following key terms means. Test yourself or ask a colleague to test you.
   - Innovation
   - Change
   - Planning
   - Social innovation
   - Order
   - Chaos
   - Paradox (tension)
   - Co-creation
   - Creativity.
2. What are the assumptions behind planned change?
3. What is emphasized by a processual view of change? Which models of change processes can you think of?
4. How do politics frame change processes?
5. Why does innovation occur between chaos and order?
6. Who are the main stakeholders in change and how do they shape the processes?
7. What does the innovation journey look like?
8. What is the innovator's dilemma?
9. What role can customers play in the innovation process?
10. What do the macro-level technological trends and paradigm shifts that underpin creative destruction look like?

TEST YOURSELF

Review what you have learned by visiting:
https://study.sagepub.com/managingandorganizations5e or your eBook

- Test yourself with multiple-choice questions.
- Revise key terms with the interactive flashcards.

REVISE KEY TERMS

TEST YOURSELF

CASE STUDY

Exploring creativity

Oil exploration is a high-risk, high-outcome endeavour. A single offshore well drilled on a geological prospect can cost over A$100 million. A single discovery can amount to over A$100 billion. All wells are based on very qualified guesswork; some may have an estimated discovery probability as low as 20 per cent. We will present three sets of empirical observations on creativity in oil exploration, all taken from a multi-year action-learning project with the exploration teams in a major oil corporation. The puzzle is this. Creativity is typically regarded as an exception, associated with stable dispositions of gifted individuals, peak experiences and intense bouts of more or less deliberate innovative efforts. What if creativity is not an exception, but a quality of forms of work, *embedded* in everyday practice? And, can one address creativity at work in settings where key personnel question the usefulness of the very concept of creativity?

'We don't call it creativity'

He was one of the first persons we interviewed, a respected manager of an exploration team and a person who had participated in many successful exploration efforts. 'I associate creativity with something that persons in fluffy garments are doing when they are painting doodles and call it art', he snuffs. 'I don't see how that kind of creativity has a place in my work. Exploration operates within basic physical laws and is about putting together data in a large puzzle, basically knowing your field and doing long-term science-based knowledge accumulation.' There is laughter. An interlude follows where we partly agree on not looking for the exploration equivalent of pottery making, partly to try to qualify how creativity is not contrary to science-based work. Then the exploration manager starts to talk passionately about the importance of seeing the big picture in small-scale prospect analysis, about seeing regional wholes, not only singular blocks or licences or prospects or wells, about being able to imagine geological processes that took place hundreds of millions of years ago, about the importance of conjuring alternative interpretations of the same data, about tectonic movements, thinking in four dimensions, seeing opportunities rather than problems, the use of sketches for zooming out, and the eternal need for persistence and

(Continued)

(Continued)

passion in exploration. Creativity as science-based imagination? We still think of this as one of our best interviews.

'Why are you not using any creativity techniques?'

We had just been rounding off a two-day workshop with exploration teams. The agenda was to develop and rank hydrocarbon prospect ideas in selected geological regions, staged as an 'exploration creativity workshop'. The workshop was led by the chief geologist, while we as external researchers had assisted in design and some of the facilitation. It was the third workshop of its kind, and the corporate word-of-mouth on the two preceding ones was quite good. One of the participants – an experienced facilitator of many development processes in the corporation and well versed in creativity techniques – had asked to join the workshop to see what was going on. At the end of day two, he popped a good question: 'Why are you not using any creativity techniques?' Indeed – why had we not? Part of the answer may seem straightforward. Geologists use a highly specialized vocabulary that will typically leave outsiders in the wild after 5–10 seconds. External facilitating of, for example, a brainstorming session on geological prospects would be very likely to slow down the process, as the many complicated combinations of ideas would have to pass the filter of an (at least partially) ignorant mind. Could this have been overcome with the use of a trained geologist as facilitator? Perhaps – the problem here seems to be that many creativity techniques presuppose a distinctness of ideas at an early stage of conception and carry the implicit assumption of the value of *steering* idea generation and combination, *and* the assumption that such techniques are more or less valid across widely different domains of activity. These are hefty assumptions. The kinds of discussions we have witnessed in exploration teams seem more like the jamming of jazz musicians than developing new dishwashers. Fragments of ideas, data, viewpoints and alternative interpretations are connected, unconnected, enriched, stripped, negated and saluted in a stream of collective efforts where no single individual has more than a temporary lead. One may try to specify the overall output of the jamming sessions and prepare the ground with communicative tools and resources. But detailed facilitation? Probably not.

'The key was understanding why the previous wells did not work'

After having interviewed more than two dozen oil finders about their successful exploration efforts, a clear pattern began to emerge. It seems that many success stories in exploration share a plot, with a breakthrough interpretation in the wake of many years of data gathering, painstaking analysis and, typically, a series of costly dry wells based on geological interpretations later found invalid. Successful exploration, then, is often based on the ability to come up with an *alternative* geological model based on the data from dry wells. What does this imply? A cynical explanation would be that prolonged exploration efforts in a region where there is oil are bound to result in a discovery, sooner or later, and that all discoveries are retrospectively justified as being based on a genius analysis rather than mere luck. More optimistically, the breakthroughs result from novel combinations of interpretations, emerging from a succession of analytical and interpretive efforts with many people and teams involved. Maybe dry wells sometimes are *necessary* as precursors to breakthrough interpretations. Maybe we should talk of *slow* creativity?

Questions

1. Starting from your own experiences, what do you think constitutes creativity at work? Can we do with one creativity concept for all kinds of work?
2. What do you think are the motivational drivers of creativity at work?
3. To what degree would you say that creativity is an individual versus a collective phenomenon, and can activities that lead to breakthrough innovations be 'routinized'?

Case prepared by Arne Carlsen, Tord F. Mortensen and Reidar Gjersvik Arne and Tord work at BI, Oslo, Norway; Reidar at tegn-3 in Oslo, part of AF consult.

ADDITIONAL RESOURCES

- There are so many books about innovation, change and creativity that it is rather hard to know where to begin but we will keep it brief. A good sourcebook on change is the text by Hardy (1995), *Managing Strategic Action: Mobilizing Change – Concepts, Readings, and Cases*. It is especially useful because it looks not just at success stories but at some failures as well. A good starting point for innovation is Christensen's (1997) book, *The Innovator's Dilemma: When New Technologies Cause Great Firms to Fail*, or the more narrative account by Wren and Greenwood (1998), *Management Innovators: The People and Ideas That Shaped Modern Business*, which tells stories about inventive managers.
- March's (1988) article, 'The technology of foolishness', is a must read.
- A fine article on the politics of innovation is written by Frost and Egri (2002), 'The political process of innovation'.
- There are many useful films on the topic of innovation, change and creativity. Perhaps the best is *Apollo 13* (Howard, 1995), especially its emphasis on the creative processes that brought the astronauts of the Apollo mission back, even in the midst of chaotic problems. It illustrates organizational learning as improvisation in action.
- As an example of how *not* to innovate, consider the film *Titanic* (Cameron, 1997), about an innovation that failed because of some of the assumptions of the designers about basic aspects of the ship and the environment in which it operated.

MANAGING SOCIAL RESPONSIBILITY ETHICALLY

STAKEHOLDERS, SUSTAINABILITY, ETHICS

LEARNING OBJECTIVES

This chapter is designed to enable you to:

- know what is constituted as corporate social responsibility (CSR)
- understand what is practised as CSR
- understand the roles played by corporate codes of ethics
- appreciate different foundations for ethical behaviour
- grasp the delicate balance between principles and profit.

BEFORE YOU GET STARTED...

'Ethics is knowing the difference between what you have a right to do and what is right to do.' (Potter Stewart, Associate Justices of the Supreme Court of the United States)

INTRODUCTION

Increasingly, ecologists urge a growing realization that although we have created a hugely successful business system for generating needs and satisfying them, one of its side-effects has been a significant growth in environmental degradation, toxic waste and species extinction. These are one aspect of a lack of ethics being exhibited in a duty of care for the environment and its species. These species include people like us and there are, unfortunately, many examples of unethical behaviour practised towards people who are employees, clients, customers, suppliers and communities with whom businesses interact.

CORPORATE SOCIAL RESPONSIBILITY (CSR)

Business organizations are bounded as systems that are open to their environment, both natural and rationally constructed. However, as open systems their effects are not contained within the organization. This is especially the case in those industries that comprise the petrochemical complex, which supplies so many modern essentials, from familiar things made of plastics, nylon and other artificial fibres, to complex compounds we have probably never heard of. Many of these chemicals are highly toxic.

Toxic chemicals are one component of what German sociologist Ulrich Beck calls the **risk society** (Beck, 2002). They cannot be contained within any one plant or nation; if they escape into the ecology, they spread through the air, rivers and rain into the environment of people who are unaware of the risks they face and unable to do much about them. The disaster at the Japanese nuclear power station Fukushima is a good example.

In a **risk society**, life-threatening disasters cannot be controlled within a specific territory.

Informed by such views, management scholars have argued that organizations need to adopt discourses and practices of corporate social responsibility and business ethics. We shall explore these themes in this chapter. We shall begin by looking at the fashionable business concept of corporate social responsibility.

Corporate social responsibility (CSR) has been adopted as a formal policy goal by many advanced society governments and businesses. Organizations that commit to CSR typically adopt sustainable development goals that take account of economic, social and environmental impacts in the way they operate. Doing so is a relatively new approach – in the past, most organizations exercised very little care for the despoliation of the environment or for sustainable development, especially those based on the exploitation of natural resources. Today, CSR is very fashionable: check the website of some favourite organizations – we would be very surprised if you did not find something that corresponds to a CSR statement.

When an organization exceeds the minimum legal obligations to stakeholders specified through regulation and corporate governance, it is called **corporate social responsibility**.

Generally, CSR is seen to be a voluntary commitment on the part of an organization to sustainable economic development that will improve the quality of life of its employees, their families, local communities and society at large. A good example of these voluntary commitments is Business for Social Responsibility, a global organization that aims to help its members be successful in a sustainable way and to respect the ethical values of stakeholders and the environment.

EXPLORE THE BSR WEBSITE

It is evident that, in pragmatic terms, the key questions for managers are *why* organizations should be concerned about CSR and *how* they should deal with the issue. Asking the *why* question can be used to differentiate ethical concerns from instrumental concerns. Ethically, at one extreme, organizations should be seen to be caring for a variety of stakeholders and the externalities that their operations create, because to do so serves ethical interests in the greater good. At the other extreme, from resource dependency and institutional perspectives, organizations also need legitimation to operate, with concern for other stakeholders being an efficient means to acquire legitimation.

There are three different levels of analysis implicit in any discussion of CSR. At the institutional level, there are assumptions about the legitimation of organizational actions in so far as they accord with institutionalized norms and values. At this level, general societal expectations and the framing and implementation of these in practice by government determine the legitimacy of a particular organization in its actions. At the organizational level, organizations must take responsibility for what they do and do not do because they can be held legally accountable for their actions and non-actions. At the individual level, the principle of managerial discretion presumes the morality and ethics of individual managers in their relationships with stakeholders. We shall begin our discussion with the latter first.

STAKEHOLDER MANAGEMENT: WHY CSR?

Why should organizations today bother with CSR, especially those that are profit oriented? After all, neo-classical economists have long argued that business owes abstractions such as 'society' nothing: shareholders are the owners of business and business's obligation is to do everything (within the law) to advance shareholder value – not to squander it on well-meaning but irrelevant CSR projects.

Milton Friedman (1982) is one of the most prominent advocates of this view. He argues that businesses are neutral instruments that have been created for the pursuit of goals of those who actually own them: the shareholders. In this perspective, an organization is a tool to maximize the returns to its owners, the shareholders.

Think of a small boulangerie: it exists to fulfil a function, which is baking good bread. If it performs this function well, loyal customers who support the business and help it to grow will reward it; if not, the business will ultimately go broke as customers cease purchasing bread from that particular bakery. However, if in the process of selling its bread the bakery were to use non-biodegradable plastic bags which then get dumped in landfill, would it still be a good bakery, as one whose rubbish can end up in landfill for infinity?

Milton Friedman argues that businesses should stay within the rules of the game and must not engage in illegal or criminal activities. That is about the only limitation he imposes on business: as long as they respect the law, they should, according to Friedman, be free to do whatever they want to increase their profits. The following quote by Friedman gained worldwide notoriety:

> The view has been gaining widespread acceptance that corporate officials and labour leaders have a 'social responsibility' that goes beyond serving the interest of their stockholders or their members. This view shows a fundamental misconception of the character and nature of a free economy. In such an economy, there is one and only one social responsibility of business – to use its resources and engage in activities designed to increase its profits so

> long as it stays within the rules of the game, which is to say, engages in open and free competition, without deception or fraud. (Friedman, 1982: 133–4)

It is easy to argue that this simple rule does not ensure that stakeholders' interests are looked after well. Think of a global fashion brand that manufactures its products in a developing country, paying minimal wages to children: according to the law of the developing countries, the sports brand may act legally. However, from an ethical perspective the behaviour of the company might be unacceptable. It can be argued that Friedman's position relies too much on a belief in the self-regulating forces of capitalism.

Not everything that is legally allowed is ethically sound (remember the quote by Justice Stewart!): just because something is not illegal does not make it automatically socially acceptable, let alone ethical. Think of your own social network: would your friends find it acceptable if you cheated on your partner and covered it up with lies? How about if you cheat in an ethics exam?

WATCH THE TED TALK

Unilever executive Harish Manwani (2013) makes an argument against this view in a TED Talk entitled 'Profit's not always the point'. His view is that there are other stakeholders apart from shareholders with interests in a firm. The stakeholder model of the firm would insist that shareholders are but one set of stakeholders; that there are plenty of other significant stakeholders, ranging from customers, NGOs, communities and civil society more generally, to activist groups claiming to articulate the interests of the environment, animals, disadvantaged people(s), or other 'mute' or muted stakeholders. The standard definition of a stakeholder is any person with an interest in the activity of an organization; in a slightly less encompassing definition, we might restrict it to those whom the organization affects with their activities, such as owners, investors, employees, the trade unions that organize the employees, customers, consumer associations, regulators, suppliers and citizens living in sufficient proximity to an organization's material presence to be affected by it.

Stakeholder theory, as a way of managing organizations, develops frameworks within which relevant stakeholders can be identified and defined. Often, these stakeholders are defined more restrictedly than their identification in broad terms would suggest. The more restricted approach limits stakeholders to those who are relevant. Relevance is defined in terms of actual investments in the organization that makes them susceptible to risk from the organization's activities. The latter approach regards stakeholders in a more restricted way by emphasizing the voluntarist basis of the relation between an organization and stakeholders. Hence, employees, investors, owners and suppliers might all be regarded as stakeholders but there might be questions about the inclusion of others. For instance, many organizations, such as Walmart, do not recognize the legitimacy of trade unions as stakeholders because they seek to maintain union-free operations. In this conception of stakeholders, the definition is barely broader than that of shareholders: it does include employees and suppliers but is silent about broader-based conceptions of stakeholding. Communities that experience a change to the amenities that they have access to because of an organization's impact would be excluded, irrespective of whether the effect was positive or negative. Stakeholders such as communities would be regarded as involuntary because they did not choose to enter into, nor can they easily withdraw from, a relationship with an organization, such as an airport whose planes fly over their houses or a toll way that divides their community with a multi-highway.

Looked at in a broader way, the question of who the relevant stakeholders should be becomes one of time periods: if businesses are alert only to interests in the short term, they will probably pay most heed to those stakeholders whose impact is most immediate on their day-to-day operations: investors and stock market analysts, especially, because they affect the share price through their perceptions of 'shareholder value' – the earnings or losses they incur on their shares in reporting periods. The problem is that if organizations only pay attention to these short-term interests they may jeopardize other interests that might claim representation or be represented which, in the long term, can boomerang back on the business by attacking its legitimacy or reputation. Thus, it becomes a matter of shareholder value to attend to broader stakeholder interests. As Vogel (2005) suggested, it may well be the standard business case that the primary responsibility of companies is to create wealth for their shareholders. But the emergence of CSR and activists associated with it adds a twist: in order for companies to do well financially, they must also act virtuously.

An article published in the *Academy of Management Review* by Hahn et al. (2014) explores how managers interpret social issues such as CSR. Typically, the approach is pragmatic, based on existing business routines; against this they recommend the importance of thinking paradoxically – sometimes launching products because they seem to offer sustainable innovation, even if they are not immediately profitable, such as hybrid cars, because in this way market share may be built on more sustainable foundations.

In some European countries, such as Austria and Germany, the notion that there is a social responsibility of business is well established. There has long been a consensus view that organizations should be seen as a 'social partnership' built upon a tacit and informal agreement between the government, the major employers' associations and various employee interest groups. In the literature, this is usually referred to as corporatism where the state encourages cooperation among these major stakeholders, who have increasingly adopted the rhetoric of CSR as it has developed in recent times.

Höllerer (2010) has thoroughly examined CSR discourse in Austrian corporate annual reports since the early 1990s. A first focus of CSR is on the sustainability of profits, people and planet – often referred to as the triple bottom line. A second focus is on good corporate governance and enhanced transparency, which, third, situates stakeholder management as a key task of managing divergent interests. Fourth, corporate values such as philanthropy and the support of societal groups in need that do not have power or voice in corporate decision-making are often deployed to demonstrate corporate responsibility for less privileged members of society. Often, this is achieved by organization members doing voluntary service – charity work – for underprivileged communities. Explicit use of CSR provides conceptual tools with which to address the varied notions of social responsibility and advance claims for enhanced legitimacy. Doing this means that CSR becomes incorporated into the strategies of the organization.

To sum up, in order to do well, a company has to do good, and that means it has to take its stakeholders' needs and interests into account. But in order to see the full picture, we have to add yet another twist to the story: in many CSR accounts, an assumption is that it is only humans that can be stakeholders. More radical views, as we shall see, suggest that the natural environment, including animals and plants, are also stakeholders.

An ethic that gives rights to animals as stakeholders is conceivable if we consider neither human beings nor animals as absolutely unique (Wise, 2000), if we consider each as a sentient living being. The uniqueness of the human condition in its capacity for symbolic reasoning and socially organized violence to all species is the reason to deny that animals deserve ethical concern. Since the community of the living forms the first universal (Singer, 2006), it ought, ethically, to impose itself upon all. The universal of being living signifies diversity and, above all, allows for individual cases or restricted ethics within systems. Singer asserts that the anthropocentrism of our vision and our ethical system prevents us from considering the possibility of moral feelings in animals: 'The moral gulf between humans and other animals appears, from our anthropocentric perspective, too wide to leap. Yet as our knowledge of the other great apes grows, they are proving to be a bridge species not only in genetic, behavioral, and cognitive senses, but also morally' (Singer, 2006: 8).

Animal ethics increasingly concern members of organizations linked to the food and pharmaceutical industries. Here the question of respect is raised; the study of unnecessary suffering supposes the possibility of empathy with animals based on the universal principle of living, which cannot absolutely be assumed (Zuzworsky, 2001: 177). For example, the case of animal rights being cruelly ignored in abattoirs raises the urgent and complex issue of an unconditional ethic, applicable to humans and all other mammals, or even extended to include invertebrates.

The animal system thus highlights both the inherent uniqueness of a code regulating animal conduct, as in the case of chimpanzees as well as the fact that the development of a restricted ethic associated with animal systems is only possible if it is based on a universal focusing on respect for the living, which supposes differentiation.

Tryggestad, Justesen and Mouristen (2013) provide one instance of where animals became enlisted as stakeholders in an ethical discourse. They tell the story of how frogs were translated from being 'non-existent' stakeholders into strategic stakeholders in a construction project. Waterholes where discovered on the site and soon their residents – 500 protected moor frogs – were identified. The project came to a halt. The frogs, hitherto leading blameless and anonymous semi-aquatic lives in obscurity other than for a few mammalian specialists, became represented as stakeholders by several spokespersons claiming to know what was in the frogs' best interests and to speak for them. The development firm hired their own frog experts as consultants who worked on determining means whereby the frogs could co-exist with the construction workers and trucks and all the noise and destruction of habitat that these would create. That meant learning to adapt to the cyclical time of the frog's life (as opposed to the linear time of project managers' charts) and constructing frog protection devices, such as corridors through which they could move without being bulldozed. The story has a happy ending, when the frogs themselves became stakeholders in the marketing campaign to sell the finished buildings – who would not want to live in a natural idyll with protected moor frogs?

One business leader who comes close to embracing the view that stakeholders can be found in non-human residents of the planet, such as moor frogs, is Steve Howard, chief sustainability officer at IKEA, who presents a cogent corporate view of sustainability and how to achieve it, through setting and achieving 100 per cent targets. As he says, IKEA has a sustainability strategy called 'people and planet positive' whose aim is to help guide the business to have a positive impact on the world. As he asks rhetorically, 'Why would we not want to have a positive impact on the world as a business?'

WATCH THE TED TALK

If only it were that easy: much of the controversy over climate science, for instance, occurs because of the inability of certain sections of business, government and the community to accept that they have responsibilities to abstract conceptions such as global warming. However, as the findings of climate science become more widely accepted as incontrovertible, the idea that the natural environment is affected by the actions of the organization and is therefore a stakeholder in the organization comes to be seen as normal. On this reasoning, we are all beholden to the future as a stakeholder in our present-day behaviours. It is for these reasons that the most critical debates about CSR tend to be about ecological and sustainability responsibilities, as we shall see towards the end of the chapter.

It is much easier to think of stakeholder theory as a form of implicit social contract between distinct and identifiable stakeholders and the organization in question. On this basis, CSR is a lot simpler than managing impacts on the future in a responsible way and comes down to identifying the distinct groups to whom the organization must accept, in social contract terms, that it has a responsibility. Stakeholder language, conceived in the form of a social contract with distinct groups, provides a way of coupling business with ethical behaviour by making a broader conception of values than that of shareholder value the benchmark for responsible managing.

Organizations that adopt a stakeholder management approach conceived on a contractarian basis first identify those that the organization has responsibilities towards and then calculate what the costs and benefits will be for these groups for any course of action decided on. Trade-offs will be inevitable. Such an approach contrasts sharply with the clarity afforded by shareholder value approaches where only one datum, the bottom line, and one set of stakeholders who own shares, have to be considered. Indeed, focusing only on shareholder value is much easier and reduces the number of competing objectives to a simple calculation of value.

Clearly, if a stakeholder model of management is to be adopted, there has to be some way of assigning differential value to all the stakeholders recognized because it is inconceivable that all can be easily satisfied without some trade-offs that affect some more adversely than others. Stakeholder approaches must rank the importance of different interests for different decisions and apportion managerial sensemaking accordingly. So the stakeholder approach is always an implicit theory of power relations in which some interests will be given a more legitimate status than others. At its best, it will be quite explicit about these rankings, using some calculus of powerfulness, legitimacy and urgency in attending to stakeholder interests. Some stakeholders will be consistently more marginal and others will be consistently more privileged.

ORGANIZATIONAL PRACTICES AND CSR CORPORATE GREENING

There are a number of ways that concerned people are seeking to limit the risks of ecological disaster and create more sustainable modes of business, giving rise to what Jermier et al. (2006: 618) term the 'new corporate environmentalism'. At the centre of this movement is the attempt by businesses and business leaders to play a leadership role in reforming the way business does business, by making it more sustainable, and to use the tools and approaches of rational management to improve ecological behaviour. Thus, the new corporate environmentalism seeks not only to comply with whatever governmental or industry regulations may be in place but also to develop more proactive sustainability approaches. This places sustainability, or as it is sometimes referred to, **corporate greening**, at the core of a firm's strategic CSR agenda.

Corporate greening involves adopting green principles and practices in as many facets of the business as it is possible to do.

Since the publication of the report of the Intergovernmental Panel on Climate Change, by UNESCO on 2 February 2007, the reality of global warming is now widely accepted (for updates, see the IPCC's website: www.ipcc.ch). Almost as widely accepted is the realization that corporate and business activity is contributing significantly to this warming. Many business leaders are now well aware of this fact and are seeking to do something about it. Corporate greening involves the espousal of 'green' values, which are becoming increasingly institutionalized with the realization that sustainable production is equivalent to more efficient production.

Corporate greening could involve green production that uses less energy, green materials that recycle and aim for zero waste, green transportation (for instance, using bicycles or pedal-powered scooters to get around the workplace or between organizations), green facilities that are designed to minimize energy waste and use, green products that use fewer non-renewable resources, and a continuing programme of educating employees and spreading learning about being green employees as widely as possible.

Here is one example of how the changing consensus of opinion has led to a concern with corporate greening. After reading Hawken's (1993) *The Ecology of Commerce: A Declaration of Sustainability*, Ray Anderson (1999), chairman of Interface Inc., the world's largest manufacturer of carpets, resolved to change his corporate ways and become more sustainable through adopting explicit CSR principles towards the ecology. Interface makes an enormous number of carpets. It also used to cause huge pollution: every year its factories produced hundreds of gallons of wastewater and nearly 900 pollutants. First, Anderson reduced waste and conserved energy by recycling. Of course, this makes great business sense. Less waste can equal more profit as you use all that you pay for rather than throw a lot of it away. Before Anderson read Hawken, his company sent 6 tonnes of carpet trimming to landfill each day. That waste was reduced to zero. New computer controls were installed on boilers to reduce carbon monoxide emissions (by 99.7 per cent), which also improved the boilers' efficiency, resulting in further decreased waste and increased profits. Anderson aimed for complete sustainability, using solar and wind power in the place of fossil fuels, planting trees to offset carbon pollution caused by trucks transporting carpets, and making carpets out of organic materials such as corn. Ray Anderson, unfortunately, is no longer with us but you can hear him espousing his views on TED Talks back in 2009, talking about 'The business logic of sustainability'.

WATCH THE TED TALK

Jermier and his colleagues (2006) suggest that several factors characterize a successful green learning organization (see also Chapter 4) that has become more socially responsible:

- *Lifelong learning*: ensuring that the organization really is a learning organization, constantly trying to find not only new ways of doing the same things better (single-loop learning) but also new things to do in innovative ways (double-loop learning).
- *Developing critical thinking skills*: helping organization members gain confidence in critical reflection on existing ways of doing things and encouraging them to voice their opinions as to how things might be done better, developing future-oriented scenarios that are more sustainable.
- *Building citizenship capabilities*: encouraging employees to think not just as employees – in terms of the firm benefit – but as concerned citizens desirous of reducing the overall ecological footprint of not only the organizations they work for and with, but also the impact that they make in their daily lives.
- *Fostering environmental literacy*: encouraging people to learn about specific environmental problems and solutions, their causes, consequences and connectedness.
- *Nurturing ecological wisdom*: sharing an eco-centred understanding of the web of life and the centrality of responsible, ethical and sustainable behaviour to a good life.

Three things need to come together to build green learning in organizations: the creation of a public sphere; the development of communicative rationality; and discursive design. A public sphere is a space in which the 'public reason of private citizens' predominates. Organizations can become actively involved in educating their members for participation in green debates in the broader society as concerned citizens and parents rather than just as employees of corporation X. Here they should be able to develop communicative rationality – a commitment to frank and open debate – as well as the capability of assessing and evaluating evidence, and reaching evidence-based ethical decisions independent of specific

WHAT WOULD YOU DO?

Think of your university. Does it have a formal commitment to being green and sustainable? Check the website to find out. How well do these claims stack up to what you see around you? Make an inventory of practices that seem to be counter-intuitive to the formal rhetoric. It could be the use of disposable polystyrene cups or hydrocarbon-based vehicles. Now - what would you do to make the reality and the rhetoric align more closely? How could you help the university to become a green learning organization? How might it be steady state or circular in its economy?

interests. They will learn to speak the language of the environment as a form of non-instrumental rationality, which is shaped not by the instrumentality of their or their organizations' interest, but by the public, ecological and ethical good.

WHEN CORPORATE GREENING FAILS

Cynics might say that it becomes a matter of shareholder value for business to appear to be concerned about CSR issues. A common critique, therefore, is that CSR is often no more than a tool of corporate 'greenwash' – a rhetorical device employed by corporations to legitimize the corporate form and accommodate the social consciences of its consumers. **Greenwashing** occurs when organizations promote themselves in the best possible light while not being consistent in their ecological commitments.

Greenwashing is the term that has been coined for espousing the rhetoric of CSR while minimizing its practice.

To be legitimate and credible, claims to CSR need to be more than greenwashing and one way of establishing this is to have these claims independently audited. Among the common range of auditors are AccountAbility's AA1000 standard, based on notions of triple bottom line (3BL) reporting; the Global Reporting Initiative's Sustainability Reporting Guidelines; Social Accountability International's SA8000 standard; and the ISO 14000 environmental management standard. The idea is that these standards will encourage a culture of compliance and adoption of them is wholly voluntary. Additionally, NGOs, such as Oxfam, often monitor the activities of transnational corporations in industries such as mining, especially with respect to the local impact that they have on communities, politics and the environment, albeit that they have no powers other than those of communication through various media with which to change the decisions of those responsible.

While organizations such as Oxfam may broadcast their views, the organizations in question broadcast theirs as well. They call this marketing. Marketing often points to the green benefits of a product and the processes taken to produce it, such as not being wasteful of paper or other resources. There is widespread use of environmental management systems and standards to structure organizational processes and behaviour; green accounting standards can be used as part of a triple bottom-line report on the environmental impact of the company or organization. The company may form green partnerships with NGOs or community organizations to extend green practices in broader society. The organization might join bodies such as the World Business Council for Sustainable Development, or align itself with something such as the United Nations Global Compact. Above all, it will seek to outdo whatever is constituted as regulatory best practice, seeking to make itself greener than it is obliged to be.

IN PRACTICE

BP – beyond petroleum?

BP's 1998 installation of solar power cells at 200 of its pumping stations looks like an example of commitment to green values. However, BP invested only 0.1 per cent of its portfolio in solar panels while simultaneously expanding its fossil fuel extraction and exploration programme. In effect, one could argue that BP has conducted a public relations campaign designed to accommodate its consumers' concerns about the effect of carbon emissions upon the world, while also expanding its fossil fuel extraction process. Critics refer to this as 'greenwashing', in an analogy with 'whitewashing'. BP has also adopted 'socially responsible' positions on global warming to mitigate regulatory risk and legitimize its operations. By defecting from the Global Climate Coalition, an association that denies global warming, it was able to take part in debates over policy prescriptions, voicing a preference for market-based and voluntary solutions.

How ethical is BP? Use the web to research arguments 'for' and 'against' the position that BP is an ethical corporation, paying particular attention to the high-profile industrial accidents that it has been involved in, especially the Deepwater Horizon disaster in the Gulf of Mexico. See, for instance, articles like this one: www.nytimes.com/2017/12/15/business/energy-environment/bp-lightsource-solar.html, which is from the *New York Times* and represents a rich source for debate.

Ethics can be used to highlight certain organizational behaviours (Gordon et al., 2009; Schweiker, 1993) and to hide others from view. We have already encountered BP's 'Beyond Petroleum' campaign. Behind the eco-image there was a different story in BP. In the past, the primary organizational ethic had been one of value engineering – or cutting costs – that in 2011 were blamed by a White House commission, together with an inadequate safety system, for the accident.[1]

Prior to the accident, the fact that the rig had not experienced any accidents, contributed to the normalization of deviance (Vaughan, 1997). BP had repeatedly opted for quicker and cheaper, rather than more secure, approaches to system safety. These seemed to work adequately and the regulators did not object. The overarching ethic was not one of safety first but cost and speed first. In this instance, the ethics in practice prior to the accident had normalized a culture in which risk taking was not recognized as such and a 'normal accident' (Perrow, 2011) was waiting to happen. Hence, once the accident occurred, the scene shifted to the civil and criminal justice systems, where different ethical systems came into play. Each of these sites of ethical decision, the rig and the courts, depend on a social code that articulates, in a fragmentary manner, any universal presumptions of a fundamental moral code. Indeed, every ethical decision 'is circumscribed by organizational rules, norms and discourses' (Clegg et al., 2007: 107) that fragment the universality of ethical discourse.

BP had to try and reset its sustainability image after the Deepwater Horizon catastrophe in the Gulf of Mexico. The firm developed a communication campaign to restore its image. This discourse insisted on the value of its future financial choices and showed how, after the catastrophe, it had reinterpreted its policies in detail to act ethically. Such a communications strategy, based on an ethics that declared future commitments, aimed to counterbalance the loss of legitimacy associated with the ecological catastrophe, the cost of which was constantly reassessed upwards (Matejek and Gössling 2014). The Deepwater Horizon catastrophe, with ethical manifestations that conformed to extremely pressing communicational constraints (Chandler, 2014), makes for a particularly clear instance of ethical opportunism, in which there is a form of disconnection between a second-order ethical discourse linked to media communication with regard to past or devalued practices and a first-order discourse focusing on current organizational practice.

EXTEND YOUR KNOWLEDGE

READ THE ARTICLES

The following two articles critically address issues around CSR and corporate greening: Patala, S., Korpivaara, I., Jalkala, A., Kuitunen, A. and Soppe, B. (2017) 'Legitimacy under institutional change: how incumbents appropriate clean rhetoric for dirty technologies', *Organization Studies*, https://doi.org/10.1177%2F0170840617736938; and Gond, J. P. and Nyberg, D. (2017) 'Materializing power to recover corporate social responsibility', *Organization Studies*, 38 (8) : 1127–48, which are both available at the companion website https://study.sagepub.com/managingandorganizations5e

THE CIRCULAR ECONOMY

ELLEN MCARTHUR FOUNDATION

READ THE FULL ARTICLE

Present-day economies, as they have been since the start of industrialization, are based on use and waste: use something or other until it is no longer useful or wanted and then consign it to waste, usually to end up as landfill. Resources are dug up to manufacture products and infrastructure, then discarded to landfill or recycled when finished with. This has been dubbed the 'take-make-dispose' economy. The circular economy, advocated by the Ellen MacArthur Foundation, addresses these unnecessary resource losses. Household names such as Unilever, Cisco, Philips and Renault are some of the Foundation's global partners. Through more recycling and design of products so that they last longer, can be repaired and upgraded, reused or resold and their materials used in remanufacture, waste can be minimized. In *The Conversation*, Suzanne Benn and Damien Giurco offer an example of the sort of switch that might be involved, such as for businesses to sell services instead of products – for example, selling 'hours behind the wheel' rather than selling cars, which is what happens with car-share schemes such as GoGet, Hertz 24/7 and GreenShareCar.

THE STEADY STATE ECONOMY

Development of steady state economics is a response to the argument that economic growth has limits of ecology, demography, and so on. While economic policies often assume that macroeconomic growth is good and progressive, the steady state theorists suggest that the costs pose biophysical limits to the desirability of continuous growth. If growth comes at the cost of species, habitat, ecology, sustainability, climate and life itself, what's the point in the long run? The International Society for Ecological Economics is a major venue for steady state ecological economics and argues that the economy is embedded in nature, such that economic processes are actually biological, physical and chemical: economics is too important to be left to the economists and their simple, single-discipline assumptions.

Degrowth economics argues that developed nations (the Global North) will have to dematerialize and detune their current economies and lifestyles as they are already in overshoot. It's major voice is Serge Latouche who argues that the pursuit of economic growth causes inequality and injustice to increase; while more people may spend more on consumer goods and services, they do so at great collective cost: the degraded quality of air, water and the environment generally; and eating food that is factory farmed in conditions that amount to the systematic torture and murder of animals denied a natural life before they enter the food chain. The costs of modern living increase as the quality of life is diminished as we need more in the way of medicine to combat the diseases of affluence, especially obesity, and we spend more and more time commuting greater distances from the suburbs to work, consuming increased numbers of products made scarcer (water, energy, open space).

READ THIS LATOUCHÉ ARTICLE

CORPORATE CODES OF ETHICS

A corporate code of ethics (CCE) is a specific document that details moral guidelines or ethical rules for employees and, on occasions, for suppliers (Helin and Sandström, 2007; Schwartz, 2001). Necessarily, it is abstracted and distinct from all and any actual ethical situations and actors that may be constituted in everyday organizational life. Thus, as a management tool, the CCE can provide ethical support, encourage dialogue about ethics at work, and promote empowerment by clarifying expectations around decision-making and thus reducing the need for delegates to refer decisions upwards because of a lack of clarity about what is or is not permitted. Codes of conduct function as a set of rules that organizations adopt; adhering to this set of rules should then ensure responsible conduct. Most of the top 1,000 US companies have a code of conduct (Nijhof et al., 2003). These codes are often referred to as statements of CSR. For instance, healthcare products manufacturer Johnson & Johnson publishes a much-cited code of ethics on its website: when at one stage in the last century one of its product lines was adversely tampered with by someone seeking to hold the company hostage by poisoning its products, the organization withdrew and replaced every instance of the product, Tylenol, in the US market. Moreover, it went on to develop tamper-proof packaging with which it replaced all the stock it rescinded and destroyed. Doing so was very much in line with Johnson & Johnson's code of conduct and won the company great legitimacy in the community as a whole as a thoroughly socially responsible organization.

Analytically, a corporation's code of ethics is the documented, formal and legal manifestation of that organization's expectations of ethical behaviours by its employees. It is the visibility that a code offers that enables an organization to be judged as ethical. Indeed, according to one institution that benchmarks codes of ethics, scoring organizations' performances against this benchmark and encouraging them to broadcast the results, the criteria for consideration as an ethical company include having an 'ethics and compliance program, governance and corporate responsibility' (Ethisphere, 2015). Implicit within such corporate prescription of employees' ethical behaviours is the organization's ability to manage any allegedly 'deviant' behaviour by organizational members (Trevino, 1986) effectively for the benefit of the organization. There is a strong normalizing function in the deployment of these codes that suggests strategic risk is being managed (Fombrun et al., 2000; Husted, 2005) although such impressions may hide a dark side of domination (Helin et al, 2011).

Ethics are complicated, however. An ethically observant company may base its business on an ethically dubious proposition. Think of fast food chains that sell sugary drinks and fatty food to young children contributing to a nationwide obesity epidemic – are they acting ethically when doing so, even if they have a code of ethics and members of the organization comply with it? Think of large multinational energy corporations that might exploit and pollute the environment they are working in (just remember the BP oil spill in the Gulf of Mexico in 2010) and cut deals with governments that do not respect human rights – are they acting responsibly? Or think of fashion brands that produce cheap shoes and clothes in developing countries, often employing children working in miserable conditions – are these companies doing the right thing? Many firms maximize profits through outsourcing production to developing countries. The unethical results of this strategy are that they employ workers who, by the standards of most of their customers, are poorly paid and oppressed. Moreover, some of them are under the age of 14 and work in 'sweatshops'. Though in the developing countries in which they work there might be considerable competition for these jobs, the cost of the labour used in production hardly compares with the millions that firms such as Nike spend on marketing their products, especially through promotional tie-ups with leading sportspeople, such as tennis champion Rafael Nadal.

Spurred by these inequities, a critical audience (Boje, 1998) picked up on these practices of Nike and protested against Nike management, successfully lobbying it to change. Nike was successful in terms of business goals but as the goals were achieved in ways that liberals in developed countries could question, the strategy turned out to be counterproductive in marketing terms.

Of course, ethical issues are rarely clear-cut: the picture is much harder to calibrate from the perspective of the developing world's workers themselves. Yes, they are exploited in global terms, and the work is demanding and detailed – but, in terms of comparable wages in their domestic economies, they are privileged. A young woman working in a factory sweatshop for a few dollars a day looks like exploitation; indeed, it is – but, in the developing world, such employment might mean the difference between starvation and survival for her family. In the light of these arguments, it is not easy to answer the question of whether Nike acted unethically or not. You might say 'yes' because it exploited workers; or you might say 'no' because it allowed workers to have a job in the first place.

APPROACHES TO CODES OF CONDUCT

The core issue in business ethics is how businesses ought to act. What is an ethically sound way for business to behave? However, as we will see, there are no simple answers to this question.

In **normative ethics**, business is generally understood as being related to the rules and/or cultural norms that govern, or should govern, organizational conduct.

For some, business ethics are conceived of as **normative ethics**.

In organizations commonly, this means that managing ethics is done through formalized codes of conduct that should govern everyday actions and decisions. Indeed, it is reported that 78 per cent of the top 1,000 US companies have a code of conduct (Nijhof et al., 2003). Theories of business ethics that develop normative models for passing ethical judgement on business practices also often use this 'codes' approach (e.g. Brass et al., 1998; Gatewood and Carroll, 1991), proposing the development of ethical rules for organizations (e.g. Beyer and Nino, 1999).

ETHICS PAYS: GOOD BUSINESS EQUALS GOOD ETHICS

One prominent normative argument is that ethics and business are, or at least can be, aligned in order to create competitive advantage. The core argument here is that ethics does not contradict the driving forces behind business organization and that there is no conflict of interest between profits and principles. Francis and Armstrong (2003), for instance, argue that an ethically informed risk management strategy increases commercial outcomes, prevents fraud and lifts corporate reputation.

In this argument, an organization's ethical commitment is driven by its self-interest: because it wants to make profits, the company will behave ethically, or, in short: ethics pays. Such a perspective dates back to Adam Smith's argument that maximizing personal advantage will lead, through self-interested actors competing in the market, to a maximum of collectively beneficial outcomes. In sum, this suggests that 'good ethics is good business'. Thus, profits and principles are mutually inclusive rather than mutually exclusive frames.

'Ethics pays' is the argument behind 'strategic philanthropy' (Seifert et al., 2003), as an 'intangible resource for competitive advantage' (Hall, 1993), as 'marketing instruments' (Maignan and Ferrell, 2004), or as means to increase organizational commitment (Cullen et al., 2003). For instance, Porter and Kramer (2002, 2011) argue that companies should use their philanthropic budget only to improve their 'competitive context' – that is, philanthropy should enhance the quality of the business environment in those locations in which businesses operate (2002: 58). The education of the workforce, the availability of economic infrastructure and the promotion of business aims would all fit the bill. Such investments are proposed as simultaneously good both for business and for the various stakeholders involved. So, for instance, McDonald's may support neighbourhood schools or provide Ronald McDonald houses for sick children, which may benefit children in the community as well as promoting McDonald's.

Such examples raise questions, however. How disinterested is this as philanthropy or how much is it a marketing exercise? And does it matter? You could argue that if it is doing good and putting resources where they would not otherwise go, if it is also marketing, so what? But, on the other hand, is it marketing food that is basically unhealthy and contributes to childhood obesity, excessive waste from the packaging, and provides a McDonaldized model for business that is uncreative and inimical to innovation? What might appear to be ethical behaviour in one dimension of an organization's remit may be counterbalanced by equally unethical action elsewhere.

Porter and Kramer argue that 'the more closely a company's philanthropy is linked to its competitive context, the greater the company's contribution to society will be' (2002; see also Handy, 2002). For example, doing something good and improving the organization's prospects are aligned. Providing good education to people is not only an altruistic act; it also ensures that the organization will have a pool of educated people that it can employ when needed. In this case, smart business thinking equals ethical behaviour. The ethical rules and the rules for organizing efficiently and profitably are positioned as being the same. Just following the rules will produce just and profitable outcomes. In sum, behaving ethically means rigorously applying the rules of good management. According to this view, there is no need to be concerned about ethics for, in the long run, good management will, by definition, be a harbinger of both profits and ethical outcomes: the two will be conjoined like Siamese twins.

ETHICS AS A POLITICAL TOOL

A more descriptive, critical approach to business ethics argues that an organizational code of ethics is a political tool for managing and controlling employee behaviours in terms that are desired by management. In their efforts to control employee behaviours, some organizations increase the numbers of business practice officers, include ethical values and compliance in performance assessments in a tick-box fashion and investigate infractions and take remedial action. For others less active, the code of ethics is assumed to provide legitimacy for an organization as a survival strategy (Long and Driscoll, 2008; Meyer and Rowan, 1977).

For instance, most organizations today profess a commitment to sustainability as a part of their overall code of ethics. The code acts as a form of insurance: should there be ethical wrongdoing then the organization can point to the ethics it publishes and endorses and observe that their breach is against organizational policy. So, for instance, an organization might subscribe to a code of ethics that seeks to minimize the organization members' ecological footprint. Individual members of the organization might be climate change sceptics who do not think that human behaviour is contributing to global warming, against the overwhelming body of scientific evidence and thus do not feel that they have any need to reduce personal energy consumption or to practise ecologically sustainable styles of working. If they are responsible for outcomes that violate the code then they, not the organization, can be held accountable, because they are in violation of the code.

If there is a conflict between the ethics of the individual and those of an organization's ethical code, then the common assumption is that the individual's preferences must be secondary and subordinate. That this is the case requires that individual employees cannot have ethical autonomy; where their preferences, values and interests conflict with those of the employing organization, whatever ethical autonomy they can exercise will be constrained by the implicit framework of their contract of employment.

Of course, ethical codes are not just concerned with recycling, energy minimization and an absence of polluting behaviour. Increasingly, in the wake of contemporary scandals from Barings Bank (1995) onwards, including Enron (2000), Lehman Bros. (2008), Barclays (2012) or the 2015 mirror trade scandal of the Deutsche Bank (for which it paid a fine of $628 million), many organizations have sought to link business interests, employee ethics and legal compliance in formal codes that seek to stipulate organizationally responsible behaviour. The motivation is to ensure that an organization's code of ethics has high visibility and enhances corporate reputation.

Codes of ethics look great on websites and on paper, slightly less good when espoused publically as an account for why some corporate malpractice is not systemic but the result of individual malfeasance. Many ethnographic studies detail the considerable cynicism and distance in 'the ranks' that such accounts encourage (Collier and Esteban, 2007; Collinson, 2003; Collinson and Ackroyd, 2005; Fleming and Spicer, 2002, 2003, 2007; Mumby, 2005; Trevino and Nelson, 2011) with respect to organizations' ethical claims. Clegg et al. (2007) conceptualize that, analytically, the gap between prescribed business codes of ethics and their subjective interpretation by organizational members hinges on mundane practices (see also Gordon et al., 2009a, 2009b). In context, ethics do not exist on paper or in a virtual space but in concrete practices: it is not what the rules stipulate but what the actors do that is important (Gordon et al., 2009a, 2009b). Daily practices by organizational members rather than executive management's dictates frame mundane organizational behaviour and it is in this mundaneity that the practice of ethics resides.

Many management and organization studies scholars, as well as students of ethics, are concerned with the way organizations deal with ethical issues through formalizing and enforcing ethical rules (see Bauman, 1993; Bowie, 1999; Jackson, 2000; Jones, C., 2003; Kjonstad and Willmott, 1995; ten Bos, 1997). Organizations typically prescribe forms of ethical behaviour through rules that focus on framing members' intentions and limiting the consequences of their actions (Rasche and Esser, 2007; Trevino et al., 1999; Trevino and Nelson, 2011). Such formal rules tend to focus exclusively on motivating employee behaviours that benefit the organization and serve to protect management from blame and legal consequences (Trevino et al., 1999: 133). Indeed, the primary objective of codes of ethics is often to minimize business risk rather than produce ethicality. The reduction of risk is sought through corporate affairs guardians monitoring and auditing compliance to enforce ethical rules (Donaldson, 2003).

Paine (1994: 106) argues that 'ethics has everything to do with management' because it reflects an organization's 'operating culture'. Culturally oriented ethics rely on managerial responsibility for ethical behaviours in combination with legal compliance, a position also argued by Christensen (2008). Paine's concern is with what ought to be done rather than what is done or may be done by organizational members. She describes various corporate initiatives, such as those related to 'diversity, quality, customer service, health and safety, the environment, legal compliance, professionalism, corporate culture, stakeholder engagement, reputation management, corporate identity' and more (Paine, 2003: 3).

Some elements of codes have the force of national regulation and law behind them. Such is the case with occupational health and safety legislation, equal employment opportunity and other areas where the state mandates acceptable behaviours. However, Paine (2003) dissolves the discursive boundaries between legal compliance (such as diversity, health and safety, and the environment) and self-governance strictures (quality, customer service, professionalism, corporate culture, reputation, corporate identity, etc.). The latter are not legally constitutive, mandated by juridical decree, as with an Act of Parliament, being locally preferential rules. These rules or structured 'guiding principles' (Paine, 2003: 111) in codes of ethics are a key part of a top-down strategy: they express strategic preferences with respect to areas of behaviour deemed significant.

In essence, reciprocity between the organization and its members is neither presumed nor left to chance. What are promoted are routines that seek to align the moral integrity of the individual with that of the organization. These routines are rarely arrived at as a result of any form of democratic participation by organizational members. Their interests are not necessarily represented in formulating a code of ethics. That the organization sets out the frame for ethical behaviour presumes a great deal about the ethicality of the organization. Moreover, it is a frame that has to deal with the extreme contingency of events; its ethicality is tested for each new event that the organization encounters (Deroy and Clegg, 2011). Indeed, ethicality is invariably tested by such events to the extent that organizational members normally predicate their ethicality on rule-following behaviour: where there is a rule, there is no necessity for decision and judgement and hence no ethicality is at stake (Clegg et al., 2007).

Codes of ethics are closely tied to organizational objectives since managerial and organizational objectives are enshrined in them. As Rasche and Esser argue, these objectives have a relation to matters of compliance both externally (compliance with the law) and internally (compliance with organizational regulations) (Rasche and Esser, 2007: 109). Christensen (2008) argues that while models of ethical decision-making typically do not include the law, its norms are implicit even if they are exogenous to moral thinking. While law and ethics may be related, they are not the same (Christensen, 2008: 451). Yet by folding both corporate rules and legal compliance into a strategic discourse concerning ethics, managerial preferences become a natural and normal part of what is constituted as legal compliance. While such compliance is stipulative, managerial preferences are not: they lack legal sanction and remit and are preferential rather than constitutive rules for conduct (Shwayder, 1965). Such strategic ethics not only require organizational members to make interpretations that management deems correct and then to take appropriate action but also that, ethically, as a matter of principle, each employee should accept the legitimacy of doing so. Corporate governance and legal compliance are entwined within the code of ethics.

EXTEND YOUR KNOWLEDGE

READ THE ARTICLE

The following article analyses how trade fair participants use pictures and movies, logos and maps, catalogues and fashion parades to define ethical fashion and frame compromises between ethics and aesthetics: Blanchet, V. (2018) 'Performing market categories through visual inscriptions: The case of ethical fashion', *Organization*, 25(3): 374-400, which is available at the companion website https://study.sagepub.com/managingandorganizations5e

ETHICS AS RISK MANAGEMENT STRATEGY

Businesses that want to move beyond a legalistic framework of risk management and Paine's (1994, 2003) organizational values-regulated-by-management approach and create empowering ethics, as suggested by Kjonstad and Willmott (1995) as well as Clegg et al. (2007), need 'to complement the construction and appreciation of moral rules with the development of moral learning and the exercise of moral judgment' (Kjonstad and Willmott, 1995: 447). Doing so requires flexibility in the way a code of ethics may be interpreted and acted on by organizational members (Clegg et al., 2007; Gordon et al., 2009a, 2009b).

Bowie (1999: 121–33) establishes a case for Kantian ethics (of doing one's duty) in business, saying that business managers – and we would argue other organizational members – should do 'the right thing' out of duty rather than personal interest. The essence of Bowie's argument is that if a manager claims to act out of duty and is later found to have acted out of self-interest, then others will be cynical about any claims made by that manager, thereby compromising both the manager's and the firm's reputations (Bowie, 1999: 135). Jones (C., 2003: 235) suggests that once a business manager begins calculating risk and benefit in making a claim or performing an action, such actions fall outside of the realm of ethics. Jones (C., 2003) reasons that ethics have a value to business because they can minimize risk, such as limiting legal responsibility, influencing employees through organizational culture and managing the firm's image and brand.

Jones (C., 2003) argues that tying ethics to risk management is problematic for ethics, since the motivations of an organization to act ethically derive neither from virtue nor moral obligation. A strategic sense of business ethics is not based on ethical intentions but on the calculated instrumental benefit to business. If being ethical is good for business, it is because business achieves success by using ethics as a tool rather than 'doing the right thing'. If a particular activity has been modified or eliminated by the code, an ethical problem arises for any employee who has pursued an activity based on their understanding of the code at a particular time, only to find subsequently, by virtue of the reaction that their actions elicit, that they have violated the code, leaving them in an untenable position with the company.

The flexibility of ethics depends on the circumstances. Minkler (1999) sees a problem when the calculability of ethical action for a business in purely economic terms is deployed as a decision-making framework, describing it as ethically questionable. He discusses motivations for action in terms of an expectation of utility (benefit), either from the external recipient of the action, or from an internalized feeling of satisfaction that will come from performing the action (Minkler, 1999: 4). Minkler (1999) argues that regardless of whether the utility of such an act provides benefits to others, the motivations serve primarily to satisfy the preferences of the doer; thus, they are hardly ethical.

WHERE ARE ETHICS TO BE FOUND?

ETHICS AS FUNDAMENTAL VALUES

In the field of ethics, many researchers see ethics as mainly constituted by the observance of fundamental values (good, evil, justice, injustice, equality, etc.) considered to be natural laws with universal scope. These are ethical codes that apply to all firms (Schwartz, 2005). These universals should make it possible to decide on ethical dilemmas by offering criteria on which to judge questionable behaviours or attitudes. Any ethical decision will necessarily be more or less disappointing with regard to expectations based on universals. Moral framing of ethical decisions is not realist in its representation of reality and is inefficient in solving local problems that require resolution by the adoption of locally embedded and subtle interpretation when solutions are required.

As a moral judgement between good and bad practice, ethics occupy a subordinate position compared with those normative social codes that regulate decisions taken in institutions. Management researchers have noted the succession of global financial, environmental and industrial scandals (Rhodes, 2016; Voliotis, 2017). They worry about their human consequences and rightly call for the strengthening of ethics in organizations; however, the continued repetition of morally unacceptable affairs raises questions about the actual scope of ethical discourse. What does a call for ethics mean, viewed as a general discourse on good and bad at a time when institutions seem to be conforming first and foremost to their conceptions of normative social codes to define and limit their operations? Many organizations are tempted to consider ethics as subsidiary compared with their practice.

Ethics define the general rules adopted in the general environment of society composed of differentiated social systems. An ethic underlines the singularity of the set of rules that prevail within *a* given social system, such as *an* institution or *an* organization composed of specific networks of actors. Every ethic is embedded into the larger environment of ethics. A great deal of research has highlighted the contextualization of ethical practice (Albert et al., 2015; Clegg et al., 2007; Deroy and Clegg, 2011; Gordon et al., 2009; Heugens et al., 2006; Ibarra-Colado et al., 2006; Iedema and Rhodes, 2010; Valentine et al., 2002; Weiskopf and Willmott, 2013). The results of this rich stream of research oppose the idea that objectified universal values exist (Kim and Donaldson, 2018). Ethical practice, instead, is seen to depend on local normative references comprising the code of the system (Durkheim, 1997; Putnam, 2009: 4–11).

Ethical codes are formally binary: what is correct is opposed to what is incorrect. *Coding* is a process that describes a practice; the practice structures a given social system. The value of any coding is only known after its enactment, which does not mean that enactment is a blind process but rather that it is a continuous process that effects and acknowledge changes within a system. For instance, changes in a highway code create new categories of deviance by motorists, whose acknowledgement of these changes drive behaviour: for instance, codes concerning the necessity of seat belts or the absence of blood alcohol readings in a driver's system create new forms of enactment. Hence, drivers who drink become unethical agents.

An institutional orientation towards ethics assimilates them to a professional norm. Ethics are seen as a part of organizational practice, although notions of the role they play differ depending on the theories specific researchers endorse (Ezzamel and Willmott, 2014; Parker, 1999; Willmott, 2009); in brief, the view is that professional have, or should have, ethical rules inscribed in their principles of action and the routines that they follow.

An agentic perspective associates ethics with notions of personal responsibility. Ethics can be used to justify resistance to organizational norms and thus oppose an ethic considered as an organizational norm if it violates a sense of personal ethics and responsibility. Ethics can be seen as the basis for a method of critical questioning by an agent, affording individuals with heuristic scope within organizational spaces (Kluver et al., 2014; Weiskopf and Willmott, 2013). Despite their differences, these two conceptions of professional and personal ethics put ethics at the heart of organizational operations and practice. Both cases involve reductionism, and focus on ethics guiding practice via morally coded judgements, whose favoured vectors are either the institutionalized norm or the responsible agent.

IN PRACTICE

Is there a set of absolute values that are not negotiable?

It has been argued that men and women should be treated equally regardless of religious belief or the culture in which they live. The Universal Declaration of Human Rights from the United Nations, written in 1948, has as Article 1 the following:

> Article 1: All human beings are born free and equal in dignity and rights. They are endowed with reason and conscience and should act towards one another in a spirit of brotherhood.

Ethically, we need to ask how consistent Article 1 is with cultures in which women's sexuality is celebrated either in advertising representations of them in scanty dress with product placement or where their whole body and face are totally covered while men's are not? When some societies embrace sexual display of parts of the body as the norm and others insist on total coverage - but only for women - is this treating everyone as free and equal in dignity? What should international businesses do ethically in their employment and advertising practices? Article 1 might be problematic if we think about it enough - but what about Article 5?

> Article 5: No one shall be subjected to torture or to cruel, inhuman or degrading treatment or punishment.

Certain countries, including the USA, engage in practices that are very close to cruel, inhuman or degrading treatment. The report on the use of torture in Guantánamo Bay prison provided evidence that the USA interprets Article 5 differently.

READ THE FULL REPORT

If not everybody agrees on such basic values as the unethicality of torture, one can imagine how hard it would be to agree on other ethical values universally. For instance, we might all agree that workers should receive a fair wage for their input. However, what constitutes a fair wage in a developing country? If it is two times more than an average local salary, could one argue it is fair? It may still be only a fraction of the market value at which the products are sold for in developed economies - so is it fair that the organization's shareholders increase their value by diminishing the wages of their employees by moving production to a cheap-wage economy?

In answering these questions, it could be argued, for instance, that it is only inward investment from more developed economies that will increase wage levels in the less developed ones. From this point of view, the relativities are not so important. As you can see, it would be very hard to develop universal rules around such issues: they very much depend on personal values and beliefs that differ from person to person.

ETHICS AS PROFESSIONAL NORMS

When ethics are assimilated as a norm, they define a system of organizational relations between functions, behaviours and problem-solving actions. Researchers in this vein have stressed the influence of the organizational context on individual ethical choices (Kluver et al., 2014). Organizations deploy norms assimilated to systemic ethical codes as they strive to appear to control individual subjectivity (Covaleski et al., 1998; Foucault, 1979: 177–84; Halsall and Brown, 2013; Miller and Rose, 1988; Townley, 1994). The utilitarian aim is clear. By using ethics as a method of control, the professional world is able to transform individuals' moral references, character and, ultimately, their values, until they accord with the organization's specific ends (Grey, 1994; McKinlay et al., 2012).

Kangas, Muotka, Huhtala, Mäkikangas and Taru Feldt (2017), in a longitudinal empirical study, looked at the positive relationship between an extremely innovative ethical frame instigated in a public hospital in Finland and agents' honesty in their sick leave declarations. Yet, in some cases, normative activity can pride itself on its ethical status while remaining fundamentally amoral, that is corrupt, as Campbell and Göritz (2014), Gordon, Kornberger and Clegg (2009), Gordon, Clegg and Kornberger (2009) and Clegg and Gordon (2012) demonstrate. For example, various Mafia have codes of ethics.

ETHICS AS INDIVIDUAL CHOICES

The ethics of responsibility stress interactions between the power of the free agent and institutional rules (Goebel and Weißenberger, 2017; Sims and Keon, 1997). In a world of norms and rules, agents' contextualize their choices with reference to organizational control and their own judgement, even if they are closely supervised (Helin and Sandström, 2010; Iedema and Rhodes, 2010). According to Moberg (2006), moral models and agents' interpretations of them introduce *blind spots* within organizations where there is a degree of disconnection between individual ethics and collective ethical action. According to professional context, the common grasp of the universality of professional norms will undergo variations, or interpretative tensions, which make it very difficult to analyse the ethics in practice, creating a multidimensional ethical climate (Wimbush et al., 1997).

The 'individualization' of ethics suggests that the individual manager is ultimately responsible for ethical behaviour and that the organizational requirement is for 'empowering ethics', which supports moral learning and development, instead of restricting ethics through codes (Kjonstad and Willmott, 1995). The heroic individual, so the argument goes, needs to listen to their inner voice or 'moral impulse' (Bauman, 1993, 1995). Such organizational members are 'morally assertive' and use their personal ethics to mediate corporate priorities (Watson, 2003). Ethics here is understood as a moral task for managers, who have personal responsibility for ethics.

If ethics essentially were a matter of individual behaviour, then organizational ethics would reside solely in the free will of the individual. In this scenario, the organization (and its rules) is a powerful framework within which an individual should act ethically. Conceived this way, an organization is an ethically questionable entity based on rules that individual members respond to, according to their own personal ethics.

ETHICS AS CEREMONIAL FACADES

CSR and formal codes of conduct can be an institutionalized rule-based system that, following Meyer and Rowan (1977), functions as a ceremonially adopted myth used to gain legitimacy, resources, stability, and to enhance survival prospects. Thus, to maintain ceremonial conformity, 'organizations that reflect institutional rules tend to buffer their formal structures from the uncertainties of technical activities by becoming loosely coupled, building gaps between their formal structures and actual work activities' (Meyer and Rowan, 1977: 340). In other words, organizations use codes of conduct in their search for legitimacy as standards to justify what they do (Brunsson and Jacobsson, 2000). In this sense, having codes of conduct becomes a 'public relation exercise' (Munro, 1992: 98).

Munro concludes that 'codes are almost useless to individual employees who are faced with their particular dilemmas' (1992: 105). When a member of an organization faces a novel situation, they must do more than merely apply a code of conduct rule in order to decide on a course of action. Rather, ruling is an activity, as the gerund demonstrates: the member has to apply the rule (interpret it) in the specific situation that can lead to a situation where two ethical rules compete with each other. As Munro (1992) has shown, it is exactly this competition that characterizes situations as dilemmas.

WHAT WOULD YOU DO?

WHAT WOULD YOU DO?

You are an employee of a global company. You learn from social media that the company is implicated in questionable employment practices in terms of your personal ethics that are occurring in subcontracted organizations in its supply chain. What would you do as an individual and as an employee?

ETHICS AS BUREAUCRACY

In sharp contrast to the above view, some have argued that the frame of the organization is more important than the individuals in it and their ethical dispositions or professional obligations. This argument is often expressed in terms of the reform of public bureaucracies in the image of market-driven organizations (du Gay, 2000). Changing bureaucracies into more entrepreneurial organizations that are 'post-bureaucratic' (Heckscher, 1994), it is argued, will shape the ability of members to behave ethically. In principle, making these organizations more flexible will allow their members to exercise more discretion. Think of a service such as a hospital. These are complex professional bureaucracies, with an extensive division of labour. Within each profession, there are strong ethical codes and a sense of the right thing to do – usually expressed in terms of an ethic of patient care. What happens if the hospital becomes a 'Trust Fund', with a budget that has to be managed by the professionals within it? It will certainly become more market-oriented, because the managers have to think about alternative uses of scarce resources. However, this may mean that they will have less time for a patient-centred ethic. They may also be urged by hospital administrators to respond more to the health issues of their wealthy and privately insured patients, than to poorer people. In this case, bureaucracy guarantees a more patient-centred ethic of care, though this may involve more waiting or queuing. Thus, the argument for bureaucracy is that it preserves 'a certain ethical dignity ... in the face of ... persistent populist, philosophical and entrepreneurial critiques' (du Gay, 2000: 9) coming from arguments for the superiority of markets. Against markets an 'ethic of personhood' is argued for. Such an ethic would stress 'autonomy, responsibility and freedom/obligation of individuals to actively make choices for themselves' (du Gay, 2004: 41).

When choice is associated with markets, the focus on individuality suggests that ethical people should be enterprising and individualistic and, above all, steadfast in their privileging of economic rationality. Markets that empower individual choice see no place for trust, mutual dependence, social bonds and honourable commitment (Sennett, 1998).

Some thinkers, such as the already cited Paul du Gay, have argued that bureaucracy may well act as a guardian of ethics. They argue that the formal rationality found in bureaucracy ensures that everybody is treated as a 'case', regardless of their status, religion, ethnic or class background (du Gay, 2000). A formally rational bureaucracy would be one in which every case is treated the same. If this formal rationality was replaced with what Max Weber called substantive rationality, where the way that a case is treated is determined by the substantive status of the people involved, then, for instance, capacity to pay, religion, gender, class or another (substantive) reason would determine the treatment that you receive. The core argument for bureaucracy is that such a substantive rationality would lead to the domination of ultimate values, such as the market capacity to pay, becoming the ethical basis of society (du Gay and Salaman, 1992). Such ethical values are dominated by notions of enterprise, economic rationality, free-market principles and individuality, conceiving of individual responsibility primarily in terms of financial accountability (du Gay, 2004).

The argument against the market is that bureaucracy's ethicality derives from the training that it provides in 'the rules' for bureaucrats, in terms of technical expertise. Through a clearly defined hierarchy, members understand everybody's responsibilities, duty and rights. They are conditioned to think of the office that they hold in terms of a 'vocation', something detached from personal privileges, passions and emotions (du Gay, 2000: 44). Bureaucratic modes of organizing provide an institutional framework for responsible governance (du Gay, 2004) in which individual responsibility and ethical conduct can be framed. According to this view, if we want ethical behaviour we should have more old-style Weberian bureaucrats who stick to their rulebook. In this view, it is not that humans would, by birth or definition, be ethically sound beings who are led astray by bureaucratic routines; rather, it is bureaucracy that provides the possibility for ethics by providing a framework beyond personal desires, needs and fantasies.

EXTEND YOUR KNOWLEDGE

READ THE ARTICLE

The following article analyses how business leaders can practically cope with ethics through irony: Rhodes, C. and Badham, R. (2018) 'Ethical irony and the relational leader: grappling with the infinity of ethics and the finitude of practice', *Business Ethics Quarterly*, 28 (1): 71–98, which is available at the companion website https://study.sagepub.com/managingandorganizations5e

ARE PROFITS AND PRINCIPLES INCOMPATIBLE?

More critical approaches to ethics in organizations question the convenience of the 'ethics pays' arguments outlined above. They are sceptical about the possibility of profit-seeking organizations, premised on the exploitation of the people that they employ, being ethical (Jones, 2004). The critical approach suggests that the core assumptions of classic management and organization theory do not position moral principles as 'a higher priority than firm profits' (Quinn and Jones, 1995: 22). Therefore, if profits are paramount, ethics will inevitably suffer: that is, if ethics potentially compromise profits, it is the former that will be sacrificed. Ethics is seen to be opposed to business rationality: their values are incompatible.

An especially public example of the opposition of ethics and business rationality has recently been paraded in Australia. In December 2017, the Australian Coalition government capitulated to sustained public pressure from whistleblowers, consumer groups, the Greens, Labor and some of its own MPs to establish a Royal Commission into the Banking Industry in Australia. The royal commission was asked to investigate whether any of Australia's financial services entities have engaged in misconduct, and if criminal or other legal proceedings should be referred to the Commonwealth. It has also been asked to consider whether sufficient mechanisms are in place to compensate victims.

Evidence has emerged in the Royal Commission of alleged bribery, forging of documents, lending practices that were conducted despite the capacity to repay of clients and the mis-selling of insurance to people who could not afford it. Companies such as AMP, a major financial institution, admitted to systematically misleading regulatory agencies through lying to them, while the Commonwealth Bank admitted some of its financial planners had been charging dead clients for financial advice, in one case for more than a decade.

The banks business model consisted of the realization that it was highly profitable to sell their customers financial advice that included purchasing the banks' financial products. Customers could be charged for financial advice that consisted of purchasing their financial products in a business model based on 'vertical integration'. The problem with this, as the corporate regulator reported, was that there was an unethical conflict of interest arising from banks providing personal financial advice to retail clients while also selling them financial products. Financial advisers failed to comply with the best interests of customers in 75 per cent of advice files reviewed, according to the corporate regulator.

Unethical conduct by the banks being investigated included the fabrication of fraudulent documents, errors in processing and administration as well as breaches of responsible lending obligations. Perhaps even more disturbing is that one bank, the Commonwealth, which had installed intelligent deposit ATMs, in which customers could deposit up to $10,000 at a time, had committed 53,700 breaches of money laundering and counter-terrorism financing laws after the bank failed to report fully $77 million worth of suspicious transactions through its machines over a number of years. The machines were being used to bank and launder the illegal gains of criminal activities.

Findings such as these lead one to ask whether business ethics is possible in a system that is driven by the pursuit of profits. A critical argument might suggest that business ethics in general and shared value in particular are both paradoxical concepts: businesses are there to make profits and making profits means maximizing one's own advantage, which more often than not will imply damaging someone else's. That has been only too evident in the hearings of the Royal Commission (see www.theguardian.com/australia-news/banking-royal-commission for a detailed discussion of the emerging evidence).

It is not just in financial institutions that unethical behaviour is deeply embedded because of the ease of making away with other people's money. Organizations can be unethical in may ways: take, for instance, a furniture manufacturer – if it wants to maximize its profits, it will pay minimum wages to its employees, buy the cheapest raw materials available (which might mean, say, illegally logged wood from rainforests in Brazil) and only implement those environmental filters that it is forced to use by law. All three practices will definitely contribute to increased profits; however, all three practices might be seen as unethical.

From this critical perspective, the essential principles of capitalist society do not value ethical behaviour. That is, commercial success and good behaviour are seen as mutually exclusive. Even where companies choose ethically sound practices, this does not mean that the companies themselves are necessarily ethically sound. For instance, The Body Shop does not rely on animal testing for its products. Whereas some might argue that this is an ethically sound decision, radical ethicists argue that The Body Shop engages in these practices only so it can promote itself. Put simply, being ethical becomes a marketing slogan that is adopted because it contributes to the bottom line. From a critical perspective, no action based on such a motivation can be called ethical. Business is by definition selfish, hence there can be no such thing as business ethics. So, this is a Catch-22 for business. If you do nothing to be seen to be ethical, then the business will be judged unethical. If, on the other hand, you do something that is seen to be ethical, you will be rebuked for 'being ethical' as a marketing ploy.

WHAT WOULD YOU DO?

Imagine you are head of the corporate social responsibility department at the NGO Oxfam (see www.oxfam.org/en). In early 2018, it was reported that some Oxfam staff were accused of sexually exploiting and abusing those that were seeking their help in the aftermath of the 2011 Haiti earthquake. Research the issue online through archives of the *Guardian* and other quality newspapers. What was the ethical wrongdoing of Oxfam staff? How could Oxfam re-build trust with donors and those it seeks to help? And how could you design an ethics toolkit or code of conduct to ensure ethical organizational behaviour?

Jones (C., 2003) suggests that business ethics may be considered analogous to law. In courts of law, it is judgment about the intentions of a defendant that play an important part in judicial decisions, including the degree of remorse shown by the defendant, when it is determined that the defendant's intentions negatively affect others. The situation is as applicable to institutional cases as it is to individuals at a personal level. Where remorse is shown, sentencing is lighter. In any potential legal case relating to unethical actions by its employees, a company with a code of ethics can show through publicly available documentary evidence that the company's intentions are ethical and that it exhorts its members not only to be ethical but also to help others to improve and to encourage their compliance with values. The company can show that its intentions are not only good but also legal and thereby minimize its potential risk exposure to actions on its behalf by its employees.

Codes of ethics afford protection: to employees who are supposed to abide by them; to customers, who know what they should expect; to investors, for whom they are a classic example of risk management and insurance against malfeasance. Codes of ethics can limit the impact of malfeasance; however, it is less likely that they can stop it. Of course, if there were a universal set of absolute values that all agreed on, the story would be different.

In the field of ethics, as we have seen, many researchers consider certain values (good, evil, justice, injustice, equality, etc.) to be natural laws with universal scope. These are ethical codes that apply to all firms (Schwartz, 2005). These universals should make it possible to decide on ethical dilemmas by offering criteria on which to judge questionable behaviours or attitudes. Yet, as we have indicated above, it is a paradox to stress the existence of universal values and to observe that, in practice, these values are not applied and can even contradict one another. This incompleteness is inherent in any ethical practice, and underlines the ideal-typical dimension of moral universals in the presence of the fragmented ethical environment within organizations.

Any ethical decision will necessarily be more or less disappointing with regard to expectations based on universals. Moral framing of ethical decisions is not realist in its representation of reality and is inefficient in solving local problems that require resolution by the adoption of locally embedded and subtle interpretation when solutions are required. A legal decision possesses a provisional universal dimension *within* the legal system, as witnessed by jurisprudence in cases of law. What the law does, albeit retrospectively, is to reaffirm ethics as universal values having a teleological dimension: they should determine action, especially in those cases where they did not. The failure of these values provides an occasion for the law to reinstate their significance and centrality. Ethical and unethical decisions, as judged in terms of legality, provide meanings that comprise a constantly unfolding meta-narrative. Hence, the practice of ethics necessarily restricts the force of these universals because such practice always displays a provisional dimension of restricted universality, situating it in local cultures, the strength of which makes it difficult to avoid the relativism of all local ethics. If culture is the way we do things around here, it is easy to see how locally embedded forms of transgression can become ethical norms, such as the police who corruptly collude with criminals (Gordon, 2007) or the bank that turns a blind eye for two years to the criminal monies being deposited into certain accounts in the sustained batching of monies being placed in its intelligent ATMs.

In practice, it seems impossible to base ethics on independent universals, since they become secondary to the different social systems in which social action is inscribed, permitting manifestly immoral practices (Parfit, 2011: 100–5). An overall ethical system with unlimited pretensions has no chance of resonating in any way with social reality because of the fact that ethical behaviour is always situated in specific practices and contexts. Even the law is a specific practice and context, albeit one that reasserts the social order on those occasions of its breaching that are apprehended. However, in extreme cases, ethics that permit manifestly immoral practices can threaten the universality of human community and thus harm the very possibility of the legality of social order. Such a danger exists when a locally embedded ethic escapes from its spatiotemporal limits to become the foundation for constructing the social world; that is, it would become totalitarian. Thus, the extermination process carried out under the Holocaust was justified by an ethical code that targeted elimination of categories of the living desired by an Aryan ethic that considered itself omnipotent.

In the presence of situations that threaten us today, we can suggest that a *common humanity* exists in the organization of the *living* that limits the potential excesses of any ethical code. Living is the common default universally and unanimously recognized by the human community *preceding* any ethic (Singer, 2006). Living is a default universal ethic against extreme historical practices and situations in which life is denied. The notion of humanity, which was called on after the Second World War by the tribunal responsible for judging former Nazis, seemed closer to a common than to an abstract, intangible universal, defined according to humanity's aspirations for justice by the chief prosecutor, Robert Jackson. The allied powers decided to defend the *common* right to being alive (Marti and Fernandez, 2013), even if it meant that the worst transgressors forfeited their right to life. In a world dominated by distinctive systems and norms, at least one universal may always be deferred to (Apel, 2000).

There are not just historical resonances to these points but also contemporary ones and not only those that apply to the many conflicts, wars and terrorism that dominate our headlines at the present time, especially in the Middle East. The most fundamental force that sustains life in general is that of planet Earth. The sustainability of the planet is the point at which business ethics becomes serious; to the extent that organizations, the dominant form of human activity on the planet, do not strive for sustainable practices in all their activities, they are slowly killing the earth's species, amongst which is that most destructive of creatures, the human animal.

In perhaps no other field of enquiry do opinions about the pros and cons differ as much as in the CSR and ethics debate. While the normative approach discussed above sees a possible alignment between ethics and economy, for many critical researchers the words business and ethics remain separate. As a future manager, you will need to be able to reflect critically and independently on ethics, understood as the difference between what you have a right to do and what it is right to do, as Potter Stewart recommended at our chapter's beginning.

SUMMARY

In this chapter, we have reviewed contemporary approaches to stakeholder management and corporate social responsibility (CSR), and embedded them in the broader context of ethics:

- Topics such as CSR and ethics are sometimes seen as 'soft' topics but they have become more and more important for businesses in the twenty-first century.

- The triple bottom line is increasingly the reporting standard of choice for global organizations. Organizations and their managers now have to relate to a much wider set of stakeholders, concerns and interests in a meaningful way.
- Managing without a simple bottom-line ethics implies dealing with paradoxes, ambiguities and trade-offs, rather than being a simple and easy matter of applying clear rules to identifiable cases.
- Ethics are today often codified and most significant organizations will have a code of ethics.
- Codes of ethics offer risk management and legal protection for organizations against the actions of their employees, but they cannot protect employees or customers from fundamentally unethical practice by organizations, such as those provoking the 2008 Global Financial Crisis or contributing to the death of the planet through accelerating climate change.

EXERCISES

1. Having read this chapter, you should be able to say in your own words what each of the following key terms means. Test yourself or ask a colleague to test you.
   - Shareholder value
   - Corporate social responsibility
   - Stakeholders
   - Corporate greening
   - Codes of conduct
   - Greenwashing
   - Business ethics
   - Critical views of business ethics.
2. What is corporate social responsibility?
3. What are the different types of stakeholder interests? Which are the most contested?
4. What distinguishes involuntary from voluntary stakeholders?
5. How would you differentiate CSR as 'greenwash' from other commitments?
6. What can corporate codes of ethics do?
7. What is an individual, and what is an organizational (bureaucratic) responsibility?

TEST YOURSELF

Review what you have learned by visiting:
https://study.sagepub.com/managingandorganizations5e or your eBook

- Test yourself with multiple-choice questions.
- Revise key terms with the interactive flashcards.

REVISE KEY TERMS

TEST YOURSELF

CASE STUDY

Granby Zoo

Emerging from the private menageries of royal families in Europe during the eighteenth century, public zoos remained primarily focused on entertainment until the second half of the twentieth century. Costumed chimpanzee performances, elephant rides, orang-utan tea parties and displays of human 'savages' were common spectacles in various zoos around the world during this period. From the 1960s, leading zoos increasingly concentrated on animal conservation, on breeding endangered species in more natural habitats (as their enclosures began to be called) and on eco-efficiency. Granby Zoo, one of the most popular zoos in Canada and a major economic driver in its region, is an example of the metamorphosis that such institutions have undergone.

Granby Zoo began as a private menagerie of the humanitarian, industrialist, animal lover, and charismatic mayor of Granby for 25 years, Horace Boivin. Wanting to create a beautiful city where all would feel happy, he established several parks including the celebrated Granby Zoo that officially opened in 1955. It immediately became a major tourist attraction, receiving nearly 300,000 visitors in its first season and supporting many local businesses in the process. Despite its popularity, it was a financially strapped small- and medium-sized enterprise (SME) that employed a skeleton staff with a few retired farmers as zookeepers. These zookeepers fed the restaurant scraps to the animals and allowed visitors to interact with them like they were domestic species. They were unable to recognize the animals' stress signals and were unaware of how inappropriate the animal care was or how prematurely these animals deceased. By the 1970s, with increased habitat destruction, species extinctions, the emerging environmental and animal rights movements, new conservation networks, and growing knowledge in fields such as zoology, zoo conservation efforts at Granby Zoo began. Despite several attempts by the vet to improve animal care, most calls were not heeded. Zookeepers repeatedly blocked her efforts and management was focused solely on survival following several years of financial losses (blamed on poor weather, union strikes and the subsequent negative publicity, as well as several pay rises). This vet left in the early 1980s and expressed her frustration with the lack of progress being made to improve animal care by publishing a scathing book.

Granby Zoo had returned to profit by this time, largely assisted by a new attraction that saw visitor numbers increase by 35 per cent in 1984. When the management staff left in 1985, the president hired a new vet who was also given two new responsibilities previously held by the director of infrastructure: animal curator and zookeeper manager. With this new power, the vet was able to replace rapidly half the zookeepers with trained specialists who supported his efforts to improve animal care. The vet's vision was inspired by a best-practice zoo conference he had attended in his first year, where he learned about the potential of exchanging or breeding animals with other zoos rather than purchasing them from dealers (which was increasingly difficult and expensive as wild species numbers diminished). This required good animal records and healthy specimens, so the vet began improving animal diets, care and habitats. With financial resources available and management behind him, the vet applied for accreditation from the network of leading American zoos that focus on conservation. While certification was not initially awarded, the recommendations stemming from the evaluation assisted the vet in pushing through a series of improvements, which saw Granby Zoo accepted into the prestigious

Association of American Zoos and Aquariums by the end of the 1980s. During this period, Granby Zoo began focusing on housing and breeding endangered species in international networks, supporting conservation efforts worldwide, reintroducing certain almost extinct species back into the wild, and educating thousands of visitors each year about such issues. By the 1990s, animal conservation and education were firmly anchored in the zoo's mission.

The early 1990s saw Granby Zoo enter another period of financial difficulty. Facing repeated poor weather, increased competition, union problems, bad press and ageing infrastructure, the zoo made one loss after another. No longer able to care adequately for several charismatic species, Granby Zoo decided to part with them and visitor numbers further diminished. During this period, certain employees began environmental initiatives such as recycling cans, an environmental club and saving energy. While some assisted in raising revenues or decreasing costs, the lack of follow-up and coordination of these efforts meant that they were often short-lived. With the zoo facing closure in 1996, the board members decided to recruit a new CEO who had a reputation for saving enterprises in difficulty. This individual immediately began installing a culture of 'wow' service, which saw visitor satisfaction and union relations improve considerably. Then he began championing an idea that would end the zoo's financial insecurity: an aquatic centre. While many employees were concerned that it would dilute the zoo's conservation role, they were quickly won over. When the aquatic park opened in 1999, visitor numbers and visit time increased by 39 per cent and 60 per cent, respectively, where they have remained ever since, making new investments in animal habitats, infrastructures and conservation efforts possible.

By 2003, Granby Zoo had paid back its debts and begun planning a major modernization project to celebrate its 50-year anniversary. The board chose a new CEO with a background in communication and the environment. She saw the potential to create a 'greener' zoo and immediately established green principles to guide all those involved in the modernization project. Early in 2004, she hired an environmental coordinator to organize, evaluate and follow up several projects collectively referred to as the 'Green Zoo'. By 2006, Granby Zoo had: decreased its water consumption by 70 per cent; become one of Canada's largest users of geothermal energy; built 72 per cent more energy-efficient ecological constructions; banned all non-organic cleaning products; and increased recycling substantially. While this process continues, Granby Zoo has already won several prestigious prizes, received much positive publicity and set new profit records.

Questions

1. How have criteria for measuring zoos as 'good' or 'ethical' evolved? How and why did Granby Zoo's *raison d'être* evolve?
2. When did Granby Zoo become an ethical organization? What made it so?
3. Which factors contributed to the success of ethical initiatives in Granby Zoo? Which factors limited such progress?
4. How did certain individuals (the vets, zookeepers, environmental coordinator, upper management) facilitate or hinder such change?

Case prepared by Annelies Hodge and Marie-France Turcotte, School of Management, University of Quebec at Montreal (UQAM).

ADDITIONAL RESOURCES

- We can recommend Al Gore's movie, *An Inconvenient Truth* (Guggenheim, 2006), a timely and interesting film that helps to understand the pressing need to change (corporate) behaviour.
- *Global Warming: The Signs and the Science* (Morisette, 2005) is a documentary that examines the science behind global warming and shows how people in different locales across the world are responding in different ways to the challenges of global warming.
- *Wal-Mart: The High Cost of Low Price* (Robert Greenwald, 2005) is a critical view of the world's largest employer – Walmart. It's wonderfully narrated, but a little one-sided, so perhaps discuss the dilemmas and ambiguities that Walmart faces in order to reveal the full story.
- *Thin Ice* (Lamb and Sington, 2013) is a documentary film following geologist Simon Lamb on a search to understand the science behind climate change. He travels the world and meets a range of scientists, from biologists to physicists, who are investigating the climate. The film's conclusion emphasizes the scientific consensus on human-induced climate change.

NOTE

1. www.telegraph.co.uk/finance/newsbysector/energy/oilandgas/8242557/Obama-oil-spill-commissions-final-report-blames-disaster-on-cost-cutting-by-BP-and-partners.html

Part Three

MANAGING ORGANIZATIONAL STRUCTURES AND PROCESSES

INTERACTIVE EBOOK ICON KEY

MANAGING PRINCIPLES
THINKERS, PRINCIPLES, MODELS

LEARNING OBJECTIVES

This chapter is designed to introduce you to:

- the origins, sometimes shameful, of some foundations and principles of early management approaches
- how legislative changes made larger organizations possible, initially using internal contracting principles before adopting the engineering principles of 'Taylorism' and 'Fordism'
- the debates surrounding bureaucracy and its hybrids as the most widespread principle of twentieth-century management in both private and public sectors
- some major theorists' principles of management
- Marx's argument, and its modern extensions, about the role of exploitation in the labour process.

BEFORE YOU GET STARTED...

Improvising on a statement by the English landscape painter John Constable:

> Remember that management is a science of which organizations are but the experiments!

INTRODUCTION

This chapter covers some of the most influential ideas about management. These ideas reduce management to simple principles or one-best-way models. Such ideas have had a long life in management and their legacy is still evident today in the many organizations that seek to model themselves on 'best practices'. Early ideas of management were, shamefully, to be found in manuals for the control of slaves; other ideas came to be applied in the design of buildings and in the application of engineering to management, before broadening the scope of bureaucracy to include human relations.

FOUNDATIONS FOR MANAGEMENT PRINCIPLES

SLAVERY

That the prosperity of many parts of England and the Americas was premised on the slave trade is a shameful part of European and American history. Cooke (2003) suggests that methods developed for the management of slaves in plantations anticipated many early modern management ideas. Slavery, an institution founded on human bondage and coercive control, became the source of some of the earliest ideas about how to manage large-scale organization. Many early principles of modern management, such as standardization, were explicitly developed in the context of slavery and found ready application in the management of the proletarian 'wage slaves' that voluntarily migrated to the Americas to escape the poverty of feudal and peasant life in Europe. The fact that early management has a shameful history has been well hidden, as Cooke (2003) observes.

WATCH VIDEOS ON THIS TOPIC

We tend to think of slavery as something belonging to the past but this is not the case, as a recent study by the Joseph Rowntree Foundation (Craig et al., 2007) in the UK points out. Extreme economic exploitation, absence of human rights and actual or threatened violence characterize modern slavery in areas of the economy such as prostitution, hotel, factory and dock labour. Bales (2005) estimated the contemporary number of slaves at 27 million people, globally.

PRINCIPLES OF MASTERY

In small workshops, the master's control was exercised face to face. The master owned key resources, such as a workplace, materials and distribution and manufactory networks, ownership that made them small-scale capitalists. On this basis, masters were easily able to enforce rules, to say when work was done correctly or incorrectly as they had knowledge that provided the basis for **direct management control**. The only thing employees owned and controlled were their bodies and, perhaps, those of their immediate family, which they could sell as labour power to the owners of resources.

Direct management control combines the ownership and control of resources with practical knowledge of the means of production to exercise discipline over their employees.

The owners of capital were known as capitalists because they owned capital – the social relations and resources that made them masters over other men, women and children.

In larger workshops, in contrast, managing and organization had to be less personal. Various methods of fusing discipline and surveillance over employees were tried. Early in the development of industrial capitalism, a building that had factory discipline built into it was described by Jeremy Bentham.

ARCHITECTURAL PRINCIPLES

Jeremy Bentham (1995) planned to reform work by using what he called the **panoptical principle** that he had observed in the early days of factory organization in place at a factory near Moscow that his brother managed.

The panoptical principle establishes the capacity to be all seeing of those aware that they are potentially being watched.

Successful surveillance, according to Bentham, depended on architectural principles. As Image 13.1 shows, the Panopticon was a complex architectural design. It consisted of a central observation tower (which you can see clearly in the cutaway section) from which any supervisor, without being seen, could see the bodies arranged in the various cells of the building. In each cell, the occupants were backlit (neither electric nor gas lighting had yet been invented) and isolated from one another by walls, yet subject to scrutiny by the observer in the tower. Control was to be maintained by the constant sense that unseen eyes might be watching those under surveillance. You had no way of knowing if you were being watched at any particular time but you were obliged to assume that you were. The Panopticon was a means not only for making work visible but also for making those being seen aware that they may be under scrutiny at any time.

The Panopticon was not just a system of surveillance but also a system of records and rules. The authorities would have a complete file on the behaviour of each inmate with rules governing timetables, the nature of work and the authority to exercise surveillance. The aim was to produce a self-disciplining subject. The asymmetrical nature of seeing but not being seen, of knowing you were possibly being watched but not when or if you were, was designed to produce employees labouring under the threat of constant supervision.

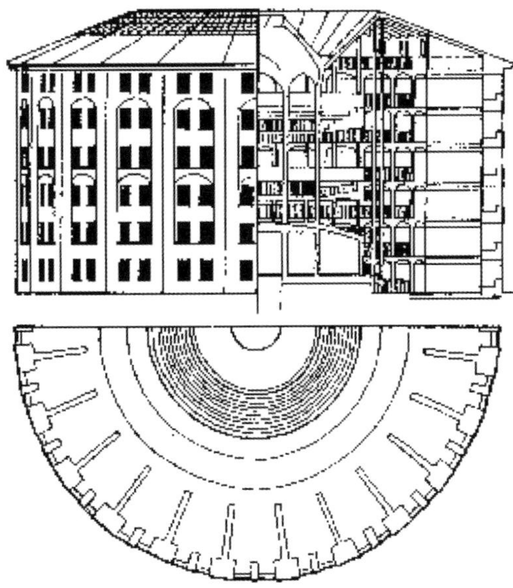

IMAGE 13.1 Plan of the Panopticon

IN PRACTICE

Today, of course, the Panopticon has become electronic. The average person in the cities of the developed world is rarely out of range of a CCTV as they move around. The average person in a busy city passes through many forms of surveillance. Think of the use of open calendars in office environments that show transparently as and when you are busy. The 'online' status of outlook360 and enterprise 'Skype for business' shows whether or not you are online at work.

Question

1. In practice, note the various kinds and number of panoptical devices that you are subject to on an average day.
2. What are they and how many are there?

EARLY MODERN PRINCIPLES EXPANDED

Early modern management was based on the principle of the efficient extraction of value from the labour that was employed.

For **early modern management**, those who were managing and being managed were expected to create more value than would be paid out to them in wages and salaries, thus ensuring that there is a return to the capital that can be invested in the enterprise. For value to be extracted in this way, the reform of both asset holding and, as a consequence, of management, was necessary.

The numbers to be supervised were not great. By the early 1850s, a factory of 300 people could still be considered very large in the British cotton industry (Hobsbawm, 1975: 21) and as late as 1871 the average British cotton factory employed only 180 people, whereas engineering works averaged only 85. One reason they were small was that finance was in scarce supply, often secured privately or on credit (Hobsbawm, 1975). Money was mostly tied up in aristocratic land holdings. Early entrepreneurs raised capital largely through credit. Merchants combined credit with rented buildings and machinery, which they utilized through employing cheap sources of labour. In this way, if the enterprise were to fail, the liability and exposure of the emergent entrepreneurs would be limited (Tribe, 1975). By keeping personal financial commitments small, fortunes might be better insured.

Limited liability legislation separated the private fortunes of entrepreneurs from investments in business, so that if the latter failed, the personal fortune was sequestered and the debtors' prison avoided.

Enterprises were enabled to grow beyond the financial capacities of their owners by the development of **limited liability legislation** from the Limited Liability Act of 1855. Such legislation was first pioneered in the UK and then widely copied internationally almost immediately thereafter. This legislation instituted the principle of incorporation of a company as a legal entity, limiting the liability of those who invest in it, such that their personal fortunes were dealt with as legally separate from their investments in the asset. Earlier, the 1844 Joint Stock Companies Act had defined the fiduciary duty of a director as the necessity of acting in good faith for the benefit of the company as a whole. The company as a whole was, in turn, defined in this legislation in terms of those who invest in its capital: shareholders. Limited liability legislation was the key factor in fuelling the formation and growth of accountancy institutes in the UK, and thus the accounting profession.

Before the 1855 Act, the situation was quite different. If the business failed, the owner's personal fortune could be seized against debtors. Not surprisingly, this limited the size of the enterprise, because a prudent investor would not want to be overexposed. Being able to risk the savings of investors freed up entrepreneurial energies and did much to prepare the ground for a widespread share market in which individuals might invest their savings in productive enterprises. A further consequence was that companies were legitimated in their obligation to enact strategies that maximize profits without regard for any other considerations or stakeholders.

The scale effects of limited liability were dramatic. For example, the Krupp works at Essen in Germany had only 72 workers in 1848, but by 1873 it employed almost 12,000. Whole regions became dominated by huge commercial ventures. Limited liability legislation was an institutional form that rapidly spread globally. Initially, it brokered a variance rather than a wholesale revision in management principles that remained based on surveillance.

INTERNAL CONTRACTING PRINCIPLES

If limited liability legislation solved the problem of how to raise capital and increase scale, it did not resolve the problem of how to manage the vastly expanded enterprise. It was the '"master" rather than the impersonal authority of the "company" [that held sway in] the enterprise, and even the company was identified with a man rather than a board of directors' (Hobsbawm, 1975: 214). But how could a single master exercise mastery over so many? How was the master to achieve effective governance over a vastly increased scale of operations?

One solution was based on the owners of previously independent business being re-employed as internal contractors to oversee the processes of labour in firms that were taken over by financiers. Financiers were individuals skilled more in the art of raising capital than executing the mundane command of work. One consequence of **internal contracting** was that quite different methods of internal control could flourish in different plants in the same industry.

In **internal contracting**, a contractor used materials, plant and equipment supplied by owners but managed the labour contracted to deliver a certain quantity of product.

Standards, machinery and other tools were highly variable, as were the principles in play. Here a benign and benevolent despot might be master, there the master might be acting on behalf of a labour-managed cooperative, while in another plant the master might be a ruthless and vicious tyrant, exploiting family members or those too weak in the market to resist downward pressure on their wages.

The system of internal contracting flourished from the late nineteenth through to the early twentieth century, with variable lags in different countries, being developed earliest and superseded fastest in the USA. Given that the internal contract was a fixed sum agreed between the internal contractor and the employers of capital, then the middleman, the internal contractor, stood to gain the most by paying the least for the quantity contracted, so there was plenty of opportunity for downward pressure on wages to occur. Not surprisingly, this fact was well understood by trade unionists as they sought to improve the lot of union members by standardizing conditions and wages (Clawson, 1980; Littler,

1982). Unionism exercised an upward pressure, standardizing the conditions of work, whereas, from the business owners and employers of finance, there was a downward pressure beginning to be exercised in the name of an efficient rate of return. The downward pressure from finance and the upward pressure from the unions led, inexorably, to an increased standardization of workplace routines, so that they became similar across workplaces, modelled on the best practice from the employees' point of view. Added to these standardizing pressures were new models of managerial control drawn from engineering.

ENGINEERING PRINCIPLES: F. W. TAYLOR

It was in steel factories in Pittsburgh in the northeast of the USA that management's founding father, F. W. Taylor, first developed the field's systematic statements from his experience as a practical engineer. Engineering was a discipline with great reach and authority. Popular engineering journals and magazines in the nineteenth century constructed the discipline as *the* locus of professional managerial expertise (Shenhav, 1999). According to the new engineering approaches to management, corporations and organizations could be managed on the basis of facts and techniques. Engineers trained in the management of things and the governance of working people sought to establish principles that aligned functions and responsibilities in a scientifically proven manner.

Management emerged as a systematic solution to the issue of how to get others 'to get things done' (Hoskin, 2004: 745). The answer, suggests Hoskin (2004), emerged initially at the Springfield Armory, in the production of muskets through 'establishing *prescribed* times required to make each musket part, and then reordering the space across which manufacture proceeded, so that the musket "took shape" following a principle of linear flow' (Hoskin, 2004: 747). Daily piece-rate targets and rates for each task were developed and a system devised for coordinating them (Hoskin, 2004).

Late in the nineteenth century, armed with a checklist and a stopwatch, F. W. Taylor (1967 [1911]) developed and popularized **scientific management** around a set of principles for making people's work more visible. He observed and timed work and then redesigned it, so that tasks could be done more efficiently.

Scientific management assumes that there is one best way to organize work and organization based on the principles of standardization of time and routinization of motion.

Taylor's four principles of management are as follows:

1. *Developing a science of work*: Observing and measuring norms of output, using a stopwatch to time human movements; on this basis, improving the design of workstations and tools, which could improve effectiveness. Given improvements in effectiveness, Taylor argued that pay could be improved.

2. *Scientifically selecting and training the employee*: Taylor believed that everyone had different aptitudes – it was really a question of fitting the worker to the job and this was the task of management. When management did this job properly, all human resources would be developed to their utmost potential.

3. *Combining the sciences of work and selecting and training of employees*: Taylor thought that workers would benefit from higher wages while

managers, who had to learn new systems of work and to give up privileges that they had, in Taylor's view, no right to, might be expected to resist.

4. *Management and workers must specialize and collaborate closely*: Management must focus on mental labour, on setting up systems, designing them and supervising them. Workers must concentrate on manual labour and leave the higher-order mental labour to the managers.

Taylor was the founding father of work-study – fitting the person to the job – and work design, as well as the pioneer of productivity-related pay systems. Taylor produced a set of principles for a political economy of the body (see Clegg et al., 2006a) that became adopted by many others (see Watts, 1991). From Taylor's point of view, the working body should be maximally productive and minimally fatigued to become more efficient.

Canguilhem (1992: 63) points out that Taylorism established a mode of work premised not only on the subjection of the workers' body to the superior intelligence of the managers' mind, but also subordinated the human body to industrial machinery. The human body was measured as if it functioned like a machine.

From Taylor's point of view, the working body should be maximally productive and minimally fatigued to become more efficient. Important followers, such as the Gilbreths, developed his practice to innovative heights through the use of time-lapsed photography, in a form of industrial futurism (Mandel, 1989). Some saw Taylor as a reformer who aimed to eliminate inefficient and excessively debilitating practices in industry (see, for example, Amar, 1920); nonetheless, Taylor's views were subject to severe criticism from several contemporary interests:

1. Internal contractors – people who provided and supervised labour to work within factories owned by remote financiers, entrepreneurs and industrialists – stood to lose their livelihoods if scientific management triumphed and replaced them with systematic managers, so they were opposed to it.
2. Owners of capital were often opposed, particularly those with small workshops. These people were already fearful of the risk of being swallowed up or driven out of business by big businesses and feared that the new knowledge would undermine their power of ownership.
3. Employers tended to adopt his ideas piecemeal; they were keen on the efficiencies from the time measurement but not as keen on the bonuses that Taylor proposed under his recommendations for the use of piece rates (Taylor, 1895).
4. From the last quarter of the nineteenth century, workers were increasingly organizing in unions that were opposed to the loss of craft skills entailed in the principles of management based on the standardization and systematization of work (Shenhav, 1999).
5. In the popular mind, Taylor's system was identified with lay-offs, due to the available work being completed faster.

Taylor's ideas had the advantage of being quite easy to grasp (see Taylor, 1995; Wrege, 1995) and to adopt but were controversial. Much of the opposition to

READ MORE FROM TAYLOR

Taylor's ideas came to a head when the US Congress, in 1912, held an inquiry into the use of his system of management, due to the association of its adoption with strikes. By the 1920s, Taylor's ideas were being implemented in a new context – that of the moving production line pioneered by Henry Ford in Detroit.

INDUSTRIAL MANAGEMENT PRINCIPLES

PRODUCTION LINE PRINCIPLES: HENRY FORD

In 1913, 30 years after Taylor installed his first system, a revolution in manufacturing occurred when Henry Ford introduced the assembly line as a new way of producing automobiles, modelled on the principles of the assembly lines in the Chicago slaughterhouses. Fordism standardized production and machine tools as well as using assembly lines but also paid higher 'living' wages designed to allow employees to become effective consumers of the products they produced. These wages were not paid to just anyone, but only those deemed fit to receive them – sober, steady fellows, with lifestyles Fordism approved after they had been inspected (see Clegg et al., 2006a). At the zenith of the Ford organization in the post-war era, it had massive handbooks of routines, rules and standardized role prescriptions written up as job descriptions. Ford developed new 'disciplinary' forms of power based on a combination of elements of Taylor's principles adapted to a moving production line rather than a static workstation.

Machinists' jobs in the new production lines had a formalized structure with rigid job description and prescription, with a high degree of work **specialization** and a clear and strict hierarchy of authority, vertical communication and a limited information network.

Specialization occurs when labour is divided and defined into smaller specific tasks rather than being seen as a general task that anyone might do.

Small spans of managerial control, long chains of command, little participation in organizational design and decision-making, high degrees of centralization of knowledge, decision-making and control, resulted in an elongated organizational structure. The organization environment was simple, stable and relatively unchanging. Jobs were repetitive, boring and exhausting and employees were often unsurprisingly resistant to the discipline imposed on them by the management system. Managers were there to control; consequently, conflict tended not to be resolved but repressed.

WHAT WOULD YOU DO?

WHAT WOULD YOU DO?

Your organization is relocating some of its manufacturing capacities to a less-developed country in South-East Asia where the wages bill will be slashed. However, the workforce in the home country is skilled and has a great deal of tacit knowledge that aids efficient manufacturing. You have to mastermind the transition between countries. What would you do to effect the transition as smoothly as possible, without the disruption of industrial strife in the home country base and in such a way as to ensure the most effective translation of practices from one site to the other? What would you do – and what would you not do?

PRINCIPLES OF AUTHORITY: HENRI FAYOL

Henri Fayol, the most significant European founder of modern management, published *Administration Industrielle et Générale* in 1916 (see Fayol, 1949). Fayol stressed management training focused on planning, organizing, commanding, coordinating and controlling for optimal performance. Fayol's training programme offered 14 principles to provide a manual for proper management, efficient organizations and happy employees.

1. *Specialization of labour*: To encourage continuous improvement in skills and the development of improvements in methods.
2. *Authority*: Establishing the right to give orders and the power to exact obedience.
3. *Discipline*: There was to be obedience.
4. *Unity of command*: Each employee was to have one and only one boss.
5. *Unity of direction*: A single mind should generate a single plan.
6. *Subordination of individual interests*: To the interests of the organization.
7. *Remuneration policy*: Employees should receive fair payment for services.
8. *Centralization*: Consolidation of management functions so that decisions will be made from the top.
9. *Scalar chain*: A clear line of authority and formal chain of command running from top to bottom of the organization, as in the military.
10. *Order*: All materials and employees have a prescribed place, where they should be found.
11. *Equity*: There should be a principle of fairness involved in the way that the organization treats employees.
12. *Personnel tenure*: Limited turnover of personnel was a good thing, and lifetime employment should be offered to good employees.
13. *Initiative*: This requires designing a plan and doing what it takes to make it happen.
14. *Esprit de corps*: There should be harmony and cohesion among organization members.

Fayol's principles were concerned with what and how managers did what they did. Fayol was not translated into English until the 1940s, so his impact on management outside the Francophone (and Latin) world was delayed.

MAX WEBER AND PRINCIPLES OF BUREAUCRACY

A military model provided the earliest template for organizational routines. By the early twentieth century, the most percipient observer of organizations, a German called Max Weber, noted that bureaucracy, modelled unambiguously on the military

READ MORE ABOUT WEBER

(Weber, 1976), was the dominant organizational model. As the economic historian Hobsbawm put it, 'Paradoxically, private enterprise in its most unrestricted and anarchic period tended to fall back on the only available model of large-scale management, the military and bureaucratic' (1975: 216), noting the railway companies, with their 'pyramid of uniformed and disciplined workers, possessing job security, often promotion by security and even pensions', as an extreme example. Weber (1948: 261) put it even more succinctly: 'No special proof is necessary to show that military discipline is the ideal model for the modern capitalist factory.'

The result of processes working towards standardization was that the blueprint for designing modern organizations was increasingly inherited from principles shaped within a framework of military discipline, even while being applied to market-based enterprises. Being disciplined and visible were the key principles. Order, discipline and authority were to become organizational watchwords, especially in the confined spaces of manufactories – or, as they became known, factories.

Bureaucracy is an organizational form consisting of a hierarchy of differentiated knowledge and expertise in which rules and disciplines are arranged not only hierarchically in regard to each other but also in parallel. In bureaucracy, action is procedurally based on formal rules. When bureaucracies are classified as being of the rational-legal type, they are supposed to apply values and principles universally, without favour or prejudice.

Bureaucratic organization, seen at the turn of the nineteenth century as the hallmark of modern organization, depended above all else on the application of 'rational' means for the achievement of specific ends. In a bureaucracy, techniques would be most rational when they were designed purely from the principle of fitness for purpose. Bureaucratic principles have endured as a dominant organizational form. Weber and subsequent theorists saw these principles as being absolutely necessary for large organizations with complex divisions of labour.

A **bureaucracy** is a form of **organizational design**.

Weber identified authority based on **rational-legal principles** as the heart of bureaucratic organizations.

An **organizational design** is the designated formal structure of the organization as a system of roles, responsibilities and decision-making.

Members of a bureaucratic organization are expected to obey the rules as general principles that can be applied to particular cases and which apply to those exercising authority as much as those who must obey the rules. In principle, members of the organization put the personal characteristics of the office holder to the side and respond purely to the demands of office. The rules are the technical basis of an ability to take appropriate action, in terms of the definitions they stipulate. Whether the bureaucracy is a public or private sector organization would be largely immaterial. Day-to-day control involves the intermediation of experts whose expertise will always be specialized, partial and fragmented. The notion of a career is essential to the practice of bureaucracy and the career is followed in a specialized area of expertise. There is differentiation of both expertise and careers.

Rational-legal principles: People obey orders as rational-legal precepts because they believe that the person giving the order is acting in accordance with a code of legal rules and regulations (Albrow, 1970: 43).

Authority was crucial to Weber's account of modern bureaucratic organizations. While leaders and managers were employed in positions of domination over employees below them – their subordinates – in practice dominance was much easier to exercise in everyday organization if it was based on legitimacy, i.e. with the consent of those being subordinated. According to Weber, three main principles of legitimacy could deliver authority in organizations:

1. *The principle of charismatic authority* meant that deference and obedience would be given because of the extraordinary attractiveness and power of the person. The person is owed homage because of their capacity to project personal magnetism, grace and bearing. For instance, a politician such as Nelson Mandela was said to have charismatic authority.

2. *The principle of traditional authority* occurs where deference and obedience are owed because of longstanding habit. Prince Charles, for instance, is not so much an authority because of his charisma but because of tradition: as oldest son of the queen, he is the future king of England because the line of descent is habitually one of primogeniture.
3. *The principle of rational-legal authority* signifies that deference and obedience are owed not to the person or the title they hold but to the role they fill. It is not the officer but the office that is owed homage because it is a part of a rational and recognized disposition of relationships in a structure of offices.

Weber saw the rational-legal bureaucracy as an instrument or tool of unrivalled technical superiority over the other bases for legitimacy. Weber defined bureaucracy as having 15 principal dimensions:

1. Power belongs to an office and is not a function of the office holder.
2. Power relations within an organization structure have a distinct authority configuration, specified by the rules of the organization.
3. Because powers are exercised in terms of the rules of office rather than the person, organizational action is impersonal.
4. Disciplinary systems of knowledge, either professionally or organizationally formulated, rather than idiosyncratic beliefs, frame organizational action.
5. The rules tend to be formally codified.
6. These rules are contained in files of written documents that, based on precedent and abstract rule, serve as standards for organizational action.
7. These rules specify tasks that are specific, distinct and done by different formal categories of personnel who specialize in these tasks and not in others. Official tasks are organized on a continuous regulated basis to ensure the smooth flow of work between discontinuous elements in its organization. Thus, there is a tendency towards specialization.
8. There is a sharp boundary between bureaucratic action and particularistic action by personnel, defining the limits of legitimacy.
9. The functional separation of tasks means that personnel must have authority and sanction available to them commensurate with their duties. Thus, organizations exhibit an authority structure.
10. Because tasks are functionally separated and because personnel charged with each function have precisely delegated powers, there is a tendency towards hierarchy.
11. The delegation of powers is expressed in terms of duties, rights, obligations and responsibilities. Thus, organizational relationships tend to have a precise contract basis.

12. Qualities required for organization positions are increasingly measured in terms of formal credentials.
13. Because different positions in the hierarchy of offices require different credentials for admission, there is a career structure in which promotion is possible either by seniority or by merit of service by individuals with similar credentials.
14. Different positions in the hierarchy are differentially paid and otherwise stratified.
15. Communication, coordination and control are centralized in the organization.

Modern bureaucratic organizations were made possible by society-wide processes of rationalization:

1. A legal system based on rules rather than personal influence.
2. An economy based on monetary exchanges.
3. A formally free labour market in which people were not bought and sold but hired for their labour time.
4. The appropriation and concentration of the physical means of production as disposable private property.
5. The representation of share rights in organizations and property ownership.
6. The 'rationalization' of various institutional areas, such as the market, technology and education.

The outcome of the process of rationalization, Weber suggests, is the production of a new type of person: the specialist or technical expert. Such experts master reality by means of increasingly precise and abstract concepts whereby all forms of magical, mystical, traditional explanation are stripped away from the world (Clegg, 1995). Meyer and Bromley (2013) see contemporary rationalization as transmitted through legal, accounting and professionalization principles, driving the creation of new organizations and the elaboration of existing ones.

CRITIQUES OF BUREAUCRACY

Many arguments have been advanced against bureaucracy. We enumerate a few before delving into more substantial discussion of later principles of management that stress the importance of informal social relations as well as formal design principles:

READ A CRITIQUE OF BUREAUCRACY

READ ABOUT OVER-BUREAUCRACY

1. In contemporary times, governments promise to reduce bureaucracy (but rarely do); consultants claim to be able to change bureaucracy (but rarely do), while ordinary citizens rail against bureaucracy and its entrapment.
2. Some of Weber's contemporaries thought market principles were much better at organizing human affairs than bureaucracies. An Austrian

economist, Ludwig Von Mises, a near contemporary of Weber, was an initial source of these views.

3. In the twentieth century, critiques of bureaucratic principles flourished. These relied on anecdote and stereotypes rather than research, including Parkinson's Law, named after historian C. Northcote Parkinson (1957), which states that work creates more work, usually to the point of filling the time available for its completion. More bureaucracy demands more bureaucrats to service the new rules and routines as well as bigger budgets.
4. The Peter Principle, named after Laurence Peter, states that employees in a bureaucracy are promoted to the level of their incompetence. In other words, competent managers continually receive promotions until they attain a position in which they are incompetent.
5. Merton (1940: 563) discusses the 'formalism, even ritualism, which ensues with an unchallenged insistence upon punctilious adherence to formalised procedures'. Merton called the primary bureaucratic dysfunction 'goal displacement', by which he meant that the members of organizations – officials – inevitably come to value rules and the behaviour required by those rules over the objectives that the rules were intended to achieve.
6. Bureaucracy begets oligarchy. Early in the century, Robert Michels (1915: 365) coined what he referred to as the 'iron law of oligarchy' as a corollary of bureaucratic organization. Oligarchy was inevitable even in representative organizations such as unions because those with superior education and expertise, dedicated to the politics of the organization, became the oligarchs, in favour of the lay members.
7. Bureaucracy inhibits enterprise. Since the late 1970s, the principles of bureaucracy have had a bad rap just about everywhere, steered politically by Thatcherism in the UK and increasing academic attacks globally, especially in the USA, led by Peters and Waterman (1982) on the private sector and Osborne and Gaebler (1992) on the public sector. The essence of the criticisms is that bureaucracy creates rule followers rather than innovators, a criticism trenchantly made by Merton (2002).

Bauman (1989), in a discussion of the Holocaust (a discussion that is extended to total institutions (Goffman, 1961) more generally, in a book by Clegg et al., 2006), made a major criticism of bureaucracy. For Bauman (1989), the apex of modernity was reached in the death camps that delivered the Holocaust, where the strengths of normal organization in delivering the efficient mass production of extinction was exemplified. Critics of his thesis, notably du Gay, have sought to preserve the notion of Weberian bureaucracy, arguing that what occurred in the camps was organization's corruption by fascism rather than an example of bureaucracy's ethos. Perhaps, but the factory efficiency of the camps as an organizational system for extermination and extraction of value was undoubtedly bureaucratic. It was, of course, not rationally legally bureaucratic; it would be better thought of as a case where decisions were made according to an absolute value or belief (*Wertrationalität*, in Weber's terms) in the absolute values of National Socialism, fealty to the Führer and the concomitant cleansing of the social order of those whom these absolute values deemed as polluting.

The death camps were undoubtedly a bureaucratic system, albeit one absent of the ethos of a vocation that Weber (1978) was at pains to point out was the hallmark of a liberal state-building character. In Bauman's terms, the death camps recorded actions in detail and in data, in rule-following, in timetables and targets, that were organized by hierarchy, rank and career in the *Schutzstaffel* (SS), which Heinrich Himmler forged into an organizational instrument of the Fascist will for the imposition of security, surveillance and terror within Germany and German-occupied Europe. A bureaucracy undoubtedly organized the Holocaust, albeit one that did not accord with a normative idealization of a Weberian bureaucracy, one that was not a rational-legal bureaucracy characterized by a professional ethic oriented to rule irrespective of persons. In fact, it was rule specifically oriented to categories of persons: Jews, Gypsies, Homosexuals, the Disabled, the Mentally Ill, and so on. In this respect, du Gay's critique of Bauman is correct, up to a point: the death camps were not a legal-rational bureaucracy that treated all cases the same according to the rules, yet to say that they were not bureaucratic is not correct.

The pertinent points of Bauman's critique of bureaucracy are the following:

1. Bureaucracy as a legitimate means can serve illegitimate ends because it is undemocratic and obedience to the rules and authority relations may enable ethically appalling behaviour to go unchecked. The Nazi war criminal Adolf Eichmann, who was one of Hitler's deputies, was the Head of the Department for Jewish Affairs. When Israeli agents finally captured Eichmann in 1960 and he was subsequently tried for crimes against humanity, Eichmann's defence when tried was that he was just a bureaucrat who had to obey because he was just following orders. Hannah Arendt (1994) wrote an account of his trial, which she captured in the memorable phrase 'the banality of evil'.

2. Bureaucratically imposed categories are not 'natural' categories but are produced by a vast organizational apparatus to appear naturalized. A fundamental organizational condition of the Holocaust was the identification of individuals as members of specific categories, and the marking of their membership categorization with devices: in the case of Jews, the Yellow Star that all those who were defined as Jews were obliged to wear.

3. Bureaucracy supports unreflexive routines. The death camps were highly routinized. Routines eliminate the need or the space for reflection. When actions that enact the organizational action in question are routinized, the acts in question become easier to enact: routine is important because it facilitates action without reflection (and responsibility), as an automatic response to a stimulus. Individuals become merely a cog in the big machinery that turns them around.

4. Bureaucracy is premised on acceptance of means without regard for the ends served. In the Holocaust, the end product was death, with many units per day marked carefully on the manager's production charts.

While engineers designed the crematoria, managers designed the system of bureaucracy that worked with a zest and efficiency more backward nations would envy.

PRAISING BUREACRACY

Against these criticisms, du Gay and colleagues have advanced arguments supporting the achievement of rational-legal principles as the basis for a just, ethical and efficient form of organization, in a related series of publications (du Gay et al, 2018; du Gay and Lopdrup-Hjorth, 2016a; du Gay, P. and Lopdrup-Hjorth, 2016b; Lopdrup-Hjorth, 2015). For these writers the attack on bureaucracy's alleged ills has been too much; the preference for informal and spontaneous modes of organizing characterized by recent political administrations, such as Tony Blair's for holding informal meetings with no notes being taken and Donald Trump's reluctance to read formal briefing notes and seek informal, often family advice, are indicative of a broader denigration of formal organization and its virtues of rationality, written records and responsible decision-making that can be transparently accounted.

The intellectual source of these recalibrations of the worth of bureaucracy lie in an important book, du Gay's (2000) *In Praise of Bureaucracy*, which defends Weber's (1978) principles of bureaucracy against their many critics. The following points, drawn in part from this work, are often advanced in praise of bureaucracy:

1. Bureaucratic organizations provide satisfaction for those working within them because you know exactly what to do and what you will have to do to get to where you want to be in the organization.
2. They are fairly predictable and they offer opportunities for careers for individual members to specialize in and develop skills in what they most enjoy.
3. They limit arbitrary power and privilege. You must follow the rules but so must everyone else.
4. If you are a client or a customer of a bureaucracy, to the extent that the bureaucracy treats you as merely a case, you can expect to be treated according to precedents established by rules, rather than the whim of an officer. Your status and identity should not matter.
5. You have a right of appeal in a bureaucracy. If the application of rules to cases were to be deemed illegitimate, then you would have rational recourse to an appeal mechanism.
6. None are above the law, none can escape rules and every office is accountable. In short, bureaucracy is a bulwark of civil liberty.
7. Bureaucracy frees people from arbitrary rule by powerful patrimonial leaders – those who personally own the instruments and offices of rule.

While du Gay praises what is essentially a Weberian model of bureaucracy, other researchers, in other contexts, welcome its mutation into hybrid forms

REDEFINING BUREAUCRACY

ELTON MAYO'S PRINCIPLES OF BUREAUCRACY

The emphasis on the formal organization has been contested in management theory, initially by Mayo, who developed what became known as Human Relations principles. The emphasis was on informal work group relations, the importance of these for sustaining the formal system and the necessity of the formal system meshing with the informal system.

As a young man in Australia just after the First World War, Mayo had helped to develop therapeutic treatments for patients with shell shock and other 'nervous' conditions. From the treatment of maladjustment on the part of veterans, it was a small step to the treatment of industrial malaises: 'Industrial unrest is not caused by mere dissatisfaction with wages and working conditions but by the fact that a conscious dissatisfaction serves to "light up" as it were the hidden fires of mental uncontrol' (Mayo, 1922: 64, cited in Bourke, 1982: 226). Treating conflict at work meant treating industrial neuroses. Most people's actions were driven by the unconscious, he thought, following Freud (1935), and this was as true of people at work as at war. Agitators and radicals were victims of neurotic fantasies that could be traced, invariably, to infantile history. If individuals could be guided by therapy in work, they would be healed of their neuroses. When he arrived in the USA, he brought these ideas with him as a highly successful public speaker on the lecture circuit. He eventually found a congenial home at Harvard, where he was invited in 1926.

At Harvard, Mayo became associated with what are known as the Hawthorne Studies. These studies have become a classic of modern management and were named thus because they were carried out in the Hawthorne Plant of the Western Electric organization in the suburbs of Chicago between 1924 and 1927. After the data had been collected and the experiments ended, Mayo joined the project in April 1928 (Henderson, with Mayo, 2002 [1936]). In a range of experiments concerning the physical determinants of productivity, illumination and other physical variables were manipulated, with the surprising result that productivity kept rising even when unexpected – when the illumination was lowered rather than increased. Why was this so?

Mayo answered the question in terms of what became known as the Hawthorne Effect: when a group realizes that it is valued and forms social relations among its members, productivity rises as a result of the group formation. The Hawthorne Effect is what happens when informal organization formation occurs. It was this finding for which the study became famous. In this instance, it was presumed that the effect was an unanticipated consequence of the experimental interest taken in workers. Such formation will often be an unanticipated consequence of academic interest in people in organizational settings: research may have unanticipated effects. The Hawthorne experiments have been widely criticized (see Carey, 2002 [1967]; Hassard, 2012; Muldoon, 2017; O'Connor, 2002; Warner and Busse, 2017).

Mayo's eight principles of management were as follows:

1. Work should be seen as a group rather than an individual activity.
2. Work is a central life interest for most people.

3. The lack of attention to human relationships was a major flaw in most other management theories.
4. In work, people find a sense of belonging to a social group and seek a need for recognition, satisfaction of which is vital for their productivity.
5. When workers complain, it may be a manifestation of some more fundamental and psychologically located issue.
6. Informal social groups at work have a profound influence on the worker's disposition and wellbeing.
7. Management can foster collaboration within informal groups to create greater cohesion and unity at work, with positive organizational benefits.
8. The workplace should be viewed as a social system made up of interdependent parts.

In the informal system, special attention was to be paid to the satisfaction of individual human needs, focusing on what motivates different people, in order to try to maximize their motivation and satisfaction. Mayo (1946) thought the manager had to be a social clinician, fostering the social skills of those with whom the manager worked. Therapeutic interviews were recommended as a management tool and training in counselling and personnel interviews was seen as an essential management skill (Trahair, 2001).

Mayo believed that people had to be shown how to collaborate in the new complex organizations and that management's task, par excellence, was to aid this. Managers were to be the new conciliators and arbitrators of an accord with rational workers based on the rationality of science (Hogan, 1978; Weiss, 1981). Many of Mayo's (2007) ideas addressed the failure of modern management to consider collaboration as integral to modern enterprise. Mayo came to the conclusion that the real problem encountered in work was the lack of 'well-knit human groups'. Too little attention was being paid to social relations at work, especially those that enable people to get on well and cooperate with others. More training in social skills was required. Just as individual members should have a cooperative attitude, the organization should have an effective system of communications to foster social skills (see also Chapter 9). Organizations should organize teams and use personnel interviews to aid members, as Mayo (1985 [1951]) suggested, to minimize useless emotional complications, encourage association between all ranks, and develop positive work attitudes in employees. Mayo's star faded fairly fast (Clegg, 1979; Clegg and Dunkerley, 1980), although it remains undoubtedly important for contemporary human resource management.

CHESTER BARNARD'S PRINCIPLES OF LEADERSHIP

The prosperous 1920s had seen modern corporate bureaucracies become legitimate. In the depression of the 1930s, however, their legitimacy came into question. The Depression of the 1930s saw many millions of people unemployed, reduced to welfare and soup kitchens. If managers were such great leaders, how come American firms were in such a mess? How could organizations be efficient and legitimate, when they also caused so much unemployment and turmoil? What good were principles of management that could not provide prosperity?

For Chester Barnard, the key issue was leadership, of which he had considerable experience – he had been the president of New Jersey Bell Telephone and the Rockefeller Foundation. Barnard thought that those lucky enough still to have jobs should buckle down to the leadership of managers schooled in the principles of leadership, for it was only these that precluded the misery of unemployment.

Barnard wrote a book on leadership that had a major impact, *The Functions of the Executive* (1936). Leadership is required, said Barnard, to ensure both managerial authority and employee obedience. Leaders should make followers' service to authority apparent by creating moral codes for subordinates to live by and strong moral values.

Barnard's five principles of management are as follows:

1. Individual behaviour is always variable and can never be easily predicted.
2. All individuals will have a 'zone of indifference' within which compliance with orders will be perceived in neutral terms without any questioning of authority. Managers should seek to extend the borders of this zone through material incentives but more especially through providing others with status, prestige and personal power.
3. Communications, especially in informal organization, are absolutely central to decision-making. Everyone should know what the channels of communication are and should have access to formal channels. Lines of communication should be as short and direct as possible.
4. Management's responsibility is to harness informal groupings and get them working for the organization, not against it.
5. Authority only exists insofar as the people are willing to accept it.

From the vantage point of his experience, Barnard saw the manager's key task as ensuring that organizational systems motivate employees towards organization goals – because where individuals work with common *values* rather than common *orders*, they would work much more effectively, he thought. The real role of the manager, he wrote, is to manage the values of the organization, which should be set by the chief executive (see also Chapter 8).

MARY PARKER FOLLETT'S PRINCIPLES OF SOCIAL JUSTICE

Not all of the original thinkers contributing to the foundations of management were men. After graduating from the Women's College at Harvard, Mary Parker Follett became involved in social work in a diverse Boston neighbourhood. What she learned in making community centres work for people lacking in the obvious resources of a wealthier society was that, with experience in 'modes of living and acting which shall teach us how to grow the social consciousness' (Follett, 1918: 363; 1924), many people were far more capable than they or others might have imagined.

Follett was the first woman to have had a book on management published, albeit after her death, called *Dynamic Administration* (1941). In this book, she argued that organizations, much as communities, could be approached as local social systems involving networks of groups. Not for her the image of the all-knowing scientific engineer in control. She believed in the full collaboration of employees and managers, and she sought their willingness to make these values compatible. Follett suggested that Taylor's ideas were incomplete. In particular, they had not been thought through for their democratic potential; Taylor's lone individuals, in a massive functional structure, under strict control, did not accord with American ideas of democracy. Something had to change in management thinking if this were to be the case. Mary Parker Follett signalled the changes. Follett was concerned to democratize power, distinguishing between power-with (coactive power) and power-over (coercive power). She argued that it is the former that needs developing and the latter that needs diminishing. She saw power as legitimate and inevitable, but it need not be authoritarian. Organizations must be developed democratically as places where people learn to be cooperative in power with others, especially managers and workers (see also pp. 267-272). Her principles of democracy stressed the experience of being participative as empowering and educative. Democratic diversity had great advantages, she said, over more authoritarian homogeneity. We should welcome difference because it feeds and enriches society, whereas differences that are ignored feed *on* society and eventually corrupt it (Follett, 1918). More modest than her male colleagues, she formulated her ideas in only three principles.

Follett's three principles of management are as follows:

1. Functions are specific task areas within organizations, which should be allocated the appropriate degree of authority and responsibility necessary for task accomplishment.
2. Responsibility is expressed in terms of an empirical duty: people should manage their responsibility on the basis of evidence and should integrate this effectively with the functions of others.
3. Authority flows from an entitlement to exercise power, which is based on legitimate authority.

Follett was a unique management academic, a woman in a world of men, and a committed democrat in a world of macho managers. Notions of legitimate authority and civic responsibility were important to her thinking. Until her revival with the publication of Graham's (1995) edited volume *Mary Parker Follett: Prophet of Management – A Celebration of Writings from the 1920s*, she was largely ignored. Follett's unique contribution and relevance to current issues are now more widely recognized and her work continues to excite contemporary interest (Boje and Rosile, 2001; Calás and Smircich, 1996; Fox, 1968; O'Connor, 1999, 2002).

The search for principles of management has produced a vast variety of organizational models to describe organizational performance. The processes through which these models are applied identify opportunities for improvement within organizations. Organizations apply management principles to areas such as quality, knowledge management, fair trade, corporate social responsibility, organizational excellence, and value chains. Today, most of these principles are represented in management models that are internally developed, by either organizations or consultancies that sell models that they have devised.

Management models are a major source of organizational change: they prescribe both changes and change as a result of their use, as they run up against the different sense that members, suppliers, customers and other stakeholders make of them (see Guillen, 1994). Hence, there is a lot of churning in management models as consultancy companies need a constant stream of new products, and organizations discover new sensemaking gaps with the use of existing models.

What is seemingly new, however, may not be as novel as it is often represented. The rise of so-called 'contemporary' models, such as ISO 9000 and its subsequent variants and the Balanced Scorecard (Kaplan and Norton, 1992) among others, represent prescriptive principles based on old ideas of task division and task allocation espoused by early bureaucratic models of management. As such, while the prescriptive demands of contemporary models may lead to different outcomes, whether they are statistical process control or other measures of performance, the managerial governance mechanisms that underpin them do not deviate from early perspectives.

Genuinely new approaches are beginning to emerge that run counter to bureaucratic principles driven by the proliferation of advanced information technology (IT) and digitalization, which endow managers and organizations with alternative governance mechanisms and IT-enabled affordances that are not bound to space or time (e.g. Yoo et al., 2012; Zammuto et al., 2007). Models such as open-source software (OSS) development, Wikipedia, Uber and other forms of online crowdsourcing or communities represent decentralized management models that are characterized by principles of fluidity, asynchronicity and self-selection by members to contribute or problem-solve. As such, IT engenders a high degree of managerial dynamism as we are just beginning to scratch the surface of the possibilities that technology offers.

WATCH A TED TALK

In practice, many managers still seem to search for the one best way to manage, almost as a 'holy grail'. They seek to 'benchmark' and yearn for 'best practice'. Theoretically, almost all management and organization scholars would tell them that, in doing so, they are likely to entrap themselves in an organizational straightjacket. There have been many organizational straitjackets in the history of management. In the very early days of management, under the tutelage of F. W. Taylor, the desire was to normalize and depersonalize work roles and employees, producing good routines out of a jumble of craft work traditions, different ethnic and linguistic identities, and early mechanization and measurement techniques. In this way, it could be claimed that there was a 'scientific' foundation for management, one that consisted of replacing the worker's knowledge of work with that of the scientific manager, rationalizing the superiority of management science over worker knowledge. These early organizations were founded on bureaucracies but this did not necessarily mean that there was a strict demarcation between work role and the worker's private life – the early days of Fordism saw attempts to produce rational homemaking, budgeting and living, as well as working.

HYBRID ORGANIZATIONS

Weber's model of bureaucracy was an ideal type – an artificially accentuated model that abstracted features of actually existing bureaucracies to make a 'pure' model that condensed the features one would find in reality. In reality, the forms that bureaucracy might take would be hybrid, blending some elements from the general model, and integrating and innovating other elements. Under communism, for instance, state socialist organizations in the USSR grew into massive industrial bureaucracies with a shadow bureaucracy of political control internalized within them to maintain the 'party line' of communism. In China, communism and bureaucracy hybridized in a different and distinct way, powering the global powerhouse that is the contemporary People's Republic of China.

IN PRACTICE

Bureaucratic hybrids: contemporary China

Ang (2017) has researched local government public administration in China and argues that it has developed a viable non-Weberian model of local government bureaucracy appropriate to a developing country context. These local government public administrations contradict a key principle of Weber's model of public administration. Public sector organizations do not have ownership rights over the income they generate; instead, any revenue should go into consolidated accounts. In China, however, it is openly acknowledged that public agencies act as if they were entrepreneurial companies. They make profits and distribute them according to their own criteria. Given this data, Ang (2017: 283) asks whether we should 'conclude that China's bureaucracy is corrupt or dysfunctional'.

If we were to apply the principles of bureaucracy that Weber outlines to the Chinese case, we would conclude that such a model of organization was indeed corrupt and certainly not functional in the sense of ensuring a public administration in which the public servant has an ethos of public service rather than the entrepreneurial pursuit of profit and exhibits a character moulded accordingly. Ang differs from the conventional view. She regards the degree of self-financing and the cultivation of personal relationships in pursuit of such financing that is evident in China not as a deviation from the Weberian model but as evidence that there are alternative ways of organizing public administration, according to context. In the context of resource scarcity in developing countries, she regards the self-financing of local government bureaucracy through extracting fees for services provided, rather than the services being available to all, to the extent that state budgets allow, as 'a high-powered incentive scheme, wherein public agents are highly motivated to finance themselves' (Ang, 2017: 283). In this context, she regards the Chinese model of personalized and revenue-generating bureaucracy to be 'a regulated and relatively disciplined mutation' of organization.

On the other hand, as Skidmore (2017) analyses, corruption is endemic to China's governing institutions (Wedeman, 2012). Not only is it well documented (Pei, 2016) as the systematic looting of state-owned property of land, natural resources and state-run enterprise assets, for which bribes and official appointments are surreptitiously but routinely traded but also Pei (2016) terms it a 'system of crony capitalism', one that is politically acknowledged by President Xi's campaign against limiting the costs of corruption. In Skidmore's view:

> Corruption fuels job promotions, the awarding of government contracts and the transfer of public assets into private hands at fire sale prices. Corruption in China is rooted

(Continued)

(Continued)

> in the blurred lines that come with a system combining weak rule of law, considerable autonomy on the part of local officials and an economic model featuring opaque relations between private enterprise and a large state-owned sector.

Ang's (2017) contrary case to Skidmore (2107), Wedeman (2012) and Pei (2016) is that what she refers to as bureau franchising occurs at the agency rather than the individual level. In China, Ang (2017: 295) states:

> [A]ctivities were carried out at the agency, rather than individual level; these activities became progressively sanctioned and regulated, rather than lawless; and local governments activate [these] high powered but risky incentives ... in order to motivate revenue-generation among state agencies, rather than ignore budgetary constraints.

The extent to which the principles of bureau franchising that Ang discusses can be kept separate from those of guanxi - the cultivation of personalized social networks for influence - and the extent to which these can easily become conduits for corruption, are a moot point.

Questions

1. In practice, what is the balance in China's bureaucracy between being corrupt and being dysfunctional?
2. Is the Weberian model the best set of principles for public administration everywhere?

Use the resources cited and any others that you can access through a web search and draw your own conclusions.

The **labour process** refers to the social relations that people enter into when they are employed.

Marx's theory of **exploitation** assumes that if labour is the source of value, profits (surplus value) must arise from labour's efforts.

Exploiting labour and retaining the surplus value produced over and above that which the labour receives in exchange defines surplus value.

CRITICAL PERSPECTIVES ON PRINCIPLES OF MANAGEMENT

PRINCIPLES OF EXPLOITATION

As a result of the joint spread of modern capitalism and modern management around the globe, common principles of the **labour process** became widely institutionalized. These were themes that had been developed in ideas about organizations that regarded Karl Marx's principles of economic **exploitation** as a point of departure. Exploitation, explains Marx, produces **surplus value**.

Marx argued that forms of capitalist organization based on exploitation produce a series of estrangements in work. Initially, there was a sense of estrangement of the worker from that which they produce. They neither design the product nor how it is produced or marketed. Estrangement from the fruits of labour occurs: no one worker creates an actual product in its totality. In seeing this as an initial estrangement, Marx was clearly contrasting capitalist relations of production with those of an idealized craftsperson. Lacking capital, out of necessity workers sell their labour in a market. They surrender a degree of self-control of the creativity that their minds, bodies and time can produce to employers who combine the powers surrendered with the means of production they own and control. A second aspect of alienation unfolds in consequence: lacking control of the use of their labour power and time, how it is deployed is hierarchically imposed through imperative commands wrapped up in the authority of control. Third, there is estrangement from others in the process of production, as labour becomes so specialized that employees can hardly relate to others as comrades but often see them as competitors in the labour market for the rewards of being employed. As such, people lose sight of their essential humanity and its capacity for fulfilment in the many creative spheres of life as they cling to their jobs, subordinate their selves to the demands of these and forgo the pleasures of life to moments of consumption that their wages service. These factors lead to an estrangement not only of the self but also of the many who experience the same sense of emotional estrangement. At this point, Marx argued, individual workers would become aware of their collective estrangement and their individual consciousness would form into a collective consciousness experienced as **alienation**. Modern management principles are regarded by labour process writers as the major means for the intensification of exploitation in search of profit.

Alienation means the experience of being isolated from a group or an activity to which one should belong or in which one should be involved.

In his early work, Marx (1844) expected that capitalism would increase levels of alienation generally and that, as collective consciousness increased, workers would increasingly resist their exploitation, leading to the emergence of a collective consciousness of their common situation of exploitation. Such an outcome has not occurred, it is argued, largely because of humanizing reforms to work organization, the development of social insurance and welfare, and the rise of a consumer culture and its media that have produced a largely instrumental attitude towards work and its discontents that can be assuaged by the inducements of consumption and pleasure bought by the yield of selling labour time and power.

EXTEND YOUR KNOWLEDGE

Exploitation

Exploitation is what happened in the bad old days of rampant capitalism, right? Wrong! Many millions of employees in advanced economies and societies and many millions more in less advanced ones are still subject to conditions of exploitation that would not be out of place in the nineteenth century. In Marquita Walker's (2016) article, 'Organizing diverse low-wage service workers', *Sage Open*, https://doi.org/10.1177%2F2158244016661749, which is available at the companion website https://study.sagepub.com/managingandorganizations5e, you can extend your knowledge by discovering more about contemporary practices of exploitation of the most vulnerable workers. The article deals with the strategic campaign of two unions organizing low-waged employees in the USA who struggled to improve the employment conditions of their members.

Later, Marx (1976) relied less on the development of a collective consciousness in his arguments about the future of capitalism and more on the tendencies of capitalism to concentration, leading to increasingly oligopolistic organizations, premised on increasing indebtedness to financial institutions that would leverage ever more forms of debt. As the fixed capital requirements of production increased as a result of advancements in production generally, the rate of profit would tend to fall, leading to inevitable crises of capitalism whose resolution would necessitate the emergence of an entirely new mode of production.

According to Marx's (1976) arguments in *Capital*, employees must receive less value in wages than they created in profits, otherwise no profits would accrue. *Capital* argues that wages are the fruits of an unequal exchange: when labourers exchange their labour for a wage, the capitalist must gain more from the exchange than the workers – a surplus value – otherwise no profit could be produced from the labour hired.

Harry Braverman (1974), in his book on the labour process, saw the role of managers as central to the realization of surplus value. In Braverman's view, managers anywhere in the world should be seen in terms of the structural role that they play as delegates of those who own capital. To ensure the efficient extraction of surplus value, they seek to increase productivity by **de-skilling** jobs to make them more controllable by managers.

De-skilling removes judgement and discretion from employees, reducing control of the work they do by separating the conception of work from its execution.

The results of de-skilling are several:

1. Increasingly routine and fragmented tasks, where individual employees lack understanding of the principles underlying their relation with others.
2. Routinization produces increasingly alienated workers.
3. The introduction of newer, simpler technologies strengthens management control over the labour process.
4. The result of de-skilling would be a downward pressure on wages and conditions of work, both within nation-states and globally.
5. Designing junk jobs makes it easier to substitute robotic machines for human labour, which are both cheaper in the long run and easier to manage.

Labour markets are complex rather than simply being subject to universal de-skilling. Not all workers compete in a single labour market, because there were many labour markets, often exhibiting characteristics of 'dual labour market segmentation' (Taubman and Wachter, 1986). Characteristically, dual labour markets divide between those segments that have some degree of career prospects, are full-time and better paid, and enjoy better conditions, and those segments composed of less skilled jobs, often casual and part-time, with worse pay, prospects and conditions. Often, labour market dualism has a gender and ethnic dimension to it; that is, the pool of employees divided into those who had secure, better paid, full-time work, largely men, whereas those who were in part-time, less secure and lower paid work were disproportionately women, often from minority backgrounds.

Braverman overlooked the role of employee resistance to the de-skilling of their jobs. Many studies of resistance developed in the wake of Braverman's work, stressing his one-sided emphasis on managerial principles without emphasizing the ingenuity and agency of those subjected to them (Spencer, 2000). Managerial control is not all of a piece. Different controls target different types of employee. Divisions make the task of control much easier because they concentrate employees' minds on the fact that they slotted into a huge hierarchy of labour, with the long-term unemployed at the bottom, and everyone competing for the minor qualitative differences available with shifting from one segment to the next – what Braverman called divide and rule prevailed. Hence, as Clegg (1981) argues, different types of control, using different principles, would be targeted at different categories of employees.

De-skilling is not undifferentiated and universal. Friedman (1977) argued that some employees, such as highly skilled and creative types, whose discretion management needs in work, mean that not all jobs could or would be de-skilled to the furthest point. Instead, some jobs would be designed to include elements of 'responsible autonomy' (also see Friedman, 1990).

Control is not just personal – the work of managers – but can be built into technology. Edwards (1979) extended Braverman's analysis by highlighting that management controlled employees through machinery and technological innovations, such as assembly lines, as well as through 'bureaucratic control'. Moreover, the role of exploitation of surplus value is overstressed in Braverman. In many contemporary organizations, labour is a small element in the overall cost structure. The scene has changed greatly since Marx's day when factories were small and labour-intensive. Patents, monopoly and innovation are all sources of profit (Pisano, 2006).

In addition, the stress on the capitalist labour process needs to be broadened to include analysis of non-capitalist organizations. A great deal of learning is translated from the private to the public sector and to the non-profit sector, and some may flow back the other way. Restricting analysis to business for profit organizations is unduly limiting when the same tendencies can be seen in the public sector (Clarke and Newman, 1997; Jones, 1999).

MARX FOR MODERN TIMES

Marx's writings are often condemned to the garbage bin of history; however, Marx's ideas have been a powerful influence on contemporary ideas of social democracy. In the wake of the financial crisis of 2008, they have been revived. For instance, Taylor (2016) suggests that the economic challenges of the 2010s cannot be solved by the 1980s' political consensus that saw economic growth being achieved by market deregulation and lower taxes and lower spending. Piketty (2014) argues that rising inequality harms growth, that social expenditures can be a revenue-boosting exercise and that governments need to intervene more not less. Even the IMF says income distribution matters for growth, linking concentration of income shares at the top of income distribution (the top 20 per cent) with GDP decline, while increases in the income share of the bottom 20 per cent are associated with higher GDP growth.

Manufacturing's share of the labour force has declined across advanced economies due to relatively strong productivity growth in countries such as China. As consumers, people in advanced economies have benefitted from cheaper goods and devices; as workers, evidence shows that where they have maintained employment they have had to accept significantly lower wages (Autor et al., 2016). Meanwhile, corporate elites have become even wealthier as they are enriched by tax cuts.

In *Class, Politics and the Economy* (Clegg et al., 1986 [2013]), an alternative basis for policy formation was proposed, based on the Swedish social democrats' active labour market policy (Esping Andersen, 1990), the Rehn–Meidner model. The elements of the model are premised on post-Keynesian economics, real wage growth, active labour market policies and state intervention to create a positive spiral as part of the business cycle. Industries should not be destroyed as in the past without any consideration for the futures of those sustained by them. Active labour market policies must focus on the many not formally educated past school, on apprenticeships, on technical education and up-skilling.

At the heart of the policy proposals is the creation of an expansive welfare state and public investment. Such measures are designed to maintain domestic demand over economic cycles, ensuring security, safety and stability to labour, capital, business and consumers. In addition, they aid low inflation by helping to prevent wage–price spirals by linking real wages with productivity growth. The government's role is to minimize inflation and maintain the social wage that, at its broadest, includes increased spending on education as well as welfare.

Today, we might add Bregman's (2016) demand for a universal basic income as a key element of such a policy. In the spirit of a solidarity wages policy, as real wages and effective demand rise, so would profits which, to the extent that they were re-invested in improving the productive capacity of corporations, should be favourably taxed where they are incentives that favour long-term investments in research and development, rather than capital gains and dividends. In the longer term, other elements of the model could be enacted, such as requiring all companies above a certain size to issue new stock shares to workers in order to redistribute the wealth created by the company, with these stock dividends to be reinvested in stock of the same company or used for employee training.

As Obstfeld (2016: 15) suggests:

> Policies that help people adjust include educational investments to create a nimble workforce, expenditure on needed infrastructure, investment in health, improved availability of housing, lowered barriers to entry for new businesses, and well-functioning financial markets. Such policies have the added benefit of also supporting growth.

Espousal of such programmes might seem strange for business school professors. Wouldn't programmes associated with a solidarity labour market policy and increasing labour costs automatically inspire the wrath of the managerial class, schooled in ideologies of managerial prerogative and its associated rights? Perhaps – ideologies should never be underestimated but neither should the experience of reality. It is not only blue-collar workers that lack skill formation but also those managers that employ and rely on cheaper labour in the face of innovative, automated competition because the necessary cycles of investment have been lacking. Many managers have seen their industries decline precisely because of the absence of such policies. As Hassard et al's (2012) research demonstrates, managers in the UK and the USA are extremely critical of the intensification effects of corporate downsizing and delayering. They see themselves as much as a 'forgotten people' as do their blue-collar colleagues. In many ways, they are correct to do so: as innovation occurs in the new centres and not the old, their knowledge and skills atrophy in terms of global relevancies. The spatial implications are evident: as specific regional and community skill formation atrophies, the lack of incentive to stay for those who can move increases. Hence, any alternative social and economic policies must also be regional policies.

EXTEND YOUR KNOWLEDGE

READ THE ARTICLE

In Courpasson, D. (2017) 'Beyond the hidden/public resistance divide: how bloggers defeated a big company', *Organization Studies*, 38 (9): 1277–1302, which is available at the companion website https://study.sagepub.com/managingandorganizations5e, you can extend your knowledge by discovering more about the ubiquitous phenomenon of resistance in organizations. The article deals with the interrelation and mutual reinforcement of hidden and public forms of resistance. The paper analyses the four-and-a-half-year struggle of a group of dismissed employees against their former employer in which the use of blogging was central.

In many respects, the purposes of management principles and designs have not changed that much. Despite changing terms and fashions, they are often oriented to making organizational behaviour predictable. They are normative and prescriptive models and, as Grant et al. (1994) noted, rarely have any explicit theory. Being simple, lacking explicit theory and being intellectually insubstantial, these models are widely grasped by hard-pressed managers searching for common-sense solutions to complex problems. The models have travelled the world, seeking to translate local variations into common models. None, perhaps, has been more globally successful than the McDonald's model.

MCDONALDIZATION'S PRINCIPLES

The American sociologist George Ritzer coined the term **McDonaldization**.

McDonaldization refers to the application of goal-oriented rationality to all areas of human life.

The model of McDonald's is a metaphor for a highly rationalized and 'cheap as chips' approach to business processes 'by which the principles of the fast food restaurants are coming to dominate more and more sectors of American society as well as the rest of the world' (Ritzer, 1993: 1). McDonaldization does not stop at the fast food store – it spreads to all areas of everyday life: to recreation, informal and interpersonal relationships, and even love and intimacy – think of 'speed dating' or the many dating apps that are now available. Even those places and activities that used to offer some release from a routinized world (such as dating) have now been rationalized through four major mechanisms:

1. *Efficiency* means utilizing the least output to gain the highest return. One way is to transfer the costs to the consumer. The McDonald's model dispenses with waitresses and offers only preformatted menus: it may not make for great choice or food but it creates a very efficient organization.

2. *Calculability* means cheapening the assembly costs of the standard product. It is calculably cheaper to make reality TV shows where there is no script development cost, no actors and agents' fees, just a bunch of people happy to try to grab their 15 minutes of 'fame' – or notoriety.
3. *Predictability* means that a McDonaldized service or product should be the same anywhere in the world every time using standardized procedures to produce standardized outputs. Every day at Disneyland should be just the same experience, irrespective of the 'team members' inside the suits, on the rides or serving in the cafeteria.
4. *Control* means minimizing variation in every ingredient in the organizational assembly of people and things: customers and employees, raw materials, labour processes and markets. It means substituting machine processes for people. Where people cannot be substituted, they can be drilled – just like the call centre operators and McDonald's staff – to always perform the same routines.

WATCH A VIDEO

The principles of McDonaldization have been widely criticized. McDonald's uses enormous quantities of grain to grow cereals to feed to cattle that will be killed in rationalized slaughterhouses (which were the original basis for Ford's idea of the moving production line). It packs the burgers in sugared bread that is unhealthy. It serves the burgers in containers that add to the planet's waste. It produces junk foods and junk jobs. At least it produces things: food, as well as waste, pollution and suburban ugliness. In 2004 Ritzer extended his argument to propose that non-things – or 'nothing' – increasingly dominate social, organizational and commercial life, such as credit cards. The globalization of nothing sees centrally conceived and controlled empty forms, relatively devoid of distinctive content, spread across the world. With your credit card you can consume McDonald's food just about anywhere if you want

IN PRACTICE

In practice, you probably eat fast food occasionally – or maybe more often. Next time that you do so, think about Ritzer's four characteristics of McDonaldization.

Questions

1. What are the aspects of what you can see in the fast food store that seem to meet the criteria of McDonaldization?
2. Think about other services you consume in places such as supermarkets, banks, gas stations, or at university. Can you identify some of the elements of McDonaldization?
3. What are some of the negatives and positives of these McDonaldized services?

WHAT WOULD YOU DO?

Imagine you are a manager with the potential capacity to make a difference to those whom you are charged with managing. Reflecting on the approaches highlighted in this section, what would you take inspiration from and why? Which ideas and theorists would you endorse and implement?

THE TIMES, ARE THEY A-CHANGING?

In the long generation after the Second World War, social democracy and Keynesianism secured an uneasy but productive peace between capitalism and democracy that has been disrupted by the aftermath of the global financial crisis, triggered in 2007–08. The changes that occurred over the post-war period were significant. National economies are no longer largely autonomous; large, centralized, vertically integrated bureaucracies no longer provide stable employment and organizational careers in the private sector; in the public sector, they are relatively deprived of resources in the name of efficiencies and deficit reduction, and today the vanguard organizations of capitalism are now largely digitally enhanced and born global, such as Facebook, Uber and Snapchat.

For more material industries that still make things, spatial and organizational decomposition and recomposition have resulted in a capitalism employing a global proletariat cheapened in costs beyond the wildest imaginings of old-time corporate managers. Liberal capitalism has flourished as liberal democracy has withered the old bargaining between capital and labour. Today, the labourers take what they can get and seek their solace in consumption while they still have the capacity to consume. Having concentrated capital in a small global financial elite, not surprisingly, asset bubbles multiply and burst, as happened in 2007–08.

Liberal democracy and liberal economics have failed to rekindle growth, failed to rekindle increasing shares of the pie to those most deprived of slices, and failed to generate an alternative economic model that is more sustainable in every sense of the word. Faced with this bleak prospect, Rogers (2015) nonetheless sees the possibility of an alternative egalitarian and democratic project, which he calls 'productive democracy'.

Productive democracy differs from social democracy in being resolutely local rather than centralized; hence, it would have at its core a notion of subsidiarity. Subsidiarity is important because it allows for local experiments rather than central prescription. Local experiments enable local learning and learning that is productive will spread, enabled in large part by digital networking. As Mary Parker Follet (1924/1951) argued, experience in local democracy deepens democracy per se. Local policies would deliver, within national frameworks, policies oriented to the quality of working life, training, career pathways and a living wage; sustainability in the provision of local goods and services; and local democracy in organization and ownership. There would be locally oriented public policies: public transport, safe cycleways, sports and recreational facilities and safe public space. Local institutions would be built through regional partnerships (among stakeholders such as business owners, their workers and the communities they are situated in) for branding, training and investment priorities; and through local community-based services for greening the environment, building citizenship and local resilience. Building democracy on organizational localism embeds and deepens what are otherwise sparsely spaced rituals of voting.

Rogers (2015) suggests that such initiatives should be conjoined with local welfare infrastructure – 'everything from early-pregnancy care to perinatal and visiting-nurse assistance to whatever else is needed, up to adulthood, by way of health, education, counseling or other support'. Centrally, a basic income guarantee would enable these services to be purchased as needed, on a 'user pays' principle. The user pays principle would be extended to organizations that benefit from local physical infrastructure.

Locally, the use of the 'commons', such as clean air, physical infrastructure, productive land and water supplies would be charged for and violations of approved standards should be substantially fined. Centrally, socially constructed rights bestowed by intellectual property rights, business law and central banking would be paid for through tithes on beneficiaries as 'a user fee, which would be distributed, in whole or in part, to all citizens on an equal per-capita basis. Alaska and Norway have long done this with their oil holdings, and California is now doing something similar with the money paid for carbon permits', as Rogers (2015) writes. Additionally, at the central level, where corporate profits are merely accumulated and not re-invested in productive activity, generating further social benefits such as wages and improved local facilities, they would be progressively taxed: stakeholders as well as stockholders would be recognized.

Internationally, measures would include some version of the Tobin tax (Persaud, 2017), the criminalization of tax-free havens and the elimination of tax arbitrage through apportioning tax liability according to the location of each corporation's production, employment, value added and sales (see https://itep.org/wp-content/uploads/pb11ssf.pdf), and meeting internationally agreed commitments to aid. In terms of governmentality across all levels, digital technology will be essential, enabling networked learning and adoption, coordination, monitoring and measuring of performance which can be displayed transparently in real time through apps developed for specific purposes. The sharing economy of peer-to-peer and open systems innovation, which already exists, may thus be a harbinger of things to come.

The future is always uncertain and there is no crystal ball available; all we can do is envisage scenarios. One scenario is that in a global economy, as we shall see in Chapter 15, it is entirely possible that some will thrive and prosper under conditions more of their own choosing, while others will suffer the degradations of labour and its exploitation, a division that is increasingly global internationally as well as regional within countries. Another scenario, sketched in terms of principles of local democracy, is possible. Neo-liberal economics is discredited; it in turn discredited the statist elements of social democracy; the time for revisiting local and productive democracy may well be now. If so, it has significant implications for managing and organizations as new and renewed principles of organizing are explored.

EXTEND YOUR KNOWLEDGE

It is an acknowledged aspect of present-day thinking about the future of work that many jobs that can be standardized and routinized are likely to be done by robotic machines before too long. It is assumed that artificial intelligence is best suited to this relatively low-level and non-managerial work. However, to quote a recent article:

> Machines are increasingly becoming a substitute for human skills and intelligence in a number of fields where decisions that are crucial to group performance have to be taken under stringent constraints – for example, when an army contingent has to devise battlefield tactics or when a medical team has to diagnose and treat a life-threatening condition or illness.

The above words open a fascinating article by Parry, Cohen and Bhattachaya (2016), which is available at the companion website https://study.sagepub.com/managingandorganizations5e, and with which you can extend your knowledge by learning about the 'Rise of the machines: a critical consideration of automated leadership decision making in organizations' that was recently published in *Group and Organization Management*, 41 (5): 571–94. The article considers the extent to which machine-based intelligent technology is available to support, and even substitute for, human decision-making in organizational leadership contexts.

READ THE ARTICLE

SUMMARY

In this chapter, we started with a discussion of two of the founders of modern management theory, F. W. Taylor and Henri Fayol:

- Taylor was an authoritarian, and believed that management's right to rule could be established scientifically, whereas for Fayol it seemed indubitable that the more rational and enlightened should lead – and lead wisely with care.
- The Taylor system was simply one aspect of a widespread movement of systematization, articulated by engineers, that was afoot in late nineteenth- and early twentieth-century management, initially in the USA and then, in the era following the First World War, spreading throughout Europe and elsewhere. Disguised, refined and altered, his ideas are still at work in many contemporary approaches.
- The idea and practice of bureaucracy were central to the development of modern industry and modern public sectors, with Max Weber pioneering academic interpretation of the concept of bureaucracy.
- Mayo's Human Relations School contributed significantly to the development of management and organization theory by stressing the importance of 'informal organization', the oil necessary to run smoothly the machine that Taylor designed.
- Follett argued for the power of democracy in organization.
- In contemporary times, major critical currents – centred on labour process

(Continued)

(Continued)

theory and the McDonaldization thesis – have re-engaged with the classic statements of management provided by early management theorists such as Taylor.

- McDonaldized and Taylorized jobs are most at risk from standardization by artificial intelligence and robotics, which may render much earlier debate redundant.
- Marx's ideas still resonate in social democratic circles, based on a reconfiguration of work and organizational designs on the basis of principles that digitalization might deliver.

EXERCISES

1. Having read this chapter, you should be able to say in your own words what each of the following key terms means. Test yourself or ask a colleague to test you.
    - Scale
    - Division of labour
    - Supervision
    - Direct management control
    - Panopticon
    - Scientific management
    - Labour process theory
    - McDonaldization
    - Exploitation
    - Alienation
    - Surplus value
    - De-skilling
    - Human relations
    - Bureaucracy
    - Traditional authority
    - Rational-legal authority
    - Iron law of oligarchy
    - Limited liability
    - Bureau franchising.
2. What are the central features of rational-legal bureaucracy?
3. Is bureau franchising a rational-legal form of organizing?
4. Why did the expansion of scale in organization activities occur in the latter half of the nineteenth century and what were its implications for management?
5. What was Bentham's unique contribution to management?
6. What was innovative about Taylor's scientific management?
7. What did Fayol add to scientific management?
8. According to Follett, what were the unanticipated consequences of highly rational (scientific) management practices?
9. What aspects of management and organization did Mayo highlight?
10. How did Barnard conceptualize leadership?
11. Why do management plans sometimes engender resistance when managers try to implement them?
12. What strikes you as problematic with the proposition that labour is the only source of value?

TEST YOURSELF

Review what you have learned by visiting:
https://study.sagepub.com/managingandorganizations5e or your eBook

- **Test yourself with multiple-choice questions.**
- **Revise key terms with the interactive flashcards.**

REVISE KEY TERMS

TEST YOURSELF

CASE STUDY

READ THE FULL ARTICLE

Guo Yongchang, party secretary of a rural county in China's Henan province, did not fit the stereotype of a corrupt Chinese official. Featured in the documentary *The Transition Period*, he was revealed as an overworked and genuinely dedicated leader. Every day, he toiled from dawn to dusk, courting investors, inspecting construction projects and resolving social conflicts, both big and small.

Yet the final seconds of the film reveal a twist: shortly before retiring, Guo was found guilty of taking bribes and sentenced to seven years in prison. Guo's story reflects a broader reality in China: economic development and corruption go hand in hand. Local leaders take on overwhelming responsibilities. They actively seek out growth opportunities for their locales, exercise power and, in the process, profit themselves too.

Once that's understood, it's clear that President Xi Jinping has set himself up with an impossible task: to keep the economy humming under state domination, while trying to eradicate corruption.

Xi's sweeping anti-corruption campaign has stalled economic growth not only by dampening the demand for luxury goods. That's just a tiny part of the story.

The larger problem is that the campaign has forced local officials to become highly risk averse and unwilling to attempt policy innovations on the ground. But China's speedy growth in the past few decades was precisely fuelled by the bold initiatives and discretionary actions of local leaders.

Take, for instance, the case of party secretary Cai, the top leader of Blessed County in Zhejiang province, featured in my book *How China Escaped the Poverty Trap* (Ang, 2016). Locals rave about this man's lasting legacy. In the early 2000s, Cai had the foresight and determination to construct a central business district from scratch, which later on spurred industrial clusters and a vibrant services economy. His forceful programme, however, did not go without friction. It met with fierce resistance from some and earned him foes.

Hence, a local entrepreneur remarked with admiration: 'Such reforms take courageous leaders, who dare to shoulder responsibilities for taking bold steps.' The current political climate does not tolerate a maverick like party secretary Cai. Today, it would be career suicide to take the risks and bold steps that he did a decade ago.

In other words, setting aside corrupt dealings, all policy innovations entail political risk. Any attempt to make unpopular decisions, try new policies or engage with businesses – even by genuinely honest politicians – may incur charges of corruption in the ongoing campaign.

Hence, it is no surprise that China's local officials now prefer to sit on their hands. Doing nothing is the safest strategy. Despite the central government's approval of trillions of yuan

(Continued)

(Continued)

worth of investment projects in a bid to stimulate the economy, local officials have dragged their feet on using these funds, for fear of exposing themselves to political risk.

As local officials become paralysed, China is inadvertently becoming increasingly centralized. Awesome as it may seem, Beijing is incapable of promoting growth by itself, let alone innovating.

What does this all mean? It means that if Xi is intent on having a strictly disciplined bureaucracy, with little room for deviance, then he cannot expect the bureaucracy to accomplish much.

In democratic countries, citizens typically complain and poke fun at lazy, paper-pushing bureaucrats. As James Wilson, a guru of the American bureaucracy once noted, the stereotypical bureaucrats are 'lethargic, incompetent hacks [who go] to great lengths to avoid the jobs they were hired to do'. This description is beginning to fit China's bureaucrats as well.

Crucially, in America, despite complaints and mockery of an unentrepreneurial bureaucracy, the market economy continues to buzz on its own. That's because the people who operate in markets and take risks are primarily private citizens, not bureaucrats. It is sufficient that the government delivers the minimum; it does not need to substitute for entrepreneurs.

In China, however, we see the reverse: while there is a sizeable private sector, state officials have traditionally played a lead role in the economy. Local governments were the primary agents of improvisation and adaptation to changing conditions. They envision, plan, publicize, allocate resources, raise funds, build infrastructure and personally mediate private conflicts.

In this context of big government, when bureaucratic entrepreneurship is suppressed, it has a serious impact on development and governance.

President Xi's campaign wants to have it all: state control over the economy, bureaucratic entrepreneurship and, at the same time, strict adherence to rules. But in politics as in life, nobody – even the most powerful leader – can have it all. In preparation for the next Party Congress, it's time for the Chinese leadership to ponder what the role of local governments ought to be, and, moving forward, to place realistic demands on its bureaucracy.

Question

1. Building on the discussion of bureaucracy in this chapter, how would you analyse the main problems of bureaucracy in this case and what would you recommend as an antidote in policy terms?

Source: The case was originally published in the article 'With its corruption crackdown, China is also stamping out innovation', in *The Conversation*, 8 November 2016, and is used under the terms of the Creative Commons Attribution No Derivatives licence.

ADDITIONAL RESOURCES

- *I, Daniel Blake*, directed by Ken Loach (2016), is a wonderful film about the dysfunctions of bureaucracy, a Kafkaesque tale of one man navigating Britain's welfare system. Daniel Blake is a carpenter living in Newcastle, England, who, having recently suffered a heart attack, is under doctor's orders not to exert himself as he recovers. A welfare bureaucracy evaluation deems him fit for work, however, and thus ineligible for disability benefits, a bureaucratic decision that slowly begins to eat away at his life. It concludes with a stirring voice for freedom and dignity against bureaucracy.

- Organization design has mostly not been oriented to the people working within the organizations in question. Magalhães (2018) reverses this formula in advocating human-centred organization design.
- The emergence of new organization designs based on self-managed teams is highly contemporary, as Annosi and colleagues (2018) discuss.
- Continuing the theme of putting people first, Alexandersson and Kalonaityte (2018) explore how to make organizations more playful spaces through office design.
- Scandinavians sometimes talk about the Viking approach to management and organizations – which is not based on looting and pillage – quite the opposite. You can explore the Viking way in a Copenhagen Business School video.

WATCH THE VIDEO

MANAGING ORGANIZATIONAL DESIGN

DESIGNING, THEORIZING, CHANGING

LEARNING OBJECTIVES

This chapter is designed to enable you to:

- understand contingency theory and the major variables that it stresses
- link different organizational contingencies to different organizational designs
- understand the transaction costs and institutional approaches to organization analysis
- realize the strong homogenizing role that factors such as professionalization, standards, fashion, culture and embeddedness play in organization designs
- be familiar with a wide range of contemporary organization designs, including the M-form, matrix organizations, shamrock organizations, networks, rhizomes, creative clusters, heterarchy and responsible autonomy, design thinking, democratic design and digital organization.

BEFORE YOU GET STARTED...

Poor organizational design and structure results in a bewildering morass of contradictions: confusion within roles, a lack of co-ordination among functions, failure to share ideas, and slow decision-making bring managers unnecessary complexity, stress, and conflict. Often those at the top of an organization are oblivious to these problems or, worse, pass them off as challenges to overcome or opportunities to develop. (Gill Corkindale, *Harvard Business Review*, 2011)

INTRODUCTION

An organizational design is the plan of an organization's rationally designed structure and mode of operation. You will probably be familiar with organization design as a formal structure of an organization as a framework of roles and procedures, often represented in an organization chart. An organizational design creates a rational model for formal organization. What should happen, of course, may not correspond to what actually happens. In this chapter, we will review a number of different approaches that explain why a particular organization design might be adopted. As we shall see, each approach suggests a different focus for analysis. We shall begin with contingency theory.

CONTINGENCY THEORY

It is all about contingencies. In management and organization theory, a contingency is something that managers cannot avoid. Contingencies arise from routines rather than from emergencies, as facts of organizational life, and have to be acknowledged and dealt with. The contingencies of environment, technology and size have been seen as the most important issues to be managed. It is argued that these are universal issues that all organizations, with similar contingencies, anywhere in the world, will have to deal with.

TABLE 14.1 Contingency effects

Contingency	Organizational effect
Organization environment	The more certain and predictable the environments in which organizations operate, the more probable it is that they will have bureaucratic structures
Organization technology	As organizations adopt more routinized technologies - technologies with repetition and routines associated with them - they tend to become more bureaucratic
Organization size	As organizations become bigger, they become more bureaucratic, in the sense of being characterized by higher scores on scales that measure the degree of formalization, standardization and centralization

Contingency theory sees all organizations as having to deal with contingencies that will shape the organization's design as it adapts to them.

Contingency theory argues that organizations, no matter where in the world they are, will have a similar design if they are similar in size and technology. It is the organizational design that is important. Thus, what gets globalized, as these organizations spread multinationally, are organizational designs. In India, China or the USA, the organizations that you work for and the way that you do your job will be essentially similar despite cultural differences.

The contingencies literature regards organizations as imperfect designs that can be improved when we know what contingencies they have to deal with. Modern organization and management theory poses a central question: how to design a structure specifically suited to the contingencies with which an organization has to deal.

Burns and Stalker (1962) were early classic writers to identify different contingencies, as we see in Table 14.2. Their chief contribution was to distinguish types of organization structure that responded to two different sets of organization environment conditions, which they termed **mechanistic** and **organic organization** design.

Mechanistic organizations' keynote is machine-like predictability and efficiency achieved by tightly prescribing job designs that employees have little or no part in creating.

Organic organizations are flexible and innovative, facing continuous and turbulent changes in markets, customer preferences, technologies and regulations. Decision-making processes are decentralized and organization design flatter.

TABLE 14.2 Mechanistic and organic design

Mechanistic design	Organic design
High standardization	Low standardization
High formalization	Low formalization
Concentrated centralization	Decentralization
Little employee discretion	Extensive delegated discretion
Many authority levels	Few authority levels - flat organization
Large administrative component	Small administrative component
Deep specialization	Breadth rather than depth of specialization
Minimal face-to-face communication	Extensive face-to-face communication

SIZE MATTERS

It is all about size. The work of the Aston school (Pugh and Hickson, 1976) was based on an extensive literature review as well as interviews with practising managers (Hickson, 2002 [1966]; Pugh et al., 1971). On this basis they designed a questionnaire whose intent was to discover the variance between different organizations in terms of the distribution of a set of systematic variables. The variables were to be found in Weber (1978):

1. *Specialization*: the extent to which the organization has highly specialized job descriptions and designs.
2. *Standardization*: the extent to which the organization has many standard manuals of procedures involving the prescription of constant and invariant ways of doing things.
3. *Formalization*: the extent to which the organization's total range of actions and procedures are covered by formal policies and agreements.
4. *Centralization*: the extent to which the organization ensures that decision-making is referred to the apex of the organization, or distributed to lower levels.
5. *Configuration*: the shape of authority structured as a system of role relationships.

The Aston researchers then used factor analysis to search statistically for patterns of variations in the data collected. These common factors were used to refine scales that aligned them more closely with statistically robust data. The scales were seen to represent real features of the empirical world as they are defined in terms of conceptual constructs. They asked the question, what are the determinants of organization structure? The answer was that structure is determined by situational contingency.

The Aston researchers regarded bureaucracy as unavoidable. They had collected extensive data on the dimensions of organization structures for 44 organizations from the West Midlands of England. After analysis, they concluded that the variable that best explained why these organization dimensions had a certain shape or pattern of association between them was the size of the organization. Basically, the larger the organization, the more bureaucratic it seemed. And this is true all over the world, they suggested, after further comparative research. They found a lack of association between size and concentration of authority/line control of workflow.

Later, Blau (2002 [1970]) researched the number of organization levels in the hierarchy, the number of departments and the number of job titles. He found that increasing size is associated with increasing differentiation of these but that the rate of differentiation decreases with increasing size. Administrative overheads are lower in larger organizations and the span of control for supervisors is greater. Administrative overheads are inversely related to size, whereas the span of control is positively related to size. Thus, larger organizations are able to achieve economies of scale *if* they can distribute delegation of authority efficiently and effectively in the organization. If they can do so, they can handle the costs of differentiation – an increased necessity for control and coordination of the differentiated activities – without piling a weighty administrative overhead on top of the hierarchy to control the complex differentiation. Thus, the larger the organization, *given that it is able effectively to delegate authority and line control of workflow*, the less necessity there is for centralized control and administrative overheads. Size increases overhead costs but also increases the scope for economies of scale, which can be deepened further by the effective delegation of authority and control.

It is all about technology. Aldrich (2002/1971) used causal path analysis to reanalyse the Aston data. He argued that the number of people employed does not precede the technologies used. The causal path that would assume so seems nonsensical. Technologies and people evolve together and the structure adapts accordingly. Aldrich gave external dependence, where top management depends on parent organizations for key resources, a high priority. In brief, the development of an organization proceeds from its initial founding and capitalization in response to perceived market opportunities, through its design based on copying and modifying other organizations' structures, and, finally, the employment of a workforce to staff the nearly completed organization. Technology is causally prior to the size of the workforce, and organization structure is, at least initially, usually prior to size (Aldrich, 2002 [1971]: 355).

In stressing technology, Aldrich was following in the footsteps of Joan Woodward, who had studied about 80 industrial firms in the southeast of England and focused on technology to make sense of the data that she collected (Woodward, 1965). She argued that the more routinized the technology, the more the firm had a structured set of organizational authority relations. Woodward's types classified technologies into:

1. *Small batch and unit production* (where the products are largely tailored designs for different customers with small runs)

2. *Large batch and mass production* (where the production runs are much larger and the customers usually many fewer)
3. *Process production* (where the system is a continuous flow on a 24/7 basis, with the major requirement being that the system stick to specifications and standards).

Firms with similar production systems were organized in a similar manner with their degree of technical complexity related to: (a) the number of levels in the organization; (b) the span of control of front-line supervisors (how many people they supervised); and (c) the ratio of managers and administrative staff to the total workforce. Organizations using the least and the most complex technologies – unit and process production, respectively – showed a number of similarities. These organizations had a low level of specialization compared with the managers in the mass production firms. Small-batch and unit production firms employed fewer specialists because these organizations required more generalist skills for more variable production runs; also, these firms tended to be smaller than mass production organizations, so staff had to be technically more competent. In process production, staff specialists had a very high status and were sometimes difficult to distinguish from technically expert management. Both process and unit and small-batch production had relatively low levels of bureaucracy compared with mass production.

Woodward related differences in organization structure and technology to the central problems that each category of organization dealt with:

1. For unit and small-batch production, it was product development – meeting specific customer requirements for single or small batches of a specialist product. Decisions tend to be made on the line with little need for authorization from on high. For the process organizations, the central issue was marketing – they had to ensure that the continually flowing output from the production process met sufficient immediate demand.
2. In a continuous process, any change to any parameter may affect all others, so decision-making has to be pooled because of the sequential and reciprocal nature of the issues involved.
3. In a mass production technology-centred firm, the central issue was efficiency in administering standardized production. Because decisions about production have major resource and related implications that tend to be referred up to functional specialists responsible for the arena within which the decision issue falls, the structure is bureaucratic.

Woodward's point was that the type of organization shapes the time span: in flow and mass production, the **time span of discretion** would be much greater than in batch and unit production, for instance. It is not only the central organizational problem that is significant but also the time span of discretion exercised in making decisions.

Time span of discretion refers to the temporal magnitude decision-making and functions as a rationale for different levels of remuneration.

Though Joan Woodward died in 1971, her ideas remain influential (Klein, 2006). Aldrich reached the conclusion, with Woodward, that technology, rather than size, might be the crucial contingency variable (Aldrich, 2002 [1971]; Mindlin and Aldrich, 2002 [1975]) after re-analysing the Aston data using a different logic of analysis. More highly structured firms – those that seem more bureaucratic – need to employ more people, Aldrich suggests. Size is an effect rather than a cause, a dependent rather than an independent variable, and the major cause of the degree of structure, according to Aldrich's re-analysis, is the technology in use in the organization.

Later research suggested that technology does not determine organizational behaviour; in fact, it is the organizational relations of power and knowledge that are significant. This finding emerged from a study by Barley (1986) into the adoption of new scanning technology in hospitals. How the technology was used as 'an occasion for structuring' and the consequences of this depended on the local politics of knowledge in the hospital, as radiologists and technicians negotiated them. Orlikowski and Yates (1994) found that both the technologies in use and the organization structure change interactively as users engage in dialogue with designers and modify technologies in practice; again, the changes in technology and structure are a result of local politics and negotiations over managerial adaptation that slowly lead to institutionalization.

Perrow (1986) regarded technology as a way of getting work done. Interested in how to minimize the chances of catastrophic failures, he investigated a near nuclear meltdown at Three Mile Island, looking at the complexity of interactions in a system and the way units in the system were coupled. The components of a tightly coupled system have an aggressive impact on each other. A system in which two or more events can interact in unexpected ways is regarded as interactively complex. Systems that are both technologically complex *and* tightly coupled are the most difficult to control. A tightly coupled complex system with little buffering or redundancy in design built into it is an accident waiting to happen because of a paradox: a complex system requires thorough diagnosis to identify what the issues are, but one that is tightly coupled requires quick action to prevent the problem from amplifying through the system. Perrow argues that large nuclear power reactors with non-routine technologies and tight coupling will lead to '*catastrophic accidents*'. The impact of the earthquake and subsequent tsunami at Fukushima in Japan, on 11 March 2011, seems to bear this out. Tightly coupled complex systems such as nuclear plants have a high potential for catastrophe.

IN PRACTICE

Fukushima

The Tōhoku earthquake on 11 March 2011 overwhelmed the Japanese city of Fukushima in a terrible tsunami, destroying many lives and property, including the nuclear power station. Fukushima should not fade from memory, any more than should Hiroshima, Nagasaki, Windscale, Chelyabinsk, Three Mile Island or Chernobyl. While some of these names – Hiroshima and Nagasaki – signify nuclear weapons and their use, the others should be seared in our collective consciousness because they were sites of nuclear accidents, of which Fukushima is not the least. Although, as Perrow (2011) argues, the extent of the ill health and deaths that will be caused by Fukushima is being occluded by the Japanese government and various other agencies, as were all the earlier nuclear accidents and as were the effects of dropping atomic bombs on civilian populations, there is a simple organizational fact to deal with: nuclear technology is far less safe than any of the alternatives. The arguments for it that are resurgent today are that nuclear energy is carbon neutral. The arguments against it are precisely those that Perrow has constructed. Any organization design that is extremely complex, tightly coupled and inherently dangerous if subject to some exogenous environmental contingency, such as an earthquake and/or a tsunami, is unsafe. Organizational design is a social fact; it is real and it should be compelling, and where it cannot be made safe it should be avoided. Students of organization theory often wonder what the pay-off is that comes from knowing the knowledge it produces: the potential for healthy life itself, in respect of Perrow's analysis of nuclear technology. If such inherently risky technologies are in use, they should be designed so that there is a great deal of loose coupling rather than tight coupling, and there should be inbuilt buffers and redundancy designed into the system so that there are back-ups and an isolation of elements if things go awry.

Question

1. In practice, can you think of some other accidents waiting to happen for which this contingency analysis might be appropriate?

STRUCTURAL ADJUSTMENT TO REGAIN FIT

It is all about strategic adjustments to regain fit. Strategic choices, such as the size of the organization, its environment and technology, may determine organization structures, and the top management team – or dominant coalition, as it is sometimes called – will exercise choice in the decisions fixing these things. The organization's products will determine the markets entered, the technologies chosen and the structural shape and size of the organization. Child (2002 [1972]) argued that strategic choice preceded any structural factors determining organizational structure. Managers choose work plans, resources and equipment. The technologies and structures that ensue will be the result of managerial decisions linking available resources with necessary tasks. The organization's competitive position and culture will constantly be adjusted.

Lex Donaldson argued that, periodically, because any organizational design would become misaligned with the contingencies with which it had to deal, a structural change to regain fit with their fit between structure and changed contingencies would be necessary (Donaldson, 2002 [1987]).

Donaldson called his approach the *SARFIT* model, in which *SARFIT* stands for Structural Adjustment to Regain Fit. Its basic premise is that as organizations' contingencies change, such as their size, technologies and environments, the design that they have adopted may become less appropriate than it was initially: hence, they have to adjust their design structurally to regain fit with the changed contingencies.

TABLE 14.3 Change management

Factors forcing change	Factors accommodating change
The business cycle of boom and bust	Diversification smoothing out market, cyclical and seasonal variations in business, making change less necessary
Competition, increasing or diminishing market share	Divisionalization spreading risks across a portfolio of products
Levels of indebtedness, either fuelling or dragging growth down	Divestment where product lines are eliminated, together with the structures supporting them, if they consistently fail
Divisional risks, as some divisions fail to meet the performance targets set, and others exceed them	Risk-management advice from non-executive directors, diminishing performance failures

An organization concentrated on a specific product range for the domestic market will typically have a structure organized around functions such as finance, sales and production. As the firm diversifies into an increased number of products aimed at different markets, such a structure will no longer be well tuned to the changing circumstances. Under such circumstances, firms will likely attempt a structural adjustment to regain fit.

WATCH A VIDEO

Donaldson argues that organizational design will shift as variables that moderate its performance change, such as its size or the tasks that it is designed to accomplish. For instance, a firm may see its performance suffering because it has ceased to be innovative. In response to this diagnosis, the organization may hire more creative and design staff; consequently, the size of the organization increases and, to justify their existence, the staff come up with new products, processes and related ideas.

Donaldson argues that changing contingencies to fit an extant structure, while feasible, is more difficult than changing structure so that it is better aligned with the changing contingencies; this will especially be the case in a competitive business environment where a firm's position is always going to be judged in relation to its competitors. Organizations and their dominant coalitions, he suggests, are more likely to readjust their structure than their contingencies to regain fit between it and the contingencies that they are obliged – by competitive pressures – to handle.

Organizations do not actually have to hire more employees to increase capabilities. They can outsource design to a creative agency, shrinking employee size. Shrinkage in size, following Donaldson's logic, creates a less bureaucratic structure and increases organizational interdependence as the firm comes to rely on the external agency. Size is a variable fixed by contracts and employing more people is not the only contractual option available: outsourcing is an alternative.

Donaldson's re-analysis of a number of well-known longitudinal studies of structural changes tests whether the straightforward contingency determinism model, the strategic choice model or the *SARFIT* model, best explains the data. He finds that changes in contingency, such as moving to new markets or products, initially lower performance. Lower performance leads to a structural adjustment to regain fit and a new cycle of matched contingencies. The process is one of trial and error. Periodically, the organization will still require additional changes to its design as contingencies continue to change. Structures overwhelmingly adjust to contingencies rather than contingencies to structures. Donaldson points out that managers have choice, but they choose to do what the contingencies would indicate.

Contingency theory of one kind or another has contributed a great deal to the theory of organization design, linking design with performance in some cases, in others with variables such as size and technology.

ECONOMIC THEORIES OF THE FIRM

It is all about efficiency. The proposition that the central concept of organizational analysis should be that of 'efficiency', in particular, as Williamson (1991a) puts it, efficiency conceived as 'economizing', has been increasingly important in analysis of all kinds of organizations, especially those in the public sector. Williamson drew on the seminal work of Coase (1937, 1960) in order to develop the project of 'Transaction Costs Economics' (TCE) (Williamson, 1975, 1985, 1991b, 1995, 1999), with such success that, eventually, he was awarded the Sveriges Riksbank Prize in Economic Sciences in Memory of Alfred Nobel. Williamson's basic concepts are quite simple. The central concept is that of **transaction costs**.

Transaction costs refer to the costs involved in market exchange, such as discovering market prices as well as the costs of writing and enforcing contracts.

Transaction costs can be divided into three broad categories:

1. *Search and information costs* such as those incurred in determining that the required good is available on the market, which offer has the lowest price, and so on.
2. *Bargaining costs* required in coming to an acceptable agreement with the other party to the transaction, drawing up an appropriate contract, and so on.
3. *Policing and enforcement costs* involved in making sure the other party sticks to the terms of the contract, as well as in taking appropriate action (often through the legal system) if this turns out not to be the case.

In terms of the transactions cost perspective, people are assumed to display bounded rationality and opportunism (interest-seeking with guile). The central unit of analysis is the transaction. Where rationality is low, highly bounded by cognitive and other factors, making perfect knowledge impossible, we should expect transactions to occur in markets rather than in organizations. Where transactions occur in organizations, they do so because the conditions that would enable market exchange are lacking. When transactions occur in organizations, efficiency is sought through the governance structure of the organization. The more asset-specific is a transaction, the greater will be the risk of guileful or untrustworthy behaviour.

Economic theories of the firm, such as Williamson (1975), are a long way from the original Weberian ideal type foundations of modern organization design. Performance is in centre frame with a concomitant stress on efficiency explaining either a market or hierarchy design. Organizations occur where transaction conditions become complex. Other approaches are not so sure about efficiency, as we consider next.

WHAT WOULD YOU DO?

WHAT WOULD YOU DO?

You have an apartment to sell. You could minimize the transaction costs by not using a real estate agent. What would be the advantages and disadvantages of doing so compared to entering into an asset-specific transaction with a real estate agent?

INSTITUTIONAL THEORY

Institutional theory focuses on how organization designs and practices become cultural capital through a coercive, mimetic or normative isomorphism that hastens their adoption elsewhere.

Isomorphism: a similarity in form, referring to a situation in which organizational designs and practices in different organizations are nonetheless similar.

It is all about culture. **Institutional theory** was developed in the 1950s and 1960s and early contributions emphasized the role of conflict and of the negotiated order between different interest groups. More recently, new institutional theory has emerged and shifted emphasis to understanding how organizations appear legitimate in the eyes of stakeholders.

DiMaggio and Powell (2002 [1983]) considered how rationalized myths lodged in institutional settings shape organizational action. These rational myths help secure organizational legitimacy in order to capture resources and mobilize support. Organizations adopt similar forms and practices because of the strength of these rational myths in a process of **isomorphism**. The adoption of particular forms and practices are a means of gaining legitimacy in the eyes of important stakeholders by projecting an *image* of rationality. The ensuing symbolic display might well be decoupled from, or loosely coupled with, 'what actually happens'.

Institutional isomorphism has become, perhaps, the key concept for much research during the past decade. According to institutional theorists, the three forms of isomorphism combine to make organizations that are subject to isomorphic pressures appear increasingly alike, at least at a surface level. Normative isomorphism works as an ideal metric of legitimacy.

Institutional theory takes legitimacy as its master concept. It sees the quest for legitimacy as the driving force in making organizations more alike. Meyer and Rowan (1977) argued that modern societies consist of many institutionalized rules, providing a framework for the creation and elaboration of formal organizations. Many of these rules are rationalized myths that are widely believed but rarely, if ever, tested. They originate and are sustained through public opinion, the educational system, laws or other institutional forms. Thus, many of the factors shaping management and organization are not based on efficiency or effectiveness but on social and cultural pressures to conform to already legitimate practices. For instance, there is a lot of pressure on organizations to adapt to new tools invented by fashionable management gurus. Institutional theory analyses the impact of this pressure on organizations and management decisions.

Failing to achieve success simply becomes further fuel for endorsing the normative model more strongly. Three ideal-type mechanisms of organizational change by institutional isomorphism have been sketched, as we can see in Table 14.4.

TABLE 14.4 Types of isomorphism

Type of isomorphism	Description	Definition
Normative	When professionalization projects shape entire occupational fields	Normative isomorphism occurs when an organization's members are normatively predisposed, perhaps through a long period of professional training and socialization, to favour certain sorts of design and practices. The widespread use of the partnership form by law and other professional firms is a case in point
Coercive	When external agencies impose changes on organizations - most obviously through practices of state regulation	Coercive isomorphism occurs when some powerful institution obliges organizations in its domain, on threat of coercion, to comply with certain practices and designs
Mimetic	Copying what is constituted as culturally valuable ways of doing or arranging things - cultural capital	In simple language, mimetic isomorphism means the process of copying. Organizational designs and practices that are seen to be successful are copied because they are associated with success

IN PRACTICE

Simulating ritual

Mimetic isomorphism is demonstrated when a particular organizational practice, such as professors and teachers dressing up in academic gowns and making a procession as part of the ceremony of awarding a degree to new graduates, becomes widely diffused because people identify it as a central part of an institution. We know of no university that has dispensed with this ceremony for, as vice chancellors have frequently been known to remark, such a ceremony is symbolically representative of the university. So, the ritual is widely adopted and diffused even in newer universities. Stewart, co-author of this book, once worked somewhere in which many of the students who did the MBA were from overseas countries. Often, they had returned home prior to being awarded their degrees in order to get back to their careers, families and friends. In leaving immediately after their studies were complete, they missed the ceremony and its photo opportunities, but nonetheless they clamoured for an opportunity to gain these mementos.

The problem was that they did not want to have the expense of flying back to Australia from India or China, for instance, to get their pictures taken. Consequently, the university instituted a pre-degree ceremony, where a senior university dignitary would speak some formal words, during which the students would be told that this was not a degree ceremony, and then hand them something that was not a degree certificate but looked just like one. The students wore gowns that they were not yet entitled to wear - as they had not graduated - but the all-important pictures could be taken 'proving' that they had been at the university and

(Continued)

(Continued)

had been 'awarded' their 'degree'. The pictures proved it! Thus, in this way their social reality was constructed. They had the pictures to prove they were graduates of, and belonged to, a specific university, with its appropriate ceremonies, rituals and photo opportunities, even though none of it had *really* happened in the sense that a due process and ritual had been enacted and the degrees actually conferred at the point at which the 'authentications' were stage-managed.

Question

In practice, what do you think of universities staging mock ceremonies as a simulacrum of events with a precise ritual, meaning and performative power, but which have none of those features?

INSTITUTIONAL ENTREPRENEURSHIP

It is all about entrepreneurship. If so much energy goes into being similar to culturally valued organizations through mimesis, how is it possible that organizations can change? This is the question the institutional entrepreneur is designed to answer.

Institutional entrepreneurs can be thought of as champions of change. Nelson Mandela was an institutional entrepreneur in South Africa, for instance, and became one of the most widely admired men on the planet in consequence. Nonetheless, as is the case for the vast majority of institutional entrepreneurs, we cannot neglect the wider organizational field in which such institutions are embedded. The organizational field is 'those organizations that, in the aggregate, constitute a recognized area of institutional life: key suppliers, resource and product customers, regulatory agencies, and other organizations that produce similar services or products' (DiMaggio and Powell, 2002 [1983]: 148). Without the long struggle, armed resistance and civil disobedience campaigns of the ANC, Mandela could not have achieved much. The ANC built support throughout many organizational fields in South Africa, from entertainment, media, public service and corporations as well as externally through the anti-apartheid movement. Of course, Mandela was a remarkable political actor but he was precisely that – a political actor tangled up in a complex web of power and political relations, including a deeply divided ANC.

Institutional entrepreneurs make strategic choices that have determinate consequences for an industry; however, these choices are limited by institutional rules that frame what are legitimate or viable strategies for action. Candace Jones' (2001) study of the early years of the American film industry from 1895 to 1920 takes from institutional theory the idea that firms' practices depend on the strategic choices that key agents make; these choices, in turn, depend on the social construction or enactment that they make of the environment in which they are operating, which frame their mental models of the institutional field. When a particular set of mental models becomes embedded in practice, a trajectory is launched for the development of an institutional field. Thus, initial conditions, especially an entrepreneur's career history as defined by their choices, help shape the frame through which subsequent choices can be made by privileging certain frames. Organizations erect barriers to imitation based on their control of either property rights or knowledge; where they are successful in terms of consumer responses to their practices, they entrench non-imitable competitive advantages that will depend on the unique mix of local resources and knowledge that they can continue to corral and control.

IN PRACTICE

Many cities are keen on dockless share-bike schemes such as oBikes or Reddy Go, and for good reason. They promote greater physical movement, help solve transport problems in congested cities, and can be fun. The advantage of dockless bikes is that users needn't find dedicated stations to pick up and return the bikes. Instead, the user leaves the bike in a public place for the next rider to use. These bikes can be tracked via in-built global positioning system (GPS) devices or Bluetooth on users' smartphones.

Bike-share schemes may not work everywhere. Certain features can make cities hostile places for bike-sharing schemes; for example, overcomplicated planning procedures, strict cycling laws (such as compulsory helmet use) and political friction over giving up parking spaces to bike docks. Inadequate infrastructure - such as limited bike lanes and unprotected cycle paths - together with traffic safety concerns, bad weather and hilly streets can also put off would-be cyclists. And if schemes suffer from poor promotion or sluggish expansion, the bikes can languish for lack of use.

Bike-share schemes have one big drawback: these bikes are littering streets or being dumped in parks and rivers. Because everyone else seems to be dumping these bikes, the implicit message is that it's OK for everyone to do the same, that this is the norm.

READ ABOUT SHARE BIKE PROBLEMS

How might we change this behaviour? Wynn suggests three ideas.

First, we could work on the perceived pay-off or instrumental attitude. Getting the user to deposit some money as a bond - say $10 before the bike was used - could encourage users to treat the bikes with a bit more care. This would also tap into the loss aversion bias that most of us suffer from, being much more motivated to avoid a loss of $10 than to gain $10. Having handed over our $10, we'll want it back. And we'll be motivated to provide proof that we've done the right thing. An education campaign to change what people do with the bikes needs to target social norms and effective deterrents.

Second, we could work on social norms, or what we think others think is the right thing to do. Most of us have a strong desire to behave as we think others want us to. A communications campaign aimed at reminding users that most others don't sling their bikes when they're finished with them could work in the same way that water-saving campaigns work. Those campaigns helped convince many consumers that it's not OK to waste water. One way this was achieved was by showing each household how their consumption compared to others.

A third suggested measure, also linked to loss aversion, would be to fine those who are found to have dumped their bike in the river or hung it from a tree, for instance. Protection

(Continued)

(Continued)

READ ABOUT DATA HARVESTING

DATA HARVESTERS

mechanisms and penalties for vandalism and theft should be in place from day one, to help minimize misuse. Market and education campaigns can be used to promote bike-sharing culture, and encourage people to take a positive attitude towards these bikes.

Questions

1. What about the cities that you frequent? How well has the institutional entrepreneurship of bike sharing worked there?
2. Where is the profit in bike sharing for entrepreneurs if so many bikes are trashed?

HOMOGENIZING DESIGNS

It is all about professions. At the core of all modern organizations of some size and complexity are professionals. Professions, Scott maintains, define, interpret and apply institutional elements such that they are the most influential contemporary creators of institutions. According to Scott (2008), professions as institutions rest on three different pillars: the regulative, normative and cultural-cognitive pillars, familiar from DiMaggio and Powell (2002 [1983]).

Cultural-cognitive agents fix ontological frameworks, distinctions, typifications and principles that range from the metaphysical realm of the theologian and philosopher to the material realm of the engineer and applied scientist. Internal professional control is largely embedded in shared sensemaking. Normative agents do moral work of various kinds that stakes out areas of legitimated action premised on professional standards, codes, precepts and rulings.

Within professions, there are distinctions between different generic categories of social action, suggests Scott. Creative professionals are lodged in universities, think tanks and research centres. Carrier professionals are those who translate professional messages and spread them to new actors, arenas and agencies: educators, trainers, consultants, and so on. The largest sub-category is comprised of the clinical professionals who deal with specific cases and clients.

All professions are a component of Florida's (2002) creative class – a somewhat elastic and amorphous category. Increasing professionalization leads to greater specialization within the primary profession, increased use of mechanization and routinization, and the consolidation and formalization of knowledge. These professionals are overwhelmingly members of organizations rather than being independent practitioners. Their clients are increasingly corporate also. The organizational form of independent professions increasingly mirrors clients: they are becoming increasingly managerial.

The world is increasingly professionalized, according to sociologist John Meyer (Krücken and Drori, 2009). He sees the major feature of the modern world as its professionalization, a process that he traces through specific areas such as education, management, the environment and science. The degree of professionalization is occurring to such an extent that it is possible to speak of a 'world society' constituted by professionals who, irrespective of where they are located in the world, have a great deal in common with other members of the same profession. For instance, scientists in a specific disciplinary community abide by similar standards and rules everywhere; the editors of prestigious scientific journals and periodicals apply similar standards, as do the organizers of conferences. Those who employ scientists do so because of the professional competence that they have mastered – they have rules built into them through the disciplines they have mastered, making their actions relatively unproblematic for managerial control because of their discipline – in every sense of the word.

STANDARDS AND INSTITUTIONALIZATION

It is all about standards. The combination of institutional entrepreneurship and the sheer centrality of professions to modern organizations have contributed to the growth of the standards industry: the spread of the ISO 9000 standard for quality management in the 1990s saw a huge growth in total quality management in organizations globally. Institutional entrepreneurs help spread fashionable ideas, because they carve out new fields that others then copy; professions do so because they are one of the major sources of legitimation of new practices that can then be globally translated and disseminated, through devices such as professional publications and international conferences.

Modern times have seen the growth of formal written international standards as a major factor working to make organizations more alike globally. As Brunsson and Jacobsson (2000) have elaborated, standards are a major mechanism of institutional isomorphism. Since the late 1980s, starting from a concern with quality, international standards bodies have issued rules on an increasing number of arenas of organizational activity, such as ecological impact. A significant industry of global consultancy, auditing, certification and accreditation accompanies these new managerial standards. Winton Higgins and Kristina Tamm Hallström (2007) have investigated 'Standardization, globalization and rationalities of government' with respect to organizations. They focus on the evolution of the national standards bodies, the participation in government of some of the pioneers of standardization, and how their relationship with public authorities developed in reference to rationally and consensually arrived-at 'technically-best' solutions, and the growing prestige of putatively independent expertise.

Standards and the regulatory routines based on them play a specific instrumental role in organizations. They construct the manager as someone who is seeking to improve constantly. Structured, standardized and similar self-assessment frameworks (Cole, 1999), such as the Malcolm Baldrige Quality Award (MBNQA), the European Foundation for Quality Management (EFQM) Excellence Model, and the Swedish Institute for Quality (SIQ) Model for Performance Excellence, act as both a coordination mechanism and a regulatory instrument; what they do is to make globally coordinated control much easier to achieve. The most important of these standards, without a doubt, is ISO 9001, dating from 1987. This standard, produced by a technical committee of the International Standards Organization (ISO), while only seven pages in length when originally produced, has been adopted globally in all sizes and forms of organizations. It is the rational management plan par excellence, being a standard for *all* management *anywhere*. In excess of one million organizations have been *certified* to ISO 9001 in over 170 countries but as insiders to the ISO world point out, it is likely that several times that number have applied the standard without seeking certification. Judged on sales of the standard alone, hundreds of millions of employees throughout the world have had contact with, or have been influenced by, ISO 9001 or one of its industry-specific derivatives, such as ISO/TS 16949:2000 and ISO 22000:2018. The role of the highly abstract ('generic') ISO 9000 quality assurance standards, and of ISO's subsequent management standards, elaborate 'practices of the self' for corporate managers to help them shape their identity as competent managers through following prescribed practices. Because these practices are subject to certification and recurring audit, the manager's and the organization's sense of legitimacy is enhanced. They must be doing the right things if they are following standards and are certified and audited as doing so! As audit never finds perfection – perfectibility is impossible – the manager must constantly live and manage with the need to constantly improve; any error or inadequacy uncovered by audit simply serves as further justification for improvements in the application of the standard.

WATCH A VIDEO ABOUT STANDARDS

Academic research has had a negligible influence on the emergence of the ISO 9001 standard. Brunsson and Jacobsson (2000), who have done the most to advance our understanding of *A World of Standards*, suggest that, in fact, research has been ignored at times when that best suited the interests of the standards writers. It is probably more accurate to say that explicit management research is something that occurs in a parallel institutional universe with very little seepage or porosity across its borders into the standards world of practice. Yet, the latter, the world of standards, has done far more to shape practice, demonstrating that in management the relation between theory and practice that is often presumed, by which ideas flow from theory to shape practice, lacks truth value. Management practice is far more likely to be shaped by standards in which theory has had little or no role to play than by the knowledge disseminated in academic journals, texts and conferences.

Such standards, much as most highly rationalized accounts of what management should do, probably have more effect on what managers represent themselves as doing rather than what they necessarily do. Standards largely shape representations rather more than practices and thus increase hypocrisy. Nonetheless, to the extent that global firms adopt global standards, such as ISO 9001, it introduces a powerful rhetorical device into management anywhere to make it more accountable in terms of the standard. In part, this is the way in which the institutionalization of ISO 9001 has been achieved, largely through a new job classification (the quality manager) that can use the tool to shape the work environment of all employees under their supervision. Especially, in the spread of global outsourcing and manufacturing, the ISO 9001 standard has been very important in translating rationalized management knowledge into local contexts far from the core of the global economy.

FASHIONS

It is all about fashion. Eric Abrahamson (1996, 1997), at Columbia University in New York, suggests that managers are followers of fashion. The argument is that the management ideas industry – a loose but powerful network of management consultancies, management gurus, software firms, business schools and the like – develops carefully packaged management initiatives, which are then commoditized and sold across the organizational world. These ideas have a shelf life of two or three years before being replaced by the next initiative. These ideas are seen as the latest fashions in management, which are then consumed by managers who can be characterized as 'dedicated followers of fashion'.

The adoption of a fashion is an example of mimetic isomorphism – copying a best practice to appear legitimate and rational in the eyes of important external stakeholders. As with any fashion, there are early adopters who are at the very height of fashion – haute couture – and those that follow when the fashion becomes more commonplace.

Management academics often look down at managers for following fashion. Barbara Czarniawska, at Gothenburg University in Sweden, and Rene ten Bos, at Nijmegen University in the Netherlands, take issue with theorists who treat fashion pejoratively or look down on fashion as trivial (Czarniawska, 2005; ten Bos, 2000). Both point out that following fashion can be a positive and exciting experience for managers and organizations alike. Czarniawska alerts us to the paradoxical nature of fashion in that it is simultaneously about 'invention and imitation, variation and uniformity, preserving the status quo' (2005: 144).

Organizations are constructions, concocted out of whatever knowledge their members deem salient in specific locales. Child and Kieser (1979) found that a sample of German organizations was consistently more centralized than was a comparable sample of British firms, which they put down to local cultural difference that proved to be even more important than the impact of models of best practice retailed by international consulting agencies. These models did not produce convergence by eroding the value basis of a German cultural predisposition for more centralized control. Such findings, of a 'societal effect', are widely established (see Maurice and Sorge, 2002).

The societal effect is particularly important for multinational organizations. They have to manage not only the cultural predispositions of their national context but also those of the contexts in which they operate. Culture influences how responsibilities are defined and distributed in organizations, as well as how they learn to address issues in different contexts. It is also a political resource, as the next extension argues.

EXTEND YOUR KNOWLEDGE

In Levy, O. and Reiche, B. S. (2018) 'The politics of cultural capital: social hierarchy and organizational architecture in the multinational corporation', *Human Relations*, 71 (6): 867–94, which is available at the companion website https://study.sagepub.com/managingandorganizations5e, the authors delineate the role of culture in reproducing and changing social hierarchy in multinational corporations (MNCs). Culture constructs social hierarchies and symbolic boundaries between individuals and groups within MNCs.

READ THE ARTICLE

When there is a contested takeover of a firm or a merger, or some other major organizational change, with the result being the appointment of a new CEO and a change in the top management team, it is often a case of 'in with the new, out with the old' – politics are a major mechanism of organizational change.

CULTURE

Rationalized myths are beliefs and practices that organizations adopt as being efficient and effective, thus granting legitimacy.

It is all about rational myths. Being against bureaucracy, being in favour of leaner, meaner organizations, became something of a **rationalized myth** in the 1980s.

A rationalized myth of modern business is that continuing competitiveness can only be achieved by a perpetual war on costs best served by 'slashing costs through mass downsizing exercises in an attempt to impress financial markets' (Hassard et al., 2009: 29). The major mechanism for translating the rationalized myth into action 'has been the substantial job cuts and reorganizations targeted specifically at managers (in addition to the long-standing threats to operatives)', as Hassard et al. (2009: 49) analyse. Some effects are easy to observe: the reduction of management layers; the outsourcing of non-core back-office functions to countries with much cheaper white-collar labour processes, such as India, and the development of international supply chains and overseas production. All of these tendencies have contributed to the growing complexity involved in managing organizations that are considerably smaller than was the case 30 or so years ago, with a greatly diminished managerial cadre whose roles and responsibilities are now stretched over many more areas of expertise.

Leaner organizations lack buffer zones and loose coupling that can contain and limit crises if things go wrong. There is consequently far more probability of crises and a need for the fire fighting that these entail. If businesses outsource, they will in the short term satisfy financial and market analysts and drive up their stock values. Rationalized myth drives restructuring, financialization, downsizing, de-layering and the removal of employee entitlements, as Hassard et al. (2009: 37) observe. Mostly, the myth seems to have spread by mimesis, by imitation. As highly regarded firms seek to ensure the maintenance of their competitive edge through these strategies, then their competitors, fearing that they will lose value in the eyes of the market if they are not seen to be doing the same things, seek to emulate their strategies.

Cuts to organizations have been unnecessarily damaging, suggest Burke and Nelson (1997), Sennett (1998) and Pfeffer (1998). Organizational knowledge that was embodied and embrained in under-valued workers has been allowed to leave the organization with insufficient regard for what was being lost; innovation has suffered as the remaining, more hard-pressed managers seek to manage a greatly intensified workload. Organizations that were once largely domiciled in their home countries now have supply chains and outsourcing arrangements that span the globe, bringing new opportunities for cost reduction into play.

Competition on the basis of price and quality has led to more demanding consumers who, in turn, maintain competitive pressure on firms. These competitive pressures are condensed and intensified within firms into expectations that middle managers can constantly manage a series of paradoxes; tighten cost control and be more innovative; deliver higher performance and greater commitment; live life through a series of projects with diminished job security and increased adherence to the corporate culture. The list of contradictions should be familiar to anybody working in major organizations today.

There are exceptions: increasingly, organizations do seek to ensure family-friendly, healthy working practices but many firms regard such 'soft stuff' as an unjustifiable cost incurred against the erosion of shareholder returns by the pressures of international competition. Senior executives in the top management team, whose income is contingently linked to performance in these terms, are unlikely to be advocates for a more caring and less uncompromising work regime for their middle managers. Moreover, such a harsh regime is functional for elite recruitment: if middle managers can manage to thrive despite the pressures, they show themselves to be the kind of people whose elevation to upper-level management may well be justified. And each time such a decision is made the vicious cycle is reinforced.

EMBEDDEDNESS

It is all about embeddedness. Rationality concerns not just technical efficiency, because it is always culturally framed. Managers seek to make their organizations similar to models that are already institutionalized as positive examples. They do not want to deviate too far from the forms that are already culturally valued. Thus, organizations end up being similar not because it is rationally efficient for them to be so but because it is institutionally rational. Sticking to legitimate forms bestows legitimacy. Hence, organizations in similar fields of activity tend to be similar in their design, functioning and structure. These are the basic insights of institutional approaches to organization analysis.

If we take institutional theory seriously, we do not deal with a singular organizational or business rationality but cultural rationalities that embed economic action, as Granovetter (2002 [1985]: 363) suggests when he writes about **embeddedness**. Granovetter focuses on the central role of networks of social relations in producing trust in economic life. Seen from this perspective, one can appreciate that 'small firms in a market setting may persist ... because a dense network of social relations is overlaid on the business relations connecting such firms' (Granovetter, 2002 [1985]: 385).

Embeddedness is the recognition that economic action is grounded in social relations.

WHAT DESIGNS MATTER?

M-FORM

It is all about the M-form of divisionalization. The **M-form** organization was one of the earliest alternatives to bureaucracy.

M-form organizations have a hub of central services linked to spokes with profit centres that are usually specialized in terms of either products or regions.

According to Alfred Chandler, the M-form facilitates growth through diversification across products, industries and markets and includes the notion of delegation of power and authority to divisional managers. The growth of firms has seen an evolution from national to multinational corporations (MNCs). These MNCs adopt an internal structuring that includes an operational and strategic integration of business functions that minimize costs and economize via internal coordination and control, and as such achieve governance economies. The M-form represents a combination of a divisional structure with hierarchical control and functional flexibility (see Figure 14.1).

Chandler (1990) argued that the M-form is more efficient due to the cost advantages that 'scale and scope' provide. Chandler defined scale as plant size, and scope as the use of many of the same raw materials to produce a variety of products. The M-form of organizing was invented by General Motors to encompass central control and ownership, vertical integration of the production, formal internal coordination through vertical and horizontal linkages between decentralized

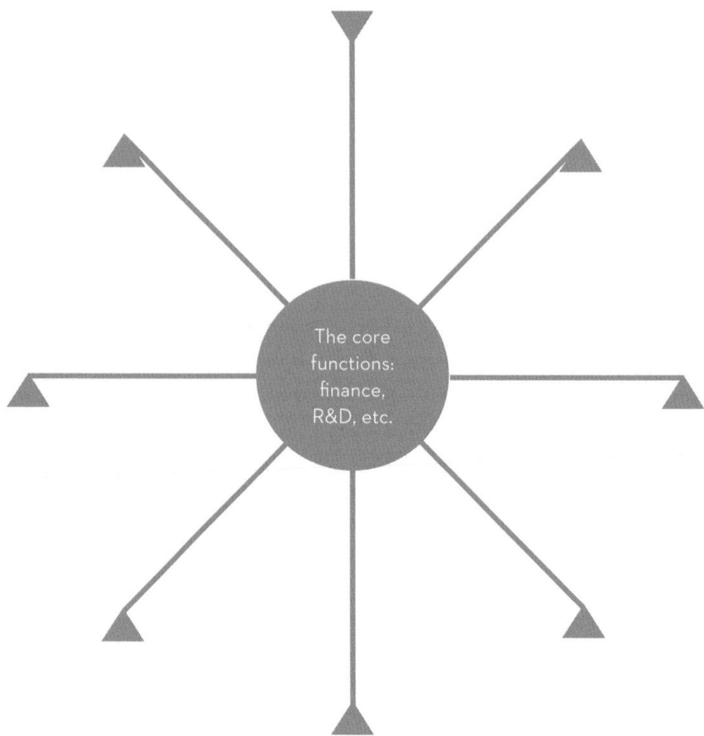

FIGURE 14.1 The multi-divisional form (MDF) structure. The many small triangles symbolize profit centres nurtured and controlled by the parental core company in the centre

divisions, and corporate head office function and specialized staff concentrated in departments and subunits. After the lead of firms such as General Motors and DuPont, it was largely firms that had strong and distinct product lines as their central strategy that made the switch early, setting up a divisional structure based on the product lines. Where the CEO of the firm had a sales, marketing or finance background, the firm was also more likely to have switched to an M-form structure early. Over time, more and more CEOs came from a finance background and such CEOs were most likely to opt for an M-form organization.

Typically, established firms were more likely to shift to the M-form rather than newer firms. However, there is an interesting mimetic effect: as other firms in an industry change to the divisional form, then any remaining firm is more likely to do so (Fligstein, 1985: 387). Overall, Fligstein concluded:

> those in control of large firms acted to change their organizational structures under three conditions: when they were pursuing a multiproduct strategy; when their competitors shifted structures and when they had a background in the organization such that their interests reflected those of the sales or finance departments. (Fligstein, 1985: 388)

Devolved geographical or product-based divisions have to perform according to criteria fixed centrally – for instance, a certain return on investment (ROI).

Thus, rules were more oriented to *outcomes* rather than to processes, unlike the classic bureaucracy.

From the 1990s onward, the M-form came under increasing pressure (Pettigrew et al., 2002 [2000]) and, especially in the USA, has been changing towards a multi-subsidiary rather than a multi-divisional form because of tax and anti-trust regimes in the USA and their effects on the ownership and control of corporate capital (Zey, 2008). The legal relationship between the parent corporation and its subsidiaries is one of capital interdependency, which is of far more importance than the notional legal independence.

Many global companies have a multidivisional structure. Overall, what an organization is designed to be affects how well it can do what it does. Pettigrew (2003; Fenton and Pettigrew, 2000; Pettigrew et al., 2002 [2000]) investigated changes in form in the top European and Japanese companies during the 1990s. A delayering of middle-management hierarchies, accompanied by increased decentralization, both operational and strategic, created more incentive-based and leaner management, often organized in cross-functional and cross-boundary project teams, sometimes with rival firms, to create a 'boundaryless organization' (Nohria and Ghoshal, 1997). What is not core can be outsourced to another organization providing the service that is cheaper, faster and more innovative – because it is its core business – or it can be delivered through an alliance (see also pp. 340–341).

MATRIX ORGANIZATIONS

It is all about the matrix. Now you might think that matrix organizations were scary and psychedelic (as in the famous movies) but you'd be wrong! **Matrix organizations** are a mixed organizational form in which traditional vertical hierarchy is overlaid by a horizontal structure consisting of projects, products and business subsidiaries or geographical areas. The key characteristic of a matrix organization is a multiple command structure in which employees experience dual or multiple lines of authority, responsibility and accountability. Jay R. Galbraith (1971) represented the matrix organization as a mixed form along the continuum of a range of organizational design alternatives. Matrix structures are best for temporary projects with designated cost, time and performance standards. Classical matrix design is specified by the choice among the authority structure, integrating mechanisms such as teams, and by the formal information system (see Table 14.5). Wherever projects are a key component in the way that products or services are delivered, then a matrix organizational design can be considered. It makes, in theory, for a more flexible organization.

In **matrix organizations**, reporting relationships are grid-like rather than traditionally hierarchical. Employees report to both a functional *and* a product manager.

TABLE 14.5 Advantages and disadvantages of matrix organizations

Advantages of a matrix organization structure	Disadvantages of a matrix organization structure
Increased frequency of communication in the organization	Creates ambiguity about resources and personnel assignments
An increase in the amount of information the organization can handle	Encourages organizational conflict between functional and project managers

(Continued)

TABLE 14.5 (Continued)

Advantages of a matrix organization structure	**Disadvantages of a matrix organization structure**
Flexibility in the use of human and capital resources	Produces conflict among individuals who must work together but have very different backgrounds
Increased motivation, job satisfaction, commitment and personal development as well as heightened ease in achieving technical excellence within the organization	Leads to insecurity for functional managers and erosion of their autonomy, making it more costly in terms of overheads and staff, more meetings, delayed decisions and information processing

Matrix organization has been adopted by multinational firms with varying degrees of success, especially in large, project-based organizations.

SHAMROCK ORGANIZATIONS

It is all about the shamrock. A shamrock organization is an organizational structure in which a core of essential executives and workers are supported by outside contractors and part-time help. We will often find this structure in design-oriented companies such as Nike. The employees in the shamrock do the designing, while the manufacture of the products is contracted out.

The shamrock leaf shape is a symbolic representation of an organization with three distinct parts, as defined by Charles Handy (1990). It is illustrated in Figure 14.2.

The first part, or leaf, represents the core staff of the organization. They are likely to be highly trained professionals who form the senior management. The second leaf consists of the contractual fringe and may include individuals who once worked for the organization but now supply services to it. These could be design professionals, for instance. These individuals operate within broad guidelines set down by the organization but have a high degree of flexibility and discretionary powers. The third leaf describes the consultancy services provided by IT specialist firms, for instance. These firms are sufficiently close to the organization to feel a degree of commitment to it, ensuring they maintain a high standard of work. The shamrock is one of many new organizational forms that have been developed in recent years.

A **network** can be understood as a long-term relationship between organizations that share resources to achieve common goals through negotiated actions.

NETWORKS

It is all about the network. In *The Rise of the Network Society*, Castells (2000) claimed that **networks** were transforming organizations.

In **networking**, independent organizations form networks in which the other organizations have complementary skills to achieve something that neither alone would be able to manage.

Networking, involving collaboration between different people or agencies such as organizations, has become a core business competence for firms in a largely technical marketing and supply chain set of relations. Certain places become magnets for particular fields of activity, like hi-tech in Silicon Valley, movie making in Hollywood or Mumbai, or creative design in Brisbane's Fortitude Valley, enabling closed and interpersonal networking to occur. Although firms can be located anywhere in cyberspace, they still seem to cluster together in specific quarters of global cities such as New York, London and Sydney (Castells, 2001).

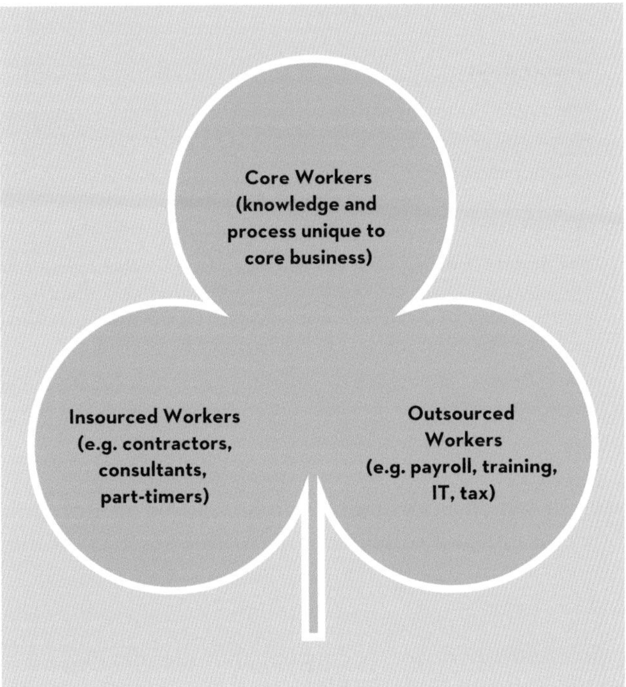

FIGURE 14.2 The shamrock organization

In a 1990 article that was highly influential, Powell challenged views that described a continuum of transaction forms from markets at one end to hierarchies at the other, with some hybrid forms such as joint ventures in between. He added networks to the dichotomy of transaction costs economics. Unlike market forms, networks involve indefinite, longer terms and sequential transactions. In networks, participants create indebtedness and reliance over a long-term basis. Networks are better than markets or hierarchies at facilitating learning and the transfer of technological know-how and they are better than hierarchies at responding to sharp fluctuations in demand and unanticipated changes. In networks, the parties gain by pooling resources and building reciprocal relations of trust. Reciprocally related know-how, trust and speediness are key characteristics of networks.

RHIZOMES

It is all about the rhizome. In terms inspired by Deleuze and Guattari (1984), organizations are open systems with no underlying structure or hierarchy, which Hardt and Negri (2000) term 'the rhizome'. The term is used metaphorically and is drawn from botanical usage, where it means a thick, underground horizontal stem that produces roots and has shoots that develop into new plants. The rhizome can be expressed in terms of four principles, suggests Munro (2008), elaborated in Table 14.6.

TABLE 14.6 Rhizomatic principles of organizing

Principle of	Description
Connection and heterogeneity	Any point in a rhizome can be connected to any other (such as a distributed network), and objects of different kinds are connected within the rhizome
Multiplicity	The rhizome is defined by its lines of flight rather than by points internal to it. As the rhizome makes connections with the outside, it undergoes a metamorphosis; like a piece of music, it transforms itself with each new note
Rupture	The rhizome can be broken at any spot, and it will either sprout a new line of growth or continue along an old line. Deleuze and Guattari described this kind of network as 'the wisdom of plants', by means of which they move, expand and develop their territory. The rhizome moves by following a flow, of wind, of rain, of water
Cartography	The rhizome does not have an underlying generative structure; intensive states and thresholds replace the idea of an underlying topology

Virtual spaces in which information can spread in an unregulated, nomadic fashion would be examples of rhizomatic networks, such as online communities.

CREATIVE CLUSTERS

It is all about the creative cluster. A concept that has developed a great deal of credibility in policy-related circles addresses not so much a new organizational form as a new way of thinking about the linkages between them. The central idea is that of the creative cluster or creative precinct, which is a concentration of organizations and talent in a specific area, with the central idea being that this concentration will enable accidental and random rhizomatic encounters to occur that are essential to fostering innovation and creativity. The notion of the creative cluster can be defined as comprising those industries that have their origin in individual creativity, skill and talent and a potential for wealth and job creation through the generation and exploitation of intellectual property.

Unified by the thread of cultural creativity, the creative cluster cuts across multiple economic sectors and does not constitute a cohesive or discrete sector in the traditional sense of an industry cluster. Three broad groups are usually recognized as forming part of the creative industries. First, there is the arts/culture cluster, comprising performing arts, visual arts, literary arts, photography, crafts, libraries, museums, galleries, archives, auctions, impresarios, heritage sites, performing arts sites, festivals and arts-supporting enterprises. Second, there is the design cluster, including advertising, architecture, web and software, graphics, industrial product, fashion, communications, interiors and environmental design. Third, there is the media/broadcast cluster comprising radio, television and cable, digital media, including software and computer services, film and video, recorded music and publishing.

HETERARCHY AND RESPONSIBLE AUTONOMY

It is all about heterarchy and responsible autonomy. For Fairtlough (2007), a rare example of a successful CEO, research biologist and organization theorist combined in one person, the alternatives to hierarchical bureaucracy are *heterarchy* and *responsible autonomy*. As he argues, heterarchy comprises dispersed leadership, dispersed power and a balance of power, with mutual accountability. A good example of heterarchy would be the structure of professional service firms, such as law firms. Although these tend to become more hierarchical as they grow in size, the advantages of partnership continue to be recognized. The procedures in many successful law firms are quasi-democratic, with voting by all partners deciding key issues. A great deal of conversation between partners takes place before a vote. However, the nature of these conversations is strongly influenced by the prospect of the subsequent vote (Fairtlough, 2007: 1274). Responsible autonomy depends on encapsulating relatively autonomous roles as responsible to rules, both explicit and tacit, which govern the interaction of autonomous actors or elements or divisions of an organization. Ross Dawson, a creative Sydney-based global consultant, has a most informative blog about heterarchy.

READ ABOUT HETERARCHY VS HIERARCHY

DESIGN THINKING

It is all about design thinking. In the last few years, the notion of **design thinking** has gained popularity outside the design professions, especially in business school circles.

Design thinking recommends a conjoined process of *inspiration, ideation* and *implementation*.

Inspiration derives from making a problem material through mock-up, sketches, scenarios, and so on. *Ideation* is the process of generating, developing and testing ideas through building prototypes, piloting and 'testing the waters' – idea work. *Implementation* is the clear development and specification of the idea, its effective communication, the enrolment of others in its support and the translation of the idea into action or practice.

Accelerating changes in organizational designs and structures over the past 30 years led to increasing calls for design thinking to be incorporated into the management curriculum. At its core, the call for design thinking seems to be a recognition that the analytical frameworks usually dominant in business schools are somewhat limited. Typically, these have stressed deduction in research that seeks to define hypotheses a priori and then test them empirically, with induction, for those researchers that prefer more grounded and ethnographic approaches where they 'induct' findings from the specifics of the empirical situation, being the opposing approach.

Design thinking stresses what the American pragmatist Peirce (1940) referred to as abduction. Abduction is 'a process of interpretation in order to develop explanations based on observation [where] the explanation arrived at is not deduced or induced but "abduced" from the variety and complexity of experiences and observations' (Iedema et al., 2006: 1115). Abduction recognizes that social reality is constantly becoming rather than being constant (Kornberger et al., 2005).

READ ABOUT DESIGN THINKING

Influenced by design thinking, the field of organization and management studies acknowledges the need to bring together practitioners and academics in order to develop knowledge that can be applied (Schön, 1992). Romme (2003) claims that organization studies should include design as one of its primary modes of thinking. A focus on design entails a set of tools, skills and epistemologies for more grounded organizational enquiry (Romme, 2003).

Drawing on the work of Herbert Simon, Schön (1992) suggests that practitioners are, of necessity, designers; the production of artefacts is essential to their business. Therefore, practitioners in the field of design sciences, including, among others, professional designers, architects and engineers, are focused on prototyping action and are solution centred (Michlewski, 2008). The idea of prototyping includes the objective of creating a physical prototype to enable organizational thinking and learning to occur more rapidly by making prototypes small and thus, by testing them, being able to minimize the impact of failures. Prototypes also encourage employees to explore new behaviour (Coughlan et al., 2007: 127). Design approaches practise interventions that are improvement- and solution-centred (Trullen and Bartunek, 2007), based on a set of fundamental values that include collaboration; a focus on solutions rather than on analysis; experiment being necessary for successful intervention processes; each situation being unique in its context and goal oriented – even if these values change in the process (Trullen and Bartunek, 2007: 27).

EXTEND YOUR KNOWLEDGE

READ THE ARTICLE

Elsbach, K. D. and Stigliani, I. (2018) 'Design thinking and organizational culture: a review and framework for future research', *Journal of Management*, 44 (6): 2274–2306, which is available at the companion website https://study.sagepub.com/managingandorganizations5e, mines recent empirical research relating the practice of design thinking to the development of culture in organizations and the production of emotional experiences and physical artefacts that help users to understand why and how specific cultures support the effective use of specific tools.

WHAT WOULD YOU DO?

Design thinking

You have been tasked with applying design thinking to the structure of your present organization. What would you do to accomplish this task over a three-month process? Use some of the resources we have suggested to work out a design thinking approach.

The focus in this section has been very much on creativity in the workplace, which is really well demonstrated in the Catherine Courage TED Talk discussion of how to make children accept MRI scans in a positive way.

WATCH THE TED TALK

DEMOCRATIC DESIGN

For much of the twentieth century, especially in Scandinavia, the dominant feature in organization design was the implementation of the principles of industrial democracy. Scandinavian industrial democracy was partly based on socio-technic systems theory, which began in the London-based Tavistock Institute in the post-war period but had its most notable take-up in Scandinavia, initially in Norway.

Socio-technical systems theory saw self-organizing teams defining their own work as the core element of organizational design, humanizing work in the process, away from the mechanism of other approaches such as Taylorism and bureaucracy. The focus was on how people and technology could interact productively and in an empowering way.

A key voice in the movement for organizational democratization, Eric Trist (1993) defined the key elements in building more democratic work and organization designs as a series of shifts in focus based on employees having responsible autonomy. The shifts would be from:

- a single jobs focus to work system
- the individual jobholder to work group
- redundancy of parts to redundancy of functions
- considering individuals as an extension of the machines to seeing them as complementary to machines
- variety decreasing to variety increasing
- external to internal regulation of individuals
- prescribed to discretionary work.

These concerns became widely espoused in Scandinavia, even becoming embedded as part of the founding principles of the tripartite union/business/government *Arbetslivscentrum* (Centre for Working Life) in Sweden, sponsoring policy innovations to improve the quality of working life. The main contours of the Scandinavian approach to organization design can be found in Klemsdal and colleagues (2017), while Battilana, Fuerstein and Lee (2017) and Lee and Edmondson (2017) also provide a contemporary overview, in the context of a discussion of post-bureaucratic organization, humanistic management and organizational democracy.

It should be noted that while Management and Organization Studies has largely intellectually been the product of North American thinking which, because of the power of its numbers, dominates global English-language discussions, there are European traditions of organizational democracy in Scandinavia, of works councils in the Netherlands, Germany and Austria, with their traditions of codetermination, that have only been lightly discussed, if at all, in the dominant English-speaking management literature of recent years (Balfour, 2018; Lecher et al., 2018; Sorge, 2018). If management's right to manage through the domination of their perspectives and the authority of their positions is assumed as a taken-for-granted feature of the English-speaking world, there is considerably more mutuality and joint decision-making between managers and employees in these European approaches. In addition, there are deep-rooted traditions of cooperative design and management evident in many sectors of the global economy, especially in producer cooperatives, discussion of which is largely neglected in the literature.

One provocative article that defends democracy in the present conjuncture in terms of design thinking is provided by Tonkinwise (2018). It stresses that the definition of who is an organizational stakeholder needs expending to include marginalized peoples, by race, class or ability, as well as a wide range of non-users, people from across the whole-of-life supply chain and delegates representing future generations and non-human actors. Together with this expanded notion of democracy, organizations should, it is suggested, be engaged in advocacy of visions for the future that the organization is working toward and prepared to evaluate its work against, as well as advocating for participation in the profits from design for all involved – from makers and maintainers to users and end-of-life disposers and recoverers. It is a profound and radical view of organizational democracy.

EXTEND YOUR KNOWLEDGE

READ THE ARTICLE

There is a classic exception to the neglect of cooperatives in the literature and that is a 2014 special issue of the journal *Organization*, 21 (5), that treats cooperatives as alternative forms of business and organization, focusing on worker-owned-and-governed forms. The special issue was entitled 'Worker cooperatives as an organizational alternative: Challenges, achievements and promise in business governance and ownership', edited by George Cheney, Iñaki Santa Cruz, Ana Maria Peredo and Elías Nazareno, which is available at the companion website https://study.sagepub.com/managingandorganizations5e

DESIGNING THE DIGITAL ORGANIZATION

Organization design today is increasingly digitally mediated. At the most elementary level, digital technologies are used by organizations to increase efficiency and effectiveness. Digital technologies augment and support work activities and decision-making, with devices such as computers and smartphones, helping manage relationships with customers, suppliers and other stakeholders in ways that extend connectivity and combinatorial possibilities (Brynjolfsson and McAfee, 2014).

Snow, Fjeldstad and Langer (2017) trace the impact of digital technologies on organization design. These technologies produce, they argue, an actor-oriented architecture composed of three elements:

1. Actors who have the capabilities and values to self-organize.
2. A digital commons of shared knowledge and databases allowing the actors to accumulate and share resources.
3. Protocols, processes and infrastructures including apps and a normative context that enable multi-actor collaboration.

The crucial distinction from a hierarchical design is that relationships are largely self-organized and lateral and reciprocal rather than being hierarchical and directed. Such an organization design requires a very different set of skills to those of more traditional organizations. Key skills for digitally designed organization will include sensemaking abilities, social intelligence and cross-cultural capabilities for handling diversities, digital fluency and transdisciplinarity, enabling a rapid switching of frames, design thinking, an ability to discriminate and filter information for importance and to understand how to maximize cognitive functioning using a variety of tools and techniques, as well as the ability to work productively, drive engagement and contribute as a member of a virtual team. Increasingly, organizing will mean working forms of artificial intelligence working with virtual teams on collaborative goals.

Digital organization produces acute issues for many who work in it, find Petriglieri, Ashford and Wrzesniewski (2018), especially as people become part of a gig economy. In the absence of organizational or professional membership, anxiety characterizes life in the precariat, which some people are able to hold at bay through finding fulfilment by creating connections to routines, places, people and a broader purpose, allowing them to define, express and develop their selves. Given the lack of anchorage in a full-time membership of an organization in which people meet face to face regularly, people become the work that they do, investing in each dramaturgical occasion of its performance. In such a context, the authors suggest that people become their work in a way that for many can be emotionally fulfilling.

Some of the discussion of digital organization stresses positive network characteristics, as in the sharing economy. Firms such as Uber, however, are really more brokers than networkers: they facilitate markets and are organized hierarchically. The algorithms that they control make it possible for some users to drive more and charge passengers for the ride and some passengers to take advantage of Uber's flexibility and generally lower costs. Thus, much of Uber is understandable through a transaction cost perspective in which it manages the terms of the transaction through the algorithm.

The widespread implementation of digital platforms such as Uber may lead, Lim (2018) suggests, to quite exploitative labour relations:

> Historically, slavery has been understood as the condition of working very hard for very little or no pay whatsoever. Going from 'gig' to 'gig' or 'micro-task' to 'micro-task' might not call slavery to mind, but gig workers are beginning to emerge as the slaves of the new economy.

The gig economy is not a new phenomenon but a resurgence of older, unregulated labour extraction methods based on job insecurity with its corrosive effects. Potential policy approaches need to address the urgent regulation of such work. An eclectic approach to using and strengthening legislation designed to safeguard the rights of consumers and providers of services, including contractors, and regardless of employment status, is required. How a successful union movement responded to the gig economy by negotiation with a digital platform to bring advertised hourly pay rates in line with the minima set within the industrial relations system for employment in the relevant industries, is discussed by Flanagan (2017).

READ THE FULL CONVERSATION ARTICLE

READ THE JOURNAL ARTICLES

EXTEND YOUR KNOWLEDGE

The title of an article in *The Conversation* by Ming Lim, from 17 January 2018, is 'Why many click farm jobs should be understood as digital slavery'. You can access it here: https://theconversation.com/why-many-click-farm-jobs-should-be-understood-as-digital-slavery-83530. Additionally, you can download Frances Flanagan's article, 'Symposium on work in the "gig" economy: introduction', from *The Economic and Labour Relations Review*, 28 (3): 378–81, which is available at the companion website, https://study.sagepub.com/managingandorganizations5e. Finally, you can download Petriglieri, G., Ashford, S. J. and Wrzesniewski, A. (2018) 'Agony and ecstasy in the gig economy: cultivating holding environments for precarious and personalized work identities', *Administrative Science Quarterly*, http://journals.sagepub.com/doi/10.1177/0001839218759646, which is available at the companion website https://study.sagepub.com/managingandorganizations5e. The last article offers more reasons to be cheerful.

SUMMARY

In this chapter, we looked at organization design:

- Bureaucracy was the dominant organizational form for much of the twentieth century.
- Initial theories of organizations built on it, using contingency theory to stress factors such as environment, size, technology and structural adjustment to regain fit.
- Economic theories, based on transaction costs, stress performance and efficiency.
- More sociologically oriented theories suggested it was all about culture, institutions, entrepreneurship, standards, fashion and embeddedness.
- The chapter concluded with a brief account of some recent approaches to design, stressing: M-forms, matrix organizations, shamrocks, networks, rhizomes, creative clusters, heterarchy, relative autonomy, design thinking, democratic design, digital organizations and the gig economy.

EXERCISES

1. Having read this chapter, you should be able to say in your own words what each of the following key terms means. Test yourself or ask a colleague to test you.
   - Economic theories of the firm
   - Transaction costs
   - Sociological theories of organizations
   - Institutional isomorphism
   - Normative isomorphism
   - Coercive isomorphism
   - Mimetic isomorphism

- Embeddedness
- Standards
- Contingencies
- M-form
- Structural contingency theory
- Strategic choice
- Heterarchy
- Networks
- Structural adjustment to regain fit
- Rhizomes
- Creative clusters
- Shamrock organizations
- Digital organization
- Gig economy.

2. What is contingency theory?
3. According to Burns and Stalker, why do organizations in stable environments have different structures than those in fast-changing and innovative environments?
4. According to the Aston School, why does an organization become more bureaucratic as its size increases? What did Aldrich argue to the contrary?
5. What were the major innovations of the multi-divisional form?
6. What does embeddedness mean?
7. Markets, hierarchies, networks and democracy have been seen as different modes of organizing: discuss their differences.
8. What are the advantages and disadvantages of the gig economy in your view?

TEST YOURSELF

Review what you have learned by visiting:
https://study.sagepub.com/managingandorganizations5e or your eBook

- **Test yourself with multiple-choice questions.**
- **Revise key terms with the interactive flashcards.**

REVISE KEY TERMS

TEST YOURSELF

CASE STUDY

Organizational democratization

Many of the alternatives to bureaucracy that have been canvassed in this chapter entail elements of organizational democratization. What are some of the consequences of such democratization where it occurs? Drawing on Clegg and van Iterson's (2013) discussion of the civilizing process in relation to organizations and management, we can consider two contrasting scenarios.

(Continued)

(Continued)

Scenario 1

One scenario sees reversing subordination and specialization as necessitating more self-regulation. Decentralization and de-specialization imply more intraorganizational linkages, such as semi-autonomous work groups and cross-functional work teams. Postmodern organizations thus represent increasingly lengthy and complex webs of interdependency that require people to take each other into greater consideration. De-specialized workers have to be proficient as 'network players'. They have to juggle anxious, disciplined behaviour and relaxed, informal behaviour. Thus, complex and lengthy interdependence chains are likely to imply a further shift toward self-regulation.

With regard to trends such as the geographical spread of organizational units, outsourcing and strategic alliances, which in part allow for a loosening of the confines of place and time, one might also assume more self-regulation of those involved. An increase in interorganizational linkages in and between contemporary organizations also represents the enhanced scope and complexity of interdependence, and this, again, requires participants to take each other into consideration more and to postpone immediate gratification. Again, complex and lengthy interdependence chains might be thought likely to imply a further shift toward self-regulation. On this scenario, democratization leads to enhanced civility.

Scenario 2

Alternatively, decentralization and de-specialization of tasks might result in less self-regulation. From this perspective, workers who participate in various cross-functional work teams will experience a fragmentation of social relations. Instead of having a fixed set of near and familiar equals, de-specialized workers now have to deal with a large variety of organizational members. De-specialized workers cooperate with many co-workers but, as a rule, only on a part-time basis, usually for limited periods of time. Proximity is ephemeral: it happens less frequently and comes to an end altogether much sooner. Why be concerned with people whom you only see once a week or month? Why be concerned with people with whom collaboration will end in the very near future? Why bother with people who hardly understand what you can do or what you actually do? If you lose face vis-à-vis such a colleague, you will only lose one face. Since authority is waning as well (because of processes of decentralization), the consequences of inconsiderate behaviour on the work floor, or in office relations, will become even less consequential.

Fading spatial and temporal concentration (as a consequence of teleworking as well as the geographical spread of organizational units, outsourcing and strategic alliances) might also lead to less self-regulation. Because many direct work contacts will disappear or occur only electronically, restraints will weaken. Why should you be concerned with people you will never see? Or rather: Why should you be concerned with a shakily moving face you know only from videoconferencing or via a webcam? Why would one curb oneself and/or take care to impress through the regulated expression of manners and of morals? In all these cases, people are likely to experience shame and repugnance less easily. Growing concerns about Internet use by employees and attempts to develop corporate rules for online etiquette may be early reactions to a trend toward the loosening of behavioural restraints and skilful expression. When employees are more isolated, literally 'distanced', from the workplace, they may be less inclined to self-regulation and possibly more inclined to feelings of estrangement, and compensation might be sought in the non-work sphere. A shorter distance to family and community, a side-effect of working from home or from a neighbourhood work centre, may produce 'civilizing' effects with indirect gains. In this scenario, bureaucratic regulation provides a framework of rules for interpersonal organizational interaction, the loosening of which may well have deleterious effects on civility and organizational manners.

The issue

The blurring of the boundaries of place, time and organizational domain may bestow organizational members with varying needs for self-regulation. How the tension between discipline and expression in postmodern organizations will affect organizational members' disposition is an intriguing issue. On the one hand, there is the possibility of an increasing tolerance for the tension between autonomy and interdependence. In relation to the aspect of differentiation of behaviour, civilizing processes in one area (e.g. meeting manners) do not rule out de-civilizing processes in another (e.g. misconduct during department outings). De-civilizing trends in corporate boardrooms may well concur with civilizing trends on the shop floor and vice versa, especially where the accountability of lower status employees is much more tightly policed than that of the upper echelons.

Questions

1. Reviewing what you have read and what you know about various schemes for organizational democratization, do you think that reversing subordination and specialization will result in an organizational good for both employees and organization?
2. What are likely to be the characteristics of the consequences of organizational democratization?

ADDITIONAL RESOURCES

- As we have seen in earlier chapters, Scandinavian organization design is distinctive, tending to be far more democratic than elsewhere. Christensen and Lægreid (2018) provide a good discussion of the Scandinavian approach in the public sector.
- Focusing in particular on Norway, Johnsen, Ennals and Holtskog (2017) argue that Scandinavian countries' culture and society embed a distinct approach to organization design. They use Norway as an example for this argument, by looking at the development of approaches to work life since the 1950s to the present day.
- Continuing the Scandinavian theme, FastCompany provides '6 Lessons We Can Learn from a Scandinavian Model of Success'. Democracy and empowerment are the key Scandinavian inputs to successful organization design.

READ ABOUT SCANDINAVIAN LESSONS

- A recent review of organization designs in a historical context and up to the present day is to be found in Schley (2018).
- Manuel Lima has an engaging video on the power of networks and rhizomatic structures.

WATCH THE LIMA VIDEO

MANAGING GLOBALIZATION

FLOWS, FINANCE, PEOPLE

LEARNING OBJECTIVES

This chapter is designed to enable you to:

- understand the characteristics of globalization and its impact on organizations
- identify some key strategic issues involved in managing the global economy
- understand who and what are the globalizers
- discuss the central role of knowledge workers in the global economy
- understand that globalization has both positive and negative effects on individuals, organizations, societies and nations, and explain why resistance to globalization occurs.

BEFORE YOU GET STARTED...

It has been said that arguing against globalization is like arguing against the laws of gravity. (Kofi Annan, ex-head of the United Nations)

INTRODUCTION

READ ABOUT GLOBALIZATION

Whereas the Cold War, the world wars or the Age of Empires shaped previous generations of managers and organizations, the contemporary scene is shaped by globalization and reactions against it. Here we debate some key themes, focusing our discussion, eventually, on the winners and losers from globalization. As a management student, you need to understand the global patterns within which your managing will be constituted. The fact is that we live in a globalizing world. What this implies is that anywhere/anything is potentially or actually linked to anywhere/anything else in the management of commerce, government, aid, or other globally exchanged goods and services. Globalization is vitally important in terms of both the factors making this connectedness possible and the consequences flowing from it. Globalization, as the enveloping context, provides the big picture within which the rest of this book should be situated. However, it is also important because globalization is the phenomenon underpinning the contemporary contexts in which you will be managing and organizing.

DEFINING GLOBALIZATION

Globalization can be thought of as worldwide integration in virtually every sphere achieved principally through markets.

Financialization means the pervasive influence of financial calculations and judgements applied to everyday life and its practices.

For some theorists, **globalization** means the **financialization** of everyday organizational life (Martin, 2002).

One consequence of widespread financialization, Harvey (1992: 194) suggests, has been the financial system's autonomy from real production, becoming dominated by an economy of signs representing immediate capital flows digitally captured rather than an economy of things being manufactured. Things are still manufactured, of course, and today many of these material things that were once produced in Japan, Western Europe and the USA, are produced in new areas that have relatively recently been incorporated into the global economy, in China and South East Asia.

Production sites may have shifted globally but the centres of power and financial calculation have, on the whole, not yet followed. The transnational elite that sits at the apex of the major organizations and institutions housing global elites is still largely centred on the world's major global cities: London, New York and Tokyo. Firms from Japan and the USA dominate the list of Global 500 firms. To the extent that the world is becoming *corporately economically* global, it is that part of the world dominated by US, East and South East Asian, Western European and allied interests. Technological, economic and cultural integration is developing within and between these three regions and is evident in the patterns of international trade and investment flows. Interfirm strategic alliances are heavily concentrated among companies from these countries.

International activities enable firms to enter new markets, exploit technological and organizational advantages, as well as reduce business costs and risks, and achieve more economic integration of their activities. **Transnational** or **multinational organizations** – the terms are often used interchangeably – have significant control over both production and consumption in more than one country. They dominate world trade. In principle, they have sufficient geographical flexibility to shift resources and operations between global locations. In practice, it may be a bit more difficult. There is a plurality of transnational corporations, which neither dominate national industrial sectors in all markets nor operate without regard for more or less sovereign states.

Transnational or **multinational organizations** routinely organize and operate beyond national space in their activities.

The power of transnational organizations can easily be overestimated. Only a small number of transnational corporations are truly global, and not all transnational corporations are necessarily large, in conventional definitions of that term. Global patterns differ markedly according to the national origin of the firms. New supplies and sources of transnational corporations evolve as the world economy evolves, so that we now have emergent market transnational corporations in newly industrializing countries.

The increasing coordination of the world's financial system emerged to some degree at the expense of the power of nation-states' public sector managers in reserve banks to control capital flows and hence fiscal and monetary policy. Instantaneous financial trading means that shocks felt in one market are communicated immediately around the world's markets, as the 2008 global financial crisis demonstrated. Contemporary financial markets are characterized by flux and flow, a constant becoming, in a system in which finitude does not exist. Of course, as we learned in the most dramatic way, with the unfolding of the 2008 global financial crisis, these markets are not self-regulating.

The mass of individual enactments change the nature of that which is being enacted in a constant process whereby a new market reality is in the process of becoming, in an endless fluidity. The process of reality constantly changing on the screen is composed of an infinite succession of data that is the market, a series of devices for managing space, in which the world is comprised of time zones rather than physical features. Global markets have their own time-reckoning systems: dates and hours set for important economic announcements and for the release of periodically calculated economic indicators and data, structuring participants' awareness and anticipation and anchoring market developments in national or regional economies' fundamental characteristics.

CHARACTERISTICS OF GLOBALIZATION

Globalization is organized in terms of flows of inputs, their transformation and outputs, organized through global supply chains and global distribution. These, in turn, are embedded in technological and logistical systems, which, in turn, are coupled with financial and governance systems. The key actors, without doubt, are transnational firms. Technological and logistical systems are contained within a financial system and a governance system of regulation, coordination and control (see Figure 15.1). Financial systems control the supply and value of the underlying key commodity, which of course is capital.

Circuits of global production have an impact in four ways:

1. *Global relations between states*, as we see states flourish as a result of globalization, such as China and India in recent times. New opportunities for managers from, and within, these countries arise, with all the challenges of international placements for HRM (Brewster et al., 2007; Sparrow et al., 2004).
2. *Sustainability*, as places such as China and India industrialize on the back of a fossil fuel industry that is ecologically damaging. The levels of pollution in the Pearl River Delta, for instance, which is China's main export route, are absolutely dreadful. Managers may manage costs by outsourcing or setting up a supply chain – but they could end up having

to manage damage that is far more than they bargained for when they made their initial assessment of the value proposition of an outsourcing or supply chain partner.

3. *Identity*: People migrate and move from one society to another as a result of globalization – the millions of 'guest workers' in the Middle East oil-rich countries of the Gulf, for instance – or the people who become informal migrants from Africa and the Middle East, often fleeing danger and instability in search of a better life, which has a considerable impact on changing conceptions of personal identity. Today, even the most remote villager can compare life in the village with life in the mirror that media project into their communities. Managers who employ such people may have to manage the contradictions that occur when the expectations of global business and local culture collide.

4. *Diversity*: In almost any of the world's great cities today there are people working with each other, competing with each other and playing with each other, whose ancestors come from villages all over the globe. Multicultural society is normal. Managers today have to be able to manage complex differentiated workforces with sensitivity and skill.

Transnational corporations often get a bad press for their subcontracting practices in the Third World. For instance, writers such as Naomi Klein are extremely critical of the role that transnationals play in the developing world. Her argument is that transnationals behave irresponsibly by employing subcontractors who pay low wages, and have poor working conditions and potentially abusive environments (Klein, 2001). She singles out the famous companies whose brands are known the world over.

On balance, it is fair to say that transnational organizations may be positive agents of change. It is clear that they have the potential to create stable, long-term jobs with decent pay and conditions. Thus, potentially, they deliver better jobs

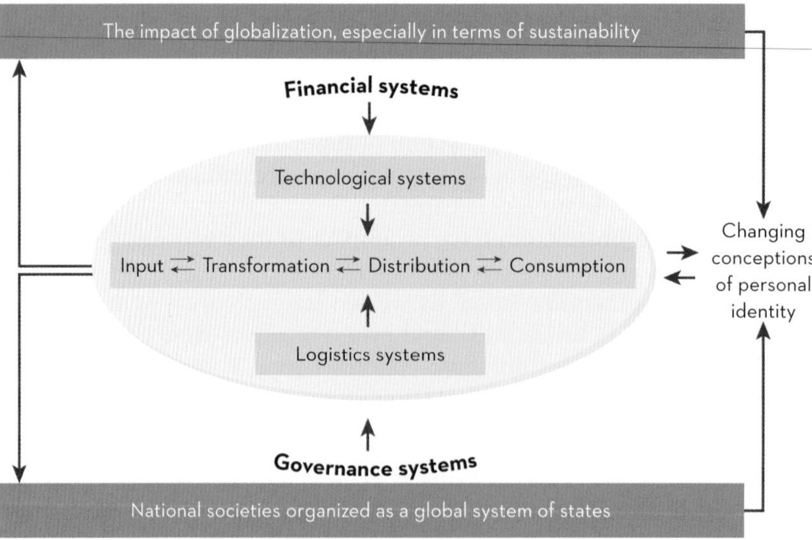

FIGURE 15.1 Global flows, systems and effects

and better wages in many economies. In addition, they set standards that local industry has to aspire to in both labour and industry practice. Those transnational organizations that do not meet global standards can expect to be subject to campaigns throughout the Western world. Their good name represents their reputational capital. If there really were 'no logos', as Naomi Klein advocates, it would be much harder to police standards, because without brand names, no reputations would suffer. There would be no brand differentia offering opportunities for discrimination between the choice of one T-shirt and another. We would expect that in such a situation, price signals would be even more sovereign and would exercise still stronger downward pressure on local wages and conditions in the Third World. Fair logos rather than no logos might be better policy.

Subcontracted manufacturing jobs also create higher export earnings domestically, which potentially enhance the tax base of less developed national governments. We say 'potentially' because often these companies are quite sophisticated in moving tax losses around their global operations and using the pricing of internally traded goods to minimize liabilities where they will attract the highest regimes of tax – something referred to as transfer pricing.

> Indeed, Freeland (2013) notes that although companies such as Amazon, Apple and Google (he also mentions Starbucks, although as coffee connoisseurs, we would prefer not to) are amongst the most admired, innovative and wealthiest companies globally, they are also some of the most lightly taxed. These companies are highly effective in their operations in using transfer pricing and licence fees for internal transactions so as to minimize their tax liability in higher taxing jurisdictions and to maximize it in in low or non-taxing jurisdictions. Their founders are extremely rich and this wealth, through lobbying, political donations and philanthropic contributions, can be a source of considerable influence effecting the ways in which their interests are represented. In some political economies, such as that of the apparatchiks that expropriated the natural resources previously controlled by the Soviet state to make themselves the oligarchs of Russia's freewheeling gangster capitalism, or their more sophisticated counterparts in the peak of the global financial services industries lacing together New York and London, influence is sufficient to change the 'rules of the game' in quite explicit ways that favour their interests.

IN PRACTICE

Shopping in a digital and global world

Not so long ago, if you were to go shopping for some new fashions you needed to go to the shops, to move from wherever you were to where the shops are. As we all know, online shopping has changed the equation of mobility and shopping. Does this mean the end of shops and shopping centres, per se? Not really, suggest two European academic specialists in technology and fashion. Céline Abecassis-Moedas and Valérie Moatti (2018) wrote in

(Continued)

(Continued)

READ THE FULL ARTICLE

The Conversation on 'Digital by design: how technology is breathing new life into the fashion business'. Shopping for fashion is a physical and emotional experience that digital technologies are intensifying rather than entirely replacing. Physical stores are not just a point of sale but also a meeting point and a recreational destination, the attractiveness of which is being digitally enhanced. New technologies can machine-store customer knowledge enhanced by the power of data analysis in terms of preferences, styles, colours, fabrics, and so on. More fundamentally, the digitization of the retail sector is transforming the entire value chain. Customer information can be analysed to customize a product in terms of style, size and general suitability. By digitizing the customer relationship, the entire manufacturing and distribution process can be shaped by the customer's involvement in the entire value chain, from the choice of raw materials through to recycling.

Questions

1. Think of your experiences as a digital shopper: what things would you not buy digitally? Why not?
2. What do you think differentiates positively and negatively the two experiences of shopping digitally and actually going somewhere to shop?

The digital revolution does not dematerialize the physical world. Things are still manufactured, shipped and designed, but increasingly these activities are globally disaggregated through globalization. Dicken (2007: 8), the foremost geographer of globalization, suggests that there is an interpenetration of four parallel processes creating globalization:

1. *Localizing processes*, geographically concentrated activities with varying degrees of functional integration, playing a key role in the global economy, define key ports such as Rotterdam, Singapore and Hong Kong or airports such as Heathrow and Frankfurt.
2. *Internationalizing processes*, with low levels of functional integration and a simple spread of economic activities across national borders. The *maquiladora* plants of Monterrey, in northern Mexico, which use cheap land and labour to service goods or produce components and goods for the US economy, would be a case in point.
3. *Globalizing processes* are characterized by both an extensive geographical spread and a high degree of functional integration. The global auto industry would be a case in point, where new models may come from any of a number of countries, despite us thinking of them as 'national' cars. German cars might be manufactured in Brazil, the USA, South Africa or the Czech Republic, for instance, as well as Germany.
4. *Regionalizing processes* take place at a regionally supranational scale such as the EU or the European Free Trade Association, or other similar common markets.

The global spread of MNCs means that in many cases corporations will have considerable potential to shape policy within nation-states. Less developed nations will sometimes compete against each other in terms of tax incentives, grants and other inducements to attract firms to their country. Within countries, regional policies operate to try and bring investment to particular regions. Corporations are often deeply embedded within specific locales, however, perhaps because of a specific infrastructure, suppliers or university research centres. Because states are spatially fixed, they are immobile compared with firms, and so governments have to struggle with the policy implications of globalization; they cannot decamp or disengage.

KEY STRATEGIC ISSUES

GLOBAL STRATEGIC ALLIANCES AND MERGERS

Major mechanisms of global integration are collaborations and strategic **alliances**. Organizations' managers engage in interorganizational arrangements such as alliances and mergers and acquisitions when they need to access resources they do not control internally. Such arrangements enable them to be more autonomous as well as more legitimate (Drees and Heugens, 2013). The major strategic objectives of alliances are maximizing value, enhancing learning, protecting core competencies and maintaining flexibility. 'The more a company becomes globalized, the more it is likely to lose its own identity within a tangle of companies, alliances and markets', suggests Petrella (1996: 76). Particularly in industries where there is a dominant worldwide market leader, strategic alliances and networks allow coalitions of smaller partners to compete against the leading companies rather than each other in several ways.

Alliances connect different organizations in a network or web that includes many transacting parties with shared control and continuing contributions by all partners.

Strategic alliances help transfer technology across borders. Access to new markets is facilitated by using the complementary resources of local firms, including distribution channels and product range extensions. Alliances allow partners to leverage specific capabilities and save the costs of duplication (see also pp. 340–341), especially where activities are outsourced through alliances or subcontracting, as well as to spread risk.

Strategic alliances are a way of focusing investments, efforts and attention only on those tasks that a company does well in its **value chain**. Activities and practices core to profit making can be differentiated from secondary aspects, such as corporate governance or human resource management.

The **value chain** allows organization transactions to be analysed with regard to the value that they add to the final product or service.

The value chain core will differ from industry to industry. Managers can analyse the value chain in their organization and outsource or procure elsewhere those elements that are not contributing positively to profitability, a process referred to as deconstruction or disintermediation of the value chain. When they do this, they establish what is often referred to as a supply chain, where rather than being created internally value is created through a network of interorganizational relations. Formalizing alliance relations helps to (a) focus participants' attention, (b) provoke articulation, deliberation and reflection, (c) instigate and maintain interaction and (d) reduce judgement errors and individual biases, and diminish the incompleteness and inconsistency of cognitive representations. Around half of all cross-border strategic alliances terminate within seven years: where one of the partners purchases the alliance, its termination signals a change in state, not failure. Managing organizational culture after a merger may not be straightforward, as it is not only systems and technologies that can prove incompatible. Mergers often under perform and lose value. The vast majority of mergers are classified as failures (Bowman et al., 1999). Excess liquidity often drives merger activity, making it possible for managers to choose poor acquisitions when they run out of good ones (Martynova and Renneboog, 2008).

DIFFERENT INSTITUTIONAL SYSTEMS

Transnational activity is not easily managed precisely because it crosses the borders of so many institutional systems. UK and US companies are stock price oriented, whereas, in contrast, Japanese, Dutch and Swiss companies are less sensitive to stock prices. Hutton (1995) argues that the primacy of finance creates an atmosphere in which a short-term orientation prevails, as companies aim to satisfy shareholders, who can easily sell their stock, which stifles innovation. German and Japanese companies, with stable and major bank investments, can plan for the medium and long term.

Geppert and Matten (2006) argue that how key actors – especially the top management team – shape the interaction of institutional pressures and, hence, manufacturing approaches, location choices and work system designs is the major factor behind differential success. Typically, they argue, managers apply a 'cherry-picking' strategy where they selectively use elements of the way in which work is normally shaped in the host country. Manufacturing strategies are highly context-specific and difficult (if not impossible) to transfer elsewhere. For instance, Japanese just-in-time manufacturing does not work very well in cities, such as Bangkok, where the traffic is gridlocked much of the time, nor did it work when the tsunami that destroyed the nuclear power station at Fukushima also broke up major roads.

EXTEND YOUR KNOWLEDGE

READ THE ARTICLE

An article available at the companion website https://study.sagepub.com/managingandorganizations5e will enable you to extend and deepen your knowledge of how politics in MNCs operate: Levy, O. and Reiche, B. S. (2018) 'The politics of cultural capital: social hierarchy and organizational architecture in the multinational corporation', *Human Relations*, 71 (6): 867–94. This article is part of a special issue of the journal dedicated to analysis of multinational organizations. If you want to extend your knowledge of multinationals and politics, the introduction and the articles collected in the special issue are well worth reading.

The rationalities of government and commerce differ greatly. Neither home base nor host-country governments necessarily share interests with the transnational organizations that straddle them. It might be remarked that in business there are no allies, only interests. Table 15.1 compares the different priorities.

TABLE 15.1 Government and business: different priorities

Government priorities	Corporate priorities
Managing changing definitions of what constitute 'citizenship rights', such as taxpayer-funded provisions of big-ticket items like health and education, or else they have to manage to persuade people who once saw themselves primarily as citizens to become consumers	Unrestricted access to resources and markets throughout the world and freedom to integrate manufacturing with other operations across national boundaries
External sources of investment, technology and knowledge that transnational organizations can supply to create global competitiveness within the national economy	Unimpeded right to try to coordinate and control all aspects of the company on a worldwide basis and global competitiveness without government barriers
Investment regulations that define specific levels of local content, technology transfer and a variety of other conditions in an effort to make transnational companies increase the extent of their local activities	Maximize shareholder value and minimize taxes by establishing corporate headquarters in low-tax regimes such as the Dutch Antilles or the Cayman Islands Tax incentives for investment in industrial R&D and technological innovations, as well as guarantees that national enterprises from the given country have a stable home base
Reduced costs of government and public administration, often producing new commercial opportunities in fields such as defence contracting and telecommunications	Lobby for light regulatory frameworks and minimal government expenditures, so less tax is paid Privileged access to the domestic market via public contracts (defence, telecommunications, health, transport, education, social services)
Efficiency drives and privatization with control of essential parts of sovereignty, such as legislation and the formation of national economic policy	Want governments to offer grants and subsidies for local investment and expect governments to cover the costs of basic infrastructure, such as funding of basic and high-risk research, universities and vocational training systems; promotion and funding of the dissemination of scientific and technical information and technology transfer; as well as ensuring economic and physical security and a communications infrastructure, such as up-to-date and high-speed international rail links and broadband
Defending state economic, political and cultural boundaries	A logic of capital mobility: if the local state does not provide the required sweeteners, mobile capitalism will simply exit the scene and set up where the benefits sought can be ensured

IN PRACTICE

Tax efficiency

Governments all over the world strive to be more efficient. In many instances, efficiency is interpreted as lower costs of government. In one country, which happens to be Australia, efficiency measures have been applied across government departments. One department that has been subject to efficiency cuts is the Australian Tax Office (ATO), responsible for overseeing the collection of the nation's tax receipts.

(Continued)

(Continued)

READ THE FULL REPORT

In a report entitled *Who Pays for Our Common Wealth?* United Voice (2014), a trade union, collaborated with the Tax Justice Network to research what Australia's 200 largest companies pay in tax. The report's analysis demonstrates large amounts of very effective and efficient tax minimization occurring for global companies. In general, looking at the largest 200 companies on the Australian Stock Exchange, nearly one-third had an average effective tax rate (ETR) of 10 per cent or less; 57 per cent disclosed that they had subsidiaries in secret jurisdictions (tax havens) and 60 per cent reported debt to equity levels above 75 per cent, which may artificially reduce taxable profits. On the United Voice web page, if you look at the tables on pages 12 and 13 you will see how much tax has been paid on average (between 0 per cent and 7 per cent for the largest 27 companies) and how much tax has been forgone, applying the standard corporate tax rate.

As tax specialists are made redundant by the ATO as an efficiency measure, they are rapidly hired by one of the major accounting firms auditing these transnational organizations or by the companies themselves, where they are able to use their insider knowledge to minimize their tax payments using smart accounting practice to profit their clients. As experienced tax professionals leave the ATO to be employed by the big four accounting firms, KPMG, PricewaterhouseCoopers, Deloitte's, and Ernst & Young, to advise transnational organizations, they can outwit the less experienced professionals who remain in the ATO's employ. These employees now work under efficiency requirements that impose case deadlines of 90 days on audit teams, providing insufficient time to do the kind of audit that might outflank the tax advice their ex-colleagues are providing. The big four accounting firms have detailed and accurate knowledge of internal ATO workings from their hiring of tax specialists: gamekeepers turned poachers.

In practice, this erosion of capability through the pursuit of government efficiency and exploitation of tax minimization by transnational organizations is widespread in governments other than Australia - it is not a uniquely Australian issue. Zirnsak (2014) identifies the problem as endemic in the OECD.

READ ABOUT GLOBALISATION & TAX

Elsewhere, in *the Guardian* online (US edition) there is a two-week report on the 'tax gap', which contains a wealth of data and analysis. In the same US edition of *the Guardian* online, there is a 27 May 2013 opinion piece by the ex-head of the World Bank, Joseph Stiglitz, entitled 'Globalisation isn't just about profits. It's about taxes too', which also addresses the issue of globalization from a tax point of view

READ MORE ABOUT TAX AVOIDANCE

In practice, as corporate tax collections decline, the balance has to be made up either in a further reduction of government services or the increased taxation of citizens. Citizens usually cannot choose where they pay taxes: companies often can and so seek the lowest tax regimes in which to establish tax liability. The tax arbitrage potential that globalization creates and the increasing mobility of corporations that own intellectual property lead to tax losses in advanced economies and put pressure on them to lower their corporate tax rates.

Questions

1. What are some of the major ethical issues attached to the organization of tax collecting, in your opinion?

WHAT WOULD YOU DO?

WHAT WOULD YOU DO?

Government has retained you on a consulting basis to advise how to raise revenue in a globalized world. The question is how to institute policies that maximize revenue in an era of globalization? What recommendations would you make? What might be the unanticipated costs as well as the anticipated benefits of the solutions that you consider?

COMPETITIVE ADVANTAGE

INNOVATION DRIVES COMPETITIVE ADVANTAGE

Globalization is driven by the strategic responses of firms as they exploit market opportunities and adapt to changes in their technological and institutional environment, and attempt to steer these changes to their advantage. The most important competitive force in the global economy is the capacity for innovation, a thesis powerfully illustrated by Porter (1990) in *The Competitive Advantage of Nations*.

Firms changing the constraints within which they and competitors operate can gain **competitive advantage**, allowing them to outperform the competition.

Porter correlates the advance of knowledge, achievement in innovation and national competitive advantage. In his search for a new paradigm of national **competitive advantage**, Porter starts from the premise that competition is dynamic and evolving, whereas traditional thinking had a static view of cost efficiency due to factor or scale advantages. But static efficiency is always being overcome by the rate of progress in the change in products, marketing, new production processes and new markets.

The crucial issue for firms, and nations, is how they 'improve the quality of the factors, raise the productivity with which they are utilized, and create new ones' (Porter, 1990: 21). The capacity to innovate successfully on a worldwide basis becomes the key competency of leading international companies. It frequently leads to substantive injustices as employees' knowledge in one part of the world is used to deliver cheaper and more efficient manufacturing in another part of the world, their jobs then being scrapped (Clegg, 1999).

Increasingly, it is **human capital** and **intellectual property** rights that lead to sustained competitive advantage.

Human capital is the stock of knowledge, habits, social and personality attributes, including creativity, embodied in the workforce at a collective, team or individual level.

Investment in human capital development comes from education. The role of human capital in economic development, productivity growth and innovation is frequently cited as justification for government investment in skill formation. Sometimes, human capital, as a concept, is broken down into different types of capital, including cultural capital, social capital, economic capital and symbolic capital. Conceived in this way, the idea of human capital and its formation links to a broader conception than just skill and educational development. Market imperfections and high transaction costs provide an incentive for firms to internalize firm-specific knowledge and expertise in the form of human capital. Intellectual property rights are bestowed on owners of ideas, inventions and creative expression that have the status of property. National laws protect intellectual property.

Intellectual property is information that derives its intrinsic value from creative ideas with a commercial value realized through sale on the market.

LOCAL CLUSTERS IN A GLOBALIZING WORLD

A paradoxical consequence of increasing globalization is the concentration of clusters of world-class expertise in specialist industries in different local economies around the world. The significant local dimension of the globalization phenomenon consists of regional economies built on interlinked networks of relations among firms, universities and other institutions in their local environment (see Storper and Scott, 1993). Early specialization is reinforced by the growth of similar firms and institutions to create highly competitive industrial and service clusters.

We can explain the rationale for the local concentration of specialist industry in terms of the advantages of being in the same location as similar firms, specialized suppliers and contractors, as well as knowledgeable customers (see also p. 480). In addition, these locations tend to provide a good technological infrastructure and specialist research institutions, as well as a highly skilled labour force, where specialization within firms enables extensive outsourcing (vertical disintegration) and encourages similar new firms to be set up in the location (horizontal disintegration). For instance, think of Hollywood and Bollywood's role in making movies, or the role of networks and clusters associated with 'Motorsport Valley', a small area north of London that accounts for most of the automotive innovation associated with Formula 1 motor racing (Tallman et al., 2004).

Local geographic concentrations of three broad groups of industrial and service activities have been noted:

1. Highly competitive, traditional, labour-intensive industries, which are highly concentrated, including textiles and clothing in Italy.
2. High-technology industries that often cluster around new activities, such as biotechnology in San Francisco, semiconductors in Silicon Valley, scientific instruments in Cambridge (UK) and musical instruments in Hamamatsu (Japan).
3. Services, notably financial and business services, such as advertising, film, fashion design, and R&D activities, concentrated in a few big global cities such as Los Angeles, Tokyo, London, Paris, Sydney and Shanghai.

Globalization increases the competitiveness of local economies by attracting international firms with their own specific advantages and enhancing established sourcing and supply relations. Local firms individually may respond to heightened competition through improving their innovative performance. Innovation may be extended through developing greater interactions between firms, suppliers, users, production support facilities and educational and other institutions in local innovation systems.

Local firms, particularly if they are highly specialized, will cooperate with international firms seeking complementary resources in the specialized assets of small firms. Some writers, following Robertson (1992), refer to the phenomenon of the interpenetration of the global in the local, and vice versa, as 'glocalization'. However, it is not only in areas of straightforward global business, such as manufacturing, that locality can become a source of competitive advantage; it can also be built from marginalized and stigmatized local cultures. Think of hip hop and grime, dominant popular music styles globally, which emerged from the marginal culture of urban youth.

WHO AND WHAT ARE THE GLOBALIZERS?

For global actions there have to be global ideas that travel and are translated widely. Over the last 25 years, there has been an emergence of a powerful management ideas industry which has successfully packaged, communicated and sold discontinuous innovation as a cultural ideal and a desirable good (Townley, 2002a, 2002b). A management ideas industry has been fuelled by the rise of business schools, especially through the provision of MBA degrees, the growth in management consultancies and the emergence of self-styled management gurus. Taken together, this amounts to an actor network that has successfully packaged and commoditized managerial initiatives. These models of 'best practice' have been disseminated throughout the organizational world. They create blueprints of what organizations 'should' look like and what managers 'should' do. Collectively, the key players of the management ideas industry have helped produce management fashions.

LARGE IT FIRMS

The major actors in the management ideas industry have been the large IT companies, such as SAP and Cap Gemini. The changes in IT have been one of the major enabling factors behind globalization. IT firms have played an important role in the development of the management ideas industry. Recent initiatives such as enterprise resource planning and knowledge management rely very heavily on IT practices. Kipping (2002) has argued that consultancies go through waves of development. According to his analysis, large IT firms are riding the most recent wave and are becoming the dominant players in the consulting industry. We may think of them as the 'fifth column' of the management ideas industry: they penetrate businesses that need the technical capabilities that IT brings, but their entry becomes a beachhead for sustained attack by management ideas. The first of these firms are usually introduced by management consultants, often called in to try and make the IT systems that millions have been expended on work better, to live up to expectations.

MANAGEMENT GURUS

The emergence of a global management project is in part a phenomenon spread through hugely influential 'guru' books. There is now a huge commercial market in popular management books and a circuit of celebrity for those who write them. They are the gurus of the modern age, the 'management gurus'. Earlier in this book we introduced Tom Peters. He is the most celebrated and, at the same time, infamous of the management gurus. Gurus are generally self-styled and known for their image and rhetoric intensity. Producing airport lounge bestsellers and conducting world lecture tours, gurus hawk their homespun nostrums throughout the corporate world.

Analysts of gurus have argued – in a McLuhan (1964) fashion – that the medium is the message: evangelical-style exhortations to change accompanied by convincing stories and snappy sound bites characterize the genre. The books follow a similar vein and, as we suggested earlier, are often taken to task for their theoretical and methodological failings, which is, perhaps, to miss the point. Even more managers are likely to listen to a guru presentation or perhaps read a guru book than are likely to attend business school (Clegg and Palmer, 1996).

Many of the gurus have enjoyed glittering corporate careers and their ideas on management are lent credibility by this corporate experience – such texts are often ghostwritten as heroic narratives that stress the unique character of doing it 'my way' (Clegg and Palmer, 1996). Often, key texts will anchor key management consultancy products.

MANAGEMENT CONSULTANCY

Large-scale management consultancy has grown exponentially and consultants have become major actors in the creation and transmission of management ideas. Management consultants simultaneously instil a sense of security and anxiety in their clients: security, because they imbue managers with a sense of certainty and control over the future or whatever organizational problem it is that the consulting is concerned with; anxiety, because the managers are in a sense emasculated – unable to manage without the guidance of consultants (Sturdy, 2006).

While many US consultancies had been in existence for much of the last century – coming out of the systematic management movement of Taylor's day – it is over the last 20 years or so that demand for their services has boomed. Organizations such as McKinsey and the Boston Consulting Group have become high-status brands in their own right. Other consultancies emerged out of the large accountancy partnerships (Hinings et al., 1999). Uniquely placed as the auditors to large firms, most major accountancy firms commercialized to the extent that their consultancy operations became at least as important as their core auditing business.

The role of the large accounting firms is pivotal to understanding the story of the rise of consultancies. By the mid-1980s, the market for financial audit was mature and had stagnated. In any case, outside of a few accounting firms in a few geographical locations, competition between these firms was frowned upon and for the most part regarded as being somewhat aggressive and ungentlemanly. What the large accounting firms possessed was a monopoly over the provision of audits to large firms, with 'full professional jurisdiction' (Abbott, 1988) protected by law. The large accounting firms developed a number of capabilities, one of which was the ability to cultivate and sustain long-term relationships with clients. These connections were often cemented by their own accountants going to work in client firms after a number of years with the accounting partnership. Accounting partnerships also possessed highly sophisticated means of charging for audits and managing large-scale interventions in organizations.

Power (1997) has argued that we increasingly live in an audit society, one in which the principles of verification and calculability underpin practices. In the UK, for instance, large accounting firms played an important role in drafting privatization and private finance initiatives from the implementation of which they were simultaneously to profit from. Accountants and management consultants now often carry out government work that was once the sole preserve

of mandarins. Audit opened the corporate door for the big accounting firms to offer additional services. Hanlon (1994) has demonstrated the way in which the large accounting firms commercialized themselves – pursuing capital accumulation strategies; also Greenwood et al. (1999) have written extensively on the unique characteristics of accounting firms that allowed them to globalize so successfully.

MANAGEMENT EDUCATION

EVOLUTION OF MANAGEMENT EDUCATION

Management education has long been a contested terrain: indeed, it could be argued that it has been such since the inception of its current form in the early twentieth century in the USA. Signs of this contestation were evident in two influential reports on management education that were released in 1959: the Carnegie Report and the Ford Report. A significant response to these reports was the deployment of the American Assembly of Collegiate Schools of Business (AACSB) in 1961 as the standards body for masters-level graduate education. As was reported shortly thereafter (Oberg, 1963), among the chief criticisms made in these reports were that education standards were low, grading too easy and the quality of research conducted in business schools poor. It was also claimed that business curricula did not prepare students properly for work: there was too much narrow vocationalism in a curriculum with an insufficient number of subjects in the humanities, liberal arts, mathematics, statistics, languages, and the natural and social sciences (Oberg, 1963).

At the same time that the American system was being challenged to make management education better quality and broader in content, it was being exported as an exemplar around the world. Indeed, the post-war phenomenon of the Americanization of management education on a global scale was instigated initially by the American involvement in the reconstruction of a devastated Europe, leading to the formation of the many new business schools. The global adoption of the MBA became the model for the advanced education of managers.

Management education dominates the Anglo-American university system to a considerable degree. Sturdy (2006) reports that '25% of US university students currently major in business or management and in the UK, 30% of undergraduates study some management'. Equally, fast-emerging economies such as China and India have embraced the MBA with great enthusiasm. A small number of business school MBAs are rich in symbolic capital, with some such as Harvard enjoying iconic status. The MBA is now offered in ever-increasing volumes across the world, fast overshadowing the traditional undergraduate domains of academic endeavour.

The MBA is the principal vehicle for normalizing the managers of tomorrow, while offering practical opportunities for the academics and consultants of today to expound influential ideas with legitimation. The consultancies seek to attract the brightest and the best from the top MBAs. The MBA-speak of PowerPoint slides and spreadsheets prepares the student of today for the consulting and management presentations of tomorrow. Thus, the MBA acts as a rationalizing device as well as a means of career advancement for individual students.

MANAGEMENT EDUCATION, THEORY AND PRACTICE

One of the fascinating features of the MBA is its link with management practice. The promissory note of the MBA is to deliver more highly paid jobs to students. While there are a host of distance and part-time programmes available, the costs of participating in a full-time programme are considerable. Students have to be fairly sure that their investment will be worthwhile by providing them with a degree of fluency in the cultural capital of managerialism: of course, whether being able to be a smooth conversationalist in a particular rhetoric makes better managers or not is an open question. What it certainly does do is to allow them to communicate with other managers in a global management context. The MBA curriculum and skills are fast becoming the Latin of the modern world, with modern accounting the grammar, spreading to become a global institutional practice, through the ubiquity of MBA and professional management education, as Yong Suk Jang (2005) argues.

Business schools have seen rumblings of disquiet about the MBA. Some authors regard the MBA as an increasingly irrelevant model based on assumptions intrinsic to a less flexible age than today. Henry Mintzberg's (2004) 'hard look at the soft practice of managing and management development' (see also Bennis and O'Toole, 2005) revealed in a popular book what other scholars such as Parker and Jary (1995) and Sturdy and Gabriel (2000) had earlier theorized more critically: the MBA does not necessarily produce either an educated workforce or good managers. Mintzberg makes a clear distinction between the practice of management and what the MBA produces (Mintzberg, 2004). His point is that (North American) MBA education is focused on an outmoded model of disciplinary business functions, analysis and technique, rather than on the practice of administering. There is a paradox here: his brief review of the series of crises that management education has faced over the years stands in stark contrast to the overwhelming international success of management education.

That the MBA should have talismanic and iconic status might seem surprising when one contrasts the market reality with the conclusions drawn by significant figures in the field such as Jeffrey Pfeffer, who suggest that, in practice, 'there is scant evidence that the MBA credential, particularly from non-elite schools, or the grades earned in business courses – a measure of the mastery of the material – are related to either salary or the attainment of higher level positions in organizations' (Pfeffer and Fong, 2002: 92). It would seem that the cultural potency of the MBA is stronger than the realities of its effects or the vigour of its critique.

In some English-speaking universities, the MBA has become a commodity to be sold to overseas students in large numbers to help keep the university afloat in an era of declining funding. One corollary has been a deflation in the value of the credential. The value of the MBA was that it was a positional good; when few people possessed it, it had a high value. When it is increasingly sold to ever more people, some of whom have few claims to any mastery of business, its positional value will be sharply eroded. Today, the MBA is increasingly global *and* ubiquitous; its ubiquity is leading to increasing attempts to differentiate products in the market, generating more specialist versions of the overall generalist qualification, in order to enhance its value proposition.

PROBLEMS WITH MANAGEMENT EDUCATION

The wave of accounting scandals and corporate collapses has led to further soul searching over the MBA. Enron was an enthusiastic recruiter of MBA graduates (Cruver, 2003). The company was originally involved in transmitting and distributing electricity and natural gas throughout the USA. Enron grew wealthy due largely to marketing, and was named 'America's Most Innovative Company' by *Fortune* magazine for six consecutive years, from 1996 to 2001. As discovered, in late 2001, when it collapsed, many of Enron's recorded assets and profits were inflated or fraudulently non-existent. Sophisticated accounting presented a picture that was far from accurate. Cruver, a Texas A&M MBA graduate, chronicles his 18 months at Enron before the company collapsed. The enduring images are of highly motivated, bright MBA graduates not asking difficult questions, not raising concerns over dubious practices and generally being socialized into the macho, competitive 'win at all costs' culture of Enron (see Gibney, 2005).

That these MBA graduates' professional education seeded ethical concerns so lightly is one thing but some writers such as Sumantra Ghoshal (2005) argue that the MBA actually made crashes such as Enron possible. By contrast with professions such as medicine and law, there is little attention paid to professional ethics and civic morals, other than those that emphasize winning at all costs, being a corporate game player and being the one who ends up with the most chips in the lottery of organizational life.

THE FUTURE OF MANAGEMENT EDUCATION

How has the MBA achieved the global significance that it has? In part, this is an outcome that is dialectically related to globalization: globalizing processes encourage the employment and utilization of the technical knowledge associated with MBAs to maintain their momentum. In part, it is precisely because of these processes of standardization.

Recently, there have been two factors that have further influenced the development of the MBA: first, the introduction of *ranking systems for business schools*; and, second, the growing pressure towards, and internationalization of, *formal accreditation systems*. Together, these have placed management education in a 'regulatory field' (Hedmo et al., 2005) that is increasingly likely to shape its future.

READ ABOUT BUSINESS SCHOOLS

There is an increasing importance of standards for the MBA as a commodity circulating at a global level. The AACSB International – a body recognized as the largest and most prestigious accrediting institution for management education in the USA (Hedmo et al., 2005) and, increasingly, the rest of the world – plays a key role in standard setting. (There is also the much smaller European-based EQUIS programme, but it does not have the same global significance.) Bodies such as the AACSB increasingly accredit MBAs. When agencies such as the AACSB subject management programmes to assessment, scrutiny and evaluation in order to accredit them (Hedmo et al., 2005), they are bearers of Americanization (Üsdiken, 2004: 89), standardizing the form of management knowledge.

While such developments can be seen as a form of decentralized cultural imitation and emulation, what is striking in recent times is the concerted attempt to impose a centralized set of standards on the geographically and culturally dispersed practice of MBA education. Most particularly, such centralization has been achieved by the way in which the AACSB has become normatively mimetic and, as such, an obligatory passage point for global legitimacy. The AACSB offers accreditation to business/management school programmes in universities across the world. Promising a guarantee of quality and credentials, the AACSB is today an important and influential force in MBA education, and is likely to be so increasingly.

GLOBAL MANAGERS AND GLOBAL JOBS

KNOWLEDGE WORK

The management ideas industry of gurus, consultants, educators and IT firms has reshaped the corporate world. They have changed the linguistic and ideational context in which organizations operate by ushering in a new grammar for organizations. Most large organizations' managers today can talk about their 'strategy', articulate their 'mission', their 'values' and their 'corporate culture'. There is no doubt that globalization spreads certain universal values and attachments through its world of global consumer products and brands. Rolex, Chivas Regal and Porsche spell success in just about every language. All young global analysts, whether working on money, films or words, recognize such symmetry.

Knowledge workers are analysts manipulating symbols to solve, identify and broker problems. They simplify reality into abstract images by rearranging, juggling, experimenting, communicating and transforming these images, using tools such as mathematical algorithms, legal arguments, financial analysis, scientific principles or psychological insights that address conceptual puzzles (Reich, 1991). They comprise the creative class who populate creative cities (Florida, 2002). They are probably who you want to be.

To what degree are these knowledge workers, comprising the creative class, different from those who have gone before? What marks out their professional identity? Management analysts such as Mats Alvesson (1993; Alvesson and Kärreman, 2001) have argued that linguistic and symbolic accomplishments in circumstances of high ambiguity and uncertainty are the hallmark of knowledge work. In such circumstances, there is no one correct answer; instead, there are a number of competing, plausible alternatives. It places the persuasive abilities of the knowledge worker to the fore, comprising both their image intensity (the suit they wear, the briefcase they carry, the sleekness of their PowerPoint presentation) and the persuasiveness of their rhetoric (the robustness of their argument, their vocabulary, their accent).

Knowledge workers are global, working for Big 4 firms or their small boutique equivalents. They regularly move between the great commercial capitals of the world, creating genuinely international corporate elites. Such transience, perhaps, fosters networking skills and alters sensibilities around risk, two other important characteristics of the symbolic analysts. In summary, they are the stressed-out but well-remunerated shifters and shapers of money, meanings and markets, doing deals, making business, moving from project to project (Garrick and Clegg, 2001).

Global business elites are easy to spot: on the one hand, those who are highly skilled and educated and employed in global organizations; on the other hand, those in the service economy of legal and financial advice – both sometimes closely related through the dependence of the former on the expertise of the latter. These expatriate and international managers comprise the globalizing elites who not only partake in similar forms of communication power flows, such as common media, technologies and messages, but they also have shared work experiences in international companies and organizations, working and living in global financial and economic centres. Expatriates are the most liquid human element in these global elites if only because they flow with and are shaped by globalizing capital. It is significant that multinational financial institutions, governments and markets all recruit individuals socialized in elite business schools.

The prominence and wealth of financial centres, from the 1980s onwards, deepened links between national elites and institutions of higher education. Business schools, especially the *Financial Times* elite, were at the core of this activity.

GLOBAL WORK

The international flow of expert migrant professional and knowledge workers helps create a global labour market in a growing number of occupations. The evidence of these jobs suggests that, despite attention to the issues of wages and the associated cost of taxes raised by journalists and politicians, transnational companies do not, by and large, necessarily invest their main facilities where wages and taxes are the lowest. If they did, the theory of comparative costs would work far better than it does. The reasons are self-evident: wages are often a minor cost factor; greater transaction costs are associated with the presence or absence of densely embedded networks for business in particular locales, such as the world cities of New York, London, Paris and Tokyo, which are likely to remain so. Creative cities act as magnets for talent, offering lifestyle and recreational attractions that draw the creative class to live there and often provide the melting pot of experiences necessary for their inspiration. In addition, many businesses reap great advantage from their cultural and geographic relationships with institutions of education, finance, government, and so on. Government–business relations typically have an exclusive rather than open character, and can be an important component in building national competitive advantage (Porter, 1990), which then attracts globally skilled knowledge workers.

KNOWLEDGE WORK AND DIRTY WORK

Globally skilled knowledge workers generate job opportunities for less skilled workers. Supporting the cars, shopping, apartments and travel of these wealthy symbolic analysts is all the dirty work done by those who cook, wash and clean up, who pack and sell convenience foods, who park and service cars, who tend to and care for appearance: the face workers, nail workers and hair workers – the necessary body maintenance to keep all the wealthy and beautiful people sweet. In global cities such as Hong Kong and Singapore, you can see street-level globalization in the form of the mainly Filipina and Sri Lankan female domestic workers who congregate in the public spaces of the central business district on Sunday, their day of rest. The rest of the week it is more likely to be thronged with global business people while the maids, chauffeurs and other domestic servants make global households run smoothly.

In addition, there is a shadow labour force of workers in the symbolic sphere – but workers who are tightly scripted, operating in unambiguous and simple environments, unlike their symbolic analyst counterpoints. Outside the confines of the corporate glitterati and the symbolic analyst elite, there is a category of disaggregated work quintessentially associated with globalization: that of call centres. Enabled by developments in technology, call centres were ushered into existence in the 1990s, the idea being particularly attractive to corporations, as it allowed them to downsize parts of the organization and establish call centres in relatively deprived areas where wage, rent and utility rates were lower and the workforce more pliable.

Call centres can be located anywhere. Work is cheapened by the routinization of existing tasks; re-engineered tasks can then be moved to places where wages are cheaper. The transaction costs associated with relocation are not great: satellites and computers can ensure virtual linkage. The blueprint is clear: rationalize parts of the organization; introduce jobs at just over minimum wage in deprived, post-industrial parts of the country or another country and institute a system of surveillance aimed at maximizing efficiency (see pp. 265–267).

In terms of globalization, there are also 'grunge jobs' (Jones, M., 2003: 256). Jones sees grunge jobs as essentially bifurcated. First, there are the semi-skilled workers who work in the lower reaches of the supply chains established by the global giants, a contingent, easily dismissible and re-employable mass of people who can be used and laid off to absorb transaction costs and cushion demand for the core transnational companies globally. In a word, these lower reaches of the supply chain are 'sweatshops' (Teal, 2008) that routinely and intensively exploit employees under labour conditions that would not be tolerated elsewhere. When these transnational companies react to signs of economic distress, it is these subcontract workers in the supply chain who bear the pain first, buffering the core company employees. These workers are low skill, add little value and are easily disposable but at least they may have social insurance and may work in the formal economy, although they have few organized rights and little representation. Many sweatshops are 'informal', meaning that they are illegal and thus evade legal requirements.

The second element in the composition of the grunge economy comprises an underclass of workers who are often illegal immigrants working sporadically in extreme conditions outside the formally regulated labour market: think of sweatshops in the garment industry or the Western world's many illegal sex workers, for instance. States often encourage the informal sector as an arena from which street-level and taxable entrepreneurs might develop in enterprises other than the marketing of drugs, prostitutes and the proceeds of crime (Deloitte & Touche, 1998; Sassen, 1998).

GLOBAL RIGHTS

Globalization in the cultural sphere has meant the global proliferation of norms of individualized values, originally of Western origin, in terms of a discourse of 'rights' (Markoff, 1996). Such discourse is not unproblematic. It meets considerable opposition from religious, political, ethnic, sexual and other rationalities tied to the specificities of local practices but it does provide a framework and set of terms through which resistance to these might be organized. Managers seeking to standardize HRM practices globally will probably follow a 'rights-based' template that will often conflict sharply with local realities.

One theorist who has realized this is Barber (1996), who has popularized the idea that the world is set on a collision between McWorld and Jihad, where convergence in the form of primarily US business interests meets stubborn and deep-seated sources of local resistance, embedded in religious worldviews. From this perspective, the trajectory of convergence produces a globalization of culture, technologies and markets against which local forms of retribalization, through Jihad, will react.

In many ways, suggests Moghadam (1999: 376), working-class and poor urban women have been the 'shock absorbers' of neo-liberal economic policies, having suffered in both domestic and industrial/productive capacities. Structural adjustment policies that increase prices, eliminate subsidies, diminish social services and increase fees for essentials hitherto provided by the state, place women at greater risk of ill health and poverty. However, to the extent that transnational organizations enter into employment in these regions, they represent unparalleled opportunities for employment outside of either the informal sector of dubious work and conditions or outside domestic service – opportunities that are often accompanied by education programmes, as governments seek to equip their human capital with the upgradeable skills that will attract further investment.

The ecosystem as a whole is now often ascribed rights and interests, in the name of sustainability. Other entities incapable of interest representation, such as foetuses, those who are on life-support systems, and so on, are also ascribed rights. Animals are ascribed rights (Singer, 1976). Whales have rights that are violated by global organizational actors from Japan; domesticated farm animals such as factory-farmed pigs, hens and turkeys are routinely treated in ways that deny their right to a 'natural' life. It matters not whether a cow is British or French in an economy where meat, sperm, livestock and meat-derived products, such as gelatine and cosmetic additives, as well as avian influenza, mad cow and foot-and-mouth disease, can move globally. Greenpeace, as an organization for expressing a standardized moral consciousness that can mobilize activists anywhere, can represent Canadian seals as easily as those that are Russian and, through global media, can act its way into the global consciousness. Local species can become global icons. Mismanage these and you will be in deep trouble!

GLOBAL SUSTAINABILITY

Economic growth and population growth place simultaneous demands on the natural environment by depleting resources, eliminating species and spreading disease. Globalization is resource hungry: the boom in the Chinese economy is swallowing finite raw materials such as wood, rubber, minerals, ores or oil from every part of the world. Global interdependence between human and ecological health is both causing and spreading global diseases such as HIV/AIDS (French, 2003; Garrett, 1994) and avian influenza.

Increasingly, we live in 'risk societies' where national and geographic boundaries cannot insulate us from human-made or natural disasters generated elsewhere (Beck, 2002). In the 2004 tsunami, whereas the Pacific had in place good management systems – in Hawaii – the Indian Ocean did not, due to the relative poverty of the region compared with the Pacific, and many thousands of people died, partially in consequence. Another example, which Beck discusses, is Chernobyl, but the examples are legion: the illegal logging of Sumatran rainforest and the burning off of waste that casts dense smoke palls all over the South-East Asian region, causing health problems in far-away Singapore. The pollution from industrial China blankets Hong Kong and occasionally drifts across the Pacific to the US West Coast. The use of cyanide in mining in Romania, at Aural Gold Plant, allowed 3.5 million cubic feet (100,000 m3) of cyanide-contaminated waste to enter the Tisza River on 30 January 2000, poisoning the Danube and infecting over 250 miles (400 km) of rivers in Hungary and Yugoslavia. Cyanide leaching is widely used in the global mining industry. That engagement ring may not only be potentially tainted with 'blood diamonds' but also cyanide-leached gold. Local actions can have global consequences.

GLOBAL WINNERS AND LOSERS

The main beneficiaries of globalization are undoubtedly the skilled employees of the transnational companies and those symbolic analyst professionals who service these companies: lawyers, researchers, consultants, IT experts, and so on. Meyer (2000: 240–1) is unequivocal that those who organize scientific and professional activity on a global scale are the real winners. Professional associations represent such people; international knowledge businesses, universities and research laboratories employ such people, as do international governmental associations and agencies. These are the people at home in airport lounges, with frequent flyer programmes and portable computers as global talismans of their universality.

The winners also include not just those whom Meyer (2000) identifies as being able to make universalistic claims about rights, science or any other form of expert knowledge, as well as the digital content providers, but also those who are experts in various global sports, representing sponsors such as Nike, Adidas and other transnational sports companies whose brands are ubiquitous, as well as the global entertainers, such as Beyoncé and Kanye. Global brands and those whom they sustain are unequivocal winners from globalization.

With the emergence of global brands, international outsourcing and supply chains, there is a natural tendency for the market leader to get further ahead, causing a monopolistic concentration of business (Arthur, 1996). Real dangers attach to winning when the losers are excluded and abandoned to their situation. The winners can come together and increasingly integrate with one another. Where such processes occur within societies, serious consequences may result in terms of increased poverty, unemployment, alienation and crime. But the consequences are of a higher order of magnitude when the processes of exclusion and alienation involve countries and whole regions of the world. The share of world trade in manufactured goods of the 102 poorest countries of the world is falling as the share of the developed world increases. There is a delinking of the less from the more developed world, particularly in Africa. The core of an increasingly globally integrated world economy tends to exclude countries from the margins.

The primary casualties of globalization appear to be low-skilled grunge workers in traditional manufacturing countries who either lose their jobs as they are moved elsewhere or experience a painful slide in their wage rates as employers strive to reduce costs. Particularly vulnerable are the relatively unskilled and undereducated, especially in labour market systems that do not develop very active and interventionist labour market policies. Wood (1994) reckons that trade with developing countries is the prime suspect for the increase in inequality *within* industrial countries. He estimates that it has reduced the demand for low-skilled workers in rich economies by more than a fifth. Against this, however, one must balance the fact that most jobs are still in spatially discrete and non-tradable sectors. A wharfie in Australia cannot easily relocate to become a longshoreman in the USA. And even for the 16 per cent of US workers who make their living in manufacturing, the overlap of production with low-wage countries is relatively small. Their main competitors in most sectors are workers in other high-wage countries, as is true of most OECD states.

In the world at large, the effects of globalization can be seen through studying the GNPs of the world of nations in the post-war eras. Those that have been phenomenally successful in lifting themselves up those tables have, by and large, engaged, and been engaged with, the world globally. The states that have not been engaged or have remained disengaged have remained poor and are the real losers from globalization.

EXTEND YOUR KNOWLEDGE

There is a very interesting talk about globalization on TED Talks from Ian Goldin (2009) that addresses both winners and losers and likely scenarios for the future. A very useful overview of globalization can be found at the Henry Stewart Talks series of online audio-visual seminars on Managing Organizations, edited by Stewart Clegg, in particular Talk #18: Transnational Corporations and Climate Change: Towards a global governance framework, by Bobby Banerjee, if your university has access to this collection. Another excellent source of information and analysis is the online journal *Globalization*. The publisher, Polity Press, maintains a website supporting several of its books in the Global Transformations series. Again, there are many links that can be easily accessed through this page.

WATCH THE TED TALK

WATCH THE HENRY STEWART TALK

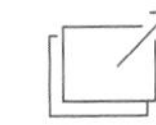
EXPLORE THE GLOBALIZATION JOURNAL

RESISTING GLOBALIZATION

Resistance to globalization began to be seen from the late 1990s onwards in the 'anti-globalization movement'. Since then, terms such as the 'social justice movement' have gained currency. The first major protests occurred in 1999, often taking the name of the date on which they occurred (e.g. J16 for 'June 16th') or the city where the protests were held (e.g. the 'Battle for Seattle'). Protests regularly occur in connection with economic policy-making institutions such as the WTO, the World Bank, the IMF, as well as conferences such as the Davos World Economic Forum and the G8 summits. The political and business elites who gather at these are seen as the chief architects of globalization by the protestors. The protests often have a libertarian and carnival quality to them. The resistance often conceives of itself as 'globalization from below' opposed to 'globalization from above', expressing a global solidarity. Since 2001, the World Social Forum has been held as a sort of annual counter-summit to the World Economic Forum. The World Social Forum has done a great deal to place issues such as environmental destruction, the need for sustainability and Third World poverty on the agenda.

New Right politicians are also against globalization; it brings people they do not want to their nation, it threatens them with ideas they do not like, and while it sells them lots of cheap goods that they can afford, it does so at the cost of vulnerable jobs in previously protected parts of the domestic economy – the heartland of their political support. They see globalization as fragmenting national identities. Those under threat demand to be protected from its adverse effects. Ethnically distinct identities (those who do not share what extremists constitute as national identity, usually because of skin colour or religion, or both) are denounced and marginalized as denying the majority of 'ordinary people' their rights to economic surplus, relief, jobs, housing, or whatever. Such figures are often enemies of free trade, instead favouring tariffs and trade wars.

Left resistance to globalization is adept at using some of its tools – such as digitalization – against it: international organizations such as the Global Justice Movement are able to influence global policy-making through their websites. Sometimes the tactics of culture jamming are used. Many anti-Nike websites have emerged, circulating information about and organizing movements against Nike, which have forced it to modify its labour practices. The management academic David Boje is particularly active in this respect.

Greenpeace created an anti-McDonald's website, developed by supporters of two British activists, Helen Steel and Dave Morris, who were sued by McDonald's for distributing leaflets denouncing the corporation's low wages, advertising practices, involvement in deforestation, cruel treatment of animals, and patronage of an unhealthy diet. With help from supporters these two fought back, organizing a McLibel campaign, creating a McSpotlight website criticizing the corporation. The three-year libel trial, the UK's longest ever, ended with the judge defending some of McDonald's claims against the activists while substantiating some criticisms. The activists sought public support to help pay their costs and the fine. The case created unprecedented adverse publicity for McDonald's and, in retrospect, the libel action could hardly be seen to have done the corporation any good.

READ ABOUT THE CASE

The New Right sometimes meets the Old Left in the shadows cast by politics. We also find many anarchists agreeing, in Sklair's (1999: 158) words, that 'globalization is often seen in terms of impersonal forces wreaking havoc on the lives of ordinary and defenceless people and communities'. As he goes on to say, it 'is not coincidental that interest in globalization over the last two decades has been accompanied by an upsurge in what has come to be known as New Social Movements (NSM) research' (Sklair, 1998; Spybey, 1996). NSM theorists argue for the importance of identity politics (of gender, sexuality, ethnicity, age, community and belief systems) in the global era.

If you are against a concept such as globalization, which seeks to capture a broad array of social detail, which bits of it are you most against? And what is the alternative to globalization? Is it protectionism? Of course, there is an argument that sometimes protectionism, especially where it preserves unique intellectual/cultural property, such as national cinema or television, is necessary if the juggernaut of cheap US mass-produced and McDonaldized products is not to eliminate cultural differences. Such arguments are common in France, for example. Increasingly, they have gained support in the USA.

THE DARK SIDE OF GLOBALIZATION

Banerjee (2008) developed the concept of necrocapitalism, which he defines as those contemporary forms of organizational accumulation that involve dispossession and the subjugation of life to the power of death. Such a process is integral to, and an essential element of, globalization, he suggests. It is a form of natural power involving violence and coercion as a substitute for the creation of social power. Organizationally, this coercive power works institutionally, materially and discursively in the political economy, resulting in violence and dispossession. Examples include the impact of the resources industry in developing countries and the privatization of war and the military. Globalization is blurring the boundary relations between states and corporations, especially in matters of warfare, where the state is increasingly outsourcing elements of war to the private sector.

Banerjee draws on contributions from classic social science discussions of colonialism and imperialism. Three characteristics of colonialism are the domination of physical space, usually to extract resources, creating not only long-standing dependency relations in economic terms but also cultural domination through the reformation of indigenous and subjugated people's minds (particularly in terms of knowledge systems and culture), and the incorporation of local economic histories into a Western perspective.

Historically, as a result of imperialism, the globe was carved up into a series of Western centres and 'other' peripheries. Organizations such as the major trading companies and mining companies played a key role in the map-making that transpired. We live with the consequences of that map-making today. For instance, the British carved Iraq out of the Ottoman Empire after the collapse of that empire as a result of the First World War. On 11 November 1920, it became a mandated protectorate of the British Empire under the imprimatur of the League of Nations with the name State of Iraq. The British government laid out the political and constitutional framework for Iraq's government, one consequence of which was that the new political system lacked legitimacy, because it was seen as an alien imposition. Britain imposed a monarchy on Iraq and defined its territorial limits with little regard for natural frontiers and traditional tribal and ethnic settlements. It was, to all intents and purposes, an artificial and puppet state in which British Petroleum interests were paramount.

READ ABOUT THE BERLIN CONFERENCE

In Africa, prior to colonization, indigenous people controlled 80 per cent of the territory. At the Berlin Conference of 1884–85, called by Bismarck, the European powers created geometric boundaries that divided Africa into 50 irregular countries. The new map of the continent was superimposed over the one thousand indigenous cultures and regions. The new countries divided coherent groups of people and merged together disparate groups who really did not get along. Nearly all of Africa's contemporary problems can be seen to have their roots in this initial map-making.

Today, Banerjee suggests, imperialism also operates in economic, political and cultural guises and is operationalized through different kinds of power: institutional power (agencies such as the IMF, WTO and the World Bank), economic power (of corporations and nation-states) and discursive power that constructs and describes uncontested notions of 'development', 'backwardness', 'subsistence economies', while disallowing other narratives from emerging. Banerjee not only traces these manifestations of power but also provides a number of examples, easily drawn from recent histories, of organizational violence committed on employees and citizens by both imperial states and imperialist corporations. Colonialism and imperialism created export-oriented, often single resource-based economies, centred on the plantation agriculture of cash crops, or resource extraction, and today it is particularly the latter arena, dominated by a few global companies, that routinely commits violence and rains down devastation, in the process of developing regions and consorting with local elites, on communities that have the misfortune to be the recipients of their investments.

READ ABOUT GLOBALIZATION & NATURE

EXTEND YOUR KNOWLEDGE

READ THE ARTICLE

Zyglidopoulos, S., Hirsch, P., de Holan, P. M. and Phillips, N. (2018) 'Expanding research on corporate corruption, management, and organizations', *Journal of Management Inquiry*, 26 (3): 247–53, which is available at the companion website https://study.sagepub.com/managingandorganizations5e, is an article well worth further exploration if you want to extend your knowledge of the dark side of organizations.

The institutional auspices of organization studies are something overwhelmingly situated in European and US universities. The hegemonic intellectualism of Western ways of knowing have been critiqued widely in the humanities and social sciences more generally in recent years, following critiques that flow from the post-colonial literature that Banerjee draws on, as they have been developed in management and organization theory by Frenkel and Shenhav (2006). They draw on theories of orientalism, associated with the work of Edward Said (1979), and hybridity as a third space, associated with the work of Homi Bhabha (1994). Orientalism is founded on a binary epistemology that necessitates a sharp distinction between colonizers and the colonized, whereas Bhabha's work represents a hybrid epistemology, taking into consideration the fusion and the mutual effects of colonizers and the colonized.

Orientalism and hybridity are often described as mutually exclusive: either as two consecutive phases in post-colonial theory or as two competing epistemologies. Their contribution examines the effect of the colonial encounter on the canonization of organization studies and management more generally as well as on the boundaries of it as a canon. Banerjee argues, theoretically, that orientalism and hybridity are neither competing nor mutually exclusive concepts but rather two complementary aspects of the same process. The argument is that the identity that has been canonized as the mainstream of management and organization studies followed two contradictory principles simultaneously at work: hybridization and purification. Hybridization refers to the mixing of practices between colonizers and the colonized, to the translation of texts and practices from the colonies to the metropolis, and vice versa. Purification refers to the mechanisms that construct colonizers and colonized as distinct and incommensurable categories.

Historically, the construction of Western management discourse was clearly based on a system of omissions and exclusions, largely of the experiences of slavery and plantation modes of production, which fed directly into early industrial practices but were excluded from formal academic accounts of the origins of management thought and practice. Similar processes are seen to be at work in the evolution of international management as a field where the good is exclusively (rational) Western and the bad (irrational) non-Western practice. At its worst, this genre lapses into pure condescension and stereotyping of non-Western practice that would not have been out of place in a 'Black Sambo' book or *Uncle Tom's Cabin*. Management has adopted an essentially colonial viewpoint, casting the non-Western as the inferior 'other' while seeing Western culture as a universal model. Much of international human resource management fits this pattern, for example. Management became the spearhead of neo-colonialism in the age of decolonization. Furthermore, it assists in the reproduction of the West's control of the global economy and culture, while at the same time increasing management's ostensibly scientific legitimacy.

EXTEND YOUR KNOWLEDGE

In Seremani, T. and Clegg, S. (2016) 'Postcolonialism, organization, and management theory: the role of "epistemological third spaces"', *Journal of Management Inquiry*, 25 (2): 171–83, which is available at the companion website https://study.sagepub.com/managingandorganizations5e, you can extend your knowledge of how ideas from outside the mainstream of management have been used and may be categorized as ways of thinking that are 'postcolonial'.

READ THE ARTICLE

Being a global manager today entails moral as well as personal responsibilities, ethical as well as financial obligations, power as well as pleasure, a commitment to the production of better lives, not just the consumption and spewing out of goods and services (Rego et al., 2012).

SUMMARY

In this chapter, we have considered the ways in which the everyday life of managing and organizations is increasingly global. Wherever we live, we cannot escape globalization:

- Globalization involves many processes interacting with each other, which are dynamic and unstable.
- Globalization occurs because of economies of scale, scope and resources acquisition.
- Managing in a globalized world means dealing with different institutional systems.
- The major agencies advancing globalization are: large IT firms, management gurus, management consultancies, MBAs and systematic management standards.
- The knowledge industries are a major component of globalization, including the education context in which you are probably reading this book.
- As well as knowledge workers, globalization also encourages the spread of dirty jobs. The good news for you is that because you are reading this book, you probably will not end up doing one of these dirty jobs!

EXERCISES

1. Having read this chapter, you should be able to say in your own words what each of the following key terms means. Test yourself or ask a colleague to test you.
   - Globalization
   - Globalization processes
   - Global finance
   - Global strategic alliances
   - Resistance to globalization
   - Global strategies
   - Transnationals
   - Global jobs
   - Grunge economy
   - Creative class
   - Dirty work
   - Global rights
   - Clusters
   - Knowledge workers
   - Necrocapitalism.
2. What are the key processes defining globalization? How do they shape the phenomenon?
3. Who are the major global actors?
4. What are the different kinds of global jobs?
5. How does globalization shape human consciousness?
6. Who are the winners and who are the losers from globalization?
7. Why is it not a paradox to say that the global is always local?

TEST YOURSELF

Review what you have learned by visiting:
https://study.sagepub.com/managingandorganizations5e or your eBook

- **Test yourself with multiple-choice questions.**
- **Revise key terms with the interactive flashcards.**

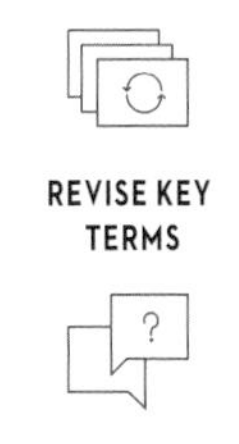

CASE STUDY

Tragedy at Rana Plaza, Bangladesh, 24 April 2013

The disastrous building collapse in Bangladesh's capital of Dhaka on 24 April 2013, at Rana Plaza, claimed at least 1,129 lives and wounded thousands, illuminating the murky business of global sweatshops. Greed, profiteering, empire building and a lack of transparency and morality underpin the rise of this industry.

With more than 5,000 garment-manufacturing factories, Bangladesh is the world's second largest exporter of ready-made garments after China, earning US$20 billion annually and employing more than 4 million workers, 90 per cent of whom are women. Demand from the West for cheaper production and supply prompted the rapid growth of industrial infrastructure in countries such as Bangladesh without proper assessment, inspection and control processes. Illegal and shoddy building design and lax safety standards are rife within the garments industry due to the complicity of corrupt engineers, officials and politicians.

Incidents of fire and collapses and appalling working conditions are commonplace. In November 2012, a fire in the Tazreen Fashions factory on the outskirts of the Bangladeshi capital, Dhaka, killed 112 people. In Chittagong on 23 February 2006, fire killed 83 garment workers – including girls aged between 12 and 14 years – at the KTS Textile Industries factory. Prior to the cataclysmic Savar collapse, several hundred people had died in numerous incidents across Bangladesh.

In the case of Rana Plaza, the building was over-stressed with machinery and up to 500 people working on each of the five 6,000-square-feet levels. The working conditions in these factories are, in most cases, horrible, with a lack of sufficient space, light and supply of drinking water. They are literally 'death traps', with workers locked inside to prevent theft, leaving no way to escape disasters such as fire.

With an average wage of less than A$37 a month, the factory work is physically demanding and emotionally draining. Workers report that physical and verbal harassment is rampant within the industry. To achieve ruthless daily targets, workers may skip meals and work long hours. The emotional impact and stress levels are extremely high among these poor workers.

Equally appalling conditions are found throughout the industry, with similar complaints in countries including Pakistan, India, China, Cambodia, Honduras, Vietnam, Indonesia and the Philippines.

(Continued)

(Continued)

The Rana Plaza case has been the subject of several articles from The Conversation, three of them by Sharif As-Saber (6 May 2013: http://theconversation.com/bangladesh-disaster-shows-why-we-must-urgently-clean-up-global-sweat-shops-13899; 17 July 2013: http://theconversation.com/will-gains-for-bangladesh-workers-founder-on-political-reality-15987; 24 April 2014: http://theconversation.com/one-year-on-from-rana-plaza-collapse-work-still-to-be-done-24710) and one by Kamal Munir (26 April 2014: http://theconversation.com/tragedy-is-inevitable-when-bangladesh-competes-on-its-own-citizens-poverty-25955). An additional link to a podcast by Kamal Munir may be found at www.jbs.cam.ac.uk/media/2014/pay-more-for-your-clothes-to-avoid-another-rana-plaza. The case has been discussed in The Conversation elsewhere by George Cairns (16 September 2013: http://theconversation.com/life-more-tragic-than-death-who-remembers-rana-plaza-18222), Annie Delaney and Rosaria Burchielli (1 July 2013: http://theconversation.com/shocking-bangladesh-reality-for-workers-highlights-key-role-for-labour-unions-15522), with related discussions by Martjin Bjoersma (13 June 2013: http://theconversation.com/mind-the-gap-company-disclosure-discrepancies-not-sustainable-15083), Rosie Findlay (8 October 2014: http://theconversation.com/do-you-know-how-your-clothes-were-made-32675), Terence Tse (1 October 2014:http://theconversation.com/speak-up-and-eliminate-forced-labour-business-can-be-ethical-and-profitable-32255), Alessandra Mezzadri (8 January 2014: http://theconversation.com/cambodian-sweatshop-protests-reveal-the-blood-on-our-clothes-21811) and Sara Bice (23 July 2013: http://theconversation.com/corporate-social-responsibility-in-asia-understanding-business-from-beginning-to-end-13928). These additional sources will be useful in considering the case. In addition, there is an ABC Four Corners report on the case (www.abc.net.au/4corners/stories/2013/06/25/3785918.htm). Searching the web will disclose many more sources.

Questions

1. You are the CEO of a major fashion brand and you have just undergone a very traumatic annual general meeting at which activists protested on behalf of young Bangladeshi women who were severely injured at Rana Plaza, many losing limbs, now without work, with little, if any, financial compensation and no social security safety net, as well as being seen as worthless burdens on their families. Having been challenged for your complicity in the disaster as a major contractor, you have promised to organize a solution for the future. You organize an industry working party, including academic researchers, representatives of NGOs and garment workers. What concrete programme of actions will you propose? Analyse the case and write a detailed report and executive summary.

ADDITIONAL RESOURCES

- The definitive text on globalization, written by an economic geographer, is Peter Dicken's (2007) *Global Shift: Mapping the Changing Contours of the World Economy*. It contains extensive discussion of a number of specific industries: clothing and textiles, automobiles, semiconductors, agro-food industry, financial services and logistics.

- An interesting guide to globalization, written by sociologist Dennis Smith (2006), *Globalization: The Hidden Agenda*, raises some quite worrying scenarios.
- Glenn Morgan's (2008) entry on 'Transnationals' in the *International Encyclopedia of Organization Studies* is a very useful introduction to key actors in globalization.
- The debate between Barbara Parker (2003) and Marc Jones (2003) in *Debating Organizations* (Westwood and Clegg, 2003) is worthwhile for those deeply interested in the topic. For others, it might be a bit heavy. Barbara Parker, together with Stewart Clegg (2006), contributed a chapter on globalization to the *Sage Handbook of Organization Studies* (edited by Clegg et al., 2006b), which is also well worth study.
- In terms of films, there are a number of good documentaries, such as *Gap and Nike: No Sweat?* (Campbell, 2000). It is a BBC *Panorama* production, focusing on Nike and Gap, both of which claim that they have strict codes of conduct for manufacturing. They claim that they do not use sweatshops or child labour. They say they routinely 'monitor' their factories, to make sure their codes are followed. But when the BBC's *Panorama* team visited Cambodia, it found severe breaches of these codes within days. By talking with workers and using hidden cameras, the team shows how one factory, used by both Gap and Nike, has sweatshop conditions and employs children. All the workers interviewed were working seven days a week, often up to 16 hours a day, and some of the employees were children as young as 12. After these findings, *Panorama* went back to speak with Gap and Nike, to hear what they had to say. The team also shows how US companies can use foreign sweatshops and still claim that the goods are made in the USA. You might want to take a look at www.oxfam.org.au/explore/workers-rights/nike.
- More commercially, there is the 2003 Stephen Frears film *Dirty Pretty Things*, which dramatizes life in the grunge jobs that illegal immigrants fill in any global city, in this case London.
- The film *Blood Diamond* (Zwick, 2006) looks at the role of transnational corporations in the troubled diamond-mining industry of Africa in Sierra Leone.

Bibliography

Abbott, A. (1988) *The System of Professions: An Essay on the Division of Expert Labor*. Chicago: Chicago University Press.

Abbott, J. D. and Moran, R. T. (2002) *Uniting North American Business: NAFTA Best Practice*. Burlington, MA: Butterworth-Heinemann.

Abecassis-Moedas, C. and Moatti, V. (2018) 'Digital by design: how technology is breathing new life into the fashion business', https://theconversation.com/digital-by-design-how-technology-is-breathing-new-life-into-the-fashion-business-93511 (accessed 7 October 2018).

Abendroth, A. K., Huffman, M. L. and Treas, J. (2014) 'The parity penalty in life course perspective: motherhood and occupational status in 13 European countries', *American Sociological Review*, *79*: 993–1014.

Abrahamson, E. (1996) 'Management fashion', *Academy of Management Review*, *21*: 254–285.

Abrahamson, E. (1997) 'The emergence and prevalence of employee management rhetorics: the effects of long waves, labour unions, and turnover, 1875 to 1992', *Academy of Management Journal*, *40* (3): 491–533.

Ackroyd, S. and Thompson, P. (1999) *Organizational Misbehavior*. London: Sage.

Adams, J. S. (1963) 'Towards an understanding of inequity', *Journal of Abnormal and Social Psychology*, *67*: 422–436.

Adler, S. (2011) 'The human experience of working: richer science, richer practice', *Industrial and Organizational Psychology*, *4* (1): 98–101.

Adner, R. (2017) 'Ecosystem as structure: an actionable construct for strategy', *Journal of Management*, *43* (1): 39–58.

Aguinas, H. and Glavas, A. (2017) 'On corporate social responsibility, sensemaking, and the search for meaningfulness through work', *Journal of Management*, https://doi.org/10.1177%2F0149206317691575.

Albert, L. S., Reynolds, S. J. and Turan, B. (2015) 'Turning inward or focusing out? Navigating theories of interpersonal and ethical cognitions to understand ethical decision-making', *Journal of Business Ethics*, *130* (2): 467–484.

Albrecht, S. (2014) *The Spatial Configuration of American Inequality: Wealth and Income Concentration through US History*. PhD thesis, University of Maryland.

Albrow, M. (1970) *Bureaucracy*. London: Pall Mall.

Aldrich, H. E. (2002) 'Technology and organizational structure: a reexamination of the findings of the Aston Group', in S. R. Clegg (ed.), *Central Currents in Organization Studies I: Frameworks and Applications*, Vol. 2. London: Sage, pp. 344–366; originally published in *Administrative Science Quarterly* (1971) 17: 26–42.

Alexandersson, A. and Kalonaityte, V. (2018) 'Playing to dissent: the aesthetics and politics of playful office design', *Organization Studies*, 39 (2–3): 297–317.

Allan, J., Fairtlough, G. and Heinzen, B. (2002) *The Power of the Tale: Using Narratives for Organisational Success*. Chichester: Wiley.

Allison, G. T. (1971) *Essence of Decision: Explaining the Cuban Missile Crisis*. Boston: Little Brown.

Allport, G. W. and Odbert, H. S. (1936) 'Trait names: a psycholexical study', *Psychological Monographs*, *47* (1): i–471.

Alter, C. (1990) 'An exploratory study of conflict and coordination in interorganizational service delivery systems', *Academy of Management Journal*, 33 (3): 478–502.

Alvesson, M. (1993) 'Organizations as rhetoric: knowledge intensive firms and the struggle with ambiguity', *Journal of Management Studies*, 30 (6): 997–1015.

Alvesson, M. (2004) *Knowledge Work and Knowledge-Intensive Firms*. Oxford: Oxford University Press.

Alvesson, M. and Kärreman, D. (2001) 'Odd couple: making sense of the curious concept of knowledge management', *Journal of Management Studies*, *38* (7): 995–1018.

Alvesson, M. and Svenningsson, S. (2008) *Changing Organizational Culture: Cultural Change Work in Progress*. London: Routledge.

Alvesson, M. and Willmott, H. (1992) 'On the idea of emancipation in management and organization studies', *Academy of Management Review*, *17* (3): 432–464.

Amabile, T. (1998) 'How to kill creativity', *Harvard Business Review*, September–October: 77–87.

Amar, J. (1920) *The Physiology of Industrial Organisation and the Re-employment of the Disabled* (trans. B. Miall). London: Routledge.

Amoore, L. (2005) *The Global Resistance Reader*. New York: Routledge.

Anandakumar, A., Pitsis, T. S. and Clegg, S. R. (2007) 'Everybody hurts, sometimes: the language of emotionality and the dysfunctional organization', in J. Langan-Fox, C. L. Cooper and R. J. Klimoski (eds), *Research Companion to the Dysfunctional Workplace: Management Challenges and Symptoms*. Cheltenham: Edward Elgar, pp. 187–215.

Anderson, P. and Tushman, M. L. (1990) 'Technological discontinuities and dominant designs: a cyclical model of technological change', *Administrative Science Quarterly*, 35 (4): 604–633.

Anderson, R. (1999) *Mid Course Correction: Toward a Sustainable Enterprise – The Interface Model*. Atlanta, GA: Peregrinzilla Press.

Ang, Y. Y. (2016) *How China Escaped the Poverty Trap*. Ithaca, NY: Cornell University Press.

Ang, Y. Y. (2017) 'Beyond Weber: conceptualizing an alternative ideal type of bureaucracy in developing contexts', *Regulation & Governance*, *11* (3): 282–298.

Annosi, M. C., Giustiniano, L., Brunetta, F. and Magnusson, M. (2018) 'The emergence of new organization designs: evidences from self-managed team-based organizations', in *Learning and Innovation in Hybrid Organizations*. London: Palgrave Macmillan, pp. 255–268.

Ansari, S., Reinecke, J. and Spaan, A. (2014) 'How are practices made to vary? Managing practice adaptation in a multinational corporation', *Organization Studies*, 35 (9): 1313–1341.

Antonakis, J. and House, R. J. (2002) 'An analysis of the full-range leadership theory: the way forward', in B. J. Avolio and F. J. Yammarino (eds), *Transformational and Charismatic Leadership: The Road Ahead*. Amsterdam: JAI Press, pp. 3–34.

Antonakis, J. and House, R. J. (2004) *'On instrumental leadership: beyond transactions and transformations'*, Paper presented at the Gallup Leadership Institute Conference, University of Nebraska.

Antonioni, D. (1998) 'Relationship between the big five personality factors and conflict management styles', *International Journal of Conflict Management*, 9 (4): 336–355.

Antorini, Y. M. (2007) 'Brand community innovation: an intrinsic case study of the adult fans of LEGO community', PhD thesis, Copenhagen Business School.

Antorini, Y. M., Muñiz, A. M. and Askildsen, T. (2012) 'Collaborating with customer communities: lessons from the Lego group', *MIT Sloan Management Review*, 53 (3): 73–79.

Appelbaum, E. and Hunter, L. (2005) 'Union participation in strategic decisions of corporations', in R. Freeman and L. Mishel (eds), *Emerging Labor Market Institutions for the 21st Century*. Cambridge, MA: National Bureau of Economic Research, pp. 265–291.

Aquino, K. (2000) 'Structural and individual determinants of workplace victimization: the effects of hierarchical status and conflict management style', *Journal of Management*, 26 (2): 171–193.

Arendt, H. (1994) *Eichmann in Jerusalem: A Report on the Banality of Evil*. New York: Penguin.

Argenti, P. and Forman, J. (2000) 'The communication advantage: a constituency-focused approach to formulating and implementing strategy', in M. Schultz, M. Hatch and M. Larsen (eds), *The Expressive Organization: Linking Identity, Reputation, and the Corporate Brand*. Oxford: Oxford University Press, pp. 233–245.

Argyris, C. and Schön, D. (1978) *Organizational Learning: A Theory of Action Perspective*. Reading, MA: Addison-Wesley.

Arieli, S., Grant, A. M. and Sagiv, L. (2014) 'Convincing yourself to care about others: an intervention for enhancing benevolence values', *Journal of Personality*, 82: 15–24.

Aritzeta, A., Ayestaran, S. and Swailes, S. (2005) 'Team role preference and conflict management styles', *International Journal of Conflict Management*, 16 (2): 157–182.

Arnold, P. E. (1995) 'Reform's changing role', *Public Administration Review*, 55 (5): 407–417.

Arntz, A. (2018) 'Schema therapy', in R. L. Leahy (ed.), *Science and Practice in Cognitive Therapy: Foundations, Mechanisms, and Applications*. New York: Guilford Press, pp. 65–86.

Aronson, E. (1960) *The Social Animal*. San Francisco: W. H. Freeman.

Aronson, E. (1969) 'The theory of cognitive dissonance: a current perspective', in L. Berkowitz (ed.), *Advances in Experimental Social Psychology*, Vol. 4. San Diego, CA: Academic Press, pp. 1–34.

Arthur, B. (1996) 'Increasing returns and the two worlds of business', *Harvard Business Review*, July–August: 100–109.

Arvey, R. D. and Murphy, K. R. (1998) 'Performance evaluation in work settings', *Annual Review of Psychology*, 49: 141–168.

As-Saber, S. (2017) 'Bangladesh disaster shows why we must urgently clean up global sweat shops', http://theconversation.com/bangladesh-disaster-shows-why-we-must-urgently-clean-up-global-sweat-shops-13899 (accessed 8 October 2018).

As-Saber, S. (2014) 'Will gains for Bangladesh workers founder on political reality?', http://theconversation.com/will-gains-for-bangladesh-workers-founder-on-political-reality-15987 (accessed 8 October 2018).

Asch, S. (1955) 'Opinions and social pressure', *Scientific American*, 193: 31–35.

Ashkanasy, N. M., Wilderom, C. P. M. and Peterson, M. F. (2011) *Handbook of Organizational Culture and Climate*, 2nd edn. London: Sage.

Ashkenasy, N. M. (2003) 'The case for culture', in R. Westwood and S. R. Clegg (eds), *Debating Organizations: Point-Counterpoint in Organization Studies*. London: Blackwell, pp. 300–310.

Assael, H. (1969) 'Constructive role of interorganizational conflict', *Administrative Science Quarterly*, *14* (4): 573–582.

Athos, A. G. and Pascale, R. T. (1981) *The Art of Japanese Management: Applications for American Executives*. New York: Simon & Schuster.

Atkin, R. S. and Conlon, E. J. (1978) 'Behaviorally anchored rating scales: some theoretical issues', *Academy of Management Review*, *3* (1): 119–128.

Augoustinos, M., Walker, I. and Donaghue, N. (2014) *Social Cognition: An Integrated Introduction*, 3rd edn. London: Sage.

Autor, D. and Dorn, D. (2013) 'The growth of low skill service jobs and the polarization of the US labor market', *American Economic Review*, *103* (5): 1553–1597.

Autor, D. H., Dorn, D. and Hanson, G. H. (2016) 'The China shock: learning from labor-market adjustment to large changes in trade', *Annual Review of Economics*, *8*: 205–240.

Ayer, D. (Director) (2014) *Fury* [Motion picture]. New York: Columbia.

Ayoko, O. B., Ashkanasy, N. M. and Jehn, K. A. (eds) (2014) *Handbook of Conflict Management Research*. Cheltenham: Edward Elgar.

Bacharach, S. A. (2005) *Get Them on Your Side: Win Support, Convert Skeptics, Get Results*. Avon, MA: Platinum Press.

Bachrach, P. and Baratz, M. S. (1962) 'Two faces of power', *American Political Science Review*, *56*: 947–952.

Bachrach, P. and Baratz, M. S. (1970) *Power and Poverty: Theory and Practice*. New York: Oxford University Press.

Badaracco, J. L. (1991) *The Knowledge Link: How Firms Compete Through Strategic Alliances*. Boston, MA: Harvard Business School Press.

Badham, R. (2013) *Short Change: An Introduction to Managing Change*. Ukraine: Business Perspectives Publishing Company.

Bagozzi, R. (2003) 'Positive and negative emotions in organizations', in K. Cameron, J. Dutton and R. Quinn (eds), *Positive Organizational Scholarship: Foundations of A New Discipline*. San Francisco: Berrett Koehler, pp. 176–193.

Baird, M. (2004) 'Orientations to paid maternity leave: understanding the Australian debate', *Journal of Industrial Relations*, *46* (3): 259–275.

Baldwin, M. W. (1992) 'Relational schemas and the processing of social information', *Psychological Bulletin*, *112*: 461–484.

Bales, K. (2005) *Understanding Global Slavery: A reader*. Berkeley, CA: University of California Press.

Balfour, C. (2018) 'Workers' participation in western Europe', in C. Balfour (ed.), *Participation in Industry*. London: Routledge, pp. 181–212.

Balogun, J. (2003) 'From blaming the middle to harnessing its potential: creating change intermediaries', *British Journal of Management*, *14* (1): 69–83.

Balogun, J. (2006) 'Managing change: steering a course between intended strategies and unanticipated outcomes', *Long Range Planning*, *39* (1): 29–49.

Balogun, J., Bartunek, J. M. and Do, B. (2015) 'Senior managers' sensemaking and responses to strategic change', *Organization Science*, *26* (4): 960–979.

Bandura, A. (1977) *Social Learning Theory*. Englewood Cliffs, NJ: Prentice Hall.

Bandura, A. (1986) *Social Foundations of Thought and Action: A Social-Cognitive Theory*. Englewood Cliffs, NJ: Prentice Hall.

Banerjee, S. B. (2008) 'Necrocapitalism', *Organization Studies*, *29* (12): 1541–1563.

Bangle, C. (2001) 'The ultimate creative machine: how BMW turns art into profit', *Harvard Business Review*, January: 47–55.

Barber, B. (1996) *Jihad vs. McWorld*. New York: Ballantine.

Barber, L., Sevastopulo, D. and Tett, G. (2018) 'Donald Trump: without Twitter, I would not be here – FT interview', *Financial Times*, 17 January, www.ft.com/content/943e322a-178a-11e7-9c35-0dd2cb31823a (accessed 7 October 2018).

Bardon, T., Clegg, S. and Josserand, E. (2012) 'Exploring identity construction from a critical management perspective: a research agenda', *M@n@gement*, *15* (4): 350–366.

Barge, J. K. and Little, M. (2002) 'Dialogical wisdom, communicative practice, and organizational life', *Communication Theory*, *12* (4): 375–397.

Barkan, S. (1986) 'Interorganizational conflict in the southern civil rights movement', *Sociological Inquiry*, *56* (2): 190–209.

Barker, J. (2002) 'Tightening the iron cage: concertive control in self-managing teams', in S. R. Clegg (ed.), *Central Currents in Organization Studies II: Contemporary Trends*, Vol. 5. London: Sage, pp. 180–210; originally published in *Administrative Science Quarterly* (1993) *38*: 408–437.

Barker, R. A. (2001) 'The nature of leadership', *Human Relations*, *54*: 469–494.

Barki, H. and Hartwick, J. (2004) 'Conceptualizing the construct of interpersonal conflict', *International Journal of Conflict Management*, *15* (3): 216–244.

Barley, S. R. (1986) 'Technology as an occasion for structuring: evidence from observations of CT scanners and the social order of radiology departments', *Administrative Science Quarterly*, *31* (1): 78–108.

Barley, S. R. (1991) 'Contextualising conflict: notes on the anthropology of disputes and negotiations', in R. J. Lewicki, B. H. Sheppard and R. Bies (eds), *Research on Negotiation in Organizations: Handbook of Negotiation Research*, Vol. 3. Greenwich, CT: JAI Press Inc., pp. 165–199.

Barley, S. R. (2007) 'Corporations, democracy, and the public good', *Journal of Management Inquiry*, *16* (3): 201–215.

Barley, S. R. and Kunda, G. (1992) 'Design and devotion: surges of rational and normative ideo-logies of control in managerial discourse', *Administrative Science Quarterly*, *37*: 363–399.

Barnard, C. (1936) *The Functions of the Executive*. Cambridge, MA: Harvard University Press.

Baron, E. (2018) 'Google to hundreds claiming age discrimination: you can't fight us together', *The Mercury News*, www.siliconvalley.com/2018/05/03/google-to-hundreds-claiming-age-discrimination-you-cant-fight-us-together (accessed 8 October 2018).

Bartholomew, S. (1998) 'National systems of biotechnology innovation: complex inter-dependence in the global system', *Journal of International Business*, 2: 241–266.

Bartunek, J. M., Kolb, D. M. and Lewicki, R. J. (1992) 'Bringing conflict out from behind the scenes: private, informal, and nonrational dimensions of conflict in organizations', in D. M. Kolb and J. M. Bartunek (eds), *Hidden Conflict in Organizations: Uncovering Behind-the-scenes Disputes*. Thousand Oaks, CA: Sage, pp. 209–228.

Bartunek, J. M., Rousseau, D. M., Rudolph, J. W. and DePalma, J. A. (2006) 'On the receiving end: sensemaking, emotion, and assessments of an organizational change initiated by others', *The Journal of Applied Behavioral Science*, *42* (2): 182–206.

Bass, B. M. and Avolio, B. (2003) *Multifactor Leadership Questionnaire: Feedback Report*. Redwood City, CA: Mind Garden.

Bass, B. M. and Avolio, B. J. (2000) *Multifactor Leadership Questionnaire*. Redwood City, CA: Mind Garden.

Battilana, J., Fuerstein, M. and Lee, M. (2017) 'New prospects for organizational democracy? How the joint pursuit of social and financial goals challenges traditional organizational designs', in R. Subramanian (ed.), *Capitalism Beyond Mutuality*. Oxford: Oxford University Press.

Bauman, Z. (1989) *Modernity and the Holocaust*. Cambridge: Polity.

Bauman, Z. (1992) *Intimations of Postmodernity*. London: Routledge.

Bauman, Z. (1993) *Postmodern Ethics*. Oxford: Blackwell.

Bauman, Z. (2013) 'Does the richness of the few benefit us all?', *Social Europe*, 28 January, www.socialeurope.eu/2013/01/does-the-richness-of-the-few-benefit-us-all/#on (accessed 14 December 2016).

Bauman, Z. (2017) *Retrotopia*. Cambridge: Polity.

Baumeister, R. F. and Leary, M. R. (1995) 'The need to belong: desire and interpersonal attachments as a fundamental human motivation', *Psychological Bulletin*, *117*: 497–529.

Baunsgaard, V. and Clegg, S. R. (2013) '"Walls and boxes": the effects of professional identity, power and rationality on strategies for cross-functional integration', *Organization Studies*, *34* (9): 1299–1325.

Becker, B. E. and Huselid, M. A. (2006) 'Strategic human resources management: where do we go from here?' *Journal of Management*: 32 (6): 898–925.

Beach, L. R. (2015) *Human Resource Management in the Public Sector: Policies and Practices*. Oxford: Routledge.

Beane, M. (2018) 'Shadow learning: building robotic surgical skill when approved means fail', *Administrative Science Quarterly*, https://doi.org/10.1177/0001839217751692.

Beck, U. (2002) *Risk Society: Towards a New Modernity*. London: Sage.

Becker, B. and Gerhart, B. (1996) 'The impact of human resource management on organizational performance: progress and prospects', *Academy of Management Journal*, 39 (4): 779–801.

Behfar, K. J., Mannix, E. A., Peterson, R. S. and Trochim, W. M. (2012) 'Conflict in small groups: the meaning and consequences of process conflict', *Small Group Research*, *42* (2): 127–176.

Belbin, R. M. (1993) *Team Roles at Work*. Oxford: Butterworth-Heinemann.

Belbin, R. M. (2000) *Beyond the Team*. Oxford: Butterworth-Heinemann.

Benard, S. and Correll, S. J. (2010) 'Normative discrimination and the motherhood penalty', *Gender & Society*, *24* (5): 616–646.

Bennis, W. G. and O'Toole, J. (2005) 'How business schools lost their way', *Harvard Business Review*, May: 96–104.

Benson, J. and Brown, M. (2011) 'Generations at work: are there differences and do they matter?', *The International Journal of Human Resource Management*, 22 (9): 1843–1865.

Berger, P. and Luckmann, T. (1967) *The Social Construction of Reality: A Treatise in the Sociology of Knowledge*. Harmondsworth: Penguin.

Berger, P. L. (1987) *The Capitalist Revolution*. Aldershot: Gower.

Berthod, O. and Müller-Seitz, G. (2017) 'Making sense in pitch darkness: an exploration of the sociomateriality of sensemaking in crises', *Journal of Management Inquiry*, 27 (1): 52–68.

Bertolotti, F., Mattarelli, E., Vignoli, M. and Macrì, D. M. (2015) 'Exploring the relationship between multiple team membership and team performance: the role of social networks and collaborative technology', *Research Policy*, *44* (4): 911–924.

Beukman, T. L. (2005) The effect of selected variables on leadership: behavior within the framework of a transformational paradigm. Doctoral dissertation, University of Pretoria.

Beyer, J. M. and Nino, D. (1999) 'Ethics and cultures in international business', *Journal of Management Inquiry*, *8* (3): 287–297.

Bhabha, H. (1994) *The Location of Culture*. London: Routledge.

Bice, S. (2013) 'Corporate social responsibility in Asia: understanding business from beginning to end', http://theconversation.com/corporate-social-responsibility-in-asia-understanding-business-from-beginning-to-end-13928 (accessed 8 October 2018).

Biggart, N. W. and Hamilton, G. G. (1992) 'On the limits of a firm-based theory to explain business networks: the Western bias of neoclassical economics', in N. Nohria and R. Eccles (eds), *Networks and Organizations: Structure, Form and Action*. Boston, MA: Harvard Business School Press, pp. 471–490.

Bjoersma, M. (2013) 'Mind the gap: company disclosure discrepancies not sustainable', http://theconversation.com/mind-the-gap-company-disclosure-discrepancies-not-sustainable-15083 (accessed 8 October 2018).

Bjørken, K., Clegg, S. R. and Pitsis, T. S. (2009) 'Becoming a practice', *Management Learning*, 40 (2): 145–159.

Björkman, I., Ehrnrooth, M., Mäkelä, K., Smale, A. and Sumelius, J. (2013) 'Talent or not? Employee reactions to talent identification', *Human Resource Management*, 52 (2): 195–214.

Björkman, I., Ehrnrooth, M., Mäkelä, K., Smale, A. and Sumelius, J. (2014) 'From HRM practices to the practice of HRM: setting a research agenda', *Journal of Organizational Effectiveness: People and Performance*, *1* (2): 122–140.

Black, J. A. and Edwards, S. (2000) 'Emergence of virtual or network organizations: fad or feature', *Journal of Organization Change Management*, *13* (6): 567–576.

Blake, R. R. and McCanse, A. A. (1991) *Leadership Dilemmas-Grid Solution*. Houston: Gulf.

Blake, R. R. and Mouton, J. S. (1985) *The Managerial Grid III*. Houston: Gulf.

Blake, R. R., Shepard, H. A. and Mouton, J. S. (1964) *Managing Intergroup Conflict in Industry*. Houston, TX: Gulf Publishing Company.

Blanchet, V. (2018) 'Performing market categories through visual inscriptions: the case of ethical fashion', *Organization*, 25(3): 374–400.

Blanchflower, D. G. and Oswald, A. J. (2011) *International Happiness*. National Bureau of Economic Research working paper series (w16668), Cambridge, MA. Available at: www.nber.org/papers/w16668 (accessed 14 July 2011).

Blau, P. M. (1955) *The Dynamics of Bureaucracy*. Chicago: University of Chicago Press.

Blau, P. M. (1964) *Exchange and Power in Social Life*. New York: Wiley.

Blau, P. M. (2002) 'A formal theory of differentiation in organizations', in S. R. Clegg (ed.), *Central Currents in Organization Studies I: Frameworks and Applications*, Vol. 2. London: Sage, pp. 276–298; originally published in *American Sociological Review* (1970) 35: 201–218.

Blau, P. M. and Schoenherr, R. (1971) *The Structure of Organizations*. New York: Basic Books.

Blau, P. M. and Scott, W. (1963) *Formal Organizations: A Comparative Approach*. London: Routledge & Kegan Paul.

Bloo, J., Artz, A. and Schouten, E. (2018) 'The borderline personality disorder checklist: psychometric evaluation and factorial structure in clinical and nonclinical samples', *Roczniki Psychologiczne/Annals of Psychology*, 20 (2): 311–336.

Bloom, D. E. and Canning, D. (2000) 'Public health: the health and wealth of nations', *Science*, *287* (5456): 1207–1209.

Bloom, J. (2018) 'Digital nomads: the new elite with no fixed abode', *BBC Business Briefing*, 2 May, www.bbc.co.uk/news/business-43927098 (accessed 19 June 2018).

Bloomfield, M. (2018) 'How activism pushes companies to be political', *The Conversation*, 17 January, https://theconversation.com/how-activism-pushes-companies-to-be-political-86892 (accessed 6 October 2018).

Bogard, W. (1996) *The Simulation of Surveillance: Hypercontrol in Telematic Societies*. Cambridge: Cambridge University Press.

Boje, D. M. (1998) 'Nike, Greek goddess of victory or cruelty? Women's stories of Asian factory life', *Journal of Organizational Change Management*, *11* (6): 461–480.

Boje, D. M. (2001) *Narrative Methods for Organizational and Communication Research*. London: Sage.

Boje, D. M. (2002) 'Stories of the storytelling organization: a postmodern analysis of Disney as "Tamara-Land"', in S. R. Clegg (ed.), *Central Currents in Organization Studies II: Contemporary Trends*, Vol. 7. London: Sage, pp. 29–66; originally published in *Academy of Management Journal* (1995) *38*: 997–1035.

Boje, D. M. (2008) *Storytelling Organizations*. London: Sage.

Boje, D. M. and Dennehey, R. (1999) *Managing in the Postmodern World*. Dubuque, IA: Kendall-Hunt. Available at: http://cbae.nmsu.edu/~dboje/pages/CHAP5LEA.html (accessed 22 July 2011).

Boje, D. M. and Rosile, G. A. (2001) 'Where's the power in empowerment? Answers from Follett and Clegg', *Journal of Applied Behavioral Science*, *37* (1): 90–117.

Bone, J. (2007) 'Black's lawyer protests at perks and privileges strategy', *The Times*, 23 May: 45.

Bordow, A. and Moore, E. (1991) *Managing Organizational Communication*. Melbourne: Longman.

Borman, W. C., Hanson, M. A. and Hedge, J. W. (1997) 'Personnel selection', *Annual Review of Psychology*, *48* (2): 299–337.

Boudreau, J. and Lawler III, E. E. (2014) 'Stubborn traditionalism in HRM: causes and consequences', *Human Resource Management Review*, *24* (3): 232–244.

Boulding, K. E. (1957) 'Organization and conflict', *Journal of Conflict Resolution*, *1* (2): 122–134.

Bourke, H. (1982) 'Industrial unrest as social pathology: the Australian writings of Elton Mayo', *Historical Studies*, 20 (79): 217–233.

Bower, J. and Paine, L. S. (2017) 'The error at the heart of corporate leadership', *Harvard Business Review*, May–June: 50–60.

Bowie, N. (1999) *Business Ethics: A Kantian Perspective*. Malden, MA: Blackwell.

Bowman, E. H., Singh, H., Useem M. and Bhadury, R. (1999) 'When does restructuring improve economic performance?', *California Management Review*, *41* (2): 33–54.

Box, R. C., Marshall, G. S., Reed, B. J. and Reed, C. (2001) 'New public management and substantive democracy', *Public Administration Review*, *61* (5): 608–619.

Boyce, A. S., Corbet, C. E. and Adler, S. (2013) 'Simulations in the selection context: considerations, challenges, and opportunities', in M. Fetzer and K. Tuzinski (eds), *Simulations for Personnel Selection*. New York: Springer, pp. 17–41.

Boyd, M. and Pikkov, D. (2005) 'Gendering migration, livelihood and entitlements: migrant women in Canada and the United States', United Nations Research Institute for Social Development (UNRISD) Occasional Paper written for the preparation of the report *Gender Equality: Striving for Justice in an Unequal World*, Occasional Paper 6: United Nations Research Institute for Social Development. Geneva, Switzerland: UNRISD. Available at: www.unrisd.org/publications/opgp6 (accessed 14 July 2011).

Bradley, B. H., Postlethwaite, B. E., Klotz, A. C., Hamdani, M. R. and Brown, K. G. (2012) 'Reaping the benefits of task conflict in teams: the critical role of team psychological safety climate', *Journal of Applied Psychology*, *97* (1): 151–158.

Brannan, M. J. (2017) 'Power, corruption and lies: mis-selling and the production of culture in financial services', *Human Relations*, *70* (6): 641–667.

Brass, D. J., Butterfield, K. D. and Skaggs, B. C. (1998) 'Relationships and unethical behavior: a social network perspective', *Academy of Management Review*, *23* (1): 14–31.

Braun, R. and Krieger, D. (2005) *Einstein – Peace Now! Visions and Ideas*. Chichester: Wiley.

Braverman, H. (1974) *Labor and Monopoly Capital*. New York: Monthly Review Press.

Braybrooke, D. and Lindblom, C. E. (1963) *A Strategy of Decision*. New York: Free Press.

Bregman, R. (2016) *Utopia for Realists: The Case for a Universal Basic Income, Open Borders, and a 15-Hour Week*. London: Bloomsbury.

Brewer, N., Mitchell, P. and Weber, N. (2002) 'Gender role, organizational status, and conflict management styles', *International Journal of Conflict Management*, *13* (1): 78–94.

Brewster, C. (1995) 'Towards a "European" model of human resource management', *Journal of International Business Studies*, *26* (1): 1–21.

Brewster, C., Sparrow, P. and Vernon, G. (2007) *International Human Resource Management: Contemporary Issues in Europe*. London: Routledge.

Bromley, P. and Meyer, J. W. (2017) '"They are all organizations": the cultural roots of blurring between the nonprofit, business, and government sectors', *Administration & Society*, *49* (7): 939–966.

Bronfenbrenner, K. (1998) *Organizing to Win: New Research on Union Strategies*. Ithaca, NY: Sage.

Brown, A. D. (2005) 'Making sense of the collapse of Barings Bank', *Human Relations*, 58 (12): 1579–1604.

Brown, A. D., Colville, I. and Pye, A. (2015) 'Making sense of sensemaking in organization studies', *Organization Studies*, 36 (2): 265–277.

Brown, A. D., Stacey, P. and Nandhakumar, J. (2008) 'Making sense of sensemaking narratives', *Human Relations*, 61 (8): 1035–1062.

Brown, D. (2012) *The Hubris Syndrome: Bush, Blair and the Intoxication of Power*. London: Methuen.

Brown, J. and Duguid, P. (2001) 'Creativity versus structure: a useful tension', *Sloan Management Review*, 42 (4): 93–94.

Brudney, J. L. and Wright, D. S. (2002) 'Revisiting administrative reform in the American states: the status of reinventing government during the 1990s', *Public Administration Review*, 62 (3): 353–361.

Brudney, J. L., Herbert, F. T. and Wright, D. S. (1999) 'Reinventing government in the American states: measuring and explaining administrative reform', *Public Administration Review*, 59 (1): 19–30.

Brummans, B. H. J. M., Putnam, L. L., Gray, B., Hanke, R., Lewicki, R. J. and Wiethoff, C. (2008) 'Making sense of intractable multiparty conflict: a study of framing in four environmental disputes', *Communication Monographs*, 75 (1): 25–51.

Brunsson, N. (1985) *The Irrational Organization*. Chichester: Wiley.

Brunsson, N. (1989) *The Organization of Hypocrisy*. Chichester: Wiley.

Brunsson, N. (2006) *Mechanisms of Hope*. Copenhagen: Copenhagen Business School Press.

Brunsson, N. and Jacobsson, B. (2000) *A World of Standards*. Oxford: Oxford University Press.

Brynjolfsson, E. and McAfee, A. (2011) *Race against the Machine: How the Digital Revolution is Accelerating Innovation, Driving Productivity, and Irreversibly Transforming Employment and the Economy*. Lexington, MA: Digital Frontier Press.

Brynjolfsson, E. and McAfee, A. (2014) *The Second Machine Age: Work, Progress, and Prosperity in a Time of Brilliant Technologies*. New York: W.W. Norton.

Buchanan, D. and Badham, R. (2008) *Power, Politics and Organizational Change: Winning the Turf Game*. London: Sage.

Buckley, S. B. (2015) 'The state, the police and the judiciary in the miners' strike: Observations and discussions, thirty years on', *Capital and Class*, 39 (3): 419–434.

Buncombe, A. (2017) 'Donald Trump one year on: how the Twitter president changed social media and the country's top office', *Independent*, 3 April, www.independent.co.uk/news/world/americas/us-politics/the-twitter-president-how-potus-changed-social-media-and-the-presidency-a8164161.html (accessed 7 October 2018).

Burawoy, M. (1979) *Manufacturing Consent: Changes in the Labor Process Under Monopoly Capitalism*. Chicago: University of Chicago Press.

Burchielli, R. (2006) 'The purpose of trade union values: an analysis of the ACTU Statement of Values', *Journal of Business Ethics*, 68 (2): 133–142.

Burke, R. J. (1994) 'Generation X: measures, sex and age differences', *Psychological Reports*, 74 (2): 555–562.

Burke, R. J. and Nelson, D. L. (1997) 'Downsizing and restructuring: lessons from the firing line for revitalizing organizations', *Leadership & Organization Development Journal*, 18 (7): 325–334.

Burns, T. and Stalker, G. M. (1961) *The Management of Innovation*. London: Tavistock.

Cairns, G. (2013) 'Life more tragic than death: who remembers Rana Plaza?', http://theconversation.com/life-more-tragic-than-death-who-remembers-rana-plaza-18222 (accessed 7 October 2018).

Calás, M. B. and Smircich, L. (1996) 'Not ahead of her time: reflections on Mary Parker Follett as a prophet of management', *Organization*, 3 (1): 147–152.

Calás, M. B. and Smircich, L. (2006) 'From the "woman's point of view" ten years later: towards a feminist organization studies', in S. R. Clegg, C. Hardy, T. B. Lawrence and W. Nord (eds), *The Sage Handbook of Organization Studies*. London: Sage, pp. 284–346.

Calista, D. J. (2002) 'A critique of reinventing government in the American states: measuring and explaining administrative reform', *Public Administration Review*, 62 (3): 347–52.

Callick, R. (2013) *The Party Forever: Inside China's Modern Communist Elite*. London: Macmillan.

Callister, R. R. and Wall Jr, J. A. (2001) 'Conflict across organizational boundaries: managed care organizations versus health care providers', *Journal of Applied Psychology*, 86 (4): 754–763.

Camelo-Ordaz, C., Garca-Cruz, J., Sousa-Ginel, E. and Valle-Cabrera, R. (2011) 'The influence of human resource management on knowledge sharing and innovation in Spain: the mediating role of affective commitment', *International Journal of Human Resource Management*, 22 (7): 1442–1463.

Cameron, J. (Director) (1997) *Titanic* [Motion picture]. United States: Paramount.

Cameron, K. S., Dutton, J. E. and Quinn, R. E. (2003) *Positive Organizational Scholarship: Foundations of a New Discipline*. San Francisco, CA: Berrett-Koehler Publishers.

Campbell, F. (Producer) (2000) *Gap and Nike: No Sweat?* [Television broadcast]. London: BBC.

Campbell, J. L. and Göritz, A. S. (2014) 'Culture corrupts! A qualitative study of organizational culture in corrupt organizations', *Journal of Business Ethics*, 120 (3): 291–311.

Campos, G. P., Ramos, C. S. and Bernal, J. J. Y. (1999) 'Emotion discourse "speaks" of involvement: commentary on Edwards', *Culture & Psychology*, 5 (3): 293–304.

Campos, J. J., Walle, E. A., Dahl, A. and Main, A. (2011) 'Reconceptualizing emotion regulation', *Emotion Review*, 3 (1): 26–35.

Canguilhem, G. (1992) 'Machine and organism', in J. Crary and S. Kwinter (eds), *Incorporations*. New York: Zone, pp. 45–69.

Carey, A. (2002) 'The Hawthorne Studies: a radical criticism', in S. R. Clegg (ed.), *Central Currents in Organization Studies I: Frameworks and Applications*, Vol. 1. London: Sage, pp. 314–322; originally published in *American Sociological Review* (1967) 32: 403–416.

Carnegie, D. (1944) *How to Win Friends and Influence People: How to Stop Worrying and Start Living*. London: Chancellor.

Carr, D. K., Hard, K. J. and Trahant, W. J. (1996) *Managing the Change Process: A Field Book for Change Agents, Consultants, Team Leaders, and Reengineering Managers*. New York: McGraw-Hill.

Carter, C., Clegg, S. R. and Kornberger, M. (2008) *A Very Short, Fairly Interesting and Reasonably Cheap Book about Studying Strategy*. London: Sage.

Casey, C. (1995) *Work, Self and Society: After Industrialism*. London: Routledge.

Castells, M. (2000) *The Rise of the Network Society: The Information Age – Economy, Society and Culture*, Vol. 1, 2nd edn. London: Blackwell.

Castles, S. and Miller, M. J. (2003) *The Age of Migration: International Population Movements in the Modern World*. London: Guilford.

Cha, S. E. and Edmondson, A. C. (2006) 'When values backfire: leadership, attribution, and disenchantment in a values-driven organization', *The Leadership Quarterly*, 17(1): 57–78.

Chadwick, S. (2013) 'Heads will roll: why it's so easy to sack a football manager', *The Conversation*, 16 August, http://theconversation.com/heads-will-roll-why-its-so-easy-to-sack-a-football-manager-16874 (accessed 1 July 2015).

Chan, A. (2003) 'Instantiative versus entitative culture: the case for culture as process', in R. Westwood and S. R. Clegg (eds), *Debating Organizations: Point-Counterpoint in Organization Studies*. Oxford: Blackwell, pp. 311–320.

Chan, A. (2008) 'Matrix organizations', in S. R. Clegg and J. R. Bailey (eds), *The Sage International Encyclopedia of Organization Studies*. Thousand Oaks, CA: Sage, pp. 884–886.

Chan, A., Clegg, S. R. and Warr, M. (2018) 'Translating intervention: when corporate culture meets Chinese socialism', *Journal of Management Inquiry*, http://journals.sagepub.com/doi/full/10.1177/1056492617696888.

Chandler, A. D. (1990) *Scale and Scope*. Cambridge, MA: Harvard University Press.

Chandler, D. (2014) 'Organizational susceptibility to institutional complexity: critical events driving the adoption and implementation of the ethics and compliance officer position', *Organization Science*, 25 (6): 1722–1743.

Chen, J. and Wang, L. (2007) 'Locus of control and the three components of commitment to change', *Personality and Individual Differences*, 42 (3): 503–512.

Cheney, G. and Christensen, L. T. (2001) 'Organizational identity: linkages between internal and external communication', in F. M. Jablin and L. L. Putnam (eds), *New Handbook of Organizational Communication*. Thousand Oaks, CA: Sage, pp. 231–270.

Chesbrough, H. (2003) *Open Innovation*. Cambridge, MA: Harvard University Press.

Child, J. (2002) 'Organizational structure, environment and performance: the role of strategic choice', in S. R. Clegg (ed.), *Central Currents in Organization Studies I: Frameworks and Applications*, Vol. 2. London: Sage, pp. 323–343; originally published in *Sociology* (1972) 6: 1–21.

Child, J. and Kieser, A. (1979) 'Organization and managerial roles in British and West German companies: an examination of the culture-free thesis', in C. J. Lammers and D. J. Hickson (eds), *Organizations Alike and Unalike: International and Inter-Institutional Studies in the Sociology of Organizations*. London: Routledge & Kegan Paul, pp. 251–271.

Christensen, C. (1997) *The Innovator's Dilemma: When New Technologies Cause Great Firms to Fail*. Boston, MA: Harvard Business School Press.

Christensen, L. and Cheney, G. (2000) 'Self-absorption and self-seduction in the corporate identity game', in M. Schultz, M. Hatch and M. Larsen (eds), *The Expressive Organization: Linking Identity, Reputation, and the Corporate Brand*. Oxford and New York: Oxford University Press, pp. 246–270.

Christensen, S. L. (2008) 'The role of law in models of ethical behaviour', *Journal of Business Ethics*, 77 (4): 451–461.

Christensen, T. and Lægreid, P. (2018) 'An organization approach to public administration', in E. Ongaro and S. Van Thiel (eds), *The Palgrave Handbook of Public Administration and Management in Europe*. London: Palgrave, pp. 1087–1104.

Cicirelli, V. G. (1987) 'Locus of control and patient role adjustment of the elderly in acute-care hospitals', *Psychology and Aging*, 2 (2): 138–143.

Clarke, J. and Newman, J. (1997) *New Managerialism, New Welfare*. London: Sage.

Clawson, D. (1980) *Bureaucracy and the Labor Process: The Transformation of US Industry 1860–1920*. New York: Monthly Review Press.

Clegg, S. R. (1979) *The Theory of Power and Organization*. London: Routledge & Kegan Paul.

Clegg, S. R. (1981) 'Organization and control', *Administrative Science Quarterly*, *26* (4): 545–562.

Clegg, S. R. (1989) *Frameworks of Power*. London: Sage.

Clegg, S. R. (1990) *Modern Organizations: Organization Studies in the Postmodern World*. London: Sage.

Clegg, S. R. (1994) 'Power and the resistant subject', in J. Jermier, D. Knights and W. R. Nord (eds), *Resistance and Power in Organizations: Agency, Subjectivity and the Labor Process*. London: Routledge.

Clegg, S. R. (1995) 'Weber and Foucault: social theory for the study of organizations', *Organization*, *1* (1): 149–178.

Clegg, S. R. (1999) 'Globalizing the intelligent organization: learning organizations, smart workers, (not so) clever countries and the sociological imagination', *Management Learning*, 30 (3): 259–280.

Clegg, S. R. (2005) 'Puritans, visionaries and survivors', *Organization Studies*, *26* (4): 527–545.

Clegg, S. R. (2009) 'Bureaucracy, the holocaust and techniques of power at work', *Management Revue*, (20) 4: 326–347.

Clegg, S. R. (2010) *SAGE Directions in Organization Studies*, Vol. 2. London: Sage.

Clegg, S. R. and Bailey, J. R. (eds) (2008) *The Sage International Encyclopedia of Organization Studies*. Thousand Oaks, CA: Sage.

Clegg, S. R. and Dunkerley, D. (1980) *Organization, Class and Control*. London: Routledge & Kegan Paul.

Clegg, S. R. and Gordon, R. (2012) 'Accounting for ethics in action: problems with localised constructions of legitimacy', *Financial and Accountability Management*, *28* (4): 417–436.

Clegg, S. R. and Hardy, C. (1996) 'Representations', in S. R. Clegg, C. Hardy and W. R. Nord (eds), *Handbook of Organization Studies*. London: Sage, pp. 676–708.

Clegg, S. R. and Kono, T. (2002) 'Trends in Japanese management: an overview of embedded continuities and disembedded discontinuities', *Asia Pacific Journal of Management*, *19* (2–3): 269–285.

Clegg, S. R. and Kornberger, M. (2003) 'Modernism, postmodernism, management and organization theory', in E. Locke (ed.), *Postmodernism in Organizational Thought: Pros, Cons and the Alternative*. Amsterdam: Elsevier, pp. 57–89.

Clegg, S. R. and Palmer, G. (1996) *The Politics of Management Knowledge*. London: Sage.

Clegg, S. R. and Rhodes, C. (2006) *Management Ethics: Contemporary Contexts*. London: Routledge.

Clegg, S. R., Schweitzer, J., Pitelis, C. and Whittle, A. (2017) *Strategy: Theory and Practice*. London: Sage.

Clegg, S. R. and Van Iterson, A. (2013) 'The effects of liquefying place, time, and organizational boundaries on employee behavior: lessons of classical sociology', *M@n@gement*, *16* (5): 621–635.

Clegg, S. R., Boreham P. and Dow, G. (1986 [2013]) *Class, Politics and the Economy*. London and Boston: Routledge & Kegan Paul, The International Library of Sociology. [Reprinted 2013 as Clegg, S. R., Boreham P. and Dow G. (2013) *Class, Politics and the Economy*. London: Routledge Revivals.]

Clegg, S. R., Carter, C. and Kornberger, M. (2004) 'Get up, I feel like being a strategy machine', *European Management Review, 1* (1): 21–28.

Clegg, S. R., Carter, C., Kornberger, M. and Schweitzer, J. (2011) *Strategy: Theory and Practice*. London: Sage.

Clegg, S. R., Courpasson, D. and Phillips, N. (2006a) *Power and Organizations*. Thousand Oaks, CA: Sage.

Clegg, S. R., Cunha, M. P e. and Rego, A. (2012) 'The theory and practice of utopia in a total institution: the pineapple panopticon', *Organization Studies*, 33 (12): 1735–1757.

Clegg, S. R., Cunha, M. P. e. and Rego, A. (2013) 'To the victor go the spoils! Distributed agencies, inhumanities and the case of Comrade Duch of the Khmer Rouge', in F. X. de Vaujany and N. Mitev (eds), *Materiality and Space: Organizations, Artefacts and Practices*. London: Palgrave Macmillan, pp. 197–215.

Clegg, S. R., Hardy, C., Lawrence, T. B. and Nord, W. R. (eds) (2006b) *The Sage Handbook of Organization Studies*, 2nd edn. London: Sage.

Clegg, S. R., Kornberger, M. and Rhodes, C. (2007) 'Business ethics as practice', *British Journal of Management, 18* (2): 107–122.

Clegg, S. R., Pitsis, T. S., Rura-Polley, T. and Marosszeky, M. (2002) 'Governmentality matters: building an alliance culture for interorganizational collaboration', *Organization Studies, 23* (3): 317–337.

Clegg, S., Mikkelsen, E. N. and Sewell, G. (2015) 'Conflict: organizational', in J. D. Wright (ed.), *The International Encyclopedia of Social and Behavioral Sciences*, 2nd edn. Oxford: Elsevier.

Coase, R. H. (1937) 'The nature of the firm', *Economica, 4* (16): 386.

Coase, R. H. (1960) 'The problem of social cost', *Journal of Law and Economics*, 3: 1–44.

Cohen, M. D., March, J. G. and Olsen, J. P. (1972) 'The garbage can model of organizational choice', *Administrative Science Quarterly, 17* (1): 1–25.

Cohen, B. and Shenk, J. (2017) [directors] *An Inconvenient Sequel: Truth to Power* [Motion Picture]. New York: Paramount.

Cole, R. E. (1999) *Managing Quality Fads*. Oxford: Oxford University Press.

Collier, J. and Esteban, R. (2007) 'Corporate social responsibility and employee commitment', *Business Ethics: A European Review, 16* (1): 19–33.

Collins, D. (1998) *Gainsharing and Power: Lessons from Six Scanlon Plans*. Ithaca, NY: Cornell University Press.

Collins, L. R. and Schneid, T. D. (2001) *Physical Hazards of the Workplace*. Boca Raton, FL: CRC Press.

Collins, R. (1975). *Conflict Sociology: Toward an Explanatory Science*. New York: Academic Press.

Collinson, D. L. (2003) 'Identities and insecurities: selves at work', *Organization, 10* (3): 527–547.

Collinson, D. L. and Ackroyd, S. (2005) 'Resistance, misbehaviour and dissent', in S. Ackroyd, P. Thompson, R. Batt and P. S. Tolbert (eds), *The Oxford Handbook of Work and Organization*. Oxford: Oxford University Press, pp. 305–326.

Colson, C. and Pearcey, N. (1999) *Shattering the Grid: How Now Shall We Live?* Wheaton, IL: Tyndall House Publishers.

Colville, I., Waterman, R. and Weick, K. (1999) 'Organizing and the search for excellence: making sense of the times in theory and practice', *Organization*, 6 (1): 129–148.

Conger, J. A. (2000) 'How generational shifts will transform organizational life', in F. Hesselbein, M. Goldsmith and R. Beckhard (eds), *The Organization of the Future*. San Francisco: Jossey-Bass, pp. 17–24.

Cooke, B. (2003) 'The denial of slavery in management studies', *Journal of Management Studies*, *40* (8): 1895–1918.

Cooney, N. (2011) *Change of Heart: What Psychology Can Teach Us About Spreading Social Change*. New York: Lantern Books.

Coppola, F. F. (Director) (1974) *The Conversation* [Motion picture]. Los Angeles, CA: Paramount.

Corley, K. G. and Gioia, D. A. (2004) 'Identity ambiguity and change in the wake of a corporate spin-off', *Administrative Science Quarterly*, *49* (2): 173–208.

Corman, S. R. and Poole, M. S. (2000) *Perspectives on Organizational Communication: Finding Common Ground*. New York: Guilford Press.

Cornelissen, J. P. (2012) 'Sensemaking under pressure: the influence of professional roles and social accountability on the creation of sense', *Organization Science*, *23* (1): 118–137.

Coser, L. (1956) *Functions of Social Conflict*. New York: Free Press.

Coser, L. (1967) *Continuities in the Study of Social Conflict*. New York: Free Press.

Costa, P. T., Jr and McCrae, R. R. (1999) *NEO Personality Inventory: Revised (NEO PI-R)*. Available from Psychological Assessment Resources, Inc. at: www.parinc.com/products_search.cfm?Search=General (accessed 12 July 2011).

Costa, P. T. and McCrae, R. R. (2017) 'The NEO inventories as instruments of psychological theory', in T. A. Widiger (ed.), *The Oxford Handbook of the Five Factor Model*. Oxford: Oxford University Press, pp. 11–37.

Coughlan, P., Fulton Surwe, J. and Canales, K. (2007) 'Prototypes as (design) ›tools for behavioral and organizational change: a design-based approach to help organizations change work behaviors', *Journal of Applied Behavioral Science*, *43*: 122–134.

Coupland, C., Brown, A., Daniels, K. and Humphreys, M. (2008) 'Saying it with feeling: analysing speakable emotions', *Human Relations*, *61* (3): 327–353.

Courpasson, D. (2002 [2000]) 'Managerial strategies of domination: power in soft bureaucracies', in S. R. Clegg (ed), *Central Currents in Organization Studies II: Contemporary Trends*, Vol. 5. London: Sage, pp. 324–345 [originally published in *Organization Studies* (2000) *21*: 141–161].

Courpasson, D. (2017) 'Beyond the hidden/public resistance divide: how bloggers defeated a big company', *Organization Studies*, *38* (9): 1277–1302.

Courpasson, D., Dany, F. and Clegg, S. (2012) 'Resisters at work: generating productive resistance in the workplace', *Organization Science*, *23* (3): 801–819.

Courpasson, D. and Younes, D. (2014) 'Double of quits: understanding the links between secrecy and creativity in a project development process', *Organization Studies*, *39* (2–3): 271–295.

Covaleski, M. A., Dirsmith, M. W., Heian, J. B. and Samuel, S. (1998) 'The calculated and the avowed: techniques of discipline and struggles over identity in Big Six public accounting firms', *Administrative Science Quarterly*, *43* (2): 293–327.

Craig, G., Gaus, A., Wilkinson, M., Skrivankova, K. and McQuade, A. (2007) 'Modern slavery in the United Kingdom', 26 February. Available at: www.jrf.org.uk/publications/modern-slavery-united-kingdom (accessed 22 July 2011).

Crosby, F. J., Iyer, A., Clayton, S. and Downing, R. A. (2003) 'Affirmative action: psychological data and the policy debates', *American Psychologist*, *58* (2): 93–115.

Crossan, M. M. and Apaydin, M. (2010) 'A multi dimensional framework of organizational innovation: a systematic review of the literature', *Journal of Management Studies*, *47* (6): 1154–1191.

Crozier, M. (1964) *The Bureaucratic Phenomenon*. London: Tavistock.

Crozier, M. and Friedberg, E. (1980) *Actors and Systems: The Politics of Collective Action*, trans. A. Goldhammer. Chicago: University of Chicago Press.

Cruver, B. (2003) *Enron: The Anatomy of Greed – The Unshredded Truth from an Enron Insider*. London: Arrow.

Cullen, J. B., Parboteeah, K. P. and Victor, B. (2003) 'The effects of ethical climates on organizational commitment: a two-study analysis', *Journal of Business Ethics*, *46*: 127–141.

Cummings, S. (2002) *Recreating Strategy*. London: Sage.

Cummings, S., Bridgman, T., Hassard, J. and Rowlinson, M. (2017) *A New History of Management*. Cambridge: Cambridge University Press.

Cunha, M. P. e. and Clegg, S. R. (2018) 'Persistence in paradox', in M. Farjoun, W. K. Smith, H. Tsoukas, et al. (eds), *Perspectives on Process Organization Studies: Dualities, Dialectics and Paradoxes in Organizational Life*. Oxford: Oxford University Press, Chapter 2.

Cunha, M. P. e., Clegg, S. R. and Rego, A. (2010) 'Obedience and evil: from Milgram and Kampuchea to normal organizations', *Journal of Business Ethics*, 97 (2): 291–309.

Cunha, M. P. e., Clegg, S. R. and Rego, A. (2015) 'The institutionalization of genocidal leadership: Pol Pot and a Cambodian dystopia', *Journal of Leadership Studies*, 9 (1): 6–18.

Cunha, M. P. e., Clegg, S. R., Rego, A. and Lancione, M. (2012) 'The organization (Ângkar) as a state of exception: the case of the S-21 extermination camp, Phnom Penh', *Journal of Political Power*, 5 (2): 279–299.

Cunha, M. P. e., Rego, A. and Clegg, S. R. (2011) 'Pol Pot, alias brother number one: leaders as instruments of history', *Management and Organizational History*, 6 (3): 268–286.

Cunha, M. P. e., Rego, A. and Clegg, S. R. (2014) 'The ethical speaking of objects: ethics and the "object-ive" world of Khmer Rouge young comrades', *Journal of Political Power*, *7* (1): 35–61.

Cunha, M. P. e., Rego, A., Silva, A. F. and Clegg, S. R. (2015) 'An institutional palimpsest? The case of Cambodia's political order, 1970 and beyond', *Journal of Political Power*, *8* (3): 431–455.

Cusumano, M. A. and Gawer, A. (2002) 'The elements of platform leadership', *MIT Sloan Management Review*, *43*: 51–58.

Cyert, R. M. and March, J. G. (1963) *A Behavioral Theory of the Firm*. Englewood Cliffs, NJ: Prentice Hall.

Czarniawska, B. (2005) 'Fashion in organizing', in B. Czarniawska and G. Sevón, *Global Ideas: How Ideas, Objects and Practices travel in the Global Economy*. Oslo/Copenhagen: Liber/Copenhagen Business School Press, pp. 129–146.

Darwin, C. (1859) *On the Origin of Species by Means of Natural Selection, or the Preservation of Favoured Races in the Struggle for Life*. London: John Murray.

Darwin, J. (2007) *After Tamerlane: The Rise and Fall of Global Empires, 1400–2000*. London: Penguin.

Das, T. K. and Teng, B. (2000) 'A resource-based theory of strategic alliances', *Journal of Management*, *26*: 31–61.

Davidson, K. and Junge, D. (2014) *Beyond the Brick: A LEGO Brickumentary*. Documentary film. Global Emerging Markets and HeLo.

Davis, A. and Mishel, L. (2014) 'CEO pay continues to rise as typical workers are paid less', *Economic Policy Institute*, 12 June, www.epi.org/publication/ceo-pay-continues-to-rise (accessed 17 May 2016).

Davis, G.F. (2016a) 'What might replace the modern corporation? Uberization and the web page enterprise', *Seattle University Law Review*, *39*: 501–515.

Davis, G.F. (2016b) *The Vanishing American Corporation*. Oakland, CA: Berrett-Koehler Publications.

Dawson, P. (2003) *Understanding Organizational Change*. London: Sage.

De Dreu, C. K. W. (2008) 'The virtue and vice of workplace conflict: food for (pessimistic) thought', *Journal of Organizational Behavior*, *29* (1): 5–18.

De Dreu, C. K. W. and Beersma, B. (2005) 'Conflict in organizations: beyond effectiveness and performance', *European Journal of Work and Organizational Psychology*, *14* (2): 105–117.

De Dreu, C. K. W. and Gelfand, M. J. (eds) (2008) *The Psychology of Conflict and Conflict Management in Organizations*. New York: Taylor Francis/Lawrence Erlbaum.

De Dreu, C. K. W. and Van de Vliert, E. (1997) *Using Conflict in Organizations*. London: Sage.

De Dreu, C. K. W. and Van Knippenberg, D. (2005) 'The possessive self as a barrier to conflict resolution: effects of mere ownership, process accountability, and self-concept clarity on competitive cognitions and behavior', *Journal of Personality and Social Psychology*, *89* (3): 345–357.

De Dreu, C. K. W. and Weingart, L. R. (2003) 'Task versus relationship conflict, team performance, and team member satisfaction: a meta-analysis', *Journal of Applied Psychology*, *88* (4): 741–749.

de Geus, A. (1988) 'Planning as learning', *Harvard Business Review*, March–April: 70–74.

de Graaf, G., Huberts, L. and Smulders, R. (2016) 'Coping with public value conflicts', *Administration & Society*, *48* (9): 1101–1127.

Devos, T., Spini, D. and Schwartz, S. H. (2002) 'Conflicts among human values and trust in institutions', *British Journal of Social Psychology*, *41* (4): 481–494.

De Wit, F. R., Greer, L. L. and Jehn, K. A. (2012) 'The paradox of intragroup conflict: a meta-analysis', *Journal of Applied Psychology*, *97* (2): 360–390.

Deal, T. E. and Kennedy, A. A. (1982) *Corporate Cultures: The Rites and Rituals of Corporate Life*. Reading, MA: Addison-Wesley.

Dean, D. and Greene, A.-M. (2017) 'How do we understand worker silence despite poor conditions – as the actress said to the woman bishop', *Human Relations*, *70* (10): 641–667.

Dean, T. (2014) 'Why research beats anecdote in our search for knowledge'. Available at: http://theconversation.com/why-research-beats-anecdote-in-our-search-for-knowledge-30654 (accessed 8 October 2015).

Deardon, J. (Director) (1999) *Rogue Trader* [Motion picture]. United Kingdom: Newmarket Capitol, Granada Film Productions.

DeCharms, R. (1968) *Personal Causation*. New York: Academic Press.

DeChurch, L., Mesmer-Magnus, J. and Doty, D. (2013) 'Moving beyond relationship and task conflict: toward a process-state perspective', *Journal of Applied Psychology*, *98* (4): 559–578.

Deci, E. L. (1975) *Intrinsic Motivation*. New York: Plenum.

Deci, E. L. and Ryan, R. M. (1985) *Intrinsic Motivation and Self-determination in Human Behavior*. New York: Plenum.

Deci, E. L. and Ryan, R. M. (1987) 'The support of autonomy and the control of behavior', *Journal of Personality and Social Psychology*, 53: 1024–1037.

Deci, E. L. and Ryan, R. M. (2000) 'The "what" and "why" of goal pursuits: human needs and the self-determination of behavior', *Psychological Inquiry*, *11* (4): 227–268.

Delaney, A. and Burchielli, R. (2013) 'Shocking Bangladesh reality for workers highlights key role for labour unions', https://theconversation.com/shocking-bangladesh-reality-for-workers-highlights-key-role-for-labour-unions-15522 (accessed 7 October 2018).

Deetz, S. A., Tracy, S. J. and Simpson, J. L. (2000) *Leading Organizations through Transition*. Thousand Oaks, CA: Sage.

Dekker, H. (2004) 'Control of inter-organizational relationships: evidence on appropriation concerns and coordination requirements', *Accounting, Organizations and Society*, *29* (1): 27–49.

Deleuze, G. and Guattari, F. (1984) *A Thousand Plateaus: Capitalism and Schizophrenia*. London: Athlone.

Deloitte & Touche (1998) *Informal Economic Activities in the EU*. Brussels: European Commission.

Denis, J. L., Lamothe, L. and Langley, A. (2001) 'The dynamics of collective leadership and strategic change in pluralistic organizations', *Academy of Management Journal*, *44* (4): 809–837.

Denison, D. (1990) *Corporate Culture and Organizational Effectiveness*. New York: Wiley.

Deroy, X. and Clegg, S. (2011) 'When events interact with business ethics', *Organization*, *18* (5): 637–653.

Deutsch, M. (1949) 'A theory of cooperation and competition', *Human Relations*, 2: 129–151.

Deutsch, M. (1973) *The Resolution of Conflict: Constructive and Destructive Processes*. New Haven, CT: Yale University Press.

Deutsch, M. (1990) 'Sixty years of conflict', *International Journal of Conflict Management*, *1*: 237–263.

Devinney, T., Auger, P., Dowling, G. R., Eckert, C. and Lin, N. (2015) 'How much does a company's reputation matter in recruiting?', *MIT Sloan Management Review*, *54* (3): 79–88.

Devos, T., Spini, D. and Schwartz, S. (2002) 'Conflicts among human values and trust in institutions', *British Journal of Social Psychology*, *41* (1): 481–494.

Dicken, P. (2007) *Global Shift: Mapping the Changing Contours of the World Economy*, 5th edn. London: Sage.

Diefendorff, J. M., Erickson, R. J., Grandey, A. A. and Dahling, J. J. (2011) 'Emotional display rules as work unit norms: a multilevel analysis of emotional labor among nurses', *Journal of Occupational Health Psychology*, *16* (2): 170–186.

Diefendorff, J., Morehart, J. and Gabriel, A. (2011) 'The influence of power and solidarity on emotional display rules at work', *Motivation & Emotion*, *34* (2): 120–132.

DiMaggio, P. and Powell, W. W. (2002 [1]983) 'The iron cage revisited: institutional isomorphism and collective rationality in organizational fields', in S. R. Clegg (ed.), *Central Currents in Organization*

Studies I: Frameworks and Applications, Vol. 3. London: Sage, pp. 324–362 [originally published in *American Journal of Sociology* (1983) *48*: 147–160].

DiStefano, T. (1984) 'Interorganizational conflict: a review of an emerging field', *Human Relations*, *37* (5): 351–366.

Dodgson, M. (2000) *The Management of Technological Innovation: An International and Strategic Approach*. Oxford: Oxford University Press.

Does, S., Derks, B. and Ellemers, N. (2011) 'Thou shalt not discriminate: how emphasizing moral ideals rather than obligations increases Whites' support for social equality', *Journal of Experimental Social Psychology*, *47* (3): 562–571.

Donaldson, L. (1999) *Performance-Driven Organizational Change: The Organizational Portfolio*. London: Sage.

Donaldson, L. (2002 [1987]) 'Strategy and structural adjustment to regain fit and performance: in defence of contingency theory', in S. R. Clegg (ed.), *Central Currents in Organization Studies I: Frameworks and Applications*, Vol. 2. London: Sage, pp. 379–389 [originally published in *Journal of Management Studies* (1987) *24*: 1–24].

Dooley, R. S., Fryxell, G. E. and Judge, W. Q. (2000) 'Belaboring the not-so-obvious: consensus, commitment, and strategy implementation speed and success', *Journal of Management Studies*, *23* (5): 501–517.

Dosi, G. (1982) 'Technological paradigms and technological trajectories: a suggested interpretation of the determinants and directions of technical change', *Research Policy*, *11* (3): 147–162.

Dosi, G. (1984) *Technical change and industrial transformation: the theory and an application to the semiconductor industry*. Berlin: Springer.

Douglas, C. and Ammeter, A. P. (2004) 'An examination of the leader political skill construct and its effect on ratings of leader effectiveness', *Leadership Quarterly*, *15*: 537–550.

Drees, J. M. and Heugens, P. P. M. A. R. (2013) 'Synthesizing and extending resource dependence theory: a meta-analysis', *Journal of Management*, *39* (6): 1666–1698.

Driskell, T., Salas, E. and Driskell, J. E. (2018) 'Teams in extreme environments: alterations in team development and teamwork', *Human Resource Management Review*, *28* (4): 434–449.

Drucker, P. (1998) *Management Challenges for the 21st Century*. Oxford: Butterworth-Heinemann.

du Gay, P., Lopdrup-Hjorth, T., Pedersen K. Z. and Obling A. R. (2018) 'Character and organization', *Journal of Cultural Economy*, https://doi.org/10.1080/17530350.2018.1481879.

du Gay, P. and Lopdrup-Hjorth, T. (2016a) 'Fear of the formal', *European Journal of Cultural and Political Sociology*, *3* (1): 6-40.

du Gay, P. and Lopdrup-Hjorth; T. (2016b) 'Reclaiming formal organization', *Human Rights and Public Life Working Paper Series*, No. 3, Whitlam Institute, pp. 57–85.

du Gay, P. (2000) *In Praise of Bureaucracy*. London: Sage.

du Gay, P. and Salaman, G. (1992) 'The cult[ure] of the customer', *Journal of Management Studies*, *29* (5): 615–633.

Dubinskas, F. A. (1992) 'Culture and conflict: the cultural roots of discords', in D. M. Kolb and J. M. Bartunek (eds), *Hidden Conflict in Organizations: Uncovering Behind-the-scenes Disputes*. Thousand Oaks, CA: Sage, pp. 187–208.

Dubrin, A. J. (2005) *Coaching and Mentoring Skills*. Englewood Cliffs, NJ: Pearson Prentice Hall.

Durkheim, E. (1997) The Division of Labour in Society (trans. W. D. Halls; intro. L. A. *Coser)*. New York: Free Press.

Dutton, J. E., Frost, P., Worline, M. C., Lilius, J. M. and Kanov, J. M. (2002) 'Leading in times of trauma', *Harvard Business Review*, *80* (1): 54–61.

Dutton, J. E., Glynn, M. A. and Spreitzer, G. M. (2006) 'Positive organizational scholarship', in J. Greenhaus and G. Callanan (eds), *Encyclopedia of Career Development*. Thousand Oaks, CA: Sage, pp. 641–644.

Dutton, J. E., Lilius, J. M. and Kanov, J. M. (2007) 'The transformative potential of compassion at work', in S. K. Piderit, R. E. Fry and D. L. Cooperrider (eds), *Handbook of Transformative Cooperation: New Designs and Dynamics*. Stanford, CA: Stanford University Press, pp. 107–124.

Dutton, J. E., Morgan Roberts, L. and Bednar, J. (2010) 'Pathways for positive identity construction at work: four types of positive identity and the building of social resources', *The Academy of Management Review*, 35 (2): 265–293.

Dylan, B. (1967) 'The Wicked Messenger', on the Long Playing Record, *John Wesley Harding*. New York: Columbia Records.

Easterby-Smith, M. (1997) 'Disciplines of organizational learning: contributions and critiques', *Human Relations*, 50 (9): 1085–1113.

Ebbers, J. J. and Wijnberg, N. M. (2017) 'Betwixt and between: role conflict, role ambiguity and role definition in project-based dual-leadership structures', *Human Relations*, *70* (11): 1342–1365.

Edelman, M. (1964) *The Symbolic Uses of Politics*. Champaign, IL: University of Illinois Press.

Edelman, M. (1971) *Political Language*. London: Academic Press.

Effron, D. A. and Knowles, E. D. (2015) 'Entitativity and intergroup bias: how belonging to a cohesive group allows people to express their prejudices', *Journal of Personality and Social Psychology*, *108* (2): 234–253.

Ehigie, B. O. and Ehigie, R. I. (2005) 'Applying qualitative methods in organizations: a note for industrial/organizational psychologists', *Qualitative Report*, *10* (3): 621–638.

Eichengreen, B. (2007) *The European Economy since 1945: Coordinated Capitalism and Beyond*. Princeton, NJ: Princeton University Press.

Eiseman, J. W. (1978) 'Reconciling "incompatible" positions', *Journal of Applied Behavioral Science*, *14* (2): 133–150.

Ekman, P. and Friesen, W. V. (1986) 'A new pan-cultural facial expression of emotion', *Motivation and Emotion*, *10* (2): 159–168.

Ellis, R. J. (1988) 'Self-monitoring and leadership emergence in groups', *Personality and Social Psychology Bulletin*, *14*: 681–693.

Elsbach, K. D. and Stigliani, I. (2018) 'Design thinking and organizational culture: a review and framework for future research', *Journal of Management*, *44* (6): 2274–2306

Emerson, R. M. (1962) 'Power-dependence relations', *American Sociological Review*, *27* (1): 31–41.

Endler, N. S. and Speer, R. L. (1998) 'Personality psychology: research trends for 1993–1995', *Journal of Personality*, *66* (5): 621–669.

Enron Code of Ethics (2000) Available at: www.thesmokinggun.com/documents/crime/enrons-code-ethics (accessed 22 April 2014).

Enz, C. A. (1988) 'The role of value congruity in interorganizational power', *Administrative Science Quarterly*, 33: 284–304.

Epstein, N. B. and Baucom, D. H. (2002) *Enhanced cognitive-Behavioral therapy for couples: A contextual approach.* Washington, DC: American Psychological Association Press.

Erickson, G. (2007) 'The day I almost sold the company'. Available at: www.clifbar.com/ourstory/document.cfm?location=journey&id=137 (accessed 2 February 2007).

Esping-Andersen, G. (1990) *The Three Worlds of Welfare Capitalism.* Cambridge: Polity.

Esser, J. K. and Lindoerfer, J. S. (1989) 'Groupthink and the Space Shuttle Challenger accident: toward a quantitative case analysis', *Journal of Behavioral Decision Making*, 2 (1): 167–177.

Ethisphere (2015) 'World's most ethical companies ranking'. Available at: http://ethisphere. com/worlds-most-ethical/wme-honorees (accessed 22 June 2015).

European Industrial Relations Observatory On-line (2004) 'Trade union membership 1993-2003'. Available at: www.eurofound.europa.eu/eiro/2004/03/update/tn0403105u.html (accessed 23 February 2007).

Evan, W. and MacDougall, J. (1967) 'Interorganizational conflict: a labor-management bargaining experiment', *The Journal of Conflict Resolution*, 11 (4): 398–413.

Ezzamel, M. and Willmott, H. (2014) 'Registering "the ethical" in organization theory formation: towards the disclosure of an "invisible force"', *Organization Studies*, 35 (7): 1013–1039.

Fairhurst, G. T. (1993) 'Echoes of the vision: when the rest of the organization talks total quality', *Management Communication Quarterly*, 6 (4): 331–371.

Fairhurst, G. T. and Sarr, R. A. (1996) *The Art of Framing.* San Francisco: Jossey-Bass.

Fairtlough, G. (1994) *Creative Compartments: A Design for Future Organization.* London: Adamantine Press.

Fairtlough, G. (2007) *Three Ways of Getting Things Done: Hierarchy, Heterarchy and Responsible Autonomy in Organizations* (International Edition). Axminster: Tricarchy Press.

Farh, J. L., Lee, C. and Farh, C. I. C. (2010) 'Task conflict and team creativity: a question of how much and when', *Journal of Applied Psychology*, 95 (6): 1173–1180.

Fayol, H. (1949) *General and Industrial Management.* London: Pitman.

Fei, F. (2018) 'How to build (and rebuild) trust', www.ted.com/talks/frances_frei_how_to_build_and_rebuild_trust/transcript?language=en, (accessed 8 October 2018).

Felin, T., Lakhani, K. R. and Tushman, M. L. (2017) 'Firms, crowds, and innovation', *Strategic Organization*, 15 (2): 119–140.

Felstiner, W. L. F., Abel, R. L. and Sarat, A. (1980) 'Emergence and transformation of disputes: naming, blaming, claiming', *Law & Society Review*, 15: 631–654.

Fenton, E. M. and Pettigrew, A. (2000) 'Theoretical perspectives on new forms of organizing', in A. M. Pettigrew and E. M. Fenton (eds), *The Innovating Organization.* London: Sage, pp. 1–46.

Ferguson, K. E. (1984). *The Feminist Case against Bureaucracy.* Philadelphia, PA: Temple University Press.

Festinger, L. (1957) *A Theory of Cognitive Dissonance.* Stanford, CA: Stanford University Press.

Festinger, L. and Carlsmith, J. M. (1959) 'Cognitive consequences of forced compliance', *Journal of Abnormal and Social Psychology*, 58: 203–210.

Fiedler, F. E. (1964) *A Theory of Leadership Effectiveness.* New York: McGraw-Hill.

Financial Times (2018) 'A dinner that demeaned both women and men', *Financial Times*, 26 January, www.ft.com/content/0b9c1ae0-01d1-11e8-9650-9c0ad2d7c5b5 (accessed 7 October 2018).

Findlay, R. (2014) 'Do you know how your clothes were made?', http://theconversation.com/do-you-know-how-your-clothes-were-made-32675 (accessed 8 October 2018).

Fink, C. F. (1968) 'Some conceptual difficulties in the theory of social conflict', *Journal of Conflict Resolution*, *12* (4): 412–460.

Fisher, S. G. (1996) 'Further evidence concerning the Belbin Team Role Self-perception Inventory', *Personnel Review*, *25* (2): 61–67.

Flanagan, F. (2017) 'Symposium on work in the "gig economy"', *Economic and Labour Relations Review*, *28* (3): 382–401.

Fleming, P. (2009) *Authenticity and the Cultural Politics of Work*. Oxford: Oxford University Press.

Fleming, P. and Spicer, A. (2002) 'Workers' playtime: cynicism, irony and humour in organisation studies', in S. Clegg (ed.), *Management and Organization Paradoxes*. Amsterdam: Benjamins, pp. 65–86.

Fleming, P. and Spicer, A. (2003) 'Working at a cynical distance: implications for power, subjectivity and resistance', *Organization*, *10* (1): 157–179.

Fleming, P. and Spicer, A. (2007) *Contesting the Corporation: Struggle, Power and Resistance in Organizations*. Cambridge: Cambridge University Press.

Fleming, P. and Spicer, A. (2008) 'Beyond power and resistance: new approaches to organizational politics', *Management Communication Quarterly*, *21* (3): 301–309.

Fleming, P. and Spicer, A. (2014) 'Power in management and organization science', *The Academy of Management Annals*, *8* (1): 237–298.

Fletcher, G. J. O. and Sydnor Clark, M. (2003) *Blackwell Handbook of Social Psychology: interpersonal processes*. Malden, MA: Blackwell Press.

Fligstein, N. (1985) 'The spread of the multidivisional form', *American Sociological Review*, 5 (3): 377–391.

Florida, R. (2002) *The Rise of the Creative Classes*. New York: Basic Books.

Flyvbjerg, B. (1998) *Rationality and Power: Democracy in Practice*. Chicago: University of Chicago Press.

Follett, M. P. (1918) *The New State: Group Organization, the Solution for Popular Government*. New York: Longman, Green.

Follett, M. P. (1924) *Creative Experience*. New York: Longman, Green.

Follett, M. P. (1924/1951) *Creative Experience*. Eastford, CT: Martino Fine Books.

Follett, M. P. (1941) *Dynamic Administration: The Collected Papers of Mary Parker Follett*, eds H. C. Metcalf and L. Urwick. New York: Harper & Bros.

Fombrun, C. J., Gardberg, N. A. and Barnett, M. L. (2000) 'Opportunity platforms and safety nets: corporate citizenship and reputational risk', *Business and Society Review*, 105 (1): 85–106.

Fong, C. T. (2006) 'The effects of emotional ambivalence on creativity', *Academy of Management Journal*, *49*: 1016–1030.

Fong, G. T. and Markus, H. (1982) 'Self-schemas and judgments about others: seeking information about others', *Social Cognition*, *1*: 191–204.

Fosfuri, A., Giarratana, M. S. and Roca, E. (2011) 'Community-focused strategies', *Strategic Organization*, 9 (3): 222–239.

Foster, M. K., Abbey, A., Callow, M. A., Zu, X. and Wilbon, A. D. (2015) 'Rethinking virtuality and its impact on teams', *Small Group Research, 46* (3): 267–299.

Foucault, M. (1979) *Discipline and Punish: The Birth of the Prison*, ed. A. Sheridan. Harmondsworth: Penguin.

Foucault, M. (1983) 'The subject and power: afterword', in H. Dreyfus and P. Rabinow (eds), *Michel Foucault: Beyond Structuralism and Hermeneutics*. Brighton: Harvester, pp. 208–226.

Fox, E. M. (1968) 'Mary Parker Follett: the enduring contribution', *Public Administration Review, 28* (6): 520–529.

Francis, R. and Armstrong, A. (2003) 'Ethics as a risk management strategy: the Australian experience', *Journal of Business Ethics, 45*: 375–385.

Frank, A. and Brownell, J. (1989) *Organizational Communication and Behaviour: Communicating to Improve Performance*. New York: Dryden.

Frears, S. (Director) (2000) *High Fidelity* [Motion picture]. United States: Buena Vista.

Frears, S. (Director) (2003) *Dirty Pretty Things* [Motion picture]. United States: Miramax.

Freedom, R. B. and Medoff, J. L. (1984) *What Do Unions Do?* New York: Basic Books.

Freeland, C. (2013) 'The rise of the new super rich'.Available at: www.ted.com/talks/chrystia_freeland_the_rise_of_the_new_global_super_rich/transcript?language=en (accessed 7 August 2017).

French, H. (2003) *Vanishing borders: Protecting the environment in the age of globalization*. New York: Norton Paperbacks.

French, J. R. P. and Raven, B. (1968) 'The bases of social power', in D. Cartwright and A. Zander (eds), *Group Dynamics*. New York: Harper & Row, pp. 150–167.

Frenkel, M. and Shenhav, Y. (2006) 'From binarism back to hybridity: a postcolonial reading of management and organization studies', *Organization Studies, 27* (6): 855–876.

Freud, S. (1935) *A General Introduction to Psychoanalysis*. New York: Carlton House.

Frey, C. B. and Osborne, M. A. (2017) 'The future of employment: how susceptible are jobs to computerisation?', *Technological Forecasting and Social Change, 114* (C): 254–280.

Frey, L. R. (2004) 'The symbolic-interpretive perspective on group dynamics', *Small Group Research, 35* (3): 277–306.

Friedman, A. (1977) 'Responsible autonomy versus direct control over the labour process', *Capital and Class, 1*: 43–57.

Friedman, A. (1990) 'Managerial strategies, activities, techniques and technology: towards a complex theory of the labour process', in D. Knights and H. Willmott (eds), *Labour Process Theory*. London: Macmillan, pp. 177–208.

Friedman, M. (1970) 'The social responsibility of business is to increase its profits', *New York Times Magazine*, 13 September: 33.

Friedman, M. (1982) *Capitalism and Freedom*. Chicago: University of Chicago Press.

Friedman, R. A. (1992) 'The culture of mediation: private understandings in the context of public conflict', in D. M. Kolb and J. M. Bartunek (eds), *Hidden Conflict in Organizations: Uncovering Behind-the-scenes Disputes*. Thousand Oaks, CA: Sage, pp. 143–164.

Friedman, V. J. and Antal, A. B. (2005) 'Negotiating reality: a theory of action approach to intercultural competence', *Management Learning, 36* (1): 69–86.

Frost, P. J. (1999) 'Why compassion counts', *Journal of Management Inquiry, 8* (2): 127–133.

Frost, P. J. (2003) *Toxic Emotions at Work: How Compassionate Managers Handle Pain and Conflict*. Cambridge, MA: Harvard Business School Press.

Frost, P. J. and Egri, C. P. (2002) 'The political process of innovation', in S. R. Clegg (ed.), *Central Currents in Organization Studies II: Contemporary Trends*, Vol. 5. London: Sage, pp. 103–161; originally published in *Research in Organizational Behaviour* (1991) 13: 229–295.

Frost, P. J. and Robinson, S. L. (1999) 'The toxic handler: organizational hero and casualty', *Harvard Business Review*, July–August: 96–106.

Frost, P. J., Dutton, J. E., Maitlis, S., Lilius, J. M., Kanov, J. M. and Worline, M. C. (2006) 'Seeing organizations differently: three lenses on compassion', in S. R. Clegg, C. Hardy, T. B. Lawrence and W. R. Nord (eds), *The Sage Handbook of Organization Studies*. London: Sage, pp. 843–866.

Fukuyama, F. (1992) *The End of History and the Last Man*. New York: Basic Books.

Fuller, B., Marler, L. EK., Hester, K. and Otondo, R. F. (2015) 'Leader reactions to follower proactive behavior: giving credit when credit is due', *Human Relations, 68*: 879–898.

Fulop, L. and Rifkin, W. (1999) 'Management knowledge and learning', in L. Fulop and S. Linstead (eds), *Management: A Critical Text*. South Yarra, Victoria: Macmillan, pp. 14–47.

Gabriel, Y., Fineman, S. and Sims, D. (2000) *Organizing and Organizations*. London: Sage.

Gahan, P. (2014) 'Why Australian workplaces need much better leaders', https://theconversation.com/why-australian-workplaces-need-much-better-leaders-23354 (accessed 8 October 2018).

Gadlin, H. (1994) 'Conflict resolution, cultural differences, and the culture of racism', *Negotiation Journal, 10* (1): 33–47.

Galbraith, J. R. (1971) 'Matrix organization designs', *Business Horizons, 14*: 29–40.

Gallie, W. B. (1956). 'Art as an essentially contested concept', *The Philosophical Quarterly (1950-)*, 6 (23): 97–114.

Gambetta, D. (2009) *Codes of the Underworld: How Criminals Communicate*. Princeton, NJ: Princeton University Press.

Gambrell, K. M., Matkin, G. S. and Burbach, M. E. (2011) 'Cultivating leadership: the need for renovating models to higher epistemic cognition', *Journal of Leadership & Organizational Studies, 18* (3): 308–317.

Gandz, J. and Murray, V. V. (1980) 'The experience of workplace politics', *Academy of Management Journal, 23* (2): 237–251.

Gardiner, L. R. and Armstrong-Wright, D. (2000) 'Employee selection under anti-discrimination law: implications for multi-criteria group decision support', *Journal of Multi-Criteria Decision Analysis*, 9 (1–3): 99–109.

Gardner, W. L., Avolio, B. J., Luthans, F., May, D. R. and Walumbwa, F. O. (2005) 'Can you see the real me? A self-based model of authentic leader and follower development', *Leadership Quarterly, 16* (3): 343–372.

Garrett, L. (1994) *The Coming Plague: Newly emerging diseases in a world out of balance*. New York: Farrar Straus and Giroux.

Garrick, J. and Clegg, S. R. (2001) 'Stressed-out knowledge workers in performative times: a postmodern take on project-based learning', *Management Learning*, 32 (1): 119–134.

Garver, E. (1978) 'Rhetoric and essentially contested arguments', *Philosophy & Rhetoric*, 156–172.

Garvin, D. A. (1984) 'What does quality really mean?' *Sloan Management Review, 26* (1): 25–43.

Gatewood, R. D. and Carroll, A. B. (1991) 'Assessment of ethical performance of organization members: a conceptual framework', *Academy of Management Review, 16* (4): 667–690.

Gawer, A. and Henderson, R. (2007) 'Platform owner entry and innovation in complementary markets: Evidence from Intel', *Journal of Economics & Management Strategy, 16* (1): 1–34.

Gehman, H. W. and the Columbia Accident Investigation Board (2003) *Columbia Accident Investigation Board Report 1*. Arlington, VA.

George, J. M. (1992) 'The role of personality in organizational life: issues and evidence', *Journal of Management, 18* (2): 185–213.

Georgopoulos, B. S., Mahoney, G. M. and Jones, N. W. (1957) 'A path goal approach to productivity', *Journal of Applied Psychology, 41*: 345–353.

Geppert, M. and Matten, D. (2006) 'Institutional influences on manufacturing organization in multinational corporations: the "cherrypicking" approach', *Organization Studies, 27* (4): 491–515.

Ghoshal, S. (2005) 'Bad management theories are destroying good management practices', *Academy of Management Learning and Education, 4* (5): 75–91.

Gibney, A. (Director) (2005) *Enron: The Smartest Guys in the Room* [Motion picture]. Los Angeles, CA: Magnolia Pictures.

Giesen-Bloo, J., van Dyck, R., Spinhoven, P., van Tilburg, W., Dirksen, C., van Asselt, T., et al. (2006) 'Outpatient psychotherapy for borderline personality disorder randomized trial of schema-focused therapy vs transference-focused psychotherapy', *Archives of General Psychiatry, 63* (6): 649–658.

Gioia, D. and Chittipeddi, K. (1991) 'Sensemaking and sensegiving in strategic change initiation', *Strategic Management Journal, 12* (6): 433–449.

Goebel, S. and Weißenberger, B. E. (2017) 'The relationship between informal controls, ethical work climates, and organizational performance', *Journal of Business Ethics, 141* (3): 505–528.

Goethals, G. R. (2017) 'Almost "nothing new under the sun": American politics and the election of Donald Trump', *Leadership*, 13 (4): 413–423.

Goffman, E. (1961) *Asylums*. Harmondsworth: Penguin.

Goldman, S. L., Nagel, R. N. and Preiss, K. (1995) *Agile Competitors and Virtual Organizations: Strategies for Enriching the Customer*. New York: Van Nostrand Reinhold.

Goleman, D. (1995) *Emotional Intelligence: Why it Can Matter More than IQ*. New York: Bantam Books.

Gond, J. P. and Nyberg, D. (2017) 'Materializing power to recover corporate social responsibility', *Organization Studies, 38* (8): 1127–1148.

Gordon, G. and DiTomaso, N. (1992) 'Predicting corporate performance from organizational culture', *Journal of Management Studies, 29* (6): 783–798.

Gordon, P. J. (2001) *Lean and Green: Profit for your Workplace and the Environment*. San Francisco: Berrett-Koehler.

Gordon, R. D. (2002) 'Conceptualizing leadership with respect to its historical-contextual antecedents to power', *Leadership Quarterly, 13*: 151–167.

Gordon, R. D. (2007) *Power, Knowledge and Domination*. Copenhagen and Oslo: CBS Press & Liber.

Gordon, R. D., Clegg, S. R. and Kornberger, M. (2009a) 'Embedded ethics: discourse and power in the New South Wales Police Service', *Organization Studies*, 30 (1): 73–99.

Gordon, R. D., Clegg, S. R. and Kornberger, M. (2009b) 'Power, rationality and legitimacy in public organizations', *Public Administration: An International Quarterly*, 27 (1): 15–34.

Gouldner, A. W. (1954) *Patterns of Industrial Bureaucracy*. New York: Free Press.

Graham, G. (2002) 'If you want honesty, break some rules', *Harvard Business Review*, April: 42–47.

Graham, P. (ed.) (1995) *Mary Parker Follett – Prophet of Management: A Celebration of Writings from the 1920s*. Boston, MA: Harvard Business School Press Classic.

Granovetter, M. (2002 [1985]) 'Economic action and social structure: the problem of embeddedness', in S. R. Clegg (ed.), *Central Currents in Organization Studies I: Frameworks and Applications*, Vol. 3. London: Sage, pp. 363–389 [originally published in *American Journal of Sociology* (1985) 93: 481–510].

Granstrom, K. and Stiwne, D. (1998) 'A bipolar model of groupthink: an expansion of Janis's concept', *Small Group Research*, 29 (1): 32–56.

Grant, R. M., Shani, R. and Khrishnan, R. (1994) 'TQM's challenge to management theory and practice', *Sloan Management Review*, 35 (2): 25–35.

Gray, B. (1985) 'Conditions facilitating interorganizational collaboration', *Human Relations*, 38 (10): 911–936.

Gray, B. (1996) 'Cross-sectoral partners: collaborative alliances among business, government and communities', in C. Huxham (ed.), *Creating Collaborative Advantage*. London: Sage, pp. 57–79.

Gray, B., Coleman, P. T. and Putnam, L. L. (2007) 'Introduction: intractable conflict – new perspectives on the causes and conditions for change', *American Behavioral Scientist*, 50 (11): 1415–1429.

Gray, C. (2005) *A Very Short, Fairly Interesting and Reasonably Cheap Book About Studying Organizations*. London: Sage.

Green, F. (1997) 'Union recognition and paid holiday entitlement', *British Journal of Industrial Relations*, 35 (2): 243–255.

Greenberg, J. and Baron, R. A. (2003) *Behavior in Organizations*, 8th edn. Englewood Cliffs, NJ: Prentice Hall.

Greenhouse, S. (2007) 'Court approves class-action suit against Wal-Mart', *New York Times*, www.nytimes.com/2007/02/07/business/07bias.html (accessed 8 October 2018).

Greenwood, R., Rose, T., Brown, J., Cooper, D. and Hinings, B. (1999) 'The global management of professional services: the example of accounting', in S. Clegg, E. Ibarra-Colado and L. Bueno-Rodriquez (eds), *Global Management: Universal Theories and Local Realities*. London: Sage, pp. 265–296.

Greer, L. L., Jehn, K. A. and Mannix, E. A. (2008) 'Conflict transformation: an exploration of the inter-relationships between task, relationship, and process conflict', *Small Group Research*, 39 (3): 278–302.

Greifeneder, R., Bless, H. and Pham, M. T. (2011) 'When do people rely on affective and cognitive feelings in judgment? A review', *Personality and Social Psychology Review*, 15 (2): 107–141.

Grey, C. (1994) 'Career as a project of the self and labour process discipline', *Sociology*, 28 (2): 479–497.

Guest, D. E. (2004) 'The psychology of the employment relationship: an analysis based on the psychological contract', *Journal of Applied Psychology*, 53 (4): 541–555.

Guest, D. E. (2011) 'Human resource management and performance: still searching for some answers', *Human Resource Management Journal, 21* (1): 3–13.

Guggenheim, D. (Director) (2006) *An Inconvenient Truth* [Motion picture]. Los Angeles, CA: Paramount.

Guillen, M. F. (1994) *Models of Management: Work, Authority, and Organization in a Comparative Perspective*. Chicago: University of Chicago Press.

Guiso, L., Sapienza, P. and Zingales, L. (2015) 'The value of corporate culture', *Journal of Financial Economics, 117* (1): 60–76.

Haggis, P. (2006) *Crash* [Motion picture]. Vancouver: Lionsgate Films.

Hahn, T., Preuss, L., Pinkse, J. and Figge, F. (2014) 'Cognitive frames in corporate sustainability: managerial sensemaking with paradoxical and business case frames', *Academy of Management Review*, 39 (4): 463–487.

Hall, R. (1993) 'A framework linking intangible resources and capabilities to sustainable competitive advantage', *Strategic Management Journal, 14*: 607–618.

Halsall, R. and Brown, M. (2013) 'Askēsis and organizational culture', *Organization*, 20 (2): 233–255.

Hamel, G. (1996) 'Strategy as revolution', *Harvard Business Review*, July–August: 69–82.

Hamel, G. (2002) *Leading the Revolution*. New York: Plume.

Hamel, G. and Prahalad, C. K. (1996) *Competing for the Future*. Boston, MA: Harvard Business School Press.

Hammer, M. and Champy, J. (1993) *Reengineering the Corporation: A Manifesto for Business Revolution*. New York: HarperBusiness.

Hancock, P. and Tyler, M. (2001) *Work, Postmodernism and Organisation: A Critical Introduction*. London: Sage.

Handy, C. (1990) *The Age of Unreason: New Thinking for a New World*. London: Business Books, Arrow.

Handy, C. (2002) *The Elephant and the Flea*. Boston, MA: Harvard Business School Press.

Haney, C., Banks, C. and Zimbardo, P. (1973) 'Interpersonal dynamics in a simulated prison', *International Journal of Criminology and Psychology*, 1: 69–97.

Hanks, P. (ed.) (1986) *Collins Dictionary of the English Language: An Extensive Coverage of Contemporary International and Australian English*. Sydney: Collins.

Hanlon, G. (1994) *Commercialisation of the Service Class*. London: Macmillan.

Hardt, M. and Negri, A. (2000) *Empire*. Cambridge, MA: Harvard University Press.

Hardt, M. and Negri, A. (2004) *Multitude*. New York: Penguin Books.

Hardy, C. and Clegg, S. R. (1999) 'Some dare call it power', in S. R. Clegg and C. Hardy (eds), *Studying Organizations: Theory and Method*. London: Sage, pp. 368–387.

Hardy, C. and Clegg, S. R. (2006) 'Some dare call it power', in S. R. Clegg, C. Hardy, T. B. Lawrence and W. R. Nord (eds), *The Sage Handbook of Organization Studies*. London: Sage, pp. 754–775.

Hardy, C. and Phillips, N. (1998) 'Strategies of engagement: lessons from the critical examination of collaboration and conflict in an interorganizational domain', *Organization Science*, 9 (2): 217–230.

Harkins, S. G. and Szymanski, K. (1989) 'Social loafing and group evaluation', *Journal of Personality and Social Psychology*, 56 (3): 934–941.

Harvey, D. (1992) *The Condition of Postmodernity*. Oxford: Blackwell.

Hassard, J. S. (2012) 'Rethinking the Hawthorne studies: the Western Electric research in its social, political and historical context', *Human Relations*, 65 (11): 1431–1461.

Hassard, J., McCann, L. and Moriss, J. (2009) *Managing in the Modern Corporation: The Intensification of Managerial Work in the USA, UK and Japan*. Cambridge: Cambridge University Press.

Hatch, M. and Schultz, M. (2001) 'Are the strategic stars aligned for your corporate brand?' *Harvard Business Review*, February: 129–134.

Hatch, M. J. and Yanow, D. (2008) 'Methodology by metaphor: ways of seeing in painting and research', *Organization Studies*, 29 (1): 23–44.

Hatcher, L. and Ross, T. L. (1991) 'From individual incentives to an organization-wide gainsharing plan: effects on teamwork and product quality', *Journal of Organizational Behavior*, 12 (3): 169–183.

Havemann, H. A. (1993) 'Ghost of managers past: managerial succession and organizational mortality', *Academy of Management Journal*, 36 (4): 864–881.

Hawes, C. (2012) *The Chinese Transformation of Corporate Culture*. London: Routledge.

Hawken, P. (1993) *The Ecology of Commerce: A Declaration of Sustainability*. New York: HarperCollins.

Hedman-Phillips, E. and Barge, J. K. (2017) 'Facilitating team reflexivity about communication', *Small Group Research*, 48 (3): 255–287.

Hedmo, T., Sahlin-Andersson, K. and Wedlin, L. (2005) 'Fields of imitation: the global expansion of management education', in B. Czarniawska and G. Sevón (eds), *Global Ideas: How Ideas, Objects and Practices Travel in the Global Economy*. Oslo: Liber, pp. 190–212.

Heffernan, M. (2012) 'Dare to disagree', www.youtube.com/watch?v=PY_kd46RfVE (accessed 7 October 2018).

Hegel, G. W. F. (1975) *Lectures on the Philosophy of World History: Introduction, Reason in History* (translated from the German edition of Johannes Hoffmeister from Hegel papers assembled by H. B. Nisbet). New York: Cambridge University Press.

Heider, F. (1958) *The Psychology of Interpersonal Relations*. New York: Wiley.

Held, B. S. (2004) 'The negative side of positive psychology', *Journal of Humanistic Psychology*, 44 (1): 9–46.

Helin, S. and Sandström, J. (2007) 'An inquiry into the study of corporate codes of ethics', *Journal of Business Ethics*, 75: 253–271.

Helin, S. and Sandström, J. (2010) 'Resisting a corporate code of ethics and the reinforcement of management control', *Organization Studies*, 31 (5): 583–604.

Helin, S., Jensen, T., Sandström, J. and Clegg, S. R. (2011) 'On the dark side of codes: domination not enlightenment', *Scandinavian Journal of Management*, 27 (1): 24–33.

Helms Mills, J., Thurlow, A. and Mills, A. J. (2010) 'Making sense of sensemaking: the critical sensemaking approach', *Qualitative Research in Organizations and Management: An International Journal*, 5 (2): 182–195.

Helpap, S. and Bekmeier-Feuerhahn, S. (2016) 'Employees' emotions in change: advancing the sensemaking approach', *Journal of Organizational Change Management*, 29 (6): 903–916.

Henderson, L. J. (2002 [1936]) 'The effects of social environment' (with Elton Mayo), in S. R. Clegg (ed.), *Central Currents in Organization Studies I: Frameworks and Applications*, Vol. 2. London:

Sage, pp. 299–313 [originally published in *Journal of Industrial Hygiene and Technology* (1936) *18*: 401–416].

Hendrickson-Eagley, A. (1987) *Sex differences in social behavior: a social-role interpretation*. Hillsdale, NJ: Lawrence Erlbaum Associates.

Hendriks, A. A. J. and Hofstee, W. K. B. (2011) *Five Factor Personality Inventory (FFPI)*. Walmolen, The Netherlands: Bohn Stafleu van Loghum.

Hendriks, A. A. J., Kuypera, H., Lubbers, M. J. and Van der Werfa, M. (2011) 'Personality as a moderator of context effects on academic achievement', *Journal of School Psychology*, *49* (2): 217–248.

Hering, E. (1977) *The Theory of Binocular Vision*. New York: Plenum Press.

Hernes, T. and Maitlis, S. (2010) *Process, Sensemaking, and Organizing*. Oxford: Oxford University Press.

Herscovitch, L. and Meyer, J. P. (2002) 'Commitment to organizational change: extension of a three-component model', *Journal of Applied Psychology*, *87*: 474–487.

Hersey, P., Blanchard, K. H. and Johnson, D. (1996) *Management of Organizational Behavior: Utilizing Human Resources*, 7th edn. Upper Saddle River, NJ: Prentice Hall.

Heugens, P. P. M. A. R., Kaptein, M. and van Oosterhout, J. H. (2006) 'The ethics of the node versus the ethics of the dyad? Reconciling virtue ethics and contractualism', *Organization Studies*, *27* (3): 391–411.

Hickson, D. J. (2002) 'A convergence in organization theory', in S. R. Clegg (ed.), *Central Currents in Organization Studies II: Contemporary Trends*, Vol. *1*. London: Sage, pp. 380–389; originally published in *Administrative Science Quarterly* (1966) *11*: 224–237.

Hickson, D. J., Butler, R. J., Cray, D., Mallory, G. R. and Wilson, D. C. (1986) *Top Decisions: Strategic Decision-Making in Organizations*. San Francisco: Jossey-Bass.

Hickson, D. J., Hinings, C. R., Lee, C. A., Schneck, R. E. and Pennings, J. M. (2002) 'A strategic contingencies theory of intra-organizational power', in S. R. Clegg (ed.), *Central Currents in Organization Studies II: Contemporary Trends*, Vol. 5. London: Sage, pp. 3–19; originally published in *Administrative Science Quarterly* (1971) *16*: 216–229.

Hickson, D. J., Miller, S. J. and Wilson, D. C. (2003) 'Planned or prioritized? Two options in managing the implementation of strategic decisions', *Journal of Management Studies*, *40* (7): 1803–1836.

Higgins, C. (1980) *Nine to Five* [Motion picture]. United States: Fox.

Higgins, W. and Hallström, K. T. (2007) 'Standardization, globalization and rationalities of government', *Organization*, *14* (5): 685–704.

Hinings, C. R., Greenwood, R. and Cooper, D. (1999) 'The dynamics of change in large accounting firms', in D. M. Brock, M. J. Powell and C. R. Hinings (eds), *Restructuring the Professional Organization: Accounting, Health Care and Law*. London: Routledge, pp. 131–153.

Hinings, C., Hickson, D., Pennings, J. and Schneck, R. (1974) 'Structural conditions of intraorganizational power', *Administrative Science Quarterly*, *19* (1): 22–44.

Hirschhorn, L. (2002) 'Campaigning for change', *Harvard Business Review*, July: 98–104.

Hirschman, A. O. (1970) *Exit, Voice, and Loyalty: Responses to Decline in Firms, Organizations, and States*. Cambridge, MA: Harvard University Press.

Hobsbawm, E. (1975) *The Age of Capital 1848–1875*. London: Weidenfeld & Nicolson.

Hocker, J. L. and Wilmot, W. W. (1991) *Interpersonal Conflict*. Dubuque, IA: Wm. C. Brown.

Hofstede, G. (1980) *Culture's Consequences: International Differences in Work-related Values*. London: Sage.

Hofstede, G. (2001) *Culture's Consequences: Comparing Values, Behaviors, Institutions and Organizations across Nations*. London: Sage.

Hofstede, G. (2006) 'What did GLOBE really measure? Researchers' minds versus respondents' minds', *Journal of International Business Studies*, *37* (6): 882–889.

Hofstede, G., Hofstede, G. J. and Minkov, M. (2010) *Cultures and Organizations: Software of the Mind*, 3rd edn. New York: McGraw-Hill.

Hogan, D. (1978) 'Education and the making of the Chicago working class, 1880-1930', *Historical Education Quarterly*, *18*: 227–270.

Hogg, M. A. (1996) 'Intragroup processes, group structure and social identity', in W. Robinson (ed.), *Social Groups and Identities: Developing the Legacy of Henri Tajfel*. Oxford: Butterworth, pp. 65–93.

Hollenbeck, J. R., Beersma, B. and Schouten, M. E. (2012) 'Beyond team types and taxonomies: a dimensional scaling conceptualization for team description', *Academy of Management Review*, *37* (1): 82–106.

Hollenbeck, J. R., DeRue, D. S. and Nahrgang, J. D. (2015) 'The opponent process theory of leadership succession', *Organizational Psychology Review*, 5 (4): 333–363.

Höllerer, M. A. (2010) *Between creed, rhetoric façade, and disregard: dissemination and theorization of corporate social responsibility (CSR) in Austrian publicly traded corporations*. Doctoral dissertation, WU Vienna University of Economics and Business.

Holt, D. B. (2003) 'What becomes an icon most?' *Harvard Business Review*, March: 43–49.

Hom, P. W., Lee, T. W., Shaw, J. D. and Hausknecht, J. P. (2017) 'One hundred years of employee turnover theory and research', *Journal of Applied Psychology*, *102* (3): 530–545.

Hope, O. (2010) 'The politics of middle management sensemaking and sensegiving', *Journal of Change Management*, *10* (2): 195–215.

Hopkins, W. E. (1997) *Ethical Dimensions of Diversity*. London: Sage.

Hornby, N. (1995) *High Fidelity*. London: Riverhead.

Horowitz, M. J. (1991) *Person Schemas and Maladaptive Interpersonal Patterns*. Chicago: University of Chicago Press.

Hoskin, K. (2004) 'Spacing, timing and the invention of management', *Organization*, *11* (6): 743–757.

House, R. J. (1971) 'A path-goal theory of leadership effectiveness', *Administrative Science Quarterly*, *16*: 321–338.

House, R. J. (1996) 'Path-goal theory of leadership: lessons, legacy, and a reformulated theory', *Leadership Quarterly*, *7*: 323–352.

House, R. J. and Mitchell, T. R. (1974) 'Path-goal theory of leadership', *Journal of Contemporary Business*, *4*: 81–97.

House, R. J., Hanges, P. J., Javidan, M., Dorfman, P. and Gupta, V. (2004) *Culture, Leadership, and Organizations: The GLOBE Study of 62 Societies*. Thousand Oaks, CA: Sage.

House, R. J., Shane, S. A. and Herold, D. M. (1996) 'Rumors of the death of dispositional research are vastly exaggerated', *Academy of Management Review*, *21*: 203–224.

Howard, G. S. (1988) 'On putting the person back into psychological research', in D. M. Deluca (ed.), *Essays on Perceiving Nature: How the Humanities, Arts, and Sciences View Our World.* Honolulu: University of Hawaii Press, pp. 207–214.

Howard, L. W. (1998) 'Validating the competing values model as a representation of organizational cultures', *International Journal of Organizational Analysis*, 6 (3): 231–250.

Howard, P. J. and Howard, J. M. (2006) *The Owner's Manual for Personality at Work: How the Big Five Personality Traits Affect Performance, Communication, Teamwork, Leadership and Sales.* Austin, TX: Bard Press.

Howard, R. (Director) (1995) *Apollo 13* [Motion picture]. United States: Universal.

Howcroft, D. and Wilson, M. (2003) 'Participation: "bounded freedom" or hidden constraints on user involvement?', *New Technology, Work, and Employment*, *18* (1): 2–19.

Howe, J. (2006) 'The rise of crowdsourcing', *Wired*, *14* (6): 1–4.

Huault, I., Perret, V. and Spicer, A. (2014) 'Beyond macro- and micro-emancipation: rethinking emancipation in organization studies', *Organization*, *21* (1): 22–49.

Hurley-Hanson, A. E. and Giannantonio, C. M. (2006) 'Recruiters' perceptions of appearance: the stigma of image norms', *Equal Opportunities International*, *25* (6): 450–463.

Husted, B. (2005) 'Risk management, real options, and corporate social responsibility', *Journal of Business Ethics*, 60 (2) (Part 2): 175–183.

Hutton, W. (1995) *The State We're In.* London: Vintage.

Huxham, C. and Macdonald, D. (1992) 'Introducing collaborative advantage: achieving inter-organizational effectiveness through meta-strategy', *Management Decision*, 30 (3): 50–56.

Huy, Q. N. (2002) 'Emotional balancing of organizational continuity and radical change: the contribution of middle managers', *Administrative Science Quarterly*, *47* (1): 31–69.

Ibarra-Colado, E., Clegg, S. R., Rhodes, C. and Kornberger, M. (2006) 'The ethics of managerial subjectivity', *Journal of Business Ethics*, *64* (1): 45–55.

Iedema, R. and Rhodes, C. (2010) 'The undecided space of ethics in organizational surveillance', *Organization Studies*, *31* (2): 199–217.

Iedema, R., Rhodes, C. and Scheeres, H. (2006) 'Surveillance, resistance, observance: exploring the teleo-affective volatility of workplace interaction', *Organization Studies*, *27* (8): 1111–1130.

Inglehart, R. (1997) *Modernization and Post-Modernization: Cultural, Economic, and Political Change in 43 Societies.* Princeton, NJ: Princeton University Press.

Ingvaldsen, J. A. (2015) 'Organizational learning: bringing the forces of production back in', *Organization Studies*, *36* (4): 423–444.

Irwin, H. and More, E. (1994) *Managing Corporate Communication.* St Leonards: Allen & Unwin.

Isaacson, W. (2011) *Steve Jobs: A Biography*. New York: Simon & Schuster.

Ivtzan, I., Lomas, T., Hefferon, K. and Worth, P. (2015) *Second Wave Positive Psychology: Embracing the Dark Side of Life*. London: Routledge.

Ivtzan, I., Lomas, T., Worth, P. and Hefferon, K. (2015) 'Challenging positive psychology: embracing the dark side of life', *British Journal of Clinical Psychology*, 53 (2): 228–244.

Iyer, A. and Ryan, M. K. (2006) 'Challenging gender inequality in the workplace: men's and women's pathways to collective action', *SPSSI-EAESP Small Group Meeting on Multiple Perspectives on Real World Helping and Social Action*, Long Beach, USA.

Iyer, A. and Ryan, M. K. (2009) 'Why do men and women challenge gender discrimination in the workplace? The role of group status and in group identification in predicting pathways to collective action', *Journal of Social Issues*, *65* (4): 791–814.

Jabri, M., Adrian, A. D. and Boje, D. (2008) 'Reconsidering the role of conversations in change communication: a contribution based on Bakhtin', *Journal of Organizational Change Management*, *21* (6): 667–685.

Jackson, A. (2011) 'Appearance, rationality and justified belief', *Philosophy and Phenomenological Research*, *82* (3): 564–593.

Jackson, S. E., Schuler, R. S. and Jiang, K. (2014) 'An aspirational framework for strategic human resource management', *The Academy of Management Annals*, *8* (1): 1–56.

Jackson, T. (2000) 'Management ethics and corporate policy: a cross-cultural comparison', *Journal of Management Studies*, *37* (3): 349–369.

Jacques, R. (1996) *Manufacturing the Employee: Management Knowledge from the 19th to 21st Century*. London: Sage.

Jang, Y. S. (2005) 'The expansion of modern accounting as a global and institutional practice', *International Journal of Comparative Sociology*, *46* (8): 297–326.

Janis, I. L. (1982) *Groupthink*. Boston: Houghton Mifflin.

Janssens, M. and Steyaert, C. (1999) 'The world in two and a third way out? The concept of duality in organization theory and practice', *Scandinavian Journal of Management*, *15* (2): 121–139.

Jehn, K. A. (1995) 'A multimethod examination of the benefits and detriments of intragroup conflict', *Administrative Science Quarterly*, *40* (2): 256–282.

Jehn, K. A. (1997) 'A qualitative analysis of conflict types and dimensions in organizational groups', *Administrative Science Quarterly*, *42* (3): 530–557.

Jehn, K. A. and Mannix, E. A. (2001) 'The dynamic nature of conflict: a longitudinal study of intragroup conflict and group performance', *Academy of Management Journal*, *44* (2): 238–251.

Jehn, K. A., Greer, L. L., Levine, S. and Szulanski, G. (2008) 'The effects of conflict types, dimensions, and emergent states on group outcomes', *Group Decision and Negotiation*, *17* (6): 465–495.

Jensen, M. C. and Meckling, W. H. (1976) 'Theory of the firm: managerial behavior, agency costs and ownership structure', *Journal of Financial Economics*, *3* (4): 305–360.

Jericho, G. (2017) 'Tax cuts for the rich don't help the rest: don't take my word for it, ask the IMF', *The Guardian*, 10 September. Available at: www.theguardian.com/business/grogonomics/2017/sep/10/tax-cuts-for-the-rich-dont-help-the-rest-dont-take-my-word-for-it-ask-the-imf (accessed 30 January 2018).

Jermier, J. M. (1996) 'The path-goal theory of leadership: a subtextual analysis', *Leadership Quarterly*, *7*: 311–316.

Jermier, J., Forbes, L. C., Benn, S. and Orsato, R. J. (2006) 'The new corporate environmentalism and green politics', in S. R. Clegg, C. Hardy, T. B. Lawrence and W. R. Nord (eds), *The Sage Handbook of Organization Studies*. London: Sage, pp. 618–650.

Jiang, Y. and Chen, C. C. (2016) 'Integrating knowledge activities for team innovation: effects of transformational leadership', *Journal of Management*, *44* (5): 1819–1847.

Joachimsthaler, E. and Aaker, D. (1997) 'Building brands without mass media', *Harvard Business Review*, January–February: 39–50.

Joffe, M. and MacKenzie-Davey, K. (2012) 'The problem of identity in hybrid managers: who are medical directors?', *International Journal of Leadership in Public Services, 8* (3): 161–174.

Johansson, A. and Vinthagen, S. S. (2016) 'Dimensions of everyday resistance', *Critical Sociology, 42* (3): 417–435.

Johnsen, H. C. G., Ennals, R. and Holtskog, H. (2017) 'Balancing organisational design principles: a pragmatic Scandinavian approach to CSR', in S. O. Idowu and S. Vertigans (eds), *Stages of Corporate Social Responsibility*. Cham: Springer, pp. 163–178.

Jones, C. (2001) 'Co-evolution of entrepreneurial careers, institutional rules and competitive dynamics in American Film, 1895–1920', *Organization Studies, 22* (6): 911–944.

Jones, C. (2003) 'As if business ethics were possible, "within such limits"', *Organization, 10* (2): 267–285.

Jones, C. (2004) 'Jacques Derrida', in S. Linstead (ed.), *Organization Theory and Postmodern Thought*. London: Sage, pp. 34–63.

Jones, D. (Director) (1993) *The Trial* [Motion picture]. United Kingdom: Angelika.

Jones, M. (2003) 'Globalization and the organization(s) of exclusion in advanced capitalism', in R. Westwood and S. R. Clegg (eds), *Debating Organizations: Point-Counterpoint in Organization Studies*. Oxford: Blackwell, pp. 252–270.

Joo-Kee, H. (2006) 'Glass ceiling or sticky floor? Exploring the Australian gender pay gap', *Economic Record, 82* (259): 408–427.

Judge, M. (Director) (1999) *Office Space* [Motion picture]. United States: 20th Century Fox.

Jupp, J. (2002) *From White Australia to Woomera: The Story of Australian Immigration*. Cambridge: Cambridge University Press.

Juris, J. S. (2008) *Networking Futures*. Durham, NC: Duke University Press.

Kahneman, D. (2011) *Thinking, Fast and Slow*. New York: Farrar, Straus and Giroux.

Kahneman, D., Krueger, A. B., Schkade, D., Schwarz, N. and Stone, A. (2006) 'Would you be happier if you were richer? A focusing illusion', *Science, 312* (5782): 1908–1910.

Kallinikos, J. (2006) *The Consequences of Information: Institutional Implications of Technological Change*. Cheltenham: Edward Elgar.

Kameda, T., Tsukasaki, T., Hastie, R. and Berg, N. (2011) 'Democracy under uncertainty: the wisdom of crowds and the free-rider problem in group decision making', *Psychological Review, 118* (1): 76–96.

Kangas, M., Muotka, J., Huhtala, M., Mäkikangas, A. and Feldt, T. (2017) 'Is the ethical culture of the organization associated with sickness absence? A multilevel analysis in a public sector organization', *Journal of Business Ethics, 140* (1): 131–145.

Kanov, J. M., Maitlis, S., Worline, M. C., Dutton, J. E., Frost, P. J. and Lilius, J. M. (2004) 'Compassion in organizational life', *American Behavioral Scientist, 47* (6): 808–827.

Kanter, R. M. (1984) *The Change Masters: Corporate Entrepreneurs at Work*. Sydney: Allen & Unwin.

Kanter, R. M. (1990) *When Giants Learn to Dance*. London: Unwin Hyman.

Kaplan, R. S. and Norton, D. P. (1992) 'The balanced scorecard: measures that drive performance', *Harvard Business Review, 70* (1): 71–79.

Kassenboehmer, S. C. and Sinning, M. G. (2014) 'Distributional changes in the gender wage gap', *Industrial and Labor Relations Review*, *67* (2): 335–361.

Katz, D. and Kahn, R. L. (1978) *The Social Psychology of Organizations*, 2nd edn. New York: Wiley.

Kaufman, P. (Director) (1983) *The Right Stuff* [Motion picture]. United States: Warner Bros.

Kawakami, K., Dion, K. L. and Dovidio, J. F. (1998) 'Racial prejudice and stereotype activation', *Personality and Social Psychology Bulletin*, *24* (4): 407–416.

Kee, H. J. (2006) 'Glass ceiling or sticky floor? Exploring the Australian gender pay gap', *Economic Record*, *82* (259): 408–427.

Keele, L. and Wolak, J. (2006) 'Value conflict and volatility in party identification', *British Journal of Political Science*, 36 (3): 671–690.

Kerr, S. and Jermier, J. M. (1978) 'Substitutes for leadership: their meaning and measurement', *Organizational Behavior and Human Performance*, *22*: 375–403.

Kettl, D. F. (1997) 'The global revolution in public management: driving themes, missing links', *Journal of Policy Analysis and Management*, *16* (3): 446–462.

Kilmann, R. H. and Thomas, K. W. (1977) 'Developing a forced-choice measure of conflict-handling behavior: the "MODE" instrument', *Educational and Psychological Measurement*, *37* (2): 309–325.

Kim, T. W. and Donaldson, T. (2018) 'Rethinking right: moral epistemology in management research', *Journal of Business Ethics*, *148* (1): 5–20.

Kim, Y. and Ployhart, R. E. (2018) 'The strategic value of selection practices: antecedents and consequences of firm-level selection practice usage', *Academy of Management Journal*, *61* (1): 46–66.

Kim, T., Wang, C., Kondo, M. and Kim, T. (2007) 'Conflict management styles: the differences among the Chinese, Japanese, and Koreans', *International Journal of Conflict Management*, *18* (1): 23–41.

Kipping, M. (2002) 'Trapped in their wave: the evolution of management consultancies', in T. Clark and R. Fincham (eds), *Critical Consulting: New Perspectives on the Management Advice Industry*. Oxford: Blackwell, pp. 28–49.

Kirkbride, P. (2006) 'Developing transformational leaders: the full range leadership model in action', *Industrial and Commercial Training*, 38 (1): 23–32.

Kirkpatrick, S. A. and Locke, E. A. (1991) 'Leadership: do traits matter?', *Academy of Management Executive*, 5: 48–60.

Kjonstad, B. and Willmott, H. (1995) 'Business ethics: restrictive or empowering?' *Journal of Business Ethics*, *14*: 445–464.

Klein, L. (2006) 'Joan Woodward Memorial Lecture: applied social science – is it just common sense?', *Human Relations*, 59 (8): 1155–1172.

Klein, N. (2001) *No Space, No Choice, No Jobs, No Logo: Taking Aim at the Brand Bullies*. New York: Picador.

Klemsdal, L., Ravn, J. E., Amble, N. and Finne, H. (2017) 'The organization theories of the industrial democracy experiments meet contemporary organizational realities', *Nordic Journal of Working Life Studies*, *7* (s2): 1–15.

Klikauer, T. (2013) *Managerialism: A Critique of Ideology*. London and New York: Palgrave-Macmillan.

Kluver, J., Frazier, R. and Haidt, J. (2014) 'Behavioral ethics for homo economicus, homo heuristicus, and homo duplex', *Organizational Behavior and Human Decision Processes*, 123 (2): 150–158.

Knafo, A., Roccas, S. and Sajiv, L. (2011) 'The value of values in cross-cultural research: a special issue in honor of Shalom Schwartz', *Journal of Cross-Cultural Psychology, 42* (2): 178–185.

Knapp, M. L., Putnam, L. L. and Davis, L. J. (1988) 'Measuring interpersonal conflict in organizations: where do we go from here?', *Management Communication Quarterly, 1* (3): 414–429.

Knapen, J., Blaker, N. and Van Vugt, M. (2018) 'The Napoleon complex: when shorter men take more', *Psychological Science, 29* (7): 1134–1144.

Knights, D. and Vurdubakis, T. (1994) 'Foucault, power and all that', in J. Jermier, D. Knights, and W. Nord (eds), *Resistance and Power in Organizations*. London: Routledge, pp. 167–198.

Knowles, M. and Knowles, H. (1972) *Introduction to Group Dynamics*. Chicago: Follett.

Kochan, T. A., Eaton, A. E., McKersie, R. B. and Adler, P. (2009) *Healing Together: The Kaiser Permanente Labor Management Partnership*. Ithaca, NY: Cornell University Press.

Kodish, S. (2017) 'Communicating organizational trust: an exploration of the link between discourse and action', *International Journal of Business Communication, 54* (4): 347–368.

Kolb, D. M. and Bartunek, J. M. (eds) (1992) *Hidden Conflict in Organizations: Uncovering Behind-the-scenes Disputes*. Thousand Oaks, CA: Sage.

Kolb, D. M. and Putnam, L. L. (1992) 'The multiple faces of conflict in organizations', *Journal of Organizational Behavior, 13* (3): 311–324.

Kono, T. and Clegg, S. R. (1998) *Transformations of Corporate Culture: Experiences of Japanese Enterprises*. Berlin and New York: de Gruyter.

Kono, T. and Clegg, S. R. (2001) *Trends in Japanese Management*. London: Palgrave.

Kornberger, M. (2010) *The Brand Society*. Cambridge: Cambridge University Press.

Kornberger, M., Carter, C. and Clegg, S. R. (2006) 'Rethinking the polyphonic organization: managing as discursive practice', *Scandinavian Journal of Management, 22*: 3–30.

Kornberger, M., Clegg, S. R. and Rhodes, C. (2005) 'Learning/becoming/organizing', *Organization, 12* (2): 147–167.

Kozlowski, S. W., Chen, G. and Salas, E. (2017) 'One hundred years of the Journal of Applied Psychology: Background, evolution, and scientific trends', *Journal of Applied Psychology, 102* (3): 237–253.

Kreiner, K. and Schultz, M. (1993) 'Informal collaboration in R&D: the formation of networks across organizations', *Organization Studies, 14*: 189–209.

Kriesberg, L. (1992) *De-escalation and Transformation of International Conflicts*. New Haven, CT: Yale University Press.

Krücken, G. and Drori, G. S. (eds) (2009) *World Society: The Writings of John Meyer*. Oxford: Oxford University Press.

Kuhn, T. and Poole, M. S. (2000) 'Do conflict management styles affect group decision making? Evidence from a longitudinal field study', *Human Communication Research, 26* (4): 558–590.

Kumar, K. and Van Dissel, H. G. (1996) 'Sustainable collaboration: managing conflict and cooperation in interorganizational systems', *Mis Quarterly, 20* (3): 279–300.

Kung, I. C. and Wang, H. Z. (2006) 'Socially constructed ethnic division of labour', *International Sociology, 21* (4): 580–601.

Kupiszewski, M. and Kupiszewska, D. (2011) '*MULTIPOLES*: a revised multiregional model for improved capture of international migration', in J. Stillwell and M. Clarke, *Population Dynamics and Projection Methods*, Vol. *4*. London: Springer, pp. 41–60.

Lakoff, G. (2014) *The All New Don't Think of an Elephant! Know Your Values and Frame the Debate*. New York: Chelsea Green Publishing.

Lamb, S., and Sington, D. (2013) *Thin Ice*. New York: PBS

Landsorganisationen I Sveirge (2006) 'The collective agreement'. Available at: www.lo.se/home/lo/home.nsf/unidView/F53218717022F344C1256E4C004F02EF (accessed 23 February 2007).

Landy, F. J. (2005) *Employment Discrimination Litigation: Behavioral, Quantitative, and Legal Perspectives*. San Francisco: Jossey-Bass.

Latané, B. (1981) 'The psychology of social impact', *American Psychologist*, *36*: 343–356.

Latané, B. and Wolf, S. (1981) 'The social impact of majorities and minorities', *Psychological Review*, *88*: 438–453.

Latusek, D. and Vlaar, P. W. (2015) 'Exploring managerial talk through metaphor: an opportunity to bridge rigour and relevance?', *Management Learning*, *46* (2): 211–232.

Laughlin, P. R. (2011) *Group Problem Solving*. Princeton, NJ: Princeton University Press.

Lauring, J. and Klitm ller, A. (2017) 'Inclusive language use in multicultural business organizations: the effect on creativity and performance', *International Journal of Business and Communication*, *54* (3): 306–324.

Lawler, III, E. E. (2005) 'Creating high performance organizations', *Asia Pacific Journal of Human Resources*, *43* (1): 10–17.

Lawler, III, E. E., Worley, C. G., Creelman, D. and Crooke, M. (2011) *Management Reset: Organizing for Sustainable Effectiveness*. San Francisco: John Wiley.

Le Carré, J. (2017) *A Legacy of Spies*. New York: Viking.

Leahy, R. L. (2011) 'Personal schemas in the negotiation process: a cognitive therapy approach', in F. Aquilar and M. Galluccio (eds), *Psychological and Political Strategies for Peace Negotiation: A Cognitive Approach*. New York: Springer, pp. 37–54.

Lecher, W., Platzer, H. W. and Weiner, K. P. (2018) *European Works Councils: Development, Types and Networking*. London: Routledge.

Lee, M. Y. and Edmondson, A. C. (2017) 'Self-managing organizations: exploring the limits of less-hierarchical organizing', *Research in Organizational Behavior*, *37*: 35–58.

Lee, Y. K., Chang, C. T., Lin, Y. and Cheng, Z. H. (2014) 'The dark side of smartphone usage: psychological traits, compulsive behavior and technostress', *Computers in Human Behavior*, *31*: 373–383.

Leon-Perez, J. M., Medina, F. J., Arenas, A. and Munduate, L. (2015) 'The relationship between interpersonal conflict and workplace bullying', *Journal of Managerial Psychology*, 30 (3): 250–263.

Leonard, D. and Sensiper, S. (1998) 'The role of tacit knowledge in group innovation', *California Management Review*, *40*: 3.

Levitt, B. and March, J. (1988) 'Organizational learning', *Annual Review of Sociology*, *14*: 319–340.

Levy, O. and Reiche, B. S. (2018) 'The politics of cultural capital: social hierarchy and organizational architecture in the multinational corporation', *Human Relations*, *71* (6): 867–894.

Lewicki, R., Gray, B. and Elliott, M. (eds) (2003) *Making Sense of Intractable Environmental Conflicts: Concepts and Cases*. Washington, DC: Island Press.

Lewin, K. (1951) *Field Theory in Social Science: Selected Theoretical Papers*. London: Tavistock.

Light, P. (2006) 'The tides of reform revisited: patterns in making government work, 1945–2002', *Public Administration Review*, 66 (1): 6–19.

Likert, R. (1979) 'From production- and employee-centeredness to systems 1–4', *Journal of Management*, 5 (2): 147–156.

Lilius, J. M., Worline, M. C., Maitlis, S., Kanov, J. M., Dutton, J. E. and Frost, P. J. (2008) 'The contours and consequences of compassion at work', *Journal of Organizational Behavior*, 29: 193–218.

Lilja, S. and Luddeckens, E. (2006) 'Women in middle management in Germany, Sweden and the United Kingdom', Masters thesis in Business, Hogskolan I Jonkoping, Internationella Handelshogskolan, Sweden. Available at: http://hj.diva-portal.org/smash/get/diva2:4150/FULLTEXT01 (accessed 22 July 2011).

Lindblom, E. (1959) 'The science of "muddling through"', *Public Administration Review*, 19 (2): 79–88.

Lindeman, M. and Verkasalo, M. (2005) 'Measuring values with the short Schwartz's value survey', *Journal of Personality Assessment*, 85 (3): 170–178.

Linstead, S., Maréchal, G. and Griffin R. W. (2014) 'Theorizing and researching the dark side of organization', *Organization Studies*, 35: 165–188.

Littlejohn, S. (1983) *Theories of Human Communication*, 2nd edn. Belmont, CA: Wadsworth.

Littlejohn, S. (1989) *Theories of Human Communication*, 6th edn. Belmont, CA: Wadsworth.

Littler, C. R. (1982) *The Development of the Labour Process in Capitalist Societies*. London: Heinemann.

Liu, F. and Maitlis, S. (2014) 'Emotional dynamics and strategizing processes: a study of strategic conversations in top team meetings', *Journal of Management Studies*, 51 (2): 202–34.

Loach, K. (2016) *I, Daniel Blake*. London: British Film Institute.

Lomas, T. and Hefferon, K. (2015) *Major Works in Positive Psychology*. London: Sage.

Long, B. S. and Driscoll, C. (2008) 'Codes of ethics and the pursuit of organizational legitimacy: theoretical and empirical contributions', *Journal of Business Ethics*, 77 (2): 173–189.

Lönnqvist, J.-E., Leikas, S., Paunonen, S. V., Nissinen, V. and Verkasalo, M. (2006) 'Conformism moderates the relations between values, anticipated regret, and behavior', *Personality and Social Psychology Bulletin*, 32 (11): 1469–1481.

Lord, R. G., Day, D. V., Zaccaro, S. J., Avolio, B. J. and Eagly, A. H. (2017) 'Leadership in applied psychology: three waves of theory and research', *Journal of Applied Psychology*, 102 (3): 434–451.

Löw, M. (2009) 'Review of *The Sociology of Spatial Inequality*, edited by Linda M. Lobao, Gregory Hooks, and Ann R. Tickamyer', *American Journal of Sociology*, 115 (1): 314–316.

Lukes, S. (1974) *Power: A Radical View*. London: Macmillan.

Lukes, S. (2005) *Power: A Radical View*, 2nd edn. London: Palgrave Macmillan.

Luthans, F. (2002) 'Positive organisational behaviour: developing and managing psychological strengths', *Academy of Management Executive*, 16 (1): 1–11.

Luthans, F. and Avolio, B. (2003) 'Authentic leadership development', in K. S. Cameron, J. E. Dutton and R. E. Quinn (eds), *Positive Organizational Scholarship: Foundations of a New Discipline*. San Francisco: Berrett-Koehler, pp. 241–258.

Luthans, F. and Youssef, C. M. (2004) 'Human, social and now positive psychological capital management: investing in people for competitive advantage', *Organizational Dynamics*, 33 (2): 143–160.

Luthans, F., Avolio, B. J., Avey, J. B. and Norman, S. M. (2007) 'Positive psychological capital: measurement and relationship with performance and satisfaction', *Personnel Psychology*, 60: 541–572.

Lvina, E., Johns, G. and Vandenberghe, C. (2018) 'Team political skill composition as a determinant of team cohesiveness and performance', *Journal of Management*, *44*: 1001–1028.

Lyon, D. (1994) *The Electronic Eye: The Rise of Surveillance Society*. Cambridge: Polity.

Lyons, S., Duxbury, L. and Higgens, C. (2005) 'Are gender differences in basic human values a generational phenomenon?' *Sex Roles*, 53 (9/10): 763–778.

Mack, R. W. and Snyder, R. C. (1957) 'The analysis of social conflict – toward an overview and synthesis', *Conflict Resolution*, *1* (2): 212–248.

Maclean, M., Harvey, C. and Chia, R. (2012) 'Sensemaking, storytelling and the legitimization of elite business careers', *Human Relations*, 65 (1): 17–40.

Maclean, M., Harvey, C., Sillince, J. A. and Golant, B. D. (2014) 'Living up to the past? Ideological sensemaking in organizational transition', *Organization*, *21* (4): 543–567.

Madden, J. (2016) *Miss Sloane*. Paris: Europa Films.

Madsen, M. (2010) *Into Eternity*. Denmark: Films Transit International.

Magalhães, R. (2018) 'Human-centred organization design', *The Design Journal*, *21* (2): 227–246.

Maignan, I. and Ferrell, O. C. (2004) 'Corporate social responsibility and marketing: an integrative framework', *Journal of the Academy of Marketing Science*, 32 (1): 3–19.

Maitlis, S. (2005) 'The social processes of organizational sensemaking', *Academy of Management Journal*, *48* (1): 21–49.

Maitlis, S. and Christianson, M. K. (2014) 'Sensemaking in organizations: taking stock and moving forward', *Academy of Management Annals*, *8* (1): 57–125.

Maitlis, S. and Lawrence, T. B. (2007) 'Triggers and enablers of sensegiving in organizations', *Academy of Management Journal*, 50 (1): 57–84.

Maitlis, S., Vogus, T. J. and Lawrence, T. B. (2013) 'Sensemaking and emotions in organizations', *Organizational Psychology Review*, 3 (3): 222–247.

Mallaby, S. (2010) *More Money than God: Hedge Funds and the Making of a New Elite*. London: Bloomsbury.

Malogiannisa, I. A., Arntzc, A., Spyropouloua, A., Tsartsaraa, E., Aggelib, A., Karvelib, S., et al. (2014) 'Schema therapy for patients with chronic depression: a single case series study', *Journal of Behavior Therapy and Experimental Psychiatry*, *45* (3): 319–329.

Mandel, M. (1989) *Making Good Time: Scientific Management; The Gilbreths; Photography and Motion; Futurism*. Riverside: California Museum of Photography.

Manwani, H. (2013) 'Profit's not always the point'. Available at: www.ted.com/talks/harish_manwani_profit_s_not_always_the_point?language=en (accessed 24 September 2015).

Manyika, J., Chui, M., Bughin, J., Dobbs, R., Bisson, P. and Marrs. A. (2013) *Disruptive technologies: advances that will transform life, business, and the global economy*. Technical report, McKinsey Global Institute. Available at: www.mckinsey.com/business-functions/digital-mckinsey/our-insights/disruptive-technologies(accessed 26 June 2018).

Manyika, J., Chui, M., Miremadi, M., Bughin, J., George, K., Wilmott, P. and Dewhurst, M. (2017) *Harnessing Automation for a Future that Works*. Sydney: McKinsey & Co.

March, J. G. (1988) 'The technology of foolishness', in J. G. March (ed.), *Decisions and Organizations*. Oxford: Blackwell, pp. 253–265.

March, J. G. (1991) 'Exploration and exploitation in organizational learning', *Organization Science*, 2 (1): 71–87.

March, J. G. (2002 [1995]) 'The future, disposable organizations and the rigidities of imagination', in S. R. Clegg (ed.), *Central Currents in Organization Studies II: Contemporary Trends*, Vol. 8. London: Sage, pp. 266–277 [originally published in *Organization* (1995) 2: 427–434].

March, J. G. and Simon, H. A. (1958) *Organizations*. New York: Wiley.

Margolis, J. (2017) 'Be careful with social media – employers are watching', *Financial Times*, www.ft.com/content/5b8bb3b0-6aca-11e7-b9c7-15af748b60d0 (accessed 8 October 2018).

Markoff, J. (1996) *Waves of Democracy: Social Movements and Political Change*. Thousand Oaks, CA: Pine Forge.

Marks, J. (2000) 'Foucault, Franks, Gauls: Il faut défendre la société – the 1976 lectures at the Collège de France', *Theory, Culture and Society*, 17 (5): 127–147.

Markus, H. R. (1977) 'Self-schemata and processing information about the self', *Journal of Personality and Social Psychology*, 35: 63–78.

Marrewijk, A. (2016) 'Conflicting subcultures in mergers and acquisitions: a longitudinal study of integrating a radical Internet firm into a bureaucratic telecoms firm', *British Journal of Management*, 27 (2): 338–354.

Marriage, M. (2018) 'Undercover reporter hostesses groped at men only event', BBC News. Available at: www.bbc.com/news/av/uk-42799595 (accessed 18 February 2018).

Martin, J. (1992) *Culture in Organizations: Three Perspectives*. New York: Oxford University Press.

Martin, J. (2000) 'Hidden gendered assumptions in mainstream organizational theory and research', *Journal of Management Inquiry*, 9 (2): 207–216.

Martin, J. (2002) *Organizational Culture: Mapping the Terrain*. Thousand Oaks, CA: Sage.

Martin, J. and Frost, P. (1996) 'The organizational culture war games: a struggle for intellectual dominance', in S. R. Clegg, C. Hardy and W. Nord (eds), *Handbook of Organization Studies*. London: Sage, pp. 599–621.

Martynova, M. and Renneboog, L. (2008) 'A century of corporate takeovers: what have we learned and where do we stand?' (previous title: 'The history of M&A activity around the world: a survey of literature'), *Journal of Banking and Finance*, ECGI – Finance Working Paper No. 97/2005. Available at SSRN: http://ssrn.com/abstract=820984 (accessed 14 May 2015).

Marx, K. (1844) 'Economic and philosophic manuscripts of 1844.' Available at: www.marxists.org/archive/marx/works/download/pdf/Economic-Philosophic-Manuscripts-1844.pdf (accessed 24 April 2018).

Marx, K. (1976 [1867]) *Capital*, Vol. 1. Harmondsworth: Penguin.

Marx, K. and Engels, F. (1998 [1848]) *The Communist Manifesto*, introduction by M. Malia. New York: Penguin; original work published 1848.

Maslow, A. (1965) *Eupsychian Management: A Journal*. Homewood, IL: Irwin.

Maslow, A. (1968) *Toward a Psychology of Being*. Princeton, NJ: Van Nostrand.

Maslow, A. (1970) *Motivation and Personality*. New York: Harper & Row.

Massola, J. (2018) 'Big surge in opposition to Adani, new polling reveals', *Sydney Morning Herald*, 1 February. Available at: www.smh.com.au/federal-politics/political-news/big-surge-in-opposition-to-adani-new-polling-reveals-20180131-p4yz4o.html (accessed 1 February 2018).

Matejek, S. and Gössling, T. (2014) 'Beyond legitimacy: a case study in BP's "green lashing"', *Journal of Business Ethics*, 120 (4): 571–584.

Maurice, M. and Sorge, A. (2002) *Embedding Organizations*. Amsterdam: Benjamins.

Mayer, J. D. (1999) 'Emotional intelligence: popular or scientific psychology?', *APA Monitor*, 30 (8). Washington, DC: APA.

Mayer, J. D., Salovey, P., Caruso, D. R. and Sitarenios, G. (2001) 'Emotional intelligence as a standard intelligence', *Emotion*, 1: 232–242.

Mayer, J. D., Salovey, P., Caruso, D. R. and Sitarenios, G. (2003) 'Measuring emotional intelligence with the MSCEIT V2.0', *Emotion*, 3 (1): 97–105.

Mayer, R. C., Davis, J. H. and Schoorman, F. D. (1995) 'An integrative model of organizational trust', *Academy of Management Review*, 20 (3): 709–734.

Mayes, B. T. and Allen, R. W. (1977) 'Towards a definition of organizational politics', *Academy of Management Review*, 2: 674–678.

Mayo, E. (1922) 'Industrial unrest and "nervous breakdowns"', *Industrial Australian and Mining Standard*, 63–64.

Mayo, E. (1946) *The Human Problems of an Industrial Civilization*. Cambridge, MA: Harvard University Press.

Mayo, E. (1985 [1951]) *The Psychology of Pierre Janet*. Westport, CT: Greenwood; original work published 1951.

Mayo, G. E. (2007) *The Social Problems of an Industrial Civilization*. London: Routledge.

McCrae, R. R. and Costa, P. T., Jr (1996) 'Toward a new generation of personality theories: theoretical contexts for the five-factor model', in J. S. Wiggins (ed.), *The Five-Factor Model of Personality: Theoretical Perspectives*. New York: Guilford, pp. 51–87.

McCrae, R. R. and Costa, P. T., Jr (1999) 'A five-factor theory of personality', *Handbook of Personality: Theory and Research*, 2: 139–153.

McGregor, D. (1960) *The Human Side of Enterprise*. New York: McGraw-Hill.

McKinsey Quarterly (2017) 'Safe enough to try: an interview with Zappos CEO Tony Hsieh', *McKinsey Quarterly*. Available at: www.mckinsey.com/business-functions/organization/our-insights/safe-enough-to-try-an-interview-with-zappos-ceo-tony-hsieh?cid=other-eml-alt-mkq-mck-oth-1710 (accessed 6 February 2018).

McLuhan, M. (1964) *Understanding Media: The Extensions of Man*. New York: McGraw-Hill.

McSweeney, B. (2002) 'Hofstede's model of national cultural differences and their consequences: a triumph of faith – a failure of analysis', *Human Relations*, 55 (1): 89–118.

McSweeney, B. (2015) 'Globe, Hofstede, Huntington, Trompenaars: common foundations, common flaws', in Y. Sánchez and C. F. Brühwiler (eds), *Transculturalism and Business in the BRIC States: A Handbook*. London: Ashgate, pp. 13–58.

Mendoza, J. L., Bard, D. E., Mumford, M. D. and Ang, S. C. (2004) 'Criterion-related validity in multiple-hurdle designs: estimation and bias', *Organizational Research Methods*, 7 (4): 418–441.

Menefee, M. L., Parnell, J. A., Powers, E. and Ziemnowicz, C. (2006) 'The role of human resources in the success of new businesses', *Southern Business Review*, 32 (1): 23–33.

Merleau-Ponty, M. (1994) *Phenomenology of Perception* (C. Smith, trans.). Evanston, IL: North Western University Press.

Merton, R. K. (1940) 'Bureaucratic structure and personality', *Social Forces, 18*: 560–568.

Merton, R. K. (1957) *Social Theory and Social Structure* (revised and expanded edn). Glencoe, NY: Free Press.

Mesch, D. J., Rooney, P. M., Steinberg, K. S. and Denton, B. (2006) 'The effects of race, gender, and marital status on giving and volunteering in Indiana', *Non-profit and Voluntary Sector Quarterly, 35* (4): 565–587.

Meusburger, P. (2006) 'Introduction: the nexus of knowledge and space, abstracts of symposia on clashes of knowledge, Ruprecht-Karls-Universität Heidelberg'. Available at: www.rzuser.uni-heidelberg.de/~bo3/symposia/1/1_abstracts.htm (accessed 9 January 2017).

Meyer, J. W. (2000) 'Globalization: sources and effects on national states and societies', *International Sociology, 15* (2): 233–248.

Meyer, J. W. and Rowan, B. (1977) 'Institutionalized organizations: formal structure as myth and ceremony', *American Journal of Sociology, 83* (2): 340–363.

Mezzadri, A. (2014) 'Cambodian sweatshop protests reveal the blood on our clothes', http://theconversation.com/cambodian-sweatshop-protests-reveal-the-blood-on-our-clothes-21811 (accessed 8 October 2018).

Meyer, J. W. and Bromley, P. (2013) 'The worldwide expansion of "organization"', *Sociological Theory, 31* (4): 366–389.

Michels, R. (1915) *Political Parties: A Sociological Study of the Oligarchical Tendencies of Modern Democracy* (translated into English by Eden Paul and Cedar Paul). New York: Free Press.

Michlewski, K. (2008) 'Uncovering design attitude: inside the culture of designers', *Organization Studies, 29* (3): 373–392.

Mihelič, K. K. and Culiberg, B. (2018) 'Reaping the fruits of another's labor: the role of moral meaningfulness, mindfulness, and motivation in social loafing', *Journal of Business Ethics*, 1–15, DOI: 10.1007/s10551-018-3933-z.

Mikkelsen, E. N. (2013) 'An analysis of the social meanings of conflict in nonprofit organizations', *Nonprofit and Voluntary Sector Quarterly, 42* (5): 923–941.

Mikkelsen, E. N. and Clegg, S. R. 'Conceptions of conflict in organizational conflict research: toward critical reflexivity', *Journal of Management Inquiry*, http://journals.sagepub.com/doi/abs/10.1177/1056492617716774.

Milgram, S. (1971) *The Individual in a Social World*. Reading, MA: Addison-Wesley.

Milgram, S. (1974) *Obedience to Authority*. New York: HarperCollins.

Miller, P. and Rose, N. (1988) 'The Tavistock programme: the government of subjectivity and social life', *Sociology, 22* (2): 171–192.

Miller, S. J. and Wilson, D. C. (2006) 'Perspectives on organizational decision-making', in S. R. Clegg, C. Hardy, T. B. Lawrence and W. R. Nord (eds), *The Sage Handbook of Organization Studies*. London: Sage, pp. 469–484.

Mindlin, S. E. and Aldrich, H. (2002 [1975]) 'Interorganizational dependence: a review of the concept and reexamination of the findings of the Aston Group', in S. R. Clegg (ed.), *Central Currents in Organization Studies I: Frameworks and Applications*, Vol. 2. London: Sage, pp. 367–378 [originally published in *Administrative Science Quarterly* (1975) 20: 382–392].

Minkler, L. (1999) 'The problem with utility: toward a non-consequentialist/utility theory synthesis', *Review of Social Economy*, 57 (1): 4–24.

Minkov, M. (2018)'A revision of Hofstede's model of national culture: old evidence and new data from 56 countries', *Cross Cultural & Strategic Management*, 25 (2): 231–256.

Mintzberg, H. (1973) *The Nature of Managerial Work*. New York: Harper & Row.

Mintzberg, H. (1983) *Power in and around Organizations*. Englewood Cliffs, NJ: Prentice-Hall.

Mintzberg, H. (1984) 'Power and organizational life cycles', *Academy of Management Review*, 9 (2): 207–224.

Mintzberg, H. (1985) 'The organization as political arena', *Journal of Management Studies*, 22: 133–154.

Mintzberg, H. (2004) *Managers Not MBAs: A Hard Look at the Soft Practice of Managing and Management Development*. San Francisco: Berrett-Koehler.

Mishel, L. (2013) 'Working as designed: high profits and stagnant wages', *Working Economics* (Economic Policy Institute blog), 28 March. Available at: www.epi.org/blog/working-designed-high-profits-stagnant-wages (accessed 6 April 2018).

Mishel, L. and Schneider, J. (2017) 'CEO pay remains high relative to the pay of typical workers and high-wage earners', *Economic Policy Institute*, 20 July. Available at: www.epi.org/publication/ceo-pay-remains-high-relative-to-the-pay-of-typical-workers-and-high-wage-earners (accessed 6 April 2018).

Mishel, L., Bivens, J., Gould, E. and Shierholz, H. (2012) *The State of Working America* (12th edn), an Economic Policy Institute book. Ithaca, NY: Cornell University Press.

Mitchell, C. (2002) 'Selling the brand inside', *Harvard Business Review*, January: 99–105.

Moberg, D. J. (2006) 'Ethics blind spots in organizations: how systematic errors in person perception undermine moral agency', *Organization Studies*, 27 (3): 413–428.

Moghadam, V. M. (1999) 'Gender and globalization: female labour and women's mobilization', *Journal of World-Systems Research*, 5 (2): 367–388.

Molnar, J. J. and Rogers, D. L. (1979) 'A comparative model of interorganizational conflict', *Administrative Science Quarterly*, 24 (3): 405–425.

Monte, C. F. (1991) *Beneath the Mask: An Introduction to Theories of Personality*. New York: Praeger.

Morgan, G. (1986) *Images of Organizations*. London: Sage.

Morgan, G. (1989) *Creative Organization Theory: A Resource Book*. London: Sage.

Morgan, G. (2008) 'Transnationals', in S. R. Clegg and J. R. Bailey (eds), *The Sage International Encyclopedia of Organization Studies*. Thousand Oaks, CA: Sage, pp. 1565–1567.

Morgan, P. (2016) *The Crown*. London: Netflix.

Morisette, A. (2005) Global Warming: The Signs and the Science. Available at: www.youtube.com/watch?v=xVQnPytgwQ0 (accessed 14 July 2015).

Morrill, C. (1989) 'The management of managers: disputing in an executive hierarchy', *Sociological Forum*, 4 (3): 387–407.

Morrill, C. (1995) *The Executive Way: Conflict Management in Corporations*. Chicago: University of Chicago Press.

Mosey, S. (2014) 'We all make mistakes but airlines are best at learning from them'. Available at: http://theconversation.com/we-all-make-mistakes-but-airlines-are-best-at-learning-from-them-28165 (accessed 8 October 2015).

Mostow, J. (Director) (2003) *Terminator 3: Rise of the Machines* [Motion picture]. United States: Warner Bros.

Mowday, R. T. (1991) 'Equity theory predictions of behavior in organizations', in R. M. Steers and L. W. Porter (eds), *Motivation and Work Behavior*. New York: McGraw-Hill, pp. 111–131.

Muldoon, J. (2017) 'The Hawthorne studies: an analysis of critical perspectives, 1936–1958', *Journal of Management History*, 23 (1): 74–94.

Müller, R., Pemsel, S. and Shao, J. (2014) 'Organizational enablers for governance and governmentality of projects: a literature review', *International Journal of Project Management*, 32 (8): 1309–1320.

Mumby, D. (1987) 'The political function of the narrative in organizations', *Communication Monograph*, 54: 113–127.

Mumby, D. K. (2005) 'Theorizing resistance in organization studies: a dialectical approach', *Management Communication Quarterly*, 19 (1): 1–26.

Mumby, D. K. and Stohl, C. (1991) 'Power and discourse in organizational studies: absence and the dialectic of control', *Discourse and Society*, 2: 313–332.

Munir, K. (2014a) 'One year on from Rana Plaza collapse, work still to be done', http://theconversation.com/one-year-on-from-rana-plaza-collapse-work-still-to-be-done-24710 (accessed 8 October 2018).

Munir, K. (2014b) 'Tragedy is inevitable when Bangladesh competes on its own citizens' poverty', http://theconversation.com/tragedy-is-inevitable-when-bangladesh-competes-on-its-own-citizens-poverty-25955 (accessed 8 October 2018).

Munir, K. (2014c) 'Want to avoid another Rana Plaza? Pay more for your clothes',www.jbs.cam.ac.uk/media/2014/pay-more-for-your-clothes-to-avoid-another-rana-plaza (accessed 8 October 2018).

Munro, I. (1992) 'Codes of ethics: some uses and abuses', in P. Davies (ed.), *Current Issues in Business Ethics*. London: Routledge, pp. 97–106.

Munro, I. (2008) 'Network society and organizations', in S. R. Clegg and J. Bailey (eds), *The Sage International Encyclopedia of Organization Studies*. Thousand Oaks, CA: Sage, pp. 971–975.

Murnighan, J. K. and Conlon, D. E. (1991) 'The dynamics of intense work groups: a study of British string quartets', *Administrative Science Quarterly*, 36: 165–186.

Murray, R., Caulier-Grice, J. and Mulgan, G. (2010) *The Open Book of Social Innovation*. London: Young Foundation. Available at: www.youngfoundation.org/publications/reports/the-open-book-social-innovation-march-2010 (accessed 21 September 2011).

Myers, D. G. (2001) *Psychology*, 6th edn. New York: Worth.

Myers, D. G. (2002) *The Pursuit of Happiness: Discovering the Pathway to Fulfillment, Well-being, and Enduring Personal Joy*. New York: HarperCollins.

Nathan, B. R. and Alexander, R. A. (1985) 'The role of inferential accuracy in performance rating', *The Academy of Management Review*, 10 (1): 109–115.

Nelson R. R. and Winter, S. (1982) *An Evolutionary Theory of Economic Change*. Cambridge, MA: Harvard University Press:

Newell, M. (1997) (Director) *Donnie Brasco* [Motion picture]. United States: Mandalay Films.

Newell, S. and Tansley, C. (2015) 'International uses of selection methods', in I. T. Robertson and C. L. Cooper (eds), *Personnel Psychology and Human Resources Management*. Chichester: Wiley.

Ng, T. W. H. and Feldman, D. C. (2011) 'Locus of control and organizational embeddedness', *Journal of Occupational and Organizational Psychology*, *84* (1): 173–190.

Nicholson, A. (2014) 'Asylum seekers: my country, my shame', *The Age*, 4 July. Available at: www.theage.com.au/comment/asylum-seekers-my-country-my-shame-20140704-zswgi.html (accessed 11 April 2018).

Nicholson, N. (2000) *Executive Instinct: Managing the Human Animal in the Information Age*. New York: Crown Business Books.

Nicol, B. (2009) *The Cambridge Introduction to Postmodern Fiction*. Cambridge: Cambridge University Press.

Nigro, L. G. and Kellough, J. E. (2008) 'Personnel reform in the states: a look at progress fifteen years after the winter commission', *Public Administration Review*, December: 550–557.

Nijhof, A., Cludts, S., Fisscher, O. and Laan, A. (2003) 'Measuring the implementation of codes of conduct: an assessment method based on a process approach of the responsible organisation', *Journal of Business Ethics*, *45*: 65–78.

Nohria, N. and Ghoshal, S. (1997) *The Differentiated Network: Organizing Multinational Corporations for Value Creation*. San Francisco: Jossey-Bass.

Nonaka, I. (1991) 'The knowledge-creating company', *Harvard Business Review*, *71* (4): 65–77.

Nonaka, I. and Takeuchi, H. (1995) *The Knowledge-creating Company: How Japanese Companies Create the Dynamics of Innovation*. Oxford: Oxford University Press.

Nowecki, M. and Summers, J. (2007) 'Changing leadership styles', *Healthcare Financial Management*, *61* (2): 118–120.

Nutt, P. C. (1984) 'Types of organizational decision processes', *Administrative Science Quarterly*, *29* (3): 414–450.

Nystrom, P. C. (1978) 'Managers and the high-high leader behavior myth', *Academy of Management Journal*, *19*: 325–331.

O'Connor, E. S. (1999) 'The politics of management thought: a case study of Harvard Business School and the Human Relations School', *Academy of Management Review*, *24* (1): 117–131.

O'Connor, E. S. (2002 [1999]) 'Minding the workers: the meaning of "human" and "human relations" in Elton Mayo', in S. R. Clegg (ed.), *Central Currents in Organization Studies I: Frameworks and Applications*, Vol. 1. London: Sage, pp. 333-356 [originally published in *Organization* (1999) 6: 223–246].

O'Doherty, J., Winston, J., Critchley, H., Perrett, D., Burt, D. M., Dolan, R. J. and Adolphs, R. (2003) 'Beauty in a smile: the role of medial orbitofrontal cortex in facial attractiveness', *Neuropsychologia*, *41* (2): 147–155.

O'Neill, T. A., Allen, N. J. and Hastings, S. E. (2013) 'Examining the "pros" and "cons" of team conflict: a team-level meta-analysis of task, relationship, and process conflict', *Human Performance*, *26* (3): 236–60.

O'Neill, T. A., McLarnon, M. J. W., Hoffart, G. C., Woodley, H. J. R. and Allen, N. J. (2018) 'The structure and function of team conflict state profiles', *Journal of Management*, *44*: 811–836.

O'Reilly, C. A. III and Tushman, M. L. (2004) 'The ambidextrous organization', *Harvard Business Review*, *82* (4): 74–81.

O'Reilly, C. and Tushman, M. (2008) 'Ambidexterity as a dynamic capability: resolving the innovator's dilemma', *Research in Organizational Behavior, 28*: 185–206.

O'Toole, J. (1996) *Leading Change: The Argument for Values-based Leadership*. New York: Ballantine Books.

Oberg, W. (1963) 'Education for business: a balanced appraisal', *American Management Association Bulletin*, No. 34.

Olekalns, M., Putnam, L. L., Weingart, L. R. and Metcalf, L. (2008) 'Communication processes and conflict management', in C. W. De Dreu and M. J. Gelfand (eds), *The Psychology of Conflict and Conflict Management in Organizations*. New York: Taylor Francis/Lawrence Erlbaum, pp. 81–114.

Olins, W. (2000) 'How brands are taking over the corporation', in M. Schultz, M. Hatch and M. Larsen (eds), *The Expressive Organization: Linking Identity, Reputation, and the Corporate Brand*. Oxford and New York: Oxford University Press, pp. 51–65.

Oliver, C. (1990) 'Determinants of interorganizational relationships', *Academy of Management Review, 15* (2): 241–265.

Olson, B. J., Parayitam, S. and Bao, Y. (2007) 'Strategic decision-making: the effects of cognitive diversity, conflict, and trust on decision outcomes', *Journal of Management, 33* (2): 196–222.

Olson, J. B. and Hulin, C. (1992) 'Information processing antecedents of rating errors in performance appraisal', *Journal of Vocational Behavior, 40* (1): 49–61.

Orlikowski, W. J. and Yates, J. (1994) 'Genre repertoire: examining the structuring of communicative practices in organizations', *Administrative Science Quarterly, 39*: 541–574.

Orsburn, J. D., Moran, L., Musselwhite, E. and Zenger, J. H. (1990) *Self-Directed Work Teams: The New American Challenge*. Homewood, IL: Irwin.

Orton, J. D. and Weick, K. E. (1990) 'Loosely coupled systems: a reconceptualization', *Academy of Management Review, 15* (2): 203–223.

Osborne, D. and Gaebler, T. (1992) *Re-inventing Government*. Reading, MA: Addison-Wesley.

Osborne, D. and Plastrik, P. (1997) *Banishing Bureaucracy: The Five Strategies for Reinventing Government*. Reading, MA: Addison Wesley.

Osbourne, S. (2018) 'Iceland make it illegal to pay men more than women', *The Independent*, 3 January. Available at: www.independent.co.uk/news/business/news/iceland-gender-pay-gap-illegal-men-pay-more-women-income-salary-earn-a8139141.html (accessed 7 October 2018).

Ostry, J. D., Loungani, P. and Furceri, D. (2016) 'Neoliberalism: oversold?', *Finance and Development*, 53 (2): 38–41.

Oxfam Canada (2016) *An Economy for the 1%*. Available at: www.oxfam.ca/our-work/publications/an-economy-for-the-1 (accessed 30 January 2018).

Paine, L. S. (1994) 'Managing for organizational integrity', *Harvard Business Review, 72* (2): 106–117.

Paine, L. S. (2003) *Value Shift: Why Companies Must Merge Social and Financial Imperatives to Achieve Superior Performance*. New York: McGraw-Hill.

Panayiotou, A., Putnam, L. L. and Kassinis, G. (2017) 'Generating tensions: a multilevel, process analysis of organizational change', *Strategic Organization*, DOI: 10.1177/147612701773446.

Panteli, N. and Sockalingam, S. (2005) 'Trust and conflict within virtual inter-organizational alliances: a framework for facilitating knowledge sharing', *Decision Support Systems, 39* (4): 599–617.

Parfit, D. (2011) *On What Matters*. New York: Oxford University Press.

Parker, B. (2003) 'The disorganization of inclusion: globalization as process', in R. Westwood and S. R. Clegg (eds), *Debating Organizations: Point-Counterpoint in Organization Studies*. Oxford: Blackwell, pp. 234–251.

Parker, B. and Clegg, S. R. (2006) 'Globalization', in S. R. Clegg, C. Hardy, T. B. Lawrence and W. R. Nord (eds), *The Sage Handbook of Organization Studies*. London: Sage, pp. 651–674.

Parker, C. (2013) 'ACCC's inquiry into supermarket bullying misses the real issue of duopoly power', *The Conversation*, 19 February. Available at: https://theconversation.com/acccs-inquiry-into-supermarket-bullying-misses-the-real-issue-of-duopoly-power-12247 (accessed 22 September 2015).

Parker, G. and Van Alstyne, M. (2017) 'Innovation, openness, and platform control', *Management Science*, *64* (7): 2973–3468.

Parker, M. and Jary, D. (1995) 'The McUniversity: organization, management and academic subjectivity', *Organization*, *2* (2): 319–338.

Parkinson, B., Totterdell, P., Briner, R. B. and Reynolds, S. (1996) *Changing Moods: The Psychology of Mood and Mood Regulation*. London and New York: Longman.

Parkinson, C. N. (1957) *Parkinson's Law*. Boston, MA: Houghton Mifflin.

Parry, E. and Urwin, P. (2011) 'Generational differences in work values: a review of theory and evidence', *International Journal of Management Reviews*, *13* (1): 79–96.

Parry, K., Cohen, M. and Bhattachaya, S. (2016) 'Rise of the machines: a critical consideration of automated leadership decision making in organizations', *Group and Organization Management*, *41* (5): 571–594.

Pascale, R. (1999) 'Surfing the edge of chaos', *Sloan Management Review*, *40* (3): 83–94.

Pascale, R. and Athos, A. (1981) *The Art of Japanese Management*. New York: Warner.

Patala, S., Korpivaara, I., Jalkala, A., Kuitunen, A. and Soppe, B. (2017) 'Legitimacy under institutional change: how incumbents appropriate clean rhetoric for dirty technologies', *Organization Studies*, https://doi.org/10.1177%2F0170840617736938.

Patty, A. (2017) 'Australian workers getting a record low share of GDP: report', *Sydney Morning Herald*, 12 June. Available at: www.smh.com.au/business/workplace-relations/share-of-australias-gdp-for-workers-hits-record-low-new-report-20170612-gwp9k5.html (accessed 26 June 2018).

Pautz, M. C. and Washington, P. (2009) 'Sarbanes-Oxley and the relentless pursuit of government accountability: the perils of 21st century reform', *Administration and Society*, *41* (6): 651–673.

Pedersen, J. S. and Dobbin, F. (2006) 'In search of identity and legitimation: bridging organizational culture and neoinstitutionalism', *American Behavioral Scientist*, *49* (7): 897–907.

Pei, M. (2016) *China's Crony Capitalism: The Dynamics of Regime Decay*. Cambridge, MA: Harvard University Press.

Peirce, C. S. (1940) *The Philosophy of Peirce: Selected Writings*. New York: Dover.

Penrose, E. (1959) *The Theory of the Growth of the Firm*. Oxford: Basil Blackwell.

Perrow, C. (1986) *Complex Organizations: A Critical Essay*, 3rd edn. New York: Random House.

Perrow, C. (2011) *Normal Accidents: Living with High Risk Technologies*. Princeton, NJ: Princeton University Press.

Perrow, C. (2013) 'Nuclear denial: from Hiroshima to Fukushima', *Bulletin of Atomic Scientists*, 69 (5): 56–67.

Persaud, A. (2017) 'Post-Brexit UK economy demands a new type of Robin Hood tax', *The Guardian*, 18 February. Available at: www.theguardian.com/business/economics-blog/2017/feb/18/post-brexit-uk-economy-demands-a-new-type-of-robin-hood-tax (accessed 7 August 2017).

Peters, M. A. (2017) 'Technological unemployment: educating for the fourth industrial revolution', *Educational Philosophy and Theory*, *49* (1): 1–6.

Peters, T. (1988) *Thriving on Chaos: Handbook for a Management Revolution*. New York: Knopf.

Peters, T. J. and Waterman Jr., R. H. (1982) In Search of Excellence: Lessons from America's Best-Run Companies. New York: Harper & Row.

Peterson, S. J., Luthans, F., Avolio, B. J., Walumbwa, F. O. and Zhang, Z. (2011) 'Psychological capital and employee performance: a latent growth modeling approach', *Personnel Psychology*, *64* (2): 427–450.

Petrella, R. (1996) 'Globalization and internationalization: the dynamics of the emerging world order', in R. Boyer and D. Drache (eds), *States Against Markets: The Limits of Globalization*. London: Routledge, pp. 62–83.

Petriglieri, G., Ashford, S. J. and Wrzesniewski, A. (2018) 'Agony and ecstasy in the gig economy: cultivating holding environments for precarious and personalized work identities', *Administrative Science Quarterly*, http://journals.sagepub.com/doi/10.1177/0001839218759646.

Pettigrew, A. (1973) *The Politics of Organizational Decision-making*. London: Tavistock.

Pettigrew, A. (1985) *Awakening Giant: Continuity and Change in ICI*. Oxford: Blackwell.

Pettigrew, A. (2002 [1977]) 'Strategy formulation as a political process', in S. R. Clegg (ed.), *Central Currents in Organization Studies II: Contemporary Trends*, Vol. 5. London: Sage, pp. 43–49 [originally published in *International Studies of Management and Organization* (1977) *1*: 78–87].

Pettigrew, A. (2003) *Innovative Forms of Organizing*. London: Sage.

Pettigrew, A., Ferlie, E. and McKee, L. (1992) *Shaping Strategic Change: Making Change in Large Organizations: The Case of the National Health Service*. London: Sage.

Pettigrew, A., Massini, S. and Numagami, T. (2002 [2000]) 'Innovative forms of organizing in Europe and Japan', in S. R. Clegg (ed.), *Central Currents in Organization Studies II: Contemporary Trends*, Vol. 8. London: Sage, pp. 323–347 [originally published in *European Management Journal* (2000) *18*: 259–273].

Pettigrew, A., Woodman, R. and Cameron, K. (2001) 'Studying organizational change and development: challenges for future research', *Academy of Management Journal*, *44* (4): 697–713.

Pfeffer, J. (1992) *Managing With Power: Politics and Influence in Organizations*. Cambridge, MA: Harvard Business School Press.

Pfeffer, J. (1998) 'Six dangerous myths about pay', *Harvard Business Review*, May–June: 108–119.

Pfeffer, J. and Fong, C. T. (2002) 'The end of the business school', *Academy of Management Learning and Education*, *1* (1): 78–95.

Pfeffer, J. and Salancik, G. (1978) *The External Control of Organizations: A Resource Dependence Perspective*. New York: Harper & Row.

Pfeffer, J. and Salancik, G. (2002 [1974]) 'The bases and uses of power in organizational decision making: the case of a university', in S. R. Clegg (ed.), *Central Currents in Organization Studies II: Contemporary Trends*, Vol. 5. London: Sage, pp. 21–42 [originally published in *Administrative Science Quarterly* (1974) *19*: 453–473].

Phillips, J. M. (1998) 'Effects of realistic job previews on multiple organizational outcomes: a meta-analysis', *Academy of Management Journal*, *41* (6): 673–690.

Pidd, H. (2014) 'Failures in Rotherham led to sexual abuse of 1,400 children'. Available at: www.the guardian.com/society/2014/aug/26/rotherham-sexual-abuse-children (accessed 3 September 2014).

Piketty, T. (2014) *Capital in the Twenty First Century*. Cambridge, MA: Harvard University Press.

Piliavin, J. A. and Unger, R. K. (1985) 'The helpful, but not helpless female: myth or reality?', in V. O'Leary, R. K. Unger and B. S. Wallston (eds), *Women, Gender, and Social Psychology*. Hillsdale, NJ: Lawrence Erlbaum Associates, pp. 149–186.

Pitsis, T. S. (2008a) 'Theory X', in S. R. Clegg and J. Bailey (eds), *The Sage International Encyclopedia of Organization Studies*. Thousand Oaks, CA: Sage, pp. 1545–1547.

Pitsis, T. S. (2008b) 'Theory Y', in S. R. Clegg and J. Bailey (eds), *The Sage International Encyclopedia of Organization Studies*. Thousand Oaks, CA: Sage, pp. 1547–1549.

Pitsis, T. S. (2008c) 'Positive psychology', in S. R. Clegg and J. Bailey (eds), *The Sage International Encyclopedia of Organization Studies*. Thousand Oaks, CA: Sage, pp. 1266–1270.

Pitsis, T. S., Clegg, S. R., Marosszeky, M. and Rura-Polley, T. (2003) 'Constructing the Olympic dream: managing innovation through the future perfect', *Organization Science*, *14* (5): 574–590.

Plato (1968) *The Republic* (trans. with notes and an interpretive essay by A. Bloom). New York: Basic Books.

Ployhart, R. E., Nyberg, A. J., Reilly, G. and Maltarich, M. A. (2014) 'Human capital is dead; long live human capital resources!', *Journal of Management*, *40* (2): 371–398.

Polanyi, M. (1962) *Personal Knowledge: Towards a Post-Critical Philosophy*. Chicago: University of Chicago Press.

Polanyi, M. (1983) *The Tacit Dimension*. Gloucester, MA: Peter Smith.

Pondy, L. R. (1967) 'Organizational conflict: concepts and models', *Administrative Science Quarterly*, *12* (2): 296–320.

Pondy, L. R. (1992) 'Reflections on organizational conflict', *Journal of Organizational Behavior*, *13* (3): 257–261.

Porter, A. J., Kuhn, T. R. and Nerlich, B. (2018) 'Organizing authority in the climate change debate: IPCC controversies and the management of dialectical tensions', *Organization Studies*, 39 (7): 873–898.

Porter, M. E. (1987) 'From competitive advantage to corporate strategy', *Harvard Business Review*, May–June: 43–59.

Porter, M. E. (1990) *The Competitive Advantage of Nations*. Basingstoke: Macmillan.

Porter, M. E. (1996) 'What is strategy?' *Harvard Business Review*, November–December: 61–78.

Porter, M. E. and Kramer, M. R. (2002) 'The competitive advantage of corporate philanthropy', in the *Harvard Business Review on Corporate Social Responsibility*. Boston: Harvard Business School Press, pp. 27–64.

Porter, M. E. and Kramer, M. R. (2011) 'The big idea: creating shared value. How to reinvent capitalism – and unleash a wave of innovation and growth', *Harvard Business Review*, *89* (1–2).

Poster, M. (1990) *The Mode of Information: Poststructuralism and Social Context*. Cambridge: Polity.

Powell, T. C. (2014) 'Strategic management and the person', *Strategic Organization*, *12* (3): 200–207.

Powell, W. W. (1990) 'Neither market nor hierarchy: network forms of organization', *Research in Organizational Behavior*, *12*: 295–336.

Powell, W. W., Koput, K. W. and Smith-Doerr, L. (1996) 'Interorganizational collaboration and the locus of innovation: networks of learning in biotechnology', *Administrative Science Quarterly*, *41*: 116–145.

Power, M. (1997) *The Audit Society: Rituals of Verification*, 2nd edn. Oxford: Oxford University Press.

Proffet-Reese, M., Rowings, L. and Sharpely, T. (2007) 'Employee benefits of the future', *Employee Benefit Plan Review*, *61* (7): 21–25.

Pruitt, D. G. (1983) 'Strategic choice in negotiation', *American Behavioral Scientist*, *27*: 167–194.

Pugh, D. S. and Hickson, D. J. (1976) *Organizational Structure in Its Context: The Aston Programme 1*. London: Saxon House.

Pugh, D. S., Hickson, D. J. and Hinings, C. R. (1971) *Writers on Organizations*. Harmondsworth: Penguin.

Putnam, L. L. (2004) 'Dialectical tensions and rhetorical tropes in negotiations', *Organization Studies*, *25* (1): 35–53.

Putnam, L. L. and Poole, M. S. (1987) 'Conflict and negotiation', in F. M. Jablin, L. L. Putnam, K. H. Roberts and L. W. Porter (eds), *Handbook of Organizational Communication: An Interdisciplinary Perspective*. Thousand Oaks, CA: Sage, pp. 549–599.

Putnam, L. L. and Wilson, C. (1982) 'Communicative strategies in organizational conflict: reliability and validity of a measurement scale', in M. Burgoon (ed.), *Communication Yearbook 6*. Newbury Park, CA: Sage, pp. 629–652.

Putnam, L. L., Fairhurst, G. T. and Banghart, S. (2016) 'Contradictions, dialectics, and paradoxes in organizations: a constitutive approach', *Academy of Management Annals*, *10* (1): 65–171.

Qiu, S., Liu, X. and Gao, T. (2017) 'Do emerging countries prefer local knowledge or distant knowledge? Spillover effect of university collaborations on local firms', *Research Policy*, *46* (7): 1299–1311.

Quinn, D. and Jones, T. M. (1995) 'An agent morality view of business policy', *Academy of Management Review*, *20*: 22–42.

Quinn, J. B. (1978) 'Strategic change: logical incrementalism', *Sloan Management Review*, *20* (Fall): 7–21.

Quinn, J. B. (1980) *Strategies for Change: Logical Incrementalism*. Homewood, IL: Irwin.

Quinn, R. E. and Cameron, K. S. (1988) 'Organizational paradox and transformation', in R. E. Quinn and K. Cameron (eds), *Paradox and Transformation: Toward a Theory of Change in Organization and Management*. Cambridge, MA: Ballinger Pub Co., pp. 1–19.

Raffns e, S., Mennicken, A. and Miller, P. (2017) 'The Foucault effect in organization studies', *Organization Studies*, http://journals.sagepub.com/doi/abs/10.1177/0170840617745110.

Rahim, M. A. (1983) 'A measure of styles of handling interpersonal conflict', *Academy of Management Journal*, *26* (2): 368–376.

Rahim, M. A. (1997) 'Relationships of stress, locus of control, and social support to psychiatric symptoms and propensity to leave a job: a field study with managers', *Journal of Business and Psychology*, *12* (2): 159–174.

Rahim, M. A. (2002) 'Toward a theory of managing organizational conflict', *International Journal of Conflict Management*, *13* (3): 206–235.

Rahim, M. A. (2010) *Managing Conflict in Organizations*, 4th edn. New York: Transaction Publishers.

Rahim, M. A., Buntzman, G. F. and White, D. (1999) 'An empirical study of the stages of moral development and conflict management styles', *International Journal of Conflict Management*, 10 (2): 154–171.

Rancière, J. (2009) *Moments politiques: interventions 1977–1999*. Paris: La Fabrique.

Rao, H. (2009) *Market Rebels: How Activists Make or Break Radical Innovations*. Princeton, NJ: Princeton University Press.

Rasche, A. and Esser, D. E. (2007) 'Managing for compliance and integrity in practice', in C. Carter, S. Clegg, M. Kornberger, S. Laske and M. Messner (eds), *Business Ethics as Practice: Representation, Reflexivity and Performance*. Cheltenham: Edward Elgar.

Ray, T. and Clegg, S. R. (2007) 'Can we make sense of knowledge management's tangible rainbow? A radical constructivist alternative', *Prometheus*, 25 (2): 161–185.

Reardon, J. (2006) 'Are labor unions consistent with the assumptions of perfect competition?' *Journal of Economic Issues*, 40 (1): 171–182.

Redding, W. C. (1985) 'Rocking boats, blowing whistles, and teaching speech communication', *Communication Education*, 34: 245–258.

Reed, S. K. (2009) *Cognition: Theory and Application*, 8th edn. Belmont, CA: Wadsworth.

Rees, H. T. and Sprecher, S. K. (2009) *Encyclopedia of Human Relationships*. Thousand Oaks, CA: Sage.

Reff Pedersen, A., Sehested, K. and S rensen, E. (2011) 'Emerging theoretical understanding of pluricentric coordination in public governance', *The American Review of Public Administration*, 41 (4): 375–394.

Rego, A., Cunha, M. P. E. and Clegg, S. R. (2012) *The Virtues of Leadership: Contemporary Challenge for Global Managers*. Oxford: Oxford University Press.

Reich, R. B. (1991) *The Work of Nations*. New York: Vintage Books.

Reis, H. T. (1994) 'Domains of experience: investigating relationship processes from three perspectives', in R. Erber and R. Gilmour (eds), *Theoretical Frameworks for Personal Relationships*. Hillsdale, NJ: Lawrence Erlbaum, pp. 87–110.

Renwick, P. A. (1975) 'Impact of topic and source of disagreement on conflict management', *Organizational Behavior and Human Performance*, 14: 416–425.

Reve, T. and Stern, L. W. (1979) 'Interorganizational relations in marketing channels', *Academy of Management Review*, 4 (3): 405–416.

Rhodes, C. (2001) 'D'Oh: *The Simpsons*, popular culture, and the organizational carnival', *Journal of Management Inquiry*, 10 (4): 374–383.

Rhodes, C. (2016) 'Democratic business ethics: Volkswagen's emissions scandal and the disruption of corporate sovereignty', *Organization Studies*, 37 (10): 1501–1518.

Rhodes, C. and Badham, R. (2018) 'Ethical irony and the relational leader: grappling with the infinity of ethics and the finitude of practice', *Business Ethics Quarterly*, 28 (1): 71–98.

Riemer, N., Simon, D. W. and Romance, J. (2013) *Challenge of Politics*. Washington, DC: Sage.

Rindova, V., Barry, D. and Ketchen, D. J. (2009) 'Entrepreneuring as emancipation', *Academy of Management Review*, 34 (3): 477–491.

Ritzer, G. (1993) *The McDonaldization of Society*. Newbury Park, CA: Pine Forge.

Ritzer, G. (2004) *The Globalization of Nothing*. Thousand Oaks, CA: Pine Forge.

Roberts, S. J., Scherer, L. L. and Bowyer, C. J. (2011) 'Job stress and incivility: what role does psychological capital play?', *Journal of Leadership & Organizational Studies*, *18* (4): 449–458.

Robertson, I. (2014) 'It's so hard going cold turkey when you're addicted to power', *The Conversation*, 28 March. Available at: https://theconversation.com/its-so-hard-going-cold-turkey-when-youre-addicted-to-power-24919 (accessed 22 September 2015).

Robertson, R. (1992) *Globalization: Social Theory and Social Culture*. London: Sage.

Robey, D. (1981) 'Computer information systems and organization structure', *Communications of the ACM*, *24*: 679–687.

Robins, K. and Webster, F. (1985) '"Revolutions of the fixed wheel": information technology and social Taylorism', in P. Drummond and R. Paterson (eds), *Television in Transition: Papers from the First International Television Studies Conference*. London: British Film Institute, pp. 36–63.

Robinson, S. L., Kraatz, M. S. and Rousseau, D. M. (1994) 'Changing obligations and the psychological contract: a longitudinal study', *Academy of Management Journal*, *37* (1): 137–152.

Roche, E. (2001) 'Words for the wise', *Harvard Business Review*, January: 26–27.

Rode, J. C., Arthaud-Day, M., Mooney, C. H., Near, J. P. and Baldwin, T. T. (2008) 'Ability and personality predictors of salary, perceived job success, and perceived career success in the initial career stage', *International Journal of Selection and Assessment*, *16* (3): 292–299.

Rodrigues, S. B. (2006) 'The political dynamics of organizational culture in an institutionalized environment', *Organization Studies*, *27* (4): 537–557.

Rogan, M. and Mors, M. L. (2017) 'Managerial networks and exploration in a professional service firm', *Organization Studies*, *38* (2): 225–249.

Rogers, C. (1967) *On Becoming a Person: A Therapist's View of Psychotherapy*. London: Constable.

Rogers, C. (1991) 'Barriers and gateways to communication', *Harvard Business Review*, November–December: 105–111.

Rogers, C. R. (2013) 'A theory of therapy and personality change: as developed in the client-centered framework', *Perspectives in Abnormal Behavior*. London: Pergamon (General Psychology Series).

Rogers, J. (2015) 'Productive democracy: It's time to embrace a new egalitarian politics', *The Nation*, 23 March. Available at: www.thenation.com/article/productive-democracy (accessed 7 August 2017).

Rohan, M. J. (2000) 'A rose by any name? The values construct', *Personality and Social Psychology Review*, *4*: 255–277.

Rokeach, M. R. (1968) *Beliefs, Attitudes and Values*. San Francisco: Jossey-Bass.

Rokeach, M. R. (1973) *The Nature of Human Values*. New York: Free Press.

Romme, A. G. L. (2003) 'Making a difference: organization as design', *Organization Science*, *14* (5): 558–573.

Ronen, S. and Shenkar, O. (1985) 'Clustering countries on attitudinal dimensions: a review and synthesis', *Academy of Management Review*, *10* (3): 435–454.

Rosenthal, R. and Jacobson, L. (1992) *Pygmalion in the Classroom: Teacher Expectation and Pupils' Intellectual Development*. New York: Irvington.

Rosenzweig, P. (2014) *The Halo Effect ... and the Eight Other Business Delusions That Deceive Managers*. New York: Simon & Schuster..

Roth, L. M. (2006) 'Because I'm worth it? Understanding inequality in a performance-based pay system', *Sociological Inquiry*, *76* (1): 116–139.

Rothausen, T. J., Henderson, K. E., Arnold, J. K. and Malshe, A. (2017) 'Should I stay or should I go? Identity and well-being in sensemaking about retention and turnover', *Journal of Management*, *43* (7): 2357–2385.

Rotter, J. B. (1966) 'Generalised expectancies for internal vs. external control of reinforcement', *Psychological Monographs*, *80*: 1–28.

Rouleau, L. (2005) 'Micro practices of strategic sensemaking and sensegiving: how middle managers interpret and sell change every day', *Journal of Management Studies*, *42* (7): 1413–41.

Rousseau, D. M. (1996) 'Changing the deal while keeping people', *Academy of Management Executive*, *10*: 50–56.

Ruiz, S. V. L., Peralta-Alva, A. and Puy, D. (2017) 'Macroeconomic and distributional effects of personal income tax reforms: a heterogeneous agent model approach for the US', *International Monetary Fund Working Paper*, 1 September. Available at: www.imf.org/en/Publications/WP/Issues/2017/09/01/Macroeconomic-and-Distributional-Effects-of-Personal-Income-Tax-Reforms-A-Heterogenous-Agent-45147 (accessed 11 September 2017).

Ryan, A. M. and Ployhart, R. E. (2014) 'A century of selection', *Annual Review of Psychology*, *65* (1): 693–717.

Ryan, K., Oestreich, D. and Orr, G., III (1996) *The Courageous Messenger: How to Successfully Speak Up at Work*. San Francisco: Jossey-Bass.

Ryan, R. M. and Deci, E. L. (2000) 'Self-determination theory and the facilitation of intrinsic motivation, social development, and well-being', *American Psychologist*, *55* (1): 68–78.

Sagiv, L. and Schwartz, S. H. (2000) 'A new look at national culture: illustrative applications to role stress and managerial behavior', in N. M. Ashkenasy, C. P. M. Wilderom and M. F. Peterson (eds), *The Handbook of Organizational Culture and Climate*. London: Sage, pp 417–436.

Sagiv, L. and Schwartz, S. H. (2000) 'Value priorities and subjective well being: direct relations and congruity effects', *European Journal of Social Psychology*, *30* (2): 177–198.

Said, E. (1979) *Orientalism*. New York: Vintage.

Samão, C. and Brauer, M. (2015) 'Beliefs about group malleability and out-group attitudes: the mediating role of perceived threat in interactions with out-group members', *European Journal of Social Psychology*, *45* (1): 1099–1992.

Sánchez, Y. and Brühwiler, C. F. (eds) (2015) *Transculturalism and Business in the BRIC States: A Handbook*. London: Ashgate.

Sandberg, J. and Targama, A. (2007) *Managing Understanding in Organizations*. London: Sage.

Sassen, S. (1998) *Globalization and Its Discontents*. New York: New Press.

Schabram, K. and Maitlis, S. (2017) 'Negotiating the challenges of a calling: emotion and enacted sensemaking in animal shelter work', *Academy of Management Journal*, *60* (2): 584–609.

Schank, R. C. and Abelson, R. P. (2013) *Scripts, Plans, Goals, and Understanding: An Inquiry into Human Knowledge Structures*. London: Psychology Press.

Schattschneider, E. E. (1960) *The Semi-sovereign People: A Realist's View of Democracy in America*. New York: Holt, Rinehart and Winston.

Schein, E. (1997) *Organizational Culture and Leadership*. San Francisco: Jossey-Bass.

Schein, E. (2002 [1990]) 'Organizational culture', in S. R. Clegg (ed.), *Central Currents in Organization Studies II: Contemporary Trends*, Vol. 7. London: Sage, pp. 196–205 [originally published in *American Psychologist* (1990) 45: 109–119].

Schein, E. (2006) 'From brainwashing to organizational therapy: a conceptual and empirical journey in search of "systemic" health and a general model of change dynamics: a drama in five acts', *Organization Studies*, 27 (2): 287–301.

Schein, E. H. (1961) *Coercive Persuasion: A Socio-psychological Analysis of the Brainwashing of American Civilian Prisoners by the Chinese Communists*. New York: W.W. Norton.

Schein, E. H. (2010). *Organizational Culture and Leadership*. London: John Wiley & Sons.

Schley, D. G. (2018) 'Origins and development of the cellular organization', in M. A. Raham, R. T. Golembiewski and K. Mackenzie (eds), *Current Topics in Management*. London: Routledge, pp. 127–156.

Schmidt, S. M. and Kochan, T. A. (1972) 'Conflict: toward conceptual clarity', *Administrative Science Quarterly*, 17 (3): 359–370.

Schmitt, D. P., Allik, J., McCrae, R. R. and Benet-Martinez, V. (2007) 'The geographic distribution of Big Five personality traits: patterns and profiles of human self-description across 56 nations', *Journal of Cross-Cultural Psychology*, 38 (2): 173–212.

Schneider, D. J. (2004) *The Psychology of Stereotyping*. New York: Guilford.

Schön, D. A. (1992) 'The theory of inquiry: Dewey's legacy to education', *Curriculum Inquiry*, 22: 119–139.

Schuler, R. S. and Jackson, S. E. (2000) 'HRM and its link with strategic management', in J. Storey (ed.), *Human Resource Management: A Critical Text*. New York: Thomson International, pp. 137–159.

Schuler, R. S. and MacMillan, I. C. (1984) 'Gaining competitive advantage through human resource management practices', *Human Resource Management*, 23 (3): 241–255.

Schulze, J. and Krumm, S. (2017) 'The "virtual team player": a review and initial model of knowledge, skills, abilities, and other characteristics for virtual collaboration', *Organizational Psychology Review*, 7: 66–95.

Schumpeter, J. A. (2006) *Capitalism, Socialism and Democracy*. London: Routledge; original work published 1942.

Schuster, M. (1983) 'The impact of union-management cooperation on productivity and employment', *Industrial and Labor Relations Review*, 36 (3): 415–430.

Schuster, M. (1984) 'The Scanlon Plan: a longitudinal analysis', *Journal of Applied Behavioral Science*, 20 (1): 23–38.

Schutz, A. (1967) *The Phenomenology of the Social World*. Evanston, IL: Northwestern University Press.

Schwartz, M. (2000) 'Why ethical codes constitute an unconscionable regression', *Journal of Business Ethics*, 23 (2): 173–184.

Schwartz, M. (2001) 'The nature of the relationship between corporate codes of ethics and behaviour', *Journal of Business Ethics*, 32 (3): 247–262.

Schwartz, M. (2005) 'Universal moral values for corporate codes of ethics', *Journal of Business Ethics*, 59 (1/2): 27–44.

Schwartz, M. S. (2017) *Corporate Social Responsibility*. London: Routledge.

Schwartz, S. (1992) 'Universals in the content and structure of values: theoretical advances and empirical tests in 20 countries', in M. P. Zanna (ed.), *Advances in Experimental Social Psychology*, Vol. *24*. San Diego, CA: Academic Press, pp. 1–65.

Schwartz, S. (1994) 'Are there universal aspects in the structure and contents of human values?' *Journal of Social Issues*, 50: 1–18.

Schwartz, S. (1996) 'Value priorities and behavior: applying a theory of integrated value systems', in C. Seligman, J. M. Olson, and M. P. Zanna (eds), *The Ontario Symposium: The Psychology of Values*, Vol. *8*. Mahwah, NJ: Lawerence Erlbaum Associates, pp. 1–24.

Schwartz, S. H. (1999) 'A theory of cultural values and some implications for work', *Applied Psychology*, *48* (1): 23–47.

Schwartz, S. H. (2012) 'An overview of the Schwartz theory of basic values', *Online Readings in Psychology and Culture*, *2* (1), http://dx.doi.org/10.9707/2307-0919.1116.

Schwartz, S. H. (2014) 'Rethinking the concept and measurement of societal culture in light of empirical findings', *Journal of Cross-Cultural Psychology*, January, *45*: 5–13.

Schwartz, S. H. (2017) 'The refined theory of basic values', in S. Roccas and L. Sagiv (eds), *Values and Behavior: Taking Cross-Cultural Perspective*. Berlin: Springer, pp. 51–72.

Schweiker, W. (1993) 'Accounting for ourselves: accounting practice and the discourse of ethics', *Accounting, Organizations and Society*, *18* (2–3): 231–252.

Schleicher, D. J., Baumann, H. M., Sullivan, D. W., Levy, P. E., Hargrove, D. C. and Barros-Rivera, B. A. (2017) 'Putting the system into performance management systems: a review and agenda for performance management research', *Journal of Management*, *44* (6): 2209–2245.

Scott, J. C. (1990) *Domination and the Arts of Resistance: Hidden Transcripts*. New Haven, CT: Yale University Press.

Scott, R. (Director) (1982) *Blade Runner* [Motion picture]. United States: Warner Bros.

Scott, R. (Director) (2000) *Gladiator* [Motion picture]. United States: Dreamworks SKG.

Scott, W. R. (2008) 'Lords of the dance: professionals as institutional agents', *Organization Studies*, *29* (2): 219–238.

Searle, T. P. and Barbuto Jr, J. E. (2011) 'Servant leadership, hope, and organizational virtuousness: a framework exploring positive micro and macro behaviors and performance impact', *Journal of Leadership & Organizational Studies*, *18* (1): 107–117.

Seifert, B., Morris, S. A. and Bartkus, B. R. (2003) 'Comparing big givers and small givers: financial correlates of corporate philanthropy', *Journal of Business Ethics*, *45* (3): 195–211.

Seligman, M. E. P. and Csikszentmihalyi, M. (2000) 'Positive psychology: an introduction', *American Psychologist*, 55: 5–14.

Semler, R. (1993) *Maverick: The Success Story Behind the World's Most Unusual Workplace*. New York: Warner Books.

Senge, P. (1990) *The Fifth Discipline: The Art and Practice of the Learning Organization*. New York: Doubleday.

Senior, B. (1997) 'Team roles and team performance: is there "really" a link?', *Journal of Occupational and Organizational Psychology*, *70* (3): 241–258.

Sennett, R. (1998) *The Corrosion of Character: The Personal Consequences of Work in the New Capitalism*. New York: W.W. Norton.

Seo, M. G. and Creed, W. D. (2002) 'Institutional contradictions, praxis, and institutional change: a dialectical perspective', *Academy of Management Review, 27* (2): 222–247.

Seremani, T. and Clegg, S. (2016) 'Postcolonialism, organization, and management theory: the role of "epistemological third spaces"', *Journal of Management Inquiry, 25* (2): 171–183.

Sewell, G. (1998) 'The discipline of teams: the control of team-based industrial work through electronic and peer surveillance', *Administrative Science Quarterly, 43* (2): 397–428.

Sewell, G. (2001) 'What goes around, comes around: inventing a mythology of teamwork and empowerment', *Journal of Applied Behavioral Science, 37* (1): 70–89.

Sewell, G. (2002 [1988]) 'The discipline of teams: the control of team-based industrial work through electronic and peer surveillance', in S. R. Clegg (ed.), *Central Currents in Organization Studies II: Contemporary Trends*, Vol. 5. London: Sage, pp. 211–245 [originally published in *Administrative Science Quarterly* (1998) *43*: 397–428].

Shah, P. and Kleiner, B. (2005) 'New developments concerning age discrimination in the workplace', *Equal Opportunities International, 24* (5/6): 15–23.

Shah, P. P. and Jehn, K. A. (1993) 'Do friends perform better than acquaintances? The interaction of friendship, conflict, and task', *Group Decision and Negotiation, 2* (2): 149–165.

Sharp, J. P., Routledge, P., Philo, C. and Paddison, R. (2000) *Entanglements of Power*. New York: Routledge.

Shaw, G. (2000) 'Planning and communicating using stories', in M. Schultz, M. Hatch and M. Larsen (eds), *The Expressive Organization: Linking Identity, Reputation, and the Corporate Brand*. Oxford and New York: Oxford University Press, pp. 182–195.

Sheehan, N. T. (2005) 'Why old tools won't work in the "new" knowledge economy', *Journal of Business Strategy, 26* (4): 53–61.

Sheldon, K. M. (1995) 'Creativity and self-determination in personality', *Creativity Research Journal, 8*: 25–36.

Sheldon, K. M., Ryan, R. M. and Reis, H. (1996) 'What makes for a good day? Competence and autonomy in the day and in the person', *Personality and Social Psychology Bulletin, 22*: 1270–1279.

Shen, J. and Edwards, V. (2004) 'Recruitment and selection in Chinese MNEs', *International Journal of Human Resource Management, 15* (4): 814–835.

Shenhav, Y. (1999) *Manufacturing Rationality: The Engineering Foundations of the Managerial Revolution*. Oxford: Oxford University Press.

Sheppard, B. H. (1992) 'Conflict research as schizophrenia: the many faces of organizational conflict', *Journal of Organizational Behavior, 13* (3): 325–334.

Sheridan, A. (1998) 'Patterns in the policies: affirmative action in Australia', *Women in Management Review, 13* (7): 243–252.

Shipka, T. A. (1969) 'Social conflict and re-construction', dissertation, Boston College.

Shwayder, D. S. (1965) *The Stratification of Behaviour: A System of Definitions Propounded and Defended*. London: Routledge & Kegan Paul.

Simmel, G. (1955) *Conflict and the Web of Group Affiliation*. New York: Free Press.

Simon, H. A. (1957) *Administrative Behavior*. New York: Macmillan.

Simon, H. A. (1960) *The New Science of Management Decisions*. New York: Harper & Row.

Simon, H. A. (1969) *The Sciences of the Artificial*. Cambridge, MA: MIT Press.

Simpson, A. V., Clegg, S. R., Lopes, M. P., Pitsis, T., Rego, A. and Cunha, M. P. e. (2014) 'Doing compassion or doing discipline? Power relations and the Magdalene Laundries', *Journal of Political Power*, *7* (2): 253–274.

Sims, R. L. and Keon, T. L. (1997) 'Ethical work climate as a factor in the development of person-organization fit', *Journal of Business Ethics*, *16* (11): 1095–1105.

Singer, P. (1976) *Animal Liberation: A New Ethics for Our Treatment of Animals*. London: Cape.

Singer, P. (2006) *In Defense of Animals: The Second Wave*. Oxford: Blackwell.

Skidmore, D. (2017) 'Understanding Chinese President Xi's anti-corruption campaign'. Available at: https://theconversation.com/understanding-chinese-president-xis-anti-corruption-campaign-86396 (accessed 27 June 2018).

Sklair, L. (1998) 'Social movements and global capitalism', in F. Jameson and M. Miyoshi (eds), *Cultures of Globalization*. Durham, NC: Duke University Press, pp. 291–308.

Sklair, L. (1999) 'Competing conceptions of globalization', *Journal of World-Systems Research*, 5 (2): 143–162.

Slaughter, J. E. and Zicker, M. J. (2006) 'A new look at the role of insiders in the newcomer socialization process', *Group & Organization Management*, *31* (2): 264–290.

Smircich, L. (2002 [1983]) 'Concepts of culture and organizational analysis', in S. R. Clegg (ed.), *Central Currents in Organization Studies II: Contemporary Trends*, Vol. 7. London: Sage, pp. 152–174 [originally published in *Administrative Science Quarterly* (1983) *28*: 393–413].

Smith, A. (1961) *An Enquiry into the Nature and Causes of the Wealth of Nations*. Indianapolis, IN: Bobbs-Merrill ; original work published 1776.

Smith, D. (2006) *Globalization: The Hidden Agenda*. Oxford: Polity Press.

Smith, K. (Director) (1994) *Clerks* [Motion picture]. United States: Miramax.

Smith, M. B., Hill, A. D., Wallace, J. C., Recendes, T. and Judge, T.A. (2017) 'Upsides to dark and downsides to bright personality: a multidomain review and future research agenda', *Journal of Management*, *44* (1): 191–217.

Smith, W., Erez, M., Lewis, M., Jarvenpaa, S. and Tracey, P. (2017) 'Adding complexity to theories of paradox, tensions, dualities of innovation and change: introduction to special issue on paradox, tensions, and dualities of innovation and change', *Organization Studies*, *38* (3–4): 303–17.

Smith, W. (2014) 'Dynamic decision-making: a model of senior leaders managing strategic paradoxes', *Academy of Management Journal*, 57 (6): 1592–1623.

Smith, W. and Lewis, M. (2011) 'Toward a theory of paradox: a dynamic equilibrium model of organizing', *Academy of Management Review*, *36* (2): 381–403.

Smither, J. W., London, M. and Reilly, R. R. (2005) 'Does performance improve following multi-source feedback? A theoretical model, meta-analysis, and review of empirical findings', *Personnel Psychology*, 58 (1): 33–66.

Smola, K. W. and Sutton, C. D. (2002) 'Generational differences: revisiting generational work values for the new millennium', *Journal of Organizational Behavior*, 23 (4): 363–382.

Snow, C. C., Fjeldstad, O. D. and Langer, A. M. (2017) 'Designing the digital organization', *Journal of Organizational Design*, 6 (7): 1–13.

Snow, C. P. (1964) *The Corridors of Power*. London: Macmillan.

Solomon, R. L. and Corbit, J. D. (1978) 'An opponent-process theory of motivation', *The American Economic Review*, *68* (6): 12–24.

Somech, A., Desivilya, H. S. and Lidogoster, H. (2009) 'Team conflict management and team effectiveness: the effects of task interdependence and team identification', *Journal of Organizational Behavior*, *30* (3): 359–378.

Sonenshein, S. and Dholakia, U. (2012) 'Explaining employee engagement with strategic change implementation: a meaning-making approach', *Organization Science*, *23* (1): 1–23.

Sontag, S. (1961) *Against Interpretation and Other Essays*. New York: Farrar, Straus and Giroux.

Sorge, A. (2018) 'Management in Germany, the dynamo of Europe', in R. Crane (ed.), *The Influence of Business Cultures in Europe: An Exploration of Central, Eastern, and Northern Economies*. London: Palgrave Macmillan, pp. 69–113.

Sparrow, P., Brewster, C. and Harris, H. (2004) *Globalization of Business: Tracking the Business Role of International HR Specialists*. London: Routledge.

Spector, P. (1982) 'Behaviour in organizations as a function of employee's locus of control', *Psychological Bulletin*, *91*: 482–497.

Spector, P. E. (1994) 'Using self-report questionnaires in OB research: a comment on the use of a controversial method', *Journal of Organizational Behavior*, *15* (5): 385–392.

Spencer, D. A. (2000) 'Braverman and the contribution of labour process analysis to the critique of capitalist production: twenty-five years on', *Work, Employment & Society*, *14* (2): 223–243.

Spicer, A. and Böhm, S. (2007) 'Moving management: theorizing struggles against the hegemony of management', *Organization Studies*, *28* (11): 1667–1698.

Sprague, J. and Rudd, G. L. (1988) 'Boat-rocking in the high-technology culture', *American Behavioral Scientist*, *32*: 169–193.

Sprinkle, T. A. and Urich, M. (2017) 'Three generational issues in organizational learning: knowledge management, perspectives on training and "low-stakes" development', *The Learning Organization*, *25* (4): DOI: 10.1108/TLO-02-2017-0021.

Spybey, T. (1996) *Globalization and World Society*. Cambridge: Polity.

Stacey, R. (1999) 'Creative organizations: the relevance of chaos and psychodynamic systems', in R. Purser and A. Montuori (eds), *Social Creativity*. Cresskill, NJ: Hampton, pp. 61–88.

Stacey, R. D. (2012) *Tools and Techniques of Leadership and Management: Meeting the Challenge of Complexity*. London: Routledge.

Starbuck, W. (1983) 'Organizations as action generators', *American Sociological Review*, *48*: 91–102.

Stark, D. (2009) *The Sense of Dissonance: Accounts of Worth in Economic Life*. Princeton, NJ: Princeton University Press.

State-Owned Assets Supervision and Administration Commission of the State Council (2005) Guiding opinion on strengthening the building of corporate culture in centrally controlled corporations. Available at: http://gqwh.sasac.gov.cn/n1870310/n1870389/n1870582/c1877540/content.html (accessed 2 March 2017).

Steigenberger, N. (2015) 'Emotions in sensemaking: a change management perspective', *Journal of Organizational Change Management*, *28* (3): 432–451.

Stein, M. (2000) 'The risk taker as shadow: a psychoanalytic view of the collapse of Barings Bank', *Journal of Management Studies*, *37* (8): 1215–1230.

Stein, M. (2007) 'Toxicity and the unconscious experience of the body at the employee–customer interface', *Organization Studies*, *28* (8): 1223–1241.

Stein, M. and Pinto, J. (2011) 'The dark side of groups: a "gang at work" in Enron', *Group & Organization Management*, 36: 692–721.

Stephens, B. (2017) 'Donald Trump's fatal culture of governance', www.afr.com/opinion/columnists/why-i-am-still-a-nevertrumper-20171230-h0bm94#ixzz5BqdReNoP (accessed 7 October 2018).

Stigliani, I. and Ravasi, D. (2012) 'Organizing thoughts and connecting brains: material practices and the transition from individual to group-level prospective sensemaking', *Academy of Management Journal*, 55 (5): 1232–1259.

Stiglitz, J. (2013) 'Globalization isn't just about profits. It's about taxes too', *Guardian*, 28 May, www.theguardian.com/commentisfree/2013/may/27/globalisation-is-about-taxes-too (accessed 8 October 2018).

Stone, O. (Director) (1986) *Platoon* [Motion picture]. United States: Orion.

Stone, O. (Director) (1987) *Wall Street* [Motion picture]. United States: Fox.

Storper, M. and Scott, A. J. (1993) 'The wealth of regions: market forces and policy imperatives in local and global context', *Lewis Center for Regional Policy Studies, Working Paper No. 7*. Los Angeles: University of California Press.

Strauss, A., Schatzman, L., Ehrlich, D., Bucher, R. and Sabshin, M. (1963) 'The hospital and its negotiated order', in E. Friedmann (ed.), *The Hospital in Modern Society*. New York: Macmillan, pp. 147–169.

Sturdy, A. (2006) 'Management education', in C. Carter and S. R. Clegg (eds), *The Encyclopedia of the Sociology of Management*. Oxford: Blackwell, pp. 2725–2728.

Sturdy, A. and Gabriel, Y. (2000) 'Missionaries, mercenaries or used car salesmen? Teaching MBA in Malaysia', *Journal of Management Studies*, 37 (4): 979–1002.

Subhabrata, B. B. and Jackson, L. (2017) 'Microfinance and the business of poverty reduction: critical perspectives from rural Bangladesh', *Human Relations*, 70 (1): 63–91.

Suchman, M. C. (1995) 'Managing legitimacy: strategic and institutional approaches', *The Academy of Management Review*, 20 (3): 571–610.

Suddaby, R. and Foster, W. M. (2017) 'History and organizational change', *Journal of Management*, 43 (1): 19–38.

Sundaramurthy, C. and Lewis, M. (2003) 'Control and collaboration: paradoxes of governance', *Academy of Management Review*, 28 (3): 397–415.

Sundback, S. (2018) 'Tradition and change in the Nordic countries', in J. W. Carroll, W. C. Roof and D. A. Roosen (eds), *The Post-War Generation and the Establishment of Religion*. London: Routledge, pp. 87–111.

Sunstein, C. R. (2006) *Infotopia: How Many Minds Produce Knowledge*. Oxford: Oxford University Press.

Sutton, R. I. and Rafaeli, A. (1988) 'Untangling the relationship between displayed emotions and organizational sales: the case of convenience stores', *Academy of Management Journal*, 31 (3): 461–487.

Swann, J., Newell, S., Scarbrough, H. and Hislop, D. (1999) 'Knowledge management and innovation: networks and networking', *Journal of Knowledge Management*, 3 (4): 262–275.

Swanton, C. (1985) 'On the "essential contestedness" of political concepts', *Ethics*, 95 (4): 811–827.

Tallman, S., Jenkins, M., Henry, N. and Pinch, S. (2004) 'Knowledge clusters and competitive advantage', *Academy of Management Review*, 29 (2): 258–271.

Tarique, I. and Schuler, R. S. (2010) 'Global talent management: literature review, integrative framework, and suggestions for further research', *Journal of World Business*, *45* (2): 122–133.

Taubman, P. and Wachter, M. L. (1986) 'Segmented labor markets', *Handbook of Labor Economics*, 2: 1183–1217.

Taylor, A. (2006) 'Call for law to help close gender pay gap', *Financial Times*, 5 January.

Taylor, F. W. (1895) *A Piece Rate System*. New York: McGraw-Hill.

Taylor, F. W. (1967) *Principles of Scientific Management*. New York: Harper; original work published 1911.

Taylor, F. W. (1995) 'Report of a lecture by and questions put to Mr. F. W. Taylor: a transcript', *Journal of Management History*, *1* (1): 8–32.

Taylor, L. (2016) 'A shift in political thinking is giving Labor a sense of purpose', *Guardian Australia*, 18 March. Available at: www.theguardian.com/australia-news/2016/mar/18/a-shift-in-political-thinking-is-giving-labor-a-sense-of-purpose (accessed 26 June 2018).

Teal, G. (2008) 'Sweatshops', in S. R. Clegg and J. R. Bailey (eds), *The Sage International Encyclopedia of Organization Studies*. Thousand Oaks, CA: Sage, pp. 1495–1498.

Teece, D. J. (2018) 'Managing the university: why "organized anarchy" is unacceptable in the age of massive open online courses', *Strategic Organization*, *16* (1): 92–102.

ten Bos, R. (1997) 'Business ethics and Bauman ethics', *Organization Studies*, *18* (6): 997–1014.

ten Bos, R. (2000) *Fashion and Utopia in Management Thinking*. Amsterdam: Benjamins.

Tesler, R., Mohammed, S., Hamilton, K., Mancuso, V. and McNeese, M. (2018) 'Mirror, mirror: guided storytelling and team reflexivity's influence on team mental models', *Small Group Research*, *49* (3): 267–305.

Tharenou, P. (1997) 'Organisational, job, and personal predictors of employee participation in training and development', *Applied Psychology*, *46* (2): 111–134.

Thayer, F. C. (1978) 'The president's management "reforms": theory X triumphant', *Public Administration Review*, July/August: 309–314.

Thomas, K. W. (1976) 'Conflict and conflict management', in M. D. Dunnette (ed.), *Handbook in Industrial and Organizational Psychology*. Chicago: Rand McNally, pp. 889–935.

Thomas, K. W. (1992) 'Conflict and conflict management: reflections and update', *Journal of Organizational Behavior*, *13* (3): 265–274.

Thompson, J. D. (1956) 'Authority and power in identical organisations', *American Journal of Sociology*, *62*: 290–301.

Thompson, J. D. (1967) *Organizations in Action: Social Science Bases of Administrative Theory*. Brunswick, NJ: Transaction Publishers.

Thorndike, E. L. (1920) 'A constant error in psychological ratings', *Journal of Applied Psychology*, *4*: 469–477.

Thrash, T. M. and Elliot, A. J. (2002) 'Implicit and self-attributed achievement motives: concordance and predictive validity', *Journal of Personality*, *70* (5): 729–755.

Tidd, J., Bessant, J. and Pavitt, K. (2001) *Managing Innovation: Integrating Technological, Market and Organizational Change*. Chichester: Wiley.

Tidström, A. (2009) 'Causes of conflict in inter-competitor cooperation', *Journal of Business & Industrial Marketing*, *24* (7): 506–518.

Tjosvold, D. (1985) 'Implications of controversy research for management', *Journal of Management*, *11* (3): 21–37.

Tjosvold, D. (2006) 'Defining conflict and making choices about its management: lighting the dark side of organizational life', *International Journal of Conflict Management*, *17* (2): 87–95.

Tjosvold, D. (2008) 'Conflicts in the study of conflict in organizations', in C. W. De Dreu and M. J. Gelfand (eds), *The Psychology of Conflict and Conflict Management in Organizations*. New York: Taylor & Francis/Lawrence Erlbaum, pp. 445–453.

Tomkins, L. and Simpson, P. (2015) 'Caring leadership: a Heideggerian perspective', *Organization Studies*, *36* (8): 1013–1031.

Tonkinwise, C. (2018) 'This time, it is really happening: democracy must be defended, by undemocratic design specifications'. Available at: www.academia.edu/35779909/Democracy_must_be_Defended_by_Undemocratic_Designs (accessed 7 October 2018).

Tourish, D. (2013) *The Dark Side of Transformational Leadership: A Critical Perspective*. London: Routledge.

Townley, B. (1993) 'Foucault, power/knowledge and its relevance for human resource management', *Academy of Management Review*, *18* (3): 518–545.

Townley, B. (1994) *Reframing Human Resource Management: Power, Ethics and the Subject at Work*. London: Sage.

Townley, B. (2002a) 'Managing with modernity', *Organization*, 9 (44): 549–573.

Townley, B. (2002b) 'The role of competing rationalities in institutional change', *Academy of Management Journal*, *45* (1): 163–179.

Trahair, R. (2001) 'George Elton Mayo', *Biographical Dictionary of Management*. Thoemmes Press. Available at: www.thoemmes.com/encyclopedia/mayo.htm (accessed 2 January 2006).

Trejo, S. J. (1993) 'Overtime pay, overtime hours, and labor unions', *Journal of Labor Economics*, *11* (2): 253–278.

Trevino, L. K. (1986) 'Ethical decision making in organizations: a person–situation interactionist model', *Academy of Management Review*, *11* (3): 607–617.

Trevino, L. K. and Nelson, K. A. (2011) *Managing Business Ethics*, 5th edn. Hoboken, NJ: John Wiley and Sons.

Trevino, L. K., Weaver, G. R., Toffler, D. G. and Ley, B. (1999) 'Managing ethics and legal compliance: what works and what hurts', *California Management Review*, *41* (2): 131–151.

Tribe, K. (1975) 'Capitalism and industrialization', *Intervention*, 5: 23–27.

Trist, E. (1983) 'Referent organizations and the development of inter-organizational domains', *Human Relations*, *36* (3): 269–284.

Trist, E. (1993) 'QWL and the 80s', in E. Trist and H. Murray (eds), *The Social Engagement of Social Science, Vol. II: The Socio-Technical Perspective*. Philadelphia: University of Pennsylvania Press, pp. 338–350.

Trullen, J. and Bartunek, J. M. (2007) 'What a design approach offers to organization development', *Journal of Applied Behavioral Science*, *43*: 23–43.

Tse, T. (2014) 'Speak up and eliminate forced labour – business can be ethical and profitable', http://theconversation.com/speak-up-and-eliminate-forced-labour-business-can-be-ethical-and-profitable-32255 (accessed 8 October 2018).

Tsui, A. S., Nifadkar, S. S. and Ou, A. Y. (2007) 'Cross-national, cross-cultural organizational behavior research: advances, gaps, and recommendations', *Journal of Management*, *33* (3): 426–478.

Tucker, J. C. (1993) 'Everyday forms of employee resistance: how temporary workers handle conflict with the employers', *Sociological Forum*, *8* (1): 25–45.

Tuckman, B. (1965) 'Developmental sequence in small groups', *Psychological Bulletin*, *63* (6): 384–399.

Tuckman, B. and Jensen, M. A. (1977) 'Stages of small group development revisited', *Group and Organisation Studies*, *2* (4): 419–427.

Turner, J. C. (1987) *Rediscovering the Social Group: A Self-Categorization Theory*. New York: Blackwell.

Tushman, M. L. and Anderson, P. (1986) 'Technological discontinuities and organizational environments', *Administrative Science Quarterly*, *31* (3): 439–465.

Tziner, A., Joanis, C. and Murphy, K. R. (2000) 'A comparison of three methods of performance appraisal with regard to goal properties', *Group Organization Management*, *25* (2): 175–190.

United Voice and the Tax Justice Network Australia, in consultation with corporate tax expert Dr Roman Lanis (2014) 'Who pays for our common wealth? Tax practices of the ASX 200', http://i.nextmedia.com.au/Assets/ASX_200_tax_practices.pdf (accessed 8 October 2018).

Urry, J. (2007) *Mobilities*. London: John Wiley and Sons.

Ury, W. (2010) 'The walk from "no" to "yes"', www.ted.com/talks/william_ury?language=en (accessed 8 October 2018).

Üsdiken, B. (2004) 'Americanization of European management education in historical and comparative perspective: a symposium', *Journal of Management Inquiry*, *13* (2): 87–89.

Vaaland, T. I. and Håkansson, H. (2003) 'Exploring interorganizational conflict in complex projects', *Industrial Marketing Management*, *32* (2): 127–138.

Valentine, S., Godkin, L. and Lucero, M. (2002) 'Ethical context, organizational commitment, and person-organization fit', *Journal of Business Ethics*, *41* (4): 349–360.

Van de Ven, A. and Poole, M. (1995) 'Explaining development and change in organizations', *Academy of Management Review*, 20 (3): 510–540.

Van de Ven, A. H., Delbecq, A. L. and Koenig Jr, R. (1976) 'Determinants of coordination modes within organizations', *American Sociological Review*, *41* (2): 322–338.

Van de Ven, A. Bechara, J. P. and Sun, K. (2018) 'How outcome agreement and power balance among parties influence processes of organizational learning and nonlearning', *Journal of Management*, http://journals.sagepub.com/doi/full/10.1177/0149206317698021.

Van de Ven, A., Polley, D., Garud, R. and Venkataraman, S. (1999) *The Innovation Journey*. Oxford: Oxford University Press.

Van Der Schalk, J., Hawk, S. T., Fischer, A. H. and Doosje, B. (2011) 'Moving faces, looking places: validation of the Amsterdam Dynamic Facial Expression Set (ADFES)', *Emotion*, *11* (4): 907–920.

Van der Schalk, J., Fischer, A., Doosje, B., Wigboldus, D., Hawk, S., Rotteveel, M. and Hess, U. (2011) 'Convergent and divergent responses to emotional displays of ingroup and outgroup', *Emotion*, *11* (2): 286–298.

Van Maanen, J. (1988) *Tales of the Field: On Writing Ethnography*. Chicago: Chicago Guides to Writing, Editing, and Publishing.

Van Maanen, J. (1992) 'Drinking our troubles away: managing conflict in a British police agency', in D. M. Kolb and J. M. Bartunek (eds), *Hidden Conflicts in Organizations: Uncovering Behind-the-scenes Disputes*. Thousand Oaks, CA: Sage, pp. 32–62.

Vanderveen, G. (2006) *Interpreting Fear, Crime, Risk and Unsafety*. Cullompton: Willan.

Vansteenkiste, M., Simons, J., Lens, W., Sheldon, K. M. and Deci, E. L. (2004) 'Motivating learning, performance, and persistence: the synergistic effects of intrinsic goal contents and autonomy-supportive contexts', *Journal of Personality and Social Psychology*, *87* (2): 246–260.

Vaughan, D. (1997) *The Challenger Launch Decision: Risky Technology, Culture, and Deviance at NASA*. Chicago: University of Chicago Press.

Veenhoven, R. (2004) 'Happiness as an aim in public policy: the greatest happiness principle', in A. Linley and S. Joseph (eds), *Positive Psychology in Practice*. Hoboken, NJ: Wiley, pp. 658–678.

Veenhoven, R. (2010) 'Capability and happiness: conceptual difference and reality links', *Journal of Socio-Economics*, *39*: 344–350.

Veenhoven, R. (2011) 'Greater happiness for a greater number: is that possible? If so, how?', in K. M. Sheldon, T. B. Kashdan and M. F. Steger (eds), *Designing Positive Psychology: Taking Stock and Moving Forward*. New York: Oxford University Press, pp. 396–409.

Verwaeren, B., Van Hoye, G. and Baeten, X. (2017) 'Getting bang for your buck: the specificity of compensation and benefits information in job advertisements', *The International Journal of Human Resource Management*, *28* (19): 2811–2830.

Vogel, D. (2005) *The Market for Virtue: The Potential and Limits of Corporate Social Responsibility*. Washington, DC: Brookings Institution Press.

Voliotis, S. (2017) 'Establishing the normative standards that determine deviance in organizational corruption: is corruption within organizations antisocial or unethical?', *Journal of Business Ethics*, *140* (1): 147–160.

Voronov, M. and Coleman, P. T. (2003) 'Organizational power practices and a "practical" critical postmodernism', *Journal of Applied Behavioral Science*, *39* (2): 169–185.

Walker, M. (2016) 'Organizing diverse low-wage service workers', *Sage Open*, https://doi.org/10.1177%2F2158244016661749 (accessed 7 October 2018).

Walker, S. (2017) *The Captain Class*. Amazon: Ebury Digital

Wall, J. A. and Callister, R. R. (1995) 'Conflict and its management', *Journal of Management*, *21* (3): 515–558.

Walton, R. E. (1969) *Interpersonal Peacemaking: Confrontations and Third-party Consultations*. Reading, MA: Addison-Wesley.

Warner, M. and Busse, R. (2017) 'The legacy of the Hawthorne experiments: a critical analysis of the Human Relations school of thought', *History of Economic Ideas*, *25* (2): 91–114.

Watkins, L. M. and Johnston, L. (2000) 'Screening job applicants: the impact of physical attractiveness and application quality', *International Journal of Selection and Assessment*, *8* (2): 76–84.

Watson, T. J. (2003) 'Ethical choice in managerial work: the scope for managerial choices in an ethically irrational world', *Human Relations*, *56* (2): 167–185.

Watts, S. L. (1991) *Order against Chaos: Business Culture and Labor Ideology in America* 1880–1915. New York: Greenwood.

Watzlawick, P., Beavin, J. and Jackson, D. (1967) *Pragmatics of Human Communication: A Study of Interactional Patterns, Pathologies, and Paradoxes*. New York: W. W. Norton.

Weber, M. (1948) *From Max Weber: Essays in Sociology* (trans., ed. and with an introduction by H. H. Gerth and C. W. Mills). London: Routledge & Kegan Paul.

Weber, M. (1976) *The Protestant Ethic and the Spirit of Capitalism*. London: Allen & Unwin.

Weber, M. (1978) *Economy and Society: An Outline of Interpretive Sociology* (G. Roth and C. Wittich, eds). Berkeley, CA: University of California Press.

Wedeman, A. (2012) *Double Paradox: Rapid Growth and Rising Corruption in China*. Ithaca, NY: Cornell University Press.

Wei, J. (2012) 'Dealing with reality: market demands, artistic integrity, and identity work in reality television production', *Poetics*, 40 (5): 444–466.

Weick, K. E. (1969) *The Social Psychology of Organizing*. Reading, MA: Addison-Wesley.

Weick, K. E. (1979) *The Social Psychology of Organizing*, 2nd edn. Reading, MA: Addison-Wesley.

Weick, K. E. (1993) 'The collapse of sensemaking in organizations: the Mann Gulch disaster', *Administrative Science Quarterly*, 38 (4): 628–652.

Weick, K. E. (1995) *Sensemaking in Organizations*. Thousand Oaks, CA: Sage.

Weick, K. E. (2004) 'Vita contemplativa: mundane poetics – searching for wisdom in organization studies', *Organization Studies*, 25 (4): 653–668.

Weick, K. E. (2008) 'Sensemaking', in S. R. Clegg and J. R. Bailey (eds), *The Sage International Encyclopedia of Organization Studies*. Thousand Oaks, CA: Sage, pp. 1403–1406.

Weick, K. E. and Westley, F. (1999) 'Organizational learning: affirming an oxymoron', in S. R. Clegg, C. Hardy and W. R. Nord (eds), *Managing Organizations*. London: Sage, pp. 190–208.

Weiner, B. (1980) *Human Motivation*. Hillsdale, NJ: Lawrence Erlbaum Associates.

Weiner, B. (1992) 'A cognitive (attribution)-emotion-action model of motivated behavior: an analysis of judgments of help-giving', *Journal of Personality and Social Psychology*, 39 (2): 186–200.

Weiner, B. (2014) 'The attribution approach to emotion and motivation: history, hypotheses, home runs, headaches/heartaches', *Emotion Review*, 6: 353–361.

Weiss, B. (1981) *American Education and the European Immigrant*. Urbana, IL: University of Illinois Press.

Weiss, H. M. and Rupp, D. E. (2011) 'Experiencing work: an essay on a person-centric work psychology', *Industrial and Organizational Psychology: Perspectives on Science and Practice*, 4: 83–97.

Wellins, R. S., Byham, W. C. and Wilson, J. M. (1991) *Empowered Teams: Creating Self-Directed Work Groups That Improve Quality, Productivity and Participation*. San Francisco: Jossey-Bass.

Wenger, E. (1998) *Communities of Practice: Learning, Meaning and Identity*. New York: Cambridge University Press.

Wenger, E. (2002 [2000]) 'Communities of practice and social learning systems', in S. R. Clegg (ed.), *Central Currents in Organization Studies II: Contemporary Trends*, Vol. 8. London: Sage, pp. 29–48 [originally published in *Organization* (2000) 7: 225–246].

West, C. and Zimmerman, D. (1987) 'Doing gender', *Gender and Society*, 1 (2): 125–151.

West, M. (2017) 'Why are we still pursuing the Adani mine?', *The Conversation*, 4 October. Available at: https://theconversation.com/why-are-we-still-pursuing-the-adani-carmichael-mine-85100(accessed1 February 2018).

West, M. A. (2003) *Effective Teamwork: Practical Lessons from Organizational Research: Psychology of Work and Organizations*. London: Blackwell.

West, M. A. (2008) 'Team performance', in S. R. Clegg and J. Bailey (eds), *The Sage International Encyclopedia of Organization Studies*. London: Sage, pp. 1522–1526.

West, M. A., Tjosvold, D. and Smith, K. (2003) *International Handbook of Organizational Teamwork and Cooperative Working*. Chichester: Wiley.

Westwood, R. and Clegg, S. R. (eds) (2003) *Debating Organisation: Point-Counterpoint in Organization Studies*. Oxford: Blackwell.

White, R. W. (1963) *Ego and Reality in Psychoanalytical Theory: Psychological Issues*, Vol. *III*, No. 3, Monograph II. New York: International Universities Press.

Whitley, R. (1999) *Divergent Capitalisms*. Oxford: Oxford University Press.

Whyte, W. H. (1956) *The Organization Man*. New York: Simon & Schuster.

Wiedow, A. and Konradt, U. (2011) 'Two-dimensional structure of team process improvement: team reflection and team adaptation', *Small Group Research*, February, *42* (1): 32–54.

Williamson, O. E. (1975) *Markets and Hierarchies, Analysis and Antitrust Implications: A Study in the Economics of Internal Organization*. New York: Free Press.

Williamson, O. E. (1985) *The Economic Institutions of Capitalism*. New York: Free Press.

Williamson, O. E. (1991a) 'Comparative economic organization: the analysis of discrete structural alternatives', *Administrative Science Quarterly*, *36*: 269–296.

Williamson, O. E. (1991b) 'Strategizing, economizing, and economic organization', *Strategic Management Journal*, *12* (S2): 75–94.

Williamson, O. E. (1995) 'Hierarchies, markets and power in the economy: an economic perspective', *Industrial and Corporate Change*, *4* (1): 21–49.

Williamson, O. E. (1999) 'Strategy research: governance and competence perspectives', *Strategic Management Journal*, 20 (12): 1087–1108.

Willmott, H. (2002 [1993]) 'Strength is ignorance; slavery is freedom: managing culture in modern organizations', in S. R. Clegg (ed.), *Central Currents in Organization Studies II: Contemporary Trends*, Vol. 7. London: Sage [originally published in *Journal of Management Studies* (1993) 30: 515–582].

Willmott, H. (2009) 'Commentary: science as intervention – recasting Weber's moral vision', *Organization*, *16* (1): 143–53.

Wilson, T. D. and Gilbert, D. T. (2005) 'Affective forecasting: knowing what to want', *Current Directions in Psychological Science*, *14* (3): 131–134.

Wimbush, J. C., Shepard, J. M. and Markham, S. E. (1997) 'An empirical examination of the multi-dimensionality of ethical climate in organizations', *Journal of Business Ethics*, *16* (1): 67–77.

Wiseman, E. (2018) 'I thought a black dress protest was too easy – but then I saw it and changed my mind'. Available at: www.theguardian.com/lifeandstyle/2018/jan/14/red-carpets-pageants-black-dresses-sneak-protests-against-harassment (accessed 24 September 2015).

Wolfe, T. (1979) *The Right Stuff*. New York: Farrar, Straus and Giroux.

Wolinsky, F. D., Vander Weg, M. W., Martin, R., Unverzagt, F. W., Willis, S. L., Marsiske, M., et al. (2010) 'Does cognitive training improve internal locus of control among older adults?', *Journal of Gerontology: Social Sciences*, 65 (5): 591-598.

Womack, D. F. (1988) 'A review of conflict instruments in organizational settings', *Management Communication*, *1* (3): 437–445.

Womack, J. P., Jones, D. T. and Roos, D. (1990) *The Machine that Changed the World*. New York: Rawson/Macmillan.

Wombacher, J. C. and Felfe, J. (2017) 'Dual commitment in the organization: effects of the interplay of team and organizational commitment on employee citizenship behavior, efficacy beliefs, and turnover intentions', *Journal of Vocational Behavior*, 102: 1–14.

Wood, A. (1994) *North-South Trade, Employment and Inequality*. Oxford: Clarendon.

Woodward, J. (1965) *Industrial Organizations: Theory and Practice*. London: Oxford University Press.

Workman, J. (1993) 'Marketing's limited role in new product development in one computer systems firm', *Journal of Marketing Research*, 30: 405–421.

Wrege, D. (1995) 'F. W. Taylor's lecture on management, 4th June 1907: an introduction', *Journal of Management History*, 1 (1): 4–7.

Wren, D. and Greenwood, R. (1998) *Management Innovators: The People and Ideas that Shaped Modern Business*. New York: Oxford University Press.

Wright, J. (2017) *Darkest Hour* [Motion picture]. London: Perfect World Pictures and Working Title Films.

Wyer, N. A. (2007) 'Motivational influences on compliance with and consequences of instructions to suppress stereotypes', *Journal of Experimental Social Psychology*, 43 (3): 417–424.

Yoo, Y., Boland Jr, R. J., Lyytinen, K. and Majchrzak, A. (2012) 'Organizing for innovation in the digitized world', *Organization Science*, 23 (5): 1398–1408.

Young, J. E., Klosko, J. S. and Weishaar, M. (2003) *Schema Therapy: A Practitioner's Guide*. New York: Guilford.

Zaccaro, S. J., Green, J. P., Dubrow, S. and Kolze, M. (2018) 'Leader individual differences, situational parameters, and leadership outcomes: a comprehensive review and integration', *The Leadership Quarterly*, 29 (1): 2–43.

Zald, M. N. and McCarthy, J. D. (1979) *The Dynamics of Social Movements: Resource Mobilization, Social Control, and Tactics*. Boston: Little Brown & Co.

Zammuto, R. F., Griffith, T. L., Majchrzak, A., Dougherty, D. J. and Faraj, S. (2007) 'Information technology and the changing fabric of organization', *Organization Science*, 18 (5): 749–762.

Zanoni, P. and Janssens, M. (2007) 'Minority employees engaging with (diversity) management: an analysis of control, agency, and micro-emancipation', *Journal of Management Studies*, 44 (8): 1371–1397.

Zey, M. (2008) 'Multisubsidiary form', in S. R. Clegg and J. R. Bailey (eds), *The Sage International Encyclopedia of Organization Studies*. Thousand Oaks, CA: Sage, pp. 934–938.

Zirnsak, M. (2017) 'Turning the corner on tackling tax cheats', *Sydney Morning Herald*, 14 January, www.smh.com.au/opinion/turning-the-corner-on-tackling-tax-cheats-20170113-gtqx5o.html (accessed 8 October 2018).

Zuboff, S. (1988) *In the Age of the Smart Machine*. New York: Basic Books.

Zwick, E. (Director) (2006) *Blood Diamond* [Motion picture]. Los Angeles, CA: Warner Bros.

Zyglidopoulos, S., Hirsch, P., de Holan, P. M. and Phillips, N. (2018) 'Expanding research on corporate corruption, management, and organizations', *Journal of Management Inquiry*, 26 (3): 247–253.

Index